INDIGENOUS SONGS OF VICTORIA

Aboriginal History Incorporated
Aboriginal History Inc. is a part of the Australian Centre for Indigenous History, Research School of Social Sciences, The Australian National University, and gratefully acknowledges the support of the School of History and the National Centre for Indigenous Studies, The Australian National University. Aboriginal History Inc. is administered by an Editorial Board which is responsible for all unsigned material. Views and opinions expressed by the author are not necessarily shared by Board members.

Contacting Aboriginal History
All correspondence should be addressed to the Editors, Aboriginal History Inc., ACIH, School of History, Research School of Social Sciences, ANU RSSS Building, The Australian National University, Canberra ACT 2600, or aboriginalhistoryinc@gmail.com.

WARNING: Readers are notified that this publication may contain names or images of deceased persons.

INDIGENOUS SONGS OF VICTORIA

STEPHEN D MOREY,
LUISE HERCUS,
EDWARD RYAN
AND GRACE KOCH

ANU PRESS

Published by ANU Press and Aboriginal History Inc.
The Australian National University
Canberra ACT 2600, Australia
Email: anupress@anu.edu.au

Available to download for free at press.anu.edu.au

The Australian National University acknowledges, celebrates and pays our respects to the Ngunnawal and Ngambri people of the Canberra region and to all First Nations Australians on whose traditional lands we meet and work, and whose cultures are among the oldest continuing cultures in human history.

ISBN (paperback): 9781760467111
ISBN (online): 9781760467128

WorldCat (paperback): 1559077664
WorldCat (online): 1559621665

DOI: 10.22459/ISV.2025

Cover design and layout by ANU Press

This book is published under the aegis of the Aboriginal History editorial board of ANU Press.

Contents

List of figures

List of tables

Acknowledgements

This book arose from a discussion back in about 2009 between the late Luise Hercus and Stephen Morey about the surviving sources for songs in Victorian Aboriginal languages. At first we thought an academic article might be appropriate, but as we have undertaken the project, we have gradually realised that there was a much greater richness of sources for songs in Victorian languages than we had imagined when the process started. Thus we have found more song texts in manuscripts coming to light; for example, those recorded for the Eastern Kulin area by William Thomas, and written down in manuscripts at the State Library of NSW MLMSS 214. We also came to know of more sound recordings, such as those made in 1914 by Felix von Luschan and now in the Berlin Phonogrammarchiv.

We quickly realised that Edward (Ted) Ryan's knowledge of the nineteenth-century sources on Victorian Aboriginal people and Grace Koch's expertise in the music of Aboriginal Australia would be essential for this book to be successful.

To fund the research in library and museum collections in Canberra, Sydney and Adelaide, the project received a grant of $16,739 in 2016 from the ARC Centre of Excellence for the Dynamics of Languages (CoEDL) (www.dynamicsoflanguage.edu.au) for the project *Songs in the Aboriginal Languages of Victoria – Linguistic and Musicological Analysis* (administered by ANU under the auspices of Prof. Jane Simpson) and two small grants of $6,500 and $2,758 from the La Trobe University *Linguistics Disciplinary Research Program* (DRP).

An important source of support for this work was an Australian Research Council Linkage Program grant, for the project entitled *Howitt & Fison's anthropology: Using new methods to reveal hidden riches.* led by Associate Professor Helen Gardner (Deakin University), with other Chief Investigators, Dr Stephen Morey (La Trobe), Dr Rachel Hendery (University of Western

Sydney), Dr Patrick McConvell (The Australian National University) and Dr Jason Gibson (Deakin University). The Howitt and Fison project led to the creation of the Howitt and Fison website.

We received further support from La Trobe University's Social Research Assistance Program and from the Centre of Excellence for the Dynamics of Language for the costs of copy-editing.

Many individuals have assisted us along the way, and we mention just a few: Barry Blake, Mary-Anne Gale, Jane Belfrage, Rob Amery, James Wafer, Graeme Skinner, Lou Bennett, Harley Dunolly-Lee, Corey Theatre, Andrew Tanner, Russell Mullett, Brendan Kennedy, Harold Koch, Jane Simpson, David Nash, Jacqui Durrant, Auntie Gail Smith, Auntie Joy Wandin Murphy, Aunty Loraine Padgham, Ian Clark, Vicki Couzens, Jesse Hodgetts, Deidre O'Sullivan and the two anonymous reviewers who took such care to examine the manuscript. We have received helpful suggestions from all of these people; any errors in this book, of course, are solely our responsibility.

A very particular thanks to Geoff Hunt whose careful copy-editing and attention to detail has very considerably improved the final version of this book.

This is an important book because it brings back into the public attention important pieces of Indigenous literature that in some cases have been hidden for a century or more. We dedicate this book to all those who created and sang these songs, and also to those who wrote them down or recorded them so that we may hear, read and be delighted by them today.

Abbreviations

AIATSIS	Australian Instititute of Aboriginal and Torres Strait Islander Studies
IPA	International Phonetic Alphabet
MLMSS	State Library of NSW, Mitchell Library Manuscripts
MS	Manuscript
MV	Museums Victoria
RAIGBI	Royal Anthropological Institute of Great Britain and Ireland
SLNSW	State Library of New South Wales
SLV	State Library of Victoria
VACL	Victorian Aboriginal Corporation for Languages
XM	Code for manuscripts in Museums Victoria

Linguistic abbreviations

1	1st person
2	2nd person
3	3rd person
ABL	ablative
ALL	allative
ALONG	along
CASE	case
CAUS	causative
DEM	demonstrative
DL	dual
EMPH	emphatic
ERG	ergative

EXCL	exclusive
FORM	formative (perhaps forming a verb from a noun)
FREQ	frequentative
FUT	future
GEN	genitive, general oblique
IMP	imperative
INCL	inclusive
INTENS	intensive
INTERR	interrogative, question word
LINK	linking morpheme
LOC	locative 'position right in'
NEG	negative
OBJ	object
OBL	oblique
ONOM	onomatopoeic
PART	participle
PARTICULAR	particularising suffix (see Hercus 1986: 84)
PL	plural
PN	proper name
POSS	possessive
POT	potential (also optative)
PRES	present
PRES.PART	present participle
PRF	perfect
PST	past
PST.PART	past participle
PURP	purposive
RECIP	reciprocal
REDUPL	reduplication
REFL	reflexive
SG	singular
SO.PART	song particle, type of vocable
WH	wh word (interrogative word)

Foreword

Vicki Couzens Keerray Wooroong Gunditjmara

My heart runs with love
for our 'Songsters'
We hear you
We will sing your songs again.
We will write songs
and sing songs
and dance songs
Continuing our Songlines

The Songsters and Songs are calling us
Our Old Peoples legacy
for us to 'find' again
To re-dream our Songlines,
reconnecting, reinvigorating Ceremony.

I too, along with the authors and community language experts, offer my deepest respect and acknowledgement to the 'Songsters' whose legacy calls to us from the pages of this book, for those of us who work in the spaces of language revitalisation and all our families and communities.

I recognise and acknowledge the care, respect and expertise of those who undertook the invaluable work that has brought about the publication of this book. To make comment is an honour.

Our languages, our Mother Tongue, are the repositories of our knowledge systems that defines our Belonging and identity. It characterises and expresses relationship with Country; tells who we are; how we Belong in kinship and family; our Stories, Songlines and Laws for Living.

Until the arrival of Europeans, our languages were wholly oral. Transmission of knowledge was through the continuum of our stories, songs and dances. The learning and acquisition of these knowledges is enabled through a sophisticated whole of life learning system that encompasses a deep symbiotic relationship with Country. This mutual symbiosis is the foundation of our learning and continuation of cultural knowledge; of our Being and living in relationship with Country; our responsibility and obligation for care, maintenance, increase and balance:

> 'yoonggama' is a Keerray Wooroong cultural value principle that encapsulates the purpose and intention of integral and inherent cultural responsibility and obligation through a promise and action in regenerative reciprocity. It is the promise of continuance, of futurity; enacted and maintained through caring for, of and with Kin and Country; transmission of Knowledge, learning and teaching. It is legacy. (Couzens 2024)

The phrase 'yoonggama' describes our reciprocal promise with Country; our interdependent and collaborative methods to ensure continuity and futurity. These methods include the development of aural listening and comprehension capacities combined with visual observations and embodied actions similar to 'touch and physical response' methodologies employed in some contemporary language revitalisation education programs.

Symbols, motifs, dance, story and song are the tools of learning. Memnonic patterning and repetition through story, song and dance ensures knowledge is embodied in living people. We are our own living archives with these knowledges embedded in our DNA, in our 'running blood' weerakaleek.

It was a wonderful moment in time those many years ago when Luise Hercus and Stephen Morey had a conversation about the music and songs they had come across in their research in archives and a wonderful idea when their considerations led them deciding to compile and make available Victorian Aboriginal Traditional Songs. This has now been done by these well-known, highly regarded linguists with specialist knowledges and experience in Victorian Aboriginal Languages.

The songs have been compiled from an extensive set of archival resources many of which have been unaccessible to our communities. The work in researching and presenting accessible language sources, musical information /interpretations here has been undertaken with highly regarded expertise in linguistics and musicology. It has been thoughtfully researched and explored and made available to us, Victorian Aboriginal people for the futurity of our languages and knowledges

While some might not agree that this work should have been undertaken by non-Aboriginal linguists (again), I think it is fair to say if this work had not been undertaken when it was, over the past two or more decades, then it would continue to remain inaccessible and unavailable to us still, and the question is how much longer would our Ancestors' legacy lie hidden among the colonial archives?

Our languages are in crisis. Language loss is a global emergency. We have the fastest attrition rate of the oldest living cultures and languages in the world. Time is of the essence and we do not have any more time to lose. Our living languages were interrupted during invasion and subsequent colonial genocidal actions where we were killed, punished and banned from language speaking.

In our language revitalisation journeys today, we have a monumental task to bring languages home, to be spoken again in our daily lives, for our children and their childrens childrens children to be First Language speakers again. We are trawling the archives, seeking knowledge still living in community with our Elders, looking at placenames and our Country finding more and more language sources. What was left by our Ancestors in the archives helps us to build our lexicon to develop our languages into spoken languages again. This collection of Traditional Songs will contribute greatly to increasing our vocabularies, our grammars and of course to our ceremonial and spiritual aspects of our living cultures.

We must celebrate what is offered in this volume. We must take these songs now and 'bring them home', sing them again, share them in our families and communities.

These Songs are a treasure; a legacy from the Old People for us to find again and to integrate into our revival continuum; in 'singing up the Songlines',

I honour the Songsters.

Pangmaar ngootapana weeng; mana ngarrakeetoong, nganto pay

Ngarrakeetoong, kaneepoorreewooka ngarrakeetoong

no one left behind hold family/community, keepfamily/community honour family/community

Dr Vicki Couzens Keerray Wooroong Gunditjmara RMIT

1

Introduction and background

The rich and diverse forms of Indigenous songs from Victoria presented in this book represent but a tiny fraction of what once was a cultural treasure, lost so casually. Yet we are able to bring together here well over 100 different songs texts, many with translations, many with musical transcriptions and analysis, that stand as an example of the rich cultural heritage of Indigenous people in Victoria.

The foundation of this book are the songs sung by Stan Day, and recorded on tape by Luise Hercus between 1962 and 1966 (see section 2.2); these were analysed from the perspective of linguistics by Hercus (1986) but to this we add the musical transcriptions and analysis undertaken by Grace Koch.

To this foundation, we have been able to add more than 100 song texts from most of the languages of Victoria, some of which were published in the nineteenth century by authors like Alfred W. Howitt (1887a, 1904) (see sections 2.3, 3.2 and 5.2) and some of which were largely found in manuscripts written by authors like Howitt and also Rev. William Thomas (see, for example, section 3.4), Rev. John Bulmer (see sections 5.3, 8.1) and Robert Hamilton Mathews (see sections 2.6, 9.6), among many others.

Where possible, we have also identified the singers and/or composers of the songs. In many cases the nineteenth-century writers did include information about the songsters, who were often ritual experts and community leaders. The nineteenth-century academic publication style did not encourage the naming of sources, so names are often omitted from publications but are found in manuscripts. On the other hand, Smyth (1878), Torrance (1887) and Howitt (1887a, 1904) do name a significant number of the songsters, but in most cases the information available in manuscripts is richer and more detailed.

For this reason, we have included full transcriptions of all parts of manuscripts from particularly Thomas, Howitt and Mathews, relating to songs. Many of these manuscripts have not been transcribed before, or if they have, those transcriptions had not yet been published.

Part of our methodology has been to share the drafts of chapters of this volume with members of the language communities whose songs are discussed in that chapter. It became clear very early in this study that these songs were not only the most substantial pieces of text in the languages of Victoria that have survived, but also were linked to deep cultural aspects of each of the communities.

Song texts, though usually quite short in length, were often written down with considerable contextual information, such as the location, timing and function of the song, as well as translations and sometimes clear word-by-word glossing. Our method in this book is to present as much of the contextual information about each song as possible, including quotes from existing published sources and full transcriptions of manuscript sources, along with whatever analysis we have been able to do.

In the case of the linguistic analysis, this has involved the use of regularisation (orthographic standardisation), in which a spelling is chosen that approximates as closely as possible to the likely phonemic structure of words. The type of regularisation varies from language to language; employing, for example, voiceless stops (**p, t, k**) in the Western Kulin chapter, but voiced stops (**b, d, g**) in the Eastern Kulin chapter, following Hercus (1992) and Blake (1991) respectively.

Thus the short text in the Wool-woork Bar-lum-bur-lin (Butterfly dance), documented by William Thomas and discussed in section 3.4.5, presents the original text in italics, the regularised spelling in bold, a gloss and then a translation, as shown in example (1.1):

(1.1)	*Yan-gee*	*yan-gee*	*ma-lar*
	yang-i	**yang-i**	**mal-a(rr)**
	go-IMP	go-IMP	let's-2SG?
	'Go! Go! (You) should (go!).'		

In the late nineteenth century, three songs were transcribed with musical notation by Rev. Dr George Torrance (see section 3.2), but as far as we know there are no surviving recordings of these for us to analyse. However, starting in around 1900, there have been five main examples of audio recordings of Indigenous songs in Victoria, as shown in (1.2):

(1.2) Wax cylinders made for A.W. Howitt (see section 2.1 for discussion of these)

Wax cylinder recordings made by Felix von Luschan (section 2.8)

Wax cylinder recordings made by Norman Tindale (sections 2.12 and 6.2)

Wax cylinder recordings made by Ronald and Catherine Berndt (sections 2.10, 8.2.2, 12.3 and 14.1)

Tape recordings made by Luise Hercus (sections 2.2 and 5.5)

Musical transcriptions are presented for all of the Hercus audio recordings, and for some of those made by von Luschan, Tindale and Berndt, depending on both the quality of the recordings and the availability of materials for research. For example, we have relied on the late Alice Moyle's transcription of the Bunganditj Song of Guichen Bay (see section 6.2.1) published in 1968 but entered into the Finale program and re-presented here. This transcription to some extent represents the musical features of all of the songs recorded by Norman Tindale and along with the notes that we were able to take when listening to these wonderful recordings gives the reader some conception of the nature of these songs.

Note: in this book we use the term 'recorded' to refer to audio recordings. These recordings were done sometimes on wax cylinders and sometimes on tape, depending on the time they were made. We may also include the word 'audio' to ensure that the reader knows that the performances can be heard.

Many of the songs discussed in this volume were intended to be sung during a dance performance, for which the Sydney language (Dharuk) word *corroboree* is generally used by all the sources. There are multiple descriptions of corroborees in the early sources, but only a small number of these have been included in this volume (particularly those documented for the Melbourne area, Eastern Kulin language group, in section 3.1.5).

For each chapter we have also included a section on musical terminology, which could otherwise be termed 'metalanguage'. This includes words for song, dance and other related terms, and any small pieces of text relating to the practice of singing and dancing. William Thomas, in particular, wrote down several 'dialogues' about corroborees in several languages (see, for example, section 3.1.8.1 for Eastern Kulin). These have been transcribed, and analysed linguistically as far as possible.

The book is divided into chapters for each of the languages as identified by Blake and Reid (1998: 3–4). We have changed the name Central Victoria as employed by Blake and Reid to 'Eastern Kulin'. Two of the languages listed by Blake and Reid (Colac and Yabula Yabula) are not represented by any song texts in this volume. A map of approximate locations the language groups referred to in the book can be found in Blake and Reid (1998: 58), or readers may like to consult the Victorian Aboriginal Corporation for Languages (VACL) map.[1]

The list of languages that are dealt with, preceded by a more general term to group the varieties, is as follows:[2]

- Western Kulin – Wemba-Wemba, Werkaya, Djadjawurrung, Tjapwurrung and Mathi-Mathi varieties (Chapter 2)
- Eastern Kulin – Woiwurrung, Boonwurrung, Thagungwurrung (Chapter 3)
- Wathawurrung (Chapter 4)
- Gippsland – Bratauolung, Brabralung, Braiakaulung, Krauatungalung and Tatungalung (Chapter 5)
- Bunganditj/Buwandik (Chapter 6)
- Warrnambool (Chapter 7)
- Paakantyi – especially Maraura (Chapter 8)
- Yorta Yorta (Chapter 9)
- Dhudhuroa (Chapter 10)
- Pallanganmiddang (Chapter 11)
- Murray River languages – including Yuyu, Keramin and Yitha-Yitha (Chapter 12).

Two language groups not included in Blake and Reid's study, but included as part of this volume, are Paakantyi (Chapter 8) and the Murray River languages (Chapter 12). In the case of Paakantyi (Maraura variety),

1 See Victorian Collections, 'Our Story', accessed 30 November 2021, victoriancollections.net.au/stories/our-story.

2 Note that the use of Kulin as a language (sub)grouping term dates back to Schmidt (1919).

the information was included because Bulmer had collected these songs in Victoria (section 8.1) and because of Luise Hercus's special expertise in Paakantyi.

The two final chapters deal with widespread songs (Chapter 13), which were sung in multiple areas and whose language the authors do not recognise and possibly come from outside of Victoria, and two songs in unknown languages associated with the areas in which the others songs were sung (Chapter 14).

This volume is not a comprehensive study of songs in Victorian languages. We have confined this volume to 'Traditional' songs and therefore not included hymns/psalms and other Christian songs translated by people like Rev. William Thomas and in some cases still in use in communities. A good example of the latter would be the Bura Fera, in Yorta Yorta language, reportedly translated by Mr Thomas Shadrack James (for a discussion of it, see Bowe and Morey 1999: 117–18). This song is widely known in Victoria and New South Wales, but like other hymns is not included in this volume (see further Chapter 9). For further information on hymns in Victorian languages, Breen (1989: 3–45) 'Part One Introduction' mentions hymns sung in Victoria. The format is that of a conversation among several people, and the comments by Marylouise Brunton are relevant to hymnody.

1.1 Types of songs

Hercus (1986: 61) categorised the songs that she was able to document as representing two types of song tradition:

i. Songs that were composed in response to a particular event, such as a song (not included in Hercus 1986) that Nyawi composed when rabbiting. He 'had hung up all his scalps on a line to dry, but had forgotten to tie up his dogs, and when he looked in the morning all the scalps were gone and so he made up a song about it'.
ii. Songs that relate to more ancient traditions, such as Nganuty-nganuty 'the bat' (section 2.2.2) 'connected with the tradition that the bat was sacred to men'.

Hercus (1986: 61) distinguishes these two types of songs from 'ritual singing' adding the following: 'Mr Stanley Day had heard ritual singing, but had never been taught any, and he recalled that in the old days the women had been enthusiastic singers and had their own songs'. She went on to add that the songs recorded on audio tape in Wemba-Wemba 'represent a negligible fragment of the original wealth of Wembawemba music and literature'.

The songs that we present in this study represent both of Hercus's types and some ritual songs. Some of the types of songs are referred to using their nineteenth-century categorisation. An example of this is the 'charm', a term that is used to describe songs like the 'Enchanting away rain' of the Boonwurrung (section 3.4.11) or some of the spells from Gippsland (see for example, the **Prewin** song in section 5.2.4 or the songs used against the **Parn** spirit discussed in sections 5.2.6 and 5.2.7). Since we are not able to discuss the categories of songs with the songsters, we will keep as much of the original nineteenth-century description of their functions as possible. In each chapter, we will separately discuss the 'classification' of songs in so far as it is possible.

Readers will also notice the use of the term *corroboree* in multiple places in this volume. In many cases, we have the Indigenous language words for dance performances, referred to as *corroboree* from the earliest written documents in the 1830s. We do not always have a clear understanding of what these dance performances consisted of, even though we often have very detailed descriptions (see for example, section 3.1.5).

Some of the songs in this volume were received by the songsters via dream; for example, Kurburu's song (3.2.2) and Wenberi's song (3.2.3). The topic of how songs were received, created or composed by the songsters is difficult to examine when we cannot speak directly to those songsters. We make note of any information that was collected about each song in the sections where each song is discussed.

Where possible we will include all the contextual information about a particular song in the discussion of it. In the chapter on songs from the 'Eastern Kulin' languages, we have included a separate section about types of songs and their context. Songs from those languages are more diverse that we have for most other parts of Victoria, partly because of the considerable cultural context noted down by William Thomas and the fact that A.W. Howitt also collected songs in the same area.

It is at least possible that the different types of songs listed in section 3.1.1, and all the different contexts in which they were sung, were present in all the language groups in Victoria; we cannot know for sure.

1.2 The songsters in Aboriginal Victoria

We are referring to the people who provided information about the songs that are discussed in this book under the heading of 'songster'. This term does not fully represent the importance of these individuals – both men and women – who created songs and who were of great significance in Indigenous society. We considered terms like *bard* or *poet* but both are laden with Western cultural ideas and neither conveyed sufficiently the importance of song in these communities. Some of the people that we include as 'songsters' were the composers or creators of the songs; others perhaps did not create them but transmitted them. We must also add that there would have been many other songsters in the nineteenth century whose names were not documented or whose expertise was not credited to them.

There are two areas in particular where we are lacking sufficient knowledge of these songsters. One is that a large majority of the songsters in this book are male, and the voices of Indigenous women from the nineteenth century were generally not heard by those researchers gathering information about Indigenous society. Some of the women whose voices were heard include Silvia Murray (sections 2.2.14 and 2.2.15), Nancy Egan (section 2.2.16), Mary Moore (section 2.9), the singers of the Wool-woork Bar-lum-bur-lin dance (section 3.4.5), the singers of the Women's lament (section 3.4.8), and Old Nanny who gave to A.W. Howitt what we have termed the Woman's answer to a **Yentjin(y)** (section 5.2.12) and the Hairy Beka chant (section 9.5.1). There are also songs in the mother's voice in the Big Eagle's Children story (section 5.3.4).

A second area of our lack of knowledge relates to the ownership of song. In some parts of Australia where song has been more thoroughly studied, there is a clear understanding of who has ownership or rights to songs. For example, O'Keeffe (2016: 12), in relation to western Arnhem land, wrote that 'a songman's sons generally inherit ownership rights to a song-set from their father, and other male relatives also have rights to sing'. In general we do not know, for Victoria, what rights of ownership and/or restriction to access there may have been.

Marett (2005: xv) wrote about the issue of researching traditional songs:

> Knowing that some songs are 'secret' and potentially harmful, people – frequently people of goodwill, who are merely trying to show proper respect – choose to avoid them completely. This has inhibited the degree in which Australians have been able to engage with Aboriginal music, and this in turn has affected the extent to which Aboriginal song is known and appreciated both within Australian and internationally. Yet my own experience is that, provided restrictions and esoteric knowledge are respected and cultural ownership of public knowledge is properly acknowledged, most Aboriginal communities, at least in the north of Australia want their music to be more widely disseminated and better understood.

We recognise that some Indigenous people in Victoria might regard some of the songs in this book as being restricted. Some Indigenous readers may choose not to engage with some of the examples presented here. And we recognise that there is incomplete knowledge about the songsters, the creators and custodians of these songs. We want to acknowledge all of the songsters, creators and custodians, both those named here and those whose names were not recorded.

We also feel it is important to compiling all the songs from this region in one place so that members of the community are better equipped to make their own decisions about which contexts particular songs can be performed in.

1.3 About the musical notations

All but one of the musicological analyses contained in this volume were based upon notations prepared either by Grace Koch or Alice Moyle, with some earlier melodies written down by Rev. Dr George Torrance (1887) (in conjunction with other texts written by A.W. Howitt), Ludwig Becker (1860) and Dr Herman Beckler (1861). Stephen Morey captured a rhythmic figure by listening to one of the Tindale recordings at the South Australian Museum. The earliest notations (Becker, Beckler and Torrance) were made on the spot from performances whereas those by Koch and by Moyle were done from recordings, including early ones on wax cylinders, that were of variable audio quality. We have included only one of the five audio recordings made by Felix von Luschan in 1914, as the sound of the others were not clear; however, with further advances in audio preservation, it may be possible for the other four to be notated at a later date.

The musical notations were made for songs in five languages/language groups: Western Kulin (see Chapter 2; 15 songs); Eastern Kulin (see Chapter 3; 3 songs); Gippsland (see Chapter 5; 1 song); Bunganditj (see Chapter 6; 1 song, based on a transcription by Alice Moyle), Maraura/Paakantyi (see Chapter 8; 2 songs); Yorta Yorta (see Chapter 9; 1 song); and two from unknown language groups. Because of the small size of the samples and the variety of types of the songs, it is not possible to make a definitive statement as to a general style of Victorian songs. Moyle's practice of creating 'pitch inventories' gives us some scope for analysis. All the pitch inventories for the songs for which there are musical notations in this book are presented in Figure 1.1. The pitch inventories (listing of notes from the lowest note to the highest note and all notes in between) for each song can be identified by title and by figure numbers corresponding to the notations in the text. Pitches are shown using the system of cents, which divides each semitone into 100 units. These pitch inventories show the closest tones to those of the diatonic scale, even though they vary from standard pitches by several cents. In interpreting the Western notation, it should not be assumed that the pitches correspond to a precise equivalent of the pitches within the system of 100 cent values. There is further information on the computer programs used for notations below. Figure 1.1 shows the pitches transposed into the key of C so that the scales of the songs can be compared.

Most of the Western Kulin songs have a fairly recognisable tonal centre, or key, even if they do not use all eight notes of a diatonic scale. The exceptions are Song 6 (Looking for dingoes, section 2.2.7) and Song 7 (Kangaroos and a dingo, section 2.2.8). Most of Stan Day's songs (section 2.2, songs 1–11) sound like they are in major keys (with a tonal centre at different pitches). For example, the pitch inventory for the first version of Nganuty-nganuty 'the bat' has the notes E, E#, F#, G#, A that, with the exception of the E# that we treat as an accidental tonal variant, make up parts of an A major scale.

While we can clearly see major scales (also termed Ionian mode) in most of Stan Day's songs, we do not encounter pentatonic scales in any of the songs presented here.

Pitch inventory transposed
(all scales beginning on C)
Fig 2.1 Song 1 Nganuty-nganuty 'the bat'(a)
Fig 2.2 Song 1 Nganuty-nganuty 'the bat' (b)
3
Fig. 2.3 Song 2 Yerrateth-kurrk 'the owlet-nightjat'
Fig. 2.4 Song 3 Going to the land of the dead
5
Fig. 2.5 Song 4 Shearing on Tulla Station
Fig. 2.6 Song 5 Jack Brown's song (Ellis)
Fig. 2.7 Song 5 Jack Brown's song (Hercus)
Fig. 2.8 Song 5a Jack Brown's Swearing song
9
Fig. 2.9 Song 6 Looking for dingoes (Ellis)
Fig. 2.10 Song 6 Looking for dingoes (Hercus)
11
Fig. 2.11 Song 7 Kangaroos and a dingo
Fig.2.12 Song 8 'Sentai' the lazy dog (Ellis)
13
Fig. 2.13 Song 8 'Sentai' the lazy dog (Hercus)
Fig. 2.14 Song 9 Escaping from justice in NSW
15
Fig. 2.15 Song 10 An ancient tale (Ellis)
Fig. 2.16 Song 10 An ancient tale (Hercus)
17
Fig. 2.17 Song 11 Bob Taylor's swearing song (a)
Fig. 2.17 Song 11 Bob Taylor's swearing song (b)

Figure 1.1: Pitch inventories transposed into the key of C

Source: Grace Koch.

For the other songs, a tonal centre cannot be identified for Mary Moore's songs and the Boat song. The Song of Guichen Bay (see Figure 5.2, and Figure 6.1 in pitch inventories) appears to be in the key of B minor. Two of the older songs, that of von Luschan and Wenberi's song, are basically chromatic scales (i.e. employing all the semitones). Wenberi's song has a pitch range within a major third, while our notation of the von Luschan song includes all the semitones across a major ninth. See Figure 2.20 and 3.2 in the pitch inventories.

In her article 'Ornamentation in Australian Vocal Music', Catherine Ellis (1962) describes various types of vocal embellishments used in songs from south-eastern Australia, referring to Tanganekald songs.[3] Although most of her references come from South Australia, she includes some generalisations about Victorian songs. Our sample shows only a few examples of ornamentation, with the most recognisable instances occurring in Laurie Moffatt's Boat song (Figure 5.2, section 5.5) where a grace note is sounded at the very first pitch and a turn near the end of the song. In the corpus of notations of the songs by Stan Day, we see a slide from one pitch to the adjacent one when the song continues after a pause in the middle of the Nganuty-nganuty 'the bat' song (Figure 2.1, section 2.2.2); however, this does not appear in the second repetition of the song. Another example can be seen in the Luise Hercus record of 'An ancient tale' (Figure 2.16, section 2.2.11) in bar 7 where the musical phrase ends on what appears to be a partial turn involving four notes. Mary Moore's Song 1 Version B (Figure 2.23, section 2.9.1) begins with a G immediately rising a minor third to the B. Finally, Laurie Moffatt (Figure 5.2, section 5.5) sings a turn on the G preceding the descent to an F. Aside from these, the notated songs do not display ornamentation.

Further generalisations about song styles of south-eastern Australia, including Victoria and New South Wales, appear in Ellis (1966). Although we agree with her observation about the songs (often) being in a free rhythm and (usually) a melodic line encompassing more than an octave (1966: 75), we disagree with her statement that there is no clear tonic, as most of Stan Day's songs do have a clear tonality and several end on the tonic pitch; however, the other notations, especially for the earlier songs, are more fluid. We have indicated the likely key in the text under musicological analysis.

Listeners may hear slight differences to what has been notated here. Koch listened to each song at least 20 times. Although listening could occur indefinitely, she chose to stop at 20 times because there had to be an endpoint for the work. The music transcriptions are included as a starting point to help people understand the musical structures and assist in the revitalisation of songs.

3 The name Tanganekald was used by Tindale (1937, 1974) to refer to one of the groups within the Ngarrindjeri.

Koch has notated the songs using several programs. First of all, audio files for each song were copied onto the program Transcribe! Version 8.63.0 for Mac, issued by Seventh String Software. The program analyses the difference for each pitch from the standard piano pitch, dividing each semitone into 100 cents and showing the deviation from the standard. Koch chose the pitches closest to the standard pitch when notating and notated the songs on staff paper.

The notations were then put onto a staff using the program Finale 2014.5. One of the most helpful features of the program is that the notation can be played back for checking both pitch and tempo.

Bar lines were inserted at places where there would be a pause or note of long duration in the melody and/or at places where the melody fell into a metrical pattern. No time signatures were shown because the metrical structure was often very complex.

The Finale notations were transferred to PDF files and inserted into the manuscript.

One of the features of Luise Hercus's original linguistic transcriptions is marking of stress or accent that was different from everyday spoken language. Hercus (1986: 22) introduced this as follows:

> In singing the accent system appears to have been utterly different from spoken speech. The speakers themselves were keenly aware of this, and often commented on it. As Mrs Egan put it: 'We could always understand what the old people said, and we could talk back to them in the language, but when they started singing, then we couldn't understand. My grandfather used to be quite cross with me because he then had to go on explaining the song over and over again'.

Hercus (1986: 22, 23) gave examples of the stress differences between the songs and spoken language. In each case, the song version had stress or accent on the final syllable, a feature that may have been present in some other songs (see, for example, the Shooting Star song in section 2.3.2). Later, Luise Hercus (pers. comm. in discussion with Grace Koch) said that when she marked stress she was thinking about a syllable of longer duration; she showed the stressed syllables as being longer than the preceding and following syllables.

In this book, for those songs recorded and translated in Hercus (1986), we will mark the stress as shown in Hercus in the phonetic line that is based on that source, as in example (2.10) in section 2.2.2, the first line of which is presented as example (1.3). These stress marks are not reflected in the musical transcriptions.

(1.3)	**kingga**	**mina**	**mayo**	**Mr Walker**	**wirra**
	ˈkiŋkɐ	mɪnɐ	ˈmajɔ	*Mr. Walker*	ˈwirɐ
	here	indeed	from.afar	Mr.Walker	hasten(PRS)
	'Here from afar hastens Mr Walker …'				

1.4 About the manuscript transcriptions

Throughout this book, there are a significant number of transcriptions from manuscripts. These transcriptions are placed inside boxes as exemplified by Box 1.1 below. Some of these transcriptions contain non-standard spellings, crossings out, insertions and words that we cannot easily read. The conventions for dealing with these issues are given in (1.4):

(1.4) Where a word cannot be read, it is transcribed in brackets with a double question mark, as [??]

Where the reading of a word in is uncertain, that word or words are in brackets with a double question mark as [shores??]

Crossed-out sections are shown with the text in brackets, followed by an en dash and then the words 'crossed out', as [make him – crossed out]. All the portion before the en dash is understood to be crossed out. In most cases the crossings out (and insertions) were done by the writers of the manuscripts as they revised their versions.

Where words are inserted, this is indicated as follows: [far away to beyond Mt Cole – inserted].

An example is given in Box 1.1, which is a transcription of a section of Howitt's notebooks, describing the initiation ceremony discussed in detail below in section 5.2.21.1.1. The original manuscript of this section of text can be seen at the Howitt and Fison Archive.[4]

4 howittandfison.org/document/XM761/10 (accessed 18 August 2021).

Box 1.1: Boys' initiation ceremony (2) Ceremony Day 2 (Friday)

Friday morning. While I was sitting with Lamby & Jonny Fidget talking about the arrangement of 1st scene we heard a distant hail from across the river and then a gunshot. The expected contingent had arrived and we all heard their shouts. Four men soon stood [??] King Charley, Big Joe, McKay & _______ But the sundown was very bright & the [shores??] too rough - our canoe both small and [useless??]. After mending it, it was decided not practicable to cross the river and the men started out to send for another - one which Old Lamby an expert canoeist [arrived??] with some tea & sugar and part of a damper. As the black with the usual improvidence had no more

Source: MV MS XM 761, p. 99; adapted by authors.

We are not using [sic] in manuscript transcriptions for non-standard or erroneous spellings, and leave the interpretation of these spellings up to the readers. In addition, we are not maintaining the original line breaks in continuous text in manuscript transcriptions, but line breaks are maintained where they are significant, such as, for example, where song texts are accompanied by glossing.

These conventions do not apply to transcriptions from Stephens (2014) or Clark (1998, 2000, 2002), which are presented as found. For example, Clark uses [...] to indicate unreadable sections.[5]

1.5 About the manuscript sources

A significant number of references in this book are to manuscripts, in particular those of William Thomas (section 1.5.1) and A.W. Howitt (section 1.5.2). The purpose of this section is to assist the reader to find images of the original manuscripts, some of which are available online.

1.5.1 William Thomas manuscripts in the State Library of NSW

The manuscripts of William Thomas are divided into three different sources. The larger part of these materials are kept in the part of the State Library of New South Wales (SLNSW) also known as the Mitchell Library. The reference for these is MLMSS 214. Another important collection of Thomas papers are in the State Library of Victoria (SLV), MS 14624 (which is not yet digitised).

5 We are very grateful to Ian Clark for providing us with a word document version of his transcriptions.

MLMSS 214 is fully digitised and all the images are available online through the SLNSW website, via the 'Digital Collections' link.[6] The manuscript consists of 26 'Volumes', in earlier times referred to as boxes. It is now divided into items, each of which has a name. Thus, the section containing the main text of the Gaiggip song (see section 3.4.1) is named as follows (1.5):

(1.5) Volume 21 Item 03 William Thomas Aboriginal song 'Gaiggip' and memorandum, 1850, 1857

This section has Record Identifier '93QV3eq1' and a full link to the section on the SLNSW website is collection.sl.nsw.gov.au/record/93QV3eq1 (accessed 23 September 2021). This section consists of several pages that are in four images. These images can be downloaded from the website as either 'JPEG small' or 'JPEG original'. The 'JPEG original' files for this section are named SLNSW_FL832691.jpg, SLNSW_FL832693.jpg, SLNSW_FL832695.jpg and SLNSW_FL832697.jpg. These file names are not sequential for reasons unclear, since it seems that both the 'small' and 'original' size files have the same names.

In our references to these manuscripts, we have included the volume and item numbers as seen in Example (1.5) and in most cases the name of the JPEG file.

To further assist those who may wish to access the Thomas papers, we include a list of the full names and record identifiers for some of the sections of this manuscript that we consulted as (1.6):

(1.6) Volume 02: William Thomas journals and associated papers, 1840–1843

Volume 02 Item 05: William Thomas journal, 1 January 1841–14 April 1842

Volume 03 Item 01: William Thomas journal, October-November 1841, and miscellaneous notes, 1830s–1840s – collection.sl.nsw.gov.au/record/9NaA7vWY

Volume 03 Item 02: Journal, notes and copy of petition to Governor George Gipps, 1838–1844

Volume 03 Item 03: Journal, including extracts from letters and notes, 16 May 1844 – 15 December 1849

6 State Library of NSW, 'Digital Collections', accessed 17 November 2021, collection.sl.nsw.gov.au/digital.

Volume 03 Item 04: William Thomas journal, 1 January–31 December 1846

Volume 03 Item 07: William Thomas journal, 1 January–15 December 1849

Volume 05 Item 02: William Thomas journal of a journey to Gippsland, 29 November–23 December 1860

Volume 09 Item 02: William Thomas correspondence, returns etc., 1843–1845 – collection.sl.nsw.gov.au/record/9NaA70mY

Volume 21 Item 03: William Thomas Aboriginal song 'Gaiggip' and memorandum, 1850, 1857 – collection.sl.nsw.gov.au/record/93QV3eq1

Volume 21 Item 05: William Thomas Brief Sketch of the Aboriginal Language of Port Phillip, 1858

Volume 21 Item 06: William Thomas 'Sacred Dances', 1858

Volume 21 Item 07: 'On the Aborigines of Australia' 1858

Volume 21 Item 11: William Thomas notes relating to Wonga, 1861

Volume 21 Item 12 William Thomas Outline of a Work on Aborigines – scraps from old Colonial papers, 1861, collection.sl.nsw.gov.au/record/1l4dKge1

Volume 22: William Thomas language and customs of Australian Aborigines, ca. 1838–ca. 1867

Volume 22 Item 05: William Thomas sketches, ca. 1838–ca. 1867

Volume 23 Item 01: William Thomas vocabularies and miscellaneous information – 'Book A', 1838-1868 – collection.sl.nsw.gov.au/record/YoldKMN9

Volume 23 Item 02: William Thomas vocabularies and miscellaneous information – 'Book B', 1838–1868 – collection.sl.nsw.gov.au/record/nZNvKeJn

Volume 23 Item 03 William Thomas vocabularies and notes, 1838–1868

Volume 24 Item 01: William Thomas Sketch of Manners and Songs & Dances, 1858 – collection.sl.nsw.gov.au/record/9PQ84mxn

Volume 26 Item 05: William Thomas loose pages of notes relating to Aborigines and extracts from journals

1.5.2 'A Lexicon of the Australian Aboriginal Tongue' in the State Library of Victoria

Ten of the songs presented in this volume are found in State Library of Victoria MS 6290, previously ascribed to William Thomas. However, recent careful research by Andrew Tanner together with Greg Gerrand from the State Library of Victoria, has established most of the history of the manuscript. Tanner has written the following (pers. comm.; forthcoming):

> The manuscript with the full title *A Lexicon of the Australian Aboriginal Tongue in the Six Dialects of Ballaarat, Bacchus Marsh, Melbourne, Gipps Land, Mount Gambier and Wonnin* is held at the State Library of Victoria and catalogued in two parts under the names J.W.C. Crouch (MS H141425) and William Thomas (MS 6290). It is a copy (with additions) of MS 38[7] held at the Royal Anthropological Institute of Great Britain and Ireland, catalogued under the name W Champ.
>
> MS 38 was exhibited by Colonel William Thomas Napier Champ at the Intercolonial Exhibition in Melbourne in 1866–67, alongside other items which were produced at Pentridge Prison (i.e. from prison labour: hats, buckets, clothing, but also Aboriginal weapons), and won a medal in the Ethnology section. Champ was the inspector general of penal establishments in Victoria (1857–68) and was the de facto superintendent of Pentridge Prison. MS 38 is not signed by the author and cannot be directly attributed to Champ, however there are two dates given – 25 December 1861 and 1 Jan 1862 – and a place: Pentridge (at the time, this name referred both to the prison and also the surrounding area, the latter being renamed Coburg in 1869). How the MS ended up at the RAI is not currently known.
>
> In 1877, Champ himself donated to the State Library of Victoria what is now referred to as MS 6290 and H141425 – a copy of MS 38 apparently made in 1864 by James Crouch, a notorious conman then in prison for fraud. Although a small part of MS 6290 comprises copied sections, incontrovertibly from William Thomas (not present in MS 38), and later published under his name in Smyth (1878, 2: 118–22), the attribution of the entirety of MS 6290 to William

7 This manuscript is available online: W. Champ, *Aboriginal vocabulary, comprising the Ballaarat, Bacchus Marsh, Melbourne and Gipps Land: dialects with a selection of dialogues and familiar phrases, 1862*, The Royal Anthropological Institute of Great Britain and Ireland, accessed 6 June 2022, WDAgo.com/b/9b79423f.

Thomas seems to be due to an unfortunate misreading of the second title page of the manuscript when it was catalogued, which has obscured the true history of the document.

The rest of the manuscript is written in a style and using an orthography for the Aboriginal languages utterly unlike Thomas's. Amongst the papers in MS 6290 there are what appear to be notes from one of the original elicitation sessions dealing with three of the six languages. The handwriting of this document matches neither Champ's nor any other candidates so far entertained (including Thomas's). At the time of writing this, the identity of the author of the document is not known, and there are strong hints that there was a deliberate attempt to maintain their anonymity. What can be stated positively is that the document was most likely produced in 1861 at Pentridge Prison under the authority of William Champ. As it happens, there were six Aboriginal prisoners at Pentridge in 1861 from tribes corresponding to the languages outlined in the document, thus it is possible to propose with some confidence the following informants, with the language varieties as listed in the document:

Peter Mungett (Bacchus Marsh, Ballaarat, Melbourne)
Billy Clarke (Gippsland)
Big Joe (Gippsland)
Monkey Neddy (Mt Gambier, but also Wonnin)
King Toms Billy (Mt Gambier, but also Wonnin)
Jackey White (Wonnin, but also Mt Gambier, Ballaarat).

Six of the songs (MS 6290, pp. 229–31) were included in the original Royal Anthropological Institute of Great Britain and Ireland MS 38 (pp. 132–33 and 357–58) but among the additions mentioned by Tanner and not found in MS 38 are three songs and a 'Suppostitious speech' [sic] that are included in a section headed 'Supplement containing words, phrases, Songs &c in the Melbourne Dialect' (MS 6290, pp. 255–57). Tanner believes that these songs were possibly written down by Crouch based on information given by Peter Mungett. There is a letter from Peter Mungett to William Thomas (MLMSS 214) that writes his name as 'Munjit the Aborigine', which suggests the name may be regularised **mandjit**. However, in rough notes in a separate booklet at the end of MS 6290 (p. 308), the words 'Wallagnary – Peter's name' appear, and this may be have been his Indigenous name (Tanner, pers. comm.) Peter Mungett's life is discussed in detail in Cahir and Clark (2009), who also mention that Peter Mungett's father's name was Oondiat. This is probably the same person listed as *Unjat, big man* in George Augustus Robinson's list of names of the '*Marpeang bulluk: Talin willum yalloke* tribe', described as 'at Backus Marsh, Malcolm's tribe'. Marpeang Bulluk is one of the clans of the Wathawurrung (G.A. Robinson papers, SLNSW A 7086 part 3, pp. 135–46; also Clark 2002: 222).

Thus Peter Mungett, a Wathawurrung man, was almost certainly the person who was the informant for the songs in section 4.2, here included as Wathawurrung because Peter Mungett was a Wathawurrung man. However, the song marked as 'Melbourne' may have been Eastern Kulin or used by multiple communities. Future research on these texts may decide that they should have been included elsewhere.

1.5.3 A.W. Howitt papers

The manuscript papers of Alfred William Howitt, which include a number of song texts discussed in sections 2.3, 3.2 and 5.2, are held in both the State Library of Victoria and Museums Victoria. Most of the manuscripts relating to Gippsland and to the Wurundjeri of the Melbourne area are available online at the Howitt and Fison Archive website (howittandfison.org/, accessed 12 December 2021).

The Howitt papers at the State Library of Victoria are listed under the identifiers 'Accession no: MS 9356' and 'Accession no: MS 10241'. However, when wishing to access the originals of the Howitt papers it is usually necessary to list the box number, and the Howitt papers are found in boxes 1049–1055.

As an example, one text that is found in these papers is the New Moon chant (section 2.3.4), which is found in Box 1053/6 (b). Box 1053 is divided into 6 folders, and within each of those folders there may be more than one part, hence (b). In 2018–19, the library made new high quality scans in colour of these materials, and the section that contains the New Moon chant was named hw0421.pdf. In our references to these documents, we will give both the Box number and folder number, as well as the PDF number and page references within both.

The Howitt papers in Museums Victoria were scanned in black and white some years ago and these scans are named according to this system, where XM761_ICDMS_lowres.pdf refers to one of Howitt's notebooks that contains a second version of the New Moon chant. In referring to the Museums Victoria manuscripts, we will use the form XM 761 and give the page number of the PDF on which the text is found.

1.5.4 R.H. Mathews papers

The manuscript papers of Robert Hamilton Mathews (1841–1918) are held at the National Library of Australia (NLA) as MS 8006 (nla.gov.au/nla.obj-416711257/findingaid). The collection is divided into eight series, of which references in this book come from five series:

(1.7) Series 2. Correspondence, 1893–1918

Series 3. Notebooks, 1872–1910

Series 4. Working notes (including Folio Box 1 containing 23 folders)

Series 5. Drafts

Series 8. Publications and reprints, 1890–1910

Referencing each of these series needs to be done in a different way. In general, though, reference to particular documents requires the manuscript number (MS 8006), the Series number and the file or box number in which the particular items are stored.

Series 2 consists of 13 files of correspondence, stored in Boxes 1, 2, 3 and 4. We will reference items from this series by file number as NLA MS 8006/2, File 9.

Series 3 consists of 32 notebooks, stored by the NLA in three different boxes, Boxes 5, 6 and 7. In Table 1.1, we list the reference to these notebooks in the NLA Finding aid (as at April 2025), the library's permanent identifier for the scans that have been made of Series 3, and our proposed reference to these three notebooks.

Table 1.1: R.H. Mathews notebooks referred to in this book

Library's description in finding aid	Library's permanent identifier for scans	Our reference
Notebook marked "1", n.d. (Item 4.1) - Box 5 (MS 8006)	07.nla.obj-416712216 - Aboriginal languages of Victoria. Notebooks marked '1'	NLA MS 8006/3/4.1, Notebook 1
Notebook marked "6. Languages NSW Victoria [& some ?]", n.d. (Item 4.2) - Box 5 (MS 8006)	08.nla.obj-828724392 - Aboriginal languages of Victoria. Notebook marked '6'	NLA MS 8006/3/4.2, Notebook 6
Notebook titled "Languages, Initiation ceremonies, organisation etc of the [Aboriginal people]", c. 1902-1903 (Item 7.2) - Box 6 (MS 8006)	14.nla.obj-416712291 - Languages, initiation ceremonies, organisation, etc	NLA MS 8006/3/7.2, Languages, initiation &c

Source: National Library of Australia; adapted by authors.

Series 4 consists of seven files that are listed in the library's Finding aid and, in addition, 23 folders that until early 2025 were stored in 'Folio Box 1'. The whole of Series 4 is now stored in Boxes 8 and 9. We will reference items from among the first seven files as 'NLA MS 8006/4/1' through to 'NLA MS 8006/4/7'.

The contents of what was once referred to as 'the Folder' or 'the Folio' are now stored in Box 9 in three files, File 8a, File 8b and File 8c. When referencing items in this section of the manuscript, we will use the form 'NLA MS 8006/4, File 8a, Folder 1'.

Series 5 consists of eight files, stored in Boxes 10 to 12. These will be referenced in the same way as the seven files in Series 4, as 'NLA MS 8006/5/1' through to 'NLA MS 8006/5/8'.

Series 8 consists more than 589 numbered items, some of which are single offprints of articles by Mathews, and some of which are multiple articles stapled together. These 589 items were numbered by the NLA in 2001 and can be referred to as follows: 'NLA MS 8006/8/1' and so on. In many cases these items contain pencil annotations by Mathews on printed documents, and also contain insertions, often scraps of paper or printed flyers on the back of which Mathews made notes. If we are referring to an inserted item, we will add that detail.

1.6 About the linguistic analysis

Apart from the texts recorded and translated by Luise Hercus (section 2.2), for which the linguistic analysis was reliable, all the other texts required considerable linguistic analysis. Some texts, like many written down by A.W. Howitt, had word-by-word glossing (for example, Song of the bottle, section 5.2.1), but it was still regarded as desirable to compare Howitt's gloss with other sources in the language. To do this, the first stage is to regularise the spellings to a consistent system (see further below section 1.6.1), so that words can be more conveniently compared.

Many texts either have a continuous 'free translation' (for example, Wak Wak 'Earthquake song', written down by John Green, section 3.8) or have a summary of the context of the song, as with the Melbourne song, written down in the SLV MS 6290 (section 4.2.1).

Still more songs had no translation at all and in many cases we have not been able to suggest one. One example that had no translation in the original, but where we have suggested a translation is the Murranawa Corroborree song (section 3.4.2). Even at the point of submission of the first draft of the book, we were unable to offer any more possible analysis than is found in Box 1.2. However, in the process of revising the book, some more words were possibly identified in this song, and a much fuller analysis is given as example (1.8) (repeated from section 3.4.2).

Box 1.2: First draft analysis of the Murranawa Corroborree song

We have not been able to make a suggested analysis or translation of this song, save that **murrunawa** is the name of the song, and the word **yinga** may be the verb 'sing' and yana may be 'go'.

The final word **murruno** would surely have been built from the same root as the word **murrunawa**. It is possible that both of these words are built on a root regularised by Blake as **murrun** 'alive'.

There is clearly parallelism in the song, with a repetition of the phrase **gabo ming(g) o nerrim**.

Source: Authors.

(1.8) *Mur-run-a-wă,*

murrun-awa

PN

'The Murrunawa'

Kar-bo	*Ming-o*	*Ner-rim*	*Nurmbul*	*Port-bo*
gab-u	**ming(g)u**	**nyirrim**	**numbul**	**burt-bu**
DEM-ABL	beginning	long	upright	smoke-ABL?

'From there, the beginning, long and upright, by smoke??.'

Yeng-ă	*Yan-ner*	*Kar-bo*	*Ming-o*	*Ner-rim*
yinga	**yana**	**gab-u**	**ming(g)u**	**nyirrim**
sing	go	DEM-ABL	beginning	long

'Singing, going, from there, the beginning, a long (way?).'

Mur-runo

murrun-u

PN-?3SG

'The Murrunawa.'

Even though the analysis suggested here is plausible, there is no way of checking with experts in this song tradition to confirm that the assumptions made in this analysis are correct. In the case of this song and many others, there may be better analysis possible in future years. Therefore, readers should treat our suggested analyses as a starting point for future discussion about the meaning of these songs.

Furthermore, while this careful analysis of the meaning of the words of the songs is an important part of this book, it must be pointed out that we do not know the extent to which those who sang songs like the Murrunawa Corroboree song had a clear understanding of its meaning. The songs recorded by Luise Hercus in section 2.2 were all in everyday language and meant to be understood. A.W. Howitt also glossed a number of songs that suggest that his consultants did have a clear concept of the word-by-word meaning of the songs, but we cannot be sure how widely this applied.

Moreover, as pointed out by one of the anonymous reviewers of this book, 'there is also evidence that song, by design, has multiple parsings (linguistic glosses) and meanings. The possibility of holding multiple possible parsings produces an aesthetic result that is pleasurable and memorable; and it is one only possible in orally transmitted traditions (like songs)'. One example of multiple possible meanings is found in the second-last word of the Wak Wak or 'Earthquake song' (section 3.8). The last word written *karwen* is glossed 'thunder' but may also refer to the echidna, who was associated with thunder in Woiwurrung culture. The use of this word may be intentionally carrying multiple meanings, the echidna's underground movement being a 'thunder' in the ground.

Probably many of the songs can have multiple interpretations. To explore all of these was beyond the intention of this volume, but is something we hope will occur as members of these communities further explore and examine these texts.

There is no clear evidence of 'non-translatable songs' of the types found in Northern Australia and discussed by Apted (2010) and O'Keeffe (2016).

1.6.1 Regularisation

As already mentioned, given the considerable diversity in spelling of what we believe are the same word between different sources, in our linguistic analyses of the songs, we present a regularisation of the spellings that is always shown in bold typeface. The discussion in the previous section showed how the data are presented with original spellings in italics and regularised spellings in bold.

One of the major challenges for the regularisation process is that that there are no voicing contrasts in any of the languages of Victoria. In other words, there is no contrast between [b] and [p] for which either **b** or **p** could be written. Some of the earlier linguistic work such as Hercus (1986) and Blake (1991) used voiced stops, whereas some more recent work such as Hercus (1992) and Blake et al. (2011) used voiceless stops. In general, throughout this volume we have used voiceless stops in the regularisations, except for the Eastern Kulin data, in which we largely follow Blake (1991) in using voiced stops except in final position.

In most cases, we follow the principles of regularisation used in the linguistic accounts of the different languages – for example, Blake, Clark and Krishna-Pillay (1998) for Wathawurrung; Bowe and Morey (1999) for Yorta Yorta; and Blake and Reid (2002) for Dhudhuroa. The regularisation followed in the chapter on Paakantyi songs (Chapter 8) was that preferred by Luise Hercus. More detailed discussion of regularisation regarding the Kulin and Gippsland languages are detailed below.

1.6.1.1 Western Kulin

In the chapter on Western Kulin (Chapter 2), the regularisations of the language will be those following Hercus (1992) for Wemba-Wemba, using voiceless consonants throughout except where there is a homorganic nasal-stop cluster. Thus we spell words like **kima** 'here' and **ngaitya** 'distant' in the Letyi-Letyi song discussed in Examples (2.60) to (2.62) in section 2.10. On the other hand, the word for 'sleep' will be spelled as **kumba** rather than a possible **kumpa**. In addition, where a distinction was recorded by Hercus, we show the retroflex tap as **r** and the alveolar trill **rr**. Where we are unsure which rhotic is intended, we will capitalise it as **R**.

1.6.1.2 Eastern Kulin

In the case of the regularisations for Eastern Kulin, example (1.3), we will use voiced stops except in final position, following Blake (1991). For example, the word for 'woman' is spelled by Thomas as *baggōōk* and *baggōōrk* in the

'Suppostitious speech' (section 3.4.6) and as *pahgoork* by McCrae in the 'Dictated message' (section 3.7.3). It is clear that these are both the same word, and we have regularised this as **bagurrk**.

Blake's analysis was based on the findings of Luise Hercus (1986:160), who suggested that the following sounds were found in Woiwurrung, based on her recordings. (Note that we have updated the spelling in these tables to follow Blake (1991), and added the 'place of articulation row'.) This inventory of consonant sounds probably contains all the different sounds found in the languages of Victoria, save that in the case of many of them, the stops are written with voiceless symbols, **p, th, d, rt, tj/ty** and **k**. Some languages do not have all of these sounds (Table 1.2).

Table 1.2: Consonant sounds in Woiwurrung

Bilabial	Dental	Alveolar	Retroflex	Palatal	Velar
b	dh	d	rd	dj	g
m	nh	n	rn	ny	ng
–	–	rr	r	–	–
–	–	l	rl	–	–
w	–	–	–	y	–

Source: Authors, after Hercus (1986: 160); Blake (1991).

Following Blake (1991), stops will be shown voiced (**b, d, g** etc.), except in final position where they will be shown voiceless. Thus the word for 'child' will be **bubup**, as also in Blake (1991). In many cases, the nineteenth-century observers were unable to distinguish dental from alveolar and retroflex stops and nasals, and in particular did not usually distinguish the two rhotics, alveolar/trill **rr** and retroflex/tap **r**. In most cases we will write **rr**, though this does suggest that all rhotics are trills.

The palatal consonants, following Blake (1991), will be **dj/tj** (the latter in final position) and **-ny**. The palatal nasal is a problem to mark for English speakers, since it is not found in final position in English and so words like **wiiny** 'fire' might be mispronounced [wi:nɪ] rather than the correct [wi:ɲ]. Blake (1991) wrote final **-ñ** and in more recent work uses **-yn** to overcome this problem. We have chosen not to do this as it would obscure the fact that this is the same phoneme pronounced in the same way whether initial, medial or final.

Another issue is with the velar nasal **ng** when it occurs in the middle of a word. In English this can either be a single velar nasal, as in most pronunciations of *singer* [sɪŋə], or velar nasal plus stop **g** as in *finger* [fɪŋgə]. In many Australian languages these are different, so in Wemba-Wemba, **pangal** is the 'clever man, ritual specialist' and **pangga** is 'to dig'. In the case of many Woiwurrung words, we do not know which sound was used. For example, in the Melbourne song in State Library of Victoria, MS 6290 (see section 4.2.1), the word we believe means 'stumble' is spelled *mang-arrōōng*. We have regularised this as **mang(g)a-rung** to indicate the uncertainty of the pronunciation.

As for the vowels in the Eastern Kulin languages, following Blake (1991) there is good evidence based on Hercus (1986) for three vowels, **a**¸**i** and **u**, and in most cases our regularisations employ these. The status of the vowels **e** and **o** is not fully established.

As with other 'regularised' spellings used in this volume, we are not suggesting that these are necessarily appropriate as practical orthographies, although ongoing work between one of the authors (Morey) and members of the Wurundjeri community in Melbourne is using a spelling similar to this, but with the possible additional use of **oo** to indicate the /u/ vowel (high back rounded vowel).

1.6.1.3 Gippsland

The ongoing revitalisation of the language (Gunnai/Kŭrnai), also spelled Kanai, has not led to adoption of a standardised orthography at the time of writing (2021). We have chosen to base our regularisation, using voiceless stops on all occasions, on the PhD thesis of Corey Theatre (2024) and also following Morey (2016). Earlier drafts of the Gippsland chapter (Chapter 5) used voiced stops.

As with other regularisations in this volume, the work of Luise Hercus is relied upon, but also to some extent R.H. Mathews in various publications. Hercus's vocabulary (1986: 240) suggests that the language varieties of Gippsland had five vowels: /i/, /e/, /a/, /o/ and /u/, and two diphthongs /au/ and /ai/. The phoneme /o/, however, is only found in a small number of words, and never in the stressed initial syllable. Note that every word recorded by Hercus has stress on the initial syllable, and we would expect this to be the pattern for the language in general. In expressing the vowels, our regularisations accord with the system as found by Hercus.

Since the most important source for songs in Gippsland is A.W. Howitt, one of the challenges is what to make of the vowels that Howitt writes as *ū* and *ŭ*. We might expect the first to be /u/ and the latter /a/, but this does not always seem to be the case. For example, in the word *mūrriwŭnda* referring to the throwing stick (woomera), we might expect from Howitt's spelling that the word was pronounced **muRiwan**, but Fesl (1985: D4, no. 38)[8] regularised this as /mariwan/ based on spellings like *marrewun*. Unfortunately, we cannot be sure of what vowel the initial syllable of this word carried, but it is (tentatively) regularised as **maRiwan** here. The use of capital **R** here is used to indicate uncertainty of the rhotic.

There are a number of other issues with the regularisation. First, there would have been variation within the Gippsland languages, as for example for the 'elopement song', **yentjin(y)** and **yen(h)in(y)**. These words are spelled by Howitt as 'Yenjin or in the Nūlit (Braiaka) language Yennin' (SLV hw0404.pdf, p. 40). Theatre (pers. comm.) has recommended the use of final **-N** where we are uncertain of the place of articulation of the final nasal, which we believe in the case of these two words may be a palatal nasal **ny** rather than the alveolar **n**.

Second, Hercus (1986) recorded that the Gippsland language had both dental and alveolar stops, which we write **th** and **t** respectively. There is some evidence that Howitt did not hear this distinction, as we see with a word like 'possum' for which he wrote *wattun* and for which Mathews wrote *waddhan* and Hercus used **wad̲an** (where the underline stands for dental). We have usually therefore written **t(h)** for elements written *t, tt, d* or *dd* by Howitt.

As mentioned, following Theatre (2024) voiceless stops are used on all occasions including for homorganic nasal clusters. Thus the word for 'dance' is regularised as **muRantha**, an alternative of which is **muntha**. Regularised spellings from Fesl (1985) and Hercus's spellings of Gippsland words are also regularised in this system.

8 Fesl (1985) does not number the pages of Appendix IV that contains the full word list that she prepared. It is divided into sections based on semantic fields, A 'Body Parts and Products', B 'Human Classification' etc. Thus the reference Fesl (1985: D4, no. 38) refers to the fourth page of section D, and no. 38, the number of the word given by Fesl.

1.7 A note on Yuin songs

A number of songs in the Yuin languages were documented by R.H. Mathews (for example, the 'chants' presented with musical notation in Mathews 1904: 240) and A.W. Howitt (those of Umbara and Mragula (1904: 423–24), and also in State Library of Victoria MS Box 1053/3 (b), hw0404.pdf, p. 16 that includes the manuscript of Umbara's song containing at least one more word not found in the published version, *ya'ral* 'water').

George Augustus Robinson also wrote down one song that was 'composed by Al.mit.gong, an Omeo Black' (Box 1.3). For the sake of completeness we are including this in the book, though we are not in a position to offer any analysis. The transcriptions here are based on Clark (2000), as we have not seen the original manuscript.

Box 1.3: Song recorded by George Augustus Robinson

New song composed by Al.mit.gong, an Omeo Black: Min.yer.mar.or.then.nay Ar.de.ning.e.o; 1. Min.yer.mar.ar.then, 2. Ar.de.ningeo and communicated to the Twofold Black by the Maneroo tribe, 16 August '44.

Note: Robinson's original transcription of this has the letter 'H' crossed out in front of the word 'Ar.de.ning.e.o'. It is assumed that this indicates an initial velar nasal **ng-** sound.

Source: SLNSW A7086, part 3, p. 80; adapted by authors.

A detailed description of the song is found in Clark (2000, 4: 170–71), dated 14 August 1844. This transcription by Clark also includes references to the various drawings made by Robinson that illustrated this description (Box 1.4).

Box 1.4: Description of corroboree in George Augustus Robinson's journals

This evening went on shore in South Twofold Bay and witnessed a very interesting corroberry by the Maneroo Natives, they were on a visit to their coast friends to introduce it, was composed and arranged by Al.mil.gong, an Omeo Black from Tongio-mungie. There were about 60 or 70 Blacks present including the Twofold Bay. Number of whales were on shore. Dance commenced late on the finest acclivity of hill, singular effect, men had a broad streak of white round small of arm and legs, women were covered [Figure 8.8] with white spots and white down of birds, cheeks and round forehead, their bodies also reddened. Three sheets of bark had been prepared – painted [Figure 8.9] the centre one represents women the two outer – men. Three women danced with boughs beside and behind the back [...] each side alternately changed side. It lasted about an hour and half. The last was by men entirely. The dancing behind the [...] and beside it and the [...] as before and lastly two men danced face to face being opposite each other [Figure 8.10] resting and residing in a stooping pose and occasionally changing sides. The Twofold Bay, like the whites, were spectators. The words were 'mun.der.rer.nar' then 'nay.ar.de.ning.e.o' and had two [...]. To courtship these men sing a rather pleasing air [Figure 8.11]. Retired to the 'Wanderer' about 10, all went off peacable [...].

Note: We were not able to recheck this transcription against the manuscript.

Source: Clark (2000, 4: 170–71); SLNSW A 7040 part 1; adapted by authors.

There are thus two versions of the song text in Clark's transcriptions, presented as (1.9):

(1.9) *Min.yer.mar.or.*then.*nay Ar.de.ning.e.o*
mun.der.rer.nar then *nay.ar.de.ning.e.o*

Besold (2012, part A: 50, 53, 61, 63) lists sources for Yuin songs, to which can be added Lhotsky (1834). Troy and Barwick (2021) offer an analysis of the 'Song of the Women of the Menero Tribe' as documented by Lhotsky. The musical characteristics of the song correspond closely with those shown in this book, especially the occasional melodic leaps and the syllabic rhythmic organisation.

It may well be that some of these Yuin songs were brought in to neighbouring areas within Victoria and were performed and understood by Victorian language speakers in Gippsland and the north-east. However, apart from this one Robinson song, we have not included any of the Yuin songs in this volume.

1.8 The study of Indigenous songs in Australia

Interest in Indigenous songs by researchers, both in the colonial period and more recently, has a long history. In this volume, we present traditional songs recorded in the very first years of the colonial period, such as those recorded by William Thomas (section 3.4). More recently, academic studies of Indigenous songs and song traditions have become more detailed and sophisticated.

We do not propose to undertake a 'literature review' of these studies here, but will mention some of the important linguistic and musicological studies of songs that have been done over the last century. In Victoria, and nearby areas, the important academic sources for songs include Tindale (1941), Berndt and Berndt (1993) and Hercus (1986); these sources are referred to frequently in this volume and are treated as primary sources along with the various manuscripts and nineteenth-century publications that we have relied on. On the musicological side, the work of Alice Moyle (1968) and Cath Ellis (1962, 1964, 1966) are but a few of the pioneering works.

Dance ceremonies, or corroborees as they are usually referred to in the earlier sources, are discussed by many academic sources, including Donaldson (1987: 20) and Wild (1987: 105). The importance of song, their relation to the ancestors and their power is discussed in Strehlow (1971) and von Sturmer (1987). The question of whether a special song language was in use and the issue of apparently meaningless words in song is discussed by Merlan (1987), Garde (2006), Apted (2010) and O'Keeffe (2016). Sutton (1987) talks in more general terms about meaning. In some varieties of English spoken in Australia, the words 'ceremony' and 'corroboree' have different meanings, with 'ceremony' referring to serious performance genres and 'corroboree' referring primarily to entertainment genres. This distinction does not necessary apply to the nineteenth-century use of 'corroboree', which was used to refer to serious performance, for example the Neur-re-ung-ern-er dance (see section 3.1.5.2).

More recent work that brings together linguistics and musicology, and looks deeply at the traditions of songs in different parts of Australia includes Dixon and Koch (1996), Barwick (2005), Marett (2005), Barwick, Birch and Evans (2007), O'Keeffe (2010), Hercus and Koch (2017), Laughren, Turpin and Turner (2017), McDonald (2017) and the many works of Turpin including (2007a, 2007b) and Turpin and Koch (2008).

1.9 Coda: Why these songs are important

Bob Edwards, quoted in Griffiths (2018: 197) writing of Aboriginal heritage, observed that 'while the Aborigines are the rightful owners of this heritage, all Australians are beneficiaries of this unique cultural tradition'.

One way in which the wider Australian community, particularly in Victoria, might come to more deeply value Indigenous culture is to become aware both of the extraordinary richness and depth of cultural heritage that is represented by these songs, and also to come to understand and acknowledge more profoundly the massive loss of culture that had occurred in the nineteenth and twentieth centuries. Although there is a terrible story of destruction that underlies the story in this volume, we can surely celebrate the poetic and musical gems that are represented by the songs discussed here.

There may be, and we hope there are, additional texts and recordings that will come to light in the coming years; we hope that the songs and other texts in this book will soon need to be enhanced by others. We also hope that the wonderful sound recordings listed in example (1.2) can be brought out into the open so that the whole community, Indigenous and non-Indigenous, can hear for themselves the extent of the extraordinary cultural heritage that is represented in this volume.

2

Western Kulin songs

2.1 Introduction

A wonderfully rich set of songs recorded by Luise Hercus from the late Stan Day between 1962 and 1966 forms the core of this collection of texts in a range of Western Kulin languages.

The various Western Kulin languages are described by Blake and Reid (1998: 4) as 'a kind of mega-language that covered an extensive area in Western Victoria from North of the Murray to Hamilton and nearly to Ballarat in the south'. This group includes the following language varieties:

Wemba-Perapa (including Wemba-Wemba and Perapa-Perapa)
Nari-Nari (see Hercus 1986: 154)
Werkaya (the Wimmera language)
Mathi-Mathi
Letyi-Letyi
Wati-Wati (Swan Hill) (including Pura-Pura)
Wati-Wati (Piangil) (probably including Weki-Weki)
Tjapwurrung
Djadjawurrung
Ngarket (spoken in South Australia).

In spelling the names of languages, we are following the spellings in recent publications, such as Blake and Reid (1998) and Blake et al. (2011), or spellings that are commonly used by communities.

Languages of the Western Kulin were the only ones that still had fluent native speakers when Luise Hercus commenced her work in 1962. The three languages that Hercus was able to document in detail were Wemba-Wemba, Werkaya and Mathi-Mathi.

Wemba-Wemba is the most deeply studied of these varieties (Hercus 1986, 1992). Hercus also taped a significant number of songs, mostly sung by the late Stan Day, which are discussed in section 2.2.

Werkaya language is also examined in detail in Hercus (1986). She wrote that '[t]he speakers of Weṛgaia and several smaller associated groups formed the Wudjubalug group of tribes,[1] called "Wotjobaluk" by Howitt (1904: 55)'. Unfortunately there were no songs collected by Hercus in Werkaya. The songs from the Wimmera area that we have are songs documented by Howitt (see section 2.3), some of which seem to have been recorded on two wax cylinders, now held at Museums Victoria, which are said to have songs sung by Sergeant Major. In addition, a single song was written down in several versions by various missionaries, the Keledia song (see section 2.5). A short song recorded by R.H. Mathews, probably in Tjapwurrung, is presented in section 2.7.

Mathi-Mathi language was also described in detail in Hercus (1986), and forms a group with Letyi-Letyi and two varieties both named Wati-Wati (or similar) in early sources. These four languages are described in detail in Blake et al. (2011). There are three songs recorded for these languages: two Mathi-Mathi songs sung by Mary Moore and recorded on audio tape by Luise Hercus (see section 2.9), and a Letyi-Letyi song documented by Berndt and Berndt (see section 2.10), for which any sound recording (if in existence) is presently not available.

Of the other Western Kulin languages, only two short songs remain. One is Tjapwurrung, written down by Dawson (1881) (see section 2.11), and the second is in a language, apparently Western Kulin, termed Marditjali by Tindale (1941) (see section 2.12).

From Djadjawurrung, which Blake treats in two varieties, Eastern and Western, there are apparently no surviving songs, although Sergeant Major, who was Djadjawurrung, appears to have been the informant for the Initiation song (see section 2.3.3), which may not be in the Western Kulin language.

1 In her 1986 volume, Hercus used voiced stops to spell all words; but later changed her practice towards using voiceless stops, spelling these two words as Werkaya and Wutjubaluk respectively.

As in other parts of Victoria, singing was used in corroborees and in a range of healing rituals and making spells. Howitt (1904: 365) records the making of spells in the Wimmera:

> In the Jupagalk tribe the method was to tie the thing, or fragment which had belonged to, or been touched by, the intended victim, to the end of a digging-stick, by a piece of cord. This was stuck in the ground in front of a fire; and as it swung there, the Bangal sang over it till it fell, which was a sign that the spell was complete.

The regularisation of the word for 'doctor' or 'clever man', given as 'medicine man' in Howitt (1904), is **pangal** (see Hercus 1986: 198 for this word). An example of a song that was almost certainly sung by a **pangal** is the Song for regaining consciousness after a kidney fat attack (see section 2.3.1), and perhaps also the song written by R.H. Mathews (section 2.7).

Dance ceremonies, more commonly referred to as corroborees in the nineteenth century, were frequently performed throughout Victoria in the early to mid-nineteenth century, and some of these were documented. One such example is the corroboree reported in *The Empire*, published in Sydney on 24 April 1869. This description includes mention of some musical instruments (see Table 2.2 in section 2.1.2). Another corroboree that is documented in detail was that held at the Bora ceremony of the *Wathi-wathi*, presumably the Wati-Wati (Piangil), where an additional musical instrument was mentioned (Cameron 1884).[2] Cahir (2012) also has numerous references to corroborees in the Goldfields areas.

Traditional songs continued to be used, for example on pastoral properties, until late in the nineteenth century. For example, at Corrong Station near Hay (run by the Tyson family) when the manager was leaving in 1891 the Aboriginal station workers sang 'a number of native songs' as part of a farewell gathering. Corrrong is a Kulin language word meaning 'big' (**kurrung** in Werkaya), so given that this event was on land where the Kulin language Nari-Nari, which was close to Werkaya and Wemba-Wemba, was spoken, it is reasonable to assume that these songs may have been in a Western Kulin language.

2 Cameron (1884: 359) writes: 'During this operation one of the tribe, who is concealed in the scrub at some distance, whirls the humming instrument round his head. This instrument is supposed to have a wonderful magic influence. By the Wathi-wathi it is called Kalari.' He adds the note 'The Ta-ta-thi call it Kalk, that is to say, word'. This use of 'word' is a misprint for 'wood'.

2.1.1 The songsters

The earliest example of a song documented in a Western Kulin language was taken down in written form by Moravian Missionary F.W. Spieseke at Ebenezer Mission on the Wimmera River in north-west Victoria in 1859. The song itself, as discussed in section 2.5, became known as 'Keledia' and came from a young man named 'Pepper'. Spieseke had been seeking songs from the mission residents that showed spiritual elements dating from before the coming of Europeans, and while he enquired widely, it appears that younger members of the community such as Pepper, his brother Charly Charly and another young man Boney were more open to discussion. As these young men became baptised 'Native Evangelists', known respectively as Nathanael and Philip Pepper and Daniel, references to traditional song became rarer in mission records. At the same time, the missionaries actively opposed the performance of 'corroboree' rituals on the mission. Traditional songs, when separated from ritual, persisted on the mission alongside religious songs in English. Traditional songs about situations new to the community were also created including one about oxen and policemen by a man called Winkel who had first guided the Moravians to the mission site.[3] Ritual practice persisted to some extent even on the mission, as shown by the singing of a 'death-song' when Br Hagenauer left Ebenezer for Gippsland. The text of this song was not written down by the Moravian missionaries (United Brethren in Christ 1861: 261).[4]

In other parts of the north-west plains away from the mission traditional practices continued and were noted by Europeans but rarely written on in any depth. An exception to the general indifference comes in an account from 1869 of a 'corroboree' on the Wimmera River sent in to the *Geelong Register* and published in *The Empire* on 24 April 1869,[5] which gave both European and 'native' names for most participants and described events. The ritual was led by King Tom (Indigenous name Brickminyarimin) who played on the 'karik mune', with his wife Wannicha singing and she and other

3 The reference to Winkel composing songs comes from Felicity Jensz's report to the Victorian Aboriginal Corporation for Languages (Jensz 2001: 19). We have not yet found any copy of the texts of Winkel's songs.

4 Brother Job Francis from Ebenezer on 10 December 1861, *Periodical Accounts relating to the Missions of the church of the United Brethren established among the Heathen*, vol. 24, 1861, 261, p. 303 of PDF, dai.mun.ca/pdfs/cns_permorv/MissionsofUnitedBrethren_V24_1861.pdf.

5 See Advertising, *Empire*, 24 April 1869, 3, accessed 30 April 2019, trove.nla.gov.au/newspaper/page/5695181. The section of interest commences: 'A correspondent writing from the Wimera [sic] River to the Geelong Register …'. This article is not yet available transcribed.

women providing percussion on the 'bilppar' (see further section 2.1.2). This is a rare instance of a song sung by a woman accompanying a dance, though the direction of events is still done by her husband and other older men. The dancers were said to be from 'Banyenong, Mt Jeffcott, Morton Plains' though others listed were local to the Wimmera River. While in many ways destructive, the pastoral economy did allow Aboriginal people, including songsters, to move across the country and continue to perform traditional rituals.

Older generation of songsters

Morton Plains Bobby

Though not listed among the 1869 performers, Morton Plains Bobby appears to have been the main consultant for Howitt's three songs in section 2.3. The Morton Plains pastoral region referred to the district between Lake Buloke and Lake Tyrell, and the local dialect of Werkaya (Wimmera) language was known as **Wutyupalak** (spelled Wotjobaluk by Howitt 1904), a different dialect from the **Tyatyala** described most fully by Hercus (1986). Hercus did mention this dialect, noting that one feature was the presence of initial consonant clusters such as **kr-**, which is exemplified in the songs (see section 2.3.1). Bobby, as he was also known, died at Ebenezer Mission in 1896,[6] at around 70 years of age, after having followed younger members of his community there early in 1884 (Ryan 1999).

While he was not a fully initiated man, and said that he was not a **pangal** (see section 2.1), he held deep cultural knowledge relating to much of north-west Victoria, including an important creation story about a pine tree reaching to the sky (recorded by Howitt, Museums Victoria XM 761, p. 66). He visited Howitt with Donald Cameron at Gippsland in 1884, at which time Howitt gave him a message stick and asked what he would do with it. Bobby listed the men he would send it out to, over a much wider area than that involved in the 1869 gathering, going as far south as Lake Condah and west as far as Tatiara (MV XM 746). While the gathering discussed by Howitt and Bobby may have been intended as a major event, it is also likely that the requisite number of learned people had been much reduced over that 15-year period, necessitating a wider 'call'.

6 Victorian Death Certificate 1896/5653.

Sergeant Major

According to Diane Barwick (1984), Sergeant Major (c. 1838–1903) was born at Inglewood[7] on the Loddon but was a 'member of his father's Wangaro-bulluk clan of Jajowrong (Djadjawurrung) at Marr near St Arnaud, adjoining the Wotjoballaiuk of the Wimmera from which his mother and paternal grandmother came'.

His Djadjawurrung clan name was spelled as *Worng-arra-gerrar* in Smyth (1878, 1: 41) and described as 'a rather numerous (tribe)' whose clan name means 'leaves of the stringybark'. This name includes the word for 'leaf' recorded by Hercus (1986) as **kirra**.[8] The Djadjawurrung word for 'stringybark' is recorded by Parker (in Smyth 1878, 2: 160) as *Wong-hurra*, and it is likely the same word was used in the Wimmera. This clan naming fits with both the local flora and regional naming practices as seen, for instance, in the west Wimmera clan name *kera-bial* 'leaves of the redgum'.

Sergeant Major spent little time at missions as a younger man and was associated with Wotjoballuk men of similar age, generally on their country. He had transferred to Coranderrk by 1894 when he married Jemima Kilmore[9] and remained there till his death[10] in 1904.

Donald Cameron

Donald Cameron, who was also born on Morton Plains, in 1850, was likely an additional informant for the Keledia song (section 2.5). He spent some years at Ebenezer as did a number of his siblings while their parents Tullum and Kitty pursued a more traditional lifestyle. Following conversion to Christianity, Donald moved as an assistant to Ramahyuck Mission in Gippsland where he married Elizabeth Flowers, a fellow Christian convert from King George's Sound, Western Australia, in 1868. Apart from periods on home country, particularly at Ebenezer, Donald spent the bulk of his life in Gippsland. In addition to his work at Ramahyuck he also spent time at Lake Tyers where John Bulmer noted cultural material from him and elsewhere in Gippsland following seasonal pastoral work. In the Howitt papers (State Library of Victoria MS Box 1053/5 (c), hw0414.pdf, p. 3), it states that 'Donald Cameron = Ngouri Warmin' adding that 'Warmin = Back'. This may be his traditional name.

7 Note that both his marriage and death certificates give his birthplace as Donald District.

8 Spelled in the original 1986 book as **gira**.

9 Victorian Marriage Certificate 1894/3216. It is assumed that this was not his first marriage.

10 Victorian Death Certificate 1904/1669.

Songsters from the time of Luise Hercus

In her general introduction to the Wemba-Wemba songs, Hercus wrote (1986: 61):

> All the songs analysed here were sung by Mr Stanley Day. He had learnt them from his grandfather Marəḍ (David Taylor). Marəḍ, like Stanley Day, was apparently a brilliant singer, but it was said of him **gadjina biṛgin** *he could not make any songs*. The author of most of the songs, particularly the more traditional ones, was a very old man (by the turn of the century), known only as 'Tommy'. He was blind and cared for by the Taylor family, but was not immediately related. The songs were composed mainly in the 1890s, but some have earlier origins.
>
> A few songs were composed by Marəḍ's brother Njaui *Sun*, 'Grandfather' Bob Taylor. Njaui's son, 'Uncle' Johnny Taylor, born in 1881, remembered a song of Njaui other than those discussed here: it could not be analysed sufficiently to be included. The subject matter was typically transitional as in Njaui's other songs: the author had been rabbiting and had hung up all his scalps on a line to dry, but had forgotten to tie up his dogs, and when he looked in the morning all the scalps had gone, and so he made up a song about it. The songs as sung by both Stanley Day and 'Uncle' Johnny Taylor were not influenced by European music. Several other informants recalled songs, but inadequately. Mr Stanley Day had heard ritual singing, but had never been taught any, and he recalled that in the old days the women had been enthusiastic singers and had their own songs. The songs translated here, therefore, represent a negligible fragment of the original wealth of Wembawemba music and literature.
>
> The songs, except 3 and 9 (and the swearing songs) consist of only one 'verse' of poetry which was always sung twice.

In the 1990s, Luise Hercus adopted a new spelling for the Wemba-Wemba language, followed in this publication, whereby she spelled the name of Stan Day's grandfather David Taylor as **Marrərt** (replacing Marəḍ) and his brother Bob Taylor as **Nyawi** (replacing Njaui). The Taylor brothers and other members of their extended family were central to the operation of Tulla and associated stations. The Wragge family took up the lease of Tulla and surrounding stations in the early 1870s, and it was here that presumably many of the songs that Stan Day sang were composed, for instance 'Shearing on Tulla Station' (see section 2.2.5).

Marrərt (David Taylor) had been born around the late 1850s and died in July 1929 aged 70.[11] His brother **Nyawi**, Robert (Bob) Taylor, was older, having been born around 1850.[12] **Nyawi**'s son, Johnny Taylor (1881–1970),[13] was the singer of a traditional song about the dingo that we have been able to partially analyse (see section 2.2.13).

Stan Day (1894[14]–1969) was the son of **Marrərt**'s daughter Maria (1872–1952). Late in her life, when listening again to Stan Day's recordings, Luise Hercus expressed her enthusiastic admiration of his great skill and expertise, noting that in many songs Stan Day had to sing so many notes in a row, but then needed to take a breath; as a younger man he would have managed the whole song.[15] Further information about Stan Day is given in section 2.2.

Jack Brown died in 1933[16] and was younger than **Marrərt** and **Nyawi**, probably born in the 1860s. Luise Hercus's note on him is reproduced in section 2.2.6.1.

Silvia Murray, also known as Tibby Clayton, was the daughter of a Wiradjuri man who learned songs from Johnny Taylor. The short songs that she sang are presented in sections 2.2.14 and 2.2.15.

Nancy Egan (1895–1965), younger sister of Stan Day, was the second major language consultant for the Wemba-Wemba language. She sang a short hymn for Luise Hercus that we have included in this volume (see section 2.2.16).

Mary Moore originally came from Ebenezer and was of Werkaya descent, but she spent a lot of her time at Balranald and married a Mathi-Mathi man, Reginald Wise. She sang two songs that are discussed below in section 2.9.

John Mack was a Letyi-Letyi man who is described in Berndt and Berndt (1993) as 'John Mack of the Munpul', which is one of the Hattah Lakes to the south-east of Mildura. John Mack's song is discussed in section 2.10.

11 New South Wales Death Certificate, NSW 1929/9301.

12 His New South Wales Death Certificate, NSW 1915/7676, states that he died in 1915 aged about 65.

13 The birth date is that given in Hercus (1986).

14 In the cemetery where he is buried, his year of birth is given as 1890.

15 Luise Hercus, pers. comm. to Stephen Morey.

16 New South Wales Death Certificate, NSW 1933/8484. In the Moonacullah Ration Book for 1920 his age was given as 43 (AIATSIS MS 5056).

His wife was the noted tradition bearer and singer Pinkie Mack, who was said to be able to sing the river from Swan Hill to the mouth of the Murray; in other words, she had knowledge of all the languages along that stretch of the river. She was one of the major consultants for Berndt and Berndt (1993) and sang several of the songs that are discussed in this volume, those in the Murray River languages (see section 12.3) as well as the Up River initiation song that is discussed below in section 14.1.

Milerum (1869–1941), shearer and Aboriginal ethnologist, also known as Clarence Long, was a member of the Tanganekald tribe (part of the Ngarrinyeri), and was a principal informant for both Norman Tindale and the Berndts. He sang songs in a range of languages discussed in this book, and there is detailed biography of him, written by Norman Tindale, in the *Australian Dictionary of Biography*.[17] Tindale described him as 'an anthropologist in his own right'. His recordings are the finest surviving of the languages of south-eastern Australia. He sang several of the Bunganditj songs presented in section 6.2, as well as the Marditjali song in section 2.12.

2.1.2 Musical terminology in Western Kulin languages

The richest data on musical terminology (metalanguage) that we have for any of the Victorian languages were recorded by Hercus for Wemba-Wemba (1986, 1992). Words related to the songs are listed in Table 2.1.

Table 2.1: Glossary of words relating to singing in Wemba-Wemba

Wemba-Wemba word	Gloss
pilp	drum, made from wood (n) (cf. **pilpa** 'to bang'); see Table 2.2 for reference to a percussion instrument called *Bilparr*
malka-pula	timesticks (two) (n); these were beaten together (and not against the ground) and were used only by men. Wembawemba women usually clapped in accompaniment to the men's singing or to their own singing
Marrərt	name of David Taylor, grandfather of the Day family and well-known for his knowledge of songs and histories
nyarrəpa, nyarrəpila	to sing, to chant a curse, to point the bone (V cont tr)

17 Norman B. Tindale, 'Milerum (1869–1941)', *Australian Dictionary of Biography*, National Centre of Biography, The Australian National University, adb.anu.edu.au/biography/milerum-7572, published first in hardcopy 1986, accessed online 30 April 2019.

Wemba-Wemba word	Gloss
pirka	to make up a song about somebody (vtr), to compose a song; **pirkak kinyam peng!** make up a song about this man!, **katyina pirkin** 'could not compose a song' – said of Marrərt
warrang-warrang	songs, corroboree (n)
woyi	song (n)

Source: Hercus (1992); adapted by authors.

Song language could vary slightly from spoken language. Hercus records two words, **nyet** 'I' and **perəpurung** 'if not', that were Perəpaperəpa words not used in everyday Wemba-Wemba but found in songs. The late Stan Day regarded Perəpaperəpa as being the same as Wemba-Wemba, except for a small number of words of which these are two examples.

Table 2.2 lists words recorded in Werkaya relating to songs and dancing. In Hercus (1986) there is only one word, **pangal** 'clever man', and no words for songs or dances.

Table 2.2: Glossary of words relating to singing in Werkaya

Werkaya word/sentence	Gloss
pangal	doctor, clever man
pilpa	*bilparr*: percussion instrument, mentioned in *The Empire* on 24 April 1869, page 3 as being similar to 'a folded opossum rug as on a tambourin', played by women
karrik mune	*karik mune*, an instrument played by King Tom, mentioned in *The Empire* on 24 April 1869, page 3

Source: Authors.

Note that some of the same musical instruments are also referred to in the Charles Officer papers (MV XM 1530),[18] see examples (2.1.4) and (2.1.5) below.

Table 2.3 lists words and phrases relating to songs and dancing from the Mathi group of languages:

18 Held at Museums Victoria; these papers relate to Mount Talbot.

Table 2.3: Glossary of words relating to singing in the Mathi group of languages

Word/ sentence	Gloss	Variety	Sources (see Blake et al. 2011 for details of the sources)
ngúinggilàtha	to hum a song (preparatory to singing it)	Mathi-Mathi	–
ngúndu	ceremonial song	Mathi-Mathi	–
pupand(j)eRi	instrument made of the fur of opossums twisted into yarn, plaited into a circular form, and fixed on a piece of thin flat wood	Wati-Wati (Piangil)	Cameron (1884)
tyawi(l)	song	Wati-Wati (Swan Hill)	*tchowie*; *tchowiel* (Beveridge)
wángilàtha, wáinggilàtha	sing	Mathi-Mathi	–
wángu	song	Mathi-Mathi	–
waRanga	sing	Wati-Wati (Swan Hill)	*warranga* (Beveridge), *warangwarane* (Mathew)
wàrrípa	dance	Mathi-Mathi	–
wiRiwa, wiRipa	dance	Wati-Wati (Swan Hill)	*wirrewa*, *wirriwa* (Beveridge)
wúigatha	sing and dance in ceremony	Mathi-Mathi	–
yarkuwi	sing	Wati-Wati (Piangil)	*yarkoi*, *yarcooie* (Davey)

Source: Authors.

The Mathi-Mathi words **ngúinggilàtha** 'hum a song' and **wáinggilàtha** 'sing' are built on the roots **ngúndu** 'ceremonial song' and **wángu** 'song' respectively, with the addition of two morphemes, **-ila** 'frequentative, continuative' and **-tha** 'stem forming suffix' (Blake et al. 2011: 102–4). The frequentative suffix is also shown in combination with the root for singing in Tjapwurrung (see Table 2.4), in Djadjawurrung in the sentences recorded by Parker (see example 2.2) and in Thomas's dialogue (see example 2.7).

For the Tjapwurrung language, Dawson (1881) records a range of words, in the Western Kulin language and in two Warrnambool varieties. The form of the word 'sing' in Tjapwurrung is based on a root **yinga-,** similar to Eastern Kulin (see section 3.1.8). The form of the word for song also includes the frequentative/continuative suffix **-ila**.

Table 2.4: Glossary of words relating to singing and dancing in the languages of the south-west of Victoria

English	Chaap wurrong (broad lip)	Regularised spelling Blake (2019)	Kuurn kopan noot (small lip)	Peek whurrong (kelp lip)
Dance, name of	Yappan nena	**yapan-**	Karweean	Kurween
Dance, to dance	Yappan neitch	**yapanyayt**	Karweean neut	Kurween
Sing	Yinglang	**yingila-ng**	Lærpeean	Lærpeen
Song, a song	Ying'elang	–	Lirpeean	Lirpeen
Stick for beating time	Tirn Tirn	**tirn tirn**	Popok	Popok

Source: From Dawson (1881); adapted by authors.

Blake (2019) also reports that George Augustus Robinson recorded the form *woripe e wot* for 'dance' for Glenelg (Clark 2002: 214), regularised with a root **waRipa**. The form is also found in Mathi-Mathi (see Table 2.3), and in the Charles Officer papers (MV XM 1530). The Officer papers contain a number of sentences relating to dancing, which are given below in Box 2.1. Officer's transcriptions[19] employ what is known as the 'ethnical alphabet' but many of the symbols are not very clear, especially those for the vowels.

Box 2.1: Sentences relating to music and dance in the Officer papers

Wɸrɛpinyun	cq?ɯŋ	I will dance tonight.
		I danced.
Wɸrɛpin	Harry	Harry danced.
Wɸrɛpin	uŋaloŋ	I danced with Harry.
Bilb pelen	Baŋbaŋgω	The lubras struck the *bilb*.
Tqrcarɩen	mɯnω	They the men struck the *mɯr*.
Wɸrepin-yɩ?	winip-p ɯinyuŋ	bɸron
They will	begin dancing	as soon as dark.

Source: Officer papers MV XM 1530; adapted by authors.

19 Transcription by Edward Ryan. Some of the symbols used in this table are representations of non-standard symbols, that were used in *The Ethnical Alphabet, or Alphabet of Nations*, that was probably sent to Officer by Redmond Barry in the 1860s. The first version of *The Ethnical Alphabet* appears to have been published in Ellis (1848).

Our tentative analysis of these is presented in examples below (2.1.1–2.1.6):

(2.1.1)

	Wφrεpinyun	*cqʔuŋ*
	I will dance tonight	
	waRipa-iny-an	**kawang**?
	dance-FUT-1SG	?
	'I will dance …'	

(2.1.2)

	Wφrεpin	*Harry*
	Harry danced	
	waRipa-in	**Harry**
	dance-PST	PN
	'Harry danced.'	

(2.1.3)

Wφrεpin uŋaloŋ
I danced with Harry
waRipa-in-angalang
dance-PST-1DL.EXCL
'We two (excl.) danced.' / 'I danced with him.'

(2.1.4)

Bilb	*pelen*	*Baŋbaŋgꝏ*
The lubras struck the bilb		
pilp(a)	**pila-in**	**bangbang-gu**
percussion instrument	strike?-PST	woman-ERG
'The women struck the *pilpa*.'		

(2.1.5)

Tqrcari̯en	*munꝏ*
They the men struck the mur	
taka-rray-in	**muno**
strike-?-PST	musical instrument
'(They) struck the *muno*.'	

(2.1.6)

Wφrepin-yi̯ʔ	*winip-p winyuŋ*	*bφron*
They will	*begin dancing*	*as soon as dark*
waRipa-iny	**winip winyung**	**purony-u**
dance-FUT	?	night-LOC
'They will dance … at night.'		

Some Djadjawurrung forms, with suggested regularisations based on Blake (2019), are presented in Table 2.5:

Table 2.5: Glossary of words relating to singing in Djadjawurrung

English	Djadjawurrung (west)		Djadjawurrung (east)	
dance	*yap pen nite* 'big corroboree' (garp); *yah-pet-nyah* (th)	**yapenya**	*yepenyun* (j)	**yapenya**
dance	*tuc er rer mite* 'little corroboree' (garp)	**takaRamayt**	–	–
dance	–	–	*kulng ga long* 'dancing' (j)	**kalng(ga)-**
sing	*yingy-lang* (th), *yayng-a-lay* (th), *ying en er lite* (garp)	**yinga-**	–	–

Source: From Blake (2019); adapted by authors.

The sources for the original spellings listed in Table 2.5 are as follows (Blake 2019):

th	Ballarat List. MS 6290 La Trobe Library, Melbourne.[20]
garp	Robinson, G.A. Grampians, Pyrenees, Mt Misery. Clark ed.: 134–57.
j	Parker, E.S. Jajawrong vocabulary. Smyth II:167–9.

There is also a short dialogue from Joseph Parker, which relates to the Eastern variety of Djadjawurrung, and this is presented as Box 2.2:

Box 2.2: Sentences from Joseph Parker

Ghee yuck-en dayne knar wharr knar kin jhal-la gee
Tell us what you saw yesterday

Knar-kin-un kulng ga long knam nu geetch goork.
Saw me dancing white women.

Source: From Smyth (1878, 2: 165); adapted by authors.

This is analysed in (2.2):

(2.2)	*Ghee yuck-en*	*dayne*	knar	wharr	knar kin	jhal-la gee
	Tell us what you saw yesterday					
	kiya-k-an	**thayn?**	**nya?**	**warr**	**ngak-in**	**tyaliki**
	speak-IMP-1SG?	?	what	2SG	see-PST	yesterday
	'Tell me … what you say yesterday.'					

20 Earlier believed to be the work of William Thomas, hence Blake used the abbreviation 'th'. This manuscript is now known not to have been written by Thomas, see section 1.5.2 for a detailed discussion.

Knar-kin-un	*kulng ga long*	*knam nu geetch goork*
Saw me dancing white women		
ngak-in-an	**kalng(g)a-ila-ang**	**ngamukiyt kurrk**
see-PST-1SG	dance-FREQ-PRES.PART	white.woman
'I saw the white women dancing.'		

This word for dance, which we regularise as **kalng(g)a**, is related to a Tjapwurrung form recorded by Dawson as *kulngaelang* 'fun' (Blake 2019). This suggests that the kind of dance referred to in these sentences was one for enjoyment, rather than a ritual.

2.1.2.1 Corroboirè dialogue from Ballarat

The compiler of SLV MS 6290 recorded, on page 228, a simple dialogue about 'Corroboirè' in the Ballarat language (Box 2.3), a source for the Western variety of Djadjawurrung (Blake 2019). A second version of this dialogue is found in the Royal Anthropological Institute of Great Britain and Ireland (RAIGBI) MS 38, pp. 131–32.

Box 2.3: Dialogue in the Ballarat dialect

Put on your pipe clay	Bēēkamil-yang-ōō
Get ready to begin	Windŷap-men
Now girls make a fire	Dōōrōī-bŭllaga-wirrika-wēē
Now, women, sit down	Balgŏt-dyee-waht-doort-doo-ee-ballŭk
You must sing	Windyak-min-yāyng-a-lay

Source: SLV MS 6290, p. 228; adapted by authors.

Our analysis of the first of these sentences is given in (2.3):

(2.3) *Put on your pipe clay*

Bēēkamil-yang-ōō

pik-am-il-angu(rr)

clay-FORM-REFL-1PL.INCL

'(Let) us put the clay on ourselves.'

Joseph Parker recorded *bee-kar-mil-leen* 'paint'. Blake (2019) suggested that **-ila** acted as a reflexive in Tjapwurrung and Djadjawurrung, stating:

> In Wergaya there is a suffix **ila** which Hercus reports as having a 'weak frequentative or continuative meaning' (Hercus 1986:91). This suffix can be found in Tjapwurrung and Djadjawurrung where it marks the reflexive. **Mutja** is 'to take' and **mutjila** is 'to marry', presumable 'take one another'. Thomas records a verb **nyurtila** 'to hide oneself', 'to lurk'. In Wergaya **nyurta** is a transitive verb meaning 'to hide something'. There is a verb **pikamila** 'to paint oneself for corroboree', which is based on **pik** 'clay', probably with a stem **pikama**.

Our analysis follows this, with the suffix **-ma** forming a verbal stem from the noun, with meaning 'put on or paint on clay'. However, in the analysis of this sentence recorded as Bacchus Marsh (Wathawurrung) language, example (4.1) in section 4.1.2 below, we point out that **-mili** is a verbal formative in Wathawurrung (Blake, Clark and Krishna-Pillay 1998: 90), found on a range of verbs.

Luise Hercus records that Mrs Jackson Stuart (Stewart)[21] always used the word *raddle* for 'red ochre', a word that originates in the shearing sheds, as in 'you raddle a sheep to mark it'.

Our analysis of the second sentence is given in (2.4):

(2.4) *Get ready to begin*

Windŷap-men

windya-ap **min**

WH-PURP EMPH

'(Are we) indeed for it, or what?'

This sentence consists of three morphemes, a WH- word, a purposive and an emphatic, which together have the meaning 'get ready' or 'let us be ready'. The translation we have given reflects both the intended overall meaning and the morphemes that make up this phrase.

21 Hercus (1986) consistently spells her family name as 'Stuart', her family uses the spelling 'Stewart'.

Our analysis of the third sentence is given in (2.5):

(2.5) *Now girls make a fire*
Dōōrōī-bŭllaga-wirrika-wēē
turoi **palak-a** **wiRka** wi
woman group-CASE? light fire
'Woman, make a fire.'

This sentence contains a bare root imperative, **wiRka** 'light a fire', and a possible case marker on the noun phrase **turoi palak** 'group of women'. Note that the form that has been regularised here as **palak** is the same as the Eastern Kulin word regularised as **buluk** and **baluk** by Blake (1991), also found throughout Western Kulin as in the tribal name Wotjobaluk. It means 'group' or 'mob'. It could be attached to words for 'man' and mean 'a group of men'.

Our analysis of the fourth sentence is given in (2.6):

(2.6) *Now, women, sit down*
Balgŏt-dyee-waht-doort-doo-ee-ballŭk
palku-tyi **wat** **turoi** **palak**
sit-IMP 2PL woman group
'Group of women, you should sit.'

Robinson (Clark 2000, 2: 133) writes *pal.go.rap* 'sit down' in the 'Vocabulary of the native language at the Grampians and Pyrenees, commencing July 1841, Mt William and Larnerjeering'.

Our analysis of the last sentence is given in (2.7):

(2.7) *You must sing*
Windyak-min-yāyng-a-lay
windya-k **min** **ying-ila-i**
WH-? EMPH sing-FREQ-IMP
'(You) should sing indeed!'

2.1.2.2 The calls of birds as represented in language

There are a couple of examples of words relating what are described in the sources as the songs and dances of birds. For example, Hercus (1992) writes the following, as part of the definition of the Wemba-Wemba word **partema** 'to wrestle':

> **partaminyangana prrityak**[22] 'I'll wrestle (with) you on the bare ground'. This is the interpretation of the song of the willie wagtail [i.e. an interpretation of the sound the bird makes], particularly when it calls in the evening time. according to the traditional story he was a cheeky fellow who challenged everybody to fight with him.

The word **partema** is related to the Gunditjmara (Warrnambool) word **parta** 'hit', which has been used in some contemporary songs in Indigenous languages discussed in Theatre (2018). Corey Theatre (pers. comm.) has raised the possibility of a connection between this phrase and traditional stories, such as the story of Bram brothers, recorded by R.H. Mathews (NLA MS 8006/3/4.1, Notebook 1), in which the willy wagtail is fighting with other animals. The connection between this Wemba-Wemba phrase and the Bram brothers story will require further research.

Dawson also records three words relating to birds, one a dance and two songs (Table 2.6). The first two words both contain the frequentative **-ila** and a final **-ang**, which may be a present participle. (See the discussion in Hercus 1986: 89 in Werkaya, where this form is described as a continuative participle.)

Table 2.6: Glossary of words relating to birds in the languages of the south-west of Victoria

English	Chaap wurrong (broad lip)	Blake's regularisation
Dance of gigantic crane	Gnuyeelang	**nguyilang**
Song of bird	G'narre pillang	**ngaRipilang**
Song of piping crow, or organ bird	Karruma	**kaRuma**

Source: From Dawson (1881); adapted by authors.

22 The spelling of initial **prr** follows Hercus (1992). In her 1986 book, where the stop was written with **b** and the alveolar trill with a single **r**, Hercus wrote that 'the only initial clusters that are found in Wembawemba are br- and gw-. Unlike the Gippsland languages which particularly favour initial br-, Wembawemba uses it only rarely and then only in the combination bri- …' (1986: 8).

While birds are sometimes the subject of songs (such as the corroboree song of the Eastern Kulin, see section 3.2.5), we do not know whether the Indigenous songsters regarded the calls of birds as a type of song.

2.2 Wemba-Wemba songs recorded on audio tape by Luise Hercus and Catherine Ellis

Hercus (1986: 61–71) gives the analysis of 12 songs including two very similar songs composed by Jack Brown (see section 2.2.6). Sound recordings of these were made, often several times, between 1962 and 1966. Several of these songs were also recorded on audio tape by the musicologist Catherine Ellis on 22 January 1963. In addition, there is a dingo song sung by Johnny Taylor (section 2.2.13), two songs sung by Silvia Murray, a frog song (section 2.2.14) and a song that seems to be some kind of love song (section 2.2.15), and finally a hymn sung by Nancy Egan (section 2.2.16). One song that we have not included is a very short song, probably a hymn translation, sung to a typically Western tune by Alf Kelly on 28 November 1969.[23]

The songs sung by Stan Day were some of the traditions longest remembered by the oldest speakers, as noted by Hercus (1965: 201). The original tapes made by both Hercus and Ellis have been digitised by the Australian Institute of Aboriginal and Torres Strait Islander Studies (AIATSIS).

In the Ellis recordings, all of Stan Day's songs are contained on a single tape, Tape 8, which was digitised by AIATSIS with the number A193B (Track B). The Hercus recordings, on the other hand, are part of a very large collection of digitisations of Luise Hercus's work, which are now divided into collections numbered L01 to L37. For most of Stan Day's songs, there are multiple recordings, often of in-depth discussions between Stan Day and Luise Hercus, in which he explains the meaning and re-sings sections of the song again. The recordings of songs that we have so far identified are all contained within the collections L04 and L08, and in particular in the recordings numbered as follows, example (2.8):

23 Ths song was recorded at the beginning of Hercus field tape 288, digitised by AIATSIS as HERCUS_L16-002108A.TMP.

(2.8) HERCUS_L04-000211A
HERCUS_L04-000211B
HERCUS_L04-000220B
HERCUS_L04-000221A
HERCUS_L04-000221B
HERCUS_L08-000997B
HERCUS_L08-000998A
HERCUS_L08-000999A
HERCUS_L08-000999B

Using the digitisations of the Hercus and Ellis tapes, we have produced audio files for each of the songs, and these are listed in Table 2.7. Some of the recordings are just of the song text, while others are of the song and the explanation of the meaning given in the discussion between Stan Day and Luise Hercus.

Table 2.7: List of digitised recordings of Wemba-Wemba songs with links

Description	Source file	Name of recording cut file	Link	Original tape no.	Date
Stan Day Song 1					
Stan Day's Song 1--Nganuty-nganuty 'the bat', recorded by Luise Hercus, 24 May 1965	HERCUS_L08-000999B.wav	HERCUS_L08-000999B_StanDaySong1_SongAndDiscussion.wav	youtu.be/L9HsZ7UOAW8	21/35	24/5/1965
Stan Day's Song 1-Nganuty-nganuty 'the bat', recorded by Luise Hercus, 25 January 1964	HERCUS_L04-000220B.wav	HERCUS_L04-000220B_StanDay_Song1_ExplanationAndSong.wav	youtu.be/17e2-OsYV3U	21/28	25/1/1964
Stan Day Song 2					
Stan Day's Song 2--Yerrateth-kurrk 'the owlet-nightjar', recorded by Luise Hercus, 9 April 1964	HERCUS_L08-000998A.wav	HERCUS_L08-000998A_StanDaySong2_SongAndDiscussion.wav	youtu.be/UtcQpnxf1GU	21/31	9/4/1964
Stan Day's Song 2--Yerrateth-kurrk 'the owlet-nightjar', recorded by Luise Hercus, 25 January 1964	HERCUS_L04-000220B.wav	HERCUS_L04-000220B_StanDay_Song2_ExplanationAndSong.wav	youtu.be/9ISA9L3VsbM	21/28	25/1/1964
Stan Day's Song 2-Yerrateth-kurrk 'the owlet-nightjar', recorded by Luise Hercus, 27 November 1965	HERCUS_L08-000997B.wav	HERCUS_L08-000997B_StanDaySong2_SongAndDiscussion.wav	youtu.be/2b-14ynmtoU	21/30	27/11/1965
Stan Day Song 3					
Stan Day's Song 3 'Going to the land of the dead', recorded by Luise Hercus, 18 April 1962	HERCUS_L04-000211B.wav	HERCUS_L04-000211B_StanDay_Song3.wav	youtu.be/OCBlfS8HYt4	21/3	18/4/1962
Stan Day's Song 3 'Going to the land of the dead', recorded by Luise Hercus, 27 November 1965	HERCUS_L04-000221B.wav	HERCUS_L04-000221B_StanDay_Song3_ExplanationAndSong.wav	youtu.be/C2YTvBmtKYM	21/29	27/11/1965

Description	Source file	Name of recording cut file	Link	Original tape no.	Date
Stan Day's Song 3 'Going to the land of the dead', recorded by Luise Hercus, 25 January 1962	HERCUS_L04-000220B.wav	HERCUS_L04-000220B_StanDay_Song3_ExplanationAndSong.wav	youtu.be/EmCNQKqPKS4	21/28	25/1/1964
Stan Day Song 4					
Stan Day's Song 4, 'Shearing on Tulla Station' recorded by Luise Hercus, 19 July 1962	HERCUS_L04-000211A.wav	HERCUS_L04-000211A_StanDay_Song4.wav	youtu.be/hISdAUhl_f0	21/2	19/7/1962
Stan Day's Song 4, 'Shearing on Tulla Station' recorded by Luise Hercus, 5 March 1966	HERCUS_L04-000221A.wav	HERCUS_L04-000221A_StanDay_Song4_Explanation.wav	youtu.be/6kTUXF5BeUU	21/28	5/3/1966
Stan Day's Song 4, 'Shearing on Tulla Station' recorded by Luise Hercus, 28 March 1965	HERCUS_L08-000997B.wav	HERCUS_L08-000997B_StanDaySong4_SongAndDiscussion.wav	youtu.be/EYQA9av_Hy8	21/30	28/3/1965
Stan Day Song 5					
Stan Day's Song 5, 'Jack Brown's song', recorded by Catherine Ellis, 22 January 1963	Ellis_193_TrackB.wav	Ellis_193_TrackB_StanDay_Song5.wav	youtu.be/5b44_R3ncfI	8	22/1/1963
Stan Day's Song 5, 'Jack Brown's song', recorded by Luise Hercus, 18 April 1965	HERCUS_L08-000998A.wav	HERCUS_L08-000998A_StanDaySong5_SongAndDiscussion.wav	youtu.be/2taiDaR0UNo	21/31	18/4/1965
Stan Day's Song 5, 'Jack Brown's song', recorded by Luise Hercus, 5 March 1966	HERCUS_L04-000220B.wav	HERCUS_L04-000220B_StanDay_Song5_Explanation.wav	youtu.be/T7BLXDRnOQU	21/27	5/3/1966
Stan Day's Song 5, 'Jack Brown's song', recorded by Luise Hercus, 5 March 1966 (2)	HERCUS_L04-000221B.wav	HERCUS_L04-000221B_StanDay_Song5_ExplanationAndSong.wav	youtu.be/QvD3AwmKO9g	21/29	5/3/1966
Stan Day's Song 5, 'Jack Brown's song', recorded by Luise Hercus, 27 November 1965	HERCUS_L08-000997B.wav; ,.	no recording cut	–	21/30	27/11/1965

Description	Source file	Name of recording cut file	Link	Original tape no.	Date
Stan Day's Song 5, 'Jack Brown's song', recorded by Luise Hercus, 26 January 1965	HERCUS_L08-000999A.wav	HERCUS_L08-000999A_StanDaySong5_SongAndDiscussion.wav	youtu.be/6SyduKfcJkE	21/34	26/1/1965
Stan Day Song 5a					
Stan Day's Song 5a, 'Jack Brown's swearing song', recorded by Luise Hercus, 27 November 1965	HERCUS_L08-000997B.wav	HERCUS_L08-000997B_StanDaySong5a_SongAndDiscussion.wav	youtu.be/L6YuCl7aJF8	21/30	27/11/1965
Stan Day's Song 5a, 'Jack Brown's swearing song', recorded by Luise Hercus, 5 March 1966	HERCUS_L04-000220B.wav	HERCUS_L04-000220B_StanDay_Song5a_Explanation.wav	youtu.be/cmxVwMyKd9A	21/27	5/3/1966
Stan Day Song 6					
Stan Day's Song 6, 'Looking for dingoes', recorded by Catherine Ellis, 22 January 1963	Ellis_193_TrackB.wav	Ellis_193_TrackB_StanDay_Song6.wav	youtu.be/XSgh_ibl9tM	8	22/1/1963
Stan Day's Song 6, 'Looking for dingoes', recorded by Luise Hercus, 28 March 1965	HERCUS_L08-000997B.wav	HERCUS_L08-000997B_StanDaySong6_SongAndDiscussion.wav	youtu.be/MDTw3VKQNaU	21/30	28/3/1965
Stan Day's Song 6, 'Looking for dingoes', recorded by Luise Hercus, 19 July 1962	HERCUS_L04-000211A.wav	HERCUS_L04-000211A_StanDay_Song6.wav	youtu.be/WYD_TwQ9sFg	21/2	19/7/1962
Stan Day's Song 6, 'Looking for dingoes', recorded by Luise Hercus, 5 March 1966	HERCUS_L04-000221A.wav	HERCUS_L04-000221A_StanDay_Song6_Explanation.wav	youtu.be/9ANzHAi76WI	21/28 and 21/29	5/3/1966
Stan Day Song 7					
Stan Day's Song 7, 'Kangaroo and a Dingo', recorded by Catherine Ellis, 22 January 1963	Ellis_193_TrackB.wav	Ellis_193_TrackB_StanDay_Song7.wav	youtu.be/ephmzfBilCY	8	22/1/1963
Stan Day's Song 7, 'Kangaroo and a Dingo', recorded by Luise Hercus, 18 April 1962	HERCUS_L04-000211B.wav	HERCUS_L04-000211B_StanDay_Song7.wav	youtu.be/X9u4KdorhJo	21/3	18/4/1962

Description	Source file	Name of recording cut file	Link	Original tape no.	Date
Stan Day's Song 7, 'Kangaroo and a Dingo', recorded by Luise Hercus, 5 March 1963	HERCUS_L04-000220B.wav	HERCUS_L04-000220B_StanDay_Song7_Explanation.wav	youtu.be/RBqalWvs55o	21/28	5/3/1966
Stan Day's Song 7, 'Kangaroo and a Dingo', recorded by Luise Hercus, 5 March 1963 (2)	HERCUS_L04-000221A.wav	no recording cut	–	21/28	5/3/1966
Stan Day's Song 7, 'Kangaroo and a Dingo', recorded by Luise Hercus, 27 November 1965	HERCUS_L04-000221A.wav	HERCUS_L04-000221A_StanDay_Song7_Explanation.wav	youtu.be/-_cOexvc5b8	21/29	27/11/1965
Stan Day's Song 7, 'Kangaroo and a Dingo', recorded by Luise Hercus, 27 November 1965 No. 2	HERCUS_L04-000221B.wav	HERCUS_L04-000221B_StanDay_Song7_ExplanationAndSong.wav	youtu.be/ITO3I93ybVE	21/29	27/11/1965
Stan Day's Song 7, 'Kangaroo and a Dingo', recorded by Luise Hercus, 24 May 1965	HERCUS_L08-000999B.wav	HERCUS_L08-000999B_StanDayUnknownSong.wav	youtu.be/jSQ3mZIMU0o	21/35	24/5/1965
Stan Day Song 8					
Stan Day's Song 8, 'Sentai, the lazy dog', recorded by Catherine Ellis, 22 January 1963	Ellis_193_TrackB.wav	Ellis_193_TrackB_StanDay_Song8.wav	youtu.be/XUU0BrVk2aM	8	22/1/1963
Stan Day's Song 8, 'Sentai, the lazy dog', recorded by Luise Hercus, 27 November 1965	HERCUS_L08-000997B.wav	HERCUS_L08-000997B_StanDaySong8_SongAndDiscussion.wav	youtu.be/HyJG6ve-TxE	21/30	27/11/1965
Stan Day's Song 8, 'Sentai, the lazy dog', recorded by Luise Hercus, 2 November 1965 (2)	HERCUS_L08-000997B.wav	no recording cut	–	21/30	27/11/1965
Stan Day's Song 8, 'Sentai, the lazy dog', recorded by Luise Hercus, 26 January 1965	HERCUS_L08-000999B.wav	HERCUS_L08-000999B_StanDaySong8_SongAndDiscussion.wav	youtu.be/ctAoe1SLBdo	21/35	26/1/1965

Description	Source file	Name of recording cut file	Link	Original tape no.	Date
Stan Day Song 9					
Stan Day's Song 9, 'Escaping from justice in N.S.W.', recorded by Catherine Ellis, 22 January 1963	Ellis_193_TrackB.wav	Ellis_193_TrackB_StanDay_Song9.wav	youtu.be/P_P0yiWF2Uk	8	22/1/1963
Stan Day's Song 9, 'Escaping from justice in N.S.W.', recorded by Luise Hercus, 19 July 1962	HERCUS_L04-000211A.wav	HERCUS_L04-000211A_StanDay_Song9.wav	youtu.be/FuBNXXSeRgs	21/2	19/7/1962
Stan Day's Song 9, 'Escaping from justice in N.S.W.', recorded by Luise Hercus, 5 March 1966	HERCUS_L04-000221A.wav	HERCUS_L04-000221A_StanDay_Song9_Explanation.wav	youtu.be/p6nPAZ_HfQQ	21/28	5/3/1966
Stan Day's Song 9, 'Escaping from justice in N.S.W.', recorded by Luise Hercus, 27 November 1965	HERCUS_L08-000997B.wav	no recording cut	-	21/30	27/11/1965
Stan Day's Song 9, 'Escaping from justice in N.S.W.', recorded by Luise Hercus, 28 March 1965	HERCUS_L08-000997B.wav	no recording cut	-	21/30	28/3/1965
Stan Day Song 10					
Stan Day's Song 10, 'An Ancient Tale', recorded by Catherine Ellis, 22 January 1963	Ellis_193_TrackB.wav	Ellis_193_TrackB_StanDay_Song10.wav	youtu.be/ZZPWR8HTzeM	8	22/1/1963
Stan Day's Song 10, 'An Ancient Tale', recorded by Luise Hercus, 28 March 1965	HERCUS_L08-000997B.wav	HERCUS_L08-000997B_StanDaySong10_SongAndDiscussion.wav	youtu.be/amZN3J2E1ZU	21/30	28/3/1965
Stan Day's Song 10, 'An Ancient Tale', recorded by Luise Hercus, 27 November 1965	HERCUS_L04-000221B.wav	HERCUS_L04-000221B_StanDay_Song10_ExplanationAndSong.wav	youtu.be/iTgcpDpAHA8	21/29	27/11/1965
Stan Day's Song 10, 'An Ancient Tale', recorded by Luise Hercus, 19 July 1962	HERCUS_L04-000211A.wav	no recording cut	-	21/2	19/7/1962

Description	Source file	Name of recording cut file	Link	Original tape no.	Date
Stan Day's Song 10, 'An Ancient Tale', recorded by Luise Hercus, 27 November 1965 (2)	HERCUS_L08-000997B.wav	no recording cut	–	21/30	27/11/1965
Stan Day's Song 10, 'An Ancient Tale', recorded by Luise Hercus, 26 January 1965	HERCUS_L08-000999B.wav	HERCUS_L08-000999B_StanDaySong10_SongAndDiscussion.wav	youtu.be/mn3FotqaT4A	21/35	26/1/1965
Stan Day Song 11					
Stan Day's Song 11, 'Bob Taylor's swearing song', recorded by Luise Hercus, 18 April 1962	HERCUS_L04-000211B.wav	HERCUS_L04-000211B_StanDay_Song11.wav	youtu.be/iSgYQKEdI7Q	21/3	18/4/1962
Stan Day's Song 11, 'Bob Taylor's swearing song', recorded by Luise Hercus, 28 March 1965	HERCUS_L08-000997B.wav	HERCUS_L08-000997B_StanDaySong11_SongAndDiscussion.wav	youtu.be/1sgfIDnM0Ss	21/30	28/3/1965
Silvia Murray's Frog song					
Silvia Murray's Frog song, recorded by Luise Hercus, 23 November 1964	HERCUS_L04-000219B.wav	HERCUS_L04-000219B_SilviaMurray_FrogSong.wav	youtu.be/3dBxQeLYbGs	21/26	23/11/1964
Silvia' Murray's song, recorded by Luise Hercus in March 1964	HERCUS_L08-000998A.wav	HERCUS_L08-000998A_SilviaMurray_Song.wav	youtu.be/25lu-V8qGwA	21/31	3/1964
Silvia Murray's Love song					
AS PREVIOUS	HERCUS_L08-000998A.wav	HERCUS_L08-000998A_SilviaMurray_Song.wav	–	21/31	3/1964
Johnny Taylor's songs					
Johnny Taylor's Songs, recorded by Luise Hercus, 26 January 1964	HERCUS_L04-000219B.wav	HERCUS_L04-000219B_JohnnyTaylorSongs_1.wav	youtu.be/FHfAa81DIKk	21/26	26/1/1964
Johnny Taylor's Songs, recorded by Luise Hercus, 23 November 1964	HERCUS_L04-000219B.wav	HERCUS_L04-000219B_JohnnyTaylorSongs_2.wav	youtu.be/1V6vRP5nCn4	21/26	23/11/1964

Source: Authors' data.

In the 1986 book, Luise Hercus presented a transcription in both an orthographic/phonemic and phonetic form, as well as glossing and translating the texts. We will be making some alterations to the form of those presentations here, updating the orthography to reflect Luise's more recent thoughts, presenting the phonetics using IPA symbols and glossing every morpheme rather than with phrases.

The method of translating these texts followed by Hercus (1986) was to note down the explanations of the text made by Stan Day. Many of these explanations have been recorded, and often he would sing a short section and then explain the meaning word by word. This is exemplified in example (2.9), a short section of the explanation of Song 3, taken from the AIATSIS recording HERCUS_L04-000221B at 14:00, with Stan Day (SD) in discussion with Luise Hercus (LH).

(2.9) SD: [sings] **winyarr kila lepuwəlang, walpukanaty! kukuminyek kukminyek** ('Who is this chasing up and disturbing the birds? You people look around and see! It is my own grandmother.')

SD: that's (who was chasing) these birds …

LH: What was it? k…

SD: [spoken] **winyarr kila lepuwəlang**

LH: **winyarr …** wínyarr kila

SD: [spoken] **winyarr kila lepuwəlang**, hunting birds up

LH: ah lep … I don't know that word, **winyarr kila**

SD: [spoken] **lepuwəlang, lepuwəlang**

LH: **lepuwəlang**

SD: mmm

LH: ah, that means hunting up birds

SD [spoken]: yeah, birds flying off when you're walking along … **lepuwəlang**

LH: oh I see

It is explanations like these that form the basis of the Hercus (1986) linguistic analysis, which we also present here. The technology in the 1960s did not allow for the easy replaying of tapes, stopping and starting and listening again to the recordings, something that is quite straightforward in the twenty-first century.

This type of quick movement from singing to explanation is a feature of some Indigenous song styles, as related, for example, by Richard Moyle (1979: 12):

> During performance of the *wangaṯa* series, one particular song was sung twice, followed each time by one singer's sung commentary on the situation described in the song text. His melody, however, bore no resemblance to that of the song … The singer claimed, and the others confirmed, that this was 'speaking' and that it was not part of the performance proper.

While the style of 'speaking' discussed by Moyle is not exactly what Stan Day was doing in the extract given in example (2.9), the ease with which he was able to do this may indicate that this type of commentary was not unknown in traditional Wemba-Wemba singing.

When discussing the difficulty of transcribing and understanding the songs and asked by Catherine Ellis what one song was about, Stan Day answered (Ellis Tape A193 Side B):

> Oh well there you are, it takes you hours to explain it, there you are, couldn't tell you, I couldn't tell you that.

Later he once said to Luise Hercus 'they're the easiest thing in the world'. At a distance of 50 years this is certainly not the case. We have spent many hours transcribing the music, listening to and comparing the multiple versions of the recordings, checking the setting of the text and the repetitions and any additional words.

Stan Day also made other observations, such as that to Catherine Ellis in January 1963 (Ellis_193_TrackB.wav, 11:40):

> but they had an idea them blacks, …. they could swing em, and they'd sing it over and over again like … and they'd swing it lovely like, you know. Different to us like, but they weren't able to make a very long song, they'd swing it over and over again.

It is interesting that while Stan Day did not talk much about the meaning of songs with Catherine Ellis, he did discuss some musicological aspects of the songs with her. Perhaps he spoke with particular researchers about the things he felt they could best understand.

The fact that Stan Day could sing a section of song and then speak it using the same words demonstrates that the language of the singing was indeed spoken language. Stan Day was able to explain the meaning of the songs with only a few exceptions, such as the words not in languages he knew in Song 10, a song in which **Marrərt** had 'put three different lingos into one song' (see section 2.2.11).

However, in many cases the text of the song as analysed by Hercus and the text as found in the musicological analysis is slightly different, perhaps in the ordering of words, in the repetitions or in some cases in the content. The musicological analysis of Stan Day's Song 6, 'Looking for dingos', is a case in point. Two musical transcriptions are presented, one based on a performance given to Catherine Ellis (Figure 2.9) and the other on a different performance of the same song recorded by Luise Hercus on field tape 21/30, AIATSIS tape HERCUS_L08-000997B.wav (Figure 2.10). In both cases there are portions of text that we cannot easily interpret. For example, the first line or section of the Hercus recording is **kiwanda yinga wirra**, which is then repeated, but there are three syllables that have words that we cannot hear after each instance of these three words. These are shown in the musical transcriptions without text.

As mentioned earlier, Hercus (1986) presents these songs in both phonemic (orthographic) and phonetic transcriptions. The 1986 phonemic transcriptions used voiced stops, and the <ŋ> symbol, underlining for dentals, dots for retroflex and single <r> for the alveolar trill/tap. The orthographic transcription used here, however, follows Hercus (1992) in using digraphs and voiceless stops. Following Hercus (1992) we also express diphthongs with semivowels, such as **telkaya**. Examples comparing the two systems are presented in Table 2.8.

Table 2.8: Comparison of orthographic transcriptions

This volume	Hercus (1986)	Gloss
kingga	**giŋga**	'here'
wirra	**wira**	'run'
tuthən	**dudən**	'put on'
ngurkity	**ŋuṛgidj**	'swallow.POT'
telkaya	**delgaia**	d'

Source: Authors.

We have updated the symbols for phonemes to reflect current practice in the twenty-first century. Printing of some phonetic symbols was more difficult to do in 1986. We have also substituted the [ɐ] symbol in place of the [ʌ] the back unrounded vowel. Hercus (1986: 19) described this sound as follows:

> In unaccented syllables a much weaker form of the phoneme a was found. This allophone appeared to be pronounced with the back of the tongue raised very slightly towards the soft palate, and the lips in a neutral position. … It has been transcribed by the symbol [ʌ] here, although it is a much more lax sound than is generally transcribed by the symbol [ʌ] in the international phonetic alphabet …

A full list of forms that have been altered in this volume from Hercus (1986) are presented in Table 2.9.[24]

Table 2.9: Hercus's phonetic transcriptions altered in this volume

This volume	Hercus (1986)
ɐ	ʌ
ɪ	I
ʊ	U
ɲ	nj
ɳ	ṇ
ʈ	ṭ
ɖ	ḍ
ɻ	ṛ
c	tj
ɟ	dj
ɲɟ	ndj
θ	θ
j	y

Source: Authors.

A further change is that we have glossed every word with each of its grammatical forms, rather than using a free translation gloss as was the case in Hercus (1986). For example, in Stan Day's Song 1, Nganuty-nganuty 'the bat', we have glossed the word **wurrengalap** as 'chase.FREQ.PURP', consisting as it does of a root **wurrenga**, the frequentative **-ila** and the purposive **-ap** (Hercus 1986: 45). The gloss in Hercus (1986) was 'for-chasing-(flies)'.

24 We are grateful to Harold Koch for suggesting some of these.

A full list of the grammatical morphemes found in the songs is given in Table 2.10 together with references to the discussion about these morphemes in Hercus (1986).

Table 2.10: Grammatical morphemes in the Stan Day songs

Abbreviation	Meaning	Form in Wemba-Wemba	Reference
1PL.INCL	1st person plural inclusive	**-angurr**	Hercus (1986: 43)
1PL.INCL.POSS	1st person plural inclusive possessive	**-angurrak**	Hercus (1986: 34)
1SG	1st person singular	**-anda**	Hercus (1986: 43)
1SG.POSS	1st person singular possessive	**-ek**	Hercus (1986: 34)
2DL	2nd person dual	**-wal**	Hercus (1986: 43)
2DLPOSS	2nd person dual posessive	**-alakang**	Hercus (1986: 34)
2PL	2nd person plural	**-aty**	Hercus (1986: 43)
2PL.POSS	2nd person plural possessive	**-atak**	Hercus (1986: 34)
2SG	2nd person singular	**-arr**	Hercus (1986: 43)
3PL	3rd person plural	**-an**	Hercus (1986: 43)
3SG.POSS	3rd person singular possessive	**-uk**	Hercus (1986: 34)
ABL	ablative	**-(k)ang**	Hercus (1986: 32, 37)
ALL	allative	–	Hercus (1986: 37)
ALONG	along	**-tawa**	See Hercus (1992)
EMPH	emphatic	**min**	Hercus (1986) glosses this as 'indeed', but in this example (2.15) it is found between the head noun and possessive suffix.
ERG	ergative	**-(k)u**	Hercus (1986: 29)
FORM	formative	**-ma**	In Songs 10 and 11, apparently not discussed by Hercus (1986)
FREQ	frequentative	**-ila**	Termed continuative in Hercus (1986: 44)
GEN	genitive, general oblique	**-a**	Termed by Hercus (1986: 30) as the 'general oblique'
IMP	imperative	**-ak**	Hercus (1986: 44)
INTENS	intensive	**-uwa**	–

Abbreviation	Meaning	Form in Wemba-Wemba	Reference
LOC	locative 'position right in'	**-ata**	Hercus (1986: 32)
POT	potential	**-ity**	Hercus (1986: 44)
PRES.PART	present participle	**-ang**	See Hercus (1992)
PST	past	**-in**	Hercus (1986: 43)
PST	past	**-in**	Hercus (1986: 44)
PST.PART	past participle	**-ən**	Hercus (1986: 43)
PURP	purposive	**-ap**	Hercus (1986: 45)
RECIP	reciprocal	**-tyerra**	Hercus (1986: 47)
REDUPL	reduplication	–	–

Source: Authors.

2.2.1 Overview of the music of Stan Day's songs

In this volume, we extend the analysis to include, for the first time, musical transcriptions prepared by Grace Koch, with the text underlaid wherever possible. As mentioned above, in the 1960s when Luise Hercus first translated these songs, her transcriptions and translations were based on the spoken words that Stan Day gave in explanation. These musical transcriptions, on the other hand, need to be taken from the sung versions and there are sometimes words that we cannot make out, repetitions and variations. In the song transcriptions, words in square brackets [ ] indicate syllables that are additional to the linguistic transcription in Hercus (1986), presented again here. Round brackets (parentheses) ( ) indicate unsure readings. Where notes have no text underlay, it is because we are unsure what words are being sung there.

The songs sung by Stan Day were composed in the 1890s, when Marəd, Tommy, Nyawi and Jack Brown spent a lot of time together. These observations are based upon Tommy's and Nyawi's songs. We will examine Jack Brown's song after showing how Tommy's and Nyawi's songs differ from one another, then move on to compare the two performances of Song 6 and Song 8.

a) Tommy's songs tend to rise a perfect fourth at the beginning whereas Nyawi's usually move stepwise.

Song 10: An ancient tale (Tommy)

Song 6: Looking for dingoes (Nyawi)

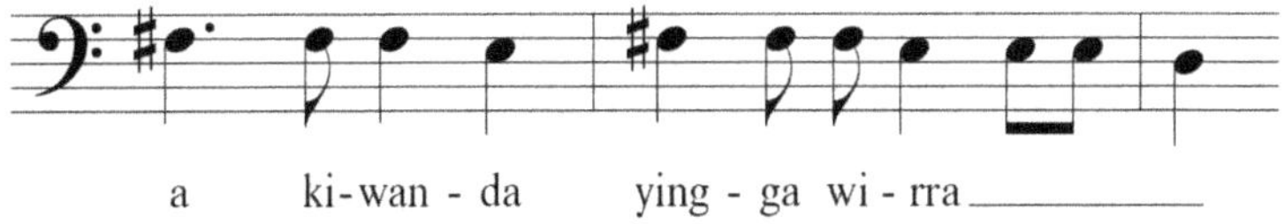

b) Two of Tommy's songs begin with a vocable 'ah', which is similar to what we find in notations made by Rev. G.W. Torrance of songs sung by Barak. According to Torrance (1887), Barak began his songs, usually on one pitch, with the syllable 'ē' or 'æ'. Tommy sings his 'ah' on two notes a minor third apart. Nyawi does not begin any of his songs in this way.

Song 2: Owlet-nightjar (Tommy)

Song 3: Going to the land of the dead (Tommy)

c) All of Tommy's songs end on multiple reiterations of one pitch. In contrast, Nyawi uses various endings, rather like musical codas.

Song 10: An ancient tale (Tommy)

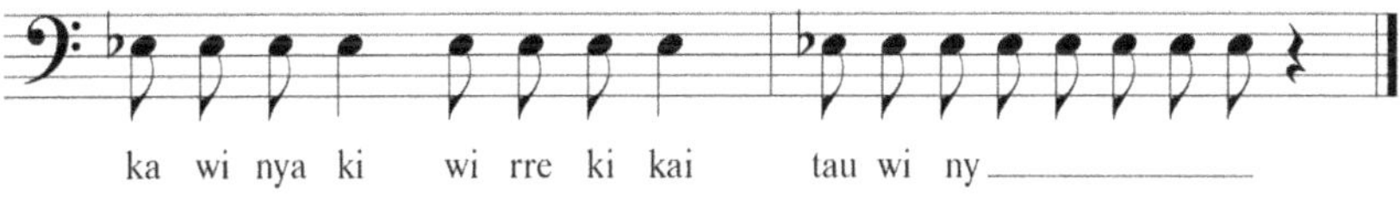

Song 8: 'Sentai', the lazy dog (Nyawi)

Song 4: Shearing on Tulla Station (Nyawi)

Song 6: Looking for dingoes (Nyawi)

kiny [ma - nyal] yau - wi - rruk

Note: Pitch descends to neighbouring note.

d) Finally, Tommy's songs may have a short middle section after which there is a large intervallic leap. Nyawi used the musical device of a leap in only two of his four songs, and there is not a short section preceding it.

Song 10: An ancient tale (Tommy)

Song 8: 'Sentai', the lazy dog

Jack Brown's song was recorded on tape by both Ellis and Hercus at different times. The bulk of the song moves stepwise within the range of a major third. The version Stan Day sang for Hercus stayed strictly between three pitches, D, E and F#, rising and falling in a wavelike motion.

Song 5: Jack Brown's song (Hercus)

When he sang it for Ellis, the bulk of the song rose and fell within a major third, but he started the song with a fourth leap.

All of the above examples show the minor differences with performances sung for both Hercus and Ellis. We now look at a song that was sung for Hercus on two occasions, Bob Taylor's swearing song, where there are major differences with the versions. Stan Day sang the text straight through for the first version, and he repeated the text three times on the second performance. We were unable to put a text underlay to the last repetition because of the speed of the rendition. The two performances are recognisable as the same song for the starting section of text 'ngathaikuny kinya Chinaman tyerrika', but the differences are worth noting. We refer to these as Version 1 and Version 2 (Table 2.11).

Table 2.11: Comparison of the musical features of the two versions of Bob Taylor's swearing song

Version 1	Version 2
Begins with an upward leap of a perfect 4th	Repeats the beginning pitch with no leap
On the text, 'wurruwilang', the melody leaps upward a minor 6th (Db–Bb) and repeats the Bb in the upper register almost to the end	At 'wurruwilang', the melody moves downwards, staying in the lower register
Text is sung straight through once	After the first verse, the last part of the text, 'kurtamilang marthang no savvy' is repeated using the melody from the opening phrase
–	After the second repetition, the text adds the word 'yakai'

Notes: See section 2.2.12, this chapter.

Source: Authors.

2.2.2 Song 1 – Nganuty-nganuty 'the bat'

The first two songs, **Nganuty-nganuty** 'the bat' and **Yerrateth-kurrk** 'the owlet-nightjar' (*Aegotheles cristatus*) (see section 2.2.3) are related to each other, composed in honour of two animals sacred to the two sexes. Hercus (1986: 61) introduces them as follows:

> The first two short songs are connected with the tradition that the bat was sacred to the men, and the owlet-nightjar sacred to the women. This tradition has been noted, among others by Howitt, who speaks of the sex-totems of the Wotjo nation (i.e. the N.W. 'Kulin' people). Stanley Day never spoke of the bat and the owlet-nightjar as ancestral beings (barəmbug), but he explained as follows:

> 'The men liked the bat, but the women were glad and would laugh if one got killed or hurt. The women loved the owlet-nightjar (yerade<u>d</u>-gurg, cf gurg *woman*). If we boys had killed a yerade<u>d</u>-gurg the old women would have been after us with a walking-stick and we would have had to run for our lives. So my grandfather made two songs about this, a good song about the bat, and a really bad song about the owlet-nightjar'.

In the recording where he explains this, Stan Day uses the term **tyilpa-tyilpa-** 'to flog' to describe the punishment that boys would receive if they hurt an owlet-nightjar (HERCUS_L08-000998A.wav, 48:35).

In discussing this particular song, Hercus added: 'The bat is here described with all the symbols of prestige known to the author. He is even given an English name, Mr Walker, as this was also the name of a much respected old Wembawemba man at Moonacullah' (1986: 62).

Howitt (1904: 148) discusses 'sex totems' in some detail, commencing with his first identification of the phenomenon, in Gippsland where *Yiirung* 'emu-wren' is the male totem, treated as an 'elder brother', and *Djiitgun* 'superb warbler' is the female totem and 'elder sister' (see section 5.1.7).

In connection with western Victoria, Howitt (1904: 148) wrote:

> The true character of the sex totem is shown by the Wotjobaluk expression, 'The life of a bat is the life of a man,' meaning that to injure a bat is to injure some man, while to kill one is to cause some man to die. The same saying applies to the Owlet-nightjar with respect to women.

Howitt (1904: 150) describes fights that arose in western Victoria relating to the bat and the owlet-nightjar, the sex totems:

> In the Wotjobaluk tribe such fights arose out of some ill-feeling, when men, for instance, would kill an owlet-nightjar and tell of doing so in the camp. The women would then in their turn kill a bat, and carry it to the camp on the point of a stick which had been thrust through it, and with a piece of wood in its mouth to keep it open. This was held up in triumph, the oldest woman walking first and the younger ones following, and all shouting 'Yeip! Yeip!' (Hurrah!)

> The men met them with clubs and boomerangs, the women being armed with their digging-sticks, and a great fight would ensue. At times the men used spears against the women, who defended themselves by turning them aside or breaking them with their sticks.
>
> In such a fight, which might last, off and on, for an hour, women have been speared; but, on the other hand, they have been known to give the men a good drubbing with their sticks.

The bat is also referred to as a male in creation stories; for example, in Howitt (1904: 484):

> The Wotjobaluk account of the creation of man says that long ago Ngunung-ngunnut, the bat, who was a man, lived on the earth, and there were others like him, but there was no difference between the sexes. Feeling lonely, he wished for a wife, and he altered himself and one other, so that he was the man and the other was the woman. Then he made fire by rubbing a stick on a log of wood.

The Wotjobaluk were speakers of Werkaya language. We presume that the 'other' who was altered into a woman was originally the owlet-nightjar.

R.H. Mathews (NLA MS 8006/3/4.1, Notebook 1, p. 155) also gives a longer story of the bat, a male character with two wives, making a note on page 157:[25]

> Yertertgurk is the night jar – greyish about size of a mainah is the sister of the woman.
>
> Ngunni-ngunnity is brother of the man

The connection between the owlet-nightjar and female and the bat and male is found all over south-east Australia, though in some places one or other of the species may be slightly altered. As evidence of this, zoologists had difficulty getting specimens of bats because the men did not want to kill them (Luise Hercus, pers. comm.).

25 Mathews makes a similar note about this bird on page 184 on one of the offprints of Mathews (1902b), NLA MS 8006/8/224, where the name of the bird is spelled *yeradaher*.

The text

The full text and translation, based on Hercus (1986: 62), is presented as Box 2.4:

Box 2.4: Song 1 – Nganuty-nganuty 'the bat'

Author: Tommy; transmitted by Marrərt (Grandfather David Taylor)	
kingga mina mayo Mr Walker wirra	Here from afar hastens Mr Walker
pilopilung goldwatchuk	all shiny, with a gold watch,
nyanyuk-min tuthən mumbelm	wearing a different hat (every day),
wurrengalap gold-yulekanən	with pieces of gold hanging down to chase away (flies).

Source: Based on Hercus (1986: 62); adapted by authors.

Recordings

There were at least two recordings of this song, both of which have been analysed musically. The first, the analysis of which is presented as Figure 2.1, was recorded on 24 May 1965 at Echuca, and is found on Hercus's field tape 21/35, which has been digitised by AIATSIS as HERCUS_L08-000999B.

The portion of the recording where this song is discussed commenced at 19:57 on the AIATSIS recording. The discussion, which continues for 7:56, consists of an explanation of the song and singing of short extracts. We have extracted this recording and named it:

HERCUS_L08-000999B_StanDaySong1_SongAndDiscussion.wav.

A second recording had been made on 25 January 1964 on Hercus field tape 21/28, digitised by AIATSIS as HERCUS_L04-000220B. A discussion of the song runs from 20:57 to 23:45, and includes a full version of the song sung with two verses (from 21:29 to 21:55), both of which have an additional line not shown in Box 2.4 or the analysis in example (2.10), then concluding with a short discussion about other birds. The musical analysis of this song is presented as Figure 2.2. We have extracted this recording and named it:

HERCUS_L04-000220B_StanDay_Song1_ExplanationAndSong.wav.

Linguistic transcription

The transcription presented here as example (2.10) follows Hercus (1986: 62), but with the orthographic phonemic spelling (in the first line) updated to follow the conventions in Hercus (1992) (see above for discussion of these changes). In the phonetic line, stress is marked as in Hercus (1986). As mentioned above, in those cases where the morphological structure of a word is clear, the glosses have been altered to reflect this, such as **pilopilung**, which contains a root, the frequentative **-ila** and the present participle -**ang**.

(2.10)	**kingga**	**mina**	**mayo**	**Mr Walker**	**wirra**
	ˈkiŋkɐ	mɪnɐ	ˈmajɔ	*Mr. Walker*	ˈwirɐ
	here	indeed	from.afar	Mr.Walker	hasten(PRS)

pilopilung	**goldwatchuk**
ˈpiloˌpɪlʊŋ	*goldwatch*-ʊk
shine.FREQ.PRES.PART	goldwatch-3SG.POSS

nyanyuk-min	**tuthən**	**mumbelm**
ˈɲɛ̃ɲuk-mɪn	ˈtʊθən	ˈmʊmbelm
different-indeed	put.on	hat

wurrengalap	**gold-yulekanən**
ˈwʊˌrɛ̃·ŋɐlɐp	*gold*-ˈju·ləkaˌnən
chase.FREQ.PURP	gold-hang.PST.PART

'Here from afar hastens Mr Walker, all shiny, with a gold watch, wearing a different hat every day, with pieces of gold hanging down (instead of cork from his hat fly-net) to chase away flies.'

Linguistic note

The word **tuthən** is not listed in Hercus (1992). It appears to include the past participle suffix **-ən**.

Version as sung, with notes on poetics

In the recording on Hercus field tape 21/35 (HERCUS_L08-000999B_StanDaySong1_SongAndDiscussion.wav), the linguistic transcription is as in example (2.11), with the word **wirra** following **mina**, rather than at the end of the line.

(2.11) kingga mina wirra mayo Mister Walker
pilpilung goldwadjuk
nyanyuk-min tuthən mumbelm
wurreng (puwanin) gold-yulekanən

The first line consists of 12 syllables, though the syllables **wirra mayo** are not easy to make out. The second line is shorter, with longer notes on the syllables of **pilopilung**. There is a clear lengthening of the first syllable of **nyanyuk** in line 3, meaning that the length of the word **nyanyuk-min** appears to match in rhythm the first four syllables of line 1, **kingga mina**.

The suffixes in the word **wurrengalap**, the frequentative **-ila** and the purposive **-ap** are not audible, and in their place a form **puwanin** of unknown meaning is heard. We speculate that he may have been intending to sing **wurreng-ap min** 'chase-PURP indeed'.

In listening repeatedly to this song, we discern a rhyme with the **-uk** of **goldwatch-uk** and of **nyanyuk**, and the **-in** of the unknown **puwanin** and **yulekanən**.

The first syllable of **nyanyuk** is sung over several notes, almost as **nyuwe-nyuk**.

The second version of the song, on Hercus field tape 21/28 (AIATSIS recording HERCUS_L04-000220B), has the full text sung twice with some additional words that we have suggested a transcription for, but cannot offer any meaning. The transcription of the words is presented as example (2.12), with uncertain readings in brackets.

(2.12) kingga mina wirra (mayo) Mister Walker
pilopilung goldwatchuk
nyanyukmin tuthən mumbelm
wurreng (puanin) goldyulekanən
(pithikingai kurra ngu a-a-a-a)

kingga mina wirra (mayo) Mister Walker
pilopilung goldwatchuk
nyanyukmin tuthən mumbelm
wurreng (puanin) goldyulekanən
(pithikingai kurra)

The word transcribed by Hercus (1986) as **mayo** sounds to us like **mika**. This is a word in Wemba-Wemba meaning 'tired', but this meaning would not be appropriate here, so we believe that it was Stan Day's intention to sing **mayo** and that perhaps he was trying to rhyme the word with the final **-ka** sound of *Walker*.

As with the first version of the song, we do not hear **wurrengalap** in the fourth line of each verse, but rather what we have transcribed as **wurreng puanin**.

This version of the song has a fifth line, which we have transcribed as **pithikingai kurra ngu**. Unfortunately, the recording of this version of the song was not identified until after Luise Hercus passed away, and we could not check this with her. The first word **pithik** is the word for 'fly' or 'blowfly' but we have not yet been able to propose an analysis for the remaining words in the transcription.

The distinctive **a-a-a-a** melody at the end of the first verse of this version is very similar to that on the last syllable of **pin-wu-rrə-rrai** in the Hercus recording of Song 10 (see Figure 2.16 in section 2.2.11).

Musical transcription and analysis (by Grace Koch)

The musical analysis of Nganuty-nganuty 'the bat' is presented as Figure 2.1.

This song has a tonal centre of E, and form similar to a major scale (Ionian mode) (see the discussion in section 2.2.1 outlining the similarity between the pitch inventories of Stan Day's songs and the major key).

The song was extremely difficult to notate due to the condition of the recording, but the transcription presented above is a close approximation. The vocal range is a minor sixth (C#–A).

Figure 2.1: Musical analysis of Stan Day, Song 1, Nganuty-nganuty 'the bat' (Version 1)

Source: Song from HERCUS_L08-000999B, analysis by Grace Koch.

There are two musical phrases in the song, separated by a breath. For the first phrase, the melody rises to an A, then descends stepwise to a C# (syllable 'gold'), rising a minor third on the same syllable to E, finishing on two rapidly enunciated Es on 'wadjuk'. The second phrase starts on the E, then stays on the F# until the word 'wuren' where in drops a perfect fourth, rising to the same E that began the phrase.

As for the text, the sung version differs somewhat from the text version above. Vowels may be drawn out; for example, the word **wúrengalap** sounded somewhat different. Most syllables are performed on separately articulated notes; an exception is the syllable, 'gold', which sounds like /gu/ sung near the end of the second line of text. Some syllables of the text as shown above may be elided, but could not be heard from the recording. The second text line begins with a vocable /a/.

Bat Song, Nganuty-Nganuty (version 2)

Song 1 recorded by Luise Hercus
sung by Stan Day

Figure 2.2: Musical analysis of Stan Day, Song 1, Nganuty-nganuty 'the bat' (Version 2)

Source: Song from HERCUS_L04-000220B, analysis by Grace Koch.

In his article 'Music of the Australian Aboriginals' (1887), Rev. G.W. Torrance analysed songs performed for him by William Barak, a Woiwurrung man. He refers to 'a curious sliding of one sound into another, not unlike the slow tuning of a violin string' (Torrance 1887: 336; also in Howitt 1904: 419). Such a pitch slide occurs in the bat song (and in several other Victorian songs) at the beginning of the third text line **nyan-yuk** and at the syllable **pua**. For subsequent songs, I shall refer to this feature as a pitch slide.

This song has a tonal centre of Eb, and form similar to a major scale.

Both melodies are generally similar for the first phrase, up to the text 'gold watchuk'. The extra text phrase, **pithikingai kurrangu** in Version 2, is sung on a single pitch, almost functioning as a type of coda. The longer rendition elaborates on the earlier version, differing in the following ways (Table 2.12):

Table 2.12: Comparison of the two versions of Song 1 – Nganuty-nganuty 'the bat'

Version 1 (from HERCUS_L08-000999B)	Version 2 (from HERCUS_L04-000220B)
Single iteration of text	Text repeated twice with some extra words: **pithikingai kurrangu**
Generally a duple metre	Repeated rhythmic pattern (♪♪♪ ♩) moves towards a compound/triple metre
Pitch slide appears on word, nyanyuk	Last phrase in bar 6 has a pitch slide on the syllable 'a' (F G D Eb). The same melodic pattern appears in bar 8 over the words, **-lo-pi-lung**, a 5th higher.
No melodic leaps larger than a 4th	Minor 7th leap in bar 7
Pitch range a minor 6th (C#–A)	Pitch range a minor 9th (D–Eb)

Source: Authors.

2.2.3 Song 2 – Yerrateth-kurrk 'the owlet-nightjar'

As already discussed in relation to the previous song, **Nganuty-nganuty** 'the bat', this song forms a pair with it, with ***Yerrateth-kurrk*** (*Aegotheles cristatus*) being the totem for women.[26] The context relating to this song and to sex totems is discussed in section 2.2.2.

Yerretgurk is a character in the story of *That-tyu-kūl*, 'a great warrior of ancient times', who chased a great cod, *Ban'-dyal.* In this chasing, the cod created the Murray River. *Yerretgurk* was the mother-in-law of *That-tyu-kūl* and like him was transformed into a star, α Eridani (Mathews 1904: 283–86). *That-tyu-kūl*'s name literally means 'arm having' but implies that

26 The use of **rr** in the spelling of this word follows Hercus (1986) who spelled this with a single <r> as *yeraded-gurg*. Corey Theatre (pers. comm.) who has listened to the Hercus recordings carefully has suggested that this sound is a glide and should perhaps be written with a single **r**.

he had only one arm. In the Mathi-Mathi language his name is spelled **Thathakwil**, discussed further in section 12.4 in connection with Pound's song, which was in one of the Murray River languages.

The text

The full text and translation, based on Hercus (1986: 62), is presented as Box 2.5:

Box 2.5: Song 2 – Yerrateth-kurrk 'the owlet-nightjar'

Author: Tommy; transmitted by Marrət (Grandfather David Taylor)	
yerrateth-kurrk bucket-wurru pen-wurru	'The owlet-nightjar, with a mouth like a bucket, a mouth like a hollow tree
ngarnity nya cook-ata	He would go cadging after the cook,
ngurkity nyula cook pileny	And he would even follow that cook as well
kathang mina pakatyerrity	After a while the people would look at each other asking
windyaluk nya cook nyunga?	"Where's the cook from around here?"
nyula malu ngurkin ngathang	"That ugly devil has swallowed him.'

Source: Based on Hercus (1986: 62); adapted by authors.

Recordings

Three recordings of this song exist. The one that we have analysed musically below as Figure 2.3 was recorded on 9 April 1964 at Echuca. It is found on Hercus field tape 21/31, which has been digitised by AIATSIS as HERCUS_L08-000998A. The discussion of this song commences at 48:15 and runs until about 52:00. The song itself is sung in full from 49:08. We have extracted this recording and named it:

HERCUS_L08-000998A_StanDaySong2_SongAndDiscussion.wav.

An earlier version of the song was recorded on 25 January 1964 on Hercus field tape 21/28, digitised by AIATSIS as HERCUS_L04-000220B, and includes a discussion of the meaning of the song with both Stan Day and Mrs Nancy Egan. The discussion of the song runs from 18:14 to 20:57 and includes a version of the song being sung. We have extracted this recording and named it:

HERCUS_L04-000220B_StanDay_Song2_ExplanationAndSong.wav.

A third recording of this song was made on 27 November 1965 on Hercus field tape 21/30, digitised by AIATSIS as HERCUS_L08-000997B.wav. The discussion of the song runs from 4:34 and one verse of the song is sung from 12:22 to about 14:00. We have extracted this recording and named it:

HERCUS_L08-000997B_StanDaySong2_SongAndDiscussion.wav.

Linguistic transcription

Hercus's (1986: 62) original transcription (with updated spelling) is presented as (2.13):

(2.13)

yerrateth-kurrk	**bucket-wurru**	**pen-wurru**
ˈjeratet̠-ˈkʊrɣ	*bucket*-wʊˈru	ˈpɛ̃ːn-wʊˈru
owlet-nightjar	bucket-mouth	hollow.tree-mouth

ngarnity	**nya**	**cook-ata**
ˈŋa·ɳɪc	ɲa	*cook*-ɐˈtɐ
cadge.POT	indeed	cook-LOC

ngurkity	**nyula**	**cook**	**pileny**
ˈŋu̟ɻkɪc	ɲʊla	*cook*	ˈpɪˌlɛ̃·ɲ
swallow.POT	that	cook	as well

kathang	**mina**	**pakatyerrity**
ˈkaθaŋ	mɪnɐ	ˈpakɐcɛˌric
later	indeed	look.enquiringly.RECIP.POT

windyaluk	**nya**	**cook**	**nyunga?**
ˈwɪndjɐˌlʊk	ɲa	*cook*	ˈɲʊŋɐ
where	indeed	cook	from.around.here

nyula	**malu**	**ngurkin**	**ngathang**
ˈɲʊlɐ	maˌlu	ˈŋu̟ɻkin	ŋaˈθaŋ
him	that.one	swallow.PST	ugly.devil

'The owlet-nightjar, with a mouth like a bucket, a mouth like a hollow tree – he would go cadging after the cook, and he would even follow that cook as well. After a while the people would look at each other asking "where's the cook from around here? That ugly devil has swallowed him".'

Linguistic notes

The word **malu** may represent an ergative form of the distal demonstrative **mala**, described by Hercus (1986: 39) as being unusual for pronouns. The ergative in Wemba-Wemba, termed operative by Hercus (1986), is marked **-u** after words ending in a consonant.

Version as sung, with notes on the poetics

In the recording on Hercus field tape 21/31 (HERCUS_L08-000998A_StanDaySong2_SongOnly), the text is sung twice, as in example (2.14), with an inserted initial word or vocable, and the last line omitted on the repeat.

(2.14) (a pa la) yeerrateth-kuurrk bucket-wurruu pen-wurruu
ngarnity nya cook-ata
ngurkity nyula cook pileny
kathang mina pakatyerrity
windyaluk nya cook nyunga?
nyula malu ngurkin ngathang

yerrateth-kurrk bucket-wurru pen-wurru
ngarnity nya cook-ata
ngurkity nyula cook pileny
kathang mina pakatyerrity
windyaluk nya cook nyunga?

There is a word that is sung before the first transcribed word **yerrateth-kurrk**, which sounds like [a pa la] or possibly [a ma la], and after listening back to the recordings several times, we suggest that it may be something like **ngathamulang**, a word that could relate to **ngathang** 'devil', which is the final word of the song text and occurs before the repetition.

The realisation of stress in this song is different from that of the spoken language, with a number of cases of stress shifting onto the final syllable. For example, in speech there would be first syllable stress on the word **wurru**, which is compounded with *bucket* and with **pen** 'hollow tree' in the first line of the song. The expected compound stress of the second compound is **pén wùrru**, but with both of these words the stress is clearly on the final syllable **-rru**. This syllable is realised with a longer note, as seen in Figure 2.3.

We observe a similar phenomenon with the word **pákatjèrrity** 'would look enquiringly at each other' in which there is final stress, on the potential marker **-ity**, also associated with a final long note.

Hercus (1986: 22) had already noted the differences between spoken language and song language in terms of stress, and gave several examples of spoken language versions of pieces of song language text, saying that 'it is impossible to draw up any definite system of rules of accentuation in singing'.

The rule '[i]f the second syllable contains the vowel **e** followed by the palatalised alveo-dental nasal **nj** or the velar nasal **ŋ** this second syllable attracts the secondary accent', discussed by Hercus (1986: 21), relates to the word **pileny** 'as well', and the secondary stress on the second syllable is clear in the singing.

The final **a** on **mina** 'indeed' also seems to be a feature of song language, because in spoken language it is a single syllable **min**. This addition of a final syllable, and shifting of stress onto final syllables even when they are inflectional suffixes, discussed earlier, may be examples of the requirements of the music affecting the stress.

The last word of the verse, **ngathang**, is based on the root **ngatha** 'ugly devil'. Hercus (1986: 30) treats this as a use of the ablative in place of the ergative (termed 'operative' in Hercus 1986). Hercus (1992) defines this word as:

> name of a mythical being, a small creature that lived in reed-beds. He was the Wembawemba equivalent of the Werkaya *ngatye* or 'little people'. The *ngatha* was regarded as harmless; he would appear at dusk and sometimes even talk to people in their own language and camp near them, particularly if they had caught lobsters, his favourite food.

Another related word is **ngathayikuny** 'my word! exclamation to arrest attention'. This seems to be a related word with a historical common origin. This is discussed in the recording HERCUS_L08-000997B at around 16:00.

Musical transcription and analysis (by Grace Koch)

The musical analysis of **Yerrateth-kurrk** 'the owlet-nightjar' is presented as Figure 2.3.

Owlet Nightjar, Yerrateth-kurrk

Song 2 recorded by Luise Hercus
sung by Stan Day

HERCUS_L08-000998_StanDaySong2

Figure 2.3: Musical analysis of Stan Day, Song 2, Yerrateth-kurrk 'the owlet-nightjar'

Source: Song from HERCUS_L08-000998A, analysis by Grace Koch.

This song has a tonal centre of Bb, and form similar to a major scale.

The melody of this song is very similar to the second version of Song 1, Nganuty-nganuty 'the bat' (see section 2.2.2), which makes sense because both are part of the same story. We can hear long repetitions of parts of the text on one pitch and a melodic leap of a minor seventh near the beginning of the second reiteration of the text. There is, however, an extra phrase added between the two text reiterations, with the form of the text being ABA.

The vocal range of this song is slightly larger than Nganuty-nganuty 'the bat', at an octave and a minor third (C–Eb).

Unlike Nganuty-nganuty 'the bat', the text fits closely to the published version in Hercus (1986). Stan Day begins singing on the possibly vocable syllable, **(ng)a** (see discussion above), which rises by a slide of a minor third (D–F). Torrance (1887) shows an 'intonation' at the start of each of his notations, matching with this performance; however, the introductory **(ng) a** does not appear on the repeat of the text. In the first iteration, F is the pitch most repeated.

The singer takes a breath after **cook nyunga**. The short phrase following the breath stays on the F, descending a tone to the Eb just at the end. This is the B section of the text as referred to earlier. This completes the first verse.

The pitch range differs dramatically in the two iterations, as the first encompasses a minor sixth (D–Bb) with the second encompassing an octave and a minor third (C–Eb). The first verse moves stepwise except for a minor third interval at the very beginning and on the word 'cook' (D–F), and leaps of a perfect fourth occur at **yerrateth-kurrk** and between **bucket-wurru** and **pen-wurru** on the top line of the notation.

The repetition begins with a leap of a perfect fourth (C–F) that rises upwards to a leap of a minor seventh (F–Eb). The melody of the repetition moves with more intervallic leaps than the first iteration. Note the pattern of leaps at **penwurru ngarnity nya** on the third system and **cook pileny** in the last system.

The pitch slide referred to by Torrance (1887) can be heard on the word **pen** on the first system and at the start of the second system on **cook**. This slide is marked by a curve or a slur mark.

2.2.4 Song 3 – Going to the land of the dead

The song is the most 'traditional' of the Stan Day's songs. Hercus (1986: 63) introduced it as follows:

> This was Tommy's favourite song, it was also his longest, and contained a number of verses. It was composed very much earlier that the other songs, shortly after the death of Tommy's own grandmother. Mr. Day regretted that he had only learnt the first verse properly. Each verse apparently told of a different trial which the dead woman would have to go through to reach the Land of the Dead; if she failed she would be 'properly dead for ever'. The first verse relates how she had to escape from being ensnared in nets. Second version was recalled in outline and involved *gaḏəl*, that is the clashing together of two big trees, and the dead person had to pass between them, just at the right moment. Other trials were described in subsequent verses. The Land of the Dead was thought of as being in the sky.
>
> This song is of particular interest and reflects ancient traditions. The belief in trials to be undergone by the dead on their way to the Land of the Dead is closely linked with what is known of the traditions of the Wiradjuri (N.S.W.) and other south-eastern Australian people. Berndt has given an excellent summary of these traditions (1964:12).

In the recording on Hercus field tape 21/3 (HERCUS_L04-000211B_StanDay_Song3.wav), Stan Day said that 'in all there were 10 verses'. This use of the numeral '10' may have implied 'many'; clearly this is a fragment of what was a much larger song.

The word **kathəl** was defined in Hercus (1992) as 'sound of knocking: limbs of trees knocking together, banging of the time-sticks, clapping of hands'.

The idea of the land of the dead being in the sky may be related to the Keledia song (see section 2.5). In Eastern Kulin, the sky to which the dead went was called *Tharangalk-bek* by Howitt, and was also a location to which the 'doctors' (**wirrarrap** in Eastern Kulin) could travel and from which they could return (Howitt 1904: 381) (see section 3.1.3.1). There seems also to have been a connection between birds, which perhaps could have brought messages about death, and the sky and death. There may have been other connections also.

Note that this song and the railway song recorded by von Luschan (see section 2.8) both commence with the question words 'what is'; this may have been a stylistic feature common to a number of songs.

The text

The full text and translation, based on Hercus (1986: 63), is presented as Box 2.6:

Box 2.6: Song 3 – Going to the land of the dead

Author: Tommy; transmitted by Marrərt (Grandfather David Taylor)	
winyarr kila lepuwəlang	Who is this chasing up and disturbing the birds?
walpukanaty! kukminyek	You people look around and see! It is my own grandmother.
pirkupirkupirkuwak	Undo the net, for heaven's sake undo it!
yukuwak moyiku tyak	Put it down on the ground this way!
kuyin-kat-min wirri tirtənayuk	Go on like mad! Run! There is a new (and bigger) one.
mala ngunum parrangguwiny-kat	That one will certainly kill you.

Source: Based on Hercus (1986: 63); adapted by authors.

Recordings

Three versions of this song were recorded, the first on 18 April 1962 on Hercus field tape 21/3, which has been digitised by AIATSIS as HERCUS_L04-000211B. The discussion of the song Going to the land of the dead commences at 30:00 on HERCUS_L04-000211B, with the song itself running from 30:34 to 31:04 and the discussion continuing up until 31:56. This is analysed musically below as Figure 2.4. We have extracted this recording and named it:

HERCUS_L04-000211B_StanDay_Song3.wav.

The second recording was made on 27 November 1965 on Hercus field tape 21/29, digitised by AIATSIS as HERCUS_L04-000221B. This recording is somewhat longer and contains the explanation of the meaning of the text. The discussion of Song 3 commences at 13:08 and runs until 21:45. There is no complete rendition of the song in this recording, rather, Stan Day sings short sections and then explains the meaning of those sections, often repeating the words in spoken language (see example (2.9)). We have extracted this recording and named it:

HERCUS_L04-000221B_StanDay_Song3_ExplanationAndSong.wav.

The third version was recorded on 24 January 1964 on Hercus field tape 21/28, digitised by AIATSIS as HERCUS_L04-000220B. The discussion runs from 24:28 to 26:30, and includes a discussion about the words for 'heaven' from Nancy Egan; one verse is sung at 25:39. We have extracted this recording and named it:

HERCUS_L04-000220B_StanDay_Song3_ExplanationAndSong.wav.

Linguistic transcription

The transcription presented here as (2.15) follows Hercus (1986: 63).

(2.15)	**wínyarr**	**kila**	**lépuwə̀lang**
	ˈwiɲar	kila	ˈlepʊəˌlaŋ
	who-(is)	now	chase up birds.FREQ.PRESPART

wálpukanàty!	**kúkminyèk**
ˈwalpʊgɐˌnac	ˈku:kmɪˌɲek
see.2PL	grandmother.indeed.1SG.POSS

pírkupírkupírkuwàk
ˈpüɻkʊˈpüɻkʊˈpüɻkʊˌwak
undo.REDUPL.REDUPL.IMP

yúkuwak	**móyiku**	**tyák**
ˈju:kʊwak	ˈmoigʊ	ˈca-k
put-down.IMP	this way	ground-

kúyin-kat-min	**wírri**	**tírtənàyuk**[27]
ˈkuin-kat-mɪn	ˈwirɪ	ˈtüʈəˌnaiʊk
go on-indeed-indeed	run	new one.3SG.POSS

27 Hercus (1986: 63) gives the orthographic form of this word as *diḍenaiug* with an /e/ vowel on the second syllable. This spelling is presented in Hercus (1992) as tirtenayuk. However the vowel in the phonetic transcription, and the vowel that we hear is the schwa, so we will spell this word with schwa in the orthography also.

mála	**ngùnum**	**párrangguwìny-kat**
ˈmalɐ	ˈŋunʊm	ˈparaŋguˌiɲ-kat
that-one	you	kill-FUT-indeed

'Who is this chasing up and disturbing the birds? You people look around and see! It is my own grandmother. Undo the net, for heaven's sake undo it! Put it down on the ground this way! Go on like mad! Run! There is a new (and bigger) one. That one will certainly kill you.'

Notes

Hercus (1986: 63) wrote:

> Line 1 is composed in accordance with what was probably a widespread literary convention. An old Wiradjuri song handed down from Fred Biggs to Charlie Kirby, and recorded by Dr Ellis and the writer, deals with quite a different subject matter (the subject of a small boy lost in the fog), and yet the beginning shows the same literary tradition: 'Who is that disturbing the cockatoos? It is your child …'
>
> Line 2 was addressed to imaginary bystanders, while the rest of the song was addressed to the dead woman.

Linguistic notes

In the word **kukminyek**, the emphatic word **min** 'indeed' is placed between the root **kuka** 'grandmother' and the 1st person singular possessive marker **-(ny)ek**. Hercus (1986: 64) explained that **kukminyek** 'apparently meant *my own grandmother* and was an emphatic possessive form, unattested elsewhere'. She added that **kukangek** was the usual form for 'my grandmother'.

The root **kuyin** 'go on' is an explanation, explained in Hercus (1992) as 'just go on! exclamation, often combined with an emphatic particle as **kuyin-kat** to mean "don't you dare!"'

Like a number of songs in this collection, it commences with a question. We also see this in Shearing on Tulla Station (see section 2.2.5) and Mary Moore's song 'Where is the Emu?' (see section 2.9.1).

Version as sung, with notes on poetics

The text is sung twice, as shown in (2.16):

(2.16) a winyarr kila lepuwəlang
walpukanaty kuk[u]minyek kuk[u]minyek
pirkupirkupirkuwak
yukuwak moyiku tyak
kuyin-kat-min wirri tirtənayuk
mala ngu(num) parrangguwiny-kat

o winyarr kila lepuwəlang
walpukanaty kuk[u]minyek kuk[u]minyek
pirkupirkupirkuwak
yukuwak moyiku tyak
kuyin-kat-min wirri tirtənayuk
mala ngunum parrangguwiny-kat

The word **kuk(u)minyek** is sung twice in both verses, in each case, there is an epenthetic [u] vowel inserted after the root **kuk**.

Each verse is sung with an initial vocalisation, here notated as **a** in the first verse and **o** in the second verse.

The syllable **num** in the word **ngunum** in the first iteration of the song is sung very softly and virtually inaudible. We have shown it in brackets.

The musical transcription of this song is given in Figure 2.4:

Going to the Land of the Dead – Song 3

recorded by Luise Hercus
sung by Stan Day
HERCUS_L04-000211B-StanDay_Song3_SongOnly

Range: Minor 9th (D# - E)

Figure 2.4: Musical analysis of Stan Day, Song 3, Going to the land of the dead

Source: From HERCUS_L04-000211B, analysis by Grace Koch.

This song has a tonal centre of B, and form similar to a major scale.

The melody and structure of this song is almost identical to the Hercus recording of the song Yerrateth-kurrk 'the owlet-nightjar' (see section 2.2.3). It is performed a semitone higher than Song 2. Similar features include an introductory syllable (a) sliding up a minor third, a short middle section on a single pitch (although Song 2 descends a tone downward at the end of the middle section), a melodic leap of a minor seventh during the second reiteration of the text, and long repetitions of a single pitch at the end of each phrase.

Song 3 differs from Song 2 in several minor ways. The short middle section is sung on part of the text at the end (**mala ngunum parranguwinykat**). The middle section for Song 2 introduces a new set of words from the first and third sections. Also, the second repetition of the text is preceded by an **o** sung on the pitch E.

Both songs differ slightly in their ranges, with Song 2 having a range of an octave and a minor third (C–Eb) while Song 3 encompasses a minor ninth (D#–E) Finally, there are a series of rests dividing the last line of the song from the preceding section. Song 2 has no such division.

2.2.5 Song 4 – Shearing on Tulla Station

This song relates to Tulla Station, earlier named Beremegad, which is between Tullakool[28] and Noorong between the Wakool and Edwards rivers. Use of the name Tulla to refer to the station only occurred in the 1870s, while the Wemba-Wemba name for the station is **Tilung** (Hercus 1992). Hercus observed that the form **talang** is a partial adaptation to the Europeanised pronunciation of *Tulla* (1986: 64). The history of Tulla is discussed in Calder (1997). It is known that Nyawi (Bob Taylor) and other members of his family and associates worked there for many years. They would have worked there as young men.

Hercus (1986: 64) says of this song that 'the shearing went on far too long and so he made a song about it'. Shearing generally commenced in this area around August and would be completed long before Christmas. This song may be about a very late shearing season, which is perhaps recorded in the Tulla Station Shearing Books. On the other hand, it may be an example of poetic licence, that Nyawi is singing about how long the season is, exaggerating it by saying it was running almost to Christmas.

28 Located at 35.3866893° South, 144.0140741° East.

The text

The full text and translation, based on Hercus (1986: 64), is presented as Box 2.7:

Box 2.7: Song 4 – Shearing on Tulla Station

Author: Nyawi (Bob Taylor)	
nyatyərruwaluk kinyam tangguwiny	When is this going to finish?
waletyuwaniny Christmas	Christmas is coming very close
tyakuinyangurr New Year's Day	And we will be having our Christmas dinner on New Year's Day.
nguwanda tyerrika kutayəlang all day	Unwillingly I stand shearing all day long
woolshedata talanga	In the woolshed on Tulla Station.

Source: Based on Hercus (1986: 64); adapted by authors.

Recordings

There are three versions of this song recorded by Luise Hercus. The first, analysed musically below as Figure 2.5, was recorded on 19 July 1962 on Hercus field tape 21/2, digitised by AIATSIS as HERCUS_L04-000211A. The discussion of the song runs from 39:38 to 41:11 with the song from 39:38 to 40:17. We have extracted this recording and named it:

HERCUS_L04-000211A_StanDay_Song4.wav.

The second version was recorded on 5 March 1966 on Hercus field tape 21/28, digitised by AIATSIS as HERCUS_L04-000221A. This consists of an explanation of the meaning, running from 15:32 to 19:37. We have extracted this recording and named it:

HERCUS_L04-000221A_StanDay_Song4_Explanation.wav.

A third version was recorded on 28 March 1965 on Hercus field tape 21/30, digitised by AIATSIS as HERCUS_L08-000997B, running from 40:30 to 42:06. We have extracted this recording and named it:

HERCUS_L08-000997B_StanDaySong4_SongAndDiscussion.

Linguistic transcription

The linguistic analysis presented here as (2.17) follows Hercus (1986: 64).

(2.17)

nyátyərruwàluk	**kínyam**	**tángguwìny**
‘ɲatʲərʊˌwalʊk	‘kiɲam	‘tɑːŋguˌiɲ
when-abouts.3SG.POSS	this	finish-FUT

wáletyùwanìny	**Christmas**
‘waleˌdjʊwaˌnɪɲ	Christmas
come near-INTENS-FUT	Christmas

tyákùwinyangùrr	**New Year’s Day**
‘tʲaˌkʊiɲaˌŋur	New Year’s Day
eat-INTENS-FUT-1PL.INCL	New Year’s Day

ngúwanda	**tyérrika**	**kútáyəlàng**	**all day**
‘ŋuandɐ	‘tʲɛrɪkɐ	‘ku’taiəˌlaŋ	all day
unwilling-1SG	stand	shear.PRES.PART	all day

woolshedata	**tálanga**
woolshed ata	‘talaŋɐ
woolshed-LOC	Tulla-GEN

‘When is this going to finish? Christmas is coming very close and we will be having our Christmas dinner on New Year’s Day. Unwillingly I stand shearing all day long in the woolshed on Tulla Station.’

Linguistic notes

In Hercus (1992), the word for Tulla Station is given as **tilung**. The root form here is **talang**.

The double marking of possessive phrases in **woolshed-ata talang-a** is very typical of the language.

Hercus (1986: 64) noted that **kinyam** was ‘one of the rare instances of the use of the object form of the pronoun as a subject’.

Version as sung

The version sung in the recording on AIATSIS tape HERCUS_L04-000211A is exactly the same as that notated linguistically in Hercus (1986), save that there is an extended **i** sung on a two notes rising a tone after the word **tangguwiny**. The version as sung is presented in (2.18):

(2.18) nyatyerruwaluk kinyam tangguwiny i
waletyuwaniny Christmas
tyakuwinyangurr New Year's Day
nguwanda tyerrika kutayəlang all day
woolshedata talanga

Musical transcription and analysis (by Grace Koch)

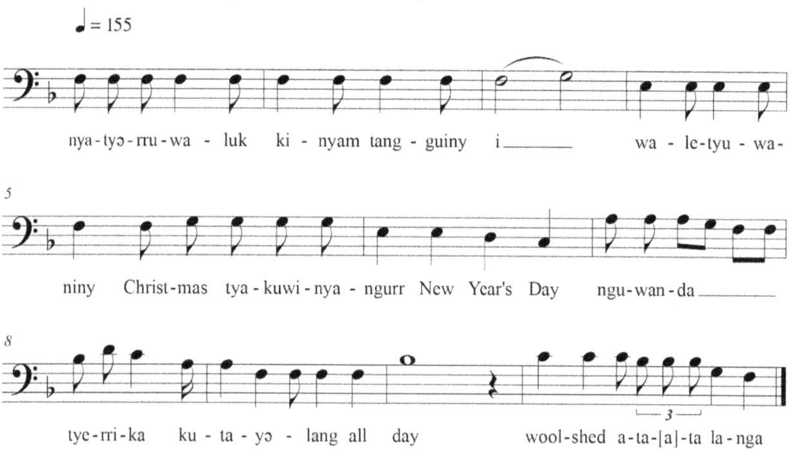

Figure 2.5: Musical analysis of Stan Day, Song 4, Shearing on Tulla Station
Source: Song from HERCUS_L04-000211A, analysis by Grace Koch.

This song has a tonal centre of F, and form similar to a major scale.

This song is totally different from the three preceding ones. Although it starts with a repetition of the pitch, F, it rises a tone on the syllable **i** (following the word **tangguwiny**), after which the melody has fewer pitch repetitions and more motion up and down. Also, the largest pitch leaps occur as a major sixth (between the words **Day** and **ngu-**) and a perfect fourth at the words **all day**.

The pitch-wise movement of the melody may display the influence of Western folk melodies. This is most apparent in the final phrase, beginning with the word **woolshed**. There is movement in the melody wherever the English words appear, such as the upward motion by a tone on the two syllables of **Christmas**, the downward stepwise progressing on **New Year's Day** and the leap of a perfect fourth on **all day** as mentioned above. Finally, the song is shorter than the preceding two, because it has one verse and a single melody.

2.2.6 Song 5 and 5a – Jack Brown's songs

In this section we present two songs, the longer version in section 2.2.6.1 and a shorter swearing song in section 2.2.6.2.

2.2.6.1 Song 5 – Jack Brown's song

Hercus (1986: 64) introduces this song as follows:

> Jack Brown was a Wembawemba man from near Deniliquin, and was not a relative but a friend of Tommy and of **Marəḑ** [**Marrərt**] and **Njaui** – 'these four old fellows were always together'. Jack Brown was younger than his friends. Stanley Day and Nancy Egan the grandchildren of **Marəḑ**, referred to him as 'poor old Jack Brown', because he always seemed to be getting into some kind of mischief.
>
> When Jack Brown was staying at Moonacullah Mission he overheard several old women saying bad things about him , and so he made up this song:

Jack Brown is photographed, with two young women, possibly his nieces, in Hercus (1986: xvi, photo 4).

The text

The full text and translation, based on Hercus (1986: 64), is presented as Box 2.8:

Box 2.8: Song 5 – Jack Brown's song

Author: Jack Brown	
kilanda wariwinyanda	I am going away now.
goodbye kuthən nguteyin kuthəp	Goodbye, you poor people, one should feel sorry for you.
nguteyin-kat tyurin yandin	You talked about me.
telkayinyan muyənatak	Your minds will be easy,
tyakinyarr Christmasatak	And you will eat your Christmas dinner (in peace),
nothinga-min nyarnapothən	Not worried about anything,
nyarnang-kat wariwin yawirrangurrak	Thinking 'he has gone, our enemy.'

Source: Based on Hercus (1986: 64); adapted by authors.

Recordings

This song is sung or discussed in five separate recordings. The first of these was made by Catherine Ellis on 22 January 1963, and recorded on her field tape No. 8, digitised by AIATSIS as Ellis_193_TrackB.wav. The discussion of the song runs from 6:58 to 8:15 on the digitisation, with the song sung from 7:00 to 7:18. The musical analysis of this song is presented as Figure 2.6. We have extracted this recording and named it:

Ellis_193_TrackB_StanDay_Song5.wav.

There are also five recordings made by Luise Hercus in which this song was sung, discussed or both. The first of these was recorded on 18 April 1965 on Hercus field tape 21/31, digitised by AIATSIS as HERCUS_L08-000998A.wav, running from 43:30 to 47:28. The musical analysis of this song is presented as Figure 2.7. We have extracted this recording and named it:

HERCUS_L08-000998A_StanDaySong5_SongAndDiscussion.wav.

Two more recordings were made by Luise Hercus on 5 March 1966. The first of these, on Hercus field tape 21/27, was digitised by AIATSIS as HERCUS_L04-000220B.wav, running from 58:18 to the end. We have extracted this recording and named it:

HERCUS_L04-000220B_StanDay_Song5_Explanation.wav.

The second of these was recorded on Hercus field tape 21/29, digitised by AIATSIS as HERCUS_L04-000221B.wav, running from 22:18 to 24:44. We have extracted this recording and named it:

HERCUS_L04-000221B_StanDay_Song5_ExplanationAndSong.wav.

A further recording, with discussion only, was made by Luise Hercus on 27 November 1965, on Hercus field tape 21/30, digitised by AIATSIS as HERCUS_L08-000997B.wav, running from 0:57 to 3:25.

The final recording listed here was made by Luise Hercus on 26 January 1965, on Hercus field tape 21/34, digitised by AIATSIS as HERCUS_L08-000999A.wav, running from 49:47 to 51:24. We have extracted this recording and named it:

HERCUS_L08-000999A_StanDaySong5_SongAndDiscussion.wav.

Linguistic transcription

The linguistic analysis, following Hercus (1986: 64–65), is presented as (2.19):

(2.19)	**kilanda**	**wariwinyanda**		
	‘ki·landɐ	‘wɔɹɪwɪɲan͵dɐ		
	now.1SG	go away.FUT.1SG		
	goodbye	**kuthən**	**nguteyin**	**kuthəp**
	goodbye	‘kʊθən	‘ŋu·te͵ɪn	‘kʊ͵θəp
	goodbye	poor people	you plural	pitying for
	nguteyin-kat	**tyurin**	**yandin**	
	‘ŋu·te͵ɪn-kat	‘cu̟ɹɪn	‘jandɪn	
	you-indeed	talk about.PST	me	
	telkayinyan	**muyənatak**		
	‘tɛl͵kaiɲan	mu:jəna͵tak		
	good.FUT.3PL	mind-2PL.POSS		
	tyakinyarr	**Christmasatak**		
	‘cakiɲar	‘Christmas a͵tak		
	eat.FUT.2SG	Christmas-2PL.POSS		

nothinga-min	**nyarnapothən**
nothing ɐmɪn	ˈɲaɳapoˌθən
nothing-indeed	worry.PST.PART

nyarnang-kat	**wariwin**	**yawirrangurrak**
ˈɲaɳaŋ-kat	ˈwɔɹɪˌwɪn	ˈjauwɪraŋʊˌrak
thinking-indeed	go away	enemy-1PL.POSS

Variant of the last line:

mala-kat	**wariwin**	**yawirrangurrak**
ˈmala-kat	ˈwɔɹɪˌwɪn	ˈjauwɪraŋʊˌrak
he-indeed	go away	enemy-1PL.POSS

‘I am going away now. Goodbye, you poor people, one should feel sorry for you. You talked about me. Your minds will be easy and you will eat your Christmas dinner (in peace), not worried about anything, thinking ‘he has gone, our enemy.’

Linguistic notes

Hercus (1986: 65) notes that **tyakinyarr** in line 5 is a singular form where one might expect a plural, which would be **tyakinyatj**.

Hercus (1992) lists the word for ‘worry’ as **nyarna** and the past participle form as **nyarnapothən**, which contains the root and also the past participle suffix **-ən**. There are several other words that have what Hercus described as an irregular past participle form in **pothən**.

Versions as sung

In the version recorded by Catherine Ellis, the musical analysis of which is presented as Figure 2.6, the text is sung as given in example (2.20). Note that in place of the last line as shown in example (2.19), the variant line is sung twice. Otherwise the text is exactly as found in the analysis presented in (2.19):

(2.20) kilanda wariwinyanda
goodbye kuthən nguteyin kuthap
nguteyin-kat tyurin yandin
telkayinyan muyənatak
tyakinyarr Christmasatak

nothinga-min nyarnapothən
mala-kat wariwin yawirrangurrak
mala-kat wariwin yawirrangurrak

In the version recorded by Luise Hercus, on AIATSIS tape HERCUS_L08-000998A.wav, the musical analysis of which is presented in Figure 2.7, the text is exactly as presented in Hercus (1986) and given as (2.19), with the exception of an initial vocable **a**, as shown in the transcription of this version given in (2.21):

(2.21) a kilanda wariwinyanda
goodbye kuthən nguteyin kuthap
nguteyin-kat tyurin yandin
telkayinyan muyənatak
tyakinyarr Christmasatak
nothinga-min nyarnapothən
nyarnang-kat wariwin yawirrangurrak
mala-kat wariwin yawirrangurrak

In both versions we can observe that there is a line-final rhyme **-atak** in the fourth and fifth lines. The first six lines of the song are slightly shorter, with eight syllables each, and in the musical transcription in Figure 2.7, each of these lines finishes with a stressed (lengthened) note, marked either with a dotted quaver, or with quaver followed by a rest, so that structure of this text as having six lines of close to equal length is very clear. The final two lines are longer, each with 11 syllables.

Hercus (1986: 22–23) discussed the 'accent' system in singing, based on these songs. Taking line 5 of this song, **tyakinyarr Christmasatak**, as an example, she observed that whereas in 'normal' speech there would be accent/stress on the first syllable of each of these two words, in the song there is stress on the last syllable of **Christmasatak** as well. We suggest that this is an indication of the fact that in this song, at least, final accent/stress is present on each of the lines.

It is possible to view the first three lines as a group and the second group of three lines (lines 4–6) as a group. Thus in Figure 2.7 the first line, **kilanda wariwinyanda** rises in pitch from D to F# and the same thing is found in the fourth line **telkayinyan muyənatak**.

Musical transcription and analysis (by Grace Koch)

Jack Brown's Song

Song 5 recorded by Cath Ellis
sung by Stan Day
ELLIS_193B_StanDay_Song5

Figure 2.6: Musical analysis of Stan Day, Song 5, Jack Brown's song

Source: Song from Ellis_193_TrackB, analysis by Grace Koch.

This song has a tonal centre of E, and form similar to a major scale.

Figure 2.7: Musical analysis of Stan Day, Song 5, Jack Brown's song

Source: Song from HERCUS_L08-000998A, analysis by Grace Koch.

This song has a tonal centre of D, and form similar to a major scale.

This song returns partially to the style of Song 1 (Nganuty-nganuty 'the bat', see section 2.2.2) and Song 2 (Yerrateth-kurrk 'the owlet-nightjar', see section 2.2.3), where much of the text is sung on one pitch, especially in the last bars. However, this song has a less complex melody that moves in a stepwise, wavelike motion within a pitch range of a major third (E–F#–G#–F#–E for the Ellis recording and D–E–F#E–D for the Hercus one). This pattern occurs three times for each rendition.

The main differences between the two versions comes at the beginning of the song and after the rest(s) close to the midpoint. When Stan Day sang the song to Ellis, he began with a leap of a perfect fourth (B–E), then began the wavelike melody until the rests, after which he sang a perfect fifth (B–F#) when he resumed the melody. The Hercus version stays within the wavelike melody with no intervallic leaps.

2.2.6.2 Song 5a – Jack Brown's swearing song

Stan Day sang a second, very short song for Luise Hercus, which she introduced as follows (1986: 66):

> Mr Day stated that this song was 'full of really bad swearing, and mind you, you could swear much worse in Wembawemba than in the whitefellow language'. He refused to sing it right through and only the first two lines could be recorded. They do not refer to the same situation as Song 5, but to some different escapade of Jack Brown's, and they were sung to an entirely different tune.

Note that although Luise says it is 'sung to an entirely different tune', the first two words, **kilanda wariwiny** are sung to a very similar tune to the first two words of Song 5 (Hercus version) in Figure 2.7.

The text

The full text and translation, based on Hercus (1986: 65), is presented as Box 2.9:

Box 2.9: Song 5a – Jack Brown's swearing song

Author: Jack Brown	
kilanda wariwinyanda kamrrandyatin	I am going away to Cummeroogunga now.
mayanda tyikipala yuminy	I'll be a cheeky fellow there.

Source: Based on Hercus (1986: 65); adapted by authors.

Recordings

There are two versions of this very short song in the Hercus recordings. The first, recorded on 27 November 1965, is on Hercus field tape 21/30, digitised by AIATSIS as HERCUS_L08-000997B.wav. The song and discussion run from 3:25 to 4:34. The musical analysis of this song is presented in Figure 2.8. We have extracted this recording and named it:

HERCUS_L08-000997B_StanDaySong5a_SongAndDiscussion.

The second recording was made on 5 March 1966 on Hercus field tape 21/27, digitised by AIATSIS as HERCUS_L04-000220B, running from 61:25 to 61:57. This is a very short discussion of the meaning of the song. We have extracted this recording and named it:

HERCUS_L04-000220B_StanDay_Song5a_Explanation.wav.

Linguistic transcription

The linguistic analysis, following Hercus (1986: 65), is presented as (2.22):

(2.22)	**kilanda**	**wariwinyanda**	**kamrrandyatin**
	‘ki·landɐ	‘wɔɻɪwɪɲan͵dɐ	‘kamraɲɟɐ͵tin
	now.1SG	go away.FUT.1SG	Cummeroogunga-to
	mayanda	**tyikipala**	**yuminy**
	‘ma·jandɐ	‘cikɪ͵pɐ͵la	‘jʊ͵miɲ
	there.1SG	cheeky fellow	be.FUT

‘I am going away to Cummeroogunga now. I’ll be a cheeky fellow there.’

Note that the usual allative in Wemba-Wemba was expressed by the general oblique **-a** (Hercus 1986: 30). The form meaning ‘to Cummeroogunga’ does not have this suffix.

Musical transcription and analysis (by Grace Koch)

Stan Day Song 5a

Recorded by Luise Hercus
Sung by Stan Day

HERCUS_L08-000997B_StanDaySong5a_SongOnly.xsc

Range: Perfect 5th (A - E)

Figure 2.8: Musical analysis of Stan Day, Song 5a, Jack Brown’s swearing song

Source: Song from HERCUS_L08-000997B, analysis by Grace Koch.

This song has a tonal centre of A, and form similar to a major scale.

This version follows the melodic line of both the Hercus and Ellis recordings of Song 5 up to the last two bars. On the words **tyiikpala yuminy**, Stan Day adds an A major triad, possibly showing a Western influence. Only two other songs that he sang, Song 4 (Shearing on Tulla Station, see section 2.2.5) and Song 8 ('Sentai', the lazy dog, see section 2.2.9), end in Western-style melodic phrases, moving with wide melodic leaps.

2.2.7 Song 6 – Looking for dingoes

This song is about dogs running along the banks of the Wakool River. It presumably refers to the need for dogs to keep dingoes away from the sheep that would have been grazing on one of the sheep stations. Hercus introduced the song as follows (1986: 66):

> Bob Taylor was out in the bush with his sons and decided he would send them back home, so that he could go on his own along the Wakool River looking for dingoes. So he made this song about it.

The text

The full text and translation, based on Hercus (1986: 66), is presented as Box 2.10:

Box 2.10: Song 6 – Looking for dingoes

Author: Nyawi (Bob Taylor)	
kiwanda yinga wirra	I'm going along this way now,
yarkuwanda wilkarr ngurrawa	And I'm looking around to see if I can spot a dingo
ngarangaranda wirra	As he runs along sniffing.
ngai nyakiny kila	Crikey! I might well see one directly
piyəlanggəlang Werkulatawa	Running along the edge of the Wakool.
nyirringdəlata kingga mala nya	Here in the creek-bed is the place
tyerrityerrawuk puyəkilang tyerrimumuk	Where the soil has been disturbed as he was licking himself, bottom upwards.
waruperpuk yarəkiny yawirruk	He won't go looking for meat again until the day after tomorrow.

Source: Based on Hercus (1986: 66); adapted by authors.

Recordings

There are four recorded versions of this song. The first two are also musically analysed. The first, recorded on 22 January 1963, was recorded by Catherine Ellis on Tape 8, and digitised by AIATSIS as Ellis_193_TrackB, with the song and discussion running from 3:33 to 5:15 on the digitised version. The musical analysis of this version is presented in Figure 2.9. We have extracted this recording and named it:

Ellis_193_TrackB_StanDay_Song6.wav.

The second recording was that made by Luise Hercus on 28 March 1965 on Hercus field tape 21/30, with the discussion running from 35:32 to 38:15. The musical analysis of this version is presented in Figure 2.10. We have extracted this recording and named it:

HERCUS_L08-000997B_StanDaySong6_SongAndDiscussion.wav.

A third version of the song, actually the earliest, was recorded on 19 July 1962 on Hercus field tape 21/2, running from 36:42 to 37:35. We have extracted this recording and named it:

HERCUS_L04-000211A_StanDay_Song6.wav.

A fourth version was recorded on 5 July 1966 on Hercus field tapes 21/29 and 21/30. These were both digitised together by AIATSIS as HERCUS_L04-000221A, with the singing and discussion of this song running from 20:00 to 20:26 (where field tape 21/29 finishes) and then running on to 30:54. We have extracted this recording and named it:

HERCUS_L04-000221A_StanDay_Song6_Explanation.wav.

Linguistic transcription

The linguistic analysis, following Hercus (1986: 66), is presented as (2.23):

(2.23)	**kiwanda**	**yinga**	**wirra**
	‘ki·wan͵dɐ	‘jiŋa	wi’ra
	right now.1SG	this way	hurry

yarkuwanda	**wilkarr**	**ngurrawa**
‘jaɻkʊwandɐ	‘wɪlkar	ŋura’wɐ
look for.1SG	dingo	?

ngarangaranda	**wirra**
‘ŋaɻɐˌŋaɻandɐ	‘wira
sniff(PRS)	run(PRS)

ngai	**nyakiny**	**kila**
‘ŋai	‘ɲakɪɲ	ki’la
crikey!	see.FUT	directly

piyəlanggəlang	**Werkulatawa**
‘piəˌlaŋgəlaŋ	‘wɛɻkʊlɐˌtawɐ
run along bank.FREQ.PRES.PART	Wakool-ALONG

nyirringdəlata	**kingga**	**mala**	**nya**
‘ɲirɪŋdəlatɐ	‘kiŋkɐ	‘malɐ	‘ɲa
creek bed.LOC	here	then	indeed

tyerrityerrawuk	**puyəkilang**	**tyerrimumuk**
‘cɛrɪˌcɛrɐwʊk	‘bu:jəkɪlaŋ	‘cɛrɪˌmumʊk
disturbed soil	lick.PRES.PART	upwards.bottom.3SG.POSS

waruperrpuk	**yarəkiny**	**yauwirruk**
‘wɔɻʊˌpɛrpʊk	‘jɛɻəkɪɲ	‘jauwɪˌrʊk
day after tomorrow.3SG.POSS	search for.FUT	meat.3SG.POSS

‘I’m going along this way now and I’m looking around to see if I can spot a dingo as he runs along sniffing. Crikey! I might well see one directly running along the edge of the Wakool. Here in the creek-bed is the place where the soil has been disturbed as he was licking himself, bottom upwards. He won’t go looking for meat again until the day after tomorrow.’

Linguistic notes

In Hercus (1992), the word for 'run along' is given as **piyalanngila**, with /a/ as the second vowel, not schwa. This form includes the frequentative particle **-ila**.

Hercus (1992) gives the word for the Wakool rivers as **Werkul**.

The word for 'disturbed soil' is listed in Hercus (1992) as being derived from **tyerrika** 'stand'.

Hercus (1992) explains the word **tyerrimumuk** as 'upside down "stand up bottom" (adverb based on verb+Npos)'. The root verb here is again **tyerrika** 'stand', while **mum** means 'bottom'.

The word **waruperrpuk** is based on the word **perrpuk** 'tomorrow', which Hercus (1992) notes is an adverb formed with the possessive marker. The root is **perrp** 'morning'. Note that we have followed Hercus's (1986, 1992) analysis of Wemba-Wemba as having two rhotic sounds, written as **rr** and **r**. Corey Theatre (2024) suggests a reanalysis of the 'rhotic' sounds in Victorian languages.

Hercus (1992) gives the word for 'search for' as '**yarka**, in song **yarəka**'.

Version as sung, with notes on poetics

There are two versions analysed musically, that recorded by Catherine Ellis, analysed in Figure 2.9, and that recorded by Luise Hercus, analysed in Figure 2.10. The musical analysis of this song proved particularly challenging, as we were in general not able to hear all of the words that were transcribed by Hercus (1986), and heard additional words that we could not transcribe. Three of the authors (Hercus, Koch and Morey) listened to this song repeatedly, together and individually, but could not make out the words more clearly than has been presented in the musical analyses below.

Because of this, we will not present a full transcription of what we heard in this section. In the version recorded by Ellis, the text was sung twice. We can make out more words in the first iteration, the text of which is presented as (2.24), with the sections that cannot be made out in [ ] square brackets:

(2.24) a kiwanda yinga wirra
[an additional word that cannot be made out] a kiwanda yinga wirra
[an additional word that cannot be made out] yarəkuwanda wilkarr ngurrawa
ngarangaranda [remainder of line cannot be made out]
[we cannot make out the words of this line]
piyəlanggəlang Werkulatawa
nyirringtelata kingga mala nya
tyerrityerrawuk puyəkilang [remainder of line cannot be made out]
waruperpuk yarəkiny yauwirruk

In this verse, and in its repeat, and also in the version recorded by Hercus, the first line is sung twice. In the Ellis version, there is a vocable **a** preceding the first word **kiwanda**. Also, in all the sung versions of this line, there is another word after **wirra** that we cannot make out. It may possibly belong to the next line. It sounds something like [kujilaŋ] and may be a verb in with a continuous **-ila** and present participle **-ang**.

The fact that the first line is made up of **kiwanda yinga wirra** is confirmed by the final stress on **wirra**. This is a line final feature that was also discussed by Hercus (1986: 22).

As can be seen in example (2.24), large portions of the text could not be made out.

Musical transcription and analysis (by Grace Koch)

The version of this song recorded by Catherine Ellis is sung twice, whereas that recorded by Luise Hercus is only sung once. Stan Day was aware that the songs made by **Nyawi** (Bob Taylor) were different from those made by Tommy and transmitted by **Marrərt** (David Taylor). He said, 'that's by a different maker altogether, you can see the difference here, can't you?' (HERCUS_L08-000997B).

The musical analysis of the song recorded by Catherine Ellis is presented as Figure 2.9:

Looking for Dingoes

Song 6 recorded by Cath Ellis
sung by Stan Day
ELLIS_193B_StanDay_Song6.wav

♩ = 183

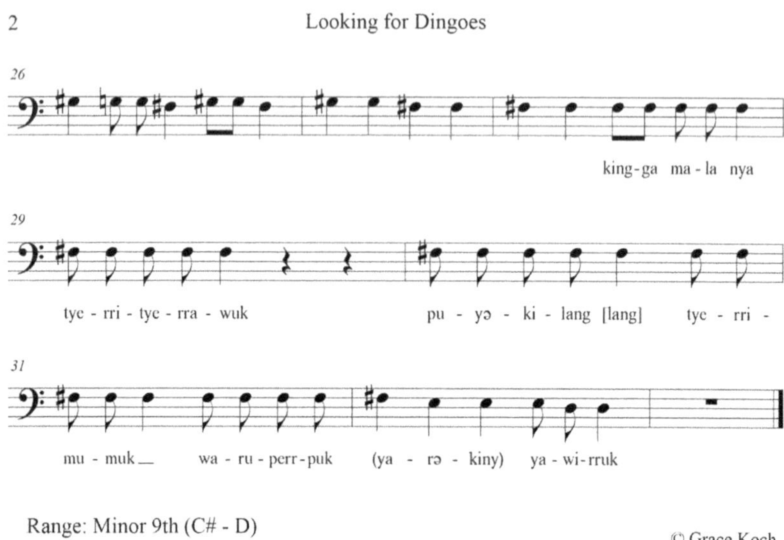

Figure 2.9: Musical analysis of Stan Day, Song 6, Looking for dingoes
Source: Song from Ellis_193_TrackB, analysis by Grace Koch.

Figure 2.9 has a tonal centre of B, and form similar to a major scale.

Figure 2.10 has a tonal centre of F, and form similar to a major scale.

These two performances of this song, originally composed by Bob Taylor, were sung for Ellis in 1963 (Figure 2.9) and for Hercus in 1965 (Figure 2.10). Stan Day sings the song twice for Ellis, with each verse beginning with the words **kiwanda yinga wirra**. When he sang it for Ellis, he began with the syllable **a** on the first pitch of the song, but he does not do this for the Hercus version, and launches straight into the word **kiwanda**. He sang the song more rapidly for Hercus (♩ = 210) than for Ellis (♩ =183), and also at a lower pitch (C as opposed to F# for Ellis). As for most of the earlier songs, both versions use long repetitions of text on single pitches, with one pitch per syllable.

For both versions, the melody moves stepwise generally downward except for an octave jump near the midpoint for Ellis and much earlier, at bar 3, for Hercus. A much smaller leap of a major third occurs the second time the word **kiwanda** is sung for both versions.

Looking for Dingoes

Song 6 recorded by Luise Hercus
sung by Stan Day
HERCUS_L08_000997B_StanDaySong6_SongOnly

Figure 2.10: Musical analysis of Stan Day, Song 6, Looking for dingoes
Source:Song from HERCUS_L08-000997B, analysis by Grace Koch.

It was very difficult to set the text as presented in Hercus (1986) to the melodic transcription, and there are large parts of the text that were unclear in the recording. As far as we can see, some of the text appears under different sections of the melody for each version. For example, in the Ellis version, the words **kingga mala** are sung for the melodic motif of F#–G#–F#–G# but the same motif at a lower pitch (C–D–C–D) was sung using the text **werkulatawa** in the Hercus version. Another example comes at the end of the song on the word **yawirruk**. As far as we can hear, Stan Day sang **yarəkiny yawirruk** at the end of each verse for Ellis and **[manyai] yawirruk** for Hercus (where **manyai** is a form for which we have no translation and is our best effort to interpret what he sings at that point). He sang the word on two pitches at the end of both verses for Ellis (E–D) and on a single pitch for Hercus (Bb).

2.2.8 Song 7 – Kangaroos and a dingo

In her introduction to this song, Hercus (1986: 66) wrote:

> One day the author saw a mob of kangaroos corning directly towards him. He was surprised until he realised that there was a dingo chasing them . He decided he would go for the dingo as it was worth more, and he made this song about it.

The fact of the dingo being worth more presumably refers to bounties paid by squatters or the government for the killing of dingoes. This places the authorship of this song clearly in the colonial period.

There is no record known to us of dingoes being killed for food in traditional Aboriginal society, and in at least parts of western Victoria the dingo was part of the totem system. Howitt (1904: 121) lists dingo as a 'sub-totem' in the Wotjobaluk tribe, which were one of the Wimmera groups speaking the Werkaya language. Therefore, the dingo was presumably a protected animal for at least some people. This demonstrates that this is a post-settlement type song.

The text

The full text and translation, based on Hercus (1986: 66), is presented as Box 2.11:

Box 2.11: Song 7 – Kangaroos and a dingo

Author: Tommy; transmitted by Marrərt (Grandfather David Taylor)	
malanda nyayin kingga kurre	The other day I saw a mob of kangaroos
pirrəpulang yerrəm tyurung-kuthəwiny	hopping towards me all in a row
moye yikeyo	one after the other straight at me.
nyinganda-min nyuməlang	I was thinking
nyanya kila	'now what is this?'
kikwanda-min nyayin wirrengən	but right then I saw a dog
ngarangaranda wirra	running along sniffing
moye yikeyo	and coming straight towards me.
wilkarr kuthəp murrənayiny yikeyang	It's a pity for you dingo but I'll kill you.

Source: Based on Hercus (1986: 66); adapted by authors.

Recordings

There are a number of versions of this song recorded, but only the first was musically analysed. This was a version recorded by Catherine Ellis on 22 January 1963 on tape 8. It was digitised by AIATSIS at Ellis_193_TrackB, and the discussion of this song runs from 10:57 to 12:28, with the song itself from 11:17 to 11:39. The musical analysis of this song is presented in Figure 2.11. We have extracted this recording and named it:

Ellis_193_TrackB_StanDay_Song7.wav.

The second version was recorded by Luise Hercus on 18 April 1962 on Hercus field tape 21/3, digitised by AIATSIS as HERCUS_L04-000211B. The song and discussion run from 28:15 to 29:36. We have extracted this recording and named it:

HERCUS_L04-000211B_StanDay_Song7.wav.

A third version was recorded on 5 March 1966 on Hercus field tape 21/28, digitised by AIATSIS as HERCUS_L04-000220B, running from 61:57 to 63:33. The digitisation of field tape 21/28 was cut partway through the discussion of this song, and continued on HERCUS_L04-000221A from 0:22 to 0:52. We have extracted the first part of this recording and named it:

HERCUS_L04-000220B_StanDay_Song7_Explanation.wav.

A fourth version was recorded on 27 November 1965 on Hercus field tape 21/29, digitised by AIATSIS as HERCUS_L04-000221A, running from 60:17 to the end at 64:34. We have extracted this recording and named it:

HERCUS_L04-000221A_StanDay_Song7_Explanation.wav.

The AIATIS digitisation of field tape 21/29 was cut in the middle of the recording of this song and continued on HERCUS_L04-000221B, running from 0:25 to 13:08, including singing a full verse from 8:36. We have extracted this recording and named it:

HERCUS_L04-000221B_StanDay_Song7_ExplanationAndSong.wav.

A further performance of the song was recorded on 24 May 1965 on Hercus field tape 21/35, digitised by AIATSIS as HERCUS_L08-000999B; this includes some discussion of this song from 31:50 to 33:48. Stan Day had partially forgotten the song, he said 'I can't get it myself now' but did explain that it was about a 'dingo driving them'; it may be an alternate version of Song 7, and we have extracted this recording and named it:

HERCUS_L08-000999B_StanDayUnknownSong.wav.

In this last recording,[29] Luise Hercus asked about the meaning of the first words of the song, which Stan Day gave as probably *kuthai kung kingga kurre*, explaining this as 'there's a big mob of kangaroos'. This discussion also includes words that sound to us like *kathap* and *nyarringin*, the second of which was explained by Stan Day as not meaning 'your name' but rather 'your forehead'. The word *nyarringin* is not found in the transcription of Song 7 given below, but we have included this recording here because of its content. Musically the style seems quite different from the version analysed in Figure 2.11.

29 This recording was only identified in early 2018, and we did not have the opportunity to discuss this with Luise Hercus before she died. Her knowledge of the language would likely have produced better transcriptions of the uncertain words than those we have presented here.

Linguistic transcription

The linguistic analysis, following Hercus (1986: 66–67), is presented as (2.25):

(2.25)

malanda	**nyain**	**kingga**	**kurre**
‘malandɐ	‘ɲaɪn	‘kiŋkɐ	kʊˌre
that one.1SG	see.PST	here	kangaroo

pirrəpulang	**yerrəm**	**tyurung-kuthəwiny**
‘pirəˌpʊlaŋ	‘jɛrəm	‘cuɻʊŋ-’kʊθəˌwiɲ
hop.FREQ.PRES.PART	1sg.ALL	lengthways

moye	**yikeo**
‘moˑje	‘jiˑkeɔ
this way	me.LOC

nyinganda-min	**nyuməlang**
‘ɲiŋandɐ-ˌmɪn	‘ɲuməˌlaŋ
then.1SG-indeed	know.FREQ.PRES.PART

nyanya	**kila**
‘ɲæɲɐ	‘kiˑlɐ
what	this

kikwanda-min	**nyain**	**wirrengən**
‘kikwandɐ-mɪn	‘ɲaɪn	‘wiˌrɛŋan
right then.1SG-indeed	see.PST	dog

ngarangaranda	**wirra**
‘ŋaɻɐˌŋaɻandɐ	‘wira
sniff.(PRES)	run.(PRES)

moye	**yikeo**
‘moˑje	‘jiˑkeɔ
this way	me.LOC

wilkarr	**kuthəp**	**murrənainy**	**yikeang**
ˈwilˌkar	kʊˈθɐp	ˈmʊrəˌnaiɲ	ˈjiˑkeˌaŋ
dingo	pity.PURP	live.FUT	me.ABL

'The other day I saw a mob of kangaroos hopping towards me all in a row one after the other straight at me. I was thinking 'now what is this?' but right then I saw a dog running along sniffing and coming straight towards me. It's a pity for you dingo but I'll kill you.'

Notes

The word **malanda** was glossed by Hercus (1986: 67) as 'the-other-day-I'.

The word **nyain** is an irregular past tense form form the root **nyaka** 'see' (see Hercus 1986: 46 for discussion of this verb).

The word **yerrəm** is an allative form of the 1st person singular pronoun. In Hercus (1986: 37) it is spelled with **e** in the second syllable, which would produce **yerrem**. The only place it was recorded is in this song.

The word **tyurung-kuthəwiny** is a compound of the word **tyurung** 'long, tall person'. Hercus (1992) does not list any gloss for **kuthəwiny**.

The word **yikeo** is listed by Hercus (1986: 37) as the locative form of the 1st person singular pronoun. The only place it was recorded is in this song. Hercus's original gloss was 'me-towards'.

The word **nyumila** meaning 'think' is the frequentative of the verb **nyuma** 'recognise, know'.

Hercus (1992) gives the form of the verb 'live' as **murrenda**, with the vowel **e** on the second syllable.

The word **yikeang** is listed by Hercus (1986: 37) as the ablative form of the 1st person singular pronoun. The only place it was recorded is in this song.

Version as sung, with notes on the poetics

The text as sung in the Ellis version is given as (2.26):

(2.26) a malanda nyayin kingga
a malanda nyayin kingga kurre
pirrəpulang yerrəm tyurung-kuthəwiny
moye yikeyo
kikwanda-min nyayin wirrengən
nyinganda-min nyuməlang
nyanya kila
wirra ngarngaranda wirra (wa mumuk)
wilkarr kuthəp murrenayiny yikeang

This differs somewhat from the analysis given by Hercus and reproduced as example (2.25). The first line is sung twice, although the word **kurre** only occurs on the repetition. Musically the first line sounds like it consists of only the words **malanda nyayin kingga** and the word **kurre** is added in an almost spoken form.

The other lines in text are not sung in the same order as in example (2.25), but rather as in (2.27):

(2.27) line 1 (twice, the first time without **kurre**)
line 2
line 3
line 6
line 4
line 5
a new line based on line 7
line 9

The line **wirra ngarngaranda wirra (wa mumuk)** is based on the line transcribed by Hercus, but repeats the word **wirra** and contains additional material that we hear as **wa mumuk**.

The eighth line in Hercus's linguistic transcription, a repetition of **moye yikeyo**, is not sung in this version.

Musical transcription and analysis (by Grace Koch)

Kangaroos and Dingo

Song 7 recorded by Cath Ellis
sung by Stan Day
ELLIS_193_StanDay_Song7

Figure 2.11: Musical analysis of Stan Day, Song 7, Kangaroos and a dingo

Source: Song from Ellis_193_TrackB, analysis by Grace Koch.

We are not able to determine a tonal centre or key for this song.

The first line of the song as shown in the notation has the same melody as the Ellis recording of Song 6 (Looking for dingoes, see section 2.2.7), differing only by the two adjacent rising pitches on the introductory **a**. The next line begins on D, which is up over an octave from the end of the first line, but the melody gradually descends after a long recitation on B, ending up on D.

The wavering pattern between two adjacent notes between bars 9 and 10 (F#–G) can be found in Song 6. Both Song 6 and Song 7 display rising and falling thirds (see bars 6, 10 and 11 in this song), but these appear as minor thirds in this song instead of the major thirds in Song 6.

The musical phrase after the rests, in bars 13 and 14, repeats the text on one note, but the final pitch drops a half tone. This can be compared to the pitch drop of a whole tone at the end of both versions of Song 6, Looking for dingoes.

2.2.9 Song 8 – 'Sentai', the lazy dog

Hercus introduced this song, composed by Nyawi, as follows (1986: 67):

> The author had a big good-natured dog, with a big head , but it was lazy and refused to hunt for its food, and so he made a song about it.

The name of the dog is Sentai, which has an initial /s/, a sound not part of traditional Wemba-Wemba phonology. Thus we can assume the song was composed well into colonial times.

The text

The full text and translation, based on Hercus (1986: 67), is presented as Box 2.12:

Box 2.12: Song 8 – 'Sentai', the lazy dog

Author: Nyawi (Bob Taylor)	
sentai nya karrinyuk murreng	Sentai, you big-headed dog,
perəpurrung werkityaliny	If you don't work,
takinyanguna panbarru tyurung-kuthəwiny	I will hit you with a wooden shovel lengthways (so that it will hurt more),
wuthak-min nya kangin nyuka tyak	So put your nose to the ground,
tyingtyingak pirkin	And wag your tail (ready for hunting)

Source: Based on Hercus (1986: 67); adapted by authors.

Recordings

There are several recorded versions of this song, of which the first two are analysed musically. The first recording was made by Catherin Ellis on 27 January 1963 on tape 8 and digitised by AIATSIS as Ellis_193_TrackB. The discussion of this song runs from 5:41 to 6:58. The musical analysis of this version is presented in Figure 2.12. We have extracted this recording and named it:

Ellis_193_TrackB_StanDay_Song8.wav.

A second version was recorded by Luise Hercus on 27 November 1965 on field tape 21/30, digitised by AIASTIS as HERCUS_L08-000997B. The discussion of this song commences at 59:09. The musical analysis of this version is presented in Figure 2.13. We have extracted this recording and named it:

HERCUS_L08-000997B_StanDaySong8_SongAndDiscussion.wav.

A further version had been recorded on the same field tape by Luise Hercus on the same day, consisting of a discussion of the meaning of the song running from 21:54 to 23:15.

The final version was recorded on 26 January 1965 on Hercus field tape 21/35, digitised by AIATSIS as HERCUS_L08-000999B, running from 15:50 to 19:57. We have extracted this recording and named it:

HERCUS_L08-000999B_StanDaySong8_SongAndDiscussion.wav.

Linguistic transcription

The linguistic analysis, following Hercus (1986: 67–68), is presented as (2.28):

(2.28)	**sentai**	**nya**	**karrinyuk**	**murreng**
	ˈsentaiˌ	ɲɐ	ˈkarɪˌɲʊk	ˈmuˌrɛ̃ŋ
	Sentai	indeed	big.3SG.POSS	head

	perəpurrung	**werkityaliny**
	ˈpɜɻəpʊˌruŋ	ˈwɜɻkɪcaˌliɲ
	if not	work.FREQ.FUT

takinyanguna	**panbarru**	**tjurung-kuthəwiny**
ˈtakɪɲaˌŋuna	ˈpanbɐru	ˈcuɻʊŋ-ˈkʊθəˌwiɲ
hit.FUT.1SG.2SG	wooden shovel.ERG	lengthways

wuthak-min	**nya**	**kangin**	**nyuka**	**tyak**
ˈwʊθak-mɪn	ɲɐ	ˈkaŋɪn	ˈɲukɐ	ˈcak
put down.IMP-indeed	indeed	nose.2SGPOSS	here	ground.OBL?

tyingtyingak	**pirkin**
ˈciŋcɪˌŋak	ˈpirˌkɪn
wag.IMP	tail.2SGPOSS

'Sentai, you big-headed dog, if you don't work, I will hit you with a wooden shovel lengthways (so that it will hurt more), so put your nose to the ground and wag your tail (ready for hunting).'

Notes

Hercus (1992) listed the word **perəpurrung** as being found 'only in song language'. A closely related form **Perəpaperəpa** is the name of the nearest related language to Wemba-Wemba and in that language **perəpa** was the word for 'no'. (See Hercus and Morey (2008) for more discussion.)

The word **takinyanguna** was glossed by Hercus (1986) as 'hit-will-I-you'. The suffix **(a)nguna** appears to subsume both a 1st person singular subject and 2nd person singular object.

The root form of the word for 'ground' is **tya**. The Hercus (1986) gloss for **tyak** was 'ground-to', although the usually allative suffix is **(k)al** (Hercus 1992). Of the case markers, Hercus (1992) wrote: 'those with initial -k- are affixed to vowel-final stems'. In this example, we have only the initial **-k** and no suffix.

Version as sung, with notes on poetics

The first version of this song was that recorded by Ellis, the musical analysis of which is presented in Figure 2.12. The words actually sung are presented here as (2.29):

(2.29) a sentai karrinyuk murreng
perəpurrung werkityaliny
takinyanguna panbarru-[a] tyurung-kuthəwiny
wuthak-min nya [nyinya] kangin nyuka tyak
tyingtyingak pirkin
[nya tyulipin kat nya tyulipin]

This differs from the version as analysed by Luise Hercus (in example (2.28)) in several ways. In the first line, there is an initial **a** vocable before the first word **sentai**, and the emphatic **nya** is omitted.

In the third line, the ergative marked word for 'wooden shovel', **panbarru**, is followed by another vocable **a**, while in the fourth line there is an additional syllable that we have read as **nyinya** following the emphatic **nya**.

The most significant difference between this version and that analysed by Hercus (1986) is that there is an additional line, consisting of a semi-repeated phrase and a very noticeable rise in pitch at the end. We read these words as **nya tyulipin, kat nya tyulipin**, where both **kat** and **nya** are emphatic ('indeed') and a word **tyulipin** which may be a noun with the 2nd person singular possessive marker **-in**. We do not know what this word may mean, but perhaps it refers to one of the dog's body parts.

The text of the version recorded by Luise Hercus, the musical analysis of which is presented as Figure 2.13, is presented as (2.30):

(2.30) sentai nya karrinyuk murreng
perəpurrung werkityaliny
takinyanguna panbarru-[a] tyurung-kuthəwiny
wirrengan nyuka[-rnin] nyuka tyak
tyingtyingak pirkin
[nya nya tyulipin kat nya tyulipin]

This version differs from that sung for Catherine Ellis in that the emphatic word **nya** is present in the first line, but as with the Ellis version, in the third line, the ergative marked word for 'wooden shovel', **panbarru**, is followed by another vocable **a**. The fourth line is very different, and contains the word **wirrengən** 'dog' in place of **wuthak-min** 'put down.IMP-indeed'.

Musical transcription and analysis (by Grace Koch)

Figure 2.12: Musical analysis of Stan Day, Song 8, 'Sentai', the lazy dog
Source: Song from from Ellis_193_TrackB, analysis by Grace Koch.

This song has a tonal centre of F, and form similar to a major scale.

Sentai the Lazy Dog

Song 8 recorded by Luise Hercus

HERCUS_L08-000997B-StanDaySong8

Figure 2.13: Musical analysis of Stan Day, Song 8, 'Sentai', the lazy dog

Source: Song from HERCUS_L08-000997B, analysis by Grace Koch.

This song has a tonal centre of A, and form similar to a major scale.

This song has a definite tonal centre or key (F for Ellis and A for Hercus), but to keep the notation consistent with the others, we show each accidental rather than displaying a key signature.

Most of Stan Day's songs tend to have a descending melodic contour. Although this one shows the same tendency, the melody rises a perfect fifth then adds a final coda that ends on the highest note in the song. This coda may have been borrowed from a folk song.

Both renditions of the song are very similar, except for a few places. In bar 1 of the Ellis version, Stan Day sings an **a** on the keynote pitch of F, then begins singing the text on the F, but he leaps up to a perfect fifth on the second pitch. In bar 8, the text **tyingtyingak pir** is sung on a single pitch for Ellis, but on two neighbouring pitches (A B A B) for Hercus.

In Bar 9, for the words **nya tyulipin** the melody rises later (on **pin**) in the Ellis version whereas for Hercus, Stan rises on the syllable, **tyu**. A summary of the differences between the two versions is given in Table 2.13:

Table 2.13: Comparison of the musical features of the two versions of 'Sentai', the lazy dog

Ellis	Hercus
Initial syllable **a**	Text begins immediately
Song begins on pitch that is repeated	First two notes encompass a perfect 5th leap
In Bar 8, first 4 notes on a repeated Bb, then rising a full tone to C	In Bar 8, first 4 notes are A B A B, then dropping a full tone to A
Perfect 4th leap at start of Bar 9	Perfect 5th leap to start of Bar 9
Bar 10 begins with a crotchet on the word, kat	Bar 10 begins with a quaver on the word, kat

Source: Authors.

2.2.10 Song 9 – Escaping from justice in N.S.W.

Hercus introduced this song as follows (1986: 68):

> This was the only song with two verses that Mr Day could recall entirely; it seemed that by the turn of the century one-verse songs were much more usual than longer ones (a really long song like [Song 3] was an exception). The song deals with a complex situation: someone is is issuing a summons against the author. The author then asks two of his friends to appear as witnesses for him, and they are scared. The matter is about to lapse when the author threatens to issue a cross-summons against the original plaintiff. The unwilling witnesses are so scared of the law altogether that they lament about what will happen to them. The author then suggests that they should cross the Murray in a canoe and go over to the Victorian side where they could not be arrested.

Aboriginal people along the Murray were aware from an early date of the differing jurisdictions on either side of the river and acted accordingly. There are examples of them issuing summons to each other from around the 1880s. For example, Old McDuff (father of Isaac McDuff), a Weki-Weki man, was sent from Victoria to court in Balranald (NSW) to appear in court there.

The text

The full text and translation, based on Hercus (1986: 68), is presented as Box 2.13:

Box 2.13: Song 9 – Escaping from justice in N.S.W.

Author: Tommy; transmitted by Marrərt (Grandfather David Taylor)	
Verse 1	
nyerrnatiyaty nya nginkuli kiyanda nyuwa	Listen you fellows, to what I am telling you,
puləminy nyet manyam	I am going to summon that man;
matemboliny courthouse-a	He will call us all into court (me as defendant and you two as witnesses).
nyakity-min nya yandin-kuli	(The two witnesses speak): 'Why all three of us?
telkaya-min manya nyarri	'That man is quite good and peaceful now,
ngin nya wakatangarr	'It is just you that is being determined and persistent.'
Verse 2	
marrangguk-min manyam nyuməlang nya	'I am going to cross-summon him, thats what I'm thinking about.'
Puləminy ngalangin nya	(The two witnesses speak): "He, (the author) is going to summon us two (to appear in court),
nyanyuk-min ngalang yuminy	"and what is going to happen to us two?"
winakuwal work-alakang	"Well, you two can just leave your jobs."
Kalputiwal Murray-watang	"And cross the Murray,"
Victorian side yuminy	"(And then you'll be all right) because that's the Victorian side over there."

Source: Based on Hercus (1986: 68); adapted by authors.

Recordings

There are several recordings of this song, the first of which is analysed musically. This was recorded by Catherine Ellis on 22 January 1963, on tape 8, and digitised by AIATSIS as Ellis_193_TrackB. The song and discussion run from 1:16 to 3:18, with the musical analysis presented below as Figure 2.14. We have extracted this recording and named it:

Ellis_193_TrackB_StanDay_Song9.wav.

A second version was recorded by Luise Hercus on 19 July 1962 on Hercus field tape 21/2, digitised by AIATSIS as HERCUS_L04-000211A, running from 37:35 to 38:33, with the song sung from 36:42. In this recording, Stan Day expressed that 'an explanation to discuss the meaning will take too long'. We have extracted this recording and named it:

HERCUS_L04-000211A_StanDay_Song9.wav.

A further version of this song was recorded on 5 March 1966 on Hercus field tape 21/28, digitised by AIATSIS as HERCUS_L04-000221A, running from 5:07 to 15:31. This consists of a detailed explanation of the meaning with small portions of singing but no complete version of the song. We have extracted this recording and named it:

HERCUS_L04-000221A_StanDay_Song9_Explanation.wav.

There are two further short discussions of the song, the first recorded on 27 November 1965, on Hercus field tape 21/30, digitised as HERCUS_L08-000997B, with discussion commencing at 18:43 and singing of part of the song at 19:25. The second of these was recorded on 28 March 1965, also on Hercus field tape 21/30 and digitised by AIATSIS as HERCUS_L08-000997B. For this version, the discussion commences at 25:35, includes fragments of singing as well as explanation, and concludes at 30:49.

Linguistic transcription

The linguistic analysis, following Hercus (1986: 68–69), is presented as (2.31):

Verse 1

(2.31)	**nyerrnatiyaty**	**nya**	**nginkuli**	**kiyanda**	**nyuwa**
	ˈɲɛrnatɪˌac	ɲa	ˈŋinkʊlɪ	ˈkiandɐ	ˈɲuɐ
	listen.2PL	indeed	2.TRIAL	tell.1SG	here

	puləminy	**nyet**	**manyam**
	ˈpuləˌmɪɲ	ˈɲet	manˌjam
	pull him in.FUT	I	him

matemboliny	**courthouse-a**
‘matɛ̃mbɔˌlɪɲ	courthouse -a
call together.FUT	courthouse.OBL

nyakity-min	**nya**	**yandin-kuli**
‘ɲakɪc-mɪn	‘ɲa	‘jandɪn’kʊli
what for-indeed	really	1.TRIAL

telkaya-min	**manya**	**nyarri**
‘tɛlˌkaijɐ-mɪn	‘maɲa	‘ɲarɪ
good-indeed	that one	now

ngin	**nya**	**wakatangarr**
‘ŋiːn	ɲa	‘wakɐtaˌŋar
you	indeed	persistent.2SG

Verse 2

marrangguk-min	**manyam**
‘maraŋˌkʊk-mɪn	‘maɲɐm
cross summon.3SGPOSS-indeed	that one

nyumәlang	**nya**
‘ɲumәˌlaŋ	‘ɲa
think.FREQ.PRES.PAST	indeed

pulәminy	**ngalangin**	**nya**
‘pulәmɪɲ	‘ŋalaŋɪn	‘ɲa
pull him in.FUT	1DL.EXCL.OBL	indeed

nyanyuk-min	**ngalang**	**yuminy**
‘ɲɛ̃bjʊk-mɪn	‘ŋalaŋ	ju’mɪɲ
what.3SGPOSS-indeed	1DL.EXCL	be.FUT

winakuwal	**work-alakang**
‘winakʊˌwal	‘work -alaˌkaŋ
leave.2DL	work.2DLPOSS

kalputiwal	**Murray-watang**
'kalpʊtɪˌwal	Murray- wa'taŋ
cross.2DL	Murray-across

Victorian side	**yuminy**
Victorian-side	'ju'mɪɲ
Victorian side	be.FUT

'Listen you fellows, to what I am telling you, I am going to summon that man; he will call us all into court (me as defendant and you two as witnesses). (The two witnesses speak): "Why all three of us? That man is quite good and peaceful now, it is just you that is being determined and persistent."'

'I am going to cross-summon him, that's what I'm thinking about.

'(The two witnesses speak): "He, (the author) is going to summon us two to appear in court, and what is going to happen to us two?"

'Well, you two can just leave your jobs and cross the Murray and then you'll be all right because that's the Victorian side over there.'

Notes

The word **nginkuli** is given in Hercus (1986: 192) as 'you three. Personal pronoun, trial'. The trial pronouns were formed 'with the addition of the word **guli** "group of people"' (Hercus 1986: 37).

Hercus (1992) explained the word **puləma** 'to issue a summons (Vtr); probably derived via the past tense **puləmin** or via the future **puləminy** from English "pull him in". This word was well assimilated and barely felt as a borrowing'.

Hercus (1992) explained the word **matembola** as 'to call as witness (Vtr), this word may be connected with English "pull (into court)" cf **puləma**'.

The word **work-alakang** contains the 2nd person dual possessive ending **-alak** which has an alternative version **-alakang** found only in songs (Hercus 1986: 34).

Version as sung, with notes on poetics

We have only analysed one version of this song, that recorded by Catherine Ellis, the musical analysis of which is presented as Figure 2.14. This song has two verses and both are sung two times. The matching of the text to the music is somewhat more difficult in the case of the first verse, and we only present the first instance of it here, as the second is very difficult to follow (and most of the musical analysis is without text). The words as we hear them in the first instance of the first verse are presented as (2.32):

(2.32) o nyerrnatiyaty nya nginkuli kiyanda nyuwa
puləminy nyet manyam
matemboliny courthouse-a
nyakity-min nya yandin-kuli
[we cannot make out this line] [tyin]
manya mala manyam
telkaya min [ngin nya] manya wakatangarr

The repetition of this first verse was very hard to make out.

The words in the second verse, as we hear them, are presented as (2.33):

Verse 2

(2.33) marrangguk-min manyam nya nyuməlang
puləminy ngalangin nya
nyanyuk-min ngalang yuminy ngalang[gu]
winakuwal work-alakang
kalputiwal Murray-watang
Victorian side yuminy

(2nd time)

o marrangguk-min manyam nya nyuməlang
nya puləminy ngalangin nya
nyanyuk-min ngalang yuminy
winakuwal work-alakang
kalputiwal Murray-watang
Victorian side yuminy

Musical transcription and analysis (by Grace Koch)

The transcription of this song is presented in Figure 2.14:

Song 9 again

Figure 2.14: Musical analysis of Stan Day, Song 9, Escaping from justice in N.S.W.

Source: Song from Ellis_193_TrackB, analysis by Grace Koch.

This song has a tonal centre of Ab, and form similar to a major scale.

The melody of this song is very similar to Song 2 (Yerrateth-kurrk 'the owlet-nightjar', section 2.2.3) and Song 10 (An ancient tale, section 2.2.11). Both this song and Song 10 were created by Tommy, and both songs repeat the text twice. This song, however, has two verses with each one being sung twice consecutively. Midway through each iteration of the text, the words are sung on one pitch, continuing until the end of the verse. The second time each verse is sung, there is a vocal upwards leap of a minor seventh near the beginning, then afterwards the melody descends gradually, settling on one pitch until the end.

2.2.11 Song 10 – An ancient tale

Hercus (1986: 69–70) introduced this song as follows:

> The authors of the songs usually spoke only Wembawemba, but they had acquired a knowledge of several other languages. Tommy, who was at least one generation older than **Marəḍ** and **Njaui** 'could understand half a dozen languages', although he did not normally speak them. Such wide linguistic knowledge was by no means uncommon, particularly among those old men who were renowned for their wisdom – for instance **King Berak** of the Woiwuru, Jacky Patchell of the Wudjubalug, and Reginald Wise of the Ma**d**ima<u>d</u>i. In Victoria and the extreme south of N.S.W., except for a few lone survivors, the last generation of such men died in 1900 or shortly after. Their linguistic knowledge was quite different from the fortunately rare superficial polyglottism of those who have a smattering of several languages, but cannot speak any accurately.
>
> It was quite natural that the knowledge of other languages should be displayed in songs, and so Tommy composed this song in three languages. Mr Day could only explain the short sections that were in Wembawemba: he did not even know which were the other two languages in the song.
>
> The story of the song concerns two small groups of men from different tribes who are at war with one another. They meet on opposite sides of a river and shout challenges to one another; but as neither party is particularly good at swimming they can't have a fight.

The connection between this song and other fight songs (for example, that in Eastern Kulin (section 3.4.10), and the Nunga Nunga song in Gippsland (section 5.2.11)) is not clear. Those songs appear to have been sung during a fight, as perhaps this also was. The text refers to the desire of the combatant to take the kidney fat of his enemy. Howitt wrote down the song used for helping a victim of a kidney-fat attack to regain consciousness (see section 2.3.1), and the Tjapwurrung song recorded by Mathews also appears to be related to kidney-fat attacks (section 2.7). A more substantial description of the recovery from kidney-fat attacks, this time in Eastern Kulin, was made by Thomas (section 3.4.9).

Multilingualism in songs is well known in other parts of Australia, such as in Western Arnhem Land (see for example, Sutton 1987; Turpin and Green 2011; O'Keeffe 2016).

The text

The full text and translation, based on Hercus (1986: 69), is presented as Box 2.14:

Box 2.14: Song 10 – An ancient tale

Author: Tommy; transmitted by Marrərt (Grandfather David Taylor)	
wurlinyula kiman kenya kungerri	?
yukwek mambulin	I wish I had your kidney-fat.
tyertamangu katina nyet	The water between us is stopping you people,
pambangin monolikayi	You are frightened ...
kawinyaki wirrekikayi	... of swimming,
tawinyangu pinwurrərrayi	I'll hit you people with a stone tomahawk.

Source: Based on Hercus (1986: 69); adapted by authors.

Recordings

There are several recordings of this song, of which the first two are analysed musically. The first was recorded on 22 January 1963 by Catherine Ellis on tape 8, and digitised by AIATSIS as Ellis_193_TrackB. The song and discussion runs from 0:45 to 1:10 and again from 3:18 to 3:33. The musical analysis of this is presented below as Figure 2.15. We have extracted this recording and named it:

Ellis_193_TrackB_StanDay_Song10.wav.

The second recording discussed here was made by Luise Hercus on 28 March 1965 on Hercus field tape 21/30, digitised by AIATSIS as HERCUS_L08-000997B, running from 33:49 to 35:32 with the song itself sung at 34:28. The musical analysis of this is presented as Figure 2.16. We have extracted this recording and named it:

HERCUS_L08-000997B_StanDaySong10_SongAndDiscussion.wav.

A third recording was made on 27 November 1965 on Hercus field tape 21/29, digitised by AIATSIS as HERCUS_L04-000221B and found at 21:45 to 22:18. In this version, the sound of which is distorted at the beginning, Stan Day comments of **Marrərt** (Marəḍ) 'how clever he was, he could put three different lingos into one song'. We have extracted this recording and named it:

HERCUS_L04-000221B_StanDay_Song10_ExplanationAndSong.wav.

A further version was recorded on 19 July 1962 on Hercus field tape 21/2, digitised by AIATSIS as HERCUS_L04-000211A, between 38:33 and 39:58. This version includes discussion of the song, but it is not sung in full. He also gives some background about children being unable to understand the songs of their grandparents. We have extracted this recording and named it:

HERCUS_L04-000211A_StanDay_Song9.wav.

Another version was recorded on 27 November 1965 on Hercus field tape 21/30, digitised as HERCUS_L08-000997B, running from 0:00 to 0:57. We have not extracted this short recording.

The final version was recorded on 26 January 1965 on Hercus field tape 21/35, digitised as HERCUS_L08-000999B, running from 34:23 to 40:43. In this version, Stan Day sings small sections and then explains the meaning; a more or less full version is sung from 36:19 to 36:50. We have extracted this recording and named it:

HERCUS_L08-000999B_StanDaySong10_SongAndDiscussion.wav.

Linguistic transcription

The linguistic analysis, following Hercus (1986: 70), is presented as example (2.34). Note that Hercus did not present an orthographic version for any of the words for which the meaning is unknown and glossed as ?. We have added the first line, the orthographic line, for consistency.

(2.34)	**wurlinyula**	**kiman**	**kenya**	**kungerri**
	ʻwuḷiɲula	gɪman	ʻgɛ̃ɲa	kuŋerɪ
	?	?	?	?

yukwek	**mambulin**
ˈjʊkwɛk	ˈmaːmbʊˌlɪn
I wish I had!	kidney fat.2SGPOSS

tyertamangu	**katina**	**nyet**
ˈcɛṯamaˌŋu	ˈkatɪnɐ	ˈɲet
stop.FORM.2PL.OBJ?	water	between

pambangin	**monolikayi**
ˈpaːmbaŋɪn	ˈmɔnɔliˌkai
frighten.2SG.POSS	?

kawinyaki	**wirrekikayi**
ˈgawiɲagi	ˈwiregigai
?	?

tawinyangu	**pinwurrərrayi**
ˈtauwɪɲaˌŋu	ˈpɪnwʊrəˌrai
hit.FUT.2PL.OBJ?	stone-tomahawk-with

'… I wish I had your kidney-fat. The water between us is stopping you people, you are frightened … of swimming … I'll hit you people with a stone tomahawk.'

Notes in Hercus (1986: 70):

> [ˈwiregigai], though in an unknown language, almost certainly refers to swimming, Wembawemba **wirraka** 'to swim'.
>
> **pinwurrərrai**; this form was not quite clear; the normal Wembawemba word for long-handled tomahawk for fighting is **pinwurrayi**.

Additional linguistic notes

The word **yukwek** is an exclamation meaning 'I wish I had!'

The word **tyertamangu** is glossed in Hercus (1986: 70) as 'stops-you-people'. The root verb here is **tyerta** 'to stop', both transitive and intransitive, and a derived form **tyertama** 'to stop, to hinder' is only transitive (Hercus 1992). The suffix **-ngu**, as with **tawinyangu**, seems to have the function of a 2nd person plural bound object.

The word **tawinyangu** is glossed by Hercus (1986) as 'hit-will-I-you-people'. It consists of a root **tawa** 'hit', the future suffix, and **-ngu**, which as with **tyertamangu** seems to have the function of a 2nd person plural bound object.

Speculation on the analysis of words in the 'other languages'

Stan Day did not suggest any analysis for the words shown glossed by ? (question mark) in example (2.34). However, we do have a number of observations about them, and speculations of their meaning.

In the first line, it is interesting to note that in the phonetic transcription Hercus (1986: 70) writes initial voiced stops [g] for the second and third words, and initial voiceless [k] for the last word of the line. This is presumed to reflect the fact that when followed by front vowels, [i] and [e], the voicing of the consonant was more pronounced. This is audible to us.

In discussions about this song, Luise Hercus speculated that perhaps **wurlinyula** is a WH- word. She also wondered if the word **kungerri** could be connected to Wemba-Wemba **kungaya** 'keep quiet', and the whole first line might mean 'why are you keeping quiet'. The suffix **-eri** may be the same as the Werkaya morpheme 'doing something to excess', as **kuperri** 'they are drinking', which was introduced into English as a general term for 'drinking plonk (cheap wine)' (Hercus 1986: 206).

Luise Hercus also wondered if the words with final **-ayi** were reflecting the 1st person singular possessive in Paakantyi (Hercus 1982: 128) also found in Mathi-Mathi (Blake et al. 2011: 90). However, we cannot suggest any meanings for these words in either of those languages.

Hercus (1986: 70) already suggested that the second word in the line **kawinyaki wirrekikayi** was related to Wemba-Wemba **wirraka** 'to swim'. The word **kawi** is 'water' in Wiradjuri and so this line would appear to relate to swimming in water. In Wati-Wati, Beveridge recorded the word *cawie kayanie* 'salt water' (see Blake et al. 2011), which also contains a root **kawi**. It may be that the syllable **kawi** is a borrowed word.

Version as sung, with notes on poetics

The text of the version as sung for Catherine Ellis, the musical analysis of which is give in Figure 2.15, is presented as example (2.35):

(2.35) o wurlinyula kiman kenya kungerri
yukwek [i] ma[r]mbulin
tyertamangu katina nyet
pambangin monolikayi
kawinyaki wirrəkikayi

o wurlinyula kiman kenya kungerri
yukwek [i] ma[r]mbulin
tyertamangu katina nyet
pambangin monolikayi
kawinyaki wirrəkikayi
tauwinyangu pinwurrərrai

The text is sung twice, but the final line, **tauwinyangu pinwurrərrai**, is only sung on the repetition. In the version recorded by Luise Hercus (Figure 2.16), also sung twice, the final line is sung both times.

In both instances, the first line is preceded by a vocable **o**. In the second line, there is an inserted syllable **i** after the word **yukwek**, which is also found in the version recorded by Luise Hercus.

A very particular feature of this song is the rendition of **mambulin**. In both the Ellis and Hercus versions, in the first singing of the verse the initial syllable is lengthened and sung on a rising melisma of a minor third. When the verse is repeated, the first syllable **mam** is either sung on a long note, or as a repetition, where we hear a faint **r**. These devices may give emphasis to the word **mambulin** 'your kidney-fat'.

Musical transcription and analysis (by Grace Koch)

ELLIS_193B_StanDay_Song10

Figure 2.15: Musical analysis of Stan Day, Song 10, An ancient tale

Source: Song from Ellis_193_TrackB, analysis by Grace Koch.

This song has a tonal centre of Db, and form similar to a major scale.

An Ancient Tale

Song 10 recorded by Luise Hercus
HERCUS_L08-000997B_StanDaySong10

Figure 2.16: Musical analysis of Stan Day, Song 10, An ancient tale.
Source: Song from HERCUS_L08-000997B, analysis by Grace Koch.

This song has a tonal centre of Eb, and form similar to a major scale.

Both performances are similar enough to identify it as the same song, and the analysis of Song 9 (Escaping from justice in N.S.W., see section 2.2.10) described some of the melodic similarities between it and the two versions of this song, An ancient tale. Both repeat the rhythmic pattern ♪♪♪♩ many times in the song, especially at the end, beginning with the text '*monoli-kayi*'.

There are significant differences, though, between the two performances of An ancient tale, as shown in Table 2.14. One of the most interesting variations comes when he omits two words of the text during the first iteration of the song for Ellis, but he catches up in matching the melody as for the Hercus version within a few bars.

Table 2.14: Comparison of the musical features of the two versions of An ancient tale

Ellis version	Hercus version
Sings a perfect 4th higher in key of Db	Sings in lower key of Eb
Begins with minim on syllable 'o' on Eb	Starts immediately with the text on Bb
In bar 2, there is the syllable [i] on the last note immediately after the word, **yukwek**	In bar 2, for the word, **yukwek** the syllable **wek** is sung over 2 crotchets
Adds an extra melodic phrase starting with o followed by **wurlinyula**, omitting the last two words **tawinyangu pinwurrə** the first time the text is sung	Sings the complete text, the first time and adds a melodic figure on **rrayi** of Bb–C–F–Ab. A similar melodic figure appears at the end of the first verse of the second performance of Song 1 (Version 2)
Melodic leap of a 7th occurs on the word 'kiman', then melody descends generally stepwise until the minor 3rd on 'katina nyet' followed by rests	Melodic leap of a 7th occurs on the words, **wurlinyula**
Texts and melody come together with the Hercus version at the word **kiman**, Melody rises and falls a tone on **kungerri**.	After the major 3rd leap on **wurlinyula**, the melody descends stepwise, differing from the variation in the Ellis version on **kungerri**
Both sing the same melody until the end.	

Source: Authors.

Although Stan Day omitted two words, **tawinyangu piwurrərayi**, in the first verse of the Ellis version, he caught up to the melody with the correct text within a bar or two, as mentioned above. The short section where he sang the **o wurlinyula** in the Ellis version is close to the duration of the words he omitted, **tawinyagu piwurrərayi** in the Hercus version. This shows a flexibility with the melody and text underlay.

2.2.12 Song 11 – Bob Taylor's swearing song

Hercus introduced this song as follows (1986: 70):

> Bob Taylor took a strong dislike to a Chinaman who happened to be shearing in the same shed with him, and so he made up a swearing song about him.

The text

The full text and translation, based on Hercus (1986: 70–71), is presented as Box 2.15:

Box 2.15: Song 11 – Bob Taylor's swearing song

Author: Nyawi (Bob Taylor)	
ngathayikuny kinya Chinaman	My word! This Chinaman.
tyerrika ?	Stands about (in the shearing shed),
wurruwilang wurruwilu	When (the others) are cleaning up and rolling the wool,
kurtəmilang mathang no savvy, no savvy	And (when) the boss comes along grumbling (because things are not being done right, all he does is say) 'no savvy, no savvy'.
tyungi-pili tyungi-wurru	He has a big belly and big lips.

Source: Based on Hercus (1986: 70–71); adapted by authors.

Recordings

There are two recordings of this song, both of which are analysed musically. One recorded by Luise Hercus on 18 April 1962 on Hercus field tape 21/3 and digitised by AIATSIS as HERCUS_L04-000211B, running from 36:04 to 37:57, with the musical analysis presented below as Figure 2.18. We have extracted this recording and named it as:

HERCUS_ L04-000211B_StanDay_Song11.wav.

A second, shorter recording of the song was recorded on 28 March 1965 on Hercus field tape 21/30, digitised by AIATSIS as HERCUS_L08-000997B, running from 54:18 to 57:09, with the musical analysis presented below as Figure 2.17. We have extracted this recording and named it:

HERCUS_L08-000997B_StanDaySong11_SongAndDiscussion.wav.

Linguistic transcription

The linguistic analysis, following Hercus (1986: 70–71), is presented as (2.36):

(2.36)	**ngathayikuny**	**kinya**	**Chinaman**
	'ŋaθaiˌkʊɲ	'kiɲɐ	Chinaman
	my word!	this	Chinaman

tyerrika	**?**
‘cɛrɪkɐ	
stand.(PRES)	?

wurruwilang	**wurruwilu**
‘wurʊwɪˌlaŋ	‘wuruwɪˌlu
clean up.PRES.PART	wool

kurtəmilang	**mathang**	**no savvy,**	**no savvy**
‘kut̪əmɪˌlaŋ	‘maˌθaŋ	no savvy,	no savvy
groan.FORM.FREQ.PRES.PART	boss.(ABL?)	no savvy,	no savvy

tyungi-pili	**tyungi-wurru**
‘cuŋgɪˌpɪlɪ	‘cuŋgɪˌwurʊ
big-belly	big-lip

‘My word! This Chinaman stands about (in the shearing shed) when (the others) are cleaning up and rolling the wool, and (when) the boss comes along grumbling (because things are not being done right, all he does is say) ‘no savvy, no savvy’. He has a big belly and big lips …’

Note in Hercus (1986: 71): ‘This was the only song, apart from the fragment of Jack Brown’s swearing song, in which words were not sung through twice. This may have been a characteristic of swearing songs. The lines of swearing at the end formed a long and fitting conclusion and took the place of the repetition’.

Linguistic notes

The root for ‘big’ is **tyunga** (Hercus 1992). The **-i** found here is perhaps related to the particularising suffix in Werkaya (Hercus 1986: 84) which has the function of being used with adjectives in exclamations and with nouns that formed the first part of a nominal compound.

The word **matha** ‘master, boss’ is borrowed from English *master*, but is sung with a final **ang**. There are two explanations for this. One, it may have been added to give the word a similar form to **ngathang** ‘ugly devil’, in other words associating this unpopular boss with the devil. Hercus (1986: 30), however, treats this as a use of the ablative in place of an expected ergative (the latter termed ‘operative’ in Hercus 1986).

Hercus (1986: 71) added at the bottom of the transcription:

> This was then followed by an array of swear-words, some in English, but only the English swearing was comprehensible and no explanation of the Wembawemba swearing was forthcoming.

This relates to the version recorded on Hercus field tape 21/3 (AIATSIS HERCUS_L04-000211B), the musical transcription of which is given in Figure 2.18. We have been able to notate the music for this section, which is marked as 'approximate notation of the melody without the text'. Stan Day knew the meaning of these words but did not wish to share them, and we will make no attempt to suggest a transcription.

Version as sung, with notes on poetics

The musical analysis of the first version of the song, sung on Hercus field tape 21/30 (AIATSIS HERCUS_L08-000997B) is presented in Figure 2.17. This is much shorter than the alternate version, and contains only the following text as given in (2.37):

(2.37) ngathaikuny kinya Chinaman
tyerrika [text not clear]
wurruwilang wurruwilu
kurtəmilang mathang no savvy

This version does not include the repetition of **no savvy** in line 4, and the fifth line is not sung at all. On this occasion, Stan Day stopped the singing, perhaps before completion, to explain the meaning of the song line by line.

The second version of the song, the musical analysis of which is presented as Figure 2.18, is longer and contains more text and several repeats. The full text is presented as (2.38):

(2.38) (ngathaikuny kinya Chinaman) [this line is very hard to hear]
tyerrika [text not clear]
wurruwilang wurruwilu
kurtəmilang mathang no savvy,
a kurtəmilang mathang no savvy,
kurtəmilang mathang no savvy, no savvy
tyungi-wurru [unclear] [yakayi]

This is followed by the untranscribed swearing.

This differs from the linguistic analysis in Hercus (1986), presented above as example (2.36), in several ways. First, the fourth line **kurtəmilang mathang no savvy** is sung three times, but only on the last of these is the **no savvy** repeated.

The last line is unclear, and we could not make out the word **tyungi-pili** 'big belly'.

Musical transcription and analysis (by Grace Koch)

The musical analyses of these songs are presented below. Note that the items marked as 'long pause here' in the transcription included discussions about the meaning of the text which are not transcribed here.

Bob Taylor's swearing song

Song 11 recorded by Luise Hercus
Sung by Stan Day
HERCUS_L08-000997B_StanDaySong11

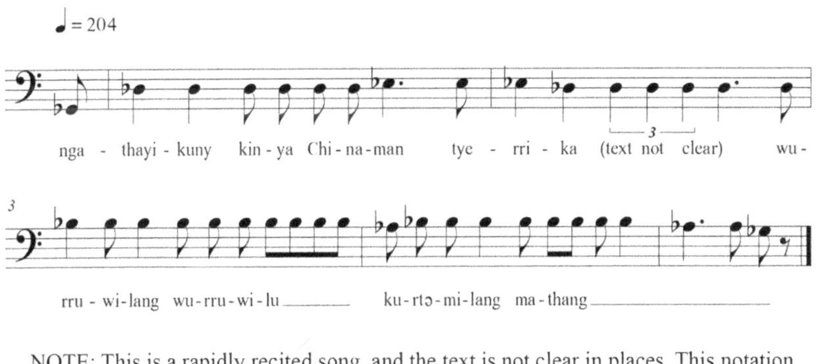

NOTE: This is a rapidly recited song, and the text is not clear in places. This notation should be seen as a close approximation of the performance.

Range: Major 10th (Gb - Bb)

©Grace Koch

Figure 2.17: Musical analysis of Stan Day, Song 11, Bob Taylor's swearing song

Source: Song from HERCUS_L08-000997B, analysis by Grace Koch.

This song has a tonal centre of Gb, and form similar to a major scale.

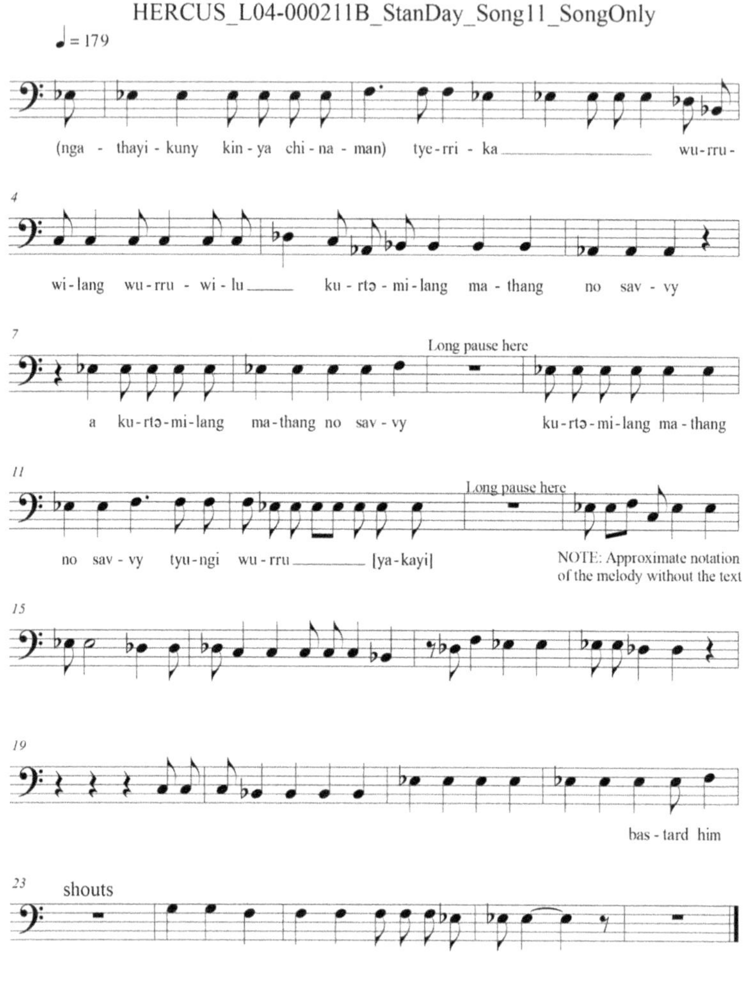

Figure 2.18: Musical analysis of Stan Day, Song 11, Bob Taylor's swearing song

Source: Song from HERCUS_L04-000211B, analysis by Grace Koch.

This song has a tonal centre of Ab, and form similar to a major scale.

A comparison of these two songs is presented as Table 2.11 in section 2.2.1.

2.2.13 Dingo song, sung by Johnny Taylor

The remaining songs recorded by Luise Hercus were not analysed linguistically in Hercus (1986). The first of these was a dingo song, sung by Johnny Taylor. Old Johnny Taylor was of an earlier generation from Stan Day. Johnny Taylor said of this song that 'the song is about dingo scalps, hanging on a line, because he got paid for dingo scalps, and he didn't lock up his dogs overnight, so by the morning they had all gone'.

Recordings

There are two recordings of this song. The first, recorded on 26 January 1964 on Hercus field tape 21/26, was digitised by AIATSIS as HERCUS_L04-000219B, running from 1:07 to 6:21. which includes several instances of the song, one from 1:17 to 1:35 which is very quiet and finishes with a characteristic 'whish' sound. The second version runs from 5:50 to 6:08. We have extracted this recording and named it:

HERCUS_L04-000219B_JohnnyTaylorSongs_1.wav.

A second recording was made on 23 November 1964 on Hercus field tape 21/26, digitised by AIATSIS as HERCUS_L04-000219B, running from 6:42 to 10:15 with the song sung from 8:18 to 8:34. At 9:20 he explains that **palengwil** means 'a dog'. We have extracted this recording and named it:

HERCUS_L04-000219B_JohnnyTaylorSongs_2.wav.

We have made a suggested transcription of the text in (2.39). This was based on the second version sung on 26 January 1964.

(2.39) **a (ng)a (ng)u(rr)i (ny)ai (y)i(rr)u (y)ai ka'tyinru wa'nha ngurru wa wurru ap**

a ngu'rrunguni yengi yowan nya yakityi munu wala-ngulu wi'reng ngulu rak

kayu ngurru rara we ngana

In 2016, Luise Hercus and Stephen Morey sat for some time listening to this with the intention of trying to identify some words. The initial consonants are particularly hard to make out in the first line, and we have therefore placed some in brackets. The vowels written as **e** tend to be mid low, more like [ɛ]. Johnny Taylor had been drinking at the time this recording was made, and his singing is thus slurred.

The four lines as written here are clearly separated by spaces, and the third line is a single syllable that we cannot fully make out but sounds like **rak**. It is either an exclamation or an unintended syllable.

We have marked stress where it occurs on what seems to be the second syllable of a word.

One word that we feel we can recognise in this text is at the end of the second line, written as **wi'reng ngulu** but perhaps intended to be **wirrenganpulu** 'two dogs'.

We might have expected to find the words **paleng-wil** and **geng-wil**. Hercus (1986: 174) wrote (using spelling with voiceless stops):

> **baleŋ-wil** ['palɛ̃ŋ,wil] dog. One of the many terms meaning a useless kind of dog; generally coupled with **geŋ-wil**. The meaning of the word **baleŋ** was not clear; it also occurred in a song, **niṇaga balenjug**, about a frog which sat on a log and jumped off and was drowned in a flood. The song was sung by one of the people who had scant knowledge of the language, and therefore not adequately translated.

Johnny Taylor Song 1

Recorded by Luise Hercus
Sung by Johnny Taylor

HERCUS_L04-000219B-JohnnyTaylorSongs_1_Version1.xsc

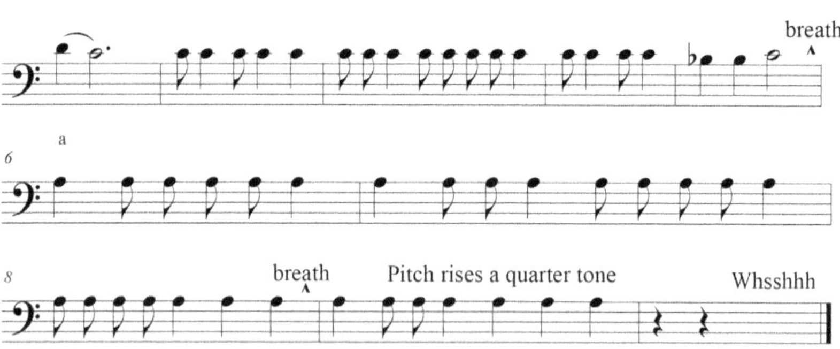

NOTE: Pitch is approximate and varies by microtones throughout.

Range: Approximately a perfect 4th (A - D)

©Grace Koch

Figure 2.19: Musical analysis of Johnny Taylor's song, Dingo song, Version 1

Source: Song from HERCUS_L04-000219B, analysis by Grace Koch.

The song about the frog was sung by Silvia Murray, and is discussed in section 2.2.14.

The musical transcription of two versions of this song, both sung on 26 January 1964, are presented as Figures 2.19 and 2.20.

The notes within this song would fit with an F major key, but the tonal centre F is not present.

Figure 2.20: Musical analysis of Johnny Taylor's song, Dingo song, Version 2

Source: Song from HERCUS_L04-000219B, analysis by Grace Koch.

This song has a tonal centre of G, and form similar to a major scale, but ends on dominant (D).

We are not sure that these two songs are the same; we cannot easily hear the text in the first version, transcribed as Figure 2.19, and our transcription of the words in example (2.39) is in any case very tentative.

Some of the musical differences between the two versions are that in Version 1, it starts with a descending interval, whereas Version 2 stays on the same pitch almost throughout the first line of the transcription. Some of the other songs do exhibit similar melodic variation, however.

There is more melodic movement in Version 2, but not significantly more. And there are two audible language features in Version 2 that we do not hear in Version 1, namely short syllables with final stop, such as **-ap** and **-ak**. Finally, Version 1 concludes with a very noticeable 'whsshhh' sound at the end which is not present in Version 2.

We do, however, hear a word that could be identified as **wirrengan** 'dog' in both versions. Unfortunately, as with so much of the material in this book, there is much that we will probably never be able to interpret.

2.2.14 Frog song, sung by Silvia Murray

Silvia Murray, also known as Tibby Clayton, was the daughter of a Wiradjuri man who learned songs from Johnny Taylor. Two of these were recorded. The first, a traditional song about a frog, can only be partly analysed. It was recorded twice.

The first recording was on 23 November 1964 on Hercus field tape 21/26, digitised by AIATSIS as HERCUS_L04-000219B, running from 16:24 to 16:58. We have extracted this recording and named it:

HERCUS_L04-000219B_SilviaMurray_FrogSong.wav.

A second version was recorded in March 1964 on Hercus field tape 21/31, digitised by AIATSIS as HERCUS_L08-000998A, running from 31:20 to 32:15. We have extracted this recording and named it:

HERCUS_L08-000998A_SilviaMurray_Song.wav.

Hercus (1992) wrote about this song in an entry in the Wemba-Wemba dictionary: '**paleng**. log, fallen timber (n), this word was recorded only from the song **nirnaka palenyuk**, which was about a frog which sat on a log and jumped off and was drowned in a flood'. See section 2.2.13 for a further use of the root **paleng-**.

Our suggested transcription of the text is given in (2.40):

(2.40) **nirnaka** **palenyuk** **tyukunduk?**
frog-? log.3SGPOSS ?

ka? **ma?** **me?**
'The frog (was) on its log …'

Notes

The word for 'frog' was recorded by Hercus as **nirnak** for both Wemba-Wemba and Werkaya. In the song, the word is clearly accompanied by a final **a** (general oblique) but it is unclear why this word is present here.

The third word sounds like **tyukunduk**. We might have expected either **puyika** 'fall' or **pirrityana** 'jump' here.

The words we have transcribed on the second line seem to be three monosyllables. We might have expected the word **ngarənga** 'drown' here.

2.2.15 Love song, sung by Silvia Murray

A second song, described as a 'love song' was sung by Silvia Murray in March 1964, recorded on Hercus field tape 21/32, digitised by AIATSIS as HERCUS_L08-000998A, running from 30:52 to 31:20. We have extracted this recording and named it as:

HERCUS_L08-000998A_SilviaMurray_Song.wav.

Our suggested transcription is given in (2.41):

(2.41) **kalinga mika natyali mika ma**
kalingi mika ma tyelinga nyukuliya ma-a
'Love …'

Notes

Only the verb **kalina** 'to love' can be clearly recognised in this song. Note that the Wemba-Wemba word **mika** means 'tired'. Perhaps she means to say 'tired of love'.

2.2.16 Hymn, sung by Nancy Egan

Luise Hercus remembered and wrote down a hymn that Nancy Egan told to her (but did not sing). We have not been able to find any recording of the discussion of this hymn on the Hercus recordings. Although we are not generally including hymns in this book, this one is included both because the language is characteristically Wemba-Wemba, and because of the similar material found in the Keledia song (see section 2.5).

The text as recorded by Luise Hercus is presented in Box 2.16:

Box 2.16: Nancy Egan's hymn

Yandang wawity kirrkundity
Yandang wawity watyipuk
Yandang wawity nya

I would follow the one from up there
I would follow his son
I would follow

Source: Luise Hercus; adapted by authors.

Our analysis is presented in (2.42):

(2.42)	**Yandang**	**wawity**	**kirrkundity**
	1SG	follow.POT	the one up there
	Yandang	**wawity**	**watyipuk**
	1SG	follow.POT	son-3SG.POSS
	Yandang	**wawity**	**nya**
	1SG	follow.POT	EMPH

'I would follow the one up there, I would follow his son, I would follow.'

Notes

The root of the word **kirrkundity** is kirrk 'sky'. This word was also recorded by the Moravian missionaries with a translation 'heaven', although unlike the Keledia song (see section 2.5), there is no record of this song by the Moravians. Similar words with final **-ity** are found as **punggandity** 'spirit' from Stone (Hercus 1992: 51).

2.3 Werkaya (Wimmera) songs recorded by Howitt

There are four songs that are given by Howitt in various sources. We believe that all four songs were given to Howitt by Morton Plains Bobby (see section 2.1.1), his main informant for what he called Wotjoballuk. In his 1904 book, Howitt specifically identifies the first two songs as being Jajaurung (Djadjawurrung), but in the manuscripts the language of the songs is not identified specifically. Since Werkaya and Djadjawurrung are both Western Kulin languages, we treat them together here. Note that the term Werkaya is used in this book to refer to the languages of the Wimmera, of which the best described is the Tyatyala variety recorded in Hercus (1986). The songs discussed here, however, were likely from varieties much further to the east, particularly the Morton Plains area, which was the homeland of Morton Plains Bobby.

Howitt had sent out a questionnaire in the form of a printed query to seek information about songs from a range of genres.[30] There does not seem to be much evidence in the Howitt papers of responses to the questionnaire, and all the songs discussed in this section (and also in section 5.2) were certainly collected personally by Howitt. He had worked together with Dr Torrance on the Eastern Kulin songs (see section 3.2). The form of the questionnaire is presented as Box 2.17:

Box 2.17: Howitt's song questionnaire

Sale, Victoria

... 188

Dear Sir

I am desirous of obtaining further information as to the songs of the Australian Aborigines. You will greatly oblige by giving replies to the following questions:-

(1) Can you give an instance of each of the following kinds of songs? A literal translation in English should be written under the words of the song, word for word:

30 Howitt used the back of this document to write notes about the Wotjo-ballŭk tribe and the manuscript version of the Initiation song presented as Box 2.21 in section 2.3.3.

(a) Songs which accompany dances (corroborees)
(b) Songs without dances
(c) Songs or incantations used by Doctors or Wizards - as, for instance, to procure rain:
(d) Songs sung to children - as, for instance, to put them to sleep;
(e) Any other songs, chaunts, or charms other than those above mentioned.

I am Dear Sir
Yours very truly,
A. W. Howitt

Source: SLV MS Box 1053/6 (a), hw0419.pdf, p. 3; adapted by authors.

The three songs are the Song for regaining consciousness after a kidney fat attack (section 2.3.1), Shooting Star song (section 2.3.2) and New Moon chant (section 2.3.4). A fourth song which we are treating as being Werkaya is the Initiation song (section 2.3.3), which, however, may have actually been Djadjawurrung.

All these songs were also sung by Sergeant Major, whose ancestry was mixed Djadjawurrung, Letyi-Letyi and Werkaya (Wimmera). Some of these may have been recorded onto the wax cylinders now held in Museums Victoria (XAV 125) of which the primary comments say:

> One of five existing cylinders recorded by Alfred Howitt. Annotation on paper wrapped around cannister: 'A.W. Howitt recording "Sergeant Major No. 1. Wax Cylinder no 36. 1 of 5 existing cylinders recorded by Howitt. See also cylinders nos 34, 35, 37, 38."'

This recording was studied by Alice Moyle who 'published an article [1959] regarding the wax cylinder collections at the National Museum of Victoria' (MV catalogue notes). Although we have been able to listen to a copy of the recording, digitised from a tape recording made by Alice Moyle from the original wax cylinder in the 1950s, we cannot make out from this recording whether one, two or all three of the songs are sung there, as we cannot make out any words. This is due to the poor audio quality of the recording we have been able to hear.

2.3.1 Song for regaining consciousness after kidney fat attack

Kidney fat attacks were much feared across the state of Victoria. Apart from this song and the next (see section 2.3.2), we also have recorded a text in Eastern Kulin that was uttered to cure a man believed to have suffered a kidney fat attack (see section 3.4.15). According to Howitt in Smyth (1878, 1: 246–47), the custom was not practised in Gippsland. Kidney fat is also referred to in the An ancient tale song of Stan Day (see section 2.2.11):

> Bulmer describes the process of a kidney fat attack in detail (Campbell 1999: 33). He notes that after taking out the kidneys, they 'afterwards began to sing his name but the man was too far gone.'

Howitt also discusses the taking of kidney fat in a section that includes the song under discussion here, headed 'Use of Human Fat in Magic' (1904: 367f). He points out (1904: 367) that:

> The practice of using human fat as a powerful magical ingredient is widely spread over Australia, and consequently the belief is universal that the medicine-men have the power of abstracting it magically from individuals, or also of actually taking it by violence accompanied by magic. This is usually spoken of by the whites as taking 'the kidney fat,' but it appears to be the caul-fat from the omentum.

Referring to the practices in north-west Victoria, particularly among the Werkaya speakers, Howitt (1904: 368) said:

> The Wotjobaluk practised this fat-taking apparently to a great extent. Here is the account of the fat-taking powers of their medicine-men (*Bangal*) as given to me by one of the old men of the tribe. As usual, the favourite plan is to sneak on the victim when asleep. As soon as the *Bangal* is near enough to see the man by the light of the fire, he swings the *Yulo* (bone) round his head, and launches it at him. It is supposed to dart into him invisibly, and compel him to come out of his camp to the medicine-man, who throws him over his shoulder and carries him to a convenient spot. Or, if he was acquainted with the man, he would manage to arrive at his camp late, so as to be asked to remain for the night. Pretending to sleep, he watches until his host is in a sound slumber, when he passes his *Yulo* under his knees, round his neck, and through the loop of the cord attached to it, and so carries him a little way from the camp.

Further details about this custom and the relationship with the shooting star is discussed below in section 2.3.2.

The linguistic terms named in this account do not always accord with other sources from the Werkaya language. Table 2.15 compares these forms with records from Hercus (1986) for Werkaya. While the words for 'medicine man' and 'club' are reported from other sources, the words for this particular 'bone', the 'shooting star' and the 'open side' were only recorded by Howitt. Comparison of the words found in this description with other sources is presented as Table 2.15.

Table 2.15: Comparison of words found in the descriptions of the taking of fat

Howitt (1904)		Werkaya (from Hercus 1986)	Notes (from Hercus 1992)
Bangal	'medicine man'	**pangal** 'doctor, clever man'	Wemba **pan-pangal** 'an assembly of witchdoctors' (Stone)
yulo	'bone'	**kalkuk** 'his bone'	–
breppen	'club with knob at the end'	**pirpiny** 'spear-pointed waddy'	–
yerigauil	'shooting star'	–	Wemba **paika turt** 'shooting star'
deking-ngalluk	'open side'	**wirpuk** 'side of a person'	–

Source: Howitt (1904) and Hercus (1986, 1992); adapted by authors.

The **pangal**, who could both take the kidney fat and cure someone after an attack, was not the only person who could take the fat. The **pangal** was an important person in the traditional society, one of his functions being to regulate society through the casting of spells.

The word for 'club with knob at the end', translated by Hercus as 'spear-pointed waddy', is probably an example of a regular sound correspondence between the dialect of Werkaya spoken by Howitt's informants (in this case Morton Plains Bobby, see section 2.1.1) and the Tyatyala variety recorded by Hercus (1986). If Howitt's transcription is to be relied upon, the regularisation of this word would be **pripiny,** which represents a metathesis of the first vowel with the /r/, between the two varieties of Werkaya. Initial clusters in Werkaya do include **pr-** and are discussed by Hercus (1986: 75), where she notes: 'The initial plosive in the Weṛgaia (eastern dialect) clusters **br-** and **gr-** was voiced'. Note that this use of clusters is evidence for associating the word recorded by Howitt with the varieties spoken around the Morton Plains.

The word for 'shooting star' in the Howitt description, which we would regularise as **yirrikawil**, differs from the word recorded by Hercus. R.H. Mathews (NLA MS 8006/3/4.2, Notebook 6) had written 'Yirri-au-ul 'α Canis major, used to catch spirit going away and stop death'. This has the same root as a word recorded by Stone (1911) – **yirri larr**, which he spelled *yere laar* and translated as 'oath stone, or charm'. Hercus (1992) adds a note that 'this must be equivalent to "that very (special) stone"'. Shooting stars were said to be observed when the spirit is leaving the body.

Howitt (1904: 369) goes on to describe how the *Yulo* bone was used by the Mukjarawaint people. The consultant here is John Connolly.

There are two versions of the song, which we believe was likely composed in the eastern areas of the Werkaya (Wimmera) language, probably around the Morton Plains. The first of these is in Howitt (1904: 369), presented as Box 2.18, and the second in the Howitt manuscripts at the State Library of Victoria (Box 2.19):

Box 2.18: Song for regaining consciousness, version 1

The song which the *Bangal* would use to make his victim regain his senses, and go away, is such a one as the following, which belongs to the Jajaurung of the St. Arnaud district. But in this case it is the man's ghost which is to get up and go away.

Moronga	*morove*	*leanijulin*	*willain-gurk*	*kroia-bangalo*
Rainbow	spirit (ghost)	like a knife cutting	swallow	curlew

If the victim were a stranger, the *Bangal* would not take the trouble to bring him back to life, but would leave him where he lay. But if he were some one whom he knew, he would do as described, and moreover he would be careful when laying him out, preparatory to operating on him, to place him in that direction in which the dead of his totem are buried.

Source: Howitt (1904: 369), adapted by authors.

The manuscript version contains some background information that slightly differs from that found in the 1904 book. This song is found on page 6 of the collection of papers in MS Box 1053/6 (a); the previous page (p. 5) is a listing of tribal names and territories and does not relate to this song. This is presented as Box 2.19:

Box 2.19: Song for regaining consciousness, version 2

When a bangal-bangal has killed some man and taken his fat, he leaves him lying on the ground and goes away if he is a stranger to him, but if he knows him he lays him out on the ground and then going about a hundred yards away he sings a song to cause the man to get up and go home. [The words of – inserted] such a song is the following:

Moronga	*morove*	*leani-gulin*
Rainbow	spirit (ghost)	knife-sharp
		(like a knife cutting)
willain-gurk	*kroia-bunglo*	
swallow	curlew	

[This is let the swallow & curlew shall wake him up to – crossed out]

This is to let his spirit (ghost) shall get up like a rainbow and the swallows and curlews [make him – crossed out] rouse him up to to go home.

When he gets up he does not know what is the matter with him but goes home and gets worse. There he dies.

His friends bury him according to his yaurin and the man who digs the grave smooths the side and bottom and waits to see the vapour of water rising up. He notes in which direction it goes and the kindred of his descent make up a party and go and kill the offender. The Bangal sees him at night sneaking about near the grave of his victim. If no vapour is seen in making the grave, the surface where the body has been buried is carefully smoothed over and next morning is watched to see any vapour rising.

The ghost finally goes to the sky land – [the – crossed out] a good country with trees and streams to which long ago the ancestors of the tribe used to climb up a pine tree to gather manna. (see p--)

Source: Howitt, SLV MS Box 1053/6 (a), p. 6, hw0419.pdf, p. 8; adapted by authors.

Note that the word *yaurin* is literally 'your flesh', with the 2nd person singular possessive suffix. Howitt (1904: 111) makes it clear that this word is used to refer to a group totem, saying that '*Yauruk*, the latter word meaning flesh, frequently expanded into *Yauruk-gologeitch*'. The form *yauruk* carries the 3rd person singular possessive suffix, **-uk**, meaning 'his, her'. The phrase 'his friends bury him according to his yaurin' refers to the direction of the burial of a person's head, discussed further in section 2.3.2.

Our linguistic analysis of this song is presented in (2.43), compared with the version from the 1904 book, which appears in the first and second rows:

(2.43)	*Moronga*	*morove*	*leanijulin*
	Rainbow	*spirit (ghost)*	*like a knife cutting*
	murrunga	**murrup-e**	**liyang-i-tyulin**
	rainbow	spirit-LOC	tooth-PARTICULAR-?

willain-gurk	*kroia-bangalo*
swallow	*curlew*
wilany-kurrk	**kruewa-pangal-u**
swallow-blood	curlew-medicine man-ERG

'(Cutting) like a …, the medicine man is making the spirit (get up) like a rainbow, like the swallow and curlew.'

It was suggested to us by Corey Theatre (pers. comm.) that the phrase **murrunga murrup-e**, literally 'rainbow spirit', could be referring to the **mirndai** 'maned snake' that is mentioned in many early sources relating to legends across many parts of western Victoria, and about which Jack Long related a story in the Mathi-Mathi language to Luise Hercus (Blake et al. 2011: 127).

Linguistic notes

One piece of evidence for this song being from an Eastern variety of Werkaya, rather than, for example Djadjawurrung, is the word for 'rainbow', **murrunga**, which is found in Werkaya sources[31] but not in Djadjawurrung.

The rainbow appears to be mentioned in a note of Howitt's (MV XM 761, unnumbered page, p. 66 of the PDF) relating to far away places and creator beings. After naming *mame'ngorak* 'our father', *gargomitch* 'a bright being' and *wŭra wŭra* 'the sky', the following is added:

> At the other side of wŭra wŭra there is the mŭrang – beyond this mŭrang there is a dark place like a mountain past which the Bangal could not get. Behind this is Mamengorak. Gargomitch comes down to the earth and goes back but they do not know what for. The blacks feared Gargomitch would take them up aloft.
>
> The Gargomitch takes the Bangal as far as wŭrk kerin and leaves them there while he goes through.

This connection between the rainbow and various powerful entities like *mamengorak* and *gargomitch* perhaps suggests that the rainbow is a place of great power, from which the **pangal** gets his power.

31 In draft versions of this chapter we wrote that 'R.H. Mathews writes "rainbow = moronga" on page 99 of one of the offprints of the Tyatyalla list (NLA MS 8006/8)'. A subsequent recheck of the sources has not found this reference, but we leave this footnote as we believe it likely that Mathews does confirm this use of the word for 'rainbow' in Western Kulin.

The word for spirit in both manuscripts has the letter <v>, rather than the expected <p>. This may represent a fricative realisation of the stop **p** in singing.

The one word that we cannot offer a full analysis of is *leanijulin* 'like a knife cutting'. In the manuscript version, an alternative reading of *leani-gulin* appears to be present. One possible related word is *tel-leen* recorded by Joseph Parker for Djadjawurrung with the meaning 'to chop' (Smyth 1878, 1: 164).

The word *leanijulin*, glossed by Howitt in the 1904 book as 'like a knife cutting', is glossed in the manuscript version as 'teeth-sharp'. It is possible that the weapon called **liyanggel** in Werkaya, a waddy or fighting club, is being referred to here, or that our regularisation of **tyulin** is correct, and this may also be related to the word for 'goanna', an animal with sharp teeth, recorded for Wemba-Wemba by Hercus (1992) as **tyuling.**[32] Note that Hartman (in Smyth 1878, 2: 55) records the form *dyoyû* for 'iguana', which is perhaps based on the same root.

Alternatively, if the initial letter of this morpheme is **g** then the text could read **kulin**, which would be the Werkaya word **kulien** 'anger, roused' ['gulɪen] (Hercus 1986: 206).[33] Donald Cameron gave information to Howitt about this word, saying (SLV MS Box 1053/6 (b), p. 13a):

> for gūlia = rage, anger; gūli woichŭp (woichŭp = belly) is also an equivalent. Donald explained as when a man is in a great rage he feels it at the pit of his stomach – hence the word

By this analysis, **liyang-i kulin** would be 'anger of the tooth', where the word for 'tooth' is marked by the -i suffix that Hercus (1986: 84) called a 'particularising suffix' that was used with nouns that formed the first part of a nominal compound. This would be an example of a body part metaphor to express emotions. Note that a full paradigm of the word **kuli-** 'enraged' is found in the Howitt papers (SLV MS Box 1053/6 (b), hw0421.pdf, p. 17), with person marked forms including the following:

> gūli-yan – I am enraged (or vexed)
> gūli-yarra thou art enraged
> guli-ya – he is enraged

32 We are grateful to Harley Dunolly Lee (pers. comm.) for this suggestion.

33 Howitt (SLV MS Box 1053/6 (b), p. 13a) also gives a paradigm for this verb, with the translation 'enraged'.

Given that Howitt was fully aware of this word, he would surely have clearly written *guli* and would have made a more transparent translation of *leanijulin*. Thus we think it more likely that this word does not contain the morpheme **kuli**.

The welcome swallow, *Hirundo neoxena*, does have red on its throat; it is literally called 'blood swallow' in Werkaya. The white-browed woodswallow (*Artamus superciliosus*) has a chestnut chest. Luise Hercus recorded the word **wila-kert** 'martin, dusky wood-swallow'. The root of the word **wila** means 'wind', and the name of the bird probably comes from the fact that it glides on the wind.

The word for 'hoary-headed grebe' (*Poliocephalus poliocephalus*) in Werkaya was recorded by Hercus as **kurrewa**. This appears to be what is meant by the spelling *kroia*. As with the word for 'club with knob at the end' in Table 2.15, there is an initial cluster in the word recorded by Howitt, perhaps **kruewa**, a metathesis of the form recorded by Hercus. This metathesis with the initial **kr**- is a feature of the Wotjobaluk dialect of the Wimmera language. It is likely that the bird referred to here is in fact the bush stone-curlew (*Burhinus grallarius*) now critically endangered in Victoria, a bird that has a powerful call[34] and does not require water in the way that the hoary-headed grebe does.[35]

2.3.2 Shooting Star song

A second song, which is connected with the Song for regaining consciousness (section 2.3.1), is presented here. Because of the reference to the *yiyi-yauw'il*, we have termed this the Shooting Star song.

Howitt (1904: 368–69) gave a detailed background relating to this custom, presumably with Morton Plains Bobby as his informant. This account seems to be based on the notes that include the text of the song presented in Box 2.20. Howitt published the entire context of this song but without the text of the song itself in the 1904 book:

34 See for example, Crikey, 'Bird of the Week: The Bush Stone Curlew', 17 September 2010, accessed 5 February 2019, www.crikey.com.au/2010/09/27/bird-of-the-week-the-bush-stone-curlew/#:~:text=The%20Bush%2DStone%20Curlew%20Burhinus,and%20modern%20land%2Dmanagement%20practices.

35 We are grateful to Paul Clyne for suggesting this.

> This old man also gave me an account of the manner in which the fat is always taken, whether the victim was noosed by the *Yulo* or knocked down by a blow on the back of the neck with the *Breppen*, that is a club with a knob at the end. The victim is laid on his back and the medicine-man sits astride of his chest, cuts him open on the right side below the ribs, and abstracts the fat. Then bringing the edges together, and singing his spell, he bites them together to make them join without a visible scar. Then he retires to a distance, leaving the man lying on his back. The medicine man then sings a song with the following effect. At the first singing the victim lifts one leg, at the second the other, at the third he turns over, at the fourth a little whirlwind comes, and blowing under his back, lifts him up. At the same time a star falls from the sky, called *Yerigauil*, with the man's heart. He thereupon rises and staggers about, wondering how he came to be sleeping there. This process is called *Deking-ngalluk*, or 'open side.'

Howitt (1904: 368) added: 'Whenever the Wotjobaluk see a falling star, they believe that it is falling with the heart of a man who has been caught by a *Bangal* and deprived of his fat'. A transcription of this short song and the context presented with it is given in Box 2.20:

Box 2.20: Shooting Star song

Long ago an old doctor – one of the cleverest who ever lived made a song

G'arnda - gall'au up above

heating affair

----

yiri-yauw'il - star

When a party has got a mans fat and left him lying they retreat 50 yd and sing a

song to make him come up the yiri yauwil falls on him (falling star) and brings him to life

1st song one leg

2nd song one leg

3rd song turn over

the [nhu...??] come & lift him up

p83

Then stand up and come to himself. Thinks he has been sleeping for long. [whatever bird – crossed out]. They have to [bear – crossed out] lay him down in the proper direction as if he were dead.

A real stranger they would kill and leave there and not bring him to life again.

Falling stars always are falling on murdered men

Source: Howitt, MV XM 761, pp. 82–83; adapted by authors.

Note that the word transcribed as [nhu…??] might be read as [nhulind?] and may be a word in language. The directions referred to here are related to the directions in which the head of person should be buried, a direction which is decided by his moiety and totem relations. Howitt (1904: 454) includes a diagram of these directions, and this diagram is reprinted and discussed in Lydon (2009: 40). R.H. Mathews has made similar diagrams from the same area (NLA MS 8006/3/4.1, Notebook 1, pp. 104, 130, 133).

Our linguistic analysis of this short song is presented as (2.44):

(2.44) *G'arnda* *gall'au* *up above*

heating *affair*

kanda **kalau**

heat? there-?

yiri yauw'il

– a star

yirriyawil

shooting star

'A shooting star'

Notes

There is a line underneath the first line separating the second line *yiri yawu'il*, and this may suggest that the song text is only that part which is contained in the first line. However, the last syllable of both lines is preceded by a small accent mark that may represent a line final accent or stress, which is a feature of the some of the songs recorded by Luise Hercus (see, for example, Jack Brown's song, section 2.2.6.1). On the basis of the apparent marking of accent or stress, we consider that the song consisted of these two lines.

That the word **kanda** relates to heat is shown by two pieces of evidence. In information that was given to Howitt by Sergeant Major, the word *kandalau* is defined as 'a place out near the narin where the sun goes down like a great fire that never goes out called kandalau'. F.W. Spieseke (*Australischer Christenbote* 1867, no. 11: 42–43) noted the form *Gautayalla* 'hell'. We think it likely that the word that Spieseke interpreted as meaning 'hell' has the same form as the words in the first line of this song. The word **karti** 'heat' is found in several related Western Kulin languages.

Corey Theatre (pers. comm.) suggested to us that the word **kalau** could be a form of the distal demonstrative, often found with a form **kil-** which is also discussed further below in connection with the Keledia song (see section 2.5).

The word for 'shooting star' is also found as **yirrikawil**, spelled in the original as *yerigauil*, discussed above in section 2.3.1. This may represent dialectal variation. Such variation between velar stop **k** and a semivowel is recorded in other words in the languages of Victoria; for example, 'his heel' in Mathi-Mathi is **kànáku**, while in Wati-Wati (Swan Hill) it is **kanawu** (Blake et al. 2011: 18).

2.3.3 Initiation song

This initiation song was used at the initiation of young boys, a ceremony that involved the knocking out of two front teeth (tooth evulsion), as mentioned by Howitt in the two passages below. There are two versions of the text of the song. The first is in a manuscript at the State Library of Victoria (MS Box 1053/6 (a), p. 3), presented in Box 2.21. In the margins of this page is written '*the garrich ceremony*'. Howitt (1904: 610) refers to the *Guritch* as 'sister's husband', and in the printed version in Box 2.22, the *guritch* is mentioned frequently.

Tooth evulsion is known to have been practised by the Djadjawurrung (as stated in Boxes 2.21 and 2.22), but may not have been practised in the Wimmera, where Werkaya language was spoken. We have included this song under the Werkaya section, because the manuscript version is found in a section that is headed 'The Wotjo-ballŭk Tribe'.

This song has the same first word, *pata*, as the Up River initiation song sung by both Albert Karloan and Pinkie Mack, and recorded by Radcliffe Brown and the Berndts respectively (see section 14.1).

Box 2.21: Initiation song, version 1

Before boys whiskers came and before he is quite grown up he is taken by his guritch (sister's husband) to this camp, Then he rubs him with red ochre and takes care of him When he goes out hunting or travelling he carries the boy when tired and he sounds the bull roarer (mānunga) to make the boy strong and sings this song continually:

pata	manunga	jirarunga
wait a while	dont touch it	growing up

This song also makes the two front top teeth easily removed when the boy is being initiated. While the song is being sung, the barn-būngal (medicine man) puts a pointed stick between the teeth to loosen them. If any blood comes from the gums either now or when the teeth are knocked out it must not be spit out -or let flow down his breast [else h -crossed out] but he must swallow it, otherwise his legs will become crooked, and he would be lame.

This was done by the Jajawrong and also by the tribes in the Murray

Source: Howitt, SLV MS 1053/6 (a), p. 3, hw0419.pdf, p. 2, adapted by authors.

Box 2.22: Initiation song, version 2

In the Jajaurung tribe the ceremonies were somewhat fuller than those of the Wurunjerri, and also illustrate them.

Before a boy was grown up and had whiskers, he was taken by his *Guritch* to his camp, where he rubbed him over with red ochre. When the *Guritch* went out hunting, or was travelling, he took the boy with him, and carried him when he was tired. He sounded the bull-roarer continually, to make the boy strong, and he sang this song:-

Pata	*mamunya*	*jira-runga*
Wait a while	don't touch it	growing up

The song also makes the two front teeth easily removable when a boy is being initiated. When the boy has grown somewhat older, so that his beard has come, his *Guritch* and the old men take him away to be made a man. He is laid down on the ground and all the hair on his face and his pubes is plucked out. If it comes out easily and without blood showing, they say, "He is a good young man," and rub him over with red ochre. The song above mentioned is then sung, and the medicine-man (*Barn-bungal*) forces a pointed stick between the teeth to loosen them. If any blood comes from the gums either now or when the teeth are knocked out, it must not be spat out or let fall on his breast; but he must swallow it, otherwise his legs would become crooked, and he would be lame. He then goes away with his *Guritch* and the old men. For a time he

[p. 614]

remains quite naked, and is rubbed with red ochre, until his oldest *Guritch* brings him an opossum rug.

If, however, blood comes when the hair is plucked out, the youth is said to have "been too much with the women", and is painted white from the waist over the head, down the back to the belt on which he wears a *Branjep*, before and behind, and he is called *Jibauk*.

Source: Howitt (1904: 613–14), adapted by authors.

Our linguistic analysis of the song is presented as (2.45):

(2.45)	*pata*	*manunga*	*jira-runga*
	wait a while	*don't touch it*	*growing up*
	pata	**mamang(g)a**	**tyiRa-Runga**
	wait	bull roarer?	tear-?
	'Wait!, the bullroarer …'		

Notes on the linguistics

The meaning of the first word, **pata**, as 'wait' is found in a quote from one of the Moravian missionaries (cited in Jensz 2000: 54[36]). This short reference related to the Moravian missionaries from the Lake Boga Mission seeing an old man passing and is dated 29 October 1851. They wrote:

> We invited him to come to us and to be instructed in the word of God; he however put off the matter, saying, 'Barta pullepea' (Wait for the present).

In another section of Jensz (2000: 8) there is an untranslated phrase *Kulli kiah: barta pulli pia* that may include the word for 'man', **kuli**, followed by an exclamation **kiya** and perhaps meant something like 'Hey, man, wait for now'. Similar phrases are found in other parts of the Moravian papers and confirm the meaning of *barta* (regularised as **pata**) as being 'wait'.

The second word in this song is glossed by Howitt as 'don't touch it' both in the manuscript and in the published version, but the spelling is different, *manunga* in the State Library of Victoria manuscript (see Box 2.21) and as *mamunya* in his 1904 book (Box 2.22). Following the latter spelling, we might speculate that *mamanya* 'don't touch it' contains the root **manya**, which is 'hand' in Wemba-Wemba.

However, in the manuscript version, the word *mānunga* is translated as 'bull roarer' in the text preceding the song, and this is perhaps a reference to the nature of the bull roarer as only being touched once someone is initiated. Perhaps, therefore, the word actually means 'bullroarer', which is an item not to be touched, but the literal translation of this word does not actually mean 'don't touch it'.

Box 2.23: Words for 'bullroarer' as recorded by R.H. Mathews

Bullroarer is mamanggurk made out of bial wood or pine,
used for bringing rain. Men only used them, but women could be in view.
Ngunnidyuk or Bumbir bumbir – bullroarer.
Mattyamuk is small roarer.

Source: NLA MS 8006/3/4.1, Notebook 1, p. 154, adapted by authors.

36 Jensz's report was based on microfilms held by AIATSIS, including AIATSIS microfilm MF 165, The Moravian Mission in Australia Papers, 1832–1916: First Mission at Lake Boga.

Words for 'bullroarer' are recorded by both Howitt and R.H. Mathews in the Werkaya language. Mathews noted several words, listed in Box 2.23, noting that only men used these, but women (and presumably uninitiated boys) could see them.

The form of the word *mamanggurk*, presumably **mamanggurrk**, looks as if it may be a compound containing **mama** 'father' and **kurrk** 'blood'. The possibility of this word being a compound including the word for blood is increased by a note in Howitt's papers (SLV MS Box 1053/2 (b), hw0391.pdf, p. 82),[37] where he writes down the words for 'bullroarer' as: '"Berbero-gumm" [possibly he meant the wood of some gum tree? or Mūnan-gurk'.[38] This discussion is in what looks to be a draft of a letter from Howitt to Baldwin Spencer, that is a page within the section containing information from William Barak. The word *Berbero-gumm* was recorded as *puber.ro gun* by Robinson for the Melbourne area language, but the word *Mūnan-gurk* appears to be an instance of the word he had recorded in the Wimmera.

In conclusion, we cannot say for sure what is the form or the meaning of the second word in this song, but it is likely to be the word for 'bullroarer'.

As regards the third word of this song, there is no word recorded for the Werkaya language meaning 'grow' resembling *jira-runga*. The closest form in Western Kulin being probably **karringa** 'grow' in Djadjawurrung.

There is a word meaning 'to tear' in Wemba-Wemba, which is **tyira**. If this is the word intended, the whole song might mean 'Wait, the bullroarer (might) tear (you)'.

2.3.4 New Moon chant

The fourth song written down by Howitt from the Wotjoballuk people is the New Moon chant, a children's song that has been found in two manuscript versions, one in the State Library of Victoria (MS Box 1053/6 (b), p. 33), presented as Box 2.24, and one from Museums Victoria (XM 761, page 86 of the PDF), presented as Box 2.25. In the SLV version, there is a small line drawing of the *ngouratch* 'petticoat' or 'apron'. The manuscript version from the museum contains more background information. Another version was published by Howitt (1887a).

37 We are grateful to Amanda Lourie for finding this page in the Howitt scans.
38 There is no closing bracket in the original.

This song appears to relate to children growing up,[39] and while the song seems to have been sung by young children (described as boys and girls), the content of it may reflect 'coming of age' or 'initiation' ceremonies. For example, in R.H. Mathews's notes headed 'Initiation of Girls' (NLA MS 8006/5/5), there is mention that in these initiation ceremonies, the mother will give a skirt or 'apron' called *nguraty*.

Box 2.24: New Moon chant, version 1

Superstitions		
A pigeon flying over a boy is likely to stop his growth.		
At every new moon the boys and girls when they see it must shout out the following in order to grow well:		
Waur -	Waur -	Waur
grow	grow	grow
Gali'mba	ge'ra	mamorek
nurse	bough	father my
Tourta	ngouretch	bapūrek
Dūrta	petticoat	mother my
wearing		
ngouratch = woman's petticoat of sinew		

Source: SLV Box 1053/6 (b), p. 33, hw0421.pdf, p. 38, adapted by authors.

Note that a rather fine drawing of the *ngouratch* is found on this page.

The Museums Victoria version is found on an unnumbered page of XM 761, commencing at page 86 of the PDF.

Box 2.25: New Moon chant, version 2

A pigeon flying over you stops you from growing.	
Ev[er]y new moon when they see it – the boys & girls sing out 3 or 4 times	
Waur waur waur – (grow grow grow)	
galim	ba | gera
[galumba – crossed out]	
[carry??] nurse	bough
mamorek	

39 We are grateful to one of our anonymous reviewers for pointing out that among the Kaytetye of Central Australia, there is a 'full moon song' for boys and a girls' song that relates to the sun/east (Thompson 2003).

father my
tūrtangouretch
babourek
my mother
dūrta
[mother - crossed out]
wearing
ngouretch
Petticoat (of sinew)
[p. 87]
mit chen = moon was a man at the time when all animals were men. When people died he used to tell them to get up. Then once another fellow called Don said let them stop dead. Then no one came to life anymore. Then the moon died and always came to life again.
The sun was a woman who left her son (little boy) to the west and then went to dig up yams left him there and went round and came up the other side. When she did she continued to do the same.

Source: MV XM 761, pp. 86–87, adapted by authors.

The association of moon with male and sun with female is found in other parts of the Howitt notebooks. This duality relates to the context of the song, which is directed at both male and female children.

Our linguistic analysis is presented as (2.46):

(2.46)

Waur -	*Waur -*	*Waur*
grow	*grow*	*grow*
wau-R	**wau-R**	**wau-R**
grow-2SG	grow-2SG	grow-2SG

'You grow, you grow, you grow!'

Gali'mba	*ge'ra*	*mamorek*
nurse	*bough*	*father my*
kalimba	**kiRa/ tyiRa**	**mam-u-R-ek**
carry/nurse	leaf	father-ERG-LINK-1SG.POSS

'My father is nursing/carrying (you) with a leaf.'

Tourta	*ngouretch*	*bapūrek*
Dūrta wear	*petticoat*	*mother my*
turta	**nguRaty**	**pap-u-R-ek**
wear	skirt	mother-ERG-LINK-1SG.POSS

'My mother wears/puts a skirt (on me). / My mother wears a skirt.'

Notes

The word for 'grow' **waur**, may be related to Mathi-Mathi **wàuwúnatha** 'swell up' which also has a root **wau-**. The **-r** is possibly a 2nd person singular suffix. Jensz (2000: 9) also notes two related words recorded in the Moravian papers: *wauinga* 'full (stomach)', German *satt*; and *wauingin* 'full (stomach)', German *gesaetteit*[?].

The Werkaya word for 'breast' or 'milk' is **kurrm**. The form **kalimba** could be a root with a similar meaning followed by a formative **-ba** creating a verb stem. This word may have as its root the word for 'carry', which may have been **kali-**. It is possibly cognate with Wati-Wati **wali-**, a word listed in the form *walliga* in the 'Swan Hill Tribe' word list in Barry (1867). This word appears to be an example of initial **k-** ~ **w-** variation.

The word for leaf is recorded as both **kira** and **tyira** in a range of Western Kulin languages. Either of these is a possible interpretation of Howitt's spelling *gera*.

In Wemba-Wemba, **tutha** means 'put on, wear' and is found in connection with the wearing of a hat in the **Nganuty-nganuty** song, sung by Stan Day (see section 2.2.2). Corey Theatre (pers. comm.) has pointed out to us that in the Djadjawurrung and Tjapwurrung languages **turta** means 'carry' (see Blake 2019).

We have regularised the spelling for the word 'skirt' as **nguRaty**, with a /u/ vowel, because of the presence of *ou* in the spelling *ngouretch*. However, it is possible that it should be realised as **ngaRaty**. In Djadjawurrung and Tjapwurrung, the word for 'sinew' is **ngaRam** with a very clear /a/ vowel recorded in multiple sources. Given that this 'skirt' is made of sinew, it would not be surprising to find the two words based on the same root.[40]

40 We are grateful to Corey Theatre for pointing this out.

The word is translated in some other sources such as R.H. Mathews as 'apron'. In his notebook (NLA MS 8006/3/4.1, Notebook 1, p. 127), on a page of information relating to Wambawamba, Mathews wrote: 'Did the girl wear Tyriburniñ or Ngūraty after she got off the log? Or at any time – what occasions for each apron?' The comment from Mathews presumably relates to a stage in a young woman's coming of age ceremony at which she starts to wear the **nguRaty**. This is suggestive that the New Moon chant is indeed a children's song that looks forward to their coming into adulthood. While it seems clear that for the females this is marked by putting on the **nguRaty**, it is less clear what it means for males.

We do not know enough about this song to say to what extent it was related to progress into adulthood, or the extent to which it might have been interpreted differently by people at different stages of their lives and cultural knowledge.[41] This song is just one more example of the great richness of cultural information that these texts hint at.

2.4 Ye-pen-ni pie-kai dance recorded by Thomas

In a list of traditional dances performed in the 1840s and 1850s, Thomas listed 'Yepene Amy Gai (by Mr Parker called Dance of Separate Spirits)' (see Box 3.1 in section 3.1.5 for the listing of other dances, all related to Central Victoria). Smyth (1878, 2: 167) gave a more detailed discussion of this dance, but no text:

> On another occasion Mr. Parker was present when the natives performed the *Yepene Amydeet,* or dance of the separated spirits. It was new to the Aborigines of the Loddon, and was conducted by an old man, who stated that it was practised by the people of the north-west, amongst whom he had learnt it. It was never introduced on any other occasion, and was soon after nearly forgotten. 'Holding boughs in each hand, which were waved in unison alternately over each shoulder, and dancing for some time in lines and semicircles, at length they gradually gathered into a compact circular body; then slowly sinking on the ground, and burying their heads under the boughs, they represented, according to the statement of the old native, who was master of the ceremonies, the approach of death,

41 We are grateful to Corey Theatre for raising this possibility.

> and in the perfectly still and motionless posture they maintained for some time the state of death itself. Then the old man, breaking suddenly into a new dance, and waving furiously his boughs over the prostrate mass, gave them the word; and, suddenly springing to their feet, they joined him in his rejoicings. This was explained to me as intended to represent the revival of the soul after death.'

The origin of this song as being further to the west and north than the Loddon River (Djadjawurrung territory) appears to be confirmed by the presence of words with initial clusters such as /pr-/, such clusters being found in the Morton Plains area in the Wimmera to the west.[42]

A.W. Howitt made a note in one of the manuscripts in the State Library of Victoria (MS Box 1054/1 (a), hw0429.pdf, p. 1) to ask Barak (see section 3.1.2) about this song, and also about the Mindi dance of the Djadjawurrung that was documented by Parker, reproduced in Smyth (1878, 1: 166). We have not found any evidence of Barak answering the questions relating to this, so perhaps by the time Howitt interviewed him in the late 1880s or 1890s, knowledge of this song and dance was lost.

This song is included in this Western Kulin chapter, as the assumption is that the song is from a Western Kulin variety. Thomas recorded it as coming from the 'far West and NWest' and the name of the dance at which this song was performed, was given as *yepene* or *yep-pen-ni*. This is certainly the same word as recorded by Robinson as *yap.pen.nite* meaning 'big corrobboree' in a section headed 'Vocabulary of Grampians and Pyrenees Blacks, commencing 19 July '41', the language presumably being Tjapwurrung (Clark 2000: 141).

The name of the dance discussed in the paragraph above is given by Smyth as *Yepene amydeet* and refers to the dance and the word also used for 'white person', which also referred to 'the soul when separated from the body'. This we can regularise as **yapani ngamadjitj**,[43] probably meaning 'dance of the white persons', where the root form of the first word is probably **yapana** combined with the particularising suffix **-i** (see Hercus 1986: 84). For Djadjawurrung, Blake (2019) regularises this word with a palatal nasal as **yapenya** (see also Table 2.5). The word *Yepene* is surely the same as *Yapeen*, written as the name of the 'Goulburn Corroboree' (see section 3.7.2).

42 We are grateful to Corey Theatre for pointing this out.

43 Howitt (SLV MS Box 1053/2 (b), hw0391, p. 37) writes that Barak told him (in connection with the Eastern Kulin language): 'White men were called by us "Ngamajet" – this word is also used to mean the bright red colors at sunset'.

This suggests that a word **yapana-** relating to dance/corroboree was in use not only in Djadjawurrung but also to the east in the Thagungwurrung variety of the Eastern Kulin.

Thomas further exemplifies this word in a newspaper article published in 1845 about burial customs:[44]

> It is remarkable that the designation given to the white inhabitants of the colony in most of the dialects of which I have heard amydeet, jajowrong, amerjig, koligan, amy gai, &c.), appears to be identical with the words used to des- cribe the soul when separated from the body. – I once, and but once, saw a singular ceremonious dance, on the Loddon station, which was called 'Yepene amy gai,' or dance of separate spirits.

We suggest that the name of the dance as given by Thomas can be regularised as **yapani payiki** 'big corroboree of rising up', suggesting the likely meaning of the dance is that some animal or entity fell to the ground and rose up again, or revived. The full text of the song sung on this occasion is given in Box 2.26:

Box 2.26: Ye-pen-ni-pie-kee dance

Sacred Dance Ye-pen-ni-pie-kee	Yea noi Wo bol Lum bool Wor bun Kor bun Mal lin uk Kur nin bang o ruk To gun ne min Yar roi Kun no muk Kun no muk Ke nu or Bul lin Ge bar Narge bar Yen erk Brun ger min then fall down like dead (Pie kee) Yan gar Yango Ungo &c – repetition. Called by Mr Parker "Yepenne a my gai. A singular dance he says never saw but once & that it has reference to the Resurrection" – Blacks from the far west and Nwest.

Source: SLNSW MLMSS 214, Volume 03 Item 01, SLNSW_FL827807.jpg; adapted by authors.

Our suggested regularisation of this song is presented as (2.47):

(2.47) **yenuwi wapul lampul wopun kopun malinuk kanin pang(g)arruk**
t(h)agunamin yarruwi kunumuk kunumuk kenuwa
palin kepa n(h)akepa yenak pranga-min … (then fall down like dead)
(payiki) yanga yanuwa-ngu

44 'Burial of the Dead among the Australian Aborigines', *South Australian Register*, Wednesday 18 June 1845, accessed 18 October 2019, trove.nla.gov.au/newspaper/article/27450374?searchTerm=burial%20of%20the%20dead%20among%20the%20australian%20aborigines&searchLimits=.

Without any translation offered by Thomas, and only the English words 'then fall down like dead' and the reference to some kind of resurrection, any suggested translation can only be very tentative.

There is some repetition of words and possible suffixes, as for example *wo bol lum bool* in the first line. This could include a dual marker **-pul**, either marking nouns as 'your (two) objects' or verbs as 'you two are doing something'. It is possible that *wo bol* is in fact the 2nd person dual pronoun **wabul** found in Woiwurrung (see Blake 1991: 70).

Several words in the text have a final **-uk**, which is perhaps the 3rd person singular possessive suffix ('his/hers').

The form *bang o ruk* that we have regularised as **pang(g)arruk** may be the Werkaya word **panggarr** 'white necked crane' (*Ardea pacifica*) (Hercus 1986: 198), combined with the 3rd person singular possessive suffix **-uk**. If this was the case, it may be that the 'white necked crane' was one of the animals referred to that fell down. There is no Djadjawurrung word for this bird recorded.

Alternatively, this could be the word for 'body', **peng**, found in many Western Kulin languages including Djadjawurrung, in combination with the 1st person plural exclusive suffix **-angurr(ak)**, meaning 'our bodies'.

We can therefore suggest a translation of the last part of the text as in (2.48):

(2.48)	*pie kee*	*yan gar yango ungo*
	payik-i	**yanga-yang-uwa-ngu**
	rise up-IMP	go-go-INTENS-1PL.INCL
	'Rise up! And we will go, go.'	

It seems that this song was interpreted by Parker and Thomas as relating to Christian Resurrection stories. However, there is no reason to suppose that this is not a fully traditional dance.

2.5 Keledia song: Werkaya (Wimmera) song recorded by Bulmer and the Moravian missionaries

This song is found in several sources from the Moravian missionaries. It was apparently recorded first by Rev. F.W. Spieseke, who wrote that when he was speaking to Pepper (Nathanael Pepper) about songs, it was he (Pepper) who came up with the song itself. The earliest version of the song is in a manuscript letter now in the archives of the Moravian missionaries at Herrnhut, dated 1859. The section relating to the Keledia song is presented in Box 2.27. Pepper was from the western part of the Wimmera, and if the language of the song was in his native variety, it was likely very similar to the Werkaya dialect recorded by Hercus (1986).

Box 2.28 presents the version of the song printed in an edition of the *Australischer Christenbote* (1861, no. 5: 23), the newsletter of the Moravian missionaries in Herrnhut. A third version is found in the Bulmer papers in Museums Victoria (MS XM 925); it is also published as Campbell (1999: 58), where the original is slightly altered. This is presented in Box 2.29, where the section in square brackets is taken from Campbell (1999). We believe that Bulmer may have learned this song from Donald Cameron who went to Ramahyuck in Gippsland in 1868 to be married.

The content of the song appears to be very Christian, but in several of the sources for this song, the missionaries who recorded it talk about this song pre-dating the conversion to Christianity. For example, it seems that Donald Cameron specifically told Bulmer that the song was known long before the arrival of missionaries (see Box 2.29).

Box 2.27: Keledia song, version 1

„Winja wallo niang a mamamuräck? Wie nahe sitzt der große Vater? Nackum „bang" in jehrero. In mich kam der Geist. wurrowim parrin. Kehledije! Reiniget den Weg. Strahlender Glanz!"
„Winja wallo niang a mamamuräck? Wie nahe sitzt der große Vater?
Nackum „bang" in jehrero. In mich kam der Geist.
wurrowim parrin. Kehledije! Reiniget den Weg. Strahlender Glanz!"

Source: Version in letter from F.W. Spieseke to his superior, Bruder Reichel, held at the archive of the Moravians at Herrnhut, Germany; transcribed by Peter Hornung.

Box 2.28: Keledia song, version 2

Winya wallo neanga mamamorek!	How near sits my great father!
Nakum bangung yereru!	In me comes his ghost!
Wurruwin parrin!	Make clear the way!
Keledia!	Great his glory!

Source: *Australischer Christenbote* (1861, no. 5: 23); adapted by authors.

Box 2.29: Keledia song, version 3

But the one I now give I must confess I have some doubts as to its genuineness – not that an Aboriginal did not compose it but I expect he had been under the influence of the missionary before he conceived the idea. However the Aboriginal who gave it me assures me that he knew it long before the missionaries went to the Wimmera. It was supposed to be composed by an old man at the prospect of death and if it is genuine I must say the composer had more light than is usually given to blacks.

Winya	*wallo*	*nganga*	*mamemerak*
How	far	sits	Our father
Whoora	*unbarring*	*killerdea*	
Who	cleared the road	so bright	
Knuk	*amba*	*ngan*	*j'il merrerak*
Feel	cheered	I	Good spirits

The old man is cheered at the prospect of death by a good spirit, [who has made the way so bright. The Aboriginal informs me that *jilmen* is a spirit, and that *jilmerak* is a spirit that helps men. The above will give a very fair idea of the songs which are among the Aborigines, and also their power of composing.]

Source: Bulmer papers, MV XM 925, adapted by authors.

In *Australischer Christenbote* there are several other references to the word *Keledia*, one of which (1862, no. 5: 23) contains the text *Jesus Mamengoruck gungee Keledia*, the source of which is given as Hagenauer. This contains the form mamangurrak, which is literally 'father-1PL.INCL'. This is also presented in a different form in Smyth (1878, 1: 465):

> The rev. Mr. Hagenauer says that the Aborigines of Gippsland believe in the existence of a good and superior Being, whom they name *Mamengorook (Mamen,* father, and *gorook,* our); but they seem to regard him but little, and are unwilling to say more than that he lives at a distance from them. He is described as being white, very clean, and in *Keledia* (great brightness or glory).

In his initial letter relating to the conversation he had with Pepper, Spieseke reports that at one point Pepper said 'ihre Gesänge sind nicht so gut', meaning 'your songs are not as good', which can perhaps be taken as meaning that he regarded this song as being part of the Indigenous culture. Spieseke later reports a conversation with 'Lady' about whether such songs pre-dated the arrival of Europeans.

Given this song text and the associated concept of *mamengorook* 'our father', and the fact that Aboriginal people denied that this song was a Christian one, it appears that some of the Moravian missionaries came to the view that this was evidence of the kind of belief found in the quote from Smyth above; namely, that at least some Aboriginal people believed in a 'father spirit'. We see some additional evidence for this from Gippsland, where Howitt in several letters discusses *Mungan-ngaura* 'our father' who was 'a great being above the sky' (e.g. Howitt to Tylor, 2 February 1884).[45]

We conclude that there is some possibility that this song is a traditional one, referring to a traditional figure, perhaps with the words and translation adjusted in view of the rapid Christianisation of Indigenous people going on at the time the song was documented. It does not appear that this text is a translation of a well-known hymn, and given that there appear to be case markers, tense markers and possessive markers in the text, this text is clearly not translated by missionaries and is perhaps a genuine traditional song.

Our linguistic analysis is presented below. The *Australischer Christenbote* version (Box 2.28) is presented in (2.49):

(2.49) *Winya-wallo* *neanga* *mamamorek!*
How near sits my great father!
wintya-walu(k) **ngenya** **mama-ngurrak**
where-3SG sit father-1SG.PL.INCL
'Where is (our) father sitting?'

Nakum *bangung* *yereru!*
In me comes his ghost!
njaka-m **peng-ang** **yirri-rru**
see?-? body-LOC spirit-ERG
'The spirit … in the body.'

45 A.W. Howitt to E.B. Tylor, 2 February 1884, 'Transcription of Box 12: Howitt correspondence Tylor papers Pitt Rivers Museum manuscript collections Part 1', Pitt Rivers Virtual Collections, accessed 6 May 2016, web.prm.ox.ac.uk/sma/index.php/primary-documents/primary-documents-index/414-howitt-tylor-papers-prm.html.

Wurruwin	*parrin!*
Make clear the way!	
warriwa-in(j)	**paring**
come-FUT	track
'He will come (by) track.'	

Keledia!
Great his glory!
kilayitya
distant (time or place)
'(From) afar.'

Linguistic notes

The word *keledia*, though always glossed by the missionary sources as 'great brightness or glory' or 'great his glory', is in fact a far distal demonstrative, recorded by Hercus (1992) for Wemba-Wemba as **kilayitya** 'long ago'. Interestingly, in one of the R.H. Mathews offprints the form *gillaity* is glossed as 'today' and *gillenadya* as 'some time ago' for Perapaperapa, termed Burraba by Mathews (NLA MS 8006/4, File 8b, Folder 9).

In Wemba-Wemba 'sit' is **ngengga**, but in Werkaya **ngenya**, hence we have used the Werkaya form.

The word **yirri** is found in the Wemba-Wemba sources (Stone 1911) in the compound **yirri larr** 'oath stone, or charm', which Hercus (1992) notes 'must be equivalent to "that very (special) stone"'. This word may also be related to the shooting star, *Yerigauil*, mentioned in connection to the Song for regaining consciousness after a kidney fat attack (see section 2.3.1).

The Bulmer version is almost identical, but with the last two lines from example (2.49) appearing before the last line. The glossing of the last line in the Bulmer version (Box 2.29) is different, as is the word for 'spirit', as we see in (2.50):

(2.50)	*knuk*	*amba*	*ngan*	*j'il merrerak*
	feel	*cheered*	*I*	*good spirits*
	ngaka	**-amba**	**ng-an**	**tyilmerr-ek**
	jump?	suffix?	?-1SG	spirit-?-1SG.POSS
	'My spirit has …'			

If the translation given by Bulmer is correct, the three forms *knuk amba ngan* would be a verb form, marked with the 1st person suffix **-an**. In Hercus's Werkaya word list (1986: 210), there are two words that may provide the root for this, **ngaka** 'jump' and **ngak** 'shadow'. Neither, however, has a meaning similar to 'feel cheered'.

As Bulmer points out, '*jilmen* is a spirit, and that *jilmerak* is a spirit that helps men' (see Box 2.29).

2.6 Corroboree song from the Wimmera, recorded by Samuel Carter

A short 'corroboree song' was written down by Samuel Carter as part of a description of a corroboree, presented here in Box 2.30. Carter had settled in 1842 at North Brighton, noting that 'Dooen was the native name for this piece of country'. Today Dooen is just to the north of Horsham and we would assume that this corroboree occurred there.

Box 2.30: Corroboree song recorded by Samuel Carter

They always painted themselves with red and white clay before a corroboree, and tied small boughs with string to their legs.

The lubras would double up a kangaroo skin and use it as a drum for heating time, and sing a weird sort of song at the same time — something to this effect: —

> "A-lip-maliah and a-ling-a ling a-ling."

It had some reference to the sky, clouds and lightning.

The men also made a burring noise whilst going through the performance.

The corroboree lasted two or three hours, and as a rule many of the men got very excited towards the end, especially if they had had a good feast beforehand. They used to make a kind of sweet intoxicating drink from honeysuckle apples by soaking them in water. This they called "Beeo," and were very fond of it.

Source: Carter (1911: 26); adapted by authors.

The language of Horsham would have been a variety of Western Kulin, possibly the Yardwadjali language. The only word that we can recognise in this text is the word for the plant that Carter calls the 'honeysuckle'. The word *Beeo* is clearly the same as that recorded by Hercus in Werkaya as 'biur-galg ['biyʊr 'galk] *sweet-drink, tree, Banksia ornata.* The flowers were soaked in water to extract the honey' (Hercus 1986: 200). This word would be regularised as **piyurr kalk**.

We suggest that this song might be regularised as (2.51):

(2.51) **(ng)alip maliya (ng)aling, (ng)aling, (ng)aling**

We are unable to suggest any translation of this song. Hercus (1986) recorded the Werkaya word for 'cloud' as **marng** (**menggi** in Mathi-Mathi). It is unlikely that this word is present in the song.

2.7 Tjapwurrung song recorded by R.H. Mathews

In a notebook in the National Library of Australia (NLA MS 8006/3/4.2, Notebook 6), R.H. Mathews wrote down a short song, with glossing and translation.

This song probably relates to a 'kidney fat' attack (see for example the Song for regaining consciousness after a kidney fat attack in section 2.3.1). Unlike that song, however, this song is warning a potential victim rather than being the curing words. On the previous page the name of an Aboriginal person is written, 'Mrs Austin', who is Mrs Rosie Austin.[46] She may have been the person who gave Mathews this text. She would have been Tjapwurrung, but the language of this song has features of several Western Kulin varieties. There are some other words on this page that are Tjapwurrung, such as *Buit buit tyappaty* 'to take everything off his body', which is given as 'strip completely' in Blake (2019), and several words translated by Mathews as 'they are turning one another' and 'they are turning around'. The full text of the song is presented in Box 2.31:

Box 2.31: Song documented by R.H. Mathews

Comeing	for thee	wild b	hit	thee
Burnala	nyai.in	yule yule	dakingatya	ngūnakngung
Song: A wild blackfellow is coming to you to kill you				

Source: NLA MS 8006/3/4.2, Notebook 6, p. 10; adapted by authors.

It is likely that the words 'take everything off this body' and 'they are turning one another' also relate to the ceremony that the song is connected to. Later on the same page (NLA MS 8006/3/4, p. 10) we find the following lines:

46 She is listed as née Francis in some sources and née Robertson in others (Victorian Marriage Certificates 1867/2622 and 1899/3909). Neither of her husbands had the surname Francis or Robertson.

The spirit has a piece of cherry tree, lighted, in his hand.

It has a peculiar smell

Carry the boys away, smoke first, tie string around several times round different parts of arm. Ringtail possum skin.

Tyipparuk gathers up wood – rubbish. p14

The page reference links to a longer description of the Tyipparuk, which has not been transcribed as yet.

Our suggested analysis of this song is presented in (2.52):

(2.52)	*Burnala*	*nyai-in*	*yule yule*	*dakingatya*	*ngūnakngung*
	come on?	*for thee*	*black to?*	*hit*	*thee*
	pirna-la	**nyai-in**	**yul yul**	**tak-iny-atya**	**nguna-k-ngang**
	come out-?	?-2SG	enemy	hit-FUT-?	2SG.OBJ-?
	'An enemy is coming out … to hit you.'				

Notes

Blake (2019) lists **pirnaka** in the meaning of 'come out' in Tjapwurrung, based on forms like *pirnaega* recorded by Dawson. This is a widespread Kulin root **pirna-**, perhaps here combined with a suffix **-la**.

The second word *nyai-in* appears to be glossed by Mathews as 'for thee'. No such form has been recorded in the Tjapwurrung and Djadjawurrung languages, where free pronouns are generally built on a base **peng**, literally 'body' or **wa-** (Blake 2019). One form that does have the initial **nyan-** is the word for 'nape of the neck', **nyani**, recorded for Djadjawurrung by William Thomas. The back of the neck was conceived of as the place from where soul departs, and is found in place names in the Wimmera such as *Towaninnie* (**tawa-nyani**), the name of 'a little creek on the Lower Avoca', in the list compiled by Chauncy (Smyth 1878, 2: 208). This name literally means 'a blow on the back of the neck, where the soul or spirit is'. It is possible that this is **nyanin** 'your neck'.

The form *yule yule* is recorded by R.H. Mathews for Djadjawurrung in the meaning 'wild man', 'enemy' (Blake 2019), and also by Dawson in the form *yuul yuul* 'wild blackfellow' (1881: 29) and as 'enemy' (1881: Vocabulary xii).

The widespread root **taka** is here combined with the Western Kulin future marker **-iny** and a final **-atya** of unknown meaning. Note that the form **tawa** in the place name *Towaninnie*, mentioned above, is an example of the same root with the variation of **k** and **w** (see also examples of this sound correspondence in Blake et al. 2011: 18).

The last word, *ngūnakngung* is probably built on the same root as the Wemba-Wemba 2nd person singular object form **ngunam**. As mentioned above, this is not the usual form of pronouns in Tjapwurrung and Djadjawurrung.

2.8. Felix von Luschan's recordings

The Austrian anthropologist Felix von Luschan (1854–1924) visited Australia in 1914 and made some audio recordings at Coranderrk. His time in Australia was cut short by the commencement of World War I, and he and his wife had to leave Australia in a hurry in August 1914.

In 1914 he had visited Coranderrk and made five recordings on wax cylinders, now in the Berlin Phonnogrammarchiv (Collection VII WS 209), listed in Box 2.32, which is a transcription of one of the documents in the archive that accompanies the recordings. *Gesang mit Bumerangschlägen* means 'song with Boomerang clapping' and *Sologesang* means 'Solo song'. There seem to have been three singers. The first, Lanki Manton, whose Indigenous name was Monmoiko, was R.H. Mathews's principal consultant for the Pura-Pura language, a variety very similar to Wati-Wati (see Blake et al. 2011, Chapter 4).

The second singer is likely to have been Willy Russell, a Yorta Yorta man who R.H. Mathews also interviewed, and who was a presence around Coranderrk for many years. He was even filmed there in the 1930s doing a corroboree. He was born between 1858 and 1862.

The third singer is named as Johnny and has not yet been identified. It could be Johnny Terrick, who was a Barapa Barapa man.

Having listened to each of the recordings, we can confirm that both recordings 1 and 3 are sung by two people, and both have accompanying boomerang clapping, although the latter is clearer in the case of Song 3. The other three songs are clearly solo. We can assume that the five recordings do indeed match the five numbered items in Box 2.32.

Box 2.32: List of recordings made at Coranderrk by Felix von Luschan, 1914

1.	Gesang mit Bumerangschlägen.		
		2 Männer Coranderk	Russel u. Lanki
2.a.	Sologesang		Mann Johnny
2.b.	Sologesang		Mann Johnny
3.	Gesang mit Bumerangschlägen.		
		2 Männer, Coranderk.	Russel u. Lanki
4.a.	Sologesang		Mann Lanki (Sprung)
4.b.	Sologesang		Mann Lanki
5.	Sologesang		Mann Russel (Sprung)

Source: Berlin Phonnogrammarchiv (Collection VII WS 209); adapted by authors.

As will be discussed in more detail shortly, it has been more difficult to clearly associate the sound recordings with the information about the songs as given in the von Luschan papers. Therefore we will present a musical notation only of Song 5 (Figure 2.21). This song was chosen for musical analysis, first because the recording is the clearest of the four and second because of the similarity of the musical line in all five songs. Although boomerang clapping is present in two of the songs, the recording is not clear enough to make a good transcription of this feature.

2.8.1 Linguistic transcriptions of the von Luschan recordings

Apart from the recordings, von Luschan also left transcriptions and in some cases translations of three songs, in fairly rough notes. These three are here reproduced as Boxes 2.33, 2.34 and 2.35. Given that the first song in the catalogue is a duet, and the first song for which there is a transcription is a solo, there is probably no direct connection between the order in which the songs are listed in Box 2.30 and the order in which the transcriptions were made. Notes at the bottom of the page contain numbers in language, with the word for '10' as 'two hands' *pulle manange*. This is very similar to the form *polite murnangin* recorded for '10' by Beveridge for the Swan Hill variety of Wati-Wati (literally 'two your (sg.) hand'),[47] and contains a typically Wati-Wati or Mathi-Mathi form **manangi** 'hand'. This suggests that the language on this page is closely similar to Wati-Wati.

47 This perhaps contains the 2nd person singular possessive suffix **-in** and might mean 'your 10 (objects)'.

We believe that Box 2.33, which contains words in Wati-Wati or a closely related language, is in fact referring to the solo song sung by Lanki (Monmoiko), Song 4, which on the recording appears to be the same text sung twice (given as 4a and 4b in Box 2.32). However, we cannot relate the words that we hear in the recording with the 'transcription' in Box 2.33. Lanki's mother was a Barapa Barapa woman, and it was through their land that the railway described in this song still travels.[48] A very tentative account of what we hear at the beginning of Song 4b is given as example (2.53) and this does not seem to relate at all to the words written in Box 2.33.

(2.53) **… na pupula we te ma o**

kalkata kalkata pili ngi …

ngurrawa o nga ngatyerri …

While we cannot say much about these words, it is possible that the word **kalkata** is the word for **kalk** 'wood', also meaning 'bone', in combination with a locative suffix **-ata.** It seems possible that kalk-ata is 'on the wood' and may refer to the way that railway tracks are placed on wooden sleepers.

The song finishes with a very clear syllable **wo** on a descending melisma.

Box 2.33: 'Transcription' and translation of a solo song by Felix von Luschan in 1914

the train go from Bendigo	Wingallak wa raireway	= railway
o Terek Terek	Terek Terek watha	→ th = δ
to Mount Hope	Wumbunga | Mount Hope	
right to Kerang	| Kalburark | kalboa wenoa Kerang kalboa warkee	
(ac)ross the big plain		

Source: Berlin Phonnogrammarchiv (Collection VII WS 209); adapted by authors.

Linguistic notes

The word *wingallak* is probably **windyala-k** 'where to'. This form *windyalo* 'where' was written down in a Pura-Pura word list collected from Lanki in the John Mathew papers (Blake et al. 2011).

48 While writing these words, Stephen Morey was sitting on a train crossing this plain, in view of the distinctive Pyramid Hill.

The second line includes the word *Terek Terek*, a place name for two hills, now a national park, from the word in Wemba-Wemba **terik-terik** 'gravel'. The names of the two hills are given in the place names list in Smyth (1878, 2: 203) as follows (Table 2.16):

Table 2.16: Names of the two Terrick hills

English name	Native name	Meaning in English
The North Terrick hill, which the largest of the two	Bullyang or Bulliyang	A cherry tree
South Terrick	Wangat	A kind of wooden spade for digging up grubs

Source: From Smyth (1878, 2: 203); adapted by authors.

These names are not found in the songs.

It is possible that the word *watha* is the negative 'no'. The name of the Piangil variety of Wati-Wati is spelled as both Wata Wata and Wathi-wathi by A.L.P. Cameron (Blake et al. 2011: 214).

So perhaps the second line means 'not (to/past) Terrick Terrick'. The railway does run a little to the west of what is now the Terrick Terrick National Park and perhaps this is what is meant.

In the third line, we might expect Wumbunga to be the word for 'Mount Hope'; however, the names of Mount Hope that we are aware of are *Yearearbil*, recorded by G.A. Robinson (Clark and Heydon 2002), and *Wirripowel* 'Part of Mt. Hope range – to west of Mt.' and *Iriyowel* 'Mt Hope' (Notes from W. Swan Urquhart's Notebook[49]).

For the last line, we can suggest an analysis as in (2.54):

(2.54) *Kalburark* *kalboa* *wenoa*

right to Kerang, (ac)ross the big plain

kalp-uwa-k? **kalp-uwa** **win-uwa**

cut-INTENS-IMP cut-INTENS leave-INTENS

49 These are part of the Surveyors' Notebooks, Black Ink Series 104_1308 W. Urquhart, 1850. These are accessible from the Victorian Land Registry Services, www.landata.vic.gov.au/. To access them it is necessary to register and then click on Central Plan Office, then Historic Crown Field Books. These Urquart books are part of the Black Ink Series.

Kerang	*kalboa*	*warkee*
kerang	**kalp-uwa**	**wa(R)ki**
PN	cut-INTENS	plain

'Cut it, cutting and leaving Kerang, (it is) cutting (across) the plain.'

We suggest that this is describing the effect of the railway line in cutting right across the wide plains of Northern Victoria.

Linguistic notes

We suggest that *kalboa* and *wenoa* are both roots in combination with an intensifier **-uwa**, recorded for Wemba-Wemba by Hercus (1986: 48).

In Mathi-Mathi, a verb **winakatha** was documented with the meaning 'leave'. This could mean a motion verb with a root **wina-**, as suggested in example (2.54).

The word for plain is **wa(R)ki** in the Swan Hill variety of Wati-Wati.

The second 'transcription' provided by von Luschan is presented in Box 2.34, and is also about the railway, but no translation was provided by von Luschan. This is one of the duet songs. It is presumably Song 3 from Box 2.32, the only one listed as a duet of Russel and Lanki.

Box 2.34: Transcription and translation of a duet song by Felix von Luschan in 1914

	Duett von Russel and Lenki [?]
Wowono railaway	
Lelelel gunde	
mungathol Barengo	→ th = δ
Crothe wu diallog	
bargánam wuarbidin	

Source: Berlin Phonnogrammarchiv (Collection VII WS 209); adapted by authors.

Our suggested analysis of the first line is presented as (2.55):

(2.55)	*wowono*	*rairaway*
	wuw-una	**railway**
	run-CAUS	railway

'The railway is making it run.'

Linguistic notes

There is a Mathi-Mathi verb recorded as **wúwatha** 'to run'. The root of this verb is **wuwa-**, and we are suggesting that here this root is combined with a causative suffix, termed 'state inducive' by Hercus (1986: 50).

In the second line, there is no word recorded in any of the languages of similar form to *lelelel*, except for **lileli** 'wife' in the Piangil variety of Wati-Wati. The only other word that can be recognised in this song is *wu diallog*, regularised as **wuti yaluk**, which includes the word **yaluk** 'creek'. This is probably the same form as the town of Woori Yallock east of Melbourne, which means 'big creek'. There is a Yaluk Yaluk creek south of Gunbower, shown on maps in the Public Records Office Victoria.[50]

The transcription of two variants of the third song, a love song, is presented in Box 2.35. We are not sure which of the five songs listed in Box 2.32 this might be, or who might have sung it. Note that the translation of the note at the bottom is '*meto* or *medo*, allegedly (means) "maid"'.

Box 2.35: Transcription and translation of a love song by Felix von Luschan in 1914

Zwei Varianten	
1. Nekadin kuenda	1. Nekadin kuinda
2. Bai barra takala	2. weipara takala
3. Jaken da wajaken	jiken tiurowha | 5 kandaradangi
4. Tjuru wanna tundawek	numelei | medo nganito [poor-crossed out]
5. Kata radangi numelei	7. poor dear my love
6. kokonderin meto	
7. poor dear my love dear	
	meto oder medo
	angeblich = maid

Source: Berlin Phonnogrammarchiv (Collection VII WS 209); adapted by authors.

50 VPRS 8168, Historical Plan Collection, Murray 10.

Linguistic notes

We cannot recognise many words in this song, but we can suggest the following:

> In line 1, it is possible that *-in* is the 2nd person singular suffix 'your'.
>
> The word *kuenda* may contain the same root as the word *guay* 'amen' documented by Peter Beveridge in his translation of the 'Lord's Prayer' and perhaps cognate with Wemba-Wemba **kwe** 'eh friend'. If so, the first line may contain an exclamation.
>
> In line 2, it may be that takala consists of **taka** 'hit' and the frequentative **-ila**.
>
> In line 3, the word *jaken* may contain the root **tjaka** 'eat'.
>
> In line 4, the word *tjuru* might be the word *tjura* found in the Moravian papers translated into German as *hoffen*, 'to hope'.
>
> The form *numelei* is clearly **numila** 'cry', also written down from Lanki by John Mathew in the form *numile* 'cry', in Mathi-Mathi **númila**.
>
> If the word *medo/meto* does mean 'maid', it might be related to the word for 'wife' in Wati-Wati, **martumi**. It may also be borrowed as the form is similar to English *maid.*

2.8.2 Musical transcriptions of the von Luschan recordings

The musical analysis of Song 5 in the von Luschan collection is presented as Figure 2.21. Note that unlike other analyses presented in this volume, time signatures have been retained as a way of expressing more clearly the metre of the song. In particular, the bars marked as 3/4 are generally found in connection with a pause or a melodic leap and indicate that more time is taken at that point in the melody.

Song 5

recorded by F. Von Luschan

Figure 2.21: Musical transcription of von Luschan's recording, Song 5

Source: Grace Koch.

Range: Minor 10th (Cb–D)

We are unable to determine a tonal centre or key.

Musical notes

There are six general instances of a sliding pattern; for example, the bars marked 17 and 18. These tend to occur within a phrase rather than at the end.

There is a noticeable rhythmic pattern consisting of what we have transcribed as four bars of ♫♩ followed by a bar of four eighth notes and then two quarter notes (♫♫ ♩♩). We see this, for example, in bars 5–10 and again in 23–28, and altogether this pattern is observed six times in the song. This rhythmic feature generally aligns with the portions of these songs where there is little or no melodic movement.

Melodically there is a wide vocal range, of a major 11th. As with a number of other songs transcribed in this volume, there are large leaps, particularly after rests, often of around an octave. For example, there is a leap of a ninth from F2 to G3.[51] Apart from that, there is a mostly downward progression of melody, nearly stepwise, from either the start or after the octave leaps.

All the von Luschan songs have noticeable vocal slides descending a full tone or a minor third on one syllable. This would appear to be the same phenomenon observed by Torrance in connection with Barak's songs (see sections 3.2 and 2.2.1), where he mentioned that there are 'curious sliding of one sound into another, not unlike the slow tuning of a violin string' (1887: 336). At least in the von Luschan songs, the speed of the song slows down noticeably when this occurs.

Note that Torrance's (1887) transcriptions have a melodic range of a third or little more, and he noted that '[t]he songs are marked throughout by sudden, frequent and ever varying inflection of voice, in compass rarely exceeding the distance of a third and minor intervals predominating'. By contrast, the von Luschan songs (1914), those of Stan Day (1962–65) (see section 2.2) and the Song of Guichen Bay (1937) (section 6.2.1) have much larger melodic range and, often, leaps of over an octave. We are unable to say whether this latter feature was one that developed after Torrance worked

51 There is a convention to name the notes in a series of octaves starting from 0 where C is always the first note of a new octave. C4 is the note known as middle C. The note termed F2 is thus the F which is an octave and a half (approximately) below middle C (C4). This is explained in the Wikipedia page 'Scientific pitch notation', accessed 7 March 2019, en.wikipedia.org/wiki/Scientific_pitch_notation.

with Barak (1887), or whether Torrance did not notate it because Barak sang only a single verse and this much larger melodic range is associated with multiple repetitions of the text.

One final point to observe is that whereas Stan Day's songs, and also the songs transcribed by Torrance, have initial introductory vocables before the commencement of text, the von Luschan songs do not appear to have this. The singer simply gets right into it!

2.9 Mathi-Mathi songs sung by Mary Moore

The two songs sung by Mary Moore were discussed and presented in Blake et al. (2011: 131–35). Both songs were recorded by Catherine Ellis on a tape that has since been digitised by AIATSIS with the name Ellis_193_TrackA.wav (full name A000193).[52]

2.9.1 'Where is the Emu?'

Of the first song, Blake et al. (2011) wrote:

> The first song is from a recording made by Mary Moore for the musicologist Catherine Ellis in December 1962. Mary originally came from Ebenezer and was of Werkaya descent, but she spent a lot of her time at Balranald and married a Mathi-Mathi man, Reginald Wise. Late in her life she lived in an old – and leaking – blue caravan at 'Murray Downs' on the New South Wales side of the Murray, at the edge of a settlement established by the Swan Hill police sergeant, Sergeant Feldtman, for Aboriginal people who until then had been simply camping by the river. It was there that Catherine Ellis recorded her. Mary subsequently sang the same song for Luise Hercus.

52 The AIATSIS call number for this collection is ELLIS_C02, and the accession number ELLIS_C02 (A000190–A000210). See AIATSIS, 'Mura Collections Catalogue: Catherine Ellis', accessed 19 June 2019, iats.ent.sirsidynix.net.au/client/en_AU/external/search/detailnonmodal/ent:$002f$002fSD_ILS$002f0$002fSD_ILS:267761/ada?qu=Catherine+Ellis&te=ILS&lm=AUDIO.

In answer to Cath Ellis's question 'Where did that song come from?', Mary answered:

> Mathi-Mathi song, that is a Balranald song
>
> if I tell you Wekiweki is further down, Canally station, it would be about about 30 miles down, they had different tribes …

In answer to Cath Ellis's question 'Where did you learn that song from?', Mary answered:

> Oh, grandmother Reynolds that lived in Balranald. For years this old lady was mainly around Balranald, she was the oldest lady around Balranald. She used to sing like … but we didn't understand she'd sing some kind of song, and sometimes you'd understand and sometimes you didn't, and she used to sing to us

The great-great-grandson of 'grandmother Reynolds', Brendan Kennedy, has told us that she died at Balranald in 1916, and was also known as Sarah Randall, and over time the name changed from Randall to Reynolds. Her husband was Tommy Randall who is buried at Canally.

The recording of this song is at 11:32 on the digitised recording Ellis_193_TrackA.wav. The transcription of the song text is given in (2.56):

(2.56) **Nhángindi wárra, nhángindi látha**
Nhángindi wárra, windha kàrríngi
Nhángindi wárra, windha panhími

When asked to sing again, she sang as follows:

Nhángindi látha, nhángindi wárra
Nhángindi windha kàrríngi
Windha panhími, nhángindi wárra,

And she explained:

nhangindi warra means what are you doing then
nhangindi latha means what are you talking about
windha karringi where is the emu, that's the meat. **yawi** is the meat

Our linguistic analysis of the first of these is presented as (2.57):

(2.57)	**nhángindi**	**wárra,**	**nhángindi**	**látha**
	what-2SG	do	what-2SG	speak
	'What are you doing, what are you talking about?'			
	nhángindi	**wárra,**	**windha**	**kàrríngi**
	what-2SG	do	where	emu
	'What are you doing, where is the emu?'			
	nhángindi	**wárra,**	**windha**	**panhími**
	what-2SG	do	where	bread
	'What are you doing, where is the bread?'			

Notes

The second version of the song differs only slightly and contains the same linguistic material in a slightly different order.

Nhangindi is a contraction of **nhangi ngindi** 'what you', which is the typical sequence in Mathi-Mathi sentences with interrogative adverbs.

Yawi 'meat' does not occur in the song and is not attested for Mathi-Mathi, it is presumably a rendering of the Werkaya **yawir** 'meat', word that Mary remembered from her youth.

When singing the song, Mary actually sang the English *where the* in place of the Mathi-Mathi **windha**. Since the English and Mathi-Mathi words are very similar both in meaning and form, the code switching here is unsurprising.

The musical analysis of the first version of the song is presented as Figure 2.22. In this transcription, the words **warra nganda** at the beginning appear to represent Mary Moore preparing to sing. The main song commences on the second line of the musical transcription.

Mary Moore Song 1a: Where's the emu?

Sung by Mary Moore to Cath Ellis

Range: Octave (F - F)

NOTE: Note the word, nhangindi, which is a contraction of nhangi ngindi. The first iteration of the word does not use the contraction, but subsequent iterations do use it.

Figure 2.22: Musical transcription of 'Where is the Emu?' Mary Moore Song 1, Version A

Source: Grace Koch.

We are unable to determine a tonal centre or key for this song.

The musical transcription of the second version is presented in Figure 2.23:

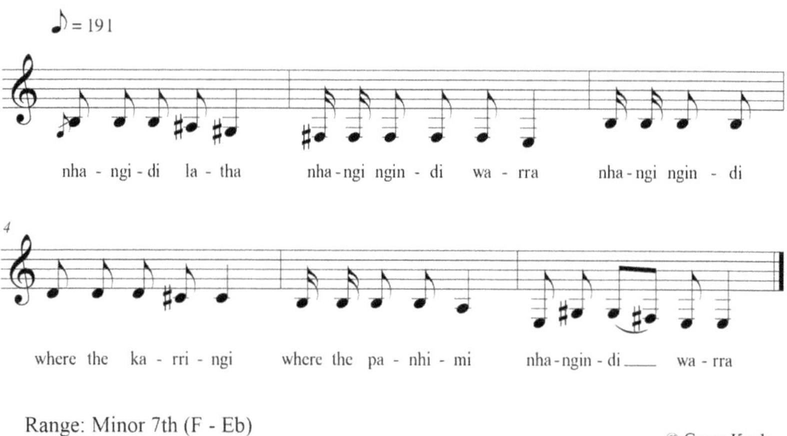

Figure 2.23: Musical transcription of 'Where is the Emu?' Mary Moore Song 1, Version B

Source: Grace Koch.

Interestingly, the range of notes in the second version is smaller than in the first. It appears that Mary Moore sang only the first part of the song in version A, then continued with the last part of the song in version B. The rhythmic pattern for the words that follow the phrase 'where the …' are basically the same, but version B has a much lower pitch range. The song seems to be influenced by Western music. There is a slight ornament at the beginning where the B is preceded by a G which is a minor third lower.

2.9.2 Fishing song

Immediately after the discussion about learning the song 'Where is the Emu?', discussed in section 2.9.1, Mary Moore sang a second song, the text of which is presented in example (2.58). The recording is at 13:30 on the digitised recording Ellis_193_TrackA.wav.

(2.58) **nhangindi warra yukani nhiyin thurri**

thanggali yukani nhiyanba nhinhi-ya

Mary Moore explained the meaning of this song as follows, in reference to grandmother Reynolds (Sarah Randall):

> She liked to go fishing and get us to get more worms for fishing and she would bring in the fish, that is Mathi-Mathi, Balranald language still. **yanggali** that is the worms and **turi** was the fish that is bream **bandyil** that is the [Murray] cod.

In discussing the meaning of this, Blake et al. (2001: 193) said:

> The word for 'worms' was given by Jack Long as **thánggali** 'worm' and a similar word was recorded for Wati-Wati (Piangil) by Davy as *tungali*. This word does not occur in the song. The Mathi-Mathi words that we can recognised from this song are **nhangi** 'what', **wíkatha** 'hungry', **thúrri** 'freshwater bream' and **nhunhi** 'that one over there'. The form **yukan-** may be related to the Wati-Wati (Swan Hill) word **yuwangila.** There are cases where Wati-Wati **w** corresponds to stops in Mathi-Mathi.

Our linguistic analysis is presented in (2.59):

(2.59)	***nhangindi***	***warra***	***yukani***	***nhiyin***	***thurri***
	nhang-in-di	**warra**	**yukan-i**	**nhiyi-n??**	**thurri**
	what-your-??	do	fish?-IMP	close by-??	bream

'What are you hungry (for)? Go and fish for bream!'

thanggali	***yukani***	***nhiyanba***	***nhi-nhi-ya***
thanggali	**yukan-i**	**nhiyi-anba**	**nhinhi-ya**
worms	fish?-IMP	close by-??	here-?

'Worms for fish over here, close by!'

Notes

The first word of the second line has been transcribed as **thanggali**, which differs from the transcription given in Blake et al. (1993: 193). Although the pronunciation of the word is not clear, the fact that in her explanation Mary Moore several times mentioned the word **thánggali** 'worm', makes us believe that this is the correct transcription.

The second last word is here written as **nhiyanba**. The first part of this word is built on the proximal **nhinhi** 'this one fairly close' (Blake et al. 2011: 99). Hercus added that '[a]nother deictic from the same base is **nhiwi** "this one close by"', where the base is **nhi-**. We do not know what the final **-anba** might mean.

The musical analysis of this song is presented in Figure 2.24:

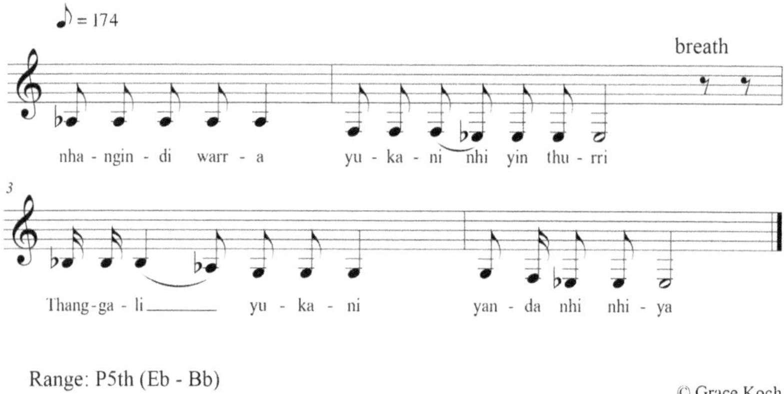

Figure 2.24: Musical transcription of the Fishing song, Mary Moore Song 2
Source: Grace Koch.

This song has a tonal centre of Eb, and form similar to a major scale.

This song appears to be of a more traditional style, rather like a chant on low pitches, than the preceding song, 'Where is the Emu?' It probably would have been sung several times to charm the fish.

2.10 Letyi-Letyi song documented by the Berndts

The following song in Berndt and Berndt (1993, Appendix 7.22) was 'composed by John Mack himself and referred to the meeting of groups of people from different areas for a large ceremony'. John Mack was a Letyi-Letyi man. This song was discussed in Blake et al. (2011: 152).

For this song there is also a sound recording of Pinkie Mack singing it, recorded by the Berndts on a wax cylinder at East Wellington in South Australia in 1943. In the 1950s, these cylinders were played and recorded onto magnetic tape at the behest of Alice Moyle, and this recording is now digitised by AIATSIS as BERNDT_RC01-004244A.wav. This consists of the recordings of 13 cylinders, of which Cylinder No. 9 contains the following (from BERNDT_RC01-004244_listing.pdf):

Box 2.36: Details of Cylinder No. 9 recorded by Berndt and Berndt

1st part: John Mack's song from ˈLaitʃum ˈBanreinʤi – Upper Murray. ˈKim ˈŋala...
2nd part: Minduk Jack's song: ˈJakəmulˈda:k tribe, Upper River Murray. ˈna:ŋgili...

Source: AIATSIS BERNDT_RC01-004244_listing.pdf; adapted by authors.

Minduk Jack's songs are discussed in section 12.3.

The section of the recording containing the two songs from Cylinder No. 9 appears to commence at 13:00 on this recording and run until 15:41, including an announcement by Alice Moyle that 'No. 9 showed very little sign of mildew but No. 10 is badly mildewed'. The words are very difficult to make out on the recordings and we cannot even be sure where the first of these songs finishes and the second commences. As a result, we have not been able to confirm the relationship between the text of this song and the recording, nor to make a musical transcription of it.

The text of the song was given by the Berndts in the following form (Box 2.37):

Box 2.37: John Mack's song

1.	Gima-ngala-gima ngala		walindjin	ngaitja		
	Stay here you and I camp		a long way	distant		
	Gima-ngala-gima		elpe-elp.			
	Stay here you and I camp		a better place.			
2.	Gima-ngala-gima		walindjin	ngaitja	gen-gima.	
	Stay here you and I camp		a long way	distant	camping here.	
3.	[first line repeated]					
4.	Urvererulk	gimainya gimainya …		walindjin	ngaitja	gima.
	Walking	you and I stay		a long way	distant	camp.
We'll camp here, we two, far away.						
We'll stay, we two, at this better place.						
We'll camp here, we two, away …						
Walking, we two, far from that distant camp, here we'll stay.						

Source: Berndt and Berndt (1993, Appendix 7.22); adapted by authors.

We can imagine that this is a song about two young people, perhaps long ago, perhaps in actual memory, whose love was forbidden and who had to go far away.

Our suggested analysis is presented as examples (2.60) to (2.62):

(2.60)	*Gima-ngala-gima ngala*				*walindjin*	*ngaitja*
	stay here you and I camp				*a long way*	*distant*
	kima	**ngali**	**kima**	**ngali**	**wali-ndyin**	**ngaitya**
	here	IDL	here	IDL	approach-?	distant
	'Let us (stay) here, let us (stay) here, approached from far'					

Gima-ngala-gima			*elpe-elp*
stay here you and I camp			*a better place*
kima	**ngali**	**kima**	**yalpi-yalp**
here	IDL	here	straight
'Let us (stay) here, straight!'			

(2.61)	*Gima-ngala-gima ngala*				*walindjin*	*ngaitja*	*gen-gima*
	stay here you and I camp				*a long way*	*distant*	*camping here*
	kima	**ngali**	**kima**	**ngali**	**wali-ndyin**	**ngaitya**	**ken?-kima**
	here	1DL	here	1DL	approach-?	distant	?-here

'Let us (stay) here, let us (stay) here, approached from far, here …'

(2.62)	*Urvererulk*	*gimainya gimainya …*				*walindjin*	*ngaitja gima*	
	walking	*you and I stay*				*a long way*	*distant camp*	
	yuwa-ri-rak	**kima**	**nga(li)**	**kima**	**nga(li)**	**wali-ndyin**	**ngaitya**	**kima**
	walk	here	1DL	here	1DL	approach-?	distant	here

'Walking … let us (stay) here, approached from far.'

Notes

In this song we can recognise the Letyi-Letyi demonstrative **kima** 'here' and the 1st person dual pronoun **ngal(i)** (see Blake et al. 2011: 141, 142).

The word *walindjin* may be a verb 'to approach'. Consider Wemba-Wemba **waletya** 'to approach' and Wati-Wati (Swan Hill) **walowal** 'near'. For Letyi-Letyi, Thomas records **wali pundyi** (*warlee poondjee*) 'another day', which appears to be also related.

The word *ngaitja* is presumed to mean 'distant'; it is possible that the **-a** ending is the general oblique case.

The word *elpe-elp* could be be **yalpi** 'straight' (Wati-Wati Swan Hill) related to **yulp** Wemba-Wemba 'right hand, straight'.

The word *urvererulk* may be based on **yuwa** 'go', possibly even with the nominaliser -**ri**. The final -**k** is problematic because this final does not otherwise occur in the surviving data for this language.

2.11 Tjapwurrung song documented by Dawson

This song, called by Dawson 'The Porcupine', is introduced by Dawson as follows (1881: 80):

> Many songs having appropriate airs are universally known. Very often complimentary or descriptive songs are composed on the instant, and are sung to wel-known airs, the whole company joining in the chorus. A lament called 'Mallæ malææ', composed in New South Wales in commemoration of the ravages of small-pox, is known all over the Australian colonies and is sung in a doleful strain, accompanied with groans and imitations of a dying person. The following is a song in the Chaap wurrong language, with its translation. It is said to have been composed in the neighbourhood of Sydney, and to have been translated into the different languages as it became known. In singing it the last two lines are repeated three times.

Following his description of the song, there is a detailed description of the corroboree (Dawson 1881: 81–84), which also talks about traditional games. It is not clear whether this refers to the Western Kulin Tjapwurrung speakers or the Warrnambool language speakers.

Note that the lament *Mallæ malææ* referred to is probably the same song as **Ma-le** for which Georgiana McCrae provided the text (see section 13.1).

The text and translation of the Porcupine song is given in Box 2.38:

Box 2.38: Text and translation of 'The Porcupine'

CHUUL'YUU WILL'YUU	THE PORCUPINE
Chuul'yuu Will'yuu Wallaa gnoræææ. Chillæ binnæ aa gna Kinuuaa gnuuraa jeeaa, Chiæbaa gnuutaa. Kirrægirræ, kirrægirræ, kirrægirræ Leeaa gnaa.	Porcupine spikes Burn like heat of fire. Someone pinching me When I am up high, With affection like a sister. Grinning, grinning, grinning, Teeth mine.

Source: Dawson (1881: 80–81), adapted by authors.

Our analysis is presented below (2.63):

(2.63) *Chuul'yuu Will'yuu*
Porcupine spikes
tyulyu wilyu
refers to echidna

Wallaa gnoræ.
Burn like heat of fire.
walpa ngure
burn blister?

Chillæ binnæ aa gna
Someone pinching me
tyilerp-an-nga(n)
pinch-PST-1SG.OBJ
'(Like someone) pinched me.'

Kinuuaa gnuuraa jeeaa,
When I am up high,
kinu-a ngura kiya
high?-? 1PL.INCL speak
'High up we speak.'

Chiæbaa gnuutaa.
With affection like a sister.
tyaty-ba nguta
sister-and 2PL
'And you (like) sisters.'

Kirrægirræ, kirrægirræ, kirrægirræ
Grinning grinning grinning
kirrityirri kirrityirri kirrityirri
ONOM ONOM ONOM
'*Kirrityirri, kirrityirri, kirrityirri.*'

Leeaa	*gnaa.*
Teeth	*mine*
lia	**-nga(n)**
tooth	1SG.POSS

'My teeth.'

Notes

The word **yulawil** is documented by Dawson for 'echidna', spelled by him as *yuluwill.* The form **tyulyu wilyu** seems to be a poetic rendition of **yulawil.**

Dawson wrote the form *meitch gnuurak* as 'blister from sun' that we can regularise as **mity nguRak**, where **mity** means 'skin'. The word **nguRak** may mean a blister or a boil of some kind and be cognate with Woiwurrung **nguRak** 'hill'.

Blake (2003: 43) records the 1st person singular possessive as **ngan**, usually spelled by Dawson as <gnan>. In the last line of the song, the spelling <gnaa> may either be an error for <gnan>, or an alternative form of the 1st person singular possessive used in singing. It is also possible that *aa gna* is meant to be **ngana** 'who'.

In Wemba-Wemba, **tyilerrpa** is 'to pinch, to squeeze'.

nguta is the 2nd person plural marker in Wemba-Wemba, here cognate with **ngura**.

The translation that Dawson has given suggests that *kinuuaa* is 'high', the form of these being **kiyuka** in other Tjawurrung sources (Dawson *keyukun yu puuree o* 'above' (**kiyukanyu puRio**)).

2.12 Marditjali song, recorded by Tindale

Tindale (1941: 239–40) gives a song which he describes as 'Marditjali Tribe song of Wanangan, from Wirriga'. Like other songs recorded by Tindale, it was actually recorded in the Coorong area of South Australia, but the language is clearly Western Kulin. This was sung by Milerum (see section 6.2), also known as Clarence Long. The sound quality of the recording of this song, and other songs by Milerum, is very high.

Tindale's (1941: 239–40) description of the song is as follows:

> In the [Kaŋgarabalak] language. It is sung through twice; the second time is merely a repeat to fill this disc.
>
> ['Wanaŋan 'Wiri'gar], a man of Wirriga siding [*lit.* Wanganan, of Wirigar], a place near Bordertown in the Marditjali (Kangarabalak) country, left his home intending to stay for a short while on the Coorong at Woods Well to try and obtain a wife, eventually marrying a father's sister of Milerum. He was old when Milerum was a boy and never went back to his own country. There were many quarrels with his people because of his departure and because the taking of the Tanganekald woman as wife upset arrangements for marriages in his own country. Many 'strong words' were said about him and there was a 'native court case'. The Tanganekald people would not allow their woman to be taken inland because of the trouble her marriage had aroused.
>
> 'Wanaŋan sang this song whenever he was asked why he had left his own country. From his father's sister's husband Milerum learned this and several other songs. The refrain is probably old, having been sung in the 'wild' times before the Coorong was settled by white people.

The traditional location of Wirigar is south-west of Bordertown, somewhere near to Kongal.[53] Wirrega is a present-day place name on the Dukes Highway around 12 kilometres north-west of Bordertown.[54]

Philip Chauncey's place name list in Brough Smyth (1878, 2: 209) also lists a place with this name near Warracknabeal, some distance to the east and in Victoria. His entry is given as Box 2.39:

53 Kongal is located at 36.3804826 South, 140.4007611 East. It can be found at Google Maps, accessed 27 November 2017, www.google.com.au/maps/place/Kongal+SA+5270/@-36.3804826,140.4007611,12z/data=!3m1!4b1!4m13!1m7!3m6!1s0x6ac9736c56067a3d:0x4033654628ed170!2sBordertown+SA+5268!3b1!8m2!3d-36.3139146!4d140.7666317!3m4!1s0x6ac98f1d469ca66b:0x4033654628f0770!8m2!3d-36.3759967!4d140.4635364.

54 Wirrega is at 36.1990044 South, 140.5033889 East. See Google Maps, accessed 27 November 2017, www.google.com.au/maps/place/Wirrega+SA+5267/@-36.1990044,140.5033889,12z/data=!3m1!4b1!4m13!1m7!3m6!1s0x6ac9736c56067a3d:0x4033654628ed170!2sBordertown+SA+5268!3b1!8m2!3d-36.3139146!4d140.7666317!3m4!1s0x6ac9a10779880c97:0x4033654628f0810!8m2!3d-36.2020359!4d140.5805397.

Box 2.39: Indigenous place name for Werrigar

Werrikghor (W.)	Werrigar , a village near Warraknabeal	*Werrik*, cleaning; *ghor*, the blossom of the box-tree – i.e., cleaning the ground from the fallen blossoms before encamping.

Source: Chauncey in Smyth (1878, 2: 209), adapted by authors.

The phrase ['Wanaŋan 'Wiri'gar] contains a locative suffix **-r(a)**. This is the same as the locative reported by Hercus (1986: 85) in the following sentence, example (2.64):

(2.64) **ngenya-k** **mum-r-in**

sit-IMP bottom-LOC-2SG.POSS

'Sit down on your bottom.'

Hercus (1986) pointed out that '**-r** is widespread as a locative elsewhere in Australia, but it does not occur in Wembawemba'.

The full text of the song is given in Box 2.40:

Box 2.40: Text and gloss of the Marditjali song

Original Text:			
'Gumba'wanaŋ'bere	'Gumba'wanaŋg	zbereil	(repeat)
(meaning uncertain)			
'jurupe'na	'wiri'gara	'peira'gara(ŋ)	'wanaŋan
for a little while	from Wirriga	for always	man's name
'wiri'gara			
from Wirriga			

Source: Tindale (1941: 239), adapted by authors.

Our linguistic analysis is presented in (2.65):

(2.65)

'Gumba'wanaŋg'bere	*'Gumba'wanaŋg*	*zbereil*	*(repeat)*
meaning uncertain			
kumba-wanangg(an)-peRe	**kumba-wanangg(an)**	**peRe-il**	
lie down-PN-always	lie down-PN	always	

'jurupe'na	*'wiri'gara*	*'peira'gara(ŋ)*	*'wanaŋan*
for a little while	*from Wirriga*	*for always*	*man's name*
yuRupena	**wirika-rr(a)**	**peRe-kara(ŋ)**	**wanaŋan**
little while?	PN-LOC	always-?	PN

'wiri'gara

from Wirriga

wirika-rr(a)

PN-LOC

'Wanangan is always staying, is always staying. For a little while at Wirika, always Wanangan is at Wirika.'

Linguistic notes

Our analysis uses the glosses from Tindale, not all of which can be confirmed in other sources.

Luise Hercus pointed out that the first word may be **kumba** 'sleep' because the singer is from Wirriga but staying somewhere else.

We cannot find **peRe-** in any of the sources, but it could be related to the word for **parr-uk** 'many' (which includes a 3rd person suffix).

We have not been able to do a musical analysis of this song because we were not allowed to make a copy of the song due to access restrictions and it was not possible to do a full analysis in the South Australian Museum. However, one of the authors (Morey) was able to listen to the recording at the museum in December 2018 and make some preliminary notes about the music of this song. The quality of the recording is excellent, and of much greater audibility than other recordings made before Luise Hercus's time. The clarity of Milerum's voice is very high and his expression clear. When it becomes possible to make thorough musical analyses of this and other of Milerum's songs, these analyses will add significantly to our knowledge of Indigenous songs in south-eastern Australia.

The first part of the song is sung approximately as shown in (2.66):

(2.66) **o kumba-wanangg(an)-peRe kumba-wanangg(an) peRe-il**

kumba-wanangg(an)-peRe

it is then partially repeated on a higher pitch as:

kumba-wanangg(an) peRe-il kumba-wanangg(an) peRe-il

yuRupena wirika-rr(a)

As we can see in this very tentative transcription, the textual material in the first line of example (2.65) is repeated much more frequently than the remaining materials. It appears in the recording that the whole text was sung around three times.

After singing all of the content words of this song, Milerum enunciated eight more vocable syllables in very clear rhythm. These vocable syllables seem clearly to be a dance call. Stephen Morey was able to listen to this recording in December 2018 and made some notes of the rhythm and sound of the vocables. Subsequently we were able to listen carefully to another of Milerum's songs recorded by Tindale (1941 Part 1: 118), titled Song 5 'The Meintank Answer to the Tatiara Song'. This song also contains the same or very similar final vocables to those heard by Stephen Morey in the Marditjali song. Our transcription of the final vocables in 'The Meintank Answer to the Tatiara Song' is shown in in Figure 2.25:

Figure 2.25: Musical transcription of the last few words of the Marditjali song

Source: Song from Tindale (1941: 239), transcription by Grace Koch.

These vocables may have employed a melody similar to that notated for the final vocables in the Song of Guichen Bay, as notated by Alice Moyle (1969) (see section 6.2.1).

It is certainly to be hoped that more detailed musicological analysis of this wonderful song can be undertaken in the future.

3

Eastern Kulin songs

3.1 Introduction and overview

A significant number of songs have been recorded from the tribes that spoke the Eastern Kulin languages – Woiwurrung, Boonwurrung and Taungurong (also Thagungwurrung) (see Blake 1991; Morey 1999; Tanner forthcoming for descriptions of aspects of this language, also sometimes termed Central Victorian). The full listing of songs, with the singer/composer and sources, is given in Table 3.1:

Table 3.1: Songs from Eastern Kulin groups

Name of song (section)	Songster (if known)	Person from whom the song was recorded	Language group	Original source
Kurburu's song (3.2.2)	Kurburu was taught this song by the *murup* (spirit) of a koala he killed	Barak	Boonwurrung	Howitt (1904, MSS)
Wenberi's song (3.2.3)	Wenberi's elder brother Ningolubbel's *murup* (spirit) sang it to Wenberi in his sleep	Barak	Woiwurrung	Howitt (1904, MSS)
Bundjil's song (3.2.4)	Berak heard it from his grandfather, who got it from his ancestors, who got it from *Bunjil*	Barak	Woiwurrung	Howitt (MSS)
Corroboree song (3.2.5)	unknown	Barak	Woiwurrung	Howitt (1904, MSS)

Name of song (section)	**Songster (if known)**	**Person from whom the song was recorded**	**Language group**	**Original source**
Words relating to growing up (3.2.6)	originally spoken by old Bobbery	probably Barak	Woiwurrung	Howitt (MSS)
Creation Corroborree song (3.3)	unknown	unknown	unknown	Smyth (1878)
Gaiggip (3.4.1)	the 'Druids' of the Victorian alps	possibly Kul-ler-kul-lup, a Taungurong man	possibly one of the alpine varieties, not Kulin	Thomas (MLMSS 214)
Murrunawa Corroboree song (3.4.2)	unknown	–	presumed Woiwurrung	Thomas (MLMSS 214)
Corroboree song (3.4.3)	unknown	–	presumed Woiwurrung	Thomas (MLMSS 214)
Ningolubbel's song (3.4.4)	Ningolubbel	Ningolubbel	presumed Woiwurrung	Thomas (MLMSS 214)
Wool-woork Bar-lum-bur-lin (Butterfly dance) (3.4.5)	unknown	–	presumed Woiwurrung	Thomas (MLMSS 214)
Short song: Balt-lem-be Ning-ber Bo-lar Bal-lem-bee (3.4.6)	unknown	–	presumed Woiwurrung	Thomas (MLMSS 214)
Body song (3.4.7)	unknown	–	presumed Woiwurrung	Thomas (MLMSS 214)
Women's lament (3.4.8)	unknown	–	presumed Woiwurrung	Thomas (MLMSS 214)
Text for Regaining Consciousness after a kidney fat attack (3.4.9)	the text was spoken by Malcolm	–	Woiwurrung or Taungurong	Thomas (MLMSS 214)
Fighting song (3.4.10)	unknown	–	presumed Woiwurrung	Thomas (MLMSS 214)
Enchanting away Rain (3.4.11)	unknown	–	–	Bride (1898: 91)

Name of song (section)	Songster (if known)	Person from whom the song was recorded	Language group	Original source
Supplement Song 1 (3.5.1)	–	Peter Mungett, collected in 1861	presumed Woiwurrung, but possibly Wathawurrung	SLV MS 6290
Supplement Song 2 (3.5.2)	–	Peter Mungett, collected in 1861	presumed Woiwurrung, but possibly Wathawurrung	SLV MS 6290
Hymn at funerals (3.5.3)	–	Peter Mungett, collected in 1861	presumed Woiwurrung, but possibly Wathawurrung	SLV MS 6290
Superstitious Speech of the abduction of a woman (3.5.4)	–	Peter Mungett, collected in 1861	presumed Woiwurrung, but possibly Wathawurrung	SLV MS 6290
Corroboree singing (3.6.1)	unknown	–	presumably Boonwurrung	Bunce (1857)
Requesting away rain (3.6.2)	unknown	–	perhaps Woiwurrung	Bunce in Smyth (1878)
Turee song, with lines composed by Ningolubbel (3.7.1)	Ningolubbel	Eliza	presumably Woiwurrung	McCrae
Goulburn Corroboree or 'Yapeen' (3.7.2)	–	Eliza	presumably Taungurong	McCrae
Dictated message (3.7.3)	unknown	–	presumably Boonwurrung	McCrae
Wak Wak, 'Earthquake song' (3.8)	unknown	–	presumably Woiwurrung	Green

Source: Authors.

Some of the utterances spoken during burial ceremonies are presented in section 3.9.

In addition, what we have been able to discover about songs in initiation ceremonies is listed in section 3.10.

These 23 short songs and more formal texts are probably the best surviving examples of texts that were recorded from speakers of these languages. Unfortunately, a large proportion of them cannot be fully analysed using modern linguistic methods, but in combination with important amounts of background context, these songs represent a very substantial corpus for Eastern Kulin.

3.1.1 Types of songs and the contexts of their performance

For the Eastern Kulin language groups, Woiwurrung, Taungurung, Boonwurrung, we can suggest the following types and functions of songs:

1. **Spirit songs**. Those which are given by the **murrup** 'spirit' (see section 3.1.4). Examples of this would be Kurburu's song (section 3.2.2) and Wenberi's song (section 3.2.3).
2. **Corroboree songs**. Some of these specifically celebrated the creation, such as Bundjil's song (section 3.2.4), and the Creation Corroboree song (section 3.3). Others are described as being 'corroboree songs' more generally, such as the corroboree songs in sections 3.2.5, 3.4.2 and 3.4.3, the Gaiggip (section 3.4.1), Ningolubbel's dance song (section 3.4.4), Butterfly dance (section 3.4.5) and Goulburn Corroboree or 'Yapeen' (section 3.7.2). Further descriptions of corroborees are found in section 3.1.5, including some cries and vocalisations. Smyth (1878, 1: 166) writes, probably with Thomas as his informant, that '[l]ittle is known of their mystic dances, which some regard as connected with a form of religion, but the *Ngargee*, or *Yain-yang* (corrobboree), is familiar to all who have lived in the bush'. As shown in section 3.1.5, corroborees were frequently performed in various parts of Victoria in the nineteenth century.
3. **Initiation songs**. None of these seem to have been documented for this area, though perhaps the words spoken by old Bobbery (section 3.2.6) were related to initiation.
4. **Historical songs**. These include songs written down by Thomas marking specific events and happenings (sections 3.4.1, 3.4.2, 3.4.3 and 3.4.4), the Earthquake song (section 3.8), and the Turee song, with lines composed by Ningolubbel (section 3.7.1). Relating to the historical songs, Thomas (William Thomas, undated notebook within the Robert Brough Smyth papers, State Library of Victoria (SLV) MS 8781, Box 1176/6 (b), p. 105) said:

> They have a species of historical song which enumerates to a monotonous tune, the individual beating time by striking a couple of sticks together or beating with his hand upon his breast, the most material circumstances wished to be remembered. I have known a blackfellow lie on his back and sing to himself for an hour together, or till he had fallen asleep, about the coming of white fellow, the first appearance of the horse, bullock, wheelbarrow (cart), dog, sheep, flour &c &c and a great variety of other matters, indeed it is not unusual to hear them at their various fires when encamped for the night humming these things over till sleep overcomes them.[1]

5. **Spells and healing**. In this category we can mentioned the words spoken for regaining consciousness after a kidney fat attack (section 3.4.9) and the Enchanter's song (section 3.4.11). Thomas mentions that during healing there would be 'singing and humming incantations the whole of the time' (State Library of NSW MLMSS 214, Volume 22, p. 105[2]).
6. **Songs relating to disputes**. Howitt (SLV MS Box 1053/2, pp. 35–36) mentions an arranged fight that included singing and dancing (similar to that in Gippsland, see section 5.2.11). One such example of a fight, described by Howitt as a 'blood feud' that was followed by a corroboree, is presented in section 3.1.5.6. Robinson described something similar, a fight held on 11 April 1839 (see section 3.1.5.8). Two texts relating to the abduction of women (see sections 3.4.6 and 3.7.3) are possibly connected to this type of ceremony.

There are likely to have been other types of songs. For example, Thomas (Stephens 2014, 1: 170) discussing the contact between the 'Western Port Blacks' (Boonwurrung) and the people from Twofold Bay (Eden), mentioned of the Boonwurrung 'that they have suffered severely from the Twofold Bay blacks is evident, some of their songs are upon their sufferings'. If Thomas wrote down any of these songs, they have not yet been identified. Fels (2011: 254–55) discusses this history of 'enmity' between the Boonwurrung and tribes further east in some detail.

1 We were drawn to this quote by Standfield (2015: 56).

2 This appears to have not been photographed by the State Library of NSW. It is part of a manuscript document headed by Thomas as 'Manners & Customs of Australian Aborigines', which forms the pages numbered 297–352 in MLMSS 214, Volume 22. These pages have a second series of numbers on the verso side, and the page containing that reference is numbered 105, on the verso of the page numbered 104/303.

George Gordon McCrae reported in his typescript reminiscences ('Experiences not Exploits', vol. 4, SLV MS 2523/5 (d)) as follows, including several types of songs:

> Song I learned by heart from Ben's dictation. A song to raise the wind (this in it's literal sense), a song for the full moon; a canoe song, a war or rather battle-song; queer little ditties in 'pidgin' made whether in honour of our neighbours or ourselves and in which the peculiarities likely to strike a stranger, were admirably hit off.

Fels (2011: 163) suggested that the 'song for raising the wind' was 'presumably for hunting', though we do not know on what basis this was assigned to be a hunting song. McCrae (SLV MS 12018, Box 2523/3, p. 140) identifies the **Ma-le** song (see section 13.1) as a 'canoe song'.

In addition to the songs, there were also the dances/corroborees in which songs were usually performed. These are discussed in more detail in section 3.1.5.

3.1.2 The songsters

There must have been a great number of skilled singers and composers of songs among the Eastern Kulin groups. In this section, we will give brief biographies of those who are known to or believed to have composed and sung songs, or taught them to those who wrote them down.

Barak (Berak)

Living from 1823 to 1904, he was known as Barak, Berak or William Barak and sometimes as King William or Old William. In this book we will use the spelling *Barak*, following the spelling preferred by the Wurundjeri Woi Wurrung Cultural Heritage Aboriginal Corporation,[3] except where we are using direct quotes from other sources.

Barak's father was named Bebejern and he was a nephew or great-nephew of the prominent Victorian tribal leader Billibilleri. Some sources state that he was born at Croydon or Wonga Park, but R.H. Mathews in a pencil note

3 See Wurundjeri Woi Wurrung Cultural Heritage Aboriginal Corporation, 'Ancestors and Past', accessed 24 November 2022, www.wurundjeri.com.au/our-story/ancestors-past/.

on one of his offprints writes 'Berak was a native of about Mt. Macedon, but was brought up among the Wurundyirballak' (NLA MS 8006/8/278, p. 244).

A full biography of Barak can be found online in the *Australian Dictionary of Biography*.[4]

Barak was the singer of the songs documented by Howitt and Dr George Torrance and is discussed below (section 3.2).

Photographs of him are quite common, such as one in Broome (2005: 211). Broome (2005: 38) describes how he was seen in November 1837 by the Quaker James Backhouse, dressed in a frock with a waistband, learning English at the Government Mission School. He lived until 1904 (Broome 2005: 210) and was Howitt's main informant on the culture and language of the Woiwurrung. He is quoted many times in Howitt (1904) and is the major informant for the notes in the manuscripts (SLV MS Box 1053/2, hw0390.pdf and hw0391.pdf, for example; also Museums Victoria XM 755).

Howitt (MV XM 759, p. 16), noted down Barak's own words about his ancestry:

> My name is Bairŭk grub in pine tree. Other father of my father gave me this name from a son of his when I was a baby.
>
> When my father died everyone told me you should go to your grandfather bairuk. He was waa like me.
>
> I was made a Tallangŭn when I was a big boy.

Tallangŭn refers to an intitated male. Howitt stated that 'The ceremony of initiation was called [tallŭngŭn – crossed out] tállang–gun. It was formally held ~~at~~ where are now called Melbourne, Geelong, Bacchus Marsh and Mt Macedon. The same ceremony was called at Echuka Wang-[Kūm]' (SLV MS Box 1053/2, hw0391.pdf, p. 13). (For further information about the ceremony at Echuca, see section 9.6.) Barak had been initiated at South Yarra, and Howitt further noted:

4 Patricia Marcard, 'Barak, William (1824–1903)', *Australian Dictionary of Biography*, National Centre of Biography, The Australian National University, published first in hardcopy in 1969, accessed online 30 May 2019, adb.anu.edu.au/biography/barak-william-2930.

> The only formality which he went through was that at South Yarra some blackfellows, Capt Turnbull, Billy Billary, Billy Lonsdale who were all Ngŭrŭngaeta invested him with the Berbert – ringtail possum shawl round his biceps, the gornbert = reed necklace, the illijeri = nose peg, the Mŭragalŭn = Kaiung = waiststring, and the Brandyep = apron.

Barak's name meant 'edible grub', and this word was recorded by Thomas in Smyth (1878, 2: 125) with the spelling *bear-uk*. This grub was, according to Thomas, smaller than the *Ver-ring*, a grub that was '[v]ery large and fat; blacks eat them raw. Said by Europeans to be fine eating, when roasted or fried'. This word was recorded by Hercus (1986: 234) as ['bæːrʌk]. In a regularised spelling, it would be **berrak**.

He was repeatedly quoted in newspaper articles, such as in the Melbourne *Argus* (15 January 1894, p. 6) in which it was written that he sang 'three native songs' at a presentation to Senior Constable Tevlin, and in the *Healesville Guardian* (Friday 25 June 1897, p. 2),[5] where he was said to be singing a 'corroberrie song'. This may refer to the song presented in section 3.2.5.

An important painting by Barak of a ceremony is illustrated in Broome (2005: 8), dated about 1885;[6] Vanderbyl (2019a and 2019b) also includes images of Barak's ceremonial paintings and discusses them in detail.

Bed-be-endgeer or Benbenjie

Bed-be-endgeer 'commonly called 'Benbenjie', and also known as 'Ben', together with his wife Lychitch or 'Eliza', was the main consultant for George Gordon McCrae ('Experiences not Exploits', SLV MS 12018, Box 2523/5 (d)).

George Gordon McCrae wrote of him:

> Song I learned by heart from Ben' dictation. A song to raise the wind (this in it's literal sense), a song for the full moon; a canoe song, a war or rather battle-song; queer little ditties in 'pidgin' made whether in honour of our neighbours or ourselves and in which the peculiarities likely to strike a stranger, were admirably hit off.

5 'Local and General News', *Healesville Guardian*, 25 June 1897, p. 2, accessed 30 May 2019, nla.gov.au/nla.news-article60281011.

6 La Trobe Picture Collection, State Library of Victoria, H29640.

> Through Ben and Eliza my mother and I were enabled to compile a vocabulary of the words or most of the words of the dialect spoken by the tribe. It is much to be regretted that this work should never have been wholly completed also that some of it should have been lost in our various 'movings' from one place to another. As a result of pretty regular daily communication with Ben, his wife and friends, I commenced however lamely to speak the language

His name was spelled as *Bet Banger* by Robinson (for example, SLNSW A 7086 part 1, p. 48), who also noted that he was married to *Ly.tit.* According to Robinson, his country was 'east of Bacchus Marsh'; Barwick (1984) listed him as the chief of the Kurung-jang-baluk clan, a Woiwurrung group, and that from this clan 'the few survivors of violent dispossession 1835 found refuge among various clans of the opposite moiety where they had kinship ties resulting from intermarriage'. It is not therefore fully clear whether the language data given by Benbenjie to McCrae are Woiwurrung or Boonwurrung.

The songs recorded in Georgiana McCrae's diary and in Kenyon (1917) are likely to be among those that George Gordon McCrae learned from Bed-be-endgeer and his wife Lychitch (see sections 3.7 and 13.1).

Billibilleri

Billibilleri was one of the Indigenous leaders in the earliest days of colonial Melbourne. He was a **ngarrang(g)atj(a)** (now usually spelled Ngurungaeta), and probably the person of whom Howitt (1904: 308) wrote: 'Some were great fighting-men, others were orators, and one who lived at the time when Melbourne was established, was a renowned maker of songs and was considered to be the greatest of all'.

In a census of the '*Waworong* Tribe', dated 20 November 1839, he is the first listed person, his name spelled as Billibellyear, and his age is given as 40. His two wives were named Konengurook (aged 38) and Moorourook (aged 34), with male children Turmbermrook (18), Woolregunner (10), Mengerook (6), Kulgegronung (4), and female children Burgurrer (6), Mingerrook (4), Burbenbrook (10) and Susannah (13 days) (SLNSW MLMSS 214, Volume 09 Item 02, SLNSW_FL853950.jpg).

In remarks, Thomas writes: 'Jacky Jacky's family, has 2 wives, is an intelligent man and much respected by the whites'.

He is thus one of those who signed the infamous 'treaty', where he is named as Jagajaga.[7]

Bobbinary

Bobbinary was member of the Boonwurrung (Western Port) tribe, and a prominent community leader in the early period of white occupation. He died at Munnup (7 miles from Melbourne) on 13 July 1849 (Stephens 2014, 2: 395).

He was the singer of the song for enchanting away rain (see section 3.4.17). Thomas in Bride (1898: 92) wrote of him:

> We have in the Western Port tribe a celebrated charmer-away of rain, old Bobbinary. I have known this man to be kept singing for hours. The blacks say, when Bobbinary was a child that it had been raining for some days, and ' blackfellows all sad, their bellies tied up to keep off hunger ; that the child Bobbinary began to sing, and that sun immediately came out, and no more rain. That ever since then he has been able to send rain away.'

Bobbinary may be the same as 'Old Bobbery' who was the informant for the words relating to growing up (see section 3.2.6). In the 1839 census collected by William Thomas, his age is given as 42 (born in 1792), and his family was named as Morerawrook, aged 28 (presumed to be his wife), and two sons, Kal-Kaller, aged 18 and Wadegulk, aged 15 (SLNSW MLMSS 214, Volume 09 Item 02, SLNSW_FL853952.jpg).

Budgery Tom

Budgery Tom (c. 1809–1848) was chief of the Boonwurrung (Western Port) tribe. Although Budgery Tom is not named as one of the people who told songs to Thomas, it is likely that he was one of the main consultants for language information in the William Thomas papers.

Fels (2011: 48) gives a brief biography of him, noting that he was listed, with his mark, as a signatory to Batman's 'treaty'. Fels added that '[h]is real name was Mooderrogar; his wife was Narrugrook and his two sons, both of whom distinguished themselves in the 1842 Native Police Corps were

7 See for example, City of Yarra, 'Wurundjeri History of Yarra: Treaty', accessed 20 January 2026, www.yarracity.vic.gov.au/residents/diversity-and-inclusion/aboriginal-yarra/aboriginal-history-yarra/wurundjeri-history-yarra.

Buckup and Munnite' (sourced from Thomas, SLNSW MLMSS 214). Elsewhere Thomas spelled his name as Mooduringu and stated that he had been aged about 30 in 1839.

Robinson had told Benbow that Budgery Tom's wife was called Kar.ding. gor.oke or Karn.jin.

Budgery Tom died at the Nerre Nerre Warren Aboriginal Protectorate Station (now the Police Paddocks in Endeavour Hills[8]) on 6 March 1848.

Kurburu

Kurburu was the name of a member of the Bunwurrung. He is likely to have been a young man of around 30 at the time of white men's arrival in Melbourne. He was the composer of the song presented in section 3.2.2 and likely the source for the information about traditions relating to koalas discussed in section 3.2.2.1.

Smyth (1878, 1: 447) writes the following footnote about him, citing Thomas as his source:[9]

> '*Kur-bo-roo,* a well-known Western Port black, and held in high esteem as a sorcerer, a dreamer, and diviner, was named "The Bear," under the following circumstances. *Kur-bo-roo* was born at the foot of a tree, and during his mother's trouble a bear in the tree growled and grunted until *Kur-bo-roo* was born, when he ceased his noise. By this, it was said, the bear intended to show that the male child born at the foot of the tree should have the privilege of consulting the bears, and the child was called *Kur-bo-roo. Kur-bo-roo* attained to some excellence in his profession, [p448] and was regarded by all as a very wise man and doctor. When a black man dreams of bears, it is a sad omen. All the people are afraid when any one dreams of bears. One time, when there were about two hundred blacks at *Nerre-nerre-Warreen* (on the Yarra), including about eighteen children attending the school, *Kur-bo-roo* had a dream. He dreamt that he was surrounded by bears. He awoke in a great fright about one o'clock in the morning, and at once aroused the whole encampment. It was half an hour or more before I could discover the cause of the great excitement everywhere apparent. Fires were suddenly set

8 City of Casey, 'Casey's History: Aboriginal Settlement', accessed 30 May 2019, www.casey.vic.gov.au/caseys-history.

9 A manuscript version of part of this is found in SLNSW MLMSS 214, Volume 03 Item 01, SLNSW_FL827790.jpg and has been transcribed in a footnote in Stephens (2014, 1: 404).

> ablaze. The young blacks climbed the trees, cut down boughs, and fed the fires. The men, women, and children rushed hither and thither, displaying the greatest terror. I reasoned with them, sought to soothe them, endeavoured to control them; but all my efforts were useless. They fled from the spot where they had so long lived in comfort. By eight o'clock in the morning the forest was a solitude – not a soul remained; and all because of a dream of *Kur-bo-roo.'–The late Wm. Thomas's M.S.*[10]

It is likely that the drawing of the Bunyip in Smyth (1878, 1: 436) was made by Kurburu. This drawing was described thus:

> The Western Port blacks call the Bun-yip *Toor-roo-dun,* and a picture of the animal, made by *Kurruk* many years ago, under the direction of a learned doctor, is that of a creature resembling the emu.

The Robert Brough Smyth papers (SLV MS 8781, Section III), contain a pencil drawing of Kurburu, which is listed as '"Kurborror", Pencil. 18.5 x 14 cm., Photoprint nos. 8 & 9'.

Kurburu died on 27 February 1849, which Thomas recorded as 'Kurboro dies at Kulluk near WesternPort – hear about his death from Mr Rutherford' (Stephens 2014, 2: 365). A longer examination of Kurburu is in Clark et al. (2020), where his name is spelled as Kurrburra, and he is described, among other things, as 'a *wirrirrap* and bard'.

Kul-ler-kul-lup

Kul-ler-lup-lup was a respected old man and probably one of the people who created the Gaiggip song and dance (see section 3.4.7). In Thomas's description of the Tanderrum ceremony from the State Library of NSW manuscript MLMSS 214, Volume 03 Item 01, he is described as:

> the oldest man I have yet seen (among the Aborigines) he must have been near 80 years of age, he was just on 6 feet high (in continued furrows) and so fat [with?? it – crossed out] (that I have not seen his equal among which for) his face was wrinkled especially his forehead, (continued horizontal furrows to his eyebrows) [& cheeks very furrowed - crossed out]

His role in transmitting the Gaiggip corroboree and song, and other corroborees and dances, is described in more detail below (section 3.4.1).

10 This manuscript is presumably one of those kept at the State Library of NSW.

Lychitch or 'Eliza'

Lychitch was the wife of Bed-be-endgeer commonly called 'Benbenjie', also known as Eliza. In her diaries, Georgiana McCrae writes that 'Eliza told me the words of a few native songs I noted them down'. Nothing more is known about her, although it is possible that she was the same Eliza who was Jimmy Dunbar's first wife, and may have been the same Eliza who died at Mordialloc on 28 February 1877. She was aged 55 at the time of her death, which would mean that she was around 25 in 1847 when the songs were told to Georgiana. However, as noted above in connection with Bed-be-endgeer, George Gordon McCrae said that he learned songs from Ben, and these are presumably some of the same songs from Georgiana McCrae's diary. Most probably both Lychitch and Bed-be-endgeer knew the songs.

As mentioned above, in Robinson's papers, her name is given as Ly.tit and Robinson states that her land was called Wee.nee.pe.yal Bar.ra.bul, in other words in Wathawurrung country.

Myngderrar/Malcolm

One of the most important ritual experts in the 1830s and 1840s came to be known as Malcolm; his original name, according to Thomas, was Myngderrar, also spelled Minderar. He was the **wirrarrap** 'doctor', and was known frequently as the 'the flying doctor'. It was he who performed the ritual of regaining consciousness after a kidney fat attack in August 1840 (see section 3.4.9). Thomas names him as being 'of the Mount Macedon Tribe', and talks about his power both to fly and to cure people. The full quote from Thomas is found below in section 3.1.3.1, which describes the power and function of the **wirrarrap**. (See Thomas in Bride (1898: 92); SLNSW MLMSS 214, Volume 23 Item 01, SLNSW_FL847437.jpg.)

Robinson (Clark 1998, 1: 201) noted down the name 'Min.de.rare.re: brother to Malcom', suggesting either that there was some confusion as to his name, or that perhaps the name was in fact used by several brothers. The name Myngderrar may be a combination of *myng*, likely the word for 'eye' (**mirring/mirn** in Blake 1991), and a second part that may be **djerraniñ** 'ill' or **djerrwa-** 'to kill' (from R.H. Mathews, *dherwai*, NLA MS 8006/8/286); hence, perhaps literally, 'kills with the eye'.

His importance as a leader of the Indigenous community is shown by the fact that on 27 June 1844 there was a 'Grand council of 3 bands: Goulburn, Yarra & Devils River 57; Mt Macedon & a few Loddon 23; Barrabools 26 – total of 106. Malcolm main speaker organising everything. A few from each tribe to officiate in the commencing corrobery' (Stephens 2014, 2: 23).

In 1847, Malcolm was described by Thomas as an 'old traveller', and he was brought in to try and communicate with the men that were later hanged for killing Andrew Beveridge (Ryan 2016).

There is a photograph of Malcolm, named as 'Malcolm age 67 Gindamin Loddon Tribe. Doctor',[11] dating from 1866, photographed by Carl Walter (1831–1907). We think it likely that this is not the same Malcolm who was Thomas's informant in the 1840s, and was already senior, both because he has a different Indigenous name and because it is likely that he would not have survived until the late 1860s.

Much more research on Malcolm is needed to fully appreciate the importance of this significant indigenous leader.

Ningolubbel

Another very significant figure was Ningolubbel, also known as Capt. Turnbull. His name was spelled variously but should probably be regularised as **ning(g)ulabul**, based on Howitt's spelling *Ningu-labul*, though the last vowel is the least certain, probably unstressed.

He was stated to be the elder brother of Wenberi (see below and also Box 3.18 in section 3.2.3), who was murdered in 1840. He is described in Howitt (SLV MS Box 1053/2 (b), p. 30) as follows:

> Tumbull was buried near Bacchus Marsh at Tŭllŭrwill, in the Kŭrŭng-jerŭng balluck, of the Werribigalluk. Note his country not far off – his country was Gisborne and the hill near Gisborne – [Bullanyaruk?]. Yarŭk killed him. I think from Echuca. He died about the time the Brighton raily was made and the Raily to Geelong.

11 Can be viewed and downloaded from the State Library of Victoria website, www.slv.vic.gov.au/, search for 'Gindamin'.

This suggests he died in the late 1850s, as the railway to Geelong was opened in November 1856 and the railway to Brighton was open progressively, starting in 1859.[12] Little is known about *Yarŭk* 'magic' but Howitt (1904: 381) does discuss its power for curing illness.

This quote from Howitt goes on to present Wenberi's song and specifically states that the **murrup** 'spirit' of the elder brother, i.e. Ningolubbel, 'came to his younger brother Wenbirri and sang this song in him when he slept'. Since Wenberi died long before Ningolubbel, this shows that the **murrup** of his brother was able to leave its body and visit Wenberi in his sleep, and thus inspire the song. Elsewhere Wenberi is said to be 'brother of Nerimbineck, son of old Ningologin'; perhaps Ningologin is the same as Ningolubbel or perhaps there were two different people with very similar names.

In the 1839 census collected by William Thomas (SLNSW MLMSS 214, Volume 09 Item 02, SLNSW_FL853950.jpg), 'Ningolobin' is stated as being 68 years old, which would mean he was born in about 1771. His wife is named as Woombuke aged 40, and there are three male children: Maboine (16), Yanbury (20) and Bondite (14).

One of the songs recorded by McCrae was composed by Ningolubbel when he was in jail (see section 3.7.1). He had been accused of murder, in 1844, but was subsequently found innocent, as someone else had admitted to the killing (*Geelong Advertiser*, Saturday 22 March 1845, p. 2).

Ningolubbel was the chief of the Kurnung Willam, as discussed by Howitt (1904: 310):

> Immediately adjoining the Wurunjerri country, on the west side, was that of the Kurnung-willam[1] who were also Woëworung, and whose Headman was called Ningu-labul[2], but was named by the white men 'Captain Turnbull.' He was a great maker of songs, which, as Berak said, 'made people glad when they heard them,' but when he sang one of them to me, it had the contrary effect, for it made him shed tears. Ningu-labul came of a family of gifted singers, for his father and grandfather had been renowned songmakers, and this, as well as his own poetical power, was the cause of his great authority as a Ngurungaeta, not only in his own tribe, but also in those adjoining. The case of this man shows how headmanship was hereditary in a family, whose members were gifted beyond their fellows.

12 Wikipedia, 'Geelong Railway Station', accessed 13 September 2020, en.wikipedia.org/wiki/Geelong_railway_station; Wikipedia, 'Sandringham Line', accessed 11 June 2019, en.wikipedia.org/wiki/Sandringham_railway_line.

> 1 *Kurnung* means 'creek,' and *willam* is 'camp.'
>
> 2 This name means 'shining,' as explained to me, 'like the sun shining on a smooth stone,' that is, reflected from it.

Howitt also mentions that Ningolubbel was the 'partner' of the headman of the 'Gal-gal-balluk part of the Jajaurung tribe' (Djadjawurrung) whose land was on the northern side of Mount Macedon (Howitt 1904: 313):

> In reference to the office of the man for which I have thought the expression 'henchman' not inappropriate, it may be observed that he stands a little at one side of, and to the rear of, his principal. The henchman of Ningu-labul was the brother of Berak's father, Bebejan, whose henchman was a man named Winberi.[2] These men seem to have had the same position as 'the friend,' who, Mr. Dawson says, accompanied the 'Chief' of one of the tribes described by him.
>
> 2 As to Winberi, Thomas says, op, cit. p. 74, 'the unfortunate Winberi (shot by Major Lettsom's party).'

Howitt (1904: 310) added that '[t]o the westward of Ningu-labul was the country of the Kriballuk, whose Headman was a great medicine-man called Doro-bauk mentioned in Chap. VIII'. See section 3.1.4 for a description of how Doro-bauk breathed life back into a man whose *murup* 'spirit' had left him.

He was known far and wide. On Saturday 24 July 1841, Robinson (Clark 1998, 2: 326) asked people near the Grampians about him:

> I asked them about the tribes east as well as west, north and south. The Wadowrong and Yarra blacks and the Neerebulluc section of the eastern tribes they knew. I named some of the natives and among others Ning.cal.ler.bel. This person they knew and they repeated a song about him, made by the Gal gal bulluc. At the end of each stanza Ning.caller.bel was mentioned by name.

Unfortunately, no text of this song has been written down.

Ningolubbel was also a key participant in a ceremony of adoption held on 6 July 1844, a ceremony Thomas called *Woorkurran* (Stephens 2014, 2: 26) and elsewhere described as *Brandoo* (SLNSW MLMSS 214, Volume 03 Item 01, SLNSW_FL827779.jpg and SLNSW_FL827781.jpg). There was an exchange of items at this event, but there is no record of any singing or dancing.

Wenberi

Wenberi (also spelled Winberri, Whinberry), was a younger leader, and composer of a song in which his elder brother Ningolubbel visited him in his sleep (see section 3.2.3). Howitt (1887) noted that '[t]he bard who composed this song came of a poetic stock. His father and his father's father before him are said to have been "the makers of songs which made men sad or joyful when they heard them"'.

Wenberi was killed in October 1840; Fels (2011: 114) describes him:

> Winberri was aged 23, brother of Nerimbineck, son of old Ningologin, a Yarra black. Winberri was by family connection able to pass safely through distant remote tribes (Thomas in Bride 1969[1898]: 408.), a man with a 'noble spirit' according to Thomas who wrote a three page description of the unusual mourning ritual for Winberri carried out morning and evening by his aged father and his only sister.

The 'unusual mourning ritual' is the ember days (SLNSW MLMSS 214, Volume 23 Item 01, SLNSW_FL847436.jpg; this is partially transcribed below in the coda to section 3.2.3).

Thomas (SLNSW, MLMSS 214, Volume 22, p. 343) reports his unjustified murder by Major Lettsom as follows:

> the unfortunate Whin berry who was shot in that unconstitutional proceeding of Major Lettsom at Port Phillip who taking an advantage of my absence beyound Western Port the whole of the Escapement by Melbourne was surrounded at sun rise by Mounted Police and regulary drove into a stock yard when Whinberry who had a noble spirit rose his waddy to protect himself and was immediately shot tho the breath & died on the spot.

Thomas added that:

> I need scarce remark when the report went in and forwarded to the Home Government that Lord John Russell the then Colonial Secretary condemned the whole proceeding and trusted it would not occur again …

The Colonial Secretary referred to is Lord John Russell (1792–1878), who was later Prime Minister.

Broome (2005: 27) includes an illustration of Wenberi (spelled in Broome as Winberry), sketched by William Thomas (SLV Robert Brough Smyth papers), shown in traditional dress and holding traditional hunting weapons.

Wonga

One of Thomas's most important consultants was Wonga, chief of the Yarra Tribe, and one of the leaders at Coranderrk. He was born at Arthur's Seat (Smyth 1878, 1: 55–56), hence his name, as that place was also called *Wonga*. He is not specifically named as the consultant for any of the songs here, but may have been the person who gave the Earthquake song (section 3.8) to John Green.

Wonga was the sources for William Thomas's census lists in the 1860s and it seems likely that he accompanied Thomas to Gippsland on his travels there. His wife Maria, whose Indigenous name was Toorongerrook, was named in his diary as being admitted into hospital on 6 July 1860 (Stephens 2014, 3: 273).

3.1.3 The types of ritual specialists

The various publications mention two main ritual specialists whose functions will be briefly overviewed here. Their expertise in healing also meant that these were associated with song. These are the **wirrarrap** 'doctors', discussed in section 3.1.3.1, and the **ngarrangatj** 'chief' discussed in section 3.1.3.2.

3.1.3.1 Wirrarrap 'the doctors'

The **wirrarrap** were powerful figures who could both cause harm and cure it. The word is variously spelled *Wer-reep* by Thomas (see section 3.4.15) and *We-weep* by Robinson (see section 3.5).

Howitt (1904: 365) details the power that the **wirrarrap** had to kill people using *mung* 'evil magic' of which the *thundal* or 'quartz crystals' was the most dangerous. He could also take kidney fat (1904: 375). He also had the ability to overcome evil and cure disease. Howitt (1904: 381) wrote:

> In the Wurunjerri tribe, when a man believed himself to be under some evil spell, or suspected that harm was impending to him, and if, as was likely, he felt ill, he had recourse to the *Wirrarap*. My Wurunjerri informant, speaking of this, said, 'The *Wirrarap*, looking at him, might say, "Yes, the fire is up so high," pointing to his waist.

> "It is well that you came to me, the next time they burn it, it might be up to your neck, and then you would be done for."' The next time the wind blew towards the north, the *Wirrarap* would go through the air to the place where the man was burning something belonging to that poor fellow, and where that *Yaruk* (magic) was, pull up the spear-thrower, with which the spell was being worked, and bring it home. Giving the *Yaruk* to the sick man, he would say something like this, 'You go and put this in a running stream to wash all the *Yaruk* out of it, and I will go up and put this *Murriwun* (spear-thrower) in some water up there.' The reference to the wind blowing northwards is because, in this case, the offending medicine-man belonged to some tribe in that direction, for the Wurunjerri believed that the tribes on the Murray frontage, called by them *Meymet*, were of all others the most inclined to evil magic. The 'going up' by the Kulin *Wirrarap* refers to the belief that such men could travel invisibly through space; by this means ascending through the sky to the *Tharangalk-bek* beyond it.

This suggests that *Tharangalk-bek* is indeed beyond the sky; it is elsewhere described in Howitt as 'destination of the souls of the dead' (see for example 1904: 435), and in his manuscript source (SLV MS Box 1053/2 (b), hw0391.pdf, p. 23) as follows:

> The ghosts are supposed also to be able to go up to Tharangalk (tharan = trees galk = wood) which is in fact the sky. William said the Kūlin believed there were many 'cherry trees' up there and [rivers – crossed out] streams and rivers.

In the word list published by Barry (1867), *tarrangalk* is given as meaning 'comet'. This word consists of three parts, the first of which is **dharran**. This root is explained by Howitt as 'trees', a form not otherwise recorded, although Green in Smyth (1878, 2) records *bajerrang* as the word for 'tree', which appears to be a compound of **ba** 'and' and **djerrang** 'leaf'. There are a number of words regularised by Blake on the base of **dharra-** that relate to long objects: **dharrak** 'arm' and **dharrandel** 'black snake'. The word **galk** means 'tree, stick, wood' and **biik** 'ground'.

Thomas in Bride (1898: 92) also speaks about the power of **wirrarrap** to cure and to fly, relating this skill particularly to Malcolm who performed the ceremony described below (section 3.4.9), where he is said to have ascended 'like an eagle':

> Doctors. – The blacks have various kinds of doctors for eyes, bowels, head, &c., and, like white physicians, are noted in pro-portion to the remarkable cures said to have been wrought. But the highest pitch of the profession is flying. Among the tribes who have visited the settlement there has been but one, that has come to my knowledge, possessed of this power, whose name is Malcolm, of the Mount Macedon tribe. I have known this man to be sent for 100 miles. The blacks say that he has power to soar above the clouds, and to fly like an eagle; he also can, in some cases, recover the marmbula (kidney fat) when it has been stolen. I have a most singular account of one of his serial journeys, together with the solemnity of the encampment during his two hours' flight, but cannot trace it now. This Malcolm (aboriginal name Myngderrar) is said to have inherited this power from his father, who was famous before him.

Quoting Bunce, Smyth (1878, 1: 110) also describes the curing powers of the **wirrarrap**:

> Mr. Daniel Bunce,* an intelligent observer, and a gentleman well acquainted with the habits of the blacks, says that no tribe that he has ever met with believe in the possibility of a man dying a natural death. If a man is taken ill, it is at once assumed that some member of a hostile tribe has stolen some of his hair. This is quite enough to cause serious illness. If the man continues sick and gets worse, it is assumed that the hair has been burnt by his enemy. Such an act, they say, is sufficient to imperil his life. If the man dies, it is assumed that the thief has choked his victim and taken away his kidney-fat. When the grave is being dug, one or more of the older men –generally doctors or conjurors (*Buk-na-look*) – stand by and attentively watch the laborers; and if an insect is thrown out of the ground, these old men observe the direction which it takes, and having determined the line, two of the young men, relations of the deceased, are despatched in the path indicated, with instructions to kill the first native they meet, who they are assured and believe is the person directly chargeable with the crime of causing the death of their relative.

Another example of the power of the doctors is given by Thomas in Bride (1898: 92–93). Note that the date is omitted in the manuscript:

> Murrina Kooding, or Strength Lost. In the encampment south of the Yarra, on the evening of were Goul-burn, Mount Macedon, Barrabool, Yarra, and Western Port blacks. The Goulburn lubras, quite naked, stole upon seven young men. No sooner had the women their hands on the heads of the young men than the latter appeared

helpless; they cut from each young man a lock of his hair. As soon as the hair was cut the young men fainted; the women took the ornaments from the men's heads and decamped. The young men's friends came about them to comfort them, but life apparently could scarcely be kept in them. Their friends sat with them the whole of the night.

On the following morning, the doctors assembled; a fire was made about a quarter or half a mile from the encampment, and the seven young men were brought, each borne by two friends bearing pieces of lighted bark in their hands, to the spot; the young men were placed round the large fire at some distance, and before each was the bark brought by the friends. The doctors, mumbling and humming, with a piece of glass bottle commenced scraping off all the hair from the crown of the head to the feet, and then rubbed them from head to feet with werup (red ochre). The young men lay speechless during the whole of the time the ceremony was being performed, and every muscle of their faces seemed to be keenly noticed by the doctors. This ceremony lasted from sunrise to three hours afterwards. I understand that these young men would have died had not this ceremony been performed. Strength left them as the lock fell from their heads. (Is not this some semblance to Samson's case?)

3.1.3.2 Ngarrang(g)atj(a) 'the chiefs'

The word for 'chief' is usually spelled in modern times as *ngurungaeta*, based on the spelling in Howitt (1904). However, since R.H. Mathews is a much more reliable recorder of the sounds of the language, we suggest a more reliable regularisation of this word would be **ngarrang(g)atj(a)**,[13] following a spelling found in a pencil note on an offprint of one of his articles, 'Is headman called Ngurungaeta – Ngarran'ge' (NLA MS 8006/8/6). Note that it was spelled by Howitt as *ngŭrŭng-eit* and *ngurungeit* (SLV MS Box 1053/2 (b), hw0391.pdf, p. 39).

The etymology of this term is possibly from the word **ngarrga-** 'dance'. Thomas (SLNSW MLMSS 214 Volume 23 Item 02, SLNSW_FL814566.jpg) gives the word *Ngarnurngate* defined as 'King or Chief', with a note: 'Blacks say that long time ago, Kings used to make Blacks dance to them – no doubt the word for corrobery is derived from this in a more enlightened

13 One of the anonymous reviewers suggested that we should spell this word, which has considerable cultural importance, without brackets. It is possible that spellings like *Ngarnurngate* do suggest a cluster of **ngg** but we cannot be sure and prefer to keep the brackets to show this uncertainty.

days among them'. This etymology, or explanation of the meaning of the word for 'chief', clearly links the ability to dance (and presumably also to sing and compose songs) with authority in the community.

In a manuscript of Thomas's relating to songs and dances (SLNSW MLMSS 214, Volume 24 Item 01, SLNSW_FL828679.jpg and SLNSW_FL828682.jpg), he explains this etymology a second time:

> 6th I will now commence with their common Corroberry's but before entering upon them, I would state that Corroberry is not an Aboriginal word of Victoria, a barbarism its real term is Ngargee, the old doctors state that many many generations past blacks were very very many that the chiefs used to make the young blacks dance before them, which I have no doubt was the case, more so when the name of the chief or King is Ngar-gate.

Howitt (1904: 307f) describes the functions of the **ngarrang(g)atj(a)** in detail. The connection with songs is indicated by this quote: 'Some were great fighting-men, others were orators, and one who lived at the time when Melbourne was established, was a renowned maker of songs and was considered to be the greatest of all' (Howitt 1904: 308). This probably refers to Billibilleri. Others who held the title were Ningolubbel and 'Mr DeVilliers' in Western Port (SLV MS Box 1053/2). In the manuscript at Museums Victoria, Howitt states 'some Ngūrrungait are doctors, not all' (XM 759, p. 17). In terms of ritual expertise, the **wirrarrap** may have been senior and more skilled.

3.1.4 *Murrup* 'the spirit'

A number of the songs are said to have been given to the singers by the **murrup** 'spirit', spelled *murup* and discussed in some detail by Howitt (1904: 435, for example).

There appear to have been a number of words for 'spirit' in the Eastern Kulin languages. Thomas, in his diary entry for 20 January 1847 (Stephens 2014, 2: 219), wrote about Nangkun, a Mount Macedon youth who was imprisoned because he was thought to be a 'lunatic'. He collected two words – *murrino* 'cranky' and *worwodo* 'lively' – and wrote the following:

> On the next day 'very early visit the Jail converse with Nangkun, who I find Murrino [cranky], he took me for his uncle Billbellary, & told me he had seen Yearkun, Spirit, Nerrun Kunne Billibellary …'

The word *yearkun* is an alternative word for 'spirit', which Thomas elsewhere glossed as 'spirit, of anyone', whereas *moorrup* he glossed as 'soul (departed spirit)'.

The first version is in one of Howitt's field notebooks (MV XM 759), included as part of a discussion the **murrup**, commencing on page 17. This discussion commences with the following:

> Every animal has a spirit = mūrūp. That of a possum is just like a possum – Doctors can see him.
>
> When the Doctor catches the nangkūm, he shows it to the Doctor – some Ngūrrungait are doctors, not all) – I am not.

Later, on page 21 of the same document, he added that '[o]nly the doctors can see the Mūrŭp'.

In some information gathered from Barak, Howitt (1904: 435), writes:

> 'When I sleep and snore, my Murup goes away, sometimes to the Tharangalk-bek, but it cannot get in, and it comes back. It can talk with some other Murups, for instance, with my father and others who are dead.'

It may be that Barak's Murup could not enter the Tharangalk-bek, the land beyond the sky, because he was not a 'Doctor'.

A great medicine man, Doro-bauk, was able to call back the *murup* of a very ill person, as described by Howitt (1904: 387):

> Soon after the white men came to Melbourne, a blackfellow living near where Heidelberg now is, was nearly dead. His friends sent for Doro-bauk,[1] who lived to the west of Mount Macedon. When he arrived, he found the man just breathing ever so slightly, and his *Murup* (spirit, ghost) had gone away from him, and nothing remained in him but a little wind. Doro-bauk went after the *Murup*, and after some time returned with it under his 'possum rug. He said that he had been just in time to catch it round the middle, before it got near to the *Karalk*.2 The dead man was just breathing a little wind when Doro-bauk laid himself on him and put the *Murup* back into him. After a time the man came back to life.
>
> 1. *Doro* a certain kind of grub, and *Bauk*, 'high up.'
>
> 2. Karalk is the bright colour of sunset, and is said to be caused by spirits of the dead going in and out of Ngamat, which is the receptacle of the sun just beyond the edge of the earth.

3.1.5 Corroborees documented/mentions of corroborees

Corroborees were very commonly performed in and around Melbourne and indeed across Victoria in the early years after the foundation of Melbourne in 1835. In this section, we will present information about a range of corroborees that are known to have been performed in Melbourne in the early days. Some of these descriptions, mostly by Thomas, contain very important detail about how the corroboree was performed. Traditional songs would likely have been sung at all of these, though the text of those is not always written down.

William Thomas wrote a draft article about songs and dances, all of which has been transcribed and is presented in different sections in this book. The 6th part, for example, which discusses the etymology of the word for 'chief' and its source in the word for 'dance', is discussed above (section 3.1.3.2). (The first three sections are presented later in this section.) A summary of Thomas's paper was published in Smyth (1878, 1: 167–69), in which he states: 'The ordinary dance of the natives of Victoria – the *Ngargee* or corrobboree – has been carefully described by Mr. Thomas'. The word that we will regularise as **ngarrgi** is probably an imperative form, a command 'dance!'.

Thomas also noted descriptions of dances, some of which included songs texts (see for example, section 3.4.2), and some of which did not. In his manuscript notes in the State Library of NSW (MLMMS 214, Volume 21 Item 12, c009070001h.jpg, page numbered 237), he noted the following actual dance performances in the 1840s and 1850s (Box 3.1):

Box 3.1: List of dances/corroborees and their preformance dates

Dances or Corroberry, Sacred Corroberries:
Weinnie, 1st perfmd in Encampt by Moonee Ponds 14th Jan 1851 –
Neur-re-ung-ern-er, 1st perfmd 20 Mar 1847 with figures –
Gaegape 1st saw it in Octr 1842 35 miles from Melbourne on Major Boyds Station –
Yepene Amy Gai (by Mr Parker called Dance of Separate Spirits)

Source: SLNSW MLMSS 214 Volume 21 Item 12, c009070001h.jpg, p. 237; adapted by authors.

The full texts relating to *Weinnie* and *Neur-re-ung-ern-er* are presented in sections 3.1.5.1 and 3.1.5.2 respectively. Another corroboree mentioned there is the Emu corroboree (see section 3.1.5.3).

For two of the dances listed in Box 3.1, texts of at least part of what was sung on those occasions were documented by Thomas. The Gaiggip (Gaegape) dance is described in section 3.4.1, while the 'Yepene Amy Gai' is discussed in the chapter on Western Kulin songs (section 2.4).

Another dance/corroboree, discussed in detail in section 3.1.5.4, was the Donkey dance, held at an unknown date, perhaps in the 1840s.

The first three sections of Thomas's general discussion of dances are presented here (SLNSW MLMSS 214, Volume 24 Item 01, SLNSW_FL828663.jpg, SLNSW_FL828666.jpg, SLNSW_FL828668.jpg and SLNSW_FL828671.jpg):

> 1st Songs & dances among Aborigines like among civilised are either sacred or profane, or more properly stating for pleasure or sacred and traditional, the two latter are generally accompanied by effigys which bears some seede resemblence ~~or~~ representation or hyroglyphs figure of what intended[X] to represent, the Aboriginal songs are numerous, and the modern ones go by the names of their authors or bards; tho rhyme and measure is out of the the question – the songs or drones of the leaders of their common dance is generally according to the caprice of the leaders, tho there are some of these regularly settled upn and known by least –
>
> 2nd A stranger would after seeing one of two Corroberrys look upon them as a monotonous repetition voide of sense, would not a stranger to our country dances and reels (say an Aborigine) look upon them as equally monotonous – there is as much sense in the one as the other, if the blacks orchestre is inferior his time and motion is far superior in fact defies any attempt at comparison, a recent and excellent writer[V] has well summed up their common Corroberrys thus 'All that was ever put upon the stage, in the most approved style of hideousness, whether in German Operas, or in British Pantomines sinks into utter insignificance before an Aboriginal Corroberry.'
>
> [v] John Sherrer, Adventures of a Gold Digger C.H. Clarke 23a Patternoster Row
>
> 3rd Their Common Corroberrys and other dances are taught to the rising generation – I have been amused in the En-campment by seeing a Dozen or more boys while their parents have been out for the day seeking their daily fare going thro a regular corroberry with the greatest accuracy. ---

This is followed by the Corroboree song (see section 3.4.3), description of Ningolubbel's song (section 3.4.4) and the discussion of the meaning of the word Ngargee (see section 3.1.3.2).

Sections 7 to 9 of Thomas's description follow here. While very much a description of its time, using terms like 'civilised' to refer to English culture, nevertheless, the respect that Thomas had for the people is shown by comments about the dances like 'in fact civilization can in no way compete with the Australian dance' (SLNSW MLMSS 214, Volume 24 Item 01, commencing at SLNSW_FL828682.jpg):[14]

> 7th The blacks have various kinds of Ngargess (or Corroberry's) the common corroberry generally seen and exhibitted before Europeans at night consists of a number of males 20 or 30 or more if 2 or more tribes are conregated, their persons are streaked and daubed all over according to their own taste, not 2 alike expect the face which generally has white round the eyes across the forehead, on the cheeks and down the nose – they however must all have boughs, below their knees to the ankles, & two sticks about 10, or 12 inches long, they retire to a distance in the thicket to equip themselves, and a strange spectable they present on their appearance, in fact like 20 or 30 Harlequins half cranky, without any understanding among them, if any how diversified orhi deous they should appear, this must have been the scene which the writer I have referred to must have seen and merely a casual inspector of such scenes have (which I nevertheless say is just) sum it up his account of the Aborigines Corroberry's they have however other Corroberry's some truly pleasing. –

> 8th But to return, a great fire is made, by which stands the leader who is also furnished with two sticks like those the dances use, but always appear in his opossoum rug and no way daubed like the dancers by his side is seated a number of lubras naked with their opossum rugs folder up which they hold on their left hand in their laps and beat time most accurately with their right hand striking their rugs, it is astonishing that a muffled up rug could make such a perfect sound like muffled drum, so many beating at once, and all in time, contrasted with the sonorous singing some times elevated to the highest pitch then gradually lowering as tho to give merit to the dead muffled sound of the opossum rugs, the leaders note is a more whining hum, the leader and lubras often commence 3 or 4 minutes ere the dancers make their appearance (like a flourish in an orchestre) when a loud united stroke is heard in the distance

14 This section forms the basis of the description in Smyth (1878, 1: 167–69).

upon the dancers sticks, this is a signal that they are on the move, and the lubras in an elevat ed strain as tho' vieing with each other strike up, the strange grotestique band always in a strait line may be seen knees, and legs extended and bent about half height advancing slowly towards the leader, the accuracy of their movement, altho 30 or 40 may be engaged baffled any attempt at description in fact civilization can in no way compete with the Australian dance, as to time and motion, as tho' all their feet, boughs, on their legs, and sticks in their hands were by machinery set in motion at one and the same time a body of 30 or 40 soldiers on parade marching, their feet move not near so exact as the demise-mi moves of the Aboriginal dancers, grad ually tho' with continued quick moves they approach the leader when within about 20 yards they break the strait line, gradually and in a promiscuous group all apparently as close as they can be raiseing their bodies gradually to an erect position as they draw near still dancing, beating their sticks over their heads, when they arrive at the leader the dance is turned to a united jumping which makes the very forest shake under them it is surprising how they can continue using their sticks without hitting each other, at this stage of the dance, they how ever do mysteriously not strike each other and conclude with a deliberate single knock, and then an expulsion of the breath, when they without or der fly back to the dark distance whence they came from, and will continue this sound for hours, till even to the stranger it becomes a tedious monotony, perhaps the most attractive appearance is the light of the blazing fire shining upon their strange daubed bodies – they have however in all their Corroberry's a decency, their back and their front parts, having a kind of apron made of opossum skins, but cut in narrow slips of an inch wide from about 2 inches from the top, and a girdle about the loins, and I may add that the lubras (who occasionally) if much elated will 3 or 4 of them rise up to dance, rising up, they always have a very fine girdle of emu feathers, which goes completely round them at the waist about 2 feet deep but their breasts which generally are much larger and flammy than European females flap up and down regularly disgusting. –

9th There are various other night dances but I will mention but one more called in the Aboriginal Language Koo-ite, but by Europeans the Monkey, this is a singular dance, streaked in like manner as the former, they touch and draw gradually the finger from the crown of the head to the feet which takes some few minutes, from their slow yet accurate and timely motions, one portion and them moving off others come foreward and do in like manner each as going thro' fall in behind, a spear is held in one hand and wonguim in the

> other gently move and the inclinded body body downwards it is surprising that tho' encum ber'd with wonguim & spear they touch each essential part from the crown of the head to the feeet which is the close of the dance by no means too noisy as in their common corroberry –

The boughs tied below the knees mentioned in the 7th section above are named in Smyth (1878, 1: 159), in the discussion about a fight, as 'boughs *(Murrum* or *Mooran Karrang)* just above the ankles'. These may be the word **marran** 'leaf' as regularised by Blake (1991). **Garrang** means both 'nose' and 'gum (of tree)' (Blake 1991).

The last dance is named *Koo-ite*, a term that has not been found in other sources for the Eastern Kulin languages.

Thomas then describes the Wool-woork Bar-lum-bur-lin (see section 3.4.5).

The 11th section is presented here (SLNSW MLMSS 214, Volume 24 Item 01, SLNSW_FL828727.jpg and SLNSW_FL828729.jpg):

> 11th at one of these dances, I was much annoyed when one of the husbands dancing was struck with jealousy at his lubra lifting up her opossum rug looking at a single man a spectator, which turned the whole of the Encampment of jovial amusement into a regular fighting field which lasted for two hours. –

This text is followed by the description of what seems to relate to the Butterfly dance (see section 3.4.5) and then the Murrunawa corroboree (section 3.4.2), before a final section (SLNSW MLMSS 214, Volume 24 Item 01, SLNSW_FL828753.jpg) as follows:

> Paper 6th – Sacred and Tradition dances are generally accompanied by figures cut rudely from sheets of bark [from the neighbouring trees] on which is decorated by the artist by the direction of the priests or doctors, who gravely sits smoking his pipe while giving instruction.
>
> Neur-re-ung-ern-er a Sacred Dance of the Devils River Tribe.

See section 3.1.5.2 for a further description of this 'sacred dance'.

In the following, we present detailed descriptions of the Weinnie dance (section 3.1.5.1), the Neur-re-ung-ern-er or 'Sacred Dance' of the Thagungwurrung (section 3.1.5.2), the Emu corroboree (section 3.1.5.3), and the 'Donkey dance' (section 3.1.5.4), all described by Thomas, rounding off with a brief mention of the New Moon corroboree, which was a regular event in the Melbourne area until 1846 (section 3.1.5.5). This is followed by the description of the 'Blood Feud' and subsequent corroboree described by Howitt (section 3.1.5.6), the corroboree written about by Georgiana McCrae (section 3.1.5.7), that documented by George Augustus Robinson (section 3.1.5.8), and rounded off by mentions of other corroborees (section 3.1.5.9).

3.1.5.1 Weinnie

The dance, with various spellings *Weinnie*, *Winne* and *Winnie*, was held in January 1851, perhaps in the area that is now Flemington or Ascot Vale. It was described as a 'sacred dance' that involved the holding up and reverencing of a Christian Bible. The information contained here was mostly gleaned from Ningolubbel. It is described as a new dance, brought by people from the West. As the text makes it clear (p. 357), the performers of this dance regarded the book as having come 'down from the clouds'.[15]

There are no language words in this portion of text. The name of the dance is perhaps related to the word for 'fire', which we might regularise as **wiiny**. Blake (1991) spells the word 'fire' as **wiiñ** with a long vowel and as a single syllable. We believe that the spelling of the word with final *-ie* is probably an attempt to convey a final palatal nasal [wiːɲ].

In his page containing the description of the 'Donkey dance' (see section 3.1.5.4), Thomas writes in the margin 'Dances, Effigys &c Belonging to Veinee fire', which we read to specifically associate the name of this dance with 'fire' (SLNSW MLMSS 214, Volume 03 Item 01, SLNSW_FL827802.jpg).

Wonga, who was born at *Wonga* (Arthurs Seat), explained to Thomas (SLNSWMLMSS 214, Volume 21 Item 11 William Thomas notes relating to Wonga, 1861, SLNSW_FL3270271.jpg) about the origin of fire, as:

15 We believe that A.A.C. Le Souëf also made observations of a similar event, where the Bible was held up at a corroboree on the Upper Goulburn. This reference is in his typed manuscript, 'Personal Recollections of Early Victoria', State Library of Victoria, MS 8719, available on Le Souëf Family Archives Guide to Records, University of Melbourne eScholarship Research Centre, updated 27 November 2008, accessed 30 April 2019, www.austehc.unimelb.edu.au/guides/leso/lesouef.htm.

> Wang – get em [have em – crossed out] Vien from 3 Bagrooks big Ker-rut-krook, Brook-bool, Boon-un-bool-la-rook – who were hard at work with their kan-kan killing snakes – when one stick break and come out fire, Lubra say Kye Kye – down came Wang [directly – inserted] & run away with the Fire. Lubra big one cry
>
> Wang fly to big one mountain Bill-le-vein [far away to beyond Mt Cole – inserted] in direction of Mt Cole

Wang refers to the ancestral crow.

Bill-le-vein is an alternative spelling of the name recorded as *Pilleweane* 'Victorian Ranges' (in the Grampians) in 'Native Names of Places in the Wannon District. (Compiled by Peter Learmonth, Esq.)' (in Smyth 1878, 2: 177), but also found in the form *Billawin* 'Victoria Range', *Pillawin* 'Mount Avoca' and *Billiwhin* 'Wimmera River' (Clark and Heydon 2002), as well as being the name of a 'track' in the Victoria Ranges, *Billywing*. Since the Wimmera River has its source in the Pyrenees, perhaps it is the name for that area, and Clark (1990: 118) listed the Pilawin Baluk as the Indigenous group there, presumably named after that location.

The name was translated by Massola (1968) as 'two fires', though he does not give his source for this translation, presumably with **pulety** 'two' as the first part of a compound. We suggest that it might also be literally 'fire of (in) the belly', **pili-wiiny**, as the word **pili** is well documented as meaning 'belly' in Western Kulin languages (see for example Clark 2014). The similarity of this word to English *belly* is purely coincidental (Hercus 1992).

The origin of fire[16] is also mentioned in connection with **Bundjil**'s song (see section 3.2.4). Howitt's description (1904: 430) talks about the sweeping of the ancestral beings into the sky because of the theft of fire by *Waang*, the crow. It may therefore be that **Bundjil**'s song was performed at the Weinnie dance.

16 Note, for example, Monash University, 'Yagun Gulinj Wiinj (How Man Found Fire)', 2016, accessed 13 February 2019, www.monash.edu/arts/monash-indigenous-studies/wunungu-awara/animations/yagun-gulinj-wiinj-how-man-found-fire-2016, which is an animation produced by Taungurung people. *Yagun gulinj wiinj* means literally 'find human fire'.

Thomas's full description of this dance is given in Box 3.2. Note that in this transcription sections shown in single brackets are inserts made by Thomas and uncertain readings are shown in brackets with a double question mark. Some of these uncertain readings are within the single bracketed insertions.

Box 3.2: Description of the Weinnie dance

[p. 355]

Winne, a sacred dance 1st performed [near - inserted] Melbourne in the encampt [W of-crossed out] [between-inserted] Moonie Ponds [& Salt Water R-inserted], 14th Jany 1851-The Booninyong & Leigh Blacks arrived & others from Backhouses Marsh [& the Goulbourn-inserted] with this new dance-[Ning-gollobin alias-inserted] John Bull [great notoriety among-inserted] of the Melbourne tribes who had been [away -crossed out] [coonday??-inserted] from his district near 2 years arrived with them -My blacks being collected. John Bull gave me to understand "that I should see a Corroberry like white mans Sunday." but was mystically silent respecting it. After some time an old Black of the Booninyong tribe came up to me and shook me [heartily -inserted] by the hand [most heartily-crossed out]. He then begged me to come with him [being prepared for something new I readily followed-inserted] & about 200 yards off a [small-crossed out] fire was being made and 23 [men-crossed out] [blacks-inserted] (among [whom-crossed out] [them-inserted] were some of my blacks) seated. They [all-inserted] jumped up on my approach & each shook me [hand with?? Most-inserted] heartily [by the hand-crossed out] [more heartily than on any previously meeting the?? tide??-inserted] they then shook hands with the old [man -crossed out] [black-inserted] & one another their hands going up near to their eyes then down to their knees [several times-inserted]. Then then set light to the fire. The old [man-crossed out] [black-inserted] light his pipe & [majestically-crossed out] [sedately-inserted] walked to the front of the fire & raising up his right hand at full height presented to the dancers an opens

[p. 356]

book, his thumb & little finger pressing the book wide open, while the 3 fingers sustained the back, they then commenced a simple dance with small boughs in right hand singing and looking steadfastly at the book [held by the old Dr or priest -inserted], the old man more like a statue kept the book at full height. I went up to him to see what book it was [that all seemed so intent?? upon-inserted] and to my astonishment found it a Bible. The [old man-inserted] motioned me [with his other hand-crossed out] not to disturb him [he motioned me with his hand not engaged?? - inserted] I could not supress [my] emotion on viewing the sacred oracle held up with such marked intenseness. Moses could not have more steadfastly lifted up the serpent in the wilderness [than this savage the [books-crossed out] records of eternal truth-inserted] had it not been for the fumes from his pipe & a red cap he had on his [head his-inserted] appearance was imposing & his fixed attitude solemn, they [blacks-inserted] danced for about ¾ of an hour [not more-inserted] in a crescent form opposite side of the fire to the old [??-crossed out] [leader-inserted] & at the conclusion again [most blacks-inserted] again shook hands. I was [full of-crossed out] anxi[ety-crossed out] [ious-inserted] to know [of this-inserted] [the history of this-crossed out] to me [extraordinary-inserted] pleasing [yet-inserted] exhibition as far as the world of normal life went [of-crossed out] the object of [attraction - crossed out] [deep attraction-inserted] altho those

[p. 357]

who gazed had of 2 had the book [& its contents - inserted] brought under their notice to know how they came by the Bible, more so why they so highly extolled it, knowing that I & others had often tried to bring them seriously to consider its invaluable contents - All I could [get - crossed out] [learn - inserted] [out of - crossed out] [from - inserted] the Boonningon & Leigh Blacks was "that it came down from the clouds. Weinee sent it down to Mt Emu blacks" - John Bull however gave me more detailed account. He stated "that the Mt Emu blacks were encamped [near Mt Emu - inserted] in the morning as usual they went [from the encampt - inserted] [out - crossed out] to seek [food - crossed out] [their daily food - inserted] when they returned in the evening they found these books, a pocket handkerchief & a stick of tobacco (3 bibles, 2 testaments [& - inserted] 4 prayer books) on each handkerchief was a stick of tobacco, & a book - the blacks were frightened & talked all night, in the morning the doctors [considered - crossed out] [had a council - inserted] after deliberation came to the conclusion that they had come down from [the clouds - crossed out] [above - inserted] One Dr. took the book [held by the leader of the dance - inserted] to a settler who stated that the book came down from heaven to make man good [& - inserted] to be happy and love one another, shake hands like Mess mates all men, [blacks & white - inserted] so the Doctors had

[written at the side]

drunkeness, male & female & fighting, when fighting vain cabals, this the night to the annoyance of all within the hearing of the Encampt that at night as I before [have - inserted] stated was forced to break up the Encampt & send to the bush this fraternal compact

[p. 358]

established this dance "Veinnie" & were sending the dance to all parts to establish unity & friendship among [to make as friends - inserted] all tribes [they all were like brothers for nearly a week & I in conveyed?? & made what use moved what way I could of it and referred often to my addresses to them from a copy of the same book which as the good settlers told them did come down from heaven - inserted] all tribes + whether this [sacred - inserted] dance still continues in the interior or not I [know - crossed out] [am - inserted] not [aware?? - inserted] but I [firmly - inserted] believe [its - crossed out] [that the Priests - inserted] object was to unite tribes together in one common fraternity - however not a week [had elapsed - inserted] from my 1st seeing this dance performed [several - crossed out] [before several - inserted] of these [united brotherly - inserted] blacks got drunk & their fraternity [was - crossed out] interrupted by fighting & all manner of cabals [which increase - inserted] & [till - inserted] continual complaints being made [by the white population - inserted] before 15 dys [& - crossed out] I was [forced - crossed out] [compelled - inserted] to break up the Encampt - had that poison of white men been kept from them, this dance might have had its desired effect & I had [hence - inserted] [made been - crossed out] an [forunner - crossed out] avenue in their [inmuredments??] for the reception of the gospel - This dance was truly innocent, a branch in each blacks right hand and those who had books held them in their left, facing each other.

[Written at the side]
on commencing touching each others branch, and then diverging into a crescent form continuing dancing before each other, tho they have a book in their left hand they do not look up to it, but steadfastly fixing their eyes on the old leaders book, they draw in a circle round the leader of the close of the dance, each puts his bough to the other merely touching each other at the top with [extending??] arms, which has a singular appearance as the top of the boughs meet their bodies are at least 4 or 5 feet from the centre, the break off shaking the old leader most cordially all of them retire – they had a quantity of [provis??] & a large boiler they had [borrages??] full of tea, they put down each with his pannican, touching each other, then dipping into one fraternal bowl, the old leader set down among them & remainder of the day was spent in [feasting??] & drinking of tea – the days afterwards was a different scene.

Source: MLMSS 214, Volume 22 Item 03, pp. 355–58;17 adapted by authors.

3.1.5.2 Neur-re-ung-ern-er

Another important dance noted by Thomas was the Neur-re-ung-ern-er. This dance was brought from the Devils River, in Taungurong country. Devils River is today the name of an area beside Lake Eildon. It no longer appears to be the name of an actual river, but is the name of a district in the arm of Lake Eildon that does not include the Goulburn. The information about this dance, presented below in Box 3.3, was gained from 'an old favorite black of the tribe'.

As the description below indicates, the dance arose from a dream in which one of the 'Doctors' (**wirrarrap**) had seen 'Great Pundgil (**Bundjil**) came with his big knife & cut off his left arm & then went around the encamp[t] and cut off every left arm of man, woman & child'. On waking, he consulted with other elders and they decided that to appease 'Great Pundgil', they would create these four figures representing a family – father, mother, son and daughter – and hold a corroboree, presumably once a month. The description indicates that this was performed on 20 March 1847, which was three days after the new moon and probably the first night that month in which a crescent moon would have been seen.

17 This section, MLMSS 214, Volume 22 Item 03, has not been photographed by the State Library of NSW. However, one of the authors (Morey) has taken photos of this section and checked the transcription of this dance against those photographs. The whole of this section of the manuscript is gathered into a single volume, along with other parts of 'Box 22' that have been photographed by the library.

Given the reference in the text to 'the cabalous judical proceeding some days on the topic touching the death of a young woman' and to '*Narrumbul* – used as a sign of grief' and '*Yar-kah*'s – exclamations of anguish and pain', this particular ceremony was perhaps also a mourning ceremony following this woman's death.

Box 3.3: Description of the Neur-re-ung-ern-er dance

[p. 133]

[On the side]

Paper 6th to Mr Duffy Sacred Dances Sacred [Dances or-inserted] traditional [dances -crossed out] are generally accompanied by figures cut rudely from sheets of bark [from the neighbouring tribes - inserted] on which is decorated by the artist, by the direction of the Priest or Doctors - who gravely sits smoking his pipe while givin instructions

Neur-re-ung-ern-er

[Main text]

Neur-re-ung-ern-er+, a sacred dance [of - crossed out] [brought from - inserted] the Devil River tribe, the great excitement this dance occasioned [among the blacks - inserted] led me to be very particular in arriving at the real meaning of it, the blacks come for some time desirous to keep me in the dark upon the subject [which led me to be more plersaces?? - inserted] and by bribing, importuning & bouncing [at length - inserted] was taken aside by an old favorite [black - inserted] of the that tribe who on my following him to a large gum tree, presented to my view 4 figures, 2 about 7 feet long & 2 about 4 feet, saying with a sigh "those are the meaning of the dance [by & large more?? see - inserted] like your big one Sunday", for the blacks are well aware that on a Sunday [white - inserted] man goes to church & sings to Pungil Marman, On looking at the figures they appeared without any [thing-crossed out][the could?? Meaning-inserted] in shape or form that could lead me to suppose that they represented any figure human, animal or representation of any of the heavenly bodies, as there was some judicial business to settle between 2 tribes and my remaining in the encampt indispensible, I seated myself by the old man who was a man of some celebracy in the art of interpreting dreams, by his direction those pieces of bark was painted [cut to shape - inserted] he carefully [now & then - inserted] acting the part of the mechanic [& artist - inserted] in very particularly giving them [exact - inserted] form altho the old man when he had with his tommahawk scarcely [given the forms & ??] made sand figure, it re-

+1st performed at Melbourne Ent 20th March 1847[18]

18 This is not mentioned in Thomas's journal of that date (Stephens 2014, 2: 234).

[p. 134]

remained for him to explain for what they were intended for altho I had seen many of these Hieroglyphics these [figures - inserted] were [pusslers??] that I could not even conjecture, by & bye you see, said he". [as - crossed out] the artist began to mix up his colours [just as I was getting regularly excited - inserted] a regular shindy at this [juncture - crossed out] [moment - inserted] was up [in the encamp[t] - inserted] it was the cabalous judical proceeding some days on the topic touching the death of a young [woman - crossed out] [lubra - inserted] hastening to the spot where soon commenced showers of missiles. I was detained for some hours and had [nearly - crossed out] [at the moment - inserted] [forgs??] then, the [old - inserted] interpreters figures but [for - crossed out] a young [man - crossed out] [black - inserted] of my tribe making some inquiry of me if I had seen any figures of the Devils River Blacks alluding to the big Sunday Corrobery that was to take place at night. I told him I had but could not make them out & with my stick scribed the form of them on the ground. The old man show'd great anger at the young [man - crossed out] [black - inserted] prying into myste-

[Written on the side]

Verbatim as sent to Mr

Duffy, 6th paper, Merri V [??]

8th June 1850

[p. 135]

ries that they[V] alone [should - crossed out] [could - inserted] explain, [and - crossed out] [here comes in the note v - inserted] it required some of my interference to make all right between the young inquisitive black & the old [man - crossed out] [savage - inserted] it must be understood that a sacred dance is brought & conveyed from one tribe to another [as missionary exertions to foreign ?? - inserted] [and - crossed out] the first time it is performed all those who have not seen it are supposed to be, in fact are, ignorant of its meaning, till after it is over, such is their intense anxiety to become acquainted with any supernatural thing, that altho perfectly new as it regards figure motion [posite?? it - inserted] & yet after the dance is over the strangers will remember every motion & give you a full description not a mere desultory one - after the dance is over, the old [men - crossed out] [Dr or Priest - inserted] when the blacks are all settled in their miams generally about midnight will explain to the tribe to which they belong, the cause & meaning of the dance & figures [& what led it be performed - inserted]. [It was - inserted] towards sundown when I

v for the old [men - crossed out] [priests & - inserted] doctors [be - crossed out] engross the whole [of capability - crossed out] [power - inserted] of unravelling [mysterious - inserted] things the young [men - crossed out] are supposed to be perfectly ignorant of anything but the spear & [?? - crossed out]

[p. 136]

returned to the old Devils River Doctor, who was seated with all the dignity of a man of importance around him was several children [& young men as tho he was lecturing them - inserted] & the four pieces of bark I had seen in the forenoon lay on the ground each on a layer of leaves, they had been some hours out of the hand of the artist, they [had - crossed out] struck me at once by the colours on them of being a rude record of awful bodings mingled with hope, he pointing to them that was to convey the coming night (with a divining eye) an explanation of what they represented, the up-per part of them gave my gessing imagination some rude representation of a human head, but the other part gave me no link to suppose such to be the case, my excitement & curiosity was raised [looks, height - inserted] when the old mane taking me aside said 'see you', the Narrumbul[V] border round it, with a knowing

ing

v used as sign of grief &

[p. 137]

ing sigh, I do, said I, do you see the Weerup[V], I do said I, some of his cotemporary aged savans seeing me deedy in conversation with the interpreter drew nigh the [old priest - inserted] beckoned to me with a heave of his chest [indicative of its serious importance - inserted] to cease conversation. [which confidential hint I immediately took - inserted] and as the others drew night we merely conversed on the expectation of the coming [mysterious - inserted] dance. These figures were [at night - inserted] borne in the dance by a Man, a Woman, a young lass, & a [young - crossed out] youth The dancers were all in bending position. The right hand closely pressing the right [pressur - crossed out] breast. The elbow projecting out, the feet closely together and knees projecting with a wonderful trembling, [the - crossed out] baffling even St. Vitus dance to mimic, the left arm could not be seen, as the feet were so closely kept together, while with simultaneous Yar-kah's[1], the air was sent out with yelling [Yar kah's is an exclamation of anguish or pain - inserted] while the leader's mumbling drones were occasionally heard in the intervals of the Yarkah's, this

dan

v emblematic of joy or hope

1 Exclamation of anguish & pain

[p. 138]

[sacred - crossed out] dance [went on - inserted], lasted till near 2 in the morning the misterious dance gave me fruitless surmises during the night to know what it [could - inserted] mean[t - crossed out], in the morning my old friend the diviner, when most of then of the blacks had left [for Melbourn - crossed out] [the encampment for food - inserted] or asleep from the fatigue of the past night, after begging me not to tell any other other white [person - crossed out] [man - inserted] in a most solemn grave manner, stated "that his tribe were all encamped in the ranges of their country, that one night one of the Doctors dreamed that while they all lay asleep Great Pundgil came [with his big knife - inserted] & cut off his left arm & then went around [the encamp[t] - inserted] and cut off every left arm of man woman & child, that the Encamp[t] was full of far Kah's, after cutting off all of the left arms, [he - crossed out] [Pundgyl - inserted] was going to cut off their right arms when [they - crossed out] all [the blacks - inserted] put their hand [that was - inserted] left to their breast & trembling cried no cut off right arm too, & Pundgil had pity & said well

[p. 139]

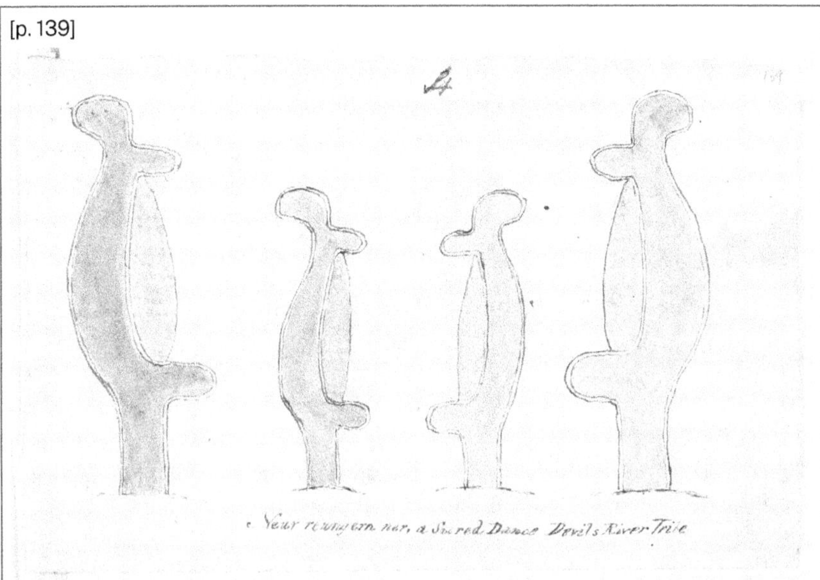

Neur reungern ner, a sacred Dance Devils River Tribe

[Note: original image is in colour.]

[p. 140]

no cut off now another time, the dreamer woke, and was so terrified that he roused the whole encampt [& no more slept - inserted] that the blacks were terribly frightened as he related the dream and that [at daybreak - inserted] the Doctors & enchanters consulted [among themselves - inserted] [at day break - crossed out] [what could this mean - inserted] during their consultation & invocations the blacks were in the greatest excitement [that - crossed out] after long consultation & invocations they brought forth the four [effigies - inserted] [figures one - crossed out] representing a man, [another his wife - crossed out] [wife or woman - inserted], [his - crossed out] son & daughter or the tribe a man woman, male and female child, informing the blacks that Pundgyl was very angry & that the only way to appease him [was - crossed out] & to keep off the [further - inserted] act of Pundgyl wrath was to corroberry for one moon every night in the attitude described by the dreamer as he found himself and [when he awoke - inserted] felt in his dream [further - inserted] that these effigies were to be borne in presence of the dancers to excite them to [their - inserted] [?? purpose - crossed out] what might have taken place had not the diviners prevented by their wisdom (in producing this dance) the wrath of Pundgyl. end

Source: SLNSW MLMSS 214, Volume 21 Item 06, commencing at SLNSW_FL841074.jpg; adapted by authors.

There are a number of Indigenous words in the text, presented in example (3.1), with regularisations in bold, including some cries.

(3.1) *Neur-re-ung-ern-er* 'name of the dance'

neyurreyungana

Narrumbul 'used as sign of grief & border around representation of the human head'

n(h)arrumbul

Weerup 'emblematic of joy or hope'

wirrap

Yar-kah 'Exclamation of anguish & pain'

ya-ga

Kah 'the cry in the dream of the "Dr" that Pundgil had come and cut off everyone'

ga

Notes

The name of this dance may derive from the word for 'gum' given as *Neureurong* in Barry (1867); this word was spelled by Thomas as Neureurong and defined as 'a kind of Terpentine eases out of stringy bark', in other words 'sap'.

The most common word for 'cut' is **galba-**, although Robinson gives the word *Pin de nung* to mean 'cut with a knife' ('Vocabulary of the languages spoken by the Waverong and Biggah Tribes', SLNSW A 7086 part 3, pp. 22–52; original transcription in Clark 2002: 165–77).

3.1.5.3 Emu corroboree

The Emu corroboree is documented by William Thomas in an undated notebook, a scan of which is found in the Robert Brough Smyth papers (SLV MS 8781, Box 1176/6, p. 116), presented here as Box 3.4. Nothing is known about what songs might have been sung in combination with this corroboree.

Box 3.4: Emu corroboree

> There are two other varieties of the Korroboery practiced by some the ... are of a more interesting kind – One of these consists of a sort of scientific representation of the manner in which the emu is captured – the bird is therefore introduced in the performance by an effigy of it as a large as life cut out of a piece of bark, & where movements are conducted by a boy behind it. – The individual personating the hunter is an Aborigl armed & as in the actual pursuit with the branch of a tree, behind which he conceals himself. – Others are engaged in endeavors to direct the attention of the bird from the designs upon its life. – A length the fatal blow is struck & the prey secured, which is indeded by a variety of evolutions & gesticulations, expressive of the great joy which such an ovation is calculated to inspire in the breast of an hungry savage. – the whole terminated with a sort of gymnastic march to a somewhat martial air & at length ends with a sudden lifting up of the arm, and a shout.

Source: Thomas, SLV MS 8781, Box 1176/6, pp. 116–17; adapted by authors.

3.1.5.4 Donkey dance

In November 1861, Thomas made a note to discuss a dance that he had either witnessed or heard about with Wonga (SLNSW MLMSS 214, Volume 21 Item 06, SLNSW_FL841095.jpg):

> Ask Wonga 24/11/61. Another Dance – near Porters on the River Plenty & Yarra – where was a large Donkey & figures like men on them &c.

This dance is also referred to again by Thomas in information collected from Wonga, where it is made clear that this was a day dance: 'Another Dance at Mr Porters Plenty & Yarra Donkey day dance & Images' (SLNSW MLMSS 214, Volume 21 Item 11).

We do not know the date of its performance, but Thomas has left a large drawing of the dance ground (see Figure 3.1). It was perhaps in the 1840s. The location was on the Yarra River near the mouth of the Plenty River. In 1838, that land was known as 'Cleveland' and was purchased by George Porter in the 1838 land sales.[19]

The full transcription of the written information on this page is presented as Box 3.5:

19 A map showing Porter's land is found in Anne Marsden and Marcus Langdon, 'George Isaac Porter: Across Two Worlds', Melbourne Mechanics Institution – 1st Committee of Management 1839, The Melbourne Athenaeum, March 2014, accessed 7 April 2024, melbourneathenaeum.org.au/wp-content/uploads/2023/06/firstcommittee_porter.pdf.

Box 3.5: Thomas's description of the Donkey dance

64 A fragment

Dances, Effigys &c

Belonging to Veinee

fire

flags, handkerchiefs of

gay colours, some 5

handkerchiefs long

5

4

3

2

& slips of *led sheits*

The flags had a very gay appear
ance – on very high gum saplings, every branch & twig cut
off, quite perpendicular, cut &
let into the ground a great depth

[written around the top of the drawing and extending down]

15 yards circumference – 20 yards in length

Two male & two females leads

the dance

Figures 3ft, 2in high & ½ man above

20 inches on the Donkey

Paget King Mt Cole Tribe
a very good man
go-up above the sky & bring em
down Book & Corrobery Kulbuli

Flags at each end

You get it netbo
what me say

[written on the left hand side of the first figure]
5 feet 8 in high

[written on the right hand side of the first figure]
5 feet 8 in high

[written sideways on the right hand side of the second figure]
All are burried when die and
the Moorup of good man
come thro. the fire

[written at the bottom]
Kunnuwurren, Queen always
go up to school
Tununderboolook Tribe beyond
Mt Cole, long long way NW

Source: SLNSW MLMSS 214, Volume 03 Item 01, SLNSW_FL827802.jpg; adapted by authors.

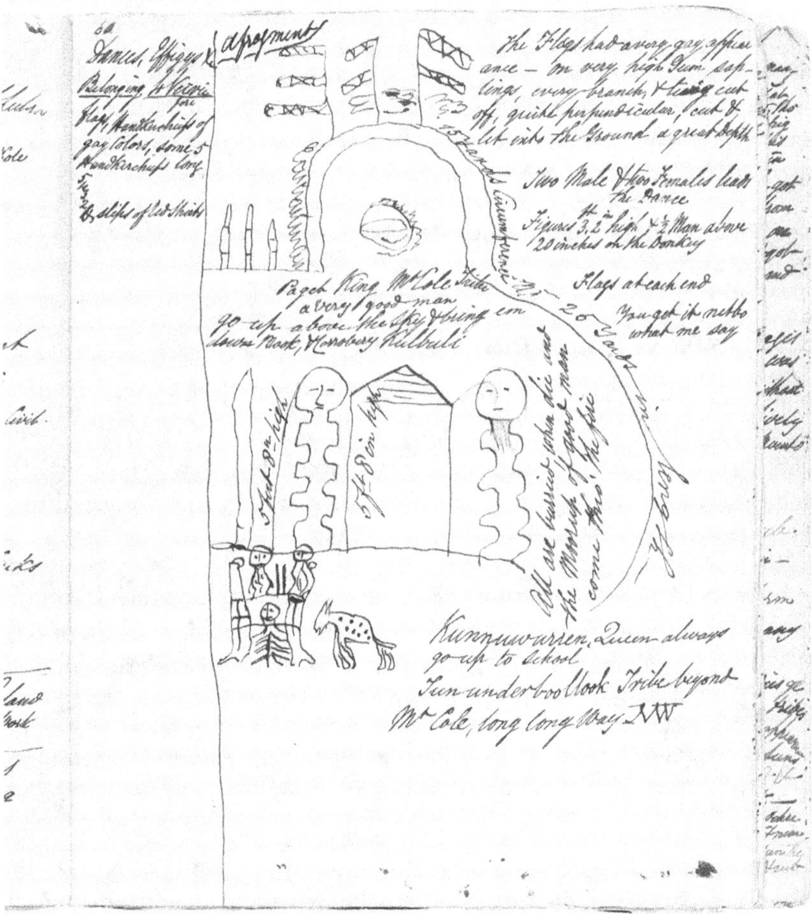

Figure 3.1: Thomas's description of the Donkey dance, 1861

Source: Courtesy of State Library of NSW (MLMSS 214, Volume 03 Item 01, SLNSW_FL827802.jpg).

Note that Mount Cole is south of the Pyrenees, in Tjapwurrung territory, and it appears that this page refers to several different events and narratives. One of them is about a king from beyond Mount Cole (in the Pyrenees, Djadjawurrung territory) going up above the sky to get 'corroberries' and one of the things he is bringing down is 'Book'; the book referred to being the Bible. It was probably viewed as a form of talisman, rather than as a religious object.

In connection with the view of the Bible as an object, it is interesting to note that when Morton Plains Bobby (see section 2.1.1) was dying at Ebenezer in 1896 the missionary approached him to read the Bible and pray. Old Bobby showed no interest in prayer but allowed the missionary to scatter holy water around and took the Bible and held it to his chest as he dismissed the missionary (Ted Ryan, pers. comm.).

Note that in the Weinnie dance (section 3.1.5.1), the 'Book' is also very prominent.

3.1.5.5 New Moon corroboree

It appears that a New Moon corroboree may have been performed every month up until 1846. In a diary entry dated Wednesday 28 January 1846, Thomas notes 'Grand Corroboree New Moon' (SLNSW MLMSS 214, Volume 03 Item 04). The new moon occurred at 9.23 a.m. Universal time on 27 January 1846, which was 7.23 p.m. Melbourne.[20]

In his diary entry for 26 February 1846, he notes 'Blacks have their last grand corroboree – New Moon' (SLNSW MLMSS 214, Volume 03 Item 04). (The actual new moon was 25 February at 7.32 p.m. Universal time or 5.32 a.m. Melbourne time on 26 February.)

The new moon would only have been visible on the day of the corroboree as a very thin sliver in the late afternoon, as the sun would have still been up at the time the moon was setting. This suggests that the New Moon corroboree was always held on the night after people observed that the moon was completely invisible. Little is known about the documentation of the phases of the moon by the Indigenous groups in Melbourne, but the accuracy of the dates of their corroborees in 1846 suggests they had a clear

20 Date and time collected from AstroPixels.com, 'Phases of the Moon: 1801 to 1900: Universal Time', accessed 30 April 2019, astropixels.com/ephemeris/phasescat/phases1801.html.

system for keeping track of the phases of the moon. Note that the Neur-re-ung-ern-er dance (section 3.1.5.2) was held at the new moon in March 1847, a full year after what Thomas described as the 'last grand corroboree'.

3.1.5.6 'Blood Feud' described in Howitt

Howitt describes what he terms a 'Blood Feud' and consequent corroboree in the manuscripts in the State Library of Victoria (MS Box 1053/2, p. 27). There are no details about any of the songs performed there. It is possible that the songs discussed in section 3.4.15 were sung on this occasion. A section of the description of the 'Blood Feud' is presented here as Box 3.6:

Box 3.6: Blood Feud

The Echuca men who were to throw at him in front of their friend in a mob. They threw so many spears and boomerangs at him that I cannot count them – there were nine to ten of the Echuca men throwing at him. At last a [spear – crossed out] a reed spear went through his side. Just then – it was about ten o'clock in the morning – a [man – crossed out] Headman from the Seymour blacks who had heard what was going to be done came up. He had followed after the Echuca men. He came in between the Echuca men and us and shouted out "Enough" "Enough" – then he said to the Echuca men – why did you come here – you should go home to your own country. The spear throwing was then stopped. They had had blood and all were friends. We had a very great corroboree after that at which all these people joined.

			Yarra Men			
			x x x x x			
Seymour				ϵ Billybellary		
King ϵ						
	x				x	
	x				x	Westernport
	x	xx		x	x	ϵ Headman
Echuca	x	xx			x	
Men	x	xx			x	
	x		ϵ Capt Turnbull			
		x x x x x x x		x x x x x x Werribee		
		Mt Macedon Geelong		ϵ Benbow		

Source: Howitt, SLV MS Box 1053/2, p. 27, hw0391.pdf, p. 40, adapted by authors.

3.1.5.7 Corroboree recorded by Georgiana McCrae

Georgiana McCrae includes a description of a corroboree in her journal (1966: 212):

> DESCRIPTION OF A CORROBOREE
>
> When there is a Corrobera or Native War Dance the men assemble to prepare for the dance, the fire being lighted (for they dance round a fire), the dancers tie wisps of straw or grass round their legs; they take their weapons in their hands and feet and wait till the Corrobera sticks begin to beat and the native songs begin, they then begin to dance with the utmost fury, beating the clubs and spears together, cooeing now and then, the clang of the weapons, the din of their songs and the trampling of their feet is enough to break the drums of one's ears. The men, women, and children each have a separate Corrobera. The Corrobera of the women is so like that of the men that it needs not be described. The Corrobera of the children ... the children light a fire and dance round it, beating time with sticks till both their arms and legs get tired. As soon as they are tired they sit down and eat their repast. Each wraps himself in his opossum rug and retires to his miamia or native hut, they then huddle themselves up in their rugs and listen to the clamour of their seniors till they fall asleep. The dance ends, the men go to their huts to sing away till day-break for the dance is kept up nearly the whole night.

3.1.5.8 Corroborees recorded by George Augustus Robinson

Robinson, starting from his 1839 journals (Clark 1998, 1), mentions a number of corroborees, some of which are mentioned here.[21] The earliest documented seems to have been on Thursday 14 March 1839. 'I paid a visit accompanied by my VDL[22] Aborigines to the corrobbery of the Port Phillip Natives.' A more substantial event was described for 28 March 1839:

> 28th March 'In the eveining corrobery and a grand display of fire works. The white inhabitants, of which there where a large assembly behaved very orderly, and the entertainment went off with exclamation. The natives highly pleased altho much difficulty was experienced in allaying their suspicions. They having been told by

21 There has never been a full study of all the records of corroborees performed in Victoria in original sources like Robinson, Thomas and newspaper accounts.

22 Van Diemen's Land.

> the depraved whites that the feast was a decoy where they would be prisoned or surrounded and sent off to VDL and be shot. This was what I had fully expected and it therefore caused me no manner of surprise.'

A ritual fight held on 11 April 1839 is described in detail (transcription from Clark 1998, 1). The figures referred to in this text are figures in Clark (1998):

> Thurs 11th April
>
> 'Am received note from Lonsdale by Billy Lonsdale informing me that the Wartowong or Barrabal Hill blacks were in the township.'
>
> 'Pm walked to the native encampment, natives all busy preparing spears and other native weapons and I was informed that the Wartowerongs had arrived and was on the encamping ground to the westward. Went and visited them. They were all seated in one group with their spears and other implements of war in their hands. These whole persons were decorated or marked in different device with a yellow earth or clay. Their heads were completely bedaubed as indicating I believe of hostile feeling. The resident tribes said they were big one sulky. They had come it appeared with the intention of redressing their wrongs done to their tribe by some of the Waverong. King Bull and Devilliers, who it appeared had murdered one of their tribe: Der.in.der.in brother. They marched to the camping ground in military way in a compact body and seated themselves on the western extremity on the bare ground. There were the men and youths 36 in number viz 25 adults and 11 lads.'
>
> 'A large assemblage of whites, many of whom were low characters, surrounding them. ½ an hour after their arrival the women and children came in carrying what we supposed at a distance spears but which proved to be sticks about seven feet long and one inch and ½ thick, called Tilbert. There were 36 individuals among the females, viz. 19 women and 17 children, total number of the tribe 72. Mr Thomas and Parker was on the ground. The women sat down about 200 yards in rear of the men at the foot of a large tree. Soon after the arrival of the women, one of the men named [blank] attended to by seven or eight others went out from the group they were divested of their garments or mantle with their waist girt and their implements of war in their hand, they took up their station on the rising ground opposite Mr Close [Clow's] house and then displayed a variety of menacing or war attitudes, a great deal of gesticulation accompanied the same. The seven or eight attendants

were also armed their position was in the following manner: [Figure 4.1]. The one that gave the challenge in front attendants a few yards in the rear. After the challenge was given they then advanced and nearby at the same time they were saluted by a loud shout or yell by the Waverongs and Tar.goon.ger.rong combined and who immediately were seen descending the hill towards the Wortowerongs and wending their way among the trees which had an imposing and pleasing effect. I advanced to meet the Waverongs and Tar.goon.ger.rongs, met Bull or [blank] who was coming down the hill by himself, told him to desist from fighting. A large party to the northward of Bull all in battle array was proceeding to the fighting ground. There were lookers on. To the south the party of Waverong and Tardoongerongs were descending and beyond them the women and children. They met on the low ground and formed in battle order thus: [Figure 4.2], and then commenced a vehement discussion, shaking their spears and clubs at each other.'

Women's fight is described 'After pacifying and separating the women I hastened to where the men were engaged. They had it appeared exchanged spears during my short absence and were in a state of great excitement brandishing their spears and making a great show of war attitudes but the principle part of their proceeding was coloqual. They, the natives, called and entreated me to get out of the way and let them fight. I said they should not. Big Jaggy Jaggy was very pert and told me to go away. I said I would not. He said buggah my eyes, but I was aware he did not understand what he was saying. Captain Baccus assisted me in some degree. Some of the whites said I was exposing myself to danger, it would not do to think of it. Mr Grills and Waterfield did not try to stop the combatants. All the whites kept at a great distance. After some considerable parley the combatants withdrew.'

'Where I shook hands with all the parties and they acknowledged that fight all gone by and by plenty at corrobbery many very interesting and affectionate scenes occurred during these occasions when the Wartowerongs came in some of the opposite party came to diferent individuals and embraced each other in the most affectionate manner. They had been at one time intimate friends or were related by marriage but the custom of their respective tribes now for a short time disavered them until the wrongs inflicted on their people or nation had been redressed. When these parties met they mutually embraced each other. In the evening I attended their corrobberies, two parties were corrobberying at the same time a large party of ruffians were on the ground but behaved in an orderly manner. A vast difference to what it was when I arrived first. The encamping ground

> presented a well lit appearance, no less than 75 fires were counted by me and I have no doubt but 100 fires or more were burning. There could not be less than 500 natives in the camp the natives wanted to know when they were to have another feast. They appeared all tolerably well contented.'

A second dance was described by Robinson from 1839 (transcription from Clark 1998, 1: 103). This names the dance as *mur.re.ne.nene*, and it was described as a religious ceremony similar to the 'White man's Sunday'. The name of this ceremony is very similar to the *Murrunawa* recorded by Thomas (see section 3.4.2), which was a daytime dance. Robinson collected his information from an Indigenous man, Mr King, who was from the Goulburn and was therefore probably a Thagungwurrung speaker. There is a photograph of Mr King taken by Carl Walter (1831–1907) and entitled '*Mr King, chief of the Goulburne* [Goulburn] *Tribe and Mary, King Billy's woman, Carngham* [Lake Burrumbeet], 1866'.[23] Robinson wrote (in Clark 1998, 1: 103):

> *Account of special ceremony closed to whites called mur.re.ne.nene. Possibly to encourage friendship b/w Pt Phillip & Goulburn blacks. Sketchy account but worth examining.*
>
> Wednesday 20 November 1839
>
> AM was informed that the natives were about having a grand ceremony. The men and women were painting themselves. That it had begun in the evening by the women cutting off the hair from the young men of the Goulburn blacks, and by their throwing about firesticks. Hastened to the spot, but they were just returning as I got to the camp. They say it is like white man's Sunday. Hence it is a religious ceremony. Mr King, a native, say they call it mur.re.ne.nene. Said they did not like white man to see it and said they could not have it again as they would all die. Said like white man's Sunday. Said they have fire in each hand and that it resembles white man's book. Mr King, I was told by my son, acted as a sort of priest. Mr King said it was like a long time ago when they were in the woods before white people came. Boy or young man named Kur.mul, also a young woman named War.er.bur.er.bine. Said they shivered like plenty cold. The men and women were painted in a fantastic manner. Their bodies red with white spots and white marks and yellow feathers of

23 The photo can be seen at Maxine Briggs, Jane Lydon and Madeleine Say, 'Collaborating: Photographs of Koories in the State Library of Victoria', *La Trobe Journal* 85: 121, 2010, latrobejournal.slv.vic.gov.au/latrobejournal/issue/latrobe-85/t1-g-t9.html.

> cockatoo and shells kangaroo teeth. The men and women marked. My son said they ran about in two or three parties as fast as they could and talking to each other. I requested the opportunity of seeing this ceremony. The men and women had a [...] appearance being painted. After the ceremony they went to Melbourne in their fancy colouring. ... Called at native camp 7pm. Thomas' man came to let me know that the natives were performing another sort of ceremony. It was all over when I arrived. It seems four women of the Waverong and Boongerong went naked to the Goulburn and cut off their hair. The Goulburn the preceding night took the Port Phillip rugs, blankets, beads &c which the others allowed and tonight the Port Phillip natives returned the compliment but it seems that the Goulburn blacks took in hand part at least some of them.

3.1.5.9 Other mentions of corroborees

Corroborees were mentioned in relation to the Melbourne area in a multitude of publications, and it is not possible to list them all here. A.W. Howitt, both in the manuscripts (State Library of Victoria, Museums Victoria) and in his publications, makes multiple references. Every time that a corroboree is mentioned relating to song, we have specifically included that in this text. There are multiple references to corroborees in Robinson's journals (Clark 1998), Thomas's journals (Stephens 2014) and in Fels (2011).

A late corroboree was documented by Frederick Revans Chapman, who arrived in Melbourne in late 1854, aged five, and lived there for 10 years. He published his reminiscences in the *Victorian Historical Magazine* in 1917 (Chapman 1917) and also in several newspaper articles, including this in the *Prahran Telegraph*, 5 January 1918:[24]

> I remember our excitement when one day, probably in 1857, 200 blacks from Gippsland arrived suddenly in Hotham street, trooping towards Elsternwick. An hour or two later a solitary gin appeared, and we gave her something to eat. She followed the tracks of the tribe in the dusty road, and when we asked her if she could see her husband's tracks, she pointed them out to us amid hundreds of others, and started away to follow them at a run, pursuing an irregular course such as he had taken when carelessly strolling with the mob. In the evening we followed the blacks, hearing that they were going to hold a corroboree, and found the whole tribe camped at a place where the

24 Frederick Revans Chapman, 'In the Fifties; South Yarra and Toorak: St. Kilda', *Prahran Telegraph*, 5 January 1918, 2. We are grateful to Ian Clark for pointing out this reference.

> trees were fairly thick. There were no residences near, save a house or two along the Brighton road, some distance away. I think the spot must have been somewhere not far from where, in later years, Sir Frederick Sargood built his fine house. [** 'Rippon Lee,' near the present railway bridge in Hotham street, Elsternwick. –Ed.] Here were [sic] stayed until midnight, mixing with the blacks, listening to their chants, and watching the strange and grave dances of the corroboree circle.

3.1.6 Invitation to the corroboree

The call to a corroboree was an important part of the process, described in Howitt (1904: 700f). This included the counting of days until the ceremony occurred using body parts (information collected for the Wotjobaluk tribe (1904: 701); also SLV MS Box 1053/6 (b), hw0421.pdf, p. 26). This body part counting probably had multiple uses.

In the State Library of Victoria (MS Box 1053/2; now photographed as hw0391.pdf, pp. 9 and 10) there is a detailed description of this process. Ball games were an important part of the corroboree, it seems:

> It was the Head man who summoned assemblies for ceremonial, or for arranged fights or for war. The messenger carried certain article which were appropriate to each kind of message as his credentials and he carried the message in his mouth. [The messenger was called Wir-i-giri and would be a young man, 'the ngŭrŭng gaeta would say to him go to ~~such~~ that mob and take the word to meet us over there' – inserted]. As an example maybe taken a message sent by a Ngŭrŭng-gaeta to assemble the people to a [ceremonial and – crossed out] festive gathering at which there would be corroborees and ball playing. The messenger would [then – crossed out] carry the [following – crossed out] yarŭk = message stick ~~&~~ the message itself was called 'Pai-ara'.
>
> The meaning of the Yarŭk is 'to bring up every man in the bush – even if a man were living with a settler he must come. If I sent such a Yarŭk I should say to the Wirigiri – take this and give it to the Ngŭrŭngaeta at such a place and tell him my Paiara. – that Ngŭrŭngaeta would then show it to his [men – crossed out] [people – inserted] and then send it on'. In company with the Yarŭk would be sent also – the Mangŭrt which is a ball of about [2½ to – inserted] 3 inches diameter made of opossum skin with fur outside sown up

> tightly. This ball is used in the favourite game of Ball play at which the different totems take different sides. With the Kulin Bunjil and Waa took opposite sides. The Mangūrt is also used to send to a friend as a token of regard. It was pointed out to me by William [that – crossed out] when I expressed a wish to send by him a small present in money to an Omeo black of my acquaintance who lived in the same hut with him that my present ought to be accompanied by a 'Mangūrt' in order to make 'Charleys heart-glad'. This was accordingly done.
>
> Together with Yarŭk and Mangūrt the messenger also carried as intimating the [full – crossed out] intended Corroboree
>
> a Brandjep = the mans apron made of a kangaroo rat skin cut into strands; a Kaiŭng = womans apron of strings [2 – written underneath] pendant [1 – written underneath] and djir-rŭn = reed which was used in some parts of the corroboree. William further said 'the Wirigirri in giving these things to the Ngŭrŭngaeta would give my Paiara and say "Kūlin send these to you to be good friends and not to grumble any more but have joy and gladness"'. —
>
> [Marginal text on p. 9 of the PDF:]
>
> The Headman makes the Yarŭk
>
> This word Yarŭk [– Yarŭk is magic – message stick is mūngū kalk or barndana]

The printed version of this information is found in Howitt (1904: 700, 701). This transcription relates to the generic invitation, but also probably refers to the Charley who was sent by Howitt to gather people for the restaging of the Gippsland initiation ceremony (see section 5.2.21.2). Note that this passage also contains reference to the 'ball', spelled *Mangūrt* by Howitt, which is probably a cognate word with Marngrook, spelled as marn-grook in Smyth (1878, 1: 176), with William Thomas given as his source. Thomas spells this word as *Man-gut* (SLNSW MLMSS 214 Volume 23 Item 02), and Robinson gives the word for 'catch it' as man.gote (SLNSW A 7086 part 4, pp. 113–48).

3.1.6.1 Welcoming words

Related to the invitation are a set of utterances recorded in Smyth (1878, 1: 133):

> If the mission is a friendly one, the stick is streaked mostly with red-ochre *(Werrup);* but if unfriendly, or for the purpose of demanding satisfaction for injuries done, or for war, then it is mostly streaked with white-ochre *(Ngarrimbul).* The principal man, in putting this stick into the hands of the messenger, and having named the tribe for which the invitation is intended, says, 'You hold this now' *(Koong-ak kinee Mirrambinerr).* 'Look out and find plenty of blackfellows' *(Yane-wat benjer oonee kolen).* 'You tell all blackfellows to come here' *(Toombooni boole-anin kolen-yan-an niool* or *Tom-buk U-mar-ko Koolin Ner-lin-go).*

Analysis of these utterances is presented in (3.2):

(3.2.1)	*Koong-ak*	*kinee*	*Mirrambinerr*
	You hold this now.		
	gunga-k	**gini**	**marrambinharr**
	take-IMP	this	you
	'You, take this!'		

(3.2.2)	*Yane-wat*	*benjer*	*oonee*	*kolen.*
	Look out and find plenty of blackfellows			
	yana-wat	**bendjeru-ni**		**guliny**
	go-2PL	several-DEM		people
	'You all go (and find) the people.'			

Note

The suffix **-ni** may be some kind of demonstrative, compare **nhinihi** 'here' in Mathi-Mathi in example (2.59).

(3.2.3)	*Toombooni*	*boole-anin*	*kolen*	*yan-an*	*niool*
	You tell all blackfellows to come here				
	dhumba-uny	**buli-anan**	**guliny**	**yana-**	**ni-yul**
	tell-?	?	person	go	DEM
	'Tell … the people to go.'				

(3.2.4) *Tom-buk U-mar-ko Koolin Ner-lin-go.*
You tell all blackfellows to come here
dhumba-k yumago kuliny nhaling(g)u
speak-IMP mob/all person return
'Tell the people to all return.'

Note

The word *umarko* is found very frequently in the Thomas papers with the meaning 'all'.

3.1.7 Learning new dances and songs

A number of the dances and songs presented here, such as the Gaiggip (section 3.4.7) and dances described in sections 3.1.5.1 and 3.1.5.2, were brought from other places and learned by the local people. Thomas noted in his diary on 22 May 1856 that this process continued well into the period of colonisation, stating that he did 'find from two blacks that I met that the Yarra blacks had all left range for the Goulbourn for 2 Moons to learn a new Corrobery' (Stephens 2014, 3: 79).

Further research into the process of learning the new songs and dances will depend on finding more sources relating to this.

3.1.8 Musical terminology in Eastern Kulin languages

Words connected with the idea of singing and the names of some types of songs are listed in Table 3.2. The regularisations in this table follow Blake (1991) but use voiceless stops, as is the practice for regularisations throughout this book.

A number of dialogues recorded by Thomas include discussion in relation to the performance of dances and songs; these are presented in section 3.1.8.2. A list of words on the relationship between corroborees and war follows in section 3.1.8.3, and decorations/ochre in section 3.1.8.4. Welcoming words were already given in section 3.1.6.1.

Table 3.2: Glossary of words relating to singing in East Kulin languages

Regularised word	Gloss	Source
yinga- **-natj** **-n/ -ny** **-in** **-k** **-ila-i** 'FREQ-IMP' **-djirri-wat** 'RECIP-2PL' **-buny**	sing	engeng 'chant' (Green), 'ditty (song)'; ying.er.net 'sing' (Robinson) Forms recorded in Thomas MSS: yengernboneit 'sing'; yeng 'hum'; yen yen; yen-gern; yeng-nyin 'hymn or song'; yengerk; yeng-erk; yen-urk 'sing, singing'; yengarbon 'you sing' yengerly 'go on sing again'; yingg-il-i; ying-derrewat 'sing all of you', ying-gahr-bay 'sing'
ngarrga **-i** 'IMP' **-un** '3SG?' **-ila-i** 'FREQ-IMP' **-ibet(j)** **-iyal** **-(w)iyn** **-natj**	dance	nar.ra.gwine rhm 'corrobbery' (Robinson); Ingargiull 'corrobboree' (Smyth 1878, 1: 425) Forms recorded in Thomas MSS: ngargee 'Corrobery, there are many kinds of corroberie'; ngargee, ngar-ri-gee 'corroboree'; ngārgoon, ngarrgohn 'corroboree, they have many kinds'; nargunile 'dance, corobory'; narraibbet 'corrobery' (MS 14624). Connected to the word of 'chief' (see section 3.1.3.2)
barran- **-dji** 'IMP'	hiss	Forms recorded in Thomas MSS: bur-ren-gee-Lyn-duk 'to hiss' bur-ren-kil-ten-dum 'hissing on passing a ... grave'
gurrinda briarr	–	Forms recorded in Thomas MSS: korindar briar 'a delightful song in memoration of an awful plague among them'
wulwuk balambalam	–	Forms recorded in Thomas MSS: Wool work bullumberlin 'a day corrobery or dance named from Butterfly'

Source: Authors.

Robinson (SLNSW A 7086 part 3, p. 35), gives the word 'one who makes a corroberry, a poet' as *yi-yote kin*. This could perhaps be regularised as **yiyud(h)gin**.

3.1.8.1 Corroboirè dialogue from Melbourne

The compiler of State Library of Victoria MS 6290 also recorded a simple dialogue about 'Corroboirè' in the Melbourne language (Box 3.7). Blake (1991) has pointed out that this source is to some extent a mixture of Eastern Kulin and Wathawurrung, but it will be treated here as Eastern Kulin, as evidenced by the use of the word **ngalamba** 'sit'. A second version of this dialogue is found in Royal Anthropological Institute of Great Britain and Ireland MS 38, pp. 131–32.

Box 3.7: Dialogue in the Melbourne dialect

Put on your pipe clay	2	Balmilly-gnŷahn
Get ready to begin	2	Win-dam-mēē
Now girls make a fire	2	Wūnga-wōōl-wēēn
Now, women, sit down	2	Ngallamby-wŏt-badgirk
You must sing	2	Yaŷn-ngāŷ

Source: SLV MS 6290; adapted by authors.

Our analysis is presented below as examples (3.3) to (3.8):

(3.3) *Put on your pipe clay*

Balmilly-gnŷahn

balmili-ngan

?

Thomas's dialogue for western Victoria (see section 2.1.2.1) also has a formative **mili**, as does the dialogue for Wathawurrung (see section 4.1.2). A root **bal-** is also found in Wathawurrung for this sentence, and the suggestion is that it may be a word **balim** 'bitter' in combination with a frequentative/continuative suffix **-ila**, or a reflexive **-il**. Thomas also records a word *bal-la-bil* 'lime' that may be related and may contain the 'having' suffix **bil** (SLNSW MLMSS 214, Volume 23 Item 02).

(3.4) *Get ready to begin*

Win-dam-mēē

wińdha-mi

WH-?

'Ready.'

The use of a WH word to mean 'ready' is also found in Thomas's dialogue for western Victoria (see section 2.1.2.1). In another part of the same dialogue, the sentence *Windamy-yannōōk-nyit* was given as 'let us proceed on our journey'. This is perhaps literally 'ready to proceed', where **yana-** is the motion verb 'go'. The suffix -mi is also found in example (3.11.4).

(3.5) *Now girls make a fire*

Wŭnga-wōōl-wēēn

wanga	**wul(u)**	**wiiny**
?	?	fire

'... fire'

The form *wulu* is not reported by Blake (1991). However, in Thomas (SLNSW MLMSS 214, Volume 23, Item 01, p. 111), there is the following sentence:

(3.6) *Molocho Kulla Wolwon ner Wein*

By & Bye then go off (or leave) and make fire

The word **mulugu** means 'later', and **wiiny** is 'fire' so it may be that the root **wulu-** means 'make fire'. The root that most closely resembles *wolwon ner* in Thomas's other records is *wool-won* 'run', which is regularised as **wurrwi-** by Blake (1991).

(3.7) *Now, women, sit down*

Ngallamby-wŏt–badgirk

ngalamb(a)-i-wat	**bagurrk**
sit-IMP-2PL	woman

'Sit down, women!'

Note that Thomas regularly glosses and translates *wat* as 'now' in SLNSW MLMSS 214, but it is clearly a 2nd person plural ending.

(3.8) *You must sing*

Yaŷn-ngāŷ

yinga-i

sing-IMP

'Sing!'

3.1.8.2 Dialogue relating to corroboree

One source of information about the corroboree, which involves dance and song, is Thomas's dialogue published in Smyth (1878, 2:127–28). After anexamination of these sentences, we consider that they probably represent actual speech, and they do give information about the attitude towards the corroboree celebration:

1. It might be cancelled due to inclement weather, and would be cancelled in view of the death of a member of the community
2. It was perhaps associated with events like the full moon.

Box 3.8: Dialogue in Smyth

Koolin ngargunner borundut.	Blackfellows' corrobboree to-night
Utur; bullito parn-min boldoneit.	No; too much tumble down rain
Tombannerreunun ngargun, bar murrumbeek umallen white money.	You tell 'em blackfellows to corrobboree, and me give them white money.
Kooliner, wongrunin bullito, borak ngargun.	Blackfellows big one stupid, no corrobboree
Kundee vener borak ngargee kooliner?	What for blackfellows no corrobboree ?
Koolin weakun ninneam werneit.	Blackfellows die last moon
Baborin borundut kooliner ngargee.	Blackfellows' corrobboree tomorrow night
Yea, ngargoon waga-bil, umarko koolin yeilve nier. Mangeit mincam uungo womon ?	Yes, big one corrobboree; all blackfellows dance. Don't you know another one moon come?

Source: Smyth (1878, 2: 127–28); adapted by authors.

Our analysis of the dialogue in Box 3.8 is presented as (3.9):

(3.9.1) *koolin* *ngargunner* *borundut*

Blackfellows' corrobboree to-night

guliny **ngarrga-nharr** **burroyn-d-uth**

person dance-2SG? night-LOC

'Blackfellow, you are dancing tonight.'

Note

In Wemba-Wemba the cognate word **kuli** always has plural reference, but if our analysis of *nner* as the 2nd person singular form -**nharr** is correct, then the form of the verb here is singular.

(3.9.2) *utur* *bullito* *parn-min* *boldoneit*

No ; too much tumble down rain -

yudha **buladu** **barnmin** **bulda-natj**

NEG much rain fall-PART?

'No, much rain is falling.'

Note

Luise Hercus reports that she witnessed a very special ceremony on a full moon in another part of Australia, so there might have been some time constraints on when these ceremonies could be held. Perhaps, if it was pouring with rain, a ceremony might have been postponed, as this sentence implies.

(3.9.3)

Tombannerreunun	*ngargun*		
You tell 'em blackfellows to corrobboree,			
dhumba-nharr-nhan	**ngarrg-uny**		
speak-2SG-1SG	dance-3SG		
bar	*murrumbeek*	*umallen*	*white money*
and me give them white money.			
ba	**marrambik**	**yumal-uny**	white money
and	1SG	give-3SG	

'You speak and say to them? that (if) they dance I will give white money.'

Notes

This text suggests that there may have been a custom of payment for performances in early colonial Melbourne.

The first word appears to have an object pronoun that is formally similar to the 1st person subject pronoun **-nhan**. This is discussed further in relation to the words relating to growing up, presented in section 3.2.6.

(3.9.4)

Kooliner	*wongrunin*	*bullito*	*borak*	*ngargun.*
Blackfellows big one stupid, no corrobboree				
guliyn-a	**wongranin**	**buladu**	**borak**	**ngarrg-uny**
man-ERG?	stupid	much	NEG	dance-3SG

'The men are foolish, there is no dance.'

Note: **borak** 'NEG' in Wathawurrung and pidgin.

(3.9.5)

Kundee	*vener*	*borak*	*ngargee*	*kooliner?*
What for blackfellows no corrobboree ? - -				
gundi	**winha**	**borak**	**ngarrga-i**	**guliny-a**
INTERR	what	NEG	dance-?IMP	man-ERG

'Why are the black men not dancing?'

Note: **kunte** is an interrogative word in Wathawurrung (Blake, Clark and Krishna-Pillay 1998).

(3.9.6) *Koolin weakun ninneam werneit.*

Blackfellows die last moon - - - -

guliny	**wiaguny**	**mirnian**	**wernatj**
man	dead	moon	last (night)

'A man died last month.'

Note: Luise Hercus (pers. comm.) felt that a ceremony would be cancelled because of a death. You would not be staying in the same place, you would head off to a different camp and that would put an end to any celebratory dance.

(3.9.7) *Baborin borundut kooliner ngargee.*

Blackfellows' corrobboree to-morrow night -

buyburruwing	**burrundj-uth**	**guliyn-a**	**ngarrga-i**
tomorrow	night-LOC	man-ERG	dance-?

'Tomorrow at night the men (will) dance.'

(3.9.8) *Yea ngargoon waga-bil umarko koolinge yeilve vier.*

Yes, big one corrobboree; all blackfellows dance.

ye	**ngarrga-uny**	**wagabil**	**yumago**	**guliny-dji**	**yulwi**	**wiya**
yes	dance-3PRES	big	all, many	person-and?	?	?

'Yes, there will be a big dancing, all the people.'

(3.9.9) *mangeit mincam uungo women?*

Don't you know another one moon come?

mangg-atj	**mirnian**	**yuwango**	**women**
make-?	moon	other	come

'?Making another moon come.'

This last line seems to suggest a belief that a dance was needed to persuade the moon to come back every month, hence a regular new moon corroboree (see section 3.1.5.5).

A somewhat different corroboree dialogue from that presented in Smyth (1878, 2:127) is found in Thomas's manuscript, presented as Box 3.9:

Box 3.9: 'On Corroberree', dialogue

Black fellow corroberee tonight	Kolingee bagrook Ngargoon Borun
Yes big one corroberre, all Blackfellows dance, don't you know another one monn kimbarly - what for stupid you	Ah Ah ngargoon wagabil, Umarko Koolinge yulve, nier naneit mineam uungo Womonx - Winda lingo wongrunin murrumbenna
Note: X a term for young male Kangaroo, Barbarista[25]	
Very good, very good where white paint me paint legs, let me paint your breast and you paint mine	Marnameek, Marnameek, Winda Narrumbul Koodywork Murrumbeek, Mullun Berkerk Brembremno Murrumbinna bar Murrumbinna Murrumbeek Brembrinno
Wantargee My stripes for bottom and privates, they are in my small bag	Wantagee murguile kihu, Euletba Billek bar boerong - kuding billing
Now where my stiicks, that will do very good blackfellows all beat em sticks	Netbo windowring nernulk, nogee marnameek tilbounoul koolin nernulk
Come come Blackfellows, you hear lubras beating their rugs, and koolin singing - Name who lead the dance tonight	Ure urebuk koolin, lubras tonboroner belp, bar koolin yengerin - nerreno koolin yengerin corroberree
Borrenuptune leads, don't you see him standing by the lubras	Borrenuptune yengerin boruin, Nelo narrin kargee terredee karbo nge lubras
Make a good large fire, cut down some boughs, and get some dry wood.	Mongan Warregut Wein, Tibunner Tarragut wyebo, bar wantagee bidderup kulk
You see them Peekaninneys how all paint themselves	Nangeit bopup monkeyn, marnameek narrumbul borkerk marnameek marnameek
Me big one stupid where my feet bands of leaves	Wongurrunin Murrumbeek, Winda murrun Tenanho
You hear Borenuptune yengerin and lubras tonboroner belp, and the fires all burning go now	Nargon Murrumbinna Borenuptune yengerin, bar lubra tonboroner belp, bar Wein yangamut - netberak
Now	

Source: SLNSW MLMSS 214, Volume 23 Item 02, SLNSW_FL814639.jpg, SLNSW_FL814641 and SLNSW_FL814642.jpg; adapted by authors.

Although this dialogue starts in a similar way to that presented in example (3.9), it contains material not found in the earlier dialogue. Our analysis is presented in (3.10).

25 We do not know what *Barbarista* refers to unless it was used for a young male kangaroo in the nineteenth century.

(3.10.1) *Kolingee bagrook Ngargoon Borun*

Black fellow corroberee tonight

guliny-dji	**bagurrk**	**ngarrg-uny**	**burruny**
man-and?	woman	dance-3SG	night

'Men and women are dancing tonight.'

Note that in example (3.9.1) the word for night carried a locative suffix, this is probably also required here.

(3.10.2) *Ah Ah ngargoon wagabil, Umarko Koolinge yulve*

Yes big one corroberre, all Blackfellows dance

nga nga	**ngarrg-uny**	**wagabil**	**yumago**	**guliny-dji**	**yulwi**
yes.REDUPL	dance-3SG	big, old	all, many	man-and?	?

'Yes (they) are dancing (a) big (one). All the men and (women) dance …'

This is similar to the line in example (3.9.8).

(3.10.3) *nier naneit mineam uungo Womon*[x]

don't you know another one monn kimbarly

ngaya	**nang-atj**	**mirnian**	**yuwango**	**wumen**
no	understand-?	moon	other	come

'(Do you) not understand that another moon (will) come?'

In the manuscript there is a note on the word *womon*, 'a term for young male Kangaroo, Barbarista'. We do not understand this note and follow the translation on example (3.9.9) where *womon* is 'come'.

(3.10.4) *winda lingo wongrunin murrumbeena*

what for stupid you?

windhalingo	**wongran-in**	**marrambinharr**
what	stupid-2SG	body-2SG

'Why are you stupid?'

(3.10.5) *Marnameek, Marnameek, Winda Narrumbul Koodywork Murrumbeek*

Very good, very good where white paint me paint legs,

manamith	**manamith**	**windha**	**ngarrambul**
good	good	WH	paint

gudiwuk	**marrambik**
?	body.1SG

'Good good, what paint … me.'

Notes

Blake regularises the word for 'good' as **manamith**, though Thomas's spelling would suggest **manamik**.

The word for 'paint, chalk' is recorded by Bunce as *N'garrambul.*

We are unable to suggest a meaning for *koodywork* at this time.

(3.10.6) *Mullun Berkuk Brembremno Murrumbinna bar Murrumbinna Murrumbeek Brembrinno*

let me paint your breast and you paint mine

mal-an	**berrka-k**	**brimbrim-(nh)u**	**marrambinharr**	**ba**
let-1SG	paint?-IMP	breast-3SG.POSS?	body.2SG	and

marrambinharr	**marrambik**	**brimbrim-(nh)u**
body.2SG	body.1SG	breast-3SG.POSS?

'Let me (put paint) on your breast and you (put it) on my breast.'

The form *berkuk* is attested by Thomas in the spellings *Ber-kerk* 'draw -write or mask' and *Ber-koneit* 'to draw' (SLNSW MLMSS 214, Volume 23 Item 02, SLNSW_FL814382.jpg).

The form for 'your breast' seems to be literally 'you – it's breast'.

(3.10.7) *Wantagee murguile kihu,*

Wantagee

wandhi-dji	**murrguyil giyu**
get.IMP	clothing for private parts

'Get my clothing for the private parts.'

Thomas defines *Murguile Kihu* as 'Stripes round males back & front parts in Corrob' (SLNSW MLMSS 214, Volume 23 Item 02, SLNSW_FL814560.jpg).

(3.10.8) *Euletba Billek bar boerong - kuding billing*

My stripes for bottom and privates, they are in my small bag

yulid(h)ba	**bilak**	**ba**	**buyurrung**	**kuding**	**bilang**
hide	bottom	and	penis	in?	bag

'(They are) for covering the bottom and penis (and are) in? (my) bag.'

Bunce (in Smyth 1878, 2) records the form *Yillertbee* with the meanings 'Cover, to hide, deposit, screen'. This is presumably an imperative form with final **-i**.

Thomas records forms *Bil-lake* and *Billake* for 'bottom'.

Bunce records the word for 'bag' as *Beelong*.

(3.10.9) *Netbo windowring nernulk*

Now where my sticks,

ned(h)bu	**windha-rra-ing**	**na(r)nalk**
now	where-?-?	corroboree sticks

'Now where are the corroboree sticks.'

Thomas defined *nernulk* as 'Sticks used in Corrobery' (SLNSW MLMSS 214, Volume 23 Item 02, SLNSW_FL814566.jpg).

(3.10.10) *nogee marnameek tilbounoul koolin nernulk*

that will do very good blackfellows all beat em sticks

nudji	**manamith**	**djilba-ngal**	**guliny**	**na(r)nalk**
enough	good	hit-1DL.INCL	man	corroboree sticks

'Enough, it is good, we two people are hitting this corroboree sticks.'

(3.10.11) *Ure urebuk koolin*

Come come Blackfellows

yarra yarra-ba-k	**guliny**
move-REDUPL-FORM-IMP	man

'Come people, move!'

(3.10.12) *lubras tonboroner belp, bar koolin yengerin*

you hear lubras beating their rugs, and koolin singing

lubras	**d(h)und(h)a-rra-nharr**	**bilp**	**ba**	**guliny**	**yinga-rr-in(y)**
lubras	knock-FORM-2SG.PRES	drum	and	person	sing-FORM-?

'Lubra, you are knocking your drum and the men are singing.'

Green records a form *Toondook* 'knock' (Smyth 1878, 2: 103) that is surely the same word. For our regularisation we assume that Thomas has incorrectly written *b* instead of *d*, as a homorganic nasal cluster is much more likely than the combination *nb*.

The **bilp** is a drum. A similar word is recorded by Hercus (1992) for Wemba-Wemba and defined as drum, made from wood (n) (cf. **pilpa** 'to bang'). See Table 1.2 and following discussion for more information about this. The word may be onomatopoeic.[26]

(3.10.13) *Borrenuptune yengerin boruin,*

Borrenuptune leads

burrun(y)abdjuny	**yinga-rra-in(y)**	**bunrun(y)**
PN	sing-?-?	night?

'Borrenuptune is singing …'

(3.10.14) *Nelo narrin kargee terredee karbo nge lubras*

don't you see him standing by the lubras

n(h)ilu	**narrin(y)**	**ga(rr)gi**	**dharra-dji**
DEM?	?	3SG.	stand-IMP?

gab-u	**nge**	lubras
here-3SG.POSS	?	lubras

'… him standing here (at) the lubras.'

Thomas records *kargee* as meaning 'He (Kargee only used when blacks don't know the parties)'.

26 We thank one of the anonymous reviewers for suggesting this.

(3.10.15) *Mongan Warregut Wein*
Make a good large fire

mungga-n	**warragat(j)**	**wiiny**
make-?	?	fire

'Mak(ing)? … fire.'

(3.10.16) *Tibunner Tarragut wyebo, bar wantagee bidderup kulk*
cut down some boughs, and get some dry wood.

djilba-na	**darra(n)g-at**	**wayibu**
cut-?	tree?-?	small

ba	**wandha-dji**	**bid(h)arrap**	**galk**
and	get-IMP	dry	wood

'Cut some small …, and get dry wood.'

(3.10.17) *Wongurrunin Murrumbeek, Winda murrun Tenanho*
Me big one stupid where my feet bands of leaves

wanga-rra-nhan	**marrambik**	**windha**	**marran**	**djinang-u**
?-FORM-1SG.PRES	body.1SG	WH	leaf	foot-CASE

'I am … where is my foot … leaves.'

Bunce (in Smyth 1878, 2) records *marron* 'leaf'.

(3.10.18) *Nargon Murrumbinna Borenuptune yengerin, bar lubra tonboroner belp,*
You hear Borenuptune yengerin and lubras tonboroner belp

ngarr(n)ga-uny	**marrambinharr**	**burrun(y)abdjuny**	**yinga-rr-in(y)**
hear-3SG	body.2SG	PN	sing-?-?

'You hear Borenuptune singing.'

ba	lubras	**d(h)und(h)a-rra-nharr**	**bilp**
and	lubras	knock-FORM-2SG.PRES	drum

'And the *lubras,* (you) are beating the drum.'

(3.10.19) *bar Wein yangamut – netberak*

and the fires all burning go now

ba	**wiiny**	**yangamat(j)**	**ned(h)bu-rra-k**
and	fire	burn?	now-?-?

'And the fires are burning?, and now …'

There are no words similar in form to *yangamut* with the meaning of 'burn' recorded in any other sources.

Unfortunately, Thomas never completed this dialogue. The final word *netberak* seems to imply that there would have been more words following.

Finally, there is a section of another short dialogue named 'Attending School' (SLNSW MLMSS 214, Volume 23 Item 02, c018660144h.jpg) that also relates to singing (Box 3.10). This dialogue goes on to talk about the Lord's Prayer, so it was perhaps hymns that were sung in the school.

Box 3.10: Extract from 'Attending School' dialogue

Call the children to come here	Kurmburgee bopul warrawe
Sit down there, first sing	Narlumby karbe, ganbony yen yen
Begin again, no you laugh	Yenerk tolo, utur garnboon murrumbinn
Now let us sing, that will do	Netbo Mal yeneerk, Nogeemee
Say the Lords Prayer	Tombak Paroogurrabun Jesus Christ

Source: SLNSW MLMSS 214, Volume 23 Item 02, SLNSW_FL814686.jpg; adapted by authors.

Our analysis is presented in (3.11):

(3.11.1) *Kurmburgee bopul warrawe*

Call the children to come here

gamba-dji	**bubup**	**warraw-i**
call-IMP	child	come-IMP

'Call the children to come!'

(3.11.2) *Narlumby karbe, ganbony yen yen*

Sit down there, first sing

ngalamb-i	**gab-i**	**ganbuny**	**yen-yen**
sit-IMP	DEM	one	sing.REDUPL

'Sit down there, first sing!'

(3.11.3) *Yenerk tolo, utur garnboon murrumbinn*

Begin again, no you laugh

yen-ak	**dhulu**	**yudha**	**garrmbu-ny**	**murrumbinharr**
sing-IMP	again	NEG	laugh-3SG	2SG

'Sing now! Don't you laugh!'

(3.11.4) *Netbo Mal yeneerk, Nogeemee*

Now let us sing, that will do

nedbu	**mal**	**yena-k**	**nudji-mi**
then	LET	sing-IMP	enough-?

'Then let (us) sing. (It) is enough.'

(3.11.5) *Tombak Paroogurrabun Jesus Christ*

Say the Lords Prayer

dhumba-k	**barr(d)-u-gurra-b-uny**	Jesus Christ
speak-IMP	knee-3SG.POSS-DO-FORM-3SG	Jesus Christ

'Speak the kneeling (to) Jesus Christ.'

Linguistic notes

Thomas shows *karbe* as 'here, and also mentions *tol-lo* as one of the words meaning 'again' (SLNSW MLMSS 214, Volume 23 Item 02, SLNSW_FL814355.jpg).

The word *Paroogurrabun* is related to forms documented by Thomas like *Par-do-gur-a-bun* and translated as both 'pray' and 'kneel'. Green wrote *Barreng-ge-gorree* for 'kneel', which we analyse as **barring-dji gurri** 'knee-PART DO', meaning literally 'do the knee-ing'. Thomas gives the word for 'knee' as *bur-din*, which we suggest can be regularised as **ba(r)rdin.** We suggest that the form in example (3.11.5) employs only the initial syllable **ba(r)rd-** and may give some insight into compounding processes in the language that involved reduction of root forms. The suffix **-dji** may be an example of what Hercus called the 'particularising suffix' for the Werkaya language, used in the creation of compounds. The translation 'the kneeling' is perhaps literally '(he) is doing the knee'.

3.1.8.3 Words relating to the relationship between corroboree and war

The following words were shown in Thomas's word lists relating to corroborees and fights (Table 3.3).

Table 3.3: Words relating to corroboree and fights

Regularisation	Original spelling	Definition	Source
ngarritj	Nar-rite	War (This is the term they use it literally means sulky–when war is declared 2 or more messengers are dispatched, their persons held sacred & take a cut stick like as used in corroberries–when peace is declared terrers are sent.)	MLMSS 214, Volume 23 Item 02
djilba-ngal 'hit-1DL.INCL'	Tilbernoul	We all knock (as in corrob duel)	MLMSS 214, Volume 23 Item 01

Source: SLNSW MLMSS 214; adapted by authors.

3.1.8.4 Decorations/ochre

Words relating to ochre and decorations noted by Thomas are presented in Table 3.4:

Table 3.4: Words relating to ochre and decorations (Thomas)

Regularisation	Original spelling	Definition	Source
d(j)errel	Terrel	A yellow clay or earth, daub in dance	MLMSS 214, Volume 23 Item 01
d(j)errelambel	Ter-rel-um-ble	Brown ochre–used in Corrob &c	MLMSS 214, Volume 21
giyalin	Kier-lin	Yellow ochre–used in Corrob &c	MLMSS 214, Volume 21
d(j)ilbanany	Til-bur-nine	Fine apron made of emu's feathers, goes all round the waist, worn by females in a single dance	Thomas in Smyth (1878, 2)
murrigal	Mur-ri-kle	Strips of opossum skin worn to hide the fundament in males when in a dance	Thomas in Smyth (1878, 2)
murrigal giyu	Murguile Kihu	Stripes round males back & front parts in Corrob	MLMSS 214, Volume 23 Item 02
na(r)nulk	Nernulk	Sticks used in Corrobery	MLMSS 214, Volume 23 Item 02

Source: Authors.

Green and Bunce gave different words for ochres (Smyth 1878, 1: 293):

> Mr. Green informs me that amongst the natives of the Yarra, white, when used for decoration in the corrobboree, is called *Trrin-in bigger-min-in;* and when used in mourning, *Trrin-in mir-rin mir-rin.* The native name for red is *Trre-barrien,* and when used in the corrobboree *Trre-barrien mirra-lin.* Black is *Woorr-karrim,* and blue (which probably means dark or dusky) is also named *Woor-karrim.*
>
> According to Mr. Bunce, red was named *Bee-bee-thu-ung,* and black *Boorooee* (meaning 'darkness' or 'night').

Green gives a detailed description of the dress for the corroboree (Smyth 1878, 1: 273):

> the full dress of an Aboriginal man, when prepared for the dance in the corrobboree, was as follows:- Around the head and crossing the forehead a piece of the skin of the ringtail opossum was worn, the ornament being called by them *Jerr-nging;* a feather of the tail of the lyre-bird was inserted between the band and the forehead (named *Kan-kano),* and around the neck and the biceps of each arm were worn ornaments made of reeds, like necklaces *(Tarr-goorrn).* Suspended from the loins by a cord, and hanging in front, was a strip of opossum skin *(Barran-jeep).* Each ankle was decorated with small boughs *(Jerrang),* and in the hands were held two sticks *(Nanalk)* for beating time. The body was painted with white clay. The double line of horizontal stripes on the chest was named *Bikamnop,* and the straight lines from the cord around the loins to the ankles were called *Beek jerrang.*
>
> The ornaments worn by a female of the Yarra tribe were few and simple. In the septum of the nose was inserted a piece of the bone of the leg of a kangaroo, called *Ellejerr;* around the neck was worn a very long reed-necklace *(Tarr-goorrn),* and around the loins was fastened the usual apron made of emu feathers and sinews, called *Jerr-barr-ning (Til-bur-nin).*

The suggested regularisations of these words are presented in Table 3.5:

Table 3.5: Words relating to dress for corroborees

Woiwurrung word as spelled by Green	Definition (based on Green in Smyth 1878, 1: 273)27	Regularisation and notes
Jerr-nging	feather of the tail of the lyre-bird, inserted between the band and the forehead and around the neck and the biceps of each arm [worn by men]	**djerranging**. This is probably based on the word **djerrang** 'leaf'
Kan-kano	forehead	**ganganu**. Blake (1991) regularises the word for 'forehead' as **minyin**, which is clearly a different word
Tarr-goorrn	a very long reed necklace, an ornaments of reeds, [worn by both men and women]	**darrgurn**. This is a compound including **gurn** 'neck'
Barran-jeep	a strip of opossum skin, suspended from the loins by a cord, and hanging in front [worn by men]	**barran-djip**
Jerrang	small boughs	**djerrang**, literally 'leaf'
Nanalk	two sticks for beating time	**nanalk**
Bikamnop	the double line of horizontal stripes on the chest	**biikamnap**. This is a compound include **biik**, earth' which also refers to the ochres
Beek jerrang	the straight lines from the cord around the loins to the ankles	**biik djerrang**. This is a compound include **biik**, 'earth' which also refers to the ochres, and with the word for 'leaf'
Ellejerr	a piece of the bone of the leg of a kangaroo, inserted in the septum of the nose [worn by women]	**(ng)iladjirr**
Jerr-barr-ning (Til-bur-nin)	apron made of emu feathers and sinews, fastened around the loins	**djirrbarrning/djilbanin**. These are probably the same word.

Source: Green in Smyth (1878, 1: 273); adapted by authors.

27 These definitions have been reordered based on the original text.

3.2 Songs documented by A.W. Howitt and Dr George Torrance

There are four songs that Howitt mentioned in the Howitt papers and/or published by Howitt and Dr George Torrance. The latter published musical transcriptions of three of the songs (Kurburu's song, Wenberi's song and the Corroboree song), which allow us to learn something about the rhythm and melody of these songs.

We do not know if Torrance had perfect pitch or if he carried a pitch pipe with him, but he begins each of the notations on the note E. We are not sure about one of the markings he uses above the staves. We recognise the accents that he indicates, but there is another marking that resembles a bowing mark. This could possibly show some type of percussion. As far as metre, he sets all of the songs to M = 100.

The sources for the songs are given in Table 3.6:

Table 3.6: Sources for Eastern Kulin songs in Howitt's manuscripts and publications

Name of song (section)	Museums Victoria	State Library of Victoria	Published versions
Kurburu's song (3.2.2)	XM 759, p. 20	Box 1053/2 (b), hw0391.jpg, pp. 26–27	Torrance (1887: 337); Howitt (1887a: 333, 1904: 420–21)
Wenberi's song (3.2.3)	–	Box 1053/2 (b), hw0391.pdf, p. 43	Torrance (1887: 337); Howitt (1887a: 331, 1904: 422)
Bundjil's song (3.2.4)	–	Box 1053/2 (c), hw0391.pdf, p. 67	Howitt (1887a: 334)
Corroboree song (3.2.5)	–	–	Torrance (1887: 339); Howitt (1904: 421)

Source: Authors.

In addition, there are the words relating to growing up, a text possibly part of the initiation process, spoken by old Bobbery (see section 3.2.6) and shown in MV XM 759, p. 27. Note that the pages are not numbered in the Museums Victoria notebook XM 759, but the reference page numbers that we employ here are the numbers of the PDF scan made by the museum.

The source for these songs is believed to have been Barak (see section 3.1.2).

3.2.1 Torrance's introduction about Barak

In his 1887 journal article, Torrance wrote a short introduction about Barak and about the quality of his singing voice. Torrance undertook a test of the compass (melodic range) of Barak's voice. Barak produced a series of pitches that Torrance (1887: 336) called an 'impromptu', which may have shown something about his concept of musical form. The full section of Torrance's discussion of this is reproduced here as Box 3.11.

Box 3.11: Torrance's discussion of the musical expertise of Barak

The native bard alluded to above (William Berak, from whom the illustrations were obtained), is an intelligent representative of his race. His voice is a baritone of average compass and not unpleasing quality. His ear also is fairly quick and accurate, though occasionally he would pause long as if trying to recall the test sounds before repeating them; and his patience, good temper, and evident pleasure at seeing his songs committed to paper, were very remarkable.

In order to ascertain the compass of this aboriginal's voice, and his power of retaining and expressing some distinct musical idea, a simple solfeggio passage was sung to him. After a brief silence, and without attempting to repeat the given sounds, he began slowly and deliberately, and with much emphasis on each note, the following impromptu:

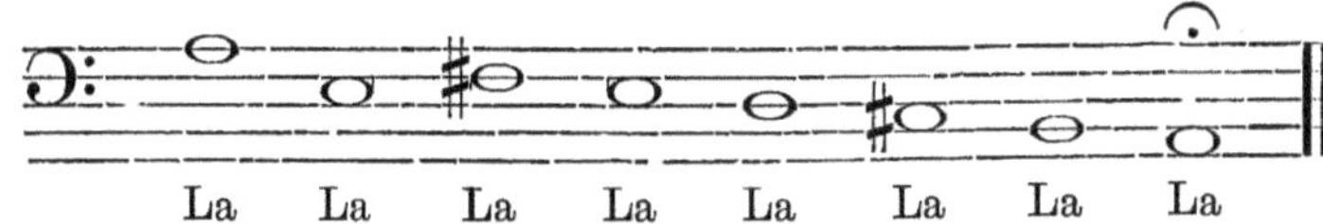

As an ear test, he then repeated accurately, pausing first as before:-

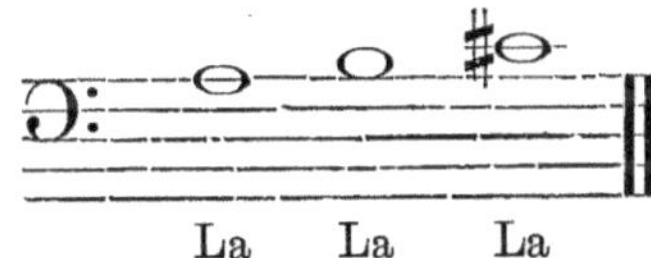

an effort which the bard voluntarily supplemented by:

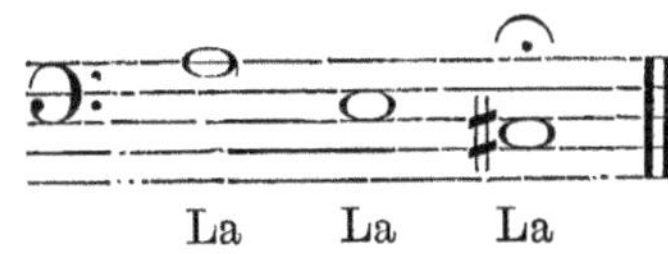

evidently much pleased with his own performance and the applause of his auditors.

Source: Torrance (1887: 336); adapted by authors.

3.2.2 Song 1 – Kurburu's song

Howitt (1904: 421) reported that this song came about after Kurburu had killed a koala (**gurrburra**), the animal after which he was named (see section 3.1.2 for the circumstances of his naming). The spirit (**murrup**) of that koala possessed him and sang this song presumably in a dream (see section 3.1.4 for a more in-depth discussion of the **murrup** or spirit). More information about traditions relating to the koala is presented in section 3.2.2.1.

The song is named by Howitt as a *gūngūrū*, a Gippsland word referring to a song that accompanied dancing (see section 5.1.2); as such we might expect it to have been performed at a corroboree, although there is no contemporary account of such a performance.

There are several versions of Kurburu's song. Probably the first version of this song was recorded in Howitt's notebook in Museums Victoria (XM 759), presented as Box 3.12:

Box 3.12: Kurburu's song, version 1

mūrūp gives the songs to doctors.

Kūrbūrū told Kūlin at Bunyip he found that Berbira coming and to keep a look out then. This man was Bunjil – Kūrbūrū the Murup of this Kurburu told him this was the man's personal name.

This bear had been killed and his murup had gone into the blackfellow. Then the murup would give him a gūngūrū.

This song is as follows

There is now

Enagourea nūng

Ngallourm ma	barrein
cut across me	track
gūrūk ba = mūrneen	
blood	
būrūn-bai	ngannūng ba
oh you hurt me	myself
chopped	tomahawk
lil-lirra	mūringa

You cut across and to coming at me on the road ahead I want to go to the foot of the range and you coming to hit

me with a tomahawk and fire me in my heart blood running to my heart

Source: MV XM 759, p. 20; adapted by authors.

The second version of this text is in manuscript drafts, in SLV MS Box 1053/2 (b). This is presented as Box 3.13:

Box 3.13: Kurburu's song, version 2

p16

Not only [is-crossed out] [was-inserted] each human individual supposed [by William-crossed out] by the Kūlin community according to King William to have a mūrŭp but each animal was also supposed to have one. For instance, as he said "The Mūrŭp if a possum is just like a possum-the Wīrriraps can see it"-

As an instance he told the following "The Mūrŭps give the coroboree tunes to the Wīriraps. A man called Kŭrbūrū who lived at Dandenong used to be able to tell the Kūlin when the Berbira were coming after there to catch them.

This man was a Būnjil (thara)-his own name was Kŭrbūrū (native bear) and he got it because when once he killed a native bear its mūrŭp enters him. After this it taught him a "gūnyūrū" which was as follows:

Enagourea	nūng	ngalourma
there is	now	cut across
barein	gurukba=	murnein
track	blood	
būrūnbai	nganūngba	
hurt	myself	
lil-lira	mŭr-ing-a	»
chopped	tomohawk	

Of this William gave the following free translation:

> "You cut across my [and-crossed out] track where I was going to the foot of the range and [you??] coming hit me and spilled my hearts blood and broke your tomohawk in my head"

Source: SLV MS Box 1053/2 (b), pages numbered 16–17, digitised as hw0391.jpg, pp. 26–27; adapted by authors.

Note that the term *Būnjil (thara)* refers to the moiety and totem of Kurburu. Howitt (1904: 126) points out that only one totem term (*thara*, the small hawk) was told to him by Barak, perhaps because this was remembered only in connection with Kurburu. Note that *thara* is also listed as one of Bundjil's sons (see Box 3.20 in section 3.2.4).

The third manuscript version of the song is in Museums Victoria (XM 759, p. 20). This is reproduced as Box 3.14.

Box 3.14: Kurburu's song, version 3

This song is as follows	
Then is now –	
Enagourea nŭng	
[–nanŭng gourdoone?? ene?? –crossed out]	
ngallourm ma	barrein
cut across me	track
	mŭrneen
gūrūk ba	= mŭrnein
blood	[dance?? –crossed out]
būrūn=bai	ngannūng ba
oh you hurt me	myself
chopped	tomahawk
lil-lirra	= mŭringa
[mŭrng –crossed out] You cut across and he coming at me in the road ahead I want to go to the foot of the ranges and you coming & hit me with a tomahawk and give me in my heart blood running to my heart	

Source: MV XM 759, p. 20; adapted by authors.

It seems that the English text commencing with 'You cut across' and running to the end of Box 3.14 might be a translation of the whole song. If this is the case, then the original song may have been somewhat longer than the texts that survive. For example, there is no mention of 'the foot of the ranges' in the text in language that we have. We are presuming that if there were mountain ranges mentioned in a fuller version of the songs, this may have referred to ranges around Mount Baw Baw.

Kurburu's song was published twice, once in the 1887 publications of Torrance and Howitt, and again in 1904, where it is given in a version together with musical notation prepared by Torrance (Howitt 1904: 420). A manuscript version of Torrance's text is found on a sheet of paper in the Howitt papers (SLV MS Box 1049/6 (a), hw0051.pdf). Howitt (1904: 421–22) writes:

> Kurburu's song serves as an example of those which are connected with the supernatural, and it brings into view a curious belief, which is found in so many Australian legends and tales, of a supernatural relation of men and beasts. It was composed and sung by a bard called Kurburu, who lived during the early settlement of the country by the whites near where the town of Berwick now stands. He was supposed to have killed a 'native bear,' and being possessed by its *Murup* or spirit, thenceforth sang its song. I was not able to obtain a verbatim translation of it, but Berak gave me the following free translation: 'You cut across my track, you spilled my blood, and you broke your tomahawk on my head.'

The song is presented without translation in the book, with the full text as in Box 3.15:

Box 3.15: Kurburu's song, version 4

ē-na gur-é-a nung ngal-úr-ma bá-reng
gūr-uk ba mirnín mirnín nge būrun bángan bödha
e-lē-re mūr-ingá : ē yam-yam mūdhan gúru bai wīrge ngū-rák

Source: Howitt (1904: 420); adapted by authors.

The musical notation in Howitt (1904: 420) is shown in Figure 3.2.

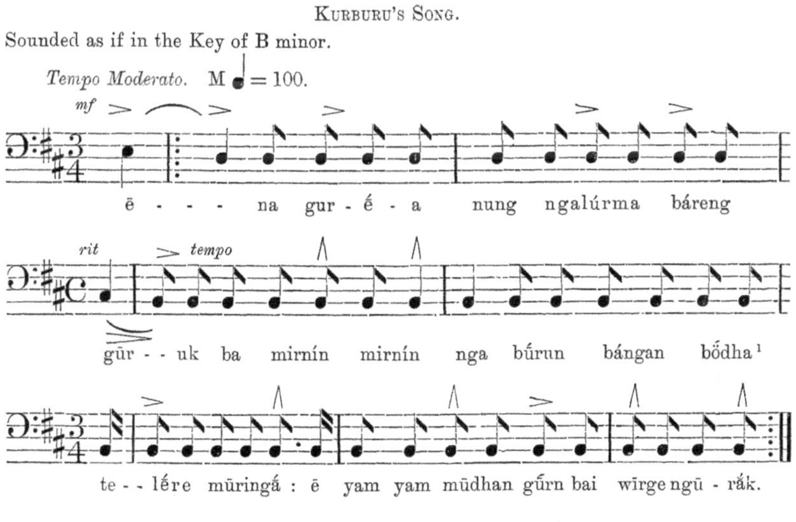

Figure 3.2: Musical notation of Kurburu's song

Source: Howitt (1904: 420); Courtesy of State Library of NSW.

The text of this song is sung in the voice of the killed koala, speaking to the singer, Kurburu. Our linguistic analysis is presented in example (3.12). The first syllable *e*, which is sung as a long note, as we see in Figure 3.2, may be a song particle, perhaps an exclamation to attract the attention of Kurburu, or a cry of despair at having been killed by him. Having a song in the voice of animal, in this case a koala, is not uncommon for Australian Indigenous songs.

(3.12)	*Enagourea*	*nŭng*	*ngalourma*	*barein*
	there is	*now*	*cut across*	*track*
	e n(g)agurr-iya	**nung**	**ngaluma**	**baring**
	SO.PRT-meet?-		cut across	track

gurukba =	*murnein*
blood	
gurrg-ba	**mu(r)niyn**
blood-and	spill?

būrūnbai	*nganūngba*
hurt	*myself*
burru-n(g)bai	**nganung-ba**
bruise-?	?-and

lil-lira	*mŭr-ing-a*
chipped	*tomohawk*
lilirra	**murring-a**
cut	tomahawk-ERG

'And so (I) met you, now, cutting across my track, (spilling) my blood … bruising me … (like) cutting with a tomahawk.'

Linguistic notes

The first two words, *Enagourea nūng*, are glossed by Howitt in MV XM 759 as 'there is' (see Box 3.12). Green recorded a word *nakorang-an-ang* 'meet', which seems to be based on a similar root **n(g)agurr-**, and we suggest that the existential 'there is' is conveyed in the language by 'met you'. This root may be related to **nganga** 'see'.

The word for 'now', which would appear to be **nung**, is not similar to other words recorded with this meaning in Eastern Kulin (see Blake 1991: 104). It may be some kind of marker of time that was attached to the previous verb.

The word **ngaluma**, with the meaning 'cut across', is not found in other sources.

The word **mu(r)niny** is perhaps the word translated in the SLV version as 'spill'; see Box 3.13 where the translation is 'spilled my hearts blood'. The word for heart is given as **durru(ng)** in Blake (1991: 83), and there is no word similar to this in the song. Nor are there any words meaning 'spilled' in other Eastern Kulin sources.

Thomas (SLNSW MLMSS 214) mentions multiple forms with a root **burru-** meaning 'break, divide, bruise'; for example, *booronganeit* 'break, bruise', *borongbun* 'broken'. The form in the song also contains a nasal followed by the labial stop.

The word **lilirra** 'cut' is not found in other Eastern Kulin sources. However, Thomas (SLNSW MLMSS 214, Volume 23 Item 03, scan page 22) includes a description of a weapon called *Lillil*, 'used by the Ovens and other blacks further north, it is a fearful weapon thrown as a Wonguim [**wan.gim** 'boomerang'] at the legs if it strikes the limb is generally broken'. Given Howitt's gloss of this word, we consider it may have been one of the verbs meaning 'cut'.

Musical analysis

The song has a range of a perfect fourth (B–E), moving stepwise downwards. Pitches are E, D, C#, B. With the exception of the downwards pitch slide at the beginning of the first two lines of music, there is a different syllable sung for each pitch with the pitch serving as a sort of reciting tone. Lines one and two show this reciting tone as being a minor third apart.

Torrance refers to the first note as an 'intonation'; this is a feature shown on each of his notations that we have included and is mentioned above, for this song, as possibly a cry from the koala as it is killed. This intonation can be found in the notations of the Western Kulin songs in this book for Songs 2 (Yerrateth-kurrk 'the owlet-nightjar', section 2.2.3); 3 (Going to the land of the dead, section 2.2.4); 5 (Jack Brown's song, section 2.2.6); 6 (Looking for dingoes – Ellis recording only, section 2.2.7); 7 (Kangaroo and dingo – Ellis version, section 2.2.8); 9 (Escaping from justice, section 2.2.10); and 10 (An ancient tale, section 2.2.11).

The pitch slides downwards a whole tone, and that pitch is repeated with one note per syllable until the end of the first 3/4 line of music. After a descent of a semitone (D–C#), the same pattern is repeated for the second line. Once the whole tone descent occurs there (C#–B), the rest of the song is sung on the B.

Torrance indicates the metre as two bars at 3/4 followed by two bars of 4/4 then back to three bars of 3/4. Each line begins with a pickup beat of a crotchet for the first two lines and a semi-quaver at the last line.

Kurburu repeated the song at least once, omitting the intonation on the E at the beginning for each repetition. Interestingly, the C# at the beginning of the second line, which follows the same pattern as the preceding intonation, is sung during the repetitions.

3.2.2.1 Traditions relating to the koala

Several texts detailing traditions relating to the koala, which are relevant to the understanding of this song, were recorded by Thomas in his October–November 1841 journals, held at the State Library of NSW. The first of these is presented as Box 3.16 and describes an altercation between the koala and humans, and an agreement that was made after, on instruction from the female spirit *Kur-ruk-ar-rook*. Her name is also spelled as Karakarook,[28] and she was a daughter of **Bundjil**, described in section 3.2.4.

Thomas speaks in more detail about Kur-ruk-ar-rook on a page of information recorded from Wonga, which includes a list of 'deities' and other supernatural beings now represented as figures in the stars/constellations (SLNSW MLMSS 214, Volume 21 Item 11 William Thomas notes relating to Wonga, 1861, c009060001h.jpg):

> Kur-rook-ur-rook – Sent wind & rain, daughter Pundgyl
>
> Tuart (stars) & Teer-reer – was 2 good blacks was caught up & made stars of and that Kur-rook-ur-rook after seeing that poor blacks had fire, went up & was a great star, NE from Melbourne
>
> Blacks always represent fire (a female) as always very good at hand in any great calamity

28 Corey Theatre (pers. comm.) has suggested to us that these might be two different entities, one whose name is based on the form **gurrk**, a root meaning 'blood' and also used to refer to females and found in the word for woman, **bagurrk**. Further research is needed to establish whether one or two female ancestral beings are referred to here.

Note that being 'caught up & made stars' is also the process described in Bundjil's song (see section 3.2.4).

The text of the agreement is given as Box 3.16:

Box 3.16: Agreement between koala and men

Superstitions agreement be tween bears & Blacks Will be found in page 74	–A Black gave me the following strange account of the altercation between the blacks and the bear – Nerlingo Yanneit Kurburu (bear) bar tombak M- maileck parn, koolin tombak utur parn, nier parn hearganner murrumbinna, molocko yanna kurboro koondee wallert bar nerlingo bar tombak, winda tarnook bar take it up all water into the tree & found the water holes all dry & for some time afraid to encamp where bears was till bears [kurukarook – inserted] told them if they would not skin him that he would no more take their tarnook. –

Source: SLNSW MLMSS 214, Volume 03 Item 01, SLNSW_FL827807.jpg; adapted by authors.

Smyth (1878, 1: 446–49) gives a number of stories about the koala and how he stole the water of the people in their buckets/drinking vessels (*tarnuk*) that include some small examples of Woiwurrung language. An extract of this text is:

> A long time ago *Kur-bo-roo* stole all the drinking vessels *(Tarnuk)* belonging to the Aborigines, and he drained the creeks, and made such a scarcity of water that all the women and young children cried aloud. The men, women, and children had no water to drink ; *Kur-bo-roo* had taken it all. Much distressed and perplexed, the Aborigines gave way at length to extreme despair, for no help came to them. *Kur-ruk-ar-ook* seeing all these things, came down from the sky, and enquired into the causes of this sorrow. *Kur-ruk-ar-ook* called all the bears to her and heard their complaints, and she heard also all that the Aborigines had to say, and she settled the quarrel thus : The blacks might eat the flesh of the bear, because it was good, but they might not skin it as they skinned common animals ; and the bears were commanded not to steal the *Tarnuk,* the *No-bean tarno,* or the waters of the creeks ; and all of them, blacks and bears, became friends by means of the counsel given *by Kur-ruk-ar-ook.* Thenceforth the bear became well disposed towards the blacks, and ever ready to give advice and help to them.

We suggest that this account is the explanation of the words in language written down by Thomas in Box 3.16, and that the words in language tell the story of Kur-ruk-ar-rook's meeting with the koalas and humans and includes some words that she spoke in language. An analysis of the Woiwurrung language portions from Box 3.16 is presented here as (3.13):

(3.13)

Nerlingo	*Yanneit*	*Kurburu*	*bar*	*tombak*
nhalinggu	**yana-(na)ty**	**gurrborra**	**ba**	**dhumba-k**
come	go-PURP?	koala	and	speak-IMP

'(She) came (down) and (told) the koala, "Speak!"'

maileck	*parn,*	*koolin*	*tombak*	*utur*	*parn,*
mayil-ek	**baany**	**guliny**	**dhumba-k**	**ngudha**	**baañ**
-1SG.POSS?	water	person	speak-IMP	NEG	water

'And (my) … the water, (told) the people "Speak!" (and they said) "there is no water".'

nier	*parn*	*hearganner*	*murrumbinna*
niya??	**baany**	**ngarga-nharr**	**marrambinherr**
NEG	water	dance-2SG	2SG

'There is no water, you should dance.'

molocko	*yanna*	*kurboro*	*koondee*	*wallert*
mulugu	**yana**	**gurrborra**	**gundi**	**walert**
later	go	koala	take.IMP	possum

'Later (she) went (and said to the) koala, "Take the possum!"'

bar	*nerlingo*	*bar*	*tombak*
ba	**nhalinggu**	**ba**	**dhumba-k**
and	come	and	speak-IMP

'And come and speak!'

winda	*tarnook*	*bar*
winda	**darnuk**	**ba**
where	bucket	and

'Where is the bucket? And …'

Linguistic notes

Only two of the words in this text are not transparent in meaning. The word *maileck* is of unknown meaning. As for the word written as *hearganner*, this may be an attempt to render the root for 'dance', **ngarrga**, with a 2nd person singular present ending **-nharr**. The 2nd person is confirmed by the presence of the free pronoun *murrumbinna* immediately following. If this is correct, these two words mean something like 'you are dancing / will dance', but dancing is not mentioned in the quote from Smyth above.

The word *koondee*, which we have regularised as **gundi**, may be related to the verb root **gunga** 'take' in an imperative form **gunga-dji** 'take-IMP'. The same form occurs in a sentence recorded in the *Koondee York Mum*[k] translated as 'Go and get me Eels' (SLNSW MLMSS 214, Volume 02 Item 01). This can be regularised as **gundi yuk marrambayik**, where the last two words are 'eel' and 'mine/for me' respectively, suggesting that *koondee* must mean 'get'. Blake (1991) regularised examples of the verb 'take' as **gunga**. For Green (in Smyth 1878, 2: 106), 'take' is *kongak*, which is **gungak** with an imperative **-k** suffix. Green (in Smyth 1878, 2: 106) translates the word *kondee* as 'to', as in the sense of purpose.

We will round out this discussion of Kurburu's song by presenting a transcription of a longer text relating to the Koala from Thomas, which is certainly the source for part of Smyth (1878, 1: 447).

Box 3.17: About the Koala

74 Superstitions Bear Kurrukerrok the Lubra's [[Grdr?]] angel	– The bear [or – inserted] (Kurboro) is [an animal – inserted] [a privileged animal – crossed out] tho [the blacks – inserted] catch it [have various superstitions respecting it – inserted] He [the bear] is not to be skinned as the Kangaroo Opossum [wombat and other animals – inserted] [??] the bear is [??] [often – inserted] consulted & his advice taken [when on a dangerous mission – inserted] in quest of the VDLand [Black – inserted] Back dangers I had an instance of this in a celebrated Western Port Black – They have a [huge – inserted [singular curious – crossed out] tradition of the bears robbing them of all their (Tarnuks) buckets [of – crossed out] [for – inserted] water & drenching a creek of water [where they were encamped – inserted] which so bewildered & distressed [them that – inserted] the [poor – inserted] black lubrars that [good – inserted] Kurrukerrok came down from the sky [& called the bears to her & draught about an amusing?? Arrangement – inserted] & it was settled [by – inserted] [between – crossed out] [good – inserted] Kurrukkerrok & the bears, that the blacks might eat them but that th[ey – crossed out] [their bodies – inserted] were not [to be – inserted] [more take their-crossed out] skin[s – inserted] [from their bodies, and the bears – crossed out] [and that the bears on this – inserted] [on this – crossed out] condition would no more molest the blacks in their water [supplies – inserted].

	Superstition [No?? -crossed out] I can vouch for him [before-crossed out] on this [head-inserted], I could mean of the bears skin which I wanted much [to obtain - inserted] - Some day, however [after much ?? - inserted] of a young black [of the Yarra tribe - inserted] who had brought in a bear early before the [red??] [to the encampt, no thu?? Blcks being in the Encampt at the time & gave him - inserted] him a good price for it stating [that - inserted] - no blacks were [present - inserted] [there -crossed out] [that - inserted] the Dr would know nothing about it - at [last - crossed out] [length - inserted] he skind it [the bear - inserted] of & I took it [away - inserted] but before
Sent to Mr Duffy paper No 15-4	the Encampt [young full?? Blcks - inserted] came in he felt very restless, his conscience [eventually - inserted] smote him, he could not put the skin on [again - inserted] nor would I give it up - he said [poor - inserted] blacks lose [em - inserted] all water [now - inserted] - frightened was he that when the first came to the Encampt - he told them [what he had done - inserted] the excitement [in the Enct which followed - inserted] was truly distressing. I tried all I could to laugh them out of it, but to no effect - [I - crossed out] [and - inserted] was forced [at length - inserted] to give up the skin, which together with the scolded bear was [by the Dr?? - inserted] ordered holie buried [as the only way of appeasing the bears & averting the calamity of loss of water - inserted].

Note: double brackets indicate uncertain readings; single brackets indicate insertions.
Source: SLNSW MLMSS 214, Volume 03 Item 01, SLNSW_FL827841.jpg; adapted by authors.

There is additional information about the Koala in the Howitt papers in Museums Victoria (XM 521, p. 3; XM 775, pp. 2–3).

3.2.3 Song 2 – Wenberi's song

This song was composed by Wenberi when the spirit of his elder brother Ningolubbel came and sang it to Wenberi in his sleep. See section 3.1.2 for more biographical information about Wenberi and Ningolubbel. Wenberi was murdered by the police in 1840, but Ningolubbel survived him by many years; if the information given by Howitt in Box 3.18 below is correct, and he died when the railway to Brighton was built, then he died in about 1859. This means that the spirit (**murrup**) of a living person could communicate a song to another living person. The background to Wenberi's song is given in Howitt (1904: 418):

> I found an interesting example of the 'inspired song' in the Wurunjerri tribe. According to Berak, it was composed by Wenberi, the henchman of the *Ngurungaeta* (Headman) Bebejan, Berak's father, to lament the death of his brother by evil magic, near

> Geelong. This is a good instance of that class of song, and also of the belief of the composer, that he was inspired by something more than mortal when composing it. In this case it is *Bunjil* himself who 'rushes down' into the breast of the singer.

No version of this song in the notebooks of field notes at Museums Victoria has yet been identified, but there is a manuscript version of this song in the State Library of Victoria. On a page headed 'The songs', after the information about Ningolubbel given above in section 3.1.2, Howitt presents the full song as follows (Box 3.18).

Box 3.18: Wenberi's song, version 1

Tumbull was buried near Bacchus Marsh at Tŭllŭrwill, in the Kŭrŭng-jerŭng balluck, of the Werribigalluk. Note his country not far off–his country was Gisborne and the hill near Gisborne–Bullanyaruck. Yarŭk killed him. I think from Echuca. He died about the time the Brighton rail[wa]y was made and the Rail[wa]y to Geelong.

His Mūrŭp came to his younger brother Wenbirri and sang this song in him when he slept:

Nge				
Tui-gar	ngal	a	ngilanba	nallūga
Let us go	then		bone	all
di'u	diru'n-ding	nga	dŭllŭr = dullur willurt	
	[gillan–crossed out] [diru'n–inserted]			
	all shining white		(this	(country)
	in that			
= willuit	[wa wein dŭn–crossed out]			
	wa-nein-dŭng			
	the rustling noise of			
[nŭng–crossed out]		Bŭnjil	mainmenngala	
		Bunjil	father of [we two–crossed out] our	
yawa-būllūk				
level				
yĕnnin	thŭllŭrmeik	nga		
singing	in my chest	this		
wūrnga'llūk		gueik		
in my inside				

This almost made me cry. Wenberri used to sing this song.

Source: SLV MS Box 1053/2 (b), hw0391.pdf, page 43; adapted by authors.

The song was later published by both Howitt and Torrance in their respective 1887 papers, itself reprinted in Howitt (1904), with musical notation from Torrance.

The version with glossing in Howitt (1904) is given in Box 3.19:

Box 3.19: Wenberi's song, version 2

Nge	tuigar	ngala	ngibenba	ngaluga
We	go	all	the bones to	all of them
diudirunding		nga	Dullur	wiluit
shining white in		this	Dullur	country
waweindung		Bunjil	mamen-ngata	yennin
the rushing noise		Bunjil	father ours	singing
thulurm-eik	nga	wur-galuk-eik		
breast mine	this	inside mine		

Berak said that this song was made on the death of Wenberi's brother, who died through evil magic in the Dullur country beyond Geelong.

Source: Howitt (1904: 422); adapted by authors.

The text and musical notation from Howitt (1904), prepared by Torrance, is given as Figure 3.3. A manuscript version of Torrance's text is found in a sheet of paper in the Howitt papers (SLV MS Box 1049/6 (a), hw0051.pdf).

Note that Torrance's comments just under the title mention that there is 'no particular key suggested. Pitched first on D# then changed abruptly to C#, D#. and B'. It is not clear if he is proposing a key when he mentions the various pitches. In any case, the notation does not display the pitch of B.

It seems clear that Torrance separately interviewed Barak to get information about songs, as we see from the following quote: 'Wenberi's song, as given by Torrance, differs slightly from it as I wrote down from Barak's dictation some time before' (1904: 422). Torrance's transcription of the text contains two more phrases, both unglossed, but on the basis of comparison with other sources for the language, we are able to suggest a translation for them.

Figure 3.3: Musical notation of Wenberi's song

Notes: [1] ñ = ny; [2] 't' in 'wurtĕin' apparently inserted or omitted at pleasure (*N.B.* –ei = 'ai' in 'rain'); [3] dh = sound of 'th' in 'this'; [4] Mueik = mweik. So also *gueik*.

Source: Torrance (1887); Courtesy of State Library of NSW.

The text of the four lines in the Torrance version is presented as (3.14). The words that do not correspond to the text in Howitt's versions are showing with underline.

(3.14) ñē … dūagḗa ngā la <u>nung ba</u> ñéllung ba
ngaluk <u>ba</u> e dèú nung ngga <u>wurtein</u> dhū̆lur wilū̆it
wā́-wundū̆n, <u>nung</u> Būngil <u>ē yā</u> mā́mengāia <u>ba yāwa bū̆lūk</u>
<u>ē</u> yern-ngen dhū̆l-lur mueik nga wū̆ru-ngā́ gueik

Our linguistic analysis of this song is given in example (3.15). The words are sung in the voice of Ningolubbel to his brother Wenberi, and the first part of the song is in the 1st person dual inclusive, singing to Wenberi and including him. The song is about the spirit of Ningolubbel going to its place of burial, and the latter part of the song shifts to the 1st person singular; that is, in Ningolubbel's voice. The burial place is conceived of as the place where the eagle, their father, and presumably moiety (**bundjil**), is singing. In this analysis (example 3.15), we present the first three lines in Italics as follows: Line 1: Text in Howitt (1904); Line 2: Gloss in Howitt (1904); Line 3: Text in Torrance (1887):

(3.15)

	Nge	*tuigar*	*ngala*	
	We	*go*	*all*	
	ñē	*dūagḗa*	*ngā la*	*nung*
	nge	**d(h)uwi-ga-ngal(a)**		**nung**
	SO.PRT	go-?-1DL.INCL		now?

	ngilanba	*ngaluga*	
	the bones to	*all of them*	
ba	*ñéllung ba*	*ngaluk*	*ba*
ba	**nyilang-ba-ngala-k**		**ba**
bone-and-1DL.INCL-?		and	

diudirunding	*nga*		*Dullur*	*wiluit*
shining white in	*this*		*Dullur*	*country*
dèú nung	*ngga*	*wurtein*	*dhū́lur*	*wilū́it*
(dha-) dharranhun	**nga**	**wurrdhun**	**dhulurrwil-uth**	
white	EMPH	many	PN-LOC	

waweindung		*Bunjil*		*mamen-ngaa*
the rushing noise		*Bunjil*		*father ours*
wā́-wundū́n	*nung*	*Būngil*	*ē yā*	*mā́mengāia*
wawind(j)-ang	**nung**	**bundjil**	**e ya**	**mama-ngal(a)**
?-PRES.PART	now?	eagle	SO.PRT	father-1PL

			yennin
			singing
ba	*yāwa bū́lūk*	*e*	*yern-ngen*
ba	**yawa buluk**	**e**	**yin(g)a-in**
and	(wide) level??	SO.PRT	sing-?

thulurm-eik	*nga*	*wur-galuk-eik*
breast mine	*this*	*inside mine*
dhū́l-lur mueik	*nga*	*wū́ru-ngā́ gueik*
dhulurr(u)m-ik	**nga**	**wurrgalug-ik**
breast-1SG.POSS	SO.PART	inside?-1SG.POSS

'*Nge*, we two are going, our bones are going, (many of them) shining white, to *thulurrwil*, … the wide level (where) *Bundyil* our father is singing inside my breast.'

Linguistic notes

The place name **dhulurrwil**, which was the burial place of Ningolubbel (see above), is clearly related to the word for 'breast', **dhulurr(u)m**, found later in the song. This is an example of word play. This word is written as *toolerum* by Green in Smyth (1878, 2: 99) where it is glossed as 'body'. The usual word for body is **marram**, and the usual word for 'breast' is **birring** or **birrm-birrm**.

The word for 'bone' was regularised by Blake as **nyilang**, with an initial palatal nasal. The word was written by Green as *nea'ling'o* (Smyth 1878, 2: 99). Howitt's manuscript is clear in having a velar nasal here, but Torrance's version indicates that *ñ* is **ny**. So we regularise this as **nyilang**.

The word *wurtein* in Torrance's version would seem likely to be **wurrdhun** 'many'. We assume this refers to the bones.

Torrance's version contains the additional words *ba yāwa bŭlŭk* after *Būngil mămengāia*. No translation is given, but in the manuscript version in the State Library, the form *yawa-būllūk* is given with a translation 'level'. McCrae (in Kenyon 1917) recorded the form *yewrarning* meaning 'wide'. It is possible that this word with a root **yawa-** refers to a wide level place where **Bundjil** is living.

If our overall translation is correct, and the last part of the song does indeed mean 'where *Bundyil* our father is singing inside my breast', then perhaps this song is using some metaphors[29] based on body parts to express emotions. In English at least, the idea of emotions is contained in statements like 'I feel [generic emotion] deep inside', and this could be what is being suggested here; however, metaphors of this kind are not so common in those Aboriginal languages that have been deeply studied from the perspective of metaphor. This translation would make sense also because the metaphor BODY PART FOR CONTAINER OF STIMULUS OF EMOTION (OF LOVE) is actually quite common in Australia.

Musical analysis

In comparing Kurburu's song (K) (section 3.2.2) and Wenberi's song (W), we will refer to each by a single letter.

29 We are grateful to Maia Ponsonnet for discussing some of the ideas in this section and for suggesting improvements to our translation.

1. The pitch slide at the beginning of the song falls a full tone (E–D) in K, whereas the pitch slide for W is a semitone (E–D#).
2. K has a range of a perfect fourth (E–B), whereas W has a minor third (E–C#).
3. W is longer than K, with 10 bars shown compared to 7 bars for K.
4. Both K and W alternate triple (3/4) and duple (4/4 or 2/4) metres.
5. The pickup notes are shown for each line of music in K, but aside from the intonation pickup note, Torrance does not show them clearly for W.
6. Both songs sing one note per syllable, with the exception of the 'gur' on line 2 in K and the 'nung' on bar 2 for W.
7. The most outstanding difference between the two songs comes during the last 2 bars of W, where, instead of repeating the lowest note, the singer goes up a semitone (C#–D).

Coda

Wenberi's life was cut sadly short, shot in an unjustified police attack, as Thomas describes in section 3.1.2. He was much mourned by his people and by his family, and some aspects of that mourning are described by Thomas in a section headed 'Ember days' (SLNSW MLMSS 214, Volume 23 Item 01, SLNSW_FL847436.jpg):

> Ember Days – the Aborigines have a [pensive?? – crossed out] [affecting – inserted] solemn custom, something similar to the ancient Christians on solemn feasts [occasions?? – inserted] – The Aborigines use it when most dire calamity have fallen upon them. I remember for a whole moon, at an hour before sun set, & about half and hour before sun rise ere was dawn, the Father & Sister and sister of the Unfortunate Whinberry taking a few embers removing a about 200 Yds from the camp [his only sister & like mourning – inserted]. After sprinkling their heads [making each a fire of bark of considerable age but no flame – inserted] sit in ashes [left of ?? fire] and pensively beholding the lighted embers till fire was extinct which generally last for 2 hours

3.2.4 Song 3 – Bundjil's song

The song presented in this section is about being blown up into the sky. It appears to be connected to both creation stories and stories of the origin of fire, and is found in Howitt's manuscript in the State Library of

Victoria, where it was discussed after some information about the stars, and names of the Pleiades, given as 'Karalgūrk, meaning a "cluster"' and the three stars in Orion's belt, given as 'Wallūng eri = the young men'. The Pleiades are associated with the 'Seven Sisters Dreaming' over a wide area of Australia extending into Victoria. The Pleiades are consistently identified as female, while the Orion Belt stars are referred to as young men, sometimes as dancing. We do not know what direct connection this song has to the Pleiades and Orion. Stories of ancestral beings being blown up into the sky are commonly found across south-eastern Australia.

We assume that this song was telling the origin of some of the stars, which Bundjil and his family became after being blown up into the sky. The stars that **Bundjil**, his wives and his six sons became are listed in Box 3.20:

Box 3.20: The stars that Bundjil, his wives and his sons became

Bunjil	Altair (α Aquilae)
His wives	γ and ε Piscis Australis
Thara	α centauri
Djŭrt Djürt	β centauri
Yukope	α crucis
Dan tun	β crucis
Tadjeri	Achernar
Turnŭng	Star in a line with Achernar & Sirius

Source: Howitt, SLV MS Box 1053/2 (b), hw0391.pdf, p. 66; adapted by authors.

Of Bundjil's six sons, Howitt also states that *Yukope* is the 'green parakeet', *Dan tun* is the 'Blue Mountain parrot' and Tadjeri is *Phascogale penicillata.*

Of *Thara* and *Djŭrt Djürt*, Howitt writes: 'These two have all red color and are the ones that burned all the country from Gippsland to beyond the Murray. Thara is being carried by Djürt Djŭrt.' And that 'Tadjeri and Turnŭng overlook the whole world and watch it'.

Note that Barak also provided information that Howitt included in several plans of the starts in a draft letter to Otto Siebert (SLV MS Box 1052/3 (a), hw0350.pdf, p. 2).

It seems that this song was sung by Woiwurrung people to commemorate **Bundjil** and his family creators being blown up into the sky. The translation we suggest is given in example (3.16), 'As a baby I stood on my legs, as a baby (I) was twisted and (brought) straight up'. The use of the word **milba** 'bend, twist' refers to the whirlwind with which the bird *Ballin Pullin* blew *Bunjil* and the people up to the sky.

Note that throughout this book, we will used the regularised **Bundjil**, where the **u** in the first syllable stands for the /u/ sound in English words like *book* and *took*. Many people now pronounce this word as if the first syllable had an /a/ vowel, rhyming with *bun* or *bungle*. Luise Hercus (1986: 234) recorded this word as **bundjil** ['bu:nɟɪl] (IPA updated from the original),[30] with the first vowel sounded as *oo* in *book*.

This song appears to relate to the Creation Corroboree song recorded in Smyth (1878, 1: 424) (see section 3.3). After relating the song of the crows that is presented there, and the creation of the crane (*Karwee*), Smyth wrote the following:

> After this, *Ballen-ballen* (the Jay), who at that time was a man, had a great many bags full of wind, and being angry, he one day opened the bags, and made such a great wind that BUND-JEL and nearly all his family were carried up into the heavens.

Howitt (1904: 430) tells a similar but more detailed version of the same story:

> According to the Wurunjerri, the Pleiades are a group of young women, the Karat-goruk[1], about whom there is a legend which recounts that they were digging up ants' eggs with their yam-sticks, at the ends of which they had coals of fire, which Waang, the crow, stole from them by a stratagem. They were ultimately swept up into the sky, when Bellin-Bellin, the musk-crow, let the whirlwind out of his bag, at the command of *Bunjil*, and remained there as the Pleiades, still carrying fire on the ends of their yamsticks. Thomas speaks of the Pleiades as Karakarook, who was the daughter of *Bunjil*. When he made two men, his son *Binbeal* caused two women to come out of the water as wives for them, and Karakarook gave each of them a *kunnan* (woman's stick).[4]
>
> 1. Karat, 'group'; goruk, feminine postfix.
>
> 4. W. Thomas, Letters of Victorian Pioneers. [In Bride 1898: 86–87]

The connection between this song and the creation of fire suggests that perhaps it was performed at the Weinnie dance (see section 3.1.5.1).

30 The original IPA transcription was ['bu:ndjIl], necessitated because of the lack of symbols :, ɪ and ɟ.

Thomas, in his long letter published in Bride, relates this to the creation story, noting that two men (*koolin*) were created by *Punjil*, and two women (*lubra*) by his brother *Pallian*, and that (Thomas in Bride 1898: 87):

> Punjil put a spear in each koolin's hand, and Karakarook, daughter to Punjil, put in each lubra's hand a kannan (woman's stick). Punjil, Pallian, and Karakarook go out with them some days, showing them how to get their food. The two men were taught to spear kangaroos, emus, &c., and the two lubras to get gum, roots, bandicoots, grubs, &c. One morning, when they awoke, they 'no see Punjil, Pallian, and Karakarook'; 'they had gone up above.' The blacks say that all this took place 'very far, far away' to the N.W., not where 'now blackfellows all about here sit down,' alluding to their belief that man and woman were first created in other countries. All agree (I mean different tribes) in stating that that country was 'far, far away,' beyond what they know to the N.W., over seas.

The whirlwind[31] and **Bundjil** are also mentioned in Thomas in an 'Outline of a Work on Aborigines' (SLNSW MLMSS 214, Volume 21 Item 12, SLNSW_FL817795.jpg and SLNSW_FL817797.jpg):

> Superstitions and religion notions. Yurren bar Yarren, when angry Pundgl cut em up all Blks [no see – inserted] Barrawang great whirlwind blow all pieces about make blks all countries all come from NW country – Tourt and Terrer Names of minor gods Agents of Bungil, 2 Young blks made conspic[uou]s by getting 1 fire from. for benefit of black man – Millowan tree where Terrer stop'd & & Tourt was burnt to death when trying to preserve fire for man on the mountn named [Munrru??] & for his exertions was caught above & made star of – [Berrul??] & Tourt – Tourt with a knife cut asunder the earth & let in all water which brought about Pt. Phillip Bay fears on loss of lock of hair, affecting tune.

While we cannot be certain, it is possible that the song that Thomas heard and described as having an 'affecting tune' is the same song as that written down by Howitt. Thomas, in his notes on a discussion with Wonga, wrote that 'Tuart (stars) & Teer-reer – was 2 good blacks was caught up & made stars' (SLNSW MLMSS 214 Volume 21 Item 11).

31 Whirlwinds are also noted in connection with other Indigenous stories, such as that of the Bram brothers from the Wimmera.

The association of **Bundjil** with stars extended well into western Victoria.[32] George Augustus Robinson wrote down the following note in a section of his notebooks headed 'Vocabulary of the Grampians and Pyrenees Blacks commencing 19 July '41' (transcribed in Clark 2002: 141):

> Punjil: a bright star which this 21 July rose in the NE. Tome and Poperchoke two small stars, one on each side of Punjil. Tome on the N and Poperchoke on the S, are said to be his wives. VDL said that fellow, i.e. that star the VDL natives said made the lakes and rivers with a flint, the + * + stars.

The reference to making lakes and rivers with a flint is another suggestion of connection between this song and the origin of fire. The origin of fire story is discussed in connection with the Weinnie dance, in section 3.1.5.1. Perhaps Bundjil's song was sung at the Weinnie dance.

The bird that caused **Bundjil** and his family to be carried up into the sky is variously described as a 'jay' or a 'musk crow'. We have not been able to establish what bird might have been referred to as a 'musk crow', but the term *jay* has been used to refer to both the 'white-winged chough' (*Corcorax melanorhamphos*) and the 'black-faced cuckooshrike' (*Coracina novaehollandiae*). The first of these is largely terrestrial and not a strong flier, and the second feeds largely on insects and other invertebrates and presents a rather docile demeanour. Both birds are thus unlikely candidates for having been able to carry **Bundjil** and family up into the heavens.

Perhaps a better choice is the 'pied currawong' (*Strepera graculina*), which according to at least one source is also called *jay*.[33] The currawongs cause greater ruckus and are a scourge to smaller birds. There are a number of species, but the pied currawong is a likely choice in Melbourne.

A further confusion with identifying this bird is the similarity of the names of two birds, given in Green (Smyth 1878, 2: 115): the 'lyrebird' *Bulinbulin* and the jay *Buleen-buleen*. These are certainly different birds, but it is tempting to regularise both as **bulin-bulin**. Hercus (1986) recorded the name of the lyrebird as ['bʊlən 'bʊlən]. However, the spelling of the name

32 Stanbridge (1858) gives the names and in some cases stories for a large number of stars and other heavenly bodies. Sirius, for example, is given as follows: 'Warepil (Male Eagle) (Sirius), a chief of the Nurrumbunguttias, and brother to War'. There is likely a connection between *Warepil* and *Bundjil*.

33 Peter Kurz, 'Minstrels in Mallacoota', Adobe Holiday Flats, October 1993, adobeholidayflats.com.au/minstrels-in-mallacoota/. Many thanks to Paul Clyne for finding this reference and also for his knowledge of the habits of the various birds and guidance as to which is the most likely candidate for this bird. Also thanks to Peter Menkhorst for similar information.

for the *jay* as *ballen-ballen* in the quote in Smyth (1878, 1: 424) and as *bellin-bellin* in the quote from Howitt (1904: 430) suggest that this bird's name was perhaps **balin-balin.**[34]

The name of bird associated with this song, the **balin-balin**, may give information as to the location of the corroboree at which it was traditionally sung. A possible location connected with this corroboree is the swampy area on the Bulleen side of the Yarra River between what is now the Eastern Freeway and the Banksia Street Bridge. The name Bulleen is believed to be taken from the name of the Bolin Bolin Swamp and some have suggested this comes from the word for lyrebird,[35] regularised by Blake as **bulen-bulen**. But perhaps the name is actually related to the 'jay' or 'pied currawong', which we will regularise as **balin-balin**, the bird that is specifically named as making the wind that blew **Bundjil** and family up into the sky.

We know that corroborees were performed nearby – see above the Donkey dance (section 3.1.5.4) that was performed near the junction of the Plenty and Yarra rivers.

Massola (1969) in his discussion of legends about **Bundjil** points to the area around Heidelberg as his dwelling place. It is also said that the Karatgurk, the five young women who had the secret of fire, lived on 'the Yarra Flats', which refers to the flat areas on both sides of the Yarra near Heidelberg. Another legend published by Massola (1969: 58) tells of the making of the Yarra. At this point we do not know the source of Massola's information, and as a result, its reliability is open to question, but it may be that the corroboree associated with Bundjil's song was traditionally performed at the Yarra Flats.

An actual example of a corroboree in which this song and perhaps also the Corroboree song (see section 3.2.5) were performed was documented by Daniel Bunce in the *Argus* of 13 April 1850, relating to a corroboree that occurred on 13 January of that year:

> The weather being very hot, I preferred performing the journey at night by moonlight. For this purpose I instructed Jemmy to call me when the constellation Orion was at a certain elevation,

34 The 'white winged chough', otherwise known as a 'jay' is called **munyukəl** in Wembawemba (Hercus 1992). No cognate form for **balin-balin** has been found in other Kulin languages.

35 See for example, Wikipedia, 'Bulleen, Victoria', accessed 13 February 2019, en.wikipedia.org/wiki/Bulleen,_Victoria.

> which would be midnight, when I intended making a start. This constellation the Melbourne blacks call Wallinjerry, which means a large man or giant. The seven stars, or the Pleiades, is called by them Moonmoondick, which word signifies a virgin. It is to the Pleiades that three of their most solemn and sacred corrobories are dedicated. They pray to her for fine weather, success in their hunting excursions &c; in fact there is scarcely a constellation or a star of the first and second magnitude which they have not a name for, and this ought to convince the more intelligent Europeans that the reasoning and discerning power of these people are of a higher order than they are generally inclined to give them credit for.

The transcription of Bundjil's song from the State Library of Victoria manuscript is given as Box 3.21:

Box 3.21: Bundjil's song, version 1

The Pleiades are called Karalgūrk, meaning a "cluster"

The three stars in Orions belt and the three other stars near are the Wallūng eri = the young men. When the Pleiades and Orion are seen it is a sign that the summer is coming.

The Blacks have a song which [has to do with Bunjil and which they sing when children are restless and cannot sleep-crossed out] [it is said was made by Bunjil and he then handed down from long age-inserted]. William says that he heard it from [his grandfather and gnouburk-inserted] the old people who said they got it from their parents who got it from theirs who got it from Bŭnjil. The song is as follows:

Bobopma	tharey thŭn	kar'eng nge
baby	leg from knees down	standing
Bobopba	melba'	ngŭrrŭ djea-nga
baby	leaning over	straight up

The Pleiades are Karalgūrk write (a cluster-a group) They are five girls. One of them has fire at the end of her yam stick. Then young women were gathering yams at the Yarra flats. They made an oven and placed them in to bake. Ballin Pallin ghost then sent the whirlwind which blew Bŭnjil up into the [a-crossed out] sky with all these people. The ovens are still for that was the last day that Karal-grūk were in the earth. A bird (a small night bird) called nari-berm-gorūk is called "the shadow" of the Karalgūrk

Source: SLV MS Box 1053/2 (b), page 45, hw0391.pdf, p. 67; adapted by authors.

Note that the word *gnouburk* is 'his grandfather', **ngaba** 'grandfather' and -**uk** '3SG.POSS'. Note also that the use of 'shadow' may relate to the many references in the moiety, totem and social organisation systems of the Western Kulin moiety where one of these is the shadow or shade of another (see for example Howitt 1904: 111 and 120f).

The song was also published in Howitt (1887a: 334), presented here as Box 3.22:

Box 3.22: Bundjil's song, version 2

Finally, I may conclude these notes by saying that there are also "lullabys" and children's songs, of which the following will serve as samples:–

The Woiwurrung had a somewhat more pretentious song, as to which my informant said he "got it from his grandfather who got it from his parents, who got it from the old people, who got it from Bunjil.

Bobópma	*tháre thŭn*	*karéngre*
baby	leg (from the knee down)	standing
Bobópma	*melba*	*ngürüjeana*
baby	lean in over	straight up

Source: Howitt (1887a: 334); adapted by authors.

Howitt (1904: 150) lists the sex totems as:

> The Wurunjerri not only had the Bat (Ngunun-ngunut) and the Owlet-nightjar (Ngari-barm-goruk), but the Kurnai totems also, under the names of Bunjil-boroin, meaning 'twilight,' for the Emu-wren, and of the Wurn-goruk for the Superb Warbler.

The bird referred to as called *nari-berm-gorūk* and described as '"the shadow" of the Karalgũrk' (Box 3.21) may be the female sex totem bird, equivalent to the **yerrateth-gurrk** of the Wemba-Wemba (see section 2.2.2 for a discussion of the sex totems).

Our analysis is presented in (3.16):

(3.16)	*Bobopma*	*tharey thŭn*	*kar'eng nge*	
	baby	*leg from knees down*	*standing*	
	bubup-ma	**dharri-dhan**	**garrang**	**nge**
	baby-?	stand-1SG.PST	(lower) leg	SO.PRT

Bobopma	*melba'*	*ngŭrrŭ djea-nga*	
baby	*leaning over*	*straight up*	
bubup-ma	**milba**	**ngirr-dji**	**nga**
baby-?	bend	up-IMP	SO.PRT

'As a baby I stood on my legs, as a baby, bring me twisting straight up!'

Notes

The word for child, **bubup**, is followed by a formative of unknown meaning **-ma**.

The word transcribed as *kar'eng nge* is interpreted here as meaning 'my leg'. Blake regularised the word for 'thigh' as **djarrang**, but the regularisation **garrang** used here is based on the form *Kal-ge-grang* given by Green in Smyth (1878, 2: 105), which would appear to be literally **galk-i garrang** 'leg of bone'.[36]

We have glossed *kar'eng nge* as **garrang nge** 'lower leg-SO.PRT'. One possible reading is that it could be **garrang-ik** with the 1st person possessive suffix **-ik**, which accords with the meaning. However, it looks as if both lines of the song have a final particle **nge/nga**.

The word for 'stand' **dharra** is also similar in form to the name of one of **Bundjil**'s sons, written by Howitt as *Thara* (see Box 3.20).

The second line of the song may be addressed to the bird *Ballin Pullin.*

3.2.5 Song 4 – Corroboree song

The fourth song documented by Howitt is described as a 'Corrobboree song' and has so far only been found in published texts: in Torrance (1887: 339), which included only the text and musical transcription, reprinted in Howitt (1904: 421). Howitt's note (1904: 422) about this song reads: 'The corrobboree song given by Dr. Torrance is one used by the Wurunjerri, but of which I have no translation'. Only the following background information was written down about it (Howitt 1904: 421):

> 'This drone or chant is repeated *ad lib.* as long as the ceremony lasts, a tone lower each time, and accompanied throughout with clapping of hands and stamping of feet.'

Torrance (1887: 336) himself wrote:

> In the 'Corroboree' the rhythmic measures are emphasized by clapping of hands and stamping of feet. When one singer or set of singers is exhausted, others in turn take up and continue the chaunt ad lib., till the wild dance is concluded.

36 The case marking with **-i** is not discussed by Blake (1991: 67) in the section on case marking. However a similar compound also with **-i** is listed for 'backbone', *galgi ngarrak* in Blake (1991: 83).

Repeated a tone lower without intonation.

Figure 3.4: The Wurundjerri 'Corrobboree' song

Source: Torrance (1887); Courtesy State Library of NSW.

We assume that this song was written down by Torrance, rather than by Howitt, but was probably also reported from Barak.

The Corroboree song as it appears in Howitt (1904) is given in Figure 3.4. A manuscript version of Torrance's text is found in a sheet of paper in the Howitt papers (SLV MS Box 1049/6 (a), hw0051.pdf).

While this song comes with musical notation, there is no gloss or translation.

The song was sung repeated, but without the initial *ē* when the version was repeated.

We have transcribed the first version of the text in Box 3.23:

Box 3.23: Text of the 'Corrobboree' song

	ē ngä	wájĕlaiya	bŭn-dĕa	gĕnunwĭl
	ngā	burdăngală	yĕlengĕa	gŏnowăra
Repeated				
	ē ngä	wăjĕlāĭya	bŭn-dĕa	&c

Source: Howitt (1904: 421); adapted by authors.

The acute accent would appear to mark accent/stress – either musical, or linguistic, or both. In our linguistic analysis of the text, presented in (91), we mark stress in the regularised line.

Although we have no information about the translation from Howitt, we suggest that it is a song giving the names of water birds. The form **gunuwarra** is well attested with the meaning 'swan'. The word recorded for 'pelican' in Eastern Kulin sources is **wadjil** whereas in Western Kulin it is **bardangal**[37] and both words appear to be in the song. Since there is only one type of pelican in Australia, *Pelecanus conspicillatus*, the use of two different words from neighbouring languages for the same bird in this song is of interest. The use of two different words from two different languages is attested in songs in other parts of Australia,[38] where it is employed for either emphasis or poetic reasons.

The song may be related to the moiety system. Although it is well known that the principal moiety division in Central Kulin was between **waang** 'crow' and **Bundjil** 'eaglehawk', it is possible that the birds mentioned in this song are totems, part of a second level/subsystem of the moiety system that was not fully recorded for the Eastern Kulin tribes. The western Victorian totem system is described by Howitt (1904: 121), and the **bardangal** 'pelican', there spelled *Batya-ngal*, is one of the 'totems' for the Wotjobaluk (Wimmera) tribe.

Our linguistic analysis is presented as (3.17):

(3.17)	*ē*	*ngä*	*wājĕlāiya*	*bŭn-dēa*	*gēnunwĭl*
	e	**nga**	**ˈwadjil-ˈaya**	**bundh-ˈaya**	**ˈdjinang-wil**
	SO.PART	SO.PART	pelican-?	bite-?	foot?-having

ngā	*burdāngalā*	*yēlengēa*	*gōnowāra*
nga	**baˈrda-ngaˈla**	**ˈyeleng-ˈaya**	**ˈgunaˈwara**
SO.PART	pelican	light-?	swan

'*E*, *nga*, (it is) the pelican, (it is) the biting one, (it is) the one legged one (crane), *nga*, (it is) the pelican, (it is) the light one, (it is) the swan.'

37 Thanks to Barry Blake for pointing this out. The spelling we have used here employs voiced consonants in keeping with Blake (1991). For Western Kulin languages, more recent sources use voiceless consonants, and the form in the Piangil varient of Wati-Wati is spelled **partangal** in Blake et al. (2011).
38 Mary Laughren, pers. comm.

Notes

Our suggestion that the song celebrates a range of birds comes from the fact that several bird names are instantly recognisable in it. We cannot know that our translation is correct, but it seems to us that a song having both forms for 'pelican' and 'swan' is likely to have meant something like what is suggested. We can assume that speakers of Eastern Kulin languages would have recognised the forms.

We think it likely that **djinang-wil**, literally 'foot having', probably meaning 'on one leg' is also a bird name, possibly referring to a crane. Howitt's manuscripts include a story about a crane called *Karwin(e)* who fought with the people. The story says that 'Bunjil came and took his wife away – there they had a corrobboree' (MV XM 775, p. 6). It is possible that this song is related to that corroboree.

The word *yēlengēa* may also have referred to a bird, literally 'the light one', or perhaps 'the morning one'. Words with initial **yeling-/yaling-** mean 'light, day, today'.

The word for 'swan', **gunawara**, is regularised with a retroflex /r/ based on cognate forms in Werkaya and Wemba-Wemba (Hercus 1986, 1992).

Musicological analysis

Torrance comments that the song is repeated 'as long as the ceremony lasts'. The range is a major third (C–E), but we do not know if subsequent repetitions would descend further. After the intonation on E, sliding downward to D, the entire text is repeated on one note, then descends a full tone to C at the syllable 'nga', which signals the next repetition of the text. The intonation is not sung at the next repetition, and Torrance says that it is not sounded any more in the performance. As for all of the songs, each pitch is sung on a separate syllable.

This song is shorter than Kurburu's song (section 3.2.2) (5 measures vs 7). As for the preceding songs, the metre shifts between duple (2/4) and triple (3/4). For this song, the syllable **nga** always appears on a crotchet, and bars 2 and 3 end with crotchets; bars 2 and 3 in Wenberi's song (section 3.2.3) also have the same rhythmic pattern. Both Kurburu's song and Wenberi's song include crotchets at the beginnings.

Unlike the other two songs, there is a distinctive dotted rhythmic figure at the end of bar 1 that is followed by 2 quavers. This pattern appears at the beginning of each repetition of the text.

This song was performed by a large group of Indigenous people at the Tanderrum ceremony, to open the Melbourne International Festival, on 3 October 2018.[39]

3.2.6 Words relating to growing up

The last of five texts that we present here may not be a song but is possibly a fragment of ritual text. It was spoken by old Bobbery, who may be the same as Bobbinary. The text is present in Howitt (1904: 255) but a more complete version was noted down in the manuscript notebook (Museums Victoria, XM 759, p. 27). The description containing this text is not obviously connected to other portions of this section of the notebook, which for example includes some information about initiation. However, the English words below the text – 'The child come from the man and the woman is only like a nurse' – suggest that it might have been used to declare that the boys, though brought up by women, were now joining their fathers and the other males. Howitt (1904: 255) explains this text as confirming the patrilineal descent among the Wurundjeri.

As such, our first feeling was that this text was a kind of 'growing up song', similar perhaps to the New Moon chant recorded in the Western Kulin languages (see section 2.3.4). The mention of 'nurse' is common to both texts. In addition, the laying out of the words in the 'line format' suggests it may have been a song/poetic text, but there is no direct evidence that this is a song text.

There are two versions of this text, the first is in Howitt's field notebook, Museums Victoria (XM 759, p. 27), presented in Box 3.24, and the second in the State Library of Victoria (MS Box 1053/2), presented in Box 3.25.

39 A version of the recording was put up on YouTube a few days later, at Dirty Pierre, 'Tanderrum Festival 2018', YouTube, accessed 10 October 2018, www.youtube.com/watch?v=B8EPgwRUr0E. As we understand it, the musical setting of this performance was done by Dr Lou Bennett, who kindly provided us with a recording of her singing it, showing the way in which the song steps up and down one full tone in melody as it is repeated.

Box 3.24: Words relating to growing up, version 1

Sometimes when the boys were grumbling old Bobbery-next to Billi Bellary-said "Why do you not listen to me-I am here-and you have my body".

Kangi mŭrrŭmbik!

Indara ngarrŭngŭn

Mŭn ngŭrlik nu nnŭn

Thŭm bŭn-murrumbik

Koy-ū-it nanthŭn narra

Murrumbik.

The child come from the man and the woman is only like a nurse.

Murrumbik = me

Indara	ngarrŭngŭn
Listen	= [language-crossed out]

Why don't you listen to this word

Source: MV XM 759, p. 27; adapted by authors.

Box 3.25: Words relating to growing up, version 2

Marriage was only allowed between Waa and Bunjil (-thara) not within the class or totem. Descent of all children through the father. The child was supposed to emanate from the male parent only as to which William made the following statements. "The child comes from the man and the woman is only like a nurse.

"I remember what Old Bobberi, who was next to Billi Billary, once said. It was at Dandenong. Some boys were grumbling and would not mind him. The old man got vexed and said: "Why do you not listen to me - I am here - and there you stand with my body" (Indara ngarŭngŭn mŭn ngŭrlik nŭnnŭn thŭmban - mŭrŭmbi-ek koy-ū-it wanthŭn-ara mŭrŭmbik)

[Indara ngarŭngŭn =listen ?-written in the margin]

Source: SLV MS Box 1053/2, page 2, hw0391.pdf, p. 3; adapted by authors.

We have not been able to make a complete linguistic analysis of this text. What we have done is presented as (3.18):

(3.18) *kangi* *mŭrŭmbik*

gang(g)i **marrambik**

DEM? 1SG

'(Here/This??) is me.'

Indara *ngarrŭngŭn*

windharra **ngarn.ga-ny**

WH listen-3.PST? PART

'For what did (s/he) listen?'

Mŭn	*ngŭrlik*	*nu nnŭn*
man	**ngarrlik**	**n(h)anhan-**
?	?-1SG.POSS	see-?1SG.PRES

'I am seeing my …?'

Thŭmbŭn –	*murrumbik*
dhumba-ny	**marrambayik**
talk-3.PST?/PART	1SG.POSS

'My talking'

Koy-ū-it	*nanthŭn*	*narra*
goy-uth	**n(h)an-dhan**	**-nharr**
?-LOC	see-1SG.PST?	-2SG.PRES

'… I saw you there.'

murrumbik
marrambik
1SG
'(Near) my body/me.'

The overall translation of this whole text seems to have been something like this:

'What is the purpose of listening to me here?
I am seeing my … my talking
I saw you there … (near) me.'

Notes

We might expect the first word *kangi* to be a deictic or a demonstrative. Green (in Smyth 1878, 2: 111) explains the demonstratives as follows: 'The same word *(Mangee)* is used thus: *-Mângee:* There in that place, or there it is; *Mang:* Here in this place, or here it is'. Earlier, he gave a form *Kon-noee* with the meaning 'that'. Thomas gives *Kar-gee* 'he', *Kar-lo* 'that or that one' and *Kun-me* 'this or this one' (SLNSW MLMSS 214, Volume 23 Item 02), which perhaps suggests a demonstrative/deictic system with initial **g-**. We suggest that **gang(g)i marrambik** can be translated as 'This is me'.

The form *murrumbik* and other forms 'based on a root **marram** "body" augmented by **b** plus pronominal suffixes' are frequently found in the records of the Eastern Kulin languages (see Blake 1991: 70). The appearance of these in genuine texts such as this confirms that these forms were used as pronouns.

The word *indara* is certainly a WH- form, meaning 'what for', based on a root **windha-**. There is a connection with phrases translated as 'I don't know', such as *indunga*, recorded by Curr (1877, 3: 526; see Blake 1991: 77). We suggest that this construction, though literally 'for what did he/she listen', actually means 'what was the purpose of hearing me if you didn't listen?'

The form *Koy-ū-it* may contain a locative **-uth** (Blake 1991: 67), and this would then suggest a place in which the boys are.

We suggest that the form *nanthŭn narra* may mean 'I saw you', where the past suffixal form of the 1st person singular **-dhan** is followed by a 2nd person singular **-nharr**, which is the form of the present tense suffix. Blake (1991: 75) gave an example of the 2nd person singular object bound pronoun as **-in**, which is the same form as the possessive. However, Thomas (SLNSW MLMSS 214, Box 23 Item 02) recorded a sentence where the 1st person subject bound pronoun, present form **-nhan** was used as an object, as *Tombarknan*, 'come and tell me', which we analyse as (3.19):

(3.19) **dhumba-k-nhan**

speak-IMP-1SG.PRES

'Tell me!'

The form **-nharr** is singular, although both manuscripts suggest that this was spoken to a group of boys, so a non-singular reference might have been expected.

The following sentences (in Box 3.26) from Thomas in Smyth (1878, 2: 127) also appear to have object pronouns, sometimes the same as the possessive form **-ik** and sometimes similar to the subject **-(nh)an**.

Box 3.26: Sentences with 1st person singular object pronouns

Give me	—	U-mar-leek.
Lend me	—	We-am-be-kan.
Bring me	—	Won-da-nun.
Send me	—	U-ro-ma-kun.

Source: Thomas in Smyth (1878, 2: 127); adapted by authors.

3.3 Creation Corroboree song in Smyth – a song of the crows

Smyth records one important song with considerable contextual information, the Creation Corroboree song. It is possible that this was sung in the same ceremonies as Bundjil's song, recorded by Howitt (see section 3.2.4).

This song comes in connection with two creation stories presented by Smyth (1878, 1: 424). The first of these is given as follows, with Smyth's footnotes, showing that the source for this is Thomas:[40]

> THE FIRST MEN.
>
> The Melbourne blacks say that PUND-JEL made of clay two males. This was in long, long ages past; and the two first breathed in a country towards the north-west *(Oodi-yul-yul wootunno per-reen N'gervein).* PUND-JEL made of *clay* two male blacks, in the following manner.-With his big knife he cut three large sheets of bark. On one of these he placed a quantity of clay, and worked it into a proper consistence with his knife. When the clay was soft, he carried a portion to one of the other pieces of bark, and he commenced to form the clay into a man , beginning at the feet; then he made the legs, then he formed the trunk and the arms and the head.* He made a man on each of the two pieces of bark. He was well pleased with his work, and he looked at the men a long time, and he danced round about them. He next took stringybark from a tree *(Eucalyptus obliqua),* made hair of it, and placed it on their heads-on one straight hair and on the other curled hair. PUND-JEL again looked at his work, much pleased *(Bul-li-to monomeeth),* and once more he danced round about them. To each he gave a name: the man with the straight hair he called *Ber-rook-boorn;* the man with the curled hair, *Koo-kin Ber-rook.* After again smoothing with his hands their bodies, from the feet upwards to their heads, he lay upon each of them, and blew his breath into their mouths, into their noses, and into their navels; and breathing very hard, they stirred. He danced round about them a third time. He then made them speak, and caused them to get up, and they rose up, and appeared as fullgrown young men-not like children,†

40 We have not yet identified where the original of this appears in Thomas's manuscripts.

> * 'In company with some blacks, I was looking at a brickmaker at work, near the new bridge over the Yarra (Prince's bridge), when a Western Port black, named "Billy Lonsdale," seeing the brickmaker smoothing the clay in the mould, said "Marminarta, like 'em that PUND-JEL make "'m Koolin."' – The *late William Thomas's MS.*

> † Some say that the first man was made at *Koorra-boort*, a place near Ballarat ; others that he was made at *Boo-err-go-en* [this is the name of PUN-JEL's brother], situated on the River Goulburn, about twelve miles above the town of Yea. He was formed, they say, of the gum of the wattle (*Acacia mollissima*), and he came out of the knot of a wattle-tree, and entered into the body of a young woman, when afterwards he appeared as a male child.

In a manuscript draft of this story (SLNSW MLMSS 214, Volume 21 Item 07, pp. 6–7, (SLNSW_FL849539.jpg and SLNSW_FL849541.jpg), Thomas wrote:

> They have a tradition of creation of man they say Pundgyl made of clay two male blacks, when pressed them to know when and where, they have invariably replied, Woody Youl Youl Wotonno, Perrin Ngervein meaning infinitely of ages [past – inserted] and distance pointing to the NW by Nth.

This story includes a line of text, referring to the creation of people in north-west Victoria. This is related to the creation stories presented in the discussion of the context of Bundjil's song (see section 3.2.4) and may be a reflection of the origins of the Kulin people in areas to the north and west of the present location of Eastern Kulin. In the manuscript version the phrase is translated as 'infinitely of ages past', with two possible interpretations, one as meaning 'plentiful winters, plentiful years', where the compound phrase **birrin(g) ngawany** may refer to winter. Thomas does give the form *per-ring-nger-wein* as 'winter' in one source (SLNSW MLMSS 214, Volume 21 Item 05). An alternative analysis is that the sentence refers not to time, but to location, a place, far away where the winter sun abounds, which is true of the north-west of Victoria in contrast to Melbourne. Our suggested analysis[41] of this sentence is presented in (3.20):

41 We are very grateful to Barry Blake (pers. comm.) and Andrew Tanner (pers. comm.) for their observations on the analysis of this line.

(3.20)	*oodi yul-yul*	*wootunno*	*per-reen*	*N'gervein*
	wudi-yal-yal	**wudhano**	**birrin(g)**	**ngawany**
	plenty	abounding	winter	sun

'Plentiful abounding winters / years' or

'The winter sun is plentiful and abounding.'

The other words in language in this text are **buladu manamith** *(Bul-li-to monomeeth)*, literally 'big good', translated by Smyth as 'much pleased', and two names of the two humans who were created, 'the man with the straight hair he called *Ber-rook-boorn*, the man with the curled hair, *Koo-kin Ber-rook*'. These can be regularised as **berruk burrn** and **gugin berruk** respectively, where the word **berr** is presumed to mean 'hair', possibly marked by the Western Kulin 3rd person singular possessor **-uk**. This word has not been found in any Eastern Kulin sources, listed in Blake (1991), but the word is probably the same root as the Wemba-Wemba word **pirrə** 'bald head with just a few tufts of hair' (Hercus 1992).[42]

Two place names are also mentioned, where the first man was made, *Koorra-boort* 'a place near Ballarat', and where the others were made, *Boo-err-go-en.* Note that this second word is clearly related to the word given by Green (in Smyth 1878, 2: 99f) for 'create', *booeegigat.*

The second creation story, which includes the Corroboree song, is as follows (Smyth 1878, 1: 425–27):

> The story is thus told by another man of the *Wa-woo-rong* or Yarra tribe :- Bund-jel was the first man. He made everything, and the second man *(Kar-ween)* he made also, as well as two wives for *Kar-ween.* But Bund-jel made no wife for himself, and after the lapse of time he came to want *Kar-ween's* wives. *Kar-ween* watched his wives very jealously, and was careful that Bund-jel should not get near them. Bund-jel, however, was clever enough to steal both of the wives in the night, and he took them away. *Kar-ween,* taking some spears with him, pursued Bundjel, but he could not find him, nor could he find his wives. But in a short time Bund-jel came back, bringing with him the two women. He asked *Kar-ween* to fight on the following day; and he proposed that if *Kar-ween* conquered he should have the women, and if Bund-jel conquered that they should be his. To this *Kar-ween* agreed. But *Kar-ween* had in his

42 Note that the form **berruk** is similar to the name of Berak, which would be regularised as **berrak**. This similarlity is probably coincidental.

> mind a different plan. And this was his plan: to make *Ingargiull* or corroboree. *Kar-ween* spoke to *Waung* (the Crow), and asked him to make a corrobboree. And many crows came, and they made a great light in the air, and they sang:
>
> Mene-Nar-in-gee,
> Targo Barra Targo,
> Burra mene long-go,
> Wah!
>
> Whilst they were thus singing, BUND-JEL danced. *Kar-ween* took a spear and threw it at him, and wounded him a little in the leg, but not in such a manner as to hurt BUND-JEL much. BUND-JEL, however, was very angry, and he seized a spear and threw it at *Kar-ween.* It was so well thrown that it went through the joint of *Kar-ween's* thigh. And *Kar-ween* could walk about no more. *Kar-ween* became sick. He became as lean as a skeleton, and thereupon BUND-JEL made *Kar-ween* a Crane, and that bird was thereafter called *Kar-ween.*
>
> BUND-JEL was the conqueror. The two women became his wives, and he had many children. After this, *Ballen-ballen* (the Jay), who at that time was a man, had a great many bags full of wind, and being angry, he one day opened the bags, and made such a great wind that BUND-JEL and nearly all his family were carried up into the heavens.

Note that this story also relates to Bundjil's song (section 3.2.4). Since the song being discussed here refers to an event that occurred before Bundjil was blown up into the sky, perhaps this was also the order in which these were performed at a corroboree?

The word *Ingargiull*, apparently the name of a type of corroboree, is based on the word **ngarrga** 'dance' (see section 3.1.8), possibly combined with the frequentative particle **-ila**.

While the words in the sentence of text in the story presented above as example (3.20), and also the name of the dance can be recognised from other sources, Smyth does not give any information at all about the possible meaning of this song but we believe we can suggest a meaning. The context as explained in Smyth is that all of the crows 'made a great light in the air' (a phrase that is difficult to interpret) and were singing while *Bund-jel* danced, while at the same time *Karween* is planning to spear *Bund-jel.* Perhaps, then, the words are an encouragement by the crows to *Bund-jel* for him to stay dancing in a particular place, to make it easier for *Karween.*

In light of this, our suggested translation of this song is presented as (3.21):

(3.21) *mene* *nar-in-gee*
minu **ngarrga-n-dji**
here dance-?-IMP
'Dance here!'

targo *barra* *targo* *burra*
dhagu **barra** **dhagu** **barra**
NEG stop NEG stop
'Don't stop! Don't stop'

mene *long-go*
minu **laang-u**
here stone?-3SG.POSS
'Here, (at) his stone.'

wah!
wa
EXCL
'Wah!'

Notes

We are grateful to Barry Blake (pers. comm.) for suggesting that *Targo* may be a negative, **dhagu**, a form found in a range of sources; for example, in Curr's *Ngooraialum* language (1887, 3: 524–29). The word *burra* (presumably **barra**) is found in both Bunce (in Smyth 1878, 2) and Haydon (1846) with the meaning 'stop, wait'.

We have assumed that since the crows were gathering in the sky, and possibly fighting, that the first line may mean 'dance here'. Thomas records **minu** as 'here' (SLNSW MLMSS 214, Volume 23 Item 02). We assume that *Nar-in-gee* is a form of the word for 'dance' (see Table 3.2).

The word *long-go* may be a 3rd person singular possessed form of the word for song, regularised as **laang**.

The final **wa!** is presumably an exclamation or cry.

3.4 Songs documented by William Thomas

Altogether, William Thomas[43] wrote down at least 11 song texts including one ritual text for regaining consciousness after a kidney fat attack. The various song texts in the Mitchell Library manuscripts, together with the song recorded in Bride (1898), are often accompanied by much more context and relate to corroborees and rituals of various types (see sections 3.4.2 to 3.4.11).

Thomas wrote a small note about the songs headed 'Miscellaneous information about songs', which is found in SLNSW MLMSS 214, Volume 23 Item 01, SLNSW_FL847436.jpg:

> Miscellaneous information about songs
>
> Songs – The Aborigines Songs tho' they may to a casual bystander appear to be composed of numerous words, such is not the case 8 to 10 words are the longest I have met with – their songs something like our dances – are generally according to the action or motion of the body – they repeat every word over the whole as they proceed and liquidate the sounds …

The songs presented here are mostly short in the number of words, and must indeed have been repeated many times. The above quote occurs immediately before the text of the second Gaiggip song (see Box 3.28 in section 3.4.1).

3.4.1 Gaiggip/Gaggip

One of the most important Indigenous songs recorded for Victoria is the Gaiggip, the text of which, in seven sections, is found in the Thomas papers (SLNSW MLMSS 214, Volume 21 Item 03, SLNSW_FL832691.jpg). It is probably the longest song text we have. The text of Gaiggip (also spelled Gaggip, Gaegape, Gageed, Gossip[44] and others) is discussed in section 3.4.7.2.

43 Thomas has been sometimes described as Rev. William Thomas, such as in Morey (1999). In his biography by Mulvaney (adb.anu.edu.au/biography/thomas-william-2727), there is no mention of him being ordained. He did certainly conduct church services in Victoria from the time he arrived in 1839.

44 In 1994, the Benalla Art Gallery had an exhibition called Sweet Damper and Gossip from which a book was produced (Fox with Phipps 1994). The word *gossip* is believed to be a mistranscription of Thomas's *gaiggip*. We are grateful to Ian Clark (pers. comm.) for pointing this out.

The importance of the Gaiggip is confirmed by the fact that it was still remembered some two generations later; Howitt stating that 'William Berak remembers some of the Kulin from the Buffalo River coming to a great meeting near Melbourne. They were the Mogullum bitch tribe, and their Head man was called Kallakallap, who had great influence and was listened to' (SLV MS Box 1053/2 (c), hw0391.jpg, p. 96). Moreover, as discussed further below, Barak made a painting of a traditional dance that is associated with the name *Gageed* (see also Vanderbyl 2019b), an alternative spelling of Gaiggip.

It seems that the Gaiggip was performed at large gatherings on two separate occasions in 1843–44 and again in March 1845. It was at the second of these the chief Kallakallap attended. The first recorded performances of it were in December 1843 to February 1844, as described in the journals of William Thomas (Stephens 2014). The background to the performance was a major gathering of tribes in Melbourne[45] in connection with the arrest and imprisonment of two Indigenous people, Polerong Billy Lonsdale and Warrodor D'Villiers, who had been accused of killing Warralim, a Western Port youth at Torridon (presumably Tooradin). Stephens (2014: 571n) notes that 'the men were released from jail on 28/12/43 and the tribes conducted their own judicial proceedings in February 1844'.

In his quarterly report for the period from 1 December 1843 to 1 March 1844, Thomas wrote (in Stephens 2014, 1: 572):

> 1843 Dec Observations on Gaggip, the purport to make Blackfellows friends. "I have every reason to believe that such is the case, one of the Devils River Blks gave me the following History of Gaggip. He stated that there are in the Australian Alps a race of Blks who live in Stone Houses made by themselves [not caves] and that some of these blacks give them, that these Blacks are very good like our Sunday, they teach Omeo, Devils River, Broken River & other Blks dances & singing, that other Blks go to these blacks & learn & when one tribe has gaggip with another from that time they are friends. This is borne out by the real Gaggip consisting of seven different Dances in each a Weapon & one is used & in each Dance a Different one, they have but 6 War implements which answers to the 6 Dances, in the 7th Dance a bough the emblem of peace, when the Dances are all finished which lasts for some days , & may be consider'd after all but as one service the barks which represent the parties engaged (each of which has a Division of seven patches of wurup (emblem of Joy & cheerfulness) are collected

45 A scan of Thomas's drawing of the encampment position of the tribes is given in Stephens (2014, 1: 571).

> together & put in the Centre of the camp in silence proclaiming good will to all around. If such a race do exist in the Australian Alps (and I see no reason to doubt there may be & many other intelligent races thro this extensive Continental island) it makes the 3rd party Civilized discovered … [He goes on to talk about stone habitations at Thorns River and Scrubby Creek, Portland district][46]

Note that the word *wurup* 'emblem of joy & cheerfulness' would probably be regularised as **wirrap**, being also written down by Thomas as *wee-reep* 'Bright red ochre (sign of Joy & Mirth)' (SLNSW MLMSS 214, Volume 21 Item 05).[47] This word is also mentioned in connection with the *Neur-re-ung-ern-er* (see section 3.1.5.2)

We do not know what language this song is, or if the word *Gaiggip* is a word in the Woiwurrung or Thagungwurrung language. As the passage above makes clear, Thomas was told by a person from the Devils River (Thagungwurrung)[48] that the dancing and singing were taught by the people from the Alps, but without information about what language they spoke. Thomas does mention the stone houses more than once in his papers, but as far as we know, there are no other contemporary references to stone houses in the Alps. In view of this we are treating this song here because it was performed in the Eastern Kulin area.

It is possible that the Gaiggip text was also sung at the Tanderrum ceremony described below (section 3.4.1.1). This was performed in March 1845 in the presence of 'old Chief Kuller Kullip' from the Mogoloombeek, a tribe who lived in the Australian Alps. The presence of this chief and the connection of the Gaiggip to the 'people from Alps' are factors that connect these two periods of performance.

Smyth (1878, 1: 136) reports that Thomas gave 'an account of a great gathering of Aborigines at the Merri Creek, near its junction with the River Yarra Yarra' and that in attendance there was a very respected old man who was named *Kul-ler-kul-lup*. Smyth (1878, 1: 137) added:

> He said that *Kul-ler-kul-lup* had informed them that there was a race living in the Alps who inhabited only the rocky parts, and had their homes in caves ; that this people rarely left their haunts but

46 This mention of stone dwellings is reminiscent of the Wati-Wati Story of the Great Stone of Balaarook (Blake et al. 2011: 224).

47 Thank you to Andrew Tanner for pointing out this reference.

48 Elsewhere Thomas notes that he got his information about the Gaiggip from two native policemen (Stephens 2014, 1: 572).

> when severely pressed by hunger, and mostly clung closely to their cave-dwellings; that to this people the Australians were indebted for corrobborees; that corrobborees were conveyed by dreams to *Kul-ler-kul-lap's* people and other Australians ; and that the men of the caves and rocks were altogether superior to the ordinary Aboriginal.

Thus it seems likely that Kul-ler-kul-lup may have been the source of the Gaiggip text, or had received it in some form from the 'Druids', even though he was not present at the 1843–44 performances. Moreover, it seems that there was some kind of connection between Gaiggip and Tanderrum. In his diary of Wednesday 7 April 1845, Thomas wrote 'take copies of the Sacred Dance of the Devils River Blacks named *New-re-ung-ern-er*' (Stephens 2014, 2: 237). This dance, which involves the use of effigies, is discussed above (section 3.1.5.2). Thomas did regard the New-re-ung-ern-er and Gaiggip as separate events, although it seems that both were brought by people from the Devils River (Taungurong) down to Melbourne. It remains unclear how New-re-ung-ern-er relates to Gaiggip, or how either of them relates to Tanderrum, but both the Gaiggip and Tanderrum include 'emblems of peace'. The seven different sections of the text are presumed to relate to these seven 'emblems'.

An important aspect of the Gaiggip is the 'Druids' who composed it. Thomas refers to these 'Druids' several times in his papers. Under the heading 'Tradition, Aboriginal Druids or inventors of Dances' (SLNSW MLMSS 214, Volume 03 Item 01, SLNSW_FL827771.jpg), he wrote:

> The Blacks say that their are in the Australian alps, who continually live in stone houses, Great wise Blacks who make blacks dream or appear to them & show them dances. I have a drawing from an old black representing one of these druids coming forth from the Rocky habitation & 6 Druids dancing.

In another part of his papers (SLNSW MLMSS 214, Volume 23 Item 02, SLNSW_FL814517.jpg) Thomas names these Druids (in language) as:

> Bul-lun-ger-me-tum – Aboriginal Druids Blacks say 1st invented songs and dances live in rocks drawn one thus:

It is likely that last two syllables of Bul-lun-ger-me-tum contain the form elsewhere spelled *middang* or *-mittung*, found as the final portion of the names of a number of Indigenous groups in the north-east of Victoria, such as the Pallanganmiddang (Blake and Reid 1999).[49]

49 Thanks to Jacqui Durrant for pointing this out.

This description is followed by a drawing to the right, which may represent the drawing referred to above ('one of the druids coming forth from the Rocky Habitation').

On Wednesday 10 January 1844, Thomas noted in his diary: 'One sketches me the ranges where Wise Black fellows make Gaggip live' (Stephens 2014, 2: 3).

Thomas (SLNSW MLMSS 214, Volume 23 Item 01, SLNSW_FL847484.jpg) adds that:

> A further race have been made known to me [by my blacks & other ?? – inserted] inhabiting the Australian alps, a portion of which people never go out to seek their food but live on what is given them and herbs. This [people the blacks say – inserted] have large stone houses very large and are always singing and making Gaggips for Black fellows.

A number of entries from Thomas's diaries (Stephens 2014, 1: 571–72; originals in SLNSW MLMSS 214, Volume 03 Item 02, c009910139h.jpg to c009910141h.jpg) at this time refer to the Gaiggip as commencing on Friday 22 December 1843, and running for at least six days:

> Saturday 23rd December 1843 … Blks have 2nd Gaiggip. Some more N. Pol[ice] arrive. Karroby at evening very grand
>
> Sunday 24 December 1843 … had much trouble in keeping them from having a Gaggip but succeeded till the Evening when they had one
>
> Wednesday 27 December 1843 … Children promise to come following day, last day of Gaggip which has now lasted 6 days [margin note: Gaggip in fear of Police].

The reference 'Gaggip in fear of Police' may mean that some White authorities in Melbourne at the time tried to ban the performance of the Gaiggip; the ceremony perhaps continued as long as the two men mentioned above were in custody.

In a further discussion about the Gaiggip, Thomas adds in his paper for Duffy (Stephens 2014, 2: 95n):

> that the Omeo, Devil River, Twofold Bay, Ovens, Murrumbidgee and other tribes send there old men Doctors there to learn what is good do sing, Gaegape like white man Sundays church big one

> Sunday, And I am informed that from these sages of the rocks or druids have sprung these new series of sacred dances with such curious effigies, altogether new from anything that have as yet been heard or seem among the Aborigines of Victoria.

A very detailed description of the ceremony at which it was performed is found in a letter from J.H. McCabe, published in the *Port Phillip Gazette*, Saturday 11 February 1843, page 3:[50]

> ORIGINAL CORRESPONDENCE.
> ABORIGINAL CEREMONY.
>
> To the Editor of the. Port Phillip Gazette.
>
> Sir – Having been eye-witness to a ceremonial of the Aborigines of which I do not remember to have seen mention in any work relating to them, I beg to send you the following account: –
>
> On Saturday morning last, I was informed by some of the blacks, that a corrobera would take place in the afternoon. This being an unusual proceeding, I walked to the Merri Creek, and fortunately reached the miam miams as the ceremony commenced. The lubras were seated, and had just commenced singing in a more plaintive manner than I can recollect to have heard them before; a few of the men were with them beating time with their sticks, and all were intently looking towards the bank of the creek (about 200 yards distant) from which, after some time, I saw a body of the men advancing, consisting of between 40 and 50. They were naked as at an ordinary corrobera – some few of them being entirely painted red, the hair also plastered with red clay – the remainder were without any ornament. Each of them had standing up from his forehead a thin twig, on the top of which was fastened a small bunch of white Cockatoo feathers; in each hand they carried green branches; they advanced very slow, their bodies slightly bent, stamping their feet to the tune of the music, and whisking the branches on alternative sides of the legs, uttering a hissing exclamation at each step. Their march was serpentine, each treading nearly in the footsteps of the foregoing, and in silence towards the spot where the singers sat; on arriving at which they formed a circle, of which the singers were in the centre, and stood keeping time to the music with their feet, but the branches were then, first with the right hand, and then with the left, advanced with a sudden motion of the arm straight out from the shoulder towards his neighbour, the effect

50 Another transcription was published by Connecting with Country on Facebook, 1 September 2020, accessed 1 December 2021, www.facebook.com/conwithco/posts/163320808711895.

of which was very pleasing. They continued this for a few minutes, when they started at full speed to the place from whence I at first saw them advance; in a short time they again came forward in a serpentine direction as before, but they had now green branches only in the left hand, while in the right they carried wands covered with the down of the cockatoo; their manner of advancing was different, as it consisted of a regular step and a bounding one, the time being carefully kept with the music, and the hissing exclamations also continued. The circle was formed round the singers as before, but at a given signal, the singers arose – the men forming the procession heading them, dancing and shouting – much in the fashion, I recollect, in old engravings of the Israelites dancing before the Ark. The whole party proceeded to the bank or creek; I followed them, and there found a bark miam miam built, the outside of which was carefully cut and painted in the same style as their shields; the singers were ranged on one side, and the men continued dancing and shouting on the opposite side, advancing reverently and touching the miam miam with the wands, which they at last threw on the roof of it with tremendous yells, and the ceremony was at end, occupying in the whole about three-quarters of an hour.

The only explanation I could get from the blacks was, that they did not call this a corrobera, but a 'gageed' – that it was black fellows Sunday, and that it was like going to church.

It should also, perhaps, be noted that a number of the natives stood at a considerable distance from the spot where the ceremony took place; and one of them told me they could not go to it, but either could not or would not, tell me the reason. I find it impossible to convey any description of the extraordinary scene; but as all circumstances connected with the customs and manner of the Aborigines are of interest, I have attempted to be as minute as possible in describing this ceremony, of which probably some of your readers may be able to give an explanation.

Yours Truly
Melbourne, Feb 8, 1843
J. H. M'CABE.

[Since receiving the above very interesting communication, we have conversed with several of the more civilized Port Phillip natives, and have ascertained that the ceremony of 'gageed' is an incantation – the intention of which is to remove the terrible epidemic under which so many of them are labouring, from their own tribe to the Goulburn tribe. They state also, that the red pigment is to represent blood. There is clearly some connection with the arrival of a great man from another tribe – probably a sort of priest. It is very interesting

> to compare this rite with that detailed in the *Port Phillip Magazine* for Feb. page 29. *Where are the grammar and dictionary of the Black Protectors!* - Ed. P.P.G.]

Some additional information is found in a book by William Hull[51] (1846) who gave some material that does not appear in McCabe's published letter:

> There are, also, some rites of a more than usually secret and solemn character occasionally practised: in the spring of 1843, *Mr. M'Cabe*, a man who had a most remarkable influence with the natives was informed (sub rosa[52]) that a very grand Coroboree – 'not for white man to see' – would take place in a secluded spot on the *Merri Creek*, about five miles from Melbourne. Mr M'Cabe, with his black guide, went out about where Mr. Dight's mill now stands, and saw a huge and rude *Temple* of stringy bark, covered with various hieroglyphics in white chalk. The only Natives present were old men, and the ceremonies altogether of a very impressive character.
>
> Hoping to obtain the materials of which the *Temple* was composed, Mr. M'Cabe hastened home and proceeded at daybreak with a bullock dray for that purpose. On his arrival the Temple had vanished; nor could he recognise the exact spot of the incantation; subsequently he ascertained that his presence had been detected, and all relics purposely destroyed.

One further description of the Gaiggip is mentioned in Howitt (1904: 492), relating the Gaiggip song to Bundjil and referencing his uncle Richard who had written a longer description of the Gaiggip many years before:

> One of the legends about Bunjil in the Woëworung tribe is perpetuated in a corrobboree which was witnessed in the early forties by Richard Howitt. The legend is that Bunjil held out his hand to the sun *(Gerer)* and warmed it, and the sun warmed the earth, which opened, and blackfellows came out and danced this corrobboree, which is called *Gayip*. At it images curiously carved in bark were exhibited.

Richard Howitt's description of the Gaiggip dance ceremony (1845: 191f) is reproduced here in full. In our view, this description links the Gaiggip song to many of the other songs and traditions already discussed here, to the role of Karakarook (section 3.2.2.1), to the Creation Corroboree song

51 Although the title of this book is *Remarks on the Probable Origin and Antiquity of the Aboriginal Natives of New South Wales*, it should be noted that at this time what is now Victoria was within the colony of New South Wales. We are grateful to Ian Clark for pointing out this reference.

52 A Latin term meaning 'happening or done in secret'.

relating to the crows (section 3.3), to Bundjil's song, the creation of fire and the ancestral spirits being blown up into the stars (section 3.2.4). Howitt (1845: 191–92) writes:

> Of their traditions the most novel is their creation. First, say they, a young man, along with others, 'quamby along a beek,' sat down in the earth, when it was '.plenty dark'. There they were, not merely two, but many people, lying or sitting unfinished, and half torpid in the ground, – this reminds us of Milton's Limbo. But Karackarock, daughter of the god Pungil, a kindly divinity, had condescended to 'yannina warreet,' walk a long way to look out for them, to clothe them comfortably with good opossum-rugs, of which no doubt she had great store. The Old Man, so they call Pungil their god, not unlike the Hebrew term, Ancient of Days, now held out his hand to 'Gerer' the Sun, and made him warm. When the sun warmed the earth it opened like a door; and then plenty of black fellows came up out of the earth. Then the black fellows 'plenty sing' like it white fellows 'big one Sunday;' which means that a day is kept sacred like our Sabbath, in commemoration of the creation; the dance on that day being of a peculiar kind called gaygip; at which time corrobory before images carved curiously in bark.
>
> For a long time after the creation, in the winter they were very cold, for they had no fire; their condition as it regarded their food was not better than their dogs for they were compelled to eat the kangaroo raw; and to add to their misery, the whole land was full of deadly snakes and guanos; but good Karackarock, their truly womanly divinity, did not forget or forsake them. Pungil her father, like a true native's god, was too much of a '.big one gentleman'. to do any thing but carry his war weapons; whilst Karackarock, a native divinity of the true feminine sort, a worker, came a long way armed with a long staff – native women carry such – and with this she went over the whole land killing the reptiles; but just before she had killed them all the staff broke, and the kind did not all perish. Misery there was in the breaking of that weapon, but there was also mercy for Karackarock had so warmed in well as herself with such a great slaughter, that when the staff snapped there came out of it fire. Fire they now had to warm themselves, and to cook with. Their condition was much improved, but did not long continue so, for Wang, the crow, a mysterious bird, regarded as superstitiously by them as the raven amongst Thor and Odin's worshippers, watched his opportunity and flew away with it. For a long time they were again in a most sad and fireless condition, until ever kind Karackarock learned their state, supplied their wants, and they have never since lost it.

> Of a great flood they speak that rose above the highest trees and hills; and how the natives were some drowned, and the rest, for a great wind blew, were caught up by a whirlwind to another similar country above them. When the flood subsided, there jumped up out of the earth, trees, kangaroos, and opossums – every thing. The old race, the antediluvians, became stars. Among them were Pungil, their principal deity; Karackarock, their female Prometheus; Teert and Teerer, songs of Pungil; Berwool and Bobinger, son and daughter of Pungil, the first pair who dwelt on earth after the flood, and from whome the present race of natives are sprung. Wang, the crow, also became a star.
>
> Pungil was still, notwithstanding his deification, and stellification, bodily often on the earth; but the coming of the white people was fraught with ruin for him as well as for his black children; for the god of the white people, was in like measure with his white children, more powerful than Pungil; and strictly ordered the old man no more to wander about the earth, which was no longer his, but to get himself into the ground. There he now is, and the white man's god does not permit him to eat or drink, not even to smoke, neither is he allowed to sit or stand, but must evermore lie down; still in his abject condition, if he has any stomach for it, to solace himself in his darkness and many griefs, he is at liberty to sing a little.

There are several pieces of language in this text. First, the words *quamby along a beek* surely include the word **gumba** 'sleep, lie down' and the word **biik** 'ground'. Haydon (1846: 169) gives the word for 'a sleeping place' as *kwomby*. This appears to be an imperative form of the verb meaning 'sleep'.

The words relating to the female creator Karakarook can be analysed as follows in (3.22):

(3.22)	*Yannina*	*warreet*
	yana-na	**warrit(j)**
	go-PART?	far
	'Going far.'	

We have been unable to relate the word *gerer* to the 'sun' or to the word for warmth. The two words in the Eastern Kulin language varieties that are similar to it in form are **djerra** 'ill' and **djirra** 'reed spear'.

Many years after the performance, Barak made several drawings that are now in the Staatliche Museen Preubischer Kulturbesitz, Museum fur Völkerkunde, Berlin, Germany. One of these drawings in pencil, dated by the museum as 1880s to 1903 (the year before Barak's death), was possibly completed before

1892, the year in which Arthur Baessler met Barak at Coranderrk. Vanderbyl (2019b: 42) describes this visit based on an examination of Baessler's notebooks, who wrote about a pencil drawing as follows:

> 'His drawings made with lead pencil always showed Corroborees, the old dances of the blacks. He drew pretty fast although different from our ways; if he had to draw a dressed man he would first draw the full body before dressing the naked person by drawing clothing over it.'

The drawing that Vanderbyl associates with these comments is termed by the museum '*Ceremony* (VI 25.160)' and described as (Vanderbyl 2019b: 42):

> 'Kangaroo three dying men, three dancing men holding a bush in the right (this dance is not a corroboree, but a different dance), but moving the upper part of the body continuously while shaking the bush. Name of the dance Gageed?'

This is illustrated in Vanderbyl (2019b: 72). Given the importance of the Gaiggip ceremony, a cross-disciplinary study to look at Barak's drawings more closely in connection with other descriptions of the Gaiggip will be very useful.

3.4.1.1 The Tanderrum ceremony

Tanderrum[53] is a ceremony described by both Joseph Parker and Thomas. Like the Gaiggip and other dances it involved the use of boughs and twigs, and ended in a peaceful gesture such as the seventh dance of the Gaiggip in which 'a bough the emblem of peace' is brought. Clark and Cahir (2004: 9) discuss this ceremony:

> Joseph Parker … recalled they were terror stricken by violent settlers and when the Aborigines first met his father they approached him carrying a green twig, something he interpreted as an emblem of peace. It was probably an attempt at enacting the ceremony of tanderrum, or 'freedom of the bush', a diplomatic rite symbolising the landholder's hospitality, in which strangers were allowed temporary access to clan resources after a ritual exchange of gifts … Boughs of different treees were cut from forests which surrounded the new comers, and these were intended to be used as seats during the tanderrum ritual.

53 Since 2013, the Tanderrum ceremony has again been performed in October as part of the opening ceremony of the Melbourne International Festival. In both 2018 and 2019, this song was performed in that ceremony.

Thomas drew a plan of the Tanderrum ground, showing directions and the places occupied by the men and the women, shown in Figure 3.5:

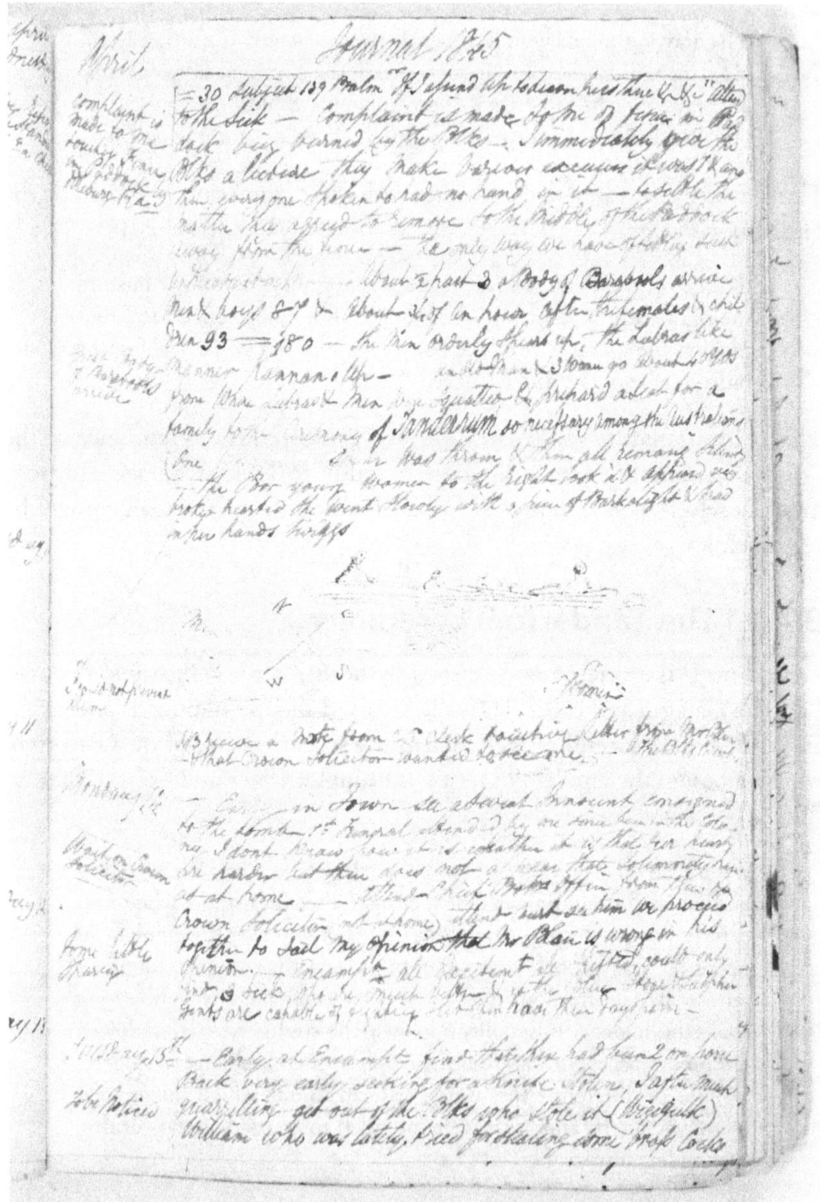

Figure 3.5: Drawing of Tanderrum ground, by William Thomas

Source: Courtesy of State Library of NSW (MLMSS 214, Volume 03 Item 03, SLNSW_FL836112.jpg).

A detailed description of the Tanderrum ceremony is found in the William Thomas papers (Volume 3 Item 01, pages numbered 94 to 96; see also Stephens 2014, 2: 98–99 for Thomas's diary entry of 13 April 1845 with some brief notes about the Tanderrum). This is dated 25 May 1858 and notes that it was sent to Mr Duffy. The portion of the text relating to Tanderrum is transcribed here as Box 3.27. Note that the date of 1844, with the 4 crossed out and replaced by 3, is an error on Thomas's part.

Box 3.27: Tanderrum ceremony

The Ceremony of Tanderrum

–16th, There is not perhaps a more pleasing sight than when blacks come into a country in which they are [perfect-inserted] strangers, where none have before trodden, each comes with fire in their hand which is supposed to purify the air, they are usher'd in by some intermedium tribe whose embassadors have previously been despatched, & [they are - inserted] made welcome, from the forest which surrounds the new comers, [is selected - crossed out] [are pick - inserted] boughs from each [different - inserted] tree, [if - crossed out] [them smaller with a great portion] & leaves, each family has a separate [seat - inserted] raised from [some - crossed out] dead log at hand about [6 or more inches - crossed out] [1 foot - inserted] from the ground, on which at one end sits the male head & his male children,

and at the other end, the female head & her female children, the male & female branches are separated. 2 fires are made one for the males, & the other for the female [branch-crossed out], - on the 1st day they are attended by those whose country they are invited to visit, not allowed to do anything for themselves, water is brought them which is carefully stirred by the attendant with a reed & the attendant takes a good draught to show that it is pure & not injurious, it is then given them to drink

–In this ceremony males attend males & females females [victuals-crossed out] [food consisting of all the varieties the bush affords - inserted] is then brought them [in the new country - inserted] during this ceremony, [during this - crossed out] the greatest silence

prevails, both by attendant & attended, you may occasionally perceive in the aged tears of gratitude [streaming-crossed out] [steal-inserted] down their murky cheeks, at night miams are made for them, the meaning of all this a hearty & cordial welcome, as the boughs on which they have set are from various trees, so they are at liberty to get from them ever after what they please, the water stired with a reed is that no weapon will be allowed to touch them

–On Saturday 22nd March 184[4-crossed out] [3-inserted] at the Encampment by my quarters [in-crossed out] Merri Creek Paddock between one & 200 strangers arrived from the countries - NW from Gipps Land Moogolumbeek & NE of Devils River tribe, the sight was truly imposing, especially their attendance upon their old Chief Kuller Kullip the oldest man I have yet seen [among the Aborigines - inserted] he must have been near 80 years of age, he was just on 6 feet high and so fat [with it - crossed out] [that I have not seen his equal among which?? for?? ?? - inserted] his face was wrinkled especially his forehead, [continued horizontal furrows to his eyebrows in continued furrows - inserted] [& cheeks very furrowed - crossed out]

-The blacks would scarce permit him to stir, attending him to idolization [invariably -inserted] early in the morning [invariably-crossed out] would be seen my blacks [with the tribes about the settlement-inserted] in [circles??-crossed out] [crescent rows-inserted] sitting [around-crossed out] [afore-inserted] him in pensive silence which the old Patriarch would be holding forth as tho' laying down some code of laws [for their guidance-inserted] or giving instructions [as hitherto they are ignorant of -inserted]
-I [have-crossed out] often endeavor'd to catch at his words [and pencil them down as well as I could but in vain-crossed out] [but-crossed out] the old [idolized-inserted] chief would immediately stop on my approach-and tho'after many days I [ventured to-inserted] endeavoured from [the hafosing??-inserted] [of??-crossed out] my blacks [Billibillary-inserted] a seat among them while the old venerable chief was giving them council [but-inserted] to no effect, they all sum'd to venerate him so much (& well they might) that whatever he objected to they
[Written on the side of the left hand column, bottom, p. 96]
seemed not to press him, but to acquiesce-however after he [his people-inserted] left [Billibillery - inserted] my Blks [Chief - inserted] informed me that he had communicated to them that a race lived in the Australian alps in rocks & caves who [never as appear??-inserted] and tho they were superior to him who made corrobery & conveyed them to Blacks [??] when sleeping.
[Written on its side on the right side of p. 95]
Kangaroo, opossum, bandicoots, [kangaroo rat-inserted], bears &c &c, [Freassol??] Eels, Fish, Gum &c &c &c in fact show off the produce of the land

Source: SLNSW MLMSS 214, Volume 03 Item 01, pages numbered 94–96; SLNSW_FL827898.jpg, SLNSW_FL827900.jpg and SLNSW_FL827902.jpg; adapted by authors.

The list of animals written on the side of page 95 of the manuscript perhaps refers to the foods that would be made available to the visitors.

A published version of this appears in Bride (1898: 97–98):

> *Ceremony of Tanderrum, or Freedom of the Bush.* – There is not, perhaps, a more pleasing sight in a native encampment than when strange blacks arrive who have never been in the country before. Each comes with fire in hand (always bark), which is supposed to purify the air the women and children in one direction, and the men and youths in another. They are ushered in generally by some of an intermediate tribe, who are friends of both parties, and have been engaged in forming an alliance or friendship between the tribes ; the aged are brought forward and introduced. The ceremony of Tanderrum is commenced ; the tribe visited may be seen lopping boughs from one tree and another, as varied as possible of each tree with leaves ; each family has a separate seat, raised about 8 or 10 inches from the ground, on which in the centre sits the male and around him his male children, and the female and her sex of children have another seat.

> Two fires are made, one for the males and the other for the females. The visitors are attended on the first day by those whose country they are come to visit, and not allowed to do anything for themselves; water is brought them which is carefully stirred by the attendant with a reed, and then given them to drink (males attend males and females females) ; victuals are then brought and laid before them, consisting of as great a variety as the bush in the new country affords, if come-at-able ; during this ceremony the greatest silence prevails, both by attendants and attended. You may sometimes perceive an aged man seated, the tear of gratitude stealing down his murky, wrinkled face. At night their mia-mias are made for them ; conversation, &c., ensue. The meaning of this is a hearty welcome. As the boughs on which they sit are from various trees, so they are welcome to every tree in the forest. The water stirred with a reed means that no weapon shall ever be raised against them. On Saturday, the 22nd March 1845, at an encampment east of Melbourne, near 200 strangers arrived. The sight was imposing and affecting, especially their attendance upon that old chief Kuller Kullup, the oldest man I have ever seen among the blacks ; he must have been near 80 years.

Elsewhere, Thomas names Kullerkulluk as chief of the Mogolum Bith, also spelled Mogooloombeek and Mogoolumbuk[54] (SLNSW MLMSS 214, Volume 23 Item 01, SLNSW_FL847450.jpg). This tribe was associated with the Australian Alps, and this is another link between the Tanderrum and the Gaiggip.

Thomas did record a few words of the Mogoollumbuk language, saying that they were 'Tribe E of Devils River. I cannot understand a word of their language'. As we can see in Table 3.7, which compares words from Yarra (Woiwurrung) and Mogolloombeek, four of the six words in this word list are clearly Dhudhuroa, and the widespread word **wurru** for 'mouth, lips' may be present in the name of the language, which as Blake and Reid (2002) point out, may be based on the word for 'no', **dhubalga**, in combination with **wurru**.

54 We are grateful to Jacqui Durrant for pointing out a number of references to the identity of the Mogullumbitj, a topic that requires further research.

Table 3.7: Words from the Mogolloombeek language

Parts of body	Yarra	Mogolloombeek	Dhudhuroa (from Blake and Reid 2002)
Head	Kowan	Morower	**marriwa**
Eyes	Myng	Wanterper	**wandjaba**
Nose	Garn	Geenguer	**dhindiwa**
Mouth	Ngarndun	Woorooer	**lendhewa, niwa niwa**
Ears	Werring	Murumboor	**marrambuwa**
Chin	Worrinun-duk	Yerree	**lendawa, yerranba** 'beard'

Source: SLNSW MLMSS 214, Volume 23 Item 03, SLNSW_FL832106.jpg; Authors.

3.4.1.2 Text of the Gaiggip and notes on the analysis

There are several versions of text that are identified as Gaiggip. The longest of these is transcribed below in Box 3.28:

Box 3.28: Gaiggip, version 1

Gaiggip

1st	Wrin-ger kun-nee mal-lin mil-le ko-mar woor-rer koit naln-but kun-nee min-nal-lo-gee par-rar-mat-ter koo-ra- -gar tal-pran-li yan-no-nee
2nd	kin-nar-ree koo-mar nurn-bien
3rd	koo-oo-thur kun-mul-lin tin-dee won-nar kal-lar pilk-e-ree
4th	nur-re-mou-ther ter-ree-mou-ther koo-yu-mar tal-lar-lar tin-ar tin-ar kroo-ther kun-mar-lee plannor-ree plan-nor-ree mur-run mur-run tin-ar kroo-thur kun-mar-lee par-rek-e-lan tal-lan-ar-tar
5th	tal-bu won-ner kul-lar woor-rar koo-mar worr-rar mal-lin
6th	nur-re-mou-ther koo-u-mar nar-re-mut-tee ting-ar ting-ar kroo-thur moy-un-ver tal- -lar-tar nur-re-mur-ree koo-u-mar
7th	tul-bee won-ner wor-rer koo-mar tin-e-ree kool-mar-ur-ree mar-lee bil-boon niam-mee U-re wor-ro boo-rar yoon-nar

Source: SLNSW MLMSS 214, Volume 21 Item 03, SLNSW_FL832691.jpg; adapted by authors.

In the margin on the next page, Thomas wrote: 'Gaggip the most important of their corroboree, intended as invented to unite Aborig[l] tribes 1837'.

As noted above, before the text in Box 3.28 (SLNSW MLMSS 214, Volume 23, Item 01, p. 59, SLNSW_FL847434.jpg, p. 28), Thomas writes:

> Songs – The Aborigines Songs tho' they may to a casual bystander appear to be composed of numerous words, such is not the case 8 to 10 words are the longest I have met with – their songs something like our dances – are generally according to the action or motion of the body – they repeat every word over the whole as they proceed and liquidate the sounds – the following are amongst their principal songs.

As an example, he gives another fraction of Ga(i)ggip, presented as Box 3.29:

Box 3.29: Gaiggip, version 2

Gaggip – Ko-ni-ar̂ Ma-lar̂
Pom-marè Ye-bar̂ Too-lar̂ Yan-beè

Source: SLNSW MLMSS 214, Volume 23 Item 01, SLNSW_FL847434.jpg; adapted by authors.

It may be that the final syllables of each of the words was stressed in this song.

A second version of this text is found in the Thomas papers on a page numbered 19, in Volume 03, Item 01 of the William Thomas papers.[55] This page has a margin heading 'Aboriginal Songs & Dances' and also includes the short song presented in Box 3.37 (section 3.4.6), the 'Body song' in section 3.4.7 and the Women's lament presented in section 3.4.8. This version of the Gaiggip song is presented as Box 3.30:

Box 3.30: Gaiggip, version 3

Ko ni are _ Boomare _ Ma.lar _ Ye-bar rar _ Kun-
ar _ Too-la _Yan-bee _ Bo-mar _ Too-lar _ U-po-mar

Source: SLNSW MLMSS 214/3/1, page numbered 19; MLMSS 214, Volume 03 Item 01, SLNSW_FL827695.jpg; adapted by authors.

Since the original Gaiggip was in seven parts, it probably relates to the following note on the same page of the Thomas manuscripts as Box 3.30 (SLNSW MLMSS 214, Volume 03 Item 01, SLNSW_FL827695.jpg):

55 The photograph of this page on the State Library of NSW website is numbered c009900025h, available at archival.sl.nsw.gov.au/Details/archive/110372954 (accessed 18 July 2018).

> Another Corrob^ee – 1st time Waddie 2nd Polloygulk (ornamented bark)
>
> 3rd Maurum (leaves) 4th Tnidee Murrong (hand) 5th Terrung (bough)
>
> 6th Swish (Kulk) – 3 or 6 turns in dance.

This is written immediately below the 'Body song' (see section 3.4.7) where the hand is also mentioned. It may be that the body song was the text for one of these dances.

The words recorded in this small note are presented in Box 3.31:

Box 3.31: Translation of terms in Thomas's note

Waddie		**wadi**	'?'
Pollygulk	ornamented bark	**buli-galk**	'?-wood'
Maurum	leaves	**marran**	'leaf'
Trindee Murrong	hand	**drindi-mar(n)ang**	'?-hand'
Terrang	bow	**djerrang**	'leaf'
Kulk	swish	**galk**	'wood'

Source: SLNSW MLMSS 214, Volume 03 Item 01, SLNSW_FL827695.jpg; adapted by authors.

A regularisation of the seven sections of the main Gaiggip text (see Box 3.29) is given in example (3.23), arranged into lines following suggestions by Harold Koch (pers. comm.). The regularisation of the other fraction (see Box 3.30) is given in example (3.24). In making these regularisations, we have assumed that words written with final *-ar* and *-er* represent a long vowel, probably /a/ and not a final rhotic. Final rhotics are not recorded at all for Dhudhuroa (Blake and Reid 2002: 185), and it is speculated by Blake and Reid (2002: 186) that 'it is likely that Dhudhuroa allowed only vowel-final words', although they are recorded for the Eastern Kulin languages. This, together with the presence of some initial clusters in the Gaiggip song, such as possible /wr/, but certainly /br/ and /gr/, makes it seem unlikely that the Gaiggip song is in the Mogolloombeek language (i.e. Dhudhuroa), which does not have initial clusters.

The Gippsland languages, on the other hand, did have initial clusters, with /br/, /gr/ and /mr/ recorded by Hercus (1986: 240–43) and /wr/ suggested by Fesl (1985), who gives the word for 'ear' as **wring**. A number of initial clusters were also recorded for Southern Ngarigu, a Yuin language (Hercus 1986: 168). It seems possible that the language of this *Gaiggip* was either Gippsland or one of the Yuin languages.

(3.23.1) **wring(g)a gani malin**
mile guma
wurra gutj
nal(i)n-bad gani minaludji
barramad(h)a gurraga
dalbranli yanuni

(3.23.2) **ginarri guma**
narnbiyn

(3.23.3) **gu(w)udhurr ganmalin**
d(h)indi wuna gala
bilgirri

(3.23.4) **narrimudha d(h)irimudha guyuma**
d(h)alala d(h)ina d(h)ina
grudha ganmali
blanurri blanurri
marran marran d(h)in(gg)a
grudha ganmali
barragilan d(h)alan-ad(h)a

(3.23.5) **d(h)albu wuna gala**
wurra guma
wurra malin

(3.23.6) **narrimud(h)a guyuma**
narrimud(h)i d(h)ing(g)a d(h)ing(g)a
grudha moyanwa d(h)al-ad(h)a
narrimurri guyuma

(3.23.7) **d(h)albi wana wurra**
guma d(h)inarri
gu(l)ma yurri mali
bilbun(y) niyami
yurri wurru burra yuna

The other fraction of Gaiggip is given as follows, example (3.24):

(3.24) **gayigip**
guniya mala
bumarre yeba
d(h)ula yanbi

We are not able to suggest any translation for the Gaiggip texts, unless perhaps the first word is in Gippsland language and is somehow connected to **wring** 'ear'. We might have expected words for war implements or weapons to be included in the songs as the description from Thomas (in Stephens 2014, 1: 572) says that 'they have but 6 War implements which answers to the 6 Dances, in the 7th Dance a bough the emblem of peace'. However, there is no sign of any Gippsland word for weapons in this text. Nor have we been able to identify any Dhudhuroa words for weapons in this text. The one possible similarity with Gippsland language is *kroo-thar*, example (3.25.2), that may be a Gippsland word recorded by Thomas as *grudba* 'destroy'.

There are a number of recurrent words in the text of the main Gaiggip, some examples of which are presented in example (3.25), where the number in brackets refers to the section of the Gaiggip.[56]

(3.25.1) **gu(yu)ma**
ko-mar (1)
koo-mar (2)
koo-mar (5)
koo-mar (7)
koo-u-mar (6)
koo-u-mar (6)
koo-yu-mar (4)

(3.25.2) **grudha**
koo-oo-thur (3)
kroo-ther (4)
kroo-thur (4)
kroo-thur (6)

56 Thanks to Harold Koch for assembling these.

(3.25.3) **gani**
kun-nee (1)
kun-nee (1)
ganmali-
kun-mul-lin (3)
kun-mar-le (4)
kun-mar-lee (4)
mali-n
mal-lin (1)
mal-lin (5)
mar-lee (7)?

(3.25.4) **narrimudha**
nur-re-mou-ther (4)
nur-re-mou-ther (6)
nar-re-mut-tee (6)
nur-re-mur-ree (6)

It is much to be regretted that we are able to say so little about this clearly very important text.

3.4.2 Murrunawa Corroboree song

A further 10 songs, and additional texts relating to the corroboree (see section 3.1.5), are found in the Thomas papers in the Mitchell Library. The first of these is described as 'another day dance called Murrunawa' (SLNSW MLMSS 214, Volume 22, pp. 353–54). This includes a detailed description of the dance and the text of the song, presented in Box 3.32.

A second version from 'Sketch of Manners and Songs & Dances, No 5 Songs & Dances, 1st June 1858' (SLNSW MLMSS 214, Volume 24 Item 01) is presented as Box 3.33.

Box 3.32: Murrunawa Corroboree song, version 1

13th = Another day Dance [called - crossed out] Murrunawa - 3 Lubras & men join in this dance, say 12 men and 12 [W-crossed out] [young girls-inserted], their faces and breasts [male & female-inserted] thinly rub'd over with red ochre [they have-crossed out] [and a - inserted] broad white circle round their naval, each has [a - inserted] bough in [their - crossed out] [both - inserted] hands [and - crossed out] they have a [male-inserted] leader who was [equiped-inserted] as the others but [had a-crossed out] [with a - inserted] wreath of slips [from boughs - inserted] round his head of the mimoza is in blosson the wrearths [form it from it which gives him a gay appearance - inserted]

-He stands [&-inserted] with his boughs [making-crossed out] begins divers motions sometimes over his head sometimes obliquely raised then obliquely falling at other times waving to & fro, the whole facing each other male and female about 30 yards off, and the leader on one side so that all could catch every motion, [and-crossed out] as he sang, they sang, the male and the female voices at one and the same time in the still forest has actually a cheering effect as the female voices are very harmonious, there is a certain hoarseness [however - inserted] in the male aboriginal voice, something like [in-inserted] seafaring men which I [have-crossed out] attributed to the same cause [being - inserted] perpetually exposed to the open air, this however does not effect the female voice [tho exposed in like manner - inserted] which is as clear as Europe - and Ladies they dance before one another till they have gone this every move that savage genius can devise the men & women [continue-crossed out] singing continuously at length the leader with both boughs up flourishing them over his head so rapidly which is performed by the others they then retrace every move but backward going thro their evolutions the males & females gradually draw back to back then gradually wheeling round form at length to near a creek save a few paces where the leader stands the leader moves as they move this dance is not much unlike at this juncture to the European peasants dance round the May Pole The greatest [astonishment-inserted] [wonder is-crossed out] in this and all their [other-inserted] dances [is - inserted] that time and motion is so exact as tho leader & all moved by one spring

The song on this occasion like all others is the rounds they move their boughs.

Mur-run-a-wă kar-bo Ming

-o Ner-rim, Nurm-bul-Port-

-bo-Yeng-ă, Yan-ner, Kar-bo,

Ming.o Ner-rim, Mur-run-o

It has been stated by some writers that their corroberrys are sacred, performed only at a New and full Moons, such however is not the case, they however generally do Corroberry at new and full moon but not in any sacred sight, [my blacks tell me it is only because glad, when new moon come and get big - they have however sacred & traditional dances which will follow in my next paper-written on side]

WT

Source: SLNSW MLMSS 214, Volume 22, pp. 353–54[57]; adapted by authors.

57 This section has not yet been photographed by the State Library of NSW. This transcription was made by checking with the original and a photograph of the page made by Stephen Morey.

Box 3.33: Murrunawa Corroboree song, version 2

13th Mur-run-a-wă another day dance, say 12 young men, and 12 young girls their faces and breasts male and female slightly rubbed over with red ochre and a broad white circle round their naval, each has a bough in both hands they have a male leader who was equiped as the others but with a wreath of slips from boughs round his head – if the Mamoza is in blossom the wreath is form'd from it which gives the leader a gay appearance, He stands and with his boughs begins divers motions sometimes oblique raised, then oblique falling at other times wavering to & fro, the whole facing each other male & female about 30 yards off, & the leader on one side so that all could catch every motion, as he sang they sung the male and the female voices at one and the same time in the still forest has actually a cheering effect as the female voices are very harmonious, there is a degree of horseness however in the male Aboriginal voice something like seafaring men which I attribute to the same cause being perpetually exposed to the open air, this however does not effect the female voice tho' exposed in like manner, which is as clear as European ladies, they dance before one another till they have gone thro' every move that savage genius can devise, the men and women singing continuously, at length the leader with both boughs up flourishing them over his head so rapidly which is performed by the others they then retrace every move but backward going thro' their evolutions the males and females gradually draw back to back then gradually wheeling round form at length to near a circle save a few paces where the leader stands the leader moving as they move, this dance is not much unlike at this juncture to the Europe-an peasants dance round the May pole

– The greatest astonishment in this and all their dances is that time and motion is so ex-act as the leader and all moved by one spring.

– The song on the occasion like all others is the rounds they move their boughs

Mur-run-a-wă, Kar-bo Ming-o, Ner-rim, Nurmbul, Port-bo, Yeng-ă Yan-ner, Kar-bo, Mingo, Ner-rim, Mur-runo

It has been stated by some writers that their corroberrys are sacred, performed only at a new and full moon, such however is not the case, they however generally do corroberry at new and full moon but not in any sacred light, my blacks tell me it is only because glad, when new moon come and get big.

– They have however sacred and traditional dances which will follow in my next paper verbatim as sent to Mr Duffy

Source: SLNSW MLMSS 214, Volume 24 Item 01, commencing on SLNSW_FL828731.jpg; adapted by authors.

Our suggested analysis of this song is given in (3.26):

(3.26) *Mur-run-a-wă,*

murrun-awa

PN

'The Murrunawa'

Kar-bo	*Ming-o*	*Ner-rim*	*Nurmbul*	*Port-bo*
gab-u	**ming(g)u**	**nyirrim**	**numbul**	**burt-bu**
DEM-ABL	beginning	long	upright	smoke-ABL?

'From there, the beginning, long and upright, by smoke??.'

Yeng-ă *Yan-ner* *Kar-bo* *Ming-o* *Ner-rim*

yinga **yana** **gab-u** **ming(g)u** **nyirrim**

sing go DEM-ABL beginning long

'Singing, going, from there, the beginning, a long (way?).'

Mur-runo

murrun-u

PN-?

'The Murrunawa.'

Linguistic notes

The translation presented here is not based on any information about the meaning of the song provided by Thomas. However, all of the words in the song are attested in Thomas's word lists, and so we suggest that they might make a meaning something like what we suggest here.

The final word **murrunu** would surely have been built from the same root as the word **murrunawa**. It is possible that both of these words are built on a root regularised by Blake as **murrun** 'alive'.

The word **gabu** may be an ablative form of a well attested demonstrative, often spelled *karbi* by Thomas and meaning 'from there'; alternatively, it may mean 'above' as Thomas, for example, gives *kar-boo* and *kar-bou* as meaning 'above'.

The word for 'long' is spelled by Thomas as *ner-rim* and by Mathews (for Thagungwurrung) as *ńiririmda* (NLA MS 8006/8/286). We suggest a regularisation of **nyirrim-**.

Thomas wrote down *mingo* 'beginning', which perhaps also contains an ablative.

Port-bo may contain the well-attested root **burt** 'smoke', since smoke would be expected to form part of such a dance.

Thomas wrote down *nurm-bull* 'upright', which may refer to the actions of the dances. The text in Box 3.33 states that the leader 'stands and with his boughs begins divers motions sometimes oblique raised, then oblique falling at other times wavering to & fro'. Perhaps, then, the words of the song describe this movement.

3.4.3 Second Corroboree song

The second corroboree song in the William Thomas papers is found in a manuscript 'Sketch of Manners and Songs & Dances', dated 1858, and presented here as Box 3.34. This section is found on the fourth to sixth pages of this unnumbered document (on blue paper).

Box 3.34: Corroboree song

-4th Their songs I at first considered nothing more than a tissue of unmeaning sounds but on more particular attention found that they were full of meaning, and from the few words in them considered them a senseless sound of repetitions-they are indeed repetitious but all in accordance, like our country dances, only that the leader sings the motion to be performed, those who understand their language will find all in perfect accordance the following are a few some named after their authors-

Ko-ro-al-bo, Yan-non-ner, Myng-gar-bro-dee, Sub-bo, Mung-ŏ

this ŏ is sung very long, till it comes down to a mere distinguished sound so peculiar to the Aboriginal cadence-this song or dance as it is used as such is merely a motion of the head, eyes backside, and feet, and which forms tho so few words a very accurate dance-

Source: SLNSW MLMSS 214, Volume 24 Item 01, SLNSW_FL828671.jpg, SLNSW_FL828674.jpg and SLNSW_FL828677.jpg; adapted by authors.

Our suggested regularisation of this song is given in (3.27):

(3.27) **gurrulbu yanana minggabrud(h)i djubu mang-u**

Although Thomas says that the songs were 'full of meaning', he does not give any meaning for this song, save the somewhat confusing statement 'some named after their authors'. The song that immediately follows this in the manuscript is specifically named as coming from Ning-gollo-bin. Since in this song there is a word *Myng-gar-bro-dee*, which has some similarity to the name of the 'famous doctor' *Myngderrar* also called Malcolm (discussed in section 3.4.15), it may be that this song is naming its composer.

The only other words in this song that might be able to be interpreted are *Yan-non-ner*, possibly a form of the verb **yana** 'go, walk' and *Mung-ŏ*, which, if the first syllable is **mang**, a demonstrative, may be an ablative form, **mang-(g)u** 'from here'.

3.4.4 Ningolubbel's song

A song composed by the expert songster Ningolubbel was documented by Thomas in the 'Sketch of Manners and Songs & Dances', in which the Corroboree song presented in section 3.4.3 was also recorded. The text of this (see Box 3.35) is presented on the sixth and seventh pages of this unnumbered document (on blue paper).

Box 3.35: Corroboree song by Ningolubbel

Ning-gollo-bins celebrated dance, a favorite among all the seven tribes, he was one of the Mount Macedon tribe originally, but on that tribe becoming near defunct joined the Melbourne tribes –

U-man-un, Koo-ree-nar, Go-la, Weing-er, Tu-un a-nun, Gee-ong-gă, Mon-ni-o, Will-lum-mee, Kor-ree-nar, Go-la, Weing-er, Tu-un-a-nun, Gee-ong-gă, Mon-ni-o, Will-lum-mee, Weing. –

Source: SLNSW MLMSS 214, Volume 24 Item 01, SLNSW_FL828677.jpg and SLNSW_FL828679.jpg; adapted by authors.

A suggested regularisation of this text is given in example (3.28). It contains two lines with similar linguistic material.

(3.28) **yuma-nhan gurri-na gula wiiny, dhuna-nhan djiyunga muniyu wilumi**
gurri-na gula wiiny, dhuna-nhan djiyunga muniyu wilumi wiiny

The first word *u-man-un* has the same form as a word elsewhere documented by Thomas with the meaning 'throw it' (SLNSW MLMSS 214, Volume 23 Item 02). We suggest that this might be a verb root **yuma** combined with the 1st person singular present form **-nhan**. Our suggested analysis of the first line from example (3.28) is presented in example (3.29). This analysis would suggest that the song is showing the power of the song maker, Ningolubbel, who was known to be a great maker of songs and a powerful individual.

(3.29)

u-man-un	*koo-ree-nar*	*go-la*	*weing-er*
yuma-nhan	**gurriñ-a?**	**gala?**	**wiiny-a**
throw-1SG	wind?-CASE?	DEM?	fire-ERG

'I am throwing the wind … (with the?) fire.'

tu-un a nun	*gee-ong-gă*	*mon-ni-o*	*will-lum-mee*
dhuna-dhan	**djiyung-a**	**muniyu**	**wilam-i**
burn-1SG	?	?	camp-?

'I am burning/cooking … (in the) camp.'

Linguistic notes

Tuununun is recorded by Thomas (MLMSS 214, Volume 23 Item 02) in the meaning 'it burns', but we suggest that the form here does include the 1st person singular present suffix **nhan**. This same verb root is also found referring to cooking as in the sentence *Tonabuk Weinna Walleat* meaning 'dress the opossum with fire', literally **dhuna-ba-k wiiny-a walert** 'cook-FORM-IMP fire-INST possum' (MLMSS 214, Volume 02).

The form *go-la* might be a demonstrative **gala**, a form already discussed in connection with the song in section 3.4.1.

The word *koo-ree-nar* may be 'wind', regularised by Blake as **gurriñ**; Thomas elsewhere records the word *coreen* as 'storm', so this may refer to a great wind.

3.4.5 Wool-woork Bar-lum-bur-lin (Butterfly dance)

Another dance performed during the daytime, and sung by women, was the butterfly dance. This is included in the 'Sketch of Manners and Songs & Dances', in which the Corroboree song presented in section 3.4.3 was also recorded. The text of this is presented on the 21st to 25th pages of this unnumbered document (on blue paper).

Thomas's original notes about this dance are found in his journal dated Tuesday 8 and Wednesday 16 June 1841. On the earlier date, Thomas noted: 'A singular ceremony takes place called Woolworkbullumberlin, the first I had particularly noticed'; adding in a margin note, 'Woolworkbullumberlin: see customs and manners in my book'.

On the latter date, 16 June 1841, he referred to this as 'a curious diversion', adding (in Stephens 2014, 1: 300, 306):[58]

> I find that the men can officiate at beating the opossum cloak as well as women, 3 beat the cloak and 4 or 5 beat gently their sticks. I stept forward & saw what I did notice before the men an amazing quick quiver of their lips made precisely the same noise as the bushes made on their legs, the almost invisible thril & quiver of the legs surpassed conception or description.

58 The manuscript with these references is to be found in MLMSS 214, Volume 02 Item 05.

The full text of this dance is presented as Box 3.36:

Box 3.36: Wool-woork Bar-lum-bur-lin (Butterfly dance)

10th Wool-woork Bar-lum-bur-lin is a day dance, in the forenoon generally, a few married lubras, 8 or 10 will make each a small fire, and their husbands also make each a small fire at a short distance within sight of each other other – the lubras seated will commence each beating their opossum rug and singing

Yan-gee, Yan-gee, Ma-lar,

as in a corroberry their husbands merely striking their sticks gently, while the men (others invited to the dance by the married) at a considerable distance prepare themselves, they are not daubed with promiscuous daubs, but thinly rubbed over with red ochre which improves their appearance much in fact gives the men a handsome look, they have leaves round just above their ankle as in common corroberry, only smaller and a wonguim or mulga in hand they approach by very short paces figuring, turning round and putting themselves in the drolest of attitudes and occasionally rushing to & fro with stern countenances as tho' leading on to combat, then suddenly stopping short and kneel,

-the singular quivering of lips of the dancers in this dance while kneeling is suprising, the lips move as a child would when pulling the fingers over the lips or [buring??] but so quiet and soft and withal the sound produced tallying precisely with the noise made by the leaves in their legs has a singular musical effect, the women now stand up, shake their breasts, and strange all sounds are alike, the lubras breasts, the lips, and leaves on the legs of the men all one simultaneous musical burr like thousands of butterflys or moths fluttering about, the lubras naked as in a corrobbery (they also being all cover'd with red ochre had really a handsome appearance) advance, when the men stop, they stop, thus by short paces they progressively proceed till they arrive altogether at the spot a group of married lubras are who are mere spectators of the scene and dance round them, and on a sudden at a sound from the married men not engaged, the actors respectfully retire to the starting point and then if inclined go thro another dance, how ever one dance seldom concluded before 20 or 30 minutes –

Source: SLNSW MLMSS 214, Volume 24 Item 01, commencing with SLNSW_FL828717.jpg; adapted by authors.

The name of the dance can be regularised as **wulwu(rr)k balam-balam**, where the second word **balam-balam** is 'butterfly'. The first word may be related to a form *Wolworgon*, recorded by Thomas (SLNSW MLMSS 214, Volume 23 Item 02) with a meaning 'let us go'.

The connection between the name of this dance and the butterfly is made explicit in the following: 'Wool work bullumberlin a day corrobery or dance named from Butter' (SLNSW MLMSS 214, Volume 23 Item 02, SLNSW_FL814705.jpg).

We assume that this dance is the same as the beautiful butterfly dance referred to in the following (SLNSW MLMSS 214, Volume 24 Item 01, commencing with SLNSW_FL828729.jpg):

> 12th This dance which is named after the moth or butterful is one of the most innocent & beautiful of all their day dances, their beautiful appearance being all over their bodies cleanly rubbed with red ochre, & the synonamous burr of the lips, leaves, and breasts of the lubras, all as one sound baffles the conception of civilized man, how such unison of sound could be produced from such different agents, but the fact is that civilized man has not the least distinct conception, of what man is his wild state cannot perform –

This may be the dance for which Thomas drew the following diagram, presented as Figure 3.6. A version of this sketch was published in Fels (2011: 171), but with the pencil images invisible. Fels (2011: 120) suggested that the sketch was done at the protectorate head station, Tubberubbabel, located at what is now Old Moorooduc Road, Mornington Peninsula. It is certainly plausible that this dance was also performed there.

This document is shown in a brown pen. At the top left there is a drawing of trees and the words: 'Blacks dress themselves in Bush for Corrob'. The centre of the area has the word 'Dancers', with the 'Leader' placed on the left and 'Fire' in front. Black and White figures appear underneath.

Figure 3.6: Corroboree plan, by William Thomas

Source: Courtesy of State Library of NSW (MLMSS 214, Volume 22 Item 05, SLNSW_FL849485.jpg).

On the left-hand side, there is another pencil drawing with the words 'Lubras beating their opossum rugs'. On the right-hand side, the words 'Blacks in groups looking on' and beneath that a drawing of the 'Protectors Tent'. Across the bottom are the words 'Let me have this again. I lay great value young productions'.

No translation was suggested for the text by Thomas, but we suggest the following possible translation, presented in (3.30):

(3.30)	*Yan-gee*	*yan-gee*	*ma-lar*
	yang-i	**yang-i**	**mal-a(rr)**
	go-IMP	go-IMP	let's-2SG?
	'Go! Go! (You) should (go!).'		

Linguistic notes

The word *ma-lar*, meaning 'let', is discussed in the notes to the translation of the superstitious speech, example (3.41) in section 3.5.4.

A possibly related song is presented next (section 3.4.6).

3.4.6 Short song: Balt-lem-be Ning-ber Bo-lar Bal-lem-bee

In a page numbered 19, SLNSW MLMSS, Volume 03 Item 01, of the William Thomas papers, there is a margin heading 'Aboriginal Songs & Dances' that includes a version of the second Gaiggip song (see Box 71 in section 3.4.1.2), the short song presented here in Box 3.37, the Body song (section 3.4.7) and the Women's lament presented in section 3.4.8. This short song is presented in Box 3.37:

Box 3.37: Short song

Balt-lem-be _ Ning-ber _ Bo-lar _ Bal-lem-bee

Source: SLNSW MLMSS 214, Volume 03 Item 01, SLNSW_FL827695.jpg; adapted by authors.

Thomas gives no information as to the meaning of this song, but it contains a form, perhaps **balambi**, which is repeated. We are tempted to suggest that this word might be related to **balam-balam** 'butterfly', which is the name of the song presented in section 3.4.5.

3.4.7 Body song

The third song on the page numbered 19, in SLNSW MLMSS Volume 03, Item 01 of the William Thomas papers, relates to actions of the body, head and eyes. As already mentioned, it is presented together with a version of the second Gaiggip song (see above Box 3.30 in section 3.4.1.2), the short song presented in section 3.4.6, and the Women's lament presented in section 3.4.8. The text of this song, for Thomas also provided a translation, is given in Box 3.38. There is also a small drawing of a human figure standing with hands in front of them and their bottom pointed backwards, perhaps an attempt to draw a dance position.

Box 3.38: Body song

Nuit-bur, Mur-po-dee, Woon-goodee, Ming-are-poo-dee	Nuitbur Murpodee, body side ways, Woon-goo-dee, to drop your head Mingarboodee up with your eyes

Source: SLNSW MLMSS 214, Volume 03 Item 01, SLNSW_FL827695.jpg; adapted by authors.

A suggested regularisation of this song is given as (3.31):

(3.31) **ngitba mu(r)badji wung(g)udji minga(r)budji**

We have not been able to present a complete analysis of this song, but we believe that the final *-dee* represents the imperative **-dji** (Blake 1991: 75). It is possible that the word *murpodee* means 'turn sideways', perhaps regularised as **mu(r)badji**. There is no word recorded in other sources for this language to which we can relate this word.

It is equally possible that the word *woon-goodee*, perhaps **wung(g)udji**, means 'drop', perhaps 'bow'. There are many words listed with meanings 'head' or 'skull' in the sources for Central Victoria, but none resemble any of the words in this song.

The word *Ming-are-poo-dee* contains the word for 'eye', which Blake regularises as both **mirn** and **mirring**. Perhaps there was a verb something like **minga(r)budji** meaning 'lift up your eyes'. There is a word in the Thomas papers meaning 'lift up', *woorunderoneit*, but this is not related to the forms found in the song.

3.4.8 Women's lament

The last of four songs on page numbered 19, SLNSW MLMSS 214, Volume 03 Item 01, of the William Thomas papers is described as 'Dirge by Lubras', but which we have here termed Women's lament. It is presented together with a version of the second Gaiggip song (see Box 3.30 in section 3.4.1.2), the short song in section 3.4.6 and the 'Body song' in section 3.4.7. The text and some other related information are presented below as Box 3.39.

In another part of the same document (SLNSW MLMSS 214, Volume 03 Item 01, SLNSW_FL827649.jpg), Thomas includes the description of funerary ceremonies occurring after the death of a Goulburn man in 1839, which is partially transcribed here:

> … they dug with sticks (as Western Port Blks) a trench round his body then commenced his grave, while being dug, a Blk Dr on his belly began incantations hold his mouth to the earth, this evidently is a regular custom & tone, after a little pause a 2nd Dr commenced opposite to him, in like manner mouth to the earth & incanting, stoping, then a lubra with a child commenced mourning dreadfully she at last paused, a 2nd a [re?? – crossed out] commenced a solemn harmonious dirge by accent harsh – at a distance under trees were body of lubras seated, mourning plaintively & so exact in tone the whole at one solemn sound which had a powerful [ef]fect on my mind – my man assisted in digging the grave, which being finished, the blacks waited till just setting of the sun, men seated round in circles, they placed the body in the tomb, covered it first with small foliage in abundance then, I should have stated that at this period everything belonged to the deceased – button, knives, &c &x clothes torn up, cap &c &c – his son at this time started …

Note that the word spelled *stoping* is surely *stooping*.

The lament that was performed by the women as 'mourning plaintively & so exact in tone the whole at one solemn sound' presumably employed the text presented here, and very likely other texts that were not written down.

Box 3.39: Women's dirge

Pigerara, Marmecar, Banbecar, Worrercar, Kootecar Tarmbucar, During her cries those of the deceased relations only scratch their faces – The Aborig^s^ believe that it is after the 3rd day that the black rises and goes to Pungil Marman above – none but D^rs^ can perform this – It is also singular that all the tribes that I have known have the same word for this ceremony – there is no distinct words for this oration, it is like all their others a kind of yell, by the purpose is supposed to [be that this dead lay still and they will avenge her death – written on the right hand side]	Dirge by Lubras

Source: SLNSW MLMSS 214, Volume 03 Item 01, SLNSW_FL827695.jpg; adapted by authors.

Thomas does not suggest any translation for this song; however, all but the first word have a final *-car*, which we suggest can be regularised as **-ga**. A suggested regularisation of the whole text of this song is presented as (3.32):

(3.32) **bi(i)gerrarra mamaga banbaga wurrega kud(j)aga d(h)ambuga**

Green in Smyth (1878, 2: 107) records 'Welcome (kind reception) – *Womin je ka.*', which is a form built on the root regularised by Blake (1991: 99) as **wumen**- meaning 'come'. It may consist of the root plus the imperative **-dji** and a final **-ga** of unknown meaning, but perhaps related to the final **-ga** on the five final words of this song. Mandy Nicholson said:[59]

> Wominjeka is commonly translated as 'welcome', but it has three parts: womin means to come, dji is a word-ending instructing you to come and ka is purpose.

This final **-ga** might also imply politeness, as suggested by Green's translation of 'kind reception', and it could be interpreted as 'please'. The word *wominjeka* is in regular use as a word of greeting or welcome in the Melbourne area.[60]

59 Mandy Nicholson in conversation with Danni Zuvela, 'If Something Is Asleep You Can Always Wake It Up', Disclaimer, accessed 6 November 2021, disclaimer.org.au/contents/if-something-is-asleep-you-can-always-wake-it-up-mandy-nicholson-in-conversation-with-danni-zuvela.

60 Wominjeka is the name of several festivals, such as annual Indigenous festival at the Footscray Community Arts Centre (footscrayarts.com/event/wominjeka-festival-2018/, site discontinued, accessed 18 July 2018), and as a name for several events/courses at universities, such as the one-hour course introducing La Trobe University students to Indigenous Australian history, culture and customs. La Trobe University, 'Wominjeka La Trobe: Indigenous Cultural Literacy for Higher Education', accessed 18 July 2018, www.latrobe.edu.au/students/your-course/subjects/current/abs0wom-wominjeka-la-trobe.

It is possible that *pigerara* is built on a root **biik** 'clay' and means something like 'paint up with clay'.

It is likely that the second word, *marmecar*, is related to the form *mamjerring* 'wailing' (Green in Smyth 1878, 2: 107). The word *mamjerring* would be a reciprocal form of a root **mama** combined with the reciprocal **djirri** (Blake 1991: 73). There is a root **mama** meaning 'hold, grab' and it is possible that the 'wailing' was associated with people holding each other, so **mamaga** could be literally 'for holding, for wailing'.

It is also possible that the last word, *tarmbucar*, is in fact the root **dhumba-** 'speak', with **dhumba-ga** perhaps meaning 'for speaking, please speak, kindly speak'.

Thus, while we do not suggest a full translation of this song, it may be that it contains sentiments such as 'Being painted up with clay, kindly wail, kindly speak'.

In the same item in the Thomas papers (SLNSW MLMSS 214, Volume 03 Item 01), there is a longer description of 'death ceremony', on the pages numbered 58 to 59.[61] This is an incomplete document describing a funeral/death ceremony and is presented below as Box 3.40. It mentions two dirges, the first on page 58 being described as 'one peculiar dirge for the dead different from any other lamentations' and a second, on page 59, described as 'the dirge of the lubras in the distance'. We presume that the text presented in Box 3.39 and discussed in this section is the second, and that no text for the 'one peculiar dirge' has yet been found.

This text mentions the name of 'perforated' hole made by the body of the dead person as *Boro Boro*. This word is related to the form for 'broken' recorded by Thomas as *Boromuk* and *Borongbun*, who also gave the form *Borungboneit* for 'break'.

61 These form the photographs 009900065h and 009900066h in Volume 03 Item 01, available on the State Library of NSW website at archival.sl.nsw.gov.au/Details/archive/110372954 (accessed 18 July 2018).

Box 3.40: Description of death ceremony

58 Death Ceremony	A Fragment cannot find other part towards the body, but collect in small groups around the adjacent trees not at a less distance one or 200 yards, proclaim by their lamentations which are not inharmonious, that a brother is dead, these lamentations affecting and solemn in [fact indeterminable?? – inserted] the still forest adds to the scene as tho' all was alike affected, there is one peculiar dirge for the dead different from any other lamentations, the men never speak but as silent as the corpse they are beside, after about an hour or less, the inner circle of mourners by the body commence grabbing the
How they discover the murderer * Wawoip, name of ceremony of that or official priest, who gives orations over the dead The dead speak	earth, with a short stick about 3 inches deep one meeting the other taking each a space of about 7 inches more or less, at last the little trench about 2 or 3 inches wide & as many deep is finished, the aged [doctors – inserted] then will examine it & if (which is always the case) a hole is found in the narrow trench it is well examined, it is believed that the dead man has perferated the earth & made this hole, & from its distance to that hole, in that direction, will be found the black who has taken his kidney fat which caused death, The Drs will then often bend their ears to the hole, & say they hear & that distinctly the dead man say no bungellarly me that is the way, – they then immediately prepare for interring the body, the relations go & select the spot which is always dry ground, the mourners still remaining round the body, head inclined & eyes rivetted to the corpse, and apart from their superstitious notions no scene can
can be more solemn or imposing). The dirge of the lubras in the distance has in the still forest an effect upon the mind, I shall or should say Rachael weeping for her children refusing to be comforted would not be more direful, the grave being finished the body is conveyed by the relations on their shoulders, no particular posession marks its progress, & when at the spot it is thrown down, as a porter would thrown down his load	59 Dirge of Lubra Boro Boro perferated hole
(fragment ... to be search for)	

Source: SLNSW MLMSS 214, Volume 03 Item 01, pages numbered 58–59, SLNSW_FL827797.jpg and SLNSW_FL827799.jpg; adapted by authors.

3.4.9 Text for regaining consciousness after a 'kidney fat attack'

A very widespread feature of Indigenous society was the belief in the life force of the kidneys, a belief that was commented on in many nineteenth-century sources relating to the taking of kidney fat and the various ceremonies associated with it. In this section, we present one ritual text that was used in this circumstance, and the context in which that ceremony was performed (see Box 3.42). The taking of kidney fat is also referred to in connection with the Fighting song in the next section (3.4.10). Smyth (1878, 1: 429) gives the following background to the beliefs relating to kidney fat:

> The Yarra blacks believe also that when the kidney-fat is taken away by sorcery, and a person dies, the spirit goes to BUND-JEL. The body will rise again if the deceased has drunk water belonging to *Menyan* (the Moon), but if the person has drunk water belonging to *Mongabarra* (the Pigeon), the body will not rise again.

A complete understanding of the role of different 'waters' requires further research.

A more detailed description of the process of healing after a kidney fat attack is given in Smyth (1878, 1: 462), where he states that '*Wer-raap* (a doctor) is made by the spirits *(Len-ba-moorr)* of deceased doctors'. This word was spelled by Thomas in MLMSS 214, Volume 23 Item 01 (Book A) as *larn-ba-moor* and translated as 'apparition of one dead', noting that it was 'a long solemn drone'. The word could be **len-ba-murr**, where the middle syllable is **ba** 'and' and the last syllable may be a shortening of **murrup** 'spirit'. Smyth also describes in some detail the way in which the doctor flies away in order to rescue a sick person (Smyth 1878, 1: 462–63):

> *Wer-raap* flies away with the *Len-ba-moorr,* who have given wings to *Wer-raap;* and sometimes *Wer-raap* does not return for two, three, or five days. When the people of the tribe see *Wer-raap* again, he is covered with feathers. He has had a long flight. He visits the sick man, and if after a time the sick man gets well, *Wer-raap* relates all the facts connected with the recovery of the kidney-fat; but if the man dies, *Wer-raap* tells them that the wicked black had eaten the kidney-fat before he could fly to him.

The description in Smyth is probably at least partly based on a manuscript of William Thomas's. A full transcription of the manuscript text is presented here as Box 3.41:

Box 3.41: Beliefs relating to kidney fat

71

Superstitions the kidney fat death

-I have before stated that the dead require a Peace offereing, & that the Aborigines have an idea (which appears universal among the tribes I have had intercourse with) that death is caused by a wild Black extracting the kidney fat from the deceased.

-A party of Blacks are order'd by the Dr. or Wise Men to go in quest of a peace offereing, the direction is given them, & distance, but they are not to fail any sacrifice in the direction beyond the hole of civilized Blks-the party-in quest go without any dinner in fact, feel it a sacred honor to have their commission, & go thro any fatigue or hardship to avenge the death of a relative, or one of their Tribe, they leave the Encampt with a kind of War War their face daubed with the emblem of sadness be daubed with white ochre, one by one in a line the Doctrs exhort them with speeches of vehemence, & they shake hands & leave, for the direction assigned them, if they have to pass thro' other tribes friendly, they explain their mission & endeavour to get some information for their guidance-when approaching the

locality, they endure great hardship live principally on bandicoots & grubs, gum &c as they are afraid to ascend tress or make any the least noise to procure food-at night they kindle a fire only of little sticks & bark, which they throw on occasionally, these fires make no blaze, before sun set, they gather a bunch of twigs with leaves, by their

side

72 side by this they can douses a blaze in a second, one or two always keep watch at night but they should be surprised, in the morning they acting with them little fire to the least spark and cover the spot with dry leaves & so disfigures the spot that no one can detect the least foot mark-Should a portion of their route on their route be sandy they will walk backward so as to deceive their direction

When coming upon their victim or victims, always at night, not at day dawn as is their general attack (unless the party come upon be too small to make resistance & that they can count upon the whole then just before day dawn they will pounce upon their unfortunate victims, in an instance spear or bludgeon their victims laying fast asleep, then hold them fast (Barndil kungark) -catch his throat (Tunnar-muk) so secure that he cannot call out (Utur Kunmin) knock him on the next (Lulbuk nunneno) cut and take out fat of the kidneys (Leurguk koomuk karnuk marmbulla) roast his kidneys (Ballanguk Marmbulla) - after having slain their victim, if they are sure of him without striking him on the next, will after taking out his kidneys raise him up (his legs being pinioned) all standing before him mocking him try to make him say who take em out your marmbulla, they have also a strong thin cord well manufactured from the sinews

of the Emu called fastened to the small leg bone of the emu, well pointed as a pincer at one end & at the other a loop with which they form a noose & strangles their victims, but this is not used unless there is some

fear of the extrication of their victim, their greatest delight is to satisfy their dead, to have a victim sound & able to agonise, as their dead agonised-and will awfully amuse the Doctors and the friends of the deceased on their return of the awful (Yar Kahs) groans of accrutiating actions of their victims

Source: SLNSW MLMSS 214, Volume 03 Item 01, SLNSW_FL827833.jpg and SLNSW_FL827836.jpg; adapted by authors.

This text contains a significant amount of language, presented as Table 3.8. Only a part of this can be interpreted. Note that some of these phrases were also written down by Thomas in connection with the 'Fighting song' in section 3.4.10.

Table 3.8: Language material from Box 3.41

Language	English gloss (Thomas)	Linguistic notes
Barndil kungark	hold them fast	**gunga** 'take'
Tunnarmuk	catch his throat	–
Utur Kunmin	cannot call out	**ngadha** 'NEG'
Lulbuk nunneno	knock him on the neck	We assume that *lulbuk* is a verb with an imperative **-k** and *nunneno* probably means 'nape of the neck'
Leurguk koomuk karnuk marmbulla	cut and take out fat of the kidneys	**ma(rr)mbul** 'kidney fat'
Ballanguk Marmbulla	roast his kidneys	**ma(rr)mbul** 'kidney fat'

Source: Authors.

The procedure for using singing to help regain health was described by Smyth (1878, 1: 463):

> If any one has a pain in the chest, the doctor examines him. He probably finds that the *Wer-raap* of another tribe, instructed by other *Len-ba-moorr,* has put a piece of opossum rug in the body. The man is taken away from the camp by the doctor, who lays him upon the ground, puts his mouth to the part affected, and at intervals sings songs taught by his own *Len -ba-moorr.* In these songs he conjures the *Len-ba-moorr* to enter into the part, and put out whatever is causing the pain or sickness. This sometimes is continued for many hours.

The above descriptions speak in general terms about overcoming a kidney fat attack. The text presented below, however, relates to a specific incident that occurred on 26 August 1840, probably on the Yarra River somewhere near Healesville, at around 7.30 p.m. The text is found on pages 81–84 of Book A in the Thomas papers (MLMSS 214, Volume 23 Item 01).

This text relates to curing a man, whose name is not given, who had suffered a kidney fat attack, and who was facing death. He was cured as a result of the intervention of Malcolm 'the celebrated flying Dr.' (see section 3.1.2). The full context of this happening, including the text of the words that revived the sick man, is presented as Box 3.42:

Box 3.42: Text for regaining consciousness after a kidney fat attack

Superstition[X] – Augt 26th 1840 [about 20 mile s of Yea I was encamped with near 200 sobbing black – inserted] A Black of the name of was out this day in search of his daily fare equiped as usual with his spears & while upon a mountain near at hand he fancied he felt the fat of kidneys go from him & that [albild??] black fellows spirit had taken it out, he immediately endeavor'd to return to the encampment which be gained according to his account with great difficulty, he informed his tribe of what had taken place, they all[V] as they came in sit around him, his brother & friend holding him in a lying position just his head raised up, – they one after another sit around him in pensive silence no quakers meeting more so – the lubras kept charge of the dogs who were muffled up in their rugs so that they could not make a noise, al tho there were upwards of 200 Blacks present the Encampment was as quiet as tho I were in the forest 100 miles from fellow man, -- I came in

X: The Mambullă

V: the males

about 1&½ hours after sun set, I was struck as I approached with surprise at not hearing noise of sticks or any sound whatever & feared that I must have taken the rong road or over that the Encampt, on ascending a rise however I found I was right by observing a faint light here & there, I drew close to them no sounds of sticks, voices dogs or anything, surely methought the blacks are gone in anxiety I hasten'd on as quick as I could – On arriving at the Encampt I felt convinced that the blacks were gone --- I made for my fire which appear'd to be the only one in life, and getting off my horse said to my men whats been the matter where are the blacks

-- My men said that the blacks were all on the other side of the creek a man was dying but that the blacks would not let them go over – I said why all was well 3 hours ago let me go & see one old man[V] who had left the morners to come over the creek & stop me from making a noise, wisper'd to me "no you gago, wild black fellow take-em out fat no you marminarta gago karberin turnit," finding me resolute however he said in a low tone me take you, no you talk, I promised him I would not (concluding some superstition was on the carpet) he wanted me to take off my shoes but I would not it was dark & many stumps, the old man conducting me I crossed the creek, he all along cautioning me to head light, he halted just before getting to the party & said now no you take wild black fellow had taken my black fellows mambula & gone off with it – I at length approached the man he was in a lying position [on the bare ground – inserted] his head a little raised not his back, the whole of the male adults & youths

V Kollorlook

in the Encampment was with him sitting in circles the aged in the nearest circle, & so on the youngsters not so regular nor so intent as those of riper years a small doused fire was on his right about 3 yds from him no other fire near him all were as silent as tho' death had taken place – At a distance of about 200 yards in the direction of the spot where he lost his fat were here & there pieces of bark set fire to which looked more[X] like sparks of fire on the ground – One Budgry Tom (a man of courage) was placing there Barks & attending to them in order that they might not only be kept up, but to douse if there should be in any the least indication to become a flame – Malcolm the celebrated Flying Dr. (hapened to be fortunately one of the Encampt) was pretending to go to & fro speaking & invoking the wild Black to return the fat, every now & then they would hear Malcolms voice, & one would answer gou gou – At last Malcolm not finding the Wild Black he was under the necessity of ascending like an eagle, a great rustling among the bushes was more evidently by the old impostor & up he went he was able at three quarters of an hour or more he returned a great rustling among the bushes at a little distance bespoke his return the silence for the first time was broken with occasionally among their principles ejaculating

> "Goa Goa Wan du duk Mo Ther Ma lar Mal la voit Marm bu la [warrumurp]"
>
> –the syllables were pronounced so slow that could be distinctly made out–the meaning of the whole is come on bring it here, make haste bring it kidney fat"–the words come articulated syllable by syllable, one taking
>
> X fires are very deceptive at night, they say fires in England look nighter than where they are–but Blacks fires look I imagine always farther off
>
> one syllable the next the following one, but to proceed at length the celebrated aerial Dr. returned & without a word comes forward catches hold of the sick man rubs in a most unmerciful manner his side & pretends to have opened it he pronounced the man all right his friends [just??] pull him upon his bottom, & all sadness was over they all jump'd up got light from the sick mans embers began to smoke their pipes, & the dying man was not backward in soliciting a smoke–the Blacks hovering round Malcolm extolling his wondrous powr & not praising God that such powers was given to man but turning round to me said Now Marminarta you see no gammon black Dr. White Doctor would give man ill like that plenty of physic, bleed him & he had one moon Malcolm tind Woroneit bar kunark marnmate, & nerling marna meek, no good white Dr. very good black Dr.–It was in vain I tried to reason with them, it was very late by the time all was over–I however the following Morn &–had some sharp work in arguing the point, & as a proof that they were all being deceived I offer'd the Flying Dr some handsome articles if he would fly in my presence.
>
> The Blacks say that Malcolm fly like a hawk in the air & turns round & when he sees the Wild Black he drops upon him, the Wild Black drops the Fat Malcolm picks it up & returns to the sick man & makes him whole–should the Wild Black have eaten any portion of the Marmbulla the sick man cannot survive[V].
>
> Thus ended this superstitious process & effect–there is no doubt but the man had what we term fainted–& encouraging his fears made him appear worn.
>
> V. This evidently is a scapegoat that when a sick man under the charge of the Flying Dr. dies he has his pleas & by that means maintains un impacted his [idle ...?].

Source: SLNSW MLMSS 214, Volume 23 Item 01, commencing from SLNSW_FL847472.jpg; adapted by authors.

Jürgen Schöpf (pers. comm.) pointed out that 'among their principles ejaculating … the words come articulated syllable by syllable, one taking one syllable the next the following one' and this suggests that multiple people knew this text and that it was uttered in a responsive manner – that people must have known what to say and how to say it.

Smyth (1878, 1: 470–71) also presented a version of this story, in a longer section headed *Marm-bu-la* (not fully reprinted here). The text from Smyth is given as Box 3.43:

Box 3.43: Extract including the text for regaining consciousness after a kidney fat attack

When, by the rustling of branches, Malcolm's return was announced, the old men seated near the sick person cried *"Goo-goo wandududuk mo-thur ma-lar-voit marm-bu-la woo-re-mup"*-each syllable being pronounced slowly, distinctly, and solemnly. They said in these words "Come, bring back the kidney-fat-make haste."

Source: Smyth (1878, 1: 470–71); adapted by authors.

The analysis of the ritual text is given in (3.33):

(3.33) *Goa goa wan du duk mo ther*

Come on bring it here

djuwa djuwa wandha-dja-k mudha

go go bring-FORM-IMP DEM?

'Move, move, bring it (here).'

Ma lar Mal la voit Marm bu la warrumurp

make haste bring it kidney fat

mala mala-wat ma(rr)mbul-a warru murrup

let let-2PL kidney fat.ERG haste? spirit

'Let, that you hasten his spirit with the kidney fat.'[62]

Linguistic notes

The first two words clearly mean 'go' or 'move'. We have regularised them as **djuwa** rather than **guwa**, because of a number of vocabulary items in the Thomas papers (SLNSW MLMSS 214, Volume 21 Item 01; see Morey 2004), such as '*Molokun Toakunna Nearlingo* "by & bye we will return"' and '*Toewangeit* "go"'. Green also recorded this root, in the form *yane-toee* 'begone' (in Symth 1878, 2: 99). Blake regularises this form as **duwi**, but if we assume that this verb in example (3.33) is the same root as these, perhaps a palatal initial is more appropriate.

The form *wan du duk* is analysed as the **wandha** 'bring' with a formative **-dj** and the imperative **-k**. The same root is very familiar with the same formative and the imperative **-i**, as **wandha-dj-i** 'bring it', which is the source of the place name *Wonthaggi*. In Wemba-Wemba, **-k** is a transitive

62 Thanks to Jane Simpson for suggesting this translation.

imperative and **-i** is intransitive (Hercus 1986: 43). Perhaps the difference in meaning here is that the object is definite or even animate here (the life spirit of a man), whereas in other cases the object is indefinite or inanimate.

The form **mal-** meaning 'let' will be discussed below in section 3.5.4; it is also found in the butterfly dance song in section 3.4.5.

Thomas gives the word *warebuk* 'make haste' (SLNSW MLMSS 214, Volume 02, source is Langhorne). We suggest this may be a verb root **warru-**.

There are two examples of code mixing between the Eastern Kulin language and a pidgin English in this text, here presented as examples (3.34) and (3.35):

(3.34) *no you gago, wild black fellow take-em out fat no you marminarta gago karberin turnit*

(3.35) *Now Marminarta you see no gammon black Dr. White Doctor would give man ill like that plenty of physic, bleed him & he had one moon Malcolm tind Woroneit bar kunark marnmate, & nerling marna meek, no good white Dr. very good black Dr.*

The Indigenous words found in these texts are as follows:

gigo 'you go' recorded by Hercus (1986)

mama-ngadha 'father-our' (for a discussion of this suffix, see Blake 1991: 70; its use as a 1st person plural inclusive possessive is also found in R.H. Mathews's annotated offprints NLA MS 8006/8/6)

gabi is a demonstrative or locational word, also found in *Kar-ber-in-Tur-nit* 'on the other side' (Thomas MLMSS 214, Volume 23 Item 02)

dind- 'gone, finished'

wurru- is perhaps the root of word recorded as *wooroneit* 'run, or pull away fast' (Thomas MLMSS 214, Volume 26, part 6)

ba 'and'

guna(rr)k 'help – Thomas records this word as '*Kunarkun* "Save or help, note great difficulty is met with, as according to the distress in – this was two instances 1 man drowning, and the other near fall from dead branch."' (MLMSS 214, Volume 23 Item 05)

manamith 'good'

nhaling(g)u 'return'.

3.4.10 Fighting song

A song performed in fighting is found in a long description that also includes other words spoken at the time of a fight or legal judgement. This song itself was sung during the part of the ceremony that involved throwing dust or dirt at enemies when they 'they get up & dance & sing all simultaneously'. A full transcription of this ceremony is transcribed in Box 3.44. The first part of this document gives the word for the process of inviting opponents to a fight in the Woiwurrung, Wathawurrung and 'Barrabool' languages.

Box 3.44: Fighting song and words relating to it

<table>
<tr><td>Scraps
for the Native
Encampt-
Declaration of
War</td><td colspan="2">-The term for kicking, stomping, throwing dust at adversaries in fighting to chalinge them</td></tr>
<tr><td></td><td>{Wawo
{Wat-
{Barr^{abl}</td><td>{Wyenolongo
{Pigenarluno
{Wyemarta</td></tr>
<tr><td></td><td colspan="2">The parties who have the bows round their legs are to receive punishment or parties who feel agrieved, ready to chalenge their accusers</td></tr>
<tr><td></td><td colspan="2">If the [deplora??] (Bin-ne kart Kur-rum) if friendly-when sulky Pe-ge-rart narnee (that will do no more fight) Wallee Marlart (that will do) Wallee-mart-boon-gart (no more sulky) tinnee-kolar-ga (only eat), bar tar-wa-gar-ry (& corroberry)</td></tr>
<tr><td></td><td colspan="2">If the meeting of tribes summoned is not friendly [& 2 bodies-inserted], there is no Corroberree-if a Corroberre but whatever beyond him or them beyond that country their stated time is to return which generally is to the day.</td></tr>
<tr><td>The messengers previous to a fight are after this fashon</td><td>Accusations English
Stand, sulky, black you killed Koolin-my friend-stand up now you & let blackfellows spear you</td><td>Aborigl
Terre paur warrer Koolin karki Terreonuk woorm Pourt warren Koolin-Pung-gu-lar Par-rir-nin</td></tr>
<tr><td></td><td colspan="2">The chief of the tribe cries out-Pat-no-Min-ner Pid-gee Nar-lun-Vein-art Port Pooling (big) put ashes over all the body & dance around the fire</td></tr>
<tr><td></td><td colspan="2">Mun-noul Mun-nup-Take up & throw at enemies dust and then they get up & dance & sing all simultaneously Yeãã Yeãã, Terre-mun-Woo-Woin-par-me-Mal-ro-ner Yeaa Yeaa Woo-ner, Gnal-pin, Tal-lert-broon, Wor-ro-me-Nar-nee-Wor-ro-me.</td></tr>
<tr><td></td><td colspan="2">If they come to a general fight, the principal offended parties condem'd ap-pear with bows on their legs, just above the ankle (Kerrunger) & stripes behind (Woorm)-the old Drs (Warwoit) in an excited</td></tr>
<tr><td></td><td colspan="2">speech to this purport-Stand Sulky Blks-if a Victim is to be sacrificed, he is seized Til-bak nun nero kow-it | hit him & hold him fast | & strike him on the neck, (Luer-gak Koo-muk Kot-nuk) cut you & take out his kidneys</td></tr>
<tr><td></td><td colspan="2">-When the victim is killed, they cry out Yeãã Yeãã</td></tr>
</table>

Yeãã Ma-ro-ner – the blacks say they only cut the right sides, put two fingers in & pull out the kidneys – before they had civilized tools, they used the Goo-an-na tooth to cut out the Marm-bulla – they roast & eat the kidney but don't the flesh till the 4th day when the victim is	
sure to be dead	
Glossary as above	English
Pallet Koounwut	2 Messengers
Nargat-Woody Woodulul Koolin	To see & fetch here all blackfellows
Bennekart Kurrum	When sulky another one
Pyerart Narnee	That will do
Warlee Narlart	Enough of it
Wellee Mort Booncart	No more sulky
Tu-wa-gee-ry	Only Corroberry
Tin-ne Ko lar-gee	Only eat

Source: SLNSW MLMSS 214, Volume 03 Item 01, SLNSW_FL827951.jpg and SLNSW_FL827953.jpg; adapted by authors.

Note that in another part of the same manuscript, Thomas writes 'Kerranger – the parties who have the [rushes??] round their legs are the parties particularly aggrieved, or to receive punishment' (SLNSW MLMSS 214, Volume 03 Item 01, SLNSW_FL827799.jpg).

There is a considerable amount of language data in this piece of text from the Woiwurrung language, presented here as Table 3.9, with some suggestions for analysis of these words and phrases.

Table 3.9: Language material from Thomas in Box 3.44

Language	English gloss	Linguistic notes
Wyenolongo	kicking, stomping, throwing dust at adversaries in fighting to chalinge them	**waya** 'hit with missile', based on sources in R.H. Mathews (e.g. 1902a)
Bin-ne kart Kur-rum	[deplora??]	–
Pe-ge-rart narnee	will do no more fight	–
Wallee Marloit	that will do	**mal(a)** 'let, perhaps'
Wallee-mart-borngut	no more sulky	–
tinnee-kat lar-ga	only eat	–
bar tar-wa-gu-ry	& corroberry	**ba** 'and'

Language	English gloss	Linguistic notes
Terre paur warrer Koolin karki Terreomuk woorm Pourt warren Koolin –Pung-gu-lar Par-rir-nin	Stand, sulky, black you killed Koolin – my friend – stand up now you & let blackfellows spear you	**d(j)arri-** 'stand' **warr** '2SG' **guliny** 'man' *Kar-ki* (Thomas MLMSS 214, Volume 23 Item 02) 'friend' **d(j)arri-ma-k** 'stand-FORM-IMP' *worrm* (is later explained as 'stripes behind') **buuk warrin** 'angry, sulky'
Pat-no-Min-ner Pid-gee Nar-lun-Vein-art Port Pooling	(big) put ashes over all the body & dance around the fire	**wiiny** 'fire' **-ooth** 'locative' (possibly Thomas meant to write *-oit*)
Mun-noul Mun-nup	Take up & throw at enemies	**manip** 'dirt, dust'
Kerrunger	bows just above the ankles	also explained as 'Kerranger – the parties who have the [rushes??] round their legs are the parties particularly aggrieved, or to receive punishment'
Woorm	stripes behind	–
Warwoit	old Drs	**wawuty** 'ritual specialist'
Til-bak nunnero kow-it	hit him hold him fast	**djilba** 'hit' **-k** 'IMP'
Luer-gak Koo-muk Kot-nuk	cut you and take out the kidneys	–
Yeāā Yeāā Ma-ro-ner	'cry when the victim is killed'	–
Pallet Koounwut	2 Messengers	**bulaty** 'two'
Nargat-Woody Woodulul Koolin	To see & fetch here all blackfellows	**nganga-** 'see' **-aty** 'subordinating marker' **wurrdi-wurrdiyalal** 'many' **guliny** 'person'
Bennekart Kurrum	When sulky another one	–
Pyerart Narnee	That will do	–
Warlee Narlart	Enough of it	–
Wellee Mort Booncart	No more sulky	–
Tu-wa-gee-ry	Only Corroberry	maybe **d(j)uwa** 'go away' **-dji** 'IMP'
Tin-ne Ko lar-gee	Only eat	–

Source: Authors.

Thomas gives the word for 'war' as *Nar-rite*, with a note: 'This is the term they use it literally means sulky – when war is declared 2 or more messengers are dispatched, their persons held sacred & take a cut stick like as used in corroberries – when peace is declared *tarrers* are sent' (*tarrer*, regularised as **djirra** 'spear') (SLNSW MLMSS 214, Volume 23 Item 02, SLNSW_FL814495.jpg).

The song that was sung during the throwing of dust (*Mun-noul Mun-nup*), when all 'get up & dance & sing all simultaneously', is regularised in example (3.36), with the original spelling shown:

(3.36) *Yeăă Yeăă, Terre-mun-Woo-Woin-par-me-Mal-ro-ner*

Yeaa Yeaa Woo-ner, Gnal-pin, Tal-lert-broon, Wor-ro-me-Nar-nee – Wor-ro-me.

yiya yiya d(j)err(w)amuny wuwunybami marruna

yiya yiya wuna ngalbin d(h)ala(r)t-brun warrami nani warrami

Notes

We cannot propose a translation of the whole of this song, but some speculations are possible.

The word Yeăă (**yiya**) is presumably a cry or exclamation.

The word *terre-mun* may contain the root **d(j)arri-** 'stand'.

The root **marru** means 'cry' and this may be an appropriate word here.

In the second line the word *wor-ro-me* is repeated, it may be related to a root **warr(a)wa** 'run'.

3.4.11 Enchanting away rain

The final song in this section is a Boonwurrung text written down by Thomas in his manuscripts and also published in Bride (1898: 91). In the manuscript this is described as a song for 'enchanting away rain'. The manuscript version of this text is presented as Box 3.45 and the version in Bride as Box 3.46, where the song's function is described as 'when a continuence of rain is desired'.

Box 3.45: Enchantment song, version 1

62 Song enchanting away rain	Won ner rer Ner wein Barn we are Won ner rer Tin der buk Koo de are. Ner wein Koo de are Tin der buk Kar-row-long Parn During the time this is sung the charmer sits in his miam & with a piece of bark about a foot or 10 in long continues throwing hot ashes from the fire into the air mumbling alternately then singing the above song in fact all their charmings are in a mumbling language not known to the rest of the blacks, even those ignorant people have an idea that something must be done or said not to be comprehended by the general mass to add to its importance like a consultation of Physicians who I think as Garth states talk together in a Dogril Latin not be comprehended by the patient even tho' a classis scholar - Bobbinary a great charm

Source: SLNSW MLMSS 214, Volume 03 Item 01, SLNSW_FL827807.jpg; adapted by authors.

Box 3.46: Enchantment song, version 2

"*Charmers or Enchanters*:– There are characters among the blacks who are supposed to possess powers according to their various qualifications. When a continuance of rain is desired, the charmer is applied to, who sings,

> "Won-ner-rer Nger-wein Barm-we-are Won-ner-rer
>
> Tin-der-buk Koo-de-are Nger-wein Koo-de-are Tin-der-buk
>
> Kar-row-lin."1

"During the time that this is sung, the charmer sits in his mia-mia, and with a piece of thin bark, about a foot or eighteen inches long, continues throwing hot dust from the fire into the air, alternately mumbling and singing the above song; in fact all their charmings are in mumbling language, not known to the rest of the blacks.

[Note]1. I have not succeeded in getting a translation of this song, *if indeed the words have any meaning at all* – Ed."

Source: Thomas in Bride (1898: 91); adapted by authors.

Thomas goes on (in Bride 1898: 92) to talk about Bobbinary, where it is made clear that this song's function is to enchant rain away:

> We have in the Western Port tribe a celebrated charmer-away of rain, old Bobbinary. I have known this man to be kept singing for hours. The blacks say, when Bobbinary was a child that it had been raining for some days, and 'blackfellows all sad, their bellies tied up to keep off hunger; that the child Bobbinary began to sing, and that sun immediately came out, and no more rain. That ever since then he has been able to send rain away.'

While it is not stated explicitly, the naming of Bobbinary in the manuscript version suggests that he was Thomas's informant for this charm.

A.W. Howitt also noted information, under a heading 'rain makers', about this chant gathered from Mr Connor J.P., who said that:

> He remembers during a very wet time that an old man endeavored to produce fine weather and to send the rain away by "muttering words to himself as he sat by his fire and at the same time throwing any ashes from the edge of the fire against the direction from which the rain was coming.

Although Thomas did not suggest a translation of this text, the presence of the word *Ner-wein* or *Nger-wein*, regularised by Blake as **ngawany** 'sun', is appropriate for this text. Our suggested analysis is presented as example (3.37). Note the version presented for analysis here is based on the manuscript version, with the additional final word *parn*. However, the separation of words is based on Bride (1898: 91).

(3.37)

won ner rer	*ner wein*
wan(h)a-rra	**ngawany**
look-up-having?	sun

'Looking far up … at the sun.'

barn we are	*won ner rer*	*tin der bak*	*koo de are*
baany-wiya	**wan(h)a-rra**	**djindi-bak**	**gurri-aya**
water-?	look-up-having?	finished-?	be?-?

'Looking far up, the rain is finished …'

ner wein	*koo de are*	*tin der buk*	*kar-row-long*	*(parn)*
ngawany	**gurri-aya**	**dindi-bak**	**garr(g)aling**	**baany**
sun	be?-?	finished-?	wet	water

'The sun (has) come wetness is finished …'

Linguistic notes

The Thomas manuscripts (MLMSS 214, Volume 23 Item 02) record two words, *Wonnunarta* 'there above, look up' and *Wonnunduk* 'look above, very high'. Given that the word for 'sun' also seems to occur in this song, these meanings seem appropriate for *won-ner-rer* and perhaps suggest a root **wan(h)a**.

The word *barm-we-are* is perhaps based on the root **baany-** 'water' and refers to rain. Many of the words recorded for rain in this language are based on **baany**, although a second word **yayal** is also recorded. Several derivations built on **baany** are found in the sources for the language: **baany(m)abil, baanymin** and **baanywin**. It is likely that **baanywiya** is another derived form meaning 'rain'.

The word *tin-der-bak* is recorded also by Thomas as *Tindeebeek* with the meaning 'all gone'.

The word *Koo-ding* is recorded by Thomas with the meaning 'in or at' (MLMSS 214, Volume 23 Item 02). This is possibly a form of the root **gurri** 'be' (Blake 1991: 76).

The word *Kar-row-lin*/*Kar-row-long* is spelled *Karrgaling* 'wet (rainy, moist)' (Green in Smyth 1878, 2: 107). We have decided to regularise this as **garr(g)aling**.

3.5 Songs in State Library of Victoria

Towards the end of the manuscript SLV MS 6290 (see section 1.5.2), the compiler of the manuscript included a supplement 'Containing additional words, phrases, Songs &c. in the Melbourne Dialect'. These four songs were almost certainly told to the compiler by Peter Mungett, a Wathawurrung man. Nevertheless, we have decided to include these here, rather than in the chapter on Wathawurrung (see section 4.2) because they are specifically identified as from Melbourne.

3.5.1 Supplement, Song 1

The transcription of the first of these songs is presented in Box 3.47:

Box 3.47: Supplement, Song 1

Song

Yū-cūm-ha-gnilla-barrom-mattina

Gnittū-barrōm-gningnūlla-gren-gnarkaŷ

mangō

Chorus: Yū-cūm-ha-gnilla-barrōm-mattīm

gningnūlla

Translation

A parrot was sitting on a tree – A Blackfellow whistled to drive him off – off they fly – then

Blackfellow gathers sticks with leaves on them (branches) on which the parrot came down & they knocked him on the head and made this song

Source: SLV MS 6290, p. 255; adapted by authors.

A suggested regularisation of the spelling is given in (3.38):

(3.38) **yugum-a ngila barrum madhina**

ngidhu barrum ngingula grengagai mangu

yugum-a ngila barrum madhim ngingula

The word for parrakeet in Eastern Kulin was recorded by Thomas (SLNSW MLMSS 214) as *Uu gup*, which can be regularised as **yugup**, and is probably the first word of the first and third lines. No other words in Eastern Kulin language can be identified here. Note that we have not been able to identify Wathawurrung words in this song; for example, **wurr-puyn** is 'whistle' in Wathawurrung (Blake, Clark and Krishna-Pillay 1998), a word not found in this song.

3.5.2 Supplement, Song 2

The transcription of the second song in the supplement is presented as Box 3.48:

Box 3.48: Supplement, Song 2

Song
Gying-gāīrana-yōōm-darrōmarek
Gying-gairana-yōōm-darrōmarek
Gniek-garrōna-gniek-garōna
Wōllōm ōmmīna-Danning-ngarrgarāding
Gēēna-gōōlygōōrk
Translation
Blackfellows saw flowers, some said they were Yam blossoms, some said no. They took
them to the old man who said they were and so they dug them up

Source: SLV MS 6290, p. 255; adapted by authors.

A suggested regularisation of this song is presented as (3.39):

(3.39) **djing gayrana yum d(h)arrumarrik**
djing gayrana yum d(h)arrumarrik
ngik garrana ngik garrana
wulumumin(h)a d(h)aning ngarrgarrading
djina guli gurrk

No analysis or translation of this song can be presented. The form *Wōllōm ōmmīna* may be the word for 'yamstick', which is regularised by Blake (1991: 89) as **wuluñ** and **wuluwañ**. The second regularisation is based on the form in Curr (1887, 3: 524), *wolo-ain*, which was from the Ngooraialum tribe. This form might be in the ergative-instrumental case with a final **-dha**.

In the Colac language, the word for 'yam daisy' is **ka(rr)** written down by George Augustus Robinson as *carr* (Blake, Clark and Reid 1998: 171). We can speculate that the words *gayrana* and *garrana* may be the word for 'yam daisy', also known as *murnong*, the roots of which were certainly eaten by Aboriginal people in Victoria.

3.5.3 Supplement, Hymn sung at funerals

The transcription of the Funeral hymn in the supplement is presented as Box 3.49:

Box 3.49: Supplement, Funeral hymn

Hymn
Sung at funerals
Blōōrgāy-gēērmah-makōnday-bōmāh
marāh-warrāh
Blōōrgāy-gēērmah-makōnday-bōmāh
marah-warrah
Blōōrgāy-gēērmah-marah-warrah
Grēēmah-rōllah-grēēnmah-marār
mārrāy-gina-gamba
Translation
There is a God – if Blackfellow has been good he will go to him, if not – he will go to the Devil

Source: SLV MS 6290, p. 256; adapted by authors.

A suggested regularisation of this song is presented in (3.40):

(3.40) **blurrgai djirrma magundai buma marra warra**
blurrgai djirrma magundai buma marra warra
blurrgai djirrma marra warra
grimarrula grima marra marrai djina gamba

No analysis or translation of this song can be suggested at this time. Given that the word **mar** is 'man' in the Warrnambool language (Blake 2003b), it may be that this word is present in this song and that the song is, consequently, not an Eastern Kulin song. It is possible that *marāh-warrāh* is a form containing the same final element as the word for 'swan', **gunawara**, or that this is the verb **warra** 'do'. No other words can be recognised. The poetic structure and parallelism of the song suggests that it was composed by an Indigenous poet or poets, rather than being the translation of a Christian hymn, but it is possibly influenced by Christian ideas.

3.5.4 Supplement, Superstitious speech

The transcription of the 'suppostitious speech' in the supplement is presented as Box 3.50:

Box 3.50: Supplement, Superstitious speech

Suppostitious speech

<u>On the abduction of a Lubra</u>

Wēē-hat-gōōlāy-yōn-gnō-net-gōōndāy-baggōōk-
gūk-garrah-mallāh-gūile-baggōōrk-
gnāllah-gneddin-dannong-gnong-wallah
mallah-yannoo-gnet-min-gōōrdōōkah
cōōlie-gnin-cabam-yannāy-yōō-gēēyōō
cōōrnday-bangōōrt-day-dŷiek

<u>Translation</u>

Let us go Lads and get that woman. If they don't give her up, we'll go to war with them and see which will be the best tribe. Then if they won't give her up, we must get [p. 257] other tribes and if they can't take her away, we must submit to her loss

Source: SLV MS 6290, pp. 256–57; adapted by authors.

Only a partial analysis of this text has so far been possible. This is presented as (3.41):

(3.41) *Wēē-hat-gōōlāy-yōn-gnō-net-gōōndāy-baggōōk-*

wiya-t	**guliyn**	**ngunitj**	**gund(a)i**	**bagurrk**
fight?-	man	?	get-?IMP	female

'Fight … men … to get the woman.'

gūk-garrah-mallāh-gūile-baggōōrk-

gu(rr)k	**garra**	**mal-a**	**guli**	**bagurrk**
?	?	let		female

'… let us … the woman.'

gnāllah-gneddin-dannong-gnong-wallah

ngalang-ad(h)an	**danung-(ng)ung**	**wala**
war-1SG.PST	?	?

'war …'

mallah-yannoo-gnet-min-gōōrdōōkah

mala	**yan-u**	**ngid(y)**	**min**	**gurduga**
let	go-?	?	EMPH?	?

'let us go …'

cōōlie-gnin-cabam-yannāy-yōō-gēēyōō

guliyn	**gabam**	**yani-yu**	**giyu**
man	?	go-away?	DEM.ABL?

'men … go away from there'

cōōrnday-bangōōrt-day-dŷiek

gund(a)i	**bangu(r)t**	**djidjik**
get-?IMP	?	younger sibling?

'to get (the woman?) …'

Notes

Parker gives a form *wialley an* 'to fight' in Smyth (1878, 2: 169) for the Ta-oungurong language. This form may include a root **wiya-** and the frequentative/continuative particle **-ila**.

The forms *gōōndāy* and *cōōnrday* have both been regularised as **gundi**. This form is discussed above in relation to Kurburu's song (section 3.2.2) and may be related to the root **gunga** 'take'.

The form **mal(a)** is found in a number of Thomas's Woiwurrung sources translated as 'let'. For example, in several locations in SLNSW MLMSS 214, Volume 02, he translates *Mal* as 'let' and in the Aboriginal–English Vocabulary (SLNSW MLMSS 214, Volume 23) he gives the form *Mullunnanger* 'let me see', which contains a root **mal(a)** and **nanga** 'see'.

The form *yannāy-yōō* is analysed as built on the root **yana** 'go'. A similar form was recorded for Woiwurrung by R.H. Mathews (NLA MS 8006/3/4.1, Notebook 1, p. 2). This is presented in example (3.42). Morey (1998) suggested that this **-yu** might be glossed as 'away', related to the **-u** ablative suffix.

(3.42) *Yan'-i-u yilamu*

'Go from the camp'

yana-i-yu **yilam-u**

go-IMP-AWAY? camp-ABL

'Go away from the camp!'

The word for 'war' is given by Green in Smyth (1878, 2: 107) as *ngalang*, a form that appears to be present in our analysis in Line 3 of example (3.41).

It is possible that the word *day-dŷiek* is a spelling of **djidjitj** 'younger sibling'.

3.6 Daniel Bunce

3.6.1 Corroboree singing

In a chapter headed 'An Excursion to Westernport', Bunce (1857)[63] wrote the following description of corroboree singing (Box 3.51):

Box 3.51: Description of corroboree singing

Proceeding upon our journey, we crossed several creeks and streams, and eventually ascended the highest part of the Western Port ranges. Each day I was enabled to add some fresh varieties to my herbarium. The western mountains abound in healthy timber. In this locality, too, there is plenty of a light, white wood, which the natives call *weenth kalk kalk* (fire stick), as they obtain a light from it, by means of friction, very readily. This kind of wood is also called *thaal kalk* (sounding stick), because a solid, ringing sound can be produced by two round billets being beaten together. When the natives hold a corroborree, a festival in which dancing forms the chief element, those who do not join in the dance beat time with the sounding stick, while they sing continually, "Yah-yabba, yah-yabba, yah."

Source: Bunce (1857, Chapter 11); adapted by authors.

We can regularise the song as (3.43):

(3.43) **ya yaba, ya yaba, ya**

These words are probably exclamatory cries. Without sound recordings we cannot know the form of these cries, but it is possible that some of these cries had extended long vowels and maybe even breathy release that could have written as **yah**. A closer examination of the cries and final utterances

63 The text is fully transcribed and readable at Project Gutenberg Australia, 'Australasiatic Reminiscences', September 2013, accessed 19 June 2019, gutenberg.net.au/ebooks13/1305271h.html.

of the songs in the sound recordings of Norman Tindale (see for example, section 6.2.1), might one day allow for more nuanced understanding of this and similar types of songs.

3.6.2 Requesting away rain

A short text relating to requesting away rain (and perhaps connected with that documented by Thomas in section 3.4.11), was written down by Bunce and republished in Smyth (1878, 1: 127–28), presented here as Box 3.52:

Box 3.52: Text for requesting away rain

Bunce describes the formation of a camp when a tribe was overtaken in a storm:– "There were signs of rain, the sky became overcast, thunder was heard in the distance, and forked lightning played amongst the branches of the trees. The women were busy with their tomahawks in stripping large flakes or sheets of bark from the stringybark trees, and setting forks and saplings whereon to place the bark for the erection of *willams*, or dwellings, as a shelter. The only parties disengaged were the blackfellows, whose duties appeared to be to pray for fine weather by a continued melancholy chant. This office they continued for a short time after the rain commenced, and when all the rest of us had retired under shelter ; but finding that their good divinity, in the present instance, was deaf to their appeals, they exclaimed – '*Marmingatha bullarto pork-wadding: quanthueeneera ?*' 'Marmingatha is very sulky-and why?'; and they commenced throwing ashes in the direction in which they believed she resided, saying '*T'see Waugh,!*' an exclamation of contempt and defiance – after which they returned to the willams." – *Australasiatic Reminiscences*, Bunce, p. 73.

Source: from Bunce in Smyth (1878, 1: 127–28); adapted by authors.

Our analysis of this text is presented in (3.44):

(3.44)	*Marmingatha*	*bullarto*	*pork-wadding*	*quanthueeneera*
	Marmingatha is very sulky and why?			
	maman-ngadha	**bulad(h)u**	**buuk-warra-ng**	**gwandhi-winharra**
	father-1PL.INCL	big	angry-PRES.PART?	?-why
	'Our great father is very angry … why?'			

Notes

In his word list, Bunce gives the meaning of the word *quanthuenera* as 'why, what for'. Based on spellings in Thomas, and others, Blake (1991) regularised this word for 'why' as **winharra**, which we suggest is the second part of the form recorded by Bunce.

Bunce translates the form *quantee* as 'how, query, to question'. This may be the same word that Green records as *qeente boordup* 'fair', where the second word is **bur(n)dap** 'good' and perhaps the first word means something like 'somewhat'.

The word *T'see waugh* is given in Bunce's word list (Smyth 1878, 2) as: 'Contempt, scorn, despise, to scorn, detest, disdain, hoot, shout of contempt, insult, jeer, to treat with scorn, nausea, feeling of disgust, pish! pshaw! interjection'.

3.7 Georgiana McCrae[64] and her son George Gordon McCrae

Georgiana McCrae (1804–1890) and her son Gordon C. McCrae (1833–1927) have left a number of song texts, versions of which are available in Georgiana's diary, dated 5 January 1847 (McCrae 1966), and republished in a slightly different form in McCrae (1917; Kenyon 1917).

According to Georgiana's diary, the songs were told to her by Eliza, who may have later been the wife of Jimmy Dunbar of the Westernport Tribe. As Georgiana wrote, 'Eliza told me the words of a few native songs I noted them down. There was one which the Goulburn black's tribe sing when one of their number is sent to jail'.

In a manuscript entitled 'Experiences not Exploits', a journal of reminiscences, George Gordon McCrae tells how Bed-be-endgeer or Benbenjie (known as Ben) taught him songs (McCrae family, Papers [not after 1958] (McCrae family papers), SLV MS 12018, Box 2523/5 (d), p. 97):

> Song I learned by heart from Ben' dictation. A song to raise the wind (this in it's literal sense), a song for the full moon; a canoe song, a war or rather battle-song; queer little ditties in 'pidgin' made whether in honour of our neighbours or ourselves and in which the peculiarities likely to strike a stranger, were admirably hit off.

Of these four songs, two song texts are found in the McCrae family papers, both of which are the same as two of the songs from Georgiana's journal. One of these is the Mah-lay (**ma-le**) song that George Gordon McCrae

64 Georgiana McCrae was a talented artist. Three of her works are held at the National Gallery of Australia.

describes as 'Australian boat or rather canoe song'. This song is discussed in detail in section 13.1. We believe that the language is probably not Woiwurrung. The second song found in the McCrae family papers is the Goulburn Corroboree or Yapeen (section 3.7.2).

The three texts that will be discussed here consist of two songs, the Turee song, with a section composed by Ningolubbel (section 3.7.1), and the Goulburn Corroboree or Yapeen (section 3.7.2). In addition, there is 'the dictated message', found only in Kenyon (1917: 170) (section 3.7.3).

3.7.1 Turee song, with section composed by Ningolubbel

Our two sources present these texts differently. In Georgiana's diary, they are a single song, but in Kenyon (1917) they are two separate songs. We propose to deal with them as one, treating this as some kind of traditional song, to which Ningolubbel added a section at the end. Note that we do not know the meaning or significance of the word *Turee*, unless it is the word **dharri** 'stand', already seen in Bundjil's song (section 3.2.4). The version in Georgiana's diary is given as Box 3.53, and the version in Kenyon is presented as Box 3.54 (the ordering of the verses is reversed).

Box 3.53: Turee song, version 1

Turee!

Turee byal turil by dthon
nanga turee pacoonbeen
booyal pacoonbeen turee wah

Arremootye, moorunmoorun,
nyinga macoonba blynturee
byrringalaca macoonba tinga
wah arremoothago ah

Unganyanganbarra poorangalpam
Jail mine pullarwaddyn
Jail wah wah

"the last three lines composed (?) by Ningolubbel when in jail. ["Hark, hark, the lark at heaven's gate sings."][65]

Source: McCrae (1966: 211); adapted by authors.

65 This last quote is in a song from William Shakespeare, *Cymbeline*, act 2, scene 3.

Box 3.54: Turee song, version 2

SONG COMPOSED BY NINGOLUBBEL* WHILE CONFINED IN

MELBOURNE GAOL, ABOUT 1842.

Ungan-yung barrah !
Pooringalpamah! tee jâl ah !
Myney-pular waddy-oo.
Tee jâl. Wah! Wah!

His lubra "Sally" used to take up the tune from outside the gaol wall.

Turee (Song)

Turee byal turil bython
Nanga turee paccoonbah
Booyal, paccoonbah Turee, Wah!

Arree-moo-tye, moorun-moorun, ying-ah,
Paccoonbah, blyn – Turee,
Poorung-alpamah paccoonbah,
Tinga! Wah! Arree-moo-tye, Ah!

* Otherwise Tsionbul (Turnbull), also McCrae

Source: Kenyon (1917: 170); adapted by authors.

Note that the song composed as a result of a visit by Ningolubbel's **murrup** 'spirit' to his younger brother was recorded by Howitt (see section 3.1.4).

(3.45) **darri bial darri bidhan**
nanga darri bagunbiny
buyal bagunbiny darri wa

ngarrimudji murrun murrun
nyinga magunba blin darri
birringalaga magunba dinga
wa ngarrimudjigu a

nganganyanbarra burrangalbam
jail mine bullawad(h)in
jail wa wa

There is no information to help us translate this song. One possible interpretation is that the word **bial** is 'red gum' and the word **darri** is the 'red parrot' (Robinson *tare.re*), in which case the first two words may mean 'the red parrot in the red gum'. It is possible that *turil bython* should be read as **darri bial-uth an** 'red.parrot red.gum-LOC ?'.

We will not suggest an analysis for the whole song, but if our idea that the song is referring to a bird, then *pacoonbeen* could be the 'beak' recorded by Green (in Smyth 1878, 2: 99) as *Bargimboon,* a root likely related to one or other of **baguna** 'hold' and **bagungga** 'gather' that seem to be the same root.

The word **murrun** maybe mean 'alive'.

If these ideas are correct, perhaps this song was made in praise of the land from which Ningolubbel came and he sang it for solace while in prison.

3.7.2 Goulburn Corroboree or 'Yapeen'

The second song recorded by Georgiana was the Yapeen or Goulburn Corroboree. The name of this song is perhaps also that of a place name near Castlemaine that is supposed to mean 'green hill' or 'valley'.[66] The word *Yapeen* is clearly related to the root form **yapana-**, presumably meaning 'dance', found in the Ye-pen-ni pie-kai dance (see section 2.4). Three versions of this text exist, that in Georgiana's diary, presented in Box 3.55, that in Kenyon 1917, presented in Box 3.56, and the manuscript version in the McCrae family papers (Box 3.57).

Box 3.55: Yapeen Corroboree song, version 1

Other Native Songs (Goulburn)

Wittimbulbah miralbanga

Thumbulbalyndia munacalebra

curriculalindula wittimbulbah

Miralbanga thumbulbalyndia

Munacalebra curricullalindula

Source: McCrae (1966: 210); adapted by authors.

66 As given in Wikipedia, 'Yapeen', accessed 28 May 2017, en.wikipedia.org/wiki/Yapeen. A word is hardly likely to mean both hill and valley so we suggest that this meaning is probably faulty. The Wikipedia page references the website www.egold.net.au/biogs/EG00274b.htm, where the same claim is made. The source of the suggested meaning may be L. Blake (1977), which is not an accurate source.

Box 3.56: Yapeen Corroboree song, version 2

GOULBURN CORROBOREE OR "YAPEEN"

(Also used by "Western Port" Tribe)

Ah! Wittimbulbah, miralbangah
Thumbubulyndya, munccalebra,
Curriculindulah wittimbullah,
Miralbanga, thumbubulyndya
Munecalebra curriculindulah
Pooroongalpama gomay Ah! ...
Corind-ye-brija. Wandary, Wandary. †

† I believe this chorus is (or was) widely used, and by remote tribes even. G.C. McC

Source: Kenyon (1917: 170); adapted by authors.

Box 3.57: Yapeen Corroboree song, version 3

Corroboree Song

[in pen:]
Thumbubalindya Wittimbulba [nyanga tetay - crossed out]
[gomay - crossed out] curriculindula nyanga gomay
[in pencil]
Coorinjebriah-nyanga curriculindula
[Moorun-moorun-yingah! nyanga! - crossed out] thumbubalindyah
Wittimbulbah [nyanga! - crossed out] curriculindula [gomay! - crossed out]
Moorun-moorun-yingah! gomay, gomay, [gomay - crossed out]
[cooindyebriah - crossed out] W.SSOO W.SSOO
find old Arthurs Seat book interleaved with red blotting paper - for right words

Source: McCrae family papers, SLV MS 12018, Box 2523/4 (b), page 74;[67] adapted by authors.

As the note at the end of this last version indicates, there were once other books that McCrae had prepared and apparently lost by the 1870s when perhaps this document was written. Thus it may be that the text was not well remembered.

67 The pages of this notebook are not numbered; but counting the first page after the inside cover as 1, and the recto of that as 2, this text is pasted onto page 74. Most of the even number (recto) pages are blank, but if there are drawings, they are pasted there.

Since the text in Kenyon (1917: 170) is longer, we will use it as the source of our analysis. Our suggested regularisation is given in (3.46):

(3.46) **(ng)a wid(h)imbula mirralbanga**
dhumba-bulandja mun.galebra
gurrigulindula wid(h)imbula
mirralbanga dhumba-bulandja
mun.galebra gurrigulindula
burrungalbama gumai a!
gurind-e-bridja wandhaji, wandhaji

Notes

It is clear that there is considerable parallelism in this song, with many of the words repeated, but without any information about the meaning, we can only guess.

The first word *Ah!* is surely a song particle.

The word *Wittimbulbah* also spelled *Wittimbullah* may contain a dual suffix **-bula**. Perhaps it is in fact the dual of the word for 'ear', **wirn-bula/wirring-bula** 'the two ears'.

The word *Thumbubulyndya* may contain the root **dhumba-** 'speak' and a suffix **bulany**, '3DL', possibly followed by an ergative, possibly meaning 'those two who are speaking are doing …'.

Finally, the last two words may be **wandhaji** 'take it'.

The order of items in the version in the McCrae family papers (Box 3.57) is different from the Kenyon (1917) version. The second last line contains the words *Moorun-moorun-yingah!*, which surely contains the root **yinga** 'sing'. Perhaps the word *moorun* here is the word for 'leaf' variously regularised by Blake (1991) as **marrin** and **murrin**. Perhaps it relates to the use of leaves as part of the corroboree ceremony.

3.7.3 The 'dictated message'

The text discussed in this section is not a song, but we have included it here because it is probably traditional in nature and perhaps had a ritual function. It is a message in the words of a man whose wife had run away from him to be with another man. Interestingly, one version of the description of this indicates that the woman 'scarcely understood two words of his dialect', referring to her first husband, and suggesting that marriages outside the language group (linguistic exogamy) was practised at times.

We have three versions of the text, the published version from Kenyon (1917: 170) presented as Box 3.58, the text from the manuscript version in the McCrae family papers presented as Box 3.59, and a version in a letter sent to Lucy Bleek in the 1870s in Box 3.60.

Box 3.58: The dictated message, version 1

According to my recollection, the following was a dictated
message from one of our blacks to another who had run away
from his wife, written down by Mr. Merrick, of Western Port:–
"Warriwi purprukki-angolen pambuner eota mirambik
pambun. Warriwi warn-wally weeriangul mammamuth.
Nu-th-waling walwaak towakyalboi telbether pahgoork
mirambike. Ngallegu wanthener pahgoork mirambike.
Eotha coongana mira."

Source: Kenyon (1917: 170); adapted by authors.

Box 3.59: The dictated message, version 2

Warriwi [pur–crossed out] prurkiangalin, pambuner
eota mirambik pambun, warriwi warn
wally weeriangul mamninnmuth nuthi waling
wal waak
Towakialboi tell bether Pagoork miram
Bike. Ngallegu wand thener pagoork mirambike
[Pur–crossed out] Eota Coongana mira

Source: SLV MS 12018, Box 2525/1(a) (f); adapted by authors.

Another version, in a manuscript at the Royal Historical Society of Victoria (Box 118-14), differs slightly from Box 3.58. On the third page of the manuscript, 'The Warriwi' has some glosses under some words: Warriwi (line 2 in Kenyon) is glossed 'to fight'; Pahgoork (lines 3 and 4) as 'wife' and Mirambike (lines 3 and 4) as 'mine'; and Eotha (line 5) as 'not'.

The third version we present here (Box 3.60) was sent in a letter sent from George Gordon McCrae to Lucy Bleek in South Africa.[68] In the original manuscript, the language words are spelled in capitals, and we have maintained this here.

Box 3.60: The dictated message, version 3

> The following is as well as I remember part of transcript of a message of defiance from one of our blacks to another who has stolen his wife. It is carelessly written, but I copy it as it stands. I can only make out the translation after this lapse of time but partially and imperfectly. It commenced in fine 'swash-buckle' style. WARRIWI 'Look out! Come on! – PERKUK ANGOLIM Fight to the death – PAMBUNUNG /yon/ coward! EOTHA MIRAMBIK PAMBUNUNG (I'm not afraid of you!) WARRIWI! WARRIWALLI, WERIANGUL, MAMMUNMUTH NUTHE COLING WAL WAAK – TOWAKEALBOI TEL-BETHER PAHGOORK MIRAMBIKE (mine wife) NGALLEGU OUANDTUR-NER PAHGOORK MIRAMBIKE EOTHA COONGANA MIRAMBIK re – you are not going to elope with my wife. I am not (something I forgot – possibly a fool, or to be trifled with &c &c).' I remember the elopement & the fight & hearing of the runaway lady having first been well clubbed about the head & then having her feet thrust into the hot ashes possibly to lame her & keep her from moving in future – It all ended however in the PAMBUNUNG craven, coward or timid one – bearing her off & making her the partner of his life. The injured husband too having exploded, a certain number of expletives & having nearly smashed two skulls retired so to speak with flying colors and thought himself possibly well rid of the faithless one. She was a member of a distant tribe whom he had stolen & clubbed & who scarcely understood two words of his dialect – taking these circumstances into consideration it is not to be wondered that it was an unhappy and preposterous match altogether. I never saw them more but I occasionally heard of them. I believe the three or four parties to this tragico-comical history are all now "under the sod".

Source: University of Capetown Library MS BC151, E3.1.14; adapted by authors.

Our analysis is presented in (3.47):

(3.47.1) *Warriwi purprukki-angolen pambuner eota mirambik pambun.*

warriwi	**berguki-ngal-in**	**bamba-nharr**
come	spear-1DL-?	fear-2SG.PRES
nyudha	**marrambik**	**bamba-n**
NEG	(body).1SG	fear-PART

'Come, let us fight …, you are afraid, I am not afraid.'

68 Thanks to Floris Solleveld for pointing out this source.

Notes

Although Bunce gives *wirraway* 'challenge', we will follow McCrae in glossing this word as 'come'.

The word **berguk** is elsewhere spelled by McCrae as *perkuk* and glossed as 'to kill'. Thomas has *bergoneit* 'to kill (spear)'.[69]

(3.47.2) *Warriwi warn-wally weeriangul mammamuth.*

warriwi	**wan**	**wali**	**wiriya-ngal**	**manamith**
come	1SG??	?	?-1DL	good

'Come, I will fight you … it is good.'

(3.47.3) *Nu-th-waling walwaak towakyalboi telbether pahgoork mirambike.*

nyudha	**waling**	**walwak**	**dhawagalbi**	**djilba-dharr**	**bagurrk**
NEG	?	?	enough?	hit-2SG.PST	woman

marram-bayik

mine

'Don't …, enough? of you hitting my woman.'

Note that *towakyalboi* is slightly reminiscent of *twarde* in the Earthquake song recorded by Green (see section 3.8). Perhaps it contains a form that has been translated as 'enough'.

(3.47.4) *Ngallegu wanthener pahgoork mirambike.*

ngaligu	**wandha-nharr**	**bagurrk**	**marram-bayik**
NEG?	get-2SG	woman	mine

'You will (not) get my wife.'

(3.47.5) *Eotha coongana mira.*

(n)yudha	**gunga-na**	**mirra**
NEG	take-??	??

'Not take her …'

69 We are grateful to Andrew Tanner for pointing this out to us.

3.8 Wak Wak, 'Earthquake song', recorded by John Green

Green recorded a single song, Wak-wak, in Smyth (1878, 2: 111), presented in Box 3.61:

Box 3.61: Wak-wak, Earthquake song

SONG – *Wak-wak*

[Very old Song, made on the occasion of an Earthquake]

Twarde kan noo toombi, jewa-to-me-me-jet Wanellima i i i inigjak barra milla brinbolene wonto ngiar-grroen bel-bel targel-booel-beek karwen mall.

LITERAL:– That will do of that kind of things. What is that noise at the back of my camp? It makes the ground shake and the gum-trees tremble.

Source: Green in Smyth (1878, 2: 111); adapted by authors.

There was a large earthquake centred at Cape Schank on 17 September 1855, which caused minor damage in Melbourne, and at first, we were tempted to think that this song related to that earthquake. However, it may be that this song is related to 'The story of Mombulark', a story of a wicked old man who stole a young boy, told by Barak and published in Ethel Shaw ([1940s]: 37). In order to free the boy trapped in a big stone:

> Bungil ordered them to get together all the strong men, Porcupine, Muskduck, Sleeping Lizard (totem names), and others. They all came to Bungil, who told them to push over a large tree nearby. After repeated attacks they pushed it over. 'That is good,' said Bungil. 'Come now to Mombulark's camp and try to smash the big stone.' This they could not do. So Bungil told Porcupine (whose native name means thunder) to go down under the ground and blow up the camp with a noise like thunder. When Porcupine did this Bungil pulled the child out of danger and gave him to his parents.

'Porcupine' here refers to the echidna, and the event described here sounds similar to an earthquake. Howitt (1887b: 35) made a reference to the same story:[70]

> the Woiworung, who believed that thunder was something which came from the *Tharangalk*, the country beyond the sky, for the purpose of smashing up trees, also thought that the *Echidna* had

70 We are very grateful to Andrew Tanner for bringing to our attention the stories noted down by Ethel Shaw and A.W. Howitt and for suggesting the connections between the echidna and thunder.

> command over it, for they have a legend of how Bunjil ordered it to smash up a rock with its thunder within which a stolen child had been hidden.

A fuller version of the story referred to here is in Howitt's manuscript (SLV MS Box 1053/2 (b), hw0391.pdf, pp. 29–31),[71] in which it is said that the boy was taken from a group of Thagungwurrung people camped near Mansfield. The boy was taken by 'a very bad old woman called Thadagŭn who was hung all round her head and neck and arms' and who placed the boy inside the Cathedral Range. The rescue of the boy is described thus:

> They said how shall he get the boy back? Būnjil said to the Porcupine 'try that tree'. He said this because the Porcupine has thunder. Then the Porcupine smashed the tree up with his thunder into little bits. Būnjil then said 'now go and put some thunder under the rock where Thadagŭn has hidden the little boy. The Porcupine dug a hole under the rock and put some thunder in it. Then he came out and the thunder burst the rock into two pieces. It also smashed Thadagŭn into bits – so that there was nothing left of her but her 'ghost' and her mūng (magic) which was very strong before was not much now, because the thunder had smashed it up into little bits also.

Perhaps this song is in the words of Mombulark and/or Thadagŭn whose camp was attacked by an earthquake that was created by the echidna?

The analysis of this song was discussed with some elders of the Wurundjeri community in November 2021 and that discussion led to adjustments to the analysis presented in example (3.48). As with other analyses in this volume, the interpretation of this song will certainly benefit from further discussions with community members in the future.

(3.48)	*Twarde*	*kan noo*	*toombi,*	*jewa-to-*
	dwadji	**gan-u**	**dhumb-i**	**djewa-d(h)u-**
	enough	that-ABL	speak-IMP	?

	me-me-jet	*Wanellima*
	me-me-djet	**wan-yelim-a**
	everything	?-house-CASE?

'Enough of that, speaking about everything in their camp.'

71 The full story can be read at Fison and Howitt Archive, hw0391/29, accessed 30 November 2021, howittandfison.org/document/hw0391/29. We are grateful to Ian Clark for pointing this out.

i i i	*inigjak*	*barra*	*milla*	*brinbolene*	*wonto*
i i i	**ngidjak**	**barra**	**milla**	**brinbiyal-iny**	**wuindhu**
EXCL	NEG?	stop	?	rainbow-?	noise

'Eh Eh Eh, (why) does that noise not stop, (made by?) **Brinbiyal,** the rainbow …'

ngiar-grroen	*bel-bel*	*targel-booel-beek*	*karwen*	*mall*
ngiyarr-grrun	**bial-bial**	**dha(rr)gal-buyal-biik**	**gawarn**	**mal**
ONOM?	red-gum-REDUPL	box tree?-?-ground	thunder	?

'*Ngiyarr*, the red gums and the box trees and the ground are thundering …'

Notes

As mentioned above in relation to the dictated message in section 3.7.3, the word *twarde* may mean 'enough'. It clearly has some kind of grammatical function. It is found in the sentence *Jelbadin twarde boop torong mirramtak* 'I killed a male kangaroo' (Green in Smyth 1878, 2: 112).

Green wrote down *kanano* with the meaning 'that one' (Smyth 1878, 2: 114), and *Kon-nooe* 'that' (Smyth 1878, 2: 114), from which we assume a root like **ganu-**.

Thomas wrote down the word for 'everything' as *mee-me-get.*

Green wrote down 'their house' as *Jew do wal ellim* in a section headed 'Yarra Tribe' (Smyth 1878, 2: 108–15). Although most of the sources for Woiwurrung give the word for 'camp' or 'house' as **wilam**, Green writes *ellim* that we regularise as **yilam**, which is the form recorded for Thagungwurrung (Taungurung). We suggest that the phrase *jewa-to-me-me-jet Wanellima* might mean something like 'everything in their camp'.

The word *brinbolene* does appear to be similar to the word for rainbow, written down by Thomas as *brin-beal.* Thomas (SLNSW, MLMSS 214, Volume 21 Item 07, p. 15) wrote the following:[72]

72 We are grateful to Andrew Tanner for pointing this out.

> Thunder and lightning they say never occurs but when Binbeal (rainbow) is sulky, this is another one of their minor deities, the clouds and elements above are under his charge and he will be obeyed, he silenced all the elements, & made the sun stand before him, he has a lubra who always accompanies him.

If **Brinbiyal** (rainbow) controls the thunder, and if the word for 'thunder', also referring to an echidna (see below), appears on the last line, then it would be appropriate for **Brinbiyal** to be mentioned in this song, though we might have expected Green to mention this in the translation.

The word for noise is given as *wooin-thdo* in Barry (1867).

The word **bial** 'red gum' is clearly present as *bel bel.*

The word *targel* has been regularised as **dha(rr)gal** and seems to be related to **dhagurn** recorded by R.H. Mathews for 'yellow box' (NLA MS 8006/5/3). Thomas gives *tar-gan* as 'box tree'.

The word spelled *karwen* may be **gawarn**, which means 'echidna'. As Ethel Shaw noted, the native name of the echidna means 'thunder'.[73]

3.9 Burial ceremonies

3.9.1 Boonwurrung burial customs as recorded by Robinson

George Augustus Robinson (SLNSW A 7086 part 4, pp. 33–40) includes a section headed 'Boonwerong burial of the dead'. This was transcribed by Clark (2002: 244). This text is presented here as Box 3.62. It includes a short cry, transcribed by Robinson as *ha-ha-ha* that was uttered by the *We-weep*, the doctor (also spelled **wirrrarrap**, see section 3.1.3.1).

The text of this description of the burial customs also includes the name of the funeral cry, *barun.bun.dul.go.dje*. We presume that the *ha-ha-ha* mentioned in this text is an example of *barun.bun.dul.go.dje*, but we do not know whether the different types of lament discussed in section 3.4.8 are examples of this.

73 We are grateful to Auntie Joy Wandin for pointing out an error in the analysis of this word in a draft version of this book.

Box 3.62: Boonwerong burial of the dead

In bur[y]ing the dead the grave is dug ranging SE and NW and not E and W. as sun rises. The head lays SE ward or to use the simple words of Benbow lays in the direction where the big ship comes from, for it is to lie in that direction ie. to the white men country the spirit flies after death.

Formerly they put their dead in trees and burnt them but since white men came they bury them because white men no like them in trees or burnt.

When the grave is dug and the corpse interred the native men all sit round the grave in silence watching, one man named [blank] sits at the foot in a recumbent posture, then one makes a noise as ha__ ha__ ha__, called we.weep. They watch for a small hole being made over the chest, it is very minute, as though made by wind, small sound like a puff of air it matters not how small, this is sufficient, a grub or insect does not come out (as said by some) at least it is never seen, they imagine it a spirit in shape of small fly but it leaves particulars of invisible, the [blank] then takes small twig and puts into the hole and the direction it points to (ie. Goulburn most frequently) are the people who have killed the deceased, subsequently a party is made up and the death is avenged on the first met. When the spirit flies off a fient puff is only heard, the puff is called win.deen, and put in stick dare.re.muk. After a man dies, the widow goes to her brother who gives her to a man friend of another tribe, never cousin in law. They expressed great abhorrence when asked if the wife went to the husband's brother. Grass is always cleared off the grave, funeral cry is called barm.bun.dul.god.je.

Source: Robinson, in Clark (2002: 244); adapted by authors.

Robinson also describes a funeral on Tuesday 10 December 1839 (Clark 1998, 1: 107).

3.9.2 Cries in burial ceremonies in 'southern Victoria' as reported in Smyth

In a detailed description of a burial ceremony relating to the 'southern tribes' of Victoria, Smyth (1878, 1: 104) mentions that at the time of the body being lowered into the grave 'the sorcerer cries aloud "Koor-re-koor!" He cries "Blood for blood!" or "Life for life!"' This cry is clearly based on the word **gurrk** 'blood'.

3.10 Initiation ceremonies

Not much information about songs in initiation ceremonies has been recorded. Thomas, in Bride (1898: 99), also quoted in Howitt (1904: 612), describes the ceremony of Tib-but, in which young males have their hair cut, are dressed in a particular way and go around the camp calling out *Tib-bo-bo-but*. The full description of this ceremony is given in Bride (1898: 99), and also in the manuscript version,[74] which is reproduced below as Box 3.63.

The only language recorded for this ceremony is the repetition of the *Tib-bo-bo-bo-bot* or *Tib-bo-bo-bo-bo-bot*, where it seems that the middle syllable *bo* of this word could be repeated multiple times. R.H. Mathews spelled the name of this ceremony as *Thibbarook* in an offprint in the National Library of Australia (NLA MS 8006/8/448). This suggests that a regularisation of this name may be **dhibarruk**. The name is likely related to the Dyibbau ceremony of the Dhudhuroa (see section 10.2) and the *Tyibbauga* of the Yorta Yorta (see section 9.6).[75]

Box 3.63: Tib-but, Male's coming of age

Tib-bo-ut - Ceremony when males are arrived at maturity - This is a most beastly custom, - the young men have all their hair cut close from their heads save a narrow streak from the pole of the neck to their forheads (thus [here a small drawing is placed]) which gives them a rawbone appearance, this is performed by a married man of influence is first act with the [sciyers??] (formally with white flint) then scraped with glass, or shaved with a razor, the head is then daubed over with clay, the streak of hair rising up amidst the clay which gives the youth a still more hideous appearance, strips of old rags strings slips of opposum skins old rope & all variety of stripes with which a fringed apron gurdles his body all round flapping round his seat (bottom) daubed over face & body with mostly daubs of clay, mud charcoal powder in fact every [mess??], to add to his beastly appearance, he is not allowed to have blankets to cover him or anything else night	79 Ceremony of Male Aborigs Coming of age Tib-bo-but

74 The photographs of these pages on the State Library of NSW website are numbered c009900086h to c009900088h, available at archival.sl.nsw.gov.au/Details/archive/110372954 (accessed 18 July 2018).
75 We are grateful to Harley Dunolly-Lee for pointing this out.

80 Tib-bo-but

night or day (and it is generally winter season selected for this purpose, he goes thro the encampment day and night calling out Tib-bo-bo-bo-bot he has a binnek (basket) under his arm which contains all the filth he can pick up not omitting soil human or animal in this prowling he goes too & fro night and day thro the Encampment – he is not molested by any one – he frightens & bedaubs all he meet with some of his beastly waist in his basket, but must not touch any in their miams, or lubras on their way getting water, but in every other case he is at liberty to annoy or frighten all he meets the children are awfully frightened at him & will fly to their miams screaming to their parents, he must however when he is on the more continualy cry out Tib-bo-bo-bo-bo-bot which is the only warning the poor creatures have to escape from him, I have been often struck at the fear created by Tib-bout, tho the Encampt knew what & who he is (& I think there must be more in the meaning that I am acquainted with) when his days of prob

tion

tion are over which lasts no small time till the appearance of hair begins to shew this the mirky day clay pate – when he is washed & the females stripe his face with certain charcoal streaks mingled with weerip (red ochre) & dance before him, his days of probation are over, & he is cart blanch to get or steal a lubra.

81 Tib-bo-ut

Source: SLNSW MLMSS 214, Volume 03 Item 01, pp. 79–81, starting at SLNSW_FL827856.jpg; adapted by authors.

R.H. Mathews also wrote extensively about the Wonga ceremony, the term related to that used for initiation in both Yorta Yorta (see section 9.6) and Dhudhuroa (see section 10.1). In NLA MS 8006/5/8, p. 6, there is a statement that 'Wm Bêrak says Wong-gûm-dhak for a made man'. We presume that this is a term also used in Eastern Kulin languages for an initiated boy, but we do not know if a term like *Wonga* was used to describe the ceremony.

Howitt (1904: 700) names the boys' initiation ceremony of the Wurundjeri as *Talangun*. We do not know how this relates to the other ceremonies here described.

Girls' initiation ceremonies were generally less well described, and perhaps less elaborate, than those of boys'. For example, in Smyth (1878, 1: 61), there is a description of a coming of age ceremony for young girls, the *Mur-rum Tur-uk-ur-uk*, probably from Eastern Kulin, probably recorded by Thomas. This ceremony included the throwing of twigs at the young girl by young men, after which the older women carefully gathered all of those twigs and:

> making a hole, bury them deeply in the ground. They are careful not to leave a single stick: each must be gathered and buried. This is done to prevent the sorcerers from taking away the girl's kidney-fat (marmbula).

No songs or cries from this ceremony have been recorded.

4

Wathawurrung songs

4.1 Background

Only three song texts connected to the Wathawurrung have come down to us, songs that were told by Peter Mungett to the compiler of State Library of Victoria MS 6290 in 1860 (see section 1.5.2). Although the three songs are from three different locations and languages, confusion between the two manuscript sources for these songs means that we have decided to group them together here, given that the person who sang the songs, Peter Mungett, was a Wathawurrung man. The three songs are presented in section 4.2. The same manuscript also provides us with the dialogue in section 4.1.2. The word list from Bacchus Marsh in that manuscript is a source for the Wathawurrrung language (for further discussion of the Wathawurrung sources, see Blake, Clark and Krishna-Pillay 1998).

There are some mentions of corroborees held in the Geelong area, such as that mentioned by Capt. Foster Fyans in Bride (1898: 122). No detailed descriptions of these corroborees of texts of songs have come down to us. A few words relating the songs are shown in the various sources for the Wathawurrung language (see section 4.1.1), as well as a dialogue from SLV MS 6290 (see section 4.1.2) and a sentence noted by Mrs Davenport in Bride (1898: 310) (see section 4.1.3).

William Thomas in Bride (1898: 96) also records a description of a fight between the Barrabool and Buninyong people on 5 December 1844 that concluded with 'chiefs of other tribes':

> rushing between the contending parties, bring the matter to a close, which is, like its commencement, ended in *wăr, wăr, wăr*, as they call it, or high words.

This is perhaps an example of a war cry, probably used by a wide range of Kulin groups, perhaps able to be regularised as **wa(rr)**, for we cannot be sure from this transcription if there was a final rhotic sound.

One aspect of music that we can mention here is the reed pipe that was used in western Victoria, in both Wathawurrung and Warrnambool areas. Robinson (in Clark 1998, 2: 121), in an entry dated 2 April 1841, wrote of a youth named Poke.o.ome.yoke (aged 23) who 'had a reed pipe, called by the Tcharcate; al.lome, Coligan; tone.done and Waddowrong; tome.dome, from which he produced pleasing sounds. I obtained it from him for a knife, they were Bullock natives. [figure 4.9]'.[1] Robinson (in Clark 1998, 2: 122) went on to add:

> I enquired of our native about the pipe or musical instrument, and was informed that the natives had it among them long before white men came among them. It appeared to me that to produce the sounds they whistled in the instrument. This was the first I had seen of the kind.

The word *tome.dome* for 'reed pipe' is not included in Blake, Clark and Krishna-Pillay's (1998) study of Wathawurrung.

4.1.1 Musical terminology in Wathawurrung

The following words related to songs and dances are found in Blake, Clark and Krishna-Pillay (1998). Following the general principle in Blake, Clark and Krishna-Pillay, we show words regularised with voiceless stops (Table 4.1).

1 Note that Clark mistakenly refers to Figure 4.9 (Clark 1998, 2: 167), which contains drawings of Mount Shadwell and Mount Elephant. The drawing of the flute is Figure 4.10 (Clark 1998, 2: 166).

Table 4.1: Glossary of words relating to singing in Wathawurrung

Regularised word	Gloss	Source spellings[2]
ying- **-ila** 'FREQ' **-ila-i** 'FREQ-IMP'	sing	*ying-ay-lay, yingile, yeanlineaati*
yeng-ying	song	*yayng-ying*
ngarri- **-ik-(y)an** 'PAST-1SG' **-mili** 'FORM'[3] **ngarrem-[ng]arrem**	dance	*kneerekeyan, gnyayry-kah, yergeh* *ngarry-milly, narimilly, ngare m il ly* *knur em ur em 'a dance'*
porrongayn	corroboree sticks	*por-ong-gine*
paapul	pipeclay	*pah-pul*
pik	pipeclay	*bik*

Source: Authors.

4.1.2 Corroboirè dialogue from Bacchus Marsh

In SLV MS 6290, there is a short dialogue about 'corroboirè'. This dialogue has already been presented for Western Kulin (section 2.1.2.1) and for Eastern Kulin (section 3.1.8.1). As discussed above, it is believed that Peter Mungett was the consultant for all these three 'dialects' (see section 1.5.2). The dialect labelled Bacchus Marsh is Wathawurrung and the 'Corroboirè' dialect is presented as Box 4.1. A second version of this dialogue is found in Royal Anthropological Institute of Great Britain and Ireland (RAIGBI) MS 38, pp. 131–32.

Box 4.1: Dialogue in the Bacchus Marsh dialect

CORROBOIRÈ		
Put on your pipe clay	2	Balmilly-wŏt
Get ready to begin	2	Wēē-ap-men
Now girls make a fire	2	Bahgŭrk-bŭllaga-wirrikak-wēēng
Now, women, sit down	2	Mōōn-gōōrip-dinang-bah-gŭrk-ballŭk
You must sing	2	We-ap-min-ying-a-lay

Source: Thomas, SLV MS 6290; adapted by authors.

2 The sources for these original spellings are found in Blake, Clark and Krishna-Pillay (1998: viii, 64).
3 See Blake, Clark and Krishna-Pillay (1998: 90).

Our analysis of the first line is presented as example (4.1):

(4.1) *Put on your pipe clay*

Balmilly-wŏt

palmili-wat

?-FORM?-2PL

'You …'

Notes

We are not able to offer a convincing analysis of this sentence. The form **wat** is a second person plural verbal suffix (Blake, Clark and Krishna-Pillay 1998: 78), and this suggests that this may be a verbal form. **Mili** is a verbal formative recorded on a range of verbs (Blake, Clark and Krishna-Pillay 1998: 90), also found on the words for 'dance' (see section 4.1.3), where the 2nd person plural suffix is also found. However, similar forms are also found in the dialogues for Melbourne (Eastern Kulin) (see section 3.1.8.1) and Ballarat (Western Kulin) (see section 2.1.2.1) where **-mili** is not found in such wide usage. This word may consist of the word for 'bitter', or 'alcohol', **palim** combined with the frequentative suffix **-ila** having a reflexive function. (See example (2.3) for the same sentence from 'Ballarat'.)

Our analysis of the second line is presented as (4.2):

(4.2) *Get ready to begin*

Wēē-ap-men

wi(nd)ya-ap	**min**
WH-PURP	EMPH

'Get ready!'

It seems likely that *Wēē-ap* is a WH word **windyap**, given that in both the Melbourne and Ballarat dialogues for the same sentence the form is spelled *Win-dam-mēē* and *Windȳap-men* respectively.

Our analysis of the third and fourth lines is presented as (4.3) and (4.4):

(4.3) *Now girls make a fire*

Bahgŭrk-bŭllaga-wirrikak-wēēng

pakurrk	**palak**	**wirrka-k**	**wiyn**
woman	group	light-imp	fire

'Group of woman, light the fire!'

(4.4) *Now, women, sit down*

Mōōn-gōōrip-dinang-bah-gŭrk-ballŭk

mun.kurri-p **tyinang** **pakurrk** **palak**

sit-PURP foot? Woman group

'Group of woman, sit down (here?)'

The reading of *dinang* as **tyinang** 'foot' is problematic as we do not clearly see why this word would be present here. But there is no other word recorded in Wathawurrung with a similar form.

Blake, Clark and Krishna-Pillay (1998: 137) regularise the word meaning 'sit down' as **mun.gurre**, with sources including G.A. Robinson.

Our analysis of the fifth line is presented as (4.5):

(4.5) *You must sing*

We-ap-min-ying-a-lay

wi(nd(ya-ap **min** **yinga-la-i**

WH-PURP EMPH sing-FREQ-IMP

'Get ready, you must sing!' (lit: Sing for thus indeed!')

4.1.3 Sentences and words documented by Mrs Davenport

Mrs Davenport, daughter of former deputy protector Sievewright, wrote some information about the Wathawurrung language in Bride (1898: 310).[4] One sentence she recorded is presented with our analysis as (4.6):

(4.6) *Will there be a "corrobery" to-night?*

Ngaré millywat morgalle u?

ngarrimili **-wat** **murrkal** **-yu**

dance 2PL tonight -ALL

'Will you all dance tonight?'

On the same page she indicated the name of a boy as '*Niramying-ying* (loud singing)'. This clearly contains two forms, **nyirrim** 'long' and **ying-** 'sing'.

4 The online version of Bride (1898) has the final digit of the date of publication crossed out and replaced with 9, hence 1899.

4.2 Three songs in the State Library of Victoria

In this section, we present the three songs that were told to the compiler of SLV MS 6290 and the manuscript on which it was originally based, RAIGBI MS 38. The story of this manuscript is discussed in detail above (section 1.5.2). The three songs were almost certainly told to the compiler by Peter Mungett (see above). Since Mungett was a Wathawurrung man, we have included all three songs that he gave in the Wathawurrung chapter, even though they are apparently in three different languages.

Each of these songs is accompanied by a 'translation' that is not a literal translation and is better treated as an explanation. In SLV MS 6290, the section containing these songs (and also those from Gippsland, Mount Gambier and Wonnin) are in a section headed 'Songs' with the name of the language listed by its location; in RAIGBI MS 38, however, the languages of different songs are indicated by coloured ink, and refer to different varieties from MS 6290, as set out in Table 4.2. Note that MS 38 also includes the name of the tribe in language. These tribal names, not found in other sources, are not further discussed here.

Table 4.2: Comparison between the language names in the two sources

Song	Language name in SLV MS 6290	Colour of ink in RAIGBI MS 38	Meaning of colour of ink in RAIGBI MS 38
Shooting star song	Melbourne	black	Bal-ah-ratý tribe (Ballarat)
Magpie song	Ballarat	brown	Boolook bah boolook tribe (Bacchus Marsh)
Parroquite song	Bacchus Marsh	blue	Bayry-birrp tribe (Melbourne)

Source: SLV MS 6290 and RAIGBI MS 38; adapted by authors.

The first two songs were clearly composed in response to particular events: seeing a shooting star or watching the magpie drink. In our regularisations of this section, we will use the voiceless stops found in Chapter 2 rather than the voiced stops found in Chapter 3.

4.2.1 Melbourne song

This song is about a boy who runs in fear from a shooting star. This fear was shared by people in western Victoria, as is shown in the Shooting star song and its description written down by A.W. Howitt (see section 2.3.2). This song, with the arrangement into lines as it appears in MS 6290, is given as Box 4.2. A check of RAIGBI MS 38, p. 133, shows no differences in the text between the two versions.

Box 4.2: Melbourne song

(Melbourne)
Gally-marr-win-wāyn-banyōōl-banyōōlāy
mah-ngah-wallōōn-yah-warrōōng-wōōrkahl
mang-arrōōng-gally-marr-win-wāyn-bānyōōl
banyōōlay-mah-ngah-wallōōn-yah-warrōōng
wōōrkahl-mang-arrōōng-gally-marr-win
wayn-banyōōl-banyōōlay-mah-ngah-wahnōōn
an-woor-woor
Translation:
There was a young boy looking up at the sky at night when he saw a falling star. He was afraid and ran back to his uncle and told him what he had seen. He stumbled over an anthill and fell. He began to cry and the bystanders in mockery made this song.

Source: SLV MS 6290, p. 229; adapted by authors.

An example of an anthill in the Yarra Ranges, part of Woiwurrung country, can be seen on the website www.warburtoninfo.com/blog/Termite-Mound-Yarra-Ranges.[5]

When the text of the song is rearranged, it can be seen that there are three lines, the first two almost identical and the third with a shortened ending. This is presented in Box 4.3.

Box 4.3: Melbourne song arranged into lines

Gally-marr-win-wāyn-banyōōl-banyōōlāy mah-ngah-wallōōn-yah-warrōōng-wōōrkahl mang-arrōōng-
gally-marr-win-wāyn-bānyōōl banyōōlay-mah-ngah-wallōōn-yah-warrōōng wōōrkahl-mang-arrōōng
gally-marr-win wayn-banyōōl-banyōōlay-mah-ngah-wahnōōn an-woor-woor

Source: SLV MS 6290, p. 229; adapted by authors.

5 Warbuton Valley, 'Termite mound beside Richards Tramway Walk', accessed 23 November 2021, www.warburtoninfo.com/blog/Termite-Mound-Yarra-Ranges.

Since this song is listed in MS 6290 as being from Melbourne, our first analysis of it assumed the language was Woiwurrung. The presence of words found in both Woiwurrung and the Western Kulin languages spoken in the area beyond Ballarat, Tjapwurrung and Djadjawurrung, such as **marru** 'cry', **panyul** 'hill' (presumed to refer to the anthill, perhaps by means of a reduplication) and **wurr-wurr** 'sky', all seem to be recognisable here; our translation works from those. The first two lines are of this form as shown in (4.7):

(4.7)	*Gally*	*marr-win*	*wāyn*	*banyōōl*	*banyōōlāy*
	kalai	**marru-ny**	**wany**	**panyul**	**panyul-ai**
	perhaps?	cry-3SG	?	hill	hill-?

mah-ngah	*wallōōn-yah*	*warrōōng*
manga	**walung-a**	**warrwu-ny**
DEM	stars in orions belt	run-3SG
wōōrkahl	*mang-arrōōng*	
wurru-kal	**mang(g)a-rung**	
sky-?	stumble-PART?	

'Maybe he (was) crying … he (was) running (to) the anthill there, (from) the Orion stars, (from) the sky, stumbling.'

As already mentioned, the last line is slightly different, and is analysed in (4.8):

(4.8)	*Gally*	*marr-win*	*wayn*	*banyōōl*	*banyōōlāy*
	kalai	**marru-ny**	**wany**	**panyul**	**panyul-ai**
	perhaps?	cry-3SG	?	hill	hill-?

mah-ngah	*wann*ōōn *an*	*woor woor*
manga	**wanhu-nhan**	**wurr-wurr**
DEM	look up-PRES-1SG.PRESS	sky

'Maybe he (was) crying, … at that anthill there, saying "I am looking up at the sky."'

Notes

We assume that the first word is **kalai**, also recorded by R.H. Mathews with the meaning 'perhaps', spelled as both *kullai* and *gullai*, in a section on verbs written on Federal Hotel notepaper (NLA MS 8006/4, File 8b, Folder 10). One sentence was given by Mathews as *ngullambŭnnan gullai* 'perhaps I will sit', **ngalamba-nhan galai** literally 'sit-1SG,PRES perhaps'. However, this word may be a demonstrative, with forms like *kalloite* 'there is' and *kullik* 'then' also noted down by Thomas. The translation might also be 'Then he was crying …'.

The usual word in Woiwurrung for 'run' is something like **warr(a)wa**, although Thomas (MLMSS 214) generally spells this word with an *l* as *Wool-won*, *Wool-woorn-eit*.

Given the meaning of the song, we think it possible that *wallōōn-yah* is the word for the 'the young men (The three stars in Orions belt and the three other stars near)', spelled by Howitt as *Wallūng eri*, his language informant being Barak.

In the word list in MS 6290, p. 189, the compiler gives the form *mangō-rang-in* for 'stumble'.

The Thomas manuscripts (SLNSW MLMSS 214, Volume 23 Item 02) record two words, *Wonnunarta* 'there above, look up' and *Wonnunduk* 'look above, very high'. Given that the word for 'sun' also seems to occur in this song, these meanings seem appropriate for *won-ner-rer* and perhaps suggest a root **wan(h)a**. If we are correct in our analysis that this combines with the 1st person singular present suffix -**nhan**, then this song was probably in Melbourne language.

4.2.2 Ballarat song

This song is listed in MS 6290 under the heading Ballarat and is presented below in Box 4.4 with the arrangement into lines as it appears in the manuscript, In RAIGBI MS 38 this song is found on page 132, and is written using red ink, which is from the Boolook bah boolook tribe (Bacchus Marsh) and is presumed to be Wathawurrung:

Box 4.4: Ballarat song

(Ballaarat)
Ngō-bŭrra-bōōdyīn-barr-wahng-ah-ahn
Bah-ngah-barra-bōōdyēēn-barr-wahng
ah-Brar-brar-ngah-mēē-ōō-mallah-
ngah-Bah-ngēēn-mee-la-wahlan-grōōnga
Dāy-ayn-ngo-barra-bōōdŷeen-barr-wahng
ah-aha-bah-ngah-barra-bōōdyēēn-barr
wahng-ah-brar-brar-ngah-mēē-ō-mallah
ngah-ngah-bah-ngēēn-mēēla-wahlan-
grōōnga
Translation:
A magpie was coming to drink. Blackfellow had a rod with a snare, and put it round the Magpies neck and pushed his head in the water. Lubra came on the hill and asked him what he was doing, he told her, and she made this song.

Source: SLV MS 6290, p. 229; adapted by authors.

The presence of the word *barr-wahng*, which is the Eastern Kulin word for 'magpie' (**barrawang**),[6] originally led us to include the song in the Eastern Kulin section of this book. This word is regularised in Wathawurrung as **parrwang** by Blake, Clark and Krishna-Pillay (1998). In light of the Corroboree song recorded by Howitt (see section 3.2.5), where both the Eastern and Western Kulin words for 'pelican' are found, it is also possible that the bird names in the song were from a language different to the bulk of the song.

The rhyme structure of the song is given in Box 4.5, in which the three lines of text are named 'a', 'b' and 'c' and follow a basic pattern of *aabc* repeated. However, some additional particles are added, including a line-initial **pa** (presumably 'and') occurring on every second line, and **tayn**, of unknown meaning, introduces the repetition.

6 A similar form is also found in the Warrnambool language, whereas in Western Kulin the form is **kurruk** (Wemba-Wemba) or **kurruki** (Mathi-Mathi).

Box 4.5: Rhyme structure of the Ballarat song

'a'	Ngō-bŭrra-bōōdyīn-barr-wahng-ah-ahn
pa + 'a'	Bah-ngah-barra-bōōdyēēn-barr-wahng ah-
'b'	Brar-brar-ngah-mēē-ōō-mallah-ngah-
pa + 'c'	Bah-ngēēn-mee-la-wahlan-grōōnga
tayn + 'a'	Dāy-ayn-ngo-barra-bōōdŷeen-barr-wahng ah-aha-
pa + 'a'	bah-ngah-barra-bōōdyēēn-barr wahng-ah-
'b'	brar-brar-ngah-mēē-ō-mallah ngah-ngah-
pa + 'c'	bah-ngēēn-mēēla-wahlan-grōōnga

Source: SLV MS 6290, p. 229; adapted by authors.

This methodology follows Donaldson's (1987: 30–35) discussion of Fred Biggs's song.

Our analysis is presented in (4.9):

(4.9)

Ngō-bŭrra	*bōōdyīn*	*barr-wahng-ah*	*aha*
ngupa-rra	**pudja-ny**	**parr(a)wang-a**	**a a**
drink-PURP	enter-3SG	magpie-ERG	EXCL

'The magpie comes in to drink, Ah! Ah!'

Bah	*ngah-barra*	*bōōdyēēn*	*barr-wahng-ah*
pa	**ngupa-rra**	**pudja-ny**	**parr(a)wang-a**
and	drink-PURP	enter-3SG	magpie-ERG

'And the magpie comes in to drink.'

Brar-brar-ngah	*mēē-ōō*	*mallah*	*ngah-*
pra-pra-nga	**miyu**	**mala**	**nga**
ONOM-SO.PRT	DEM?	let's?	SO.PRT?

'(It was crying) *bra-bra* …'

Bah	*ngēēn*	*mee-la*	*wahlan*	*grōōnga*
baany		**mala**	**walan**	**krunga**
water?		let's?	?	push into?

'And … pushed it into the water …'

Notes

We suggest that the word **pudja** 'enter' is related to the Wemba-Wemba **putheka** 'come into' and **puthekila** 'to dive into the water', and also seems to be related to a root **putj** 'stomach'.

While it seems clear that the first two lines mean 'the magpie comes in to drink', we cannot offer an analysis for the rest of the song. We might expect the word for water, **paany** in Eastern Kulin but **ngupitj** in Wathawurrung, to be present. It is possible that the form *Bah ngēēn* represents the word for 'water' in Eastern Kulin.

William Thomas records a form *Krungee* with the meaning 'come in' in Eastern Kulin (SLNSW MLMSS 214), which may account for the form *grōōnga* and may relate to the section of the translation about pushing the magpie's neck into the water, though we might expect a locative/allative marker, **-uth** in Eastern Kulin and **-o** in Wathawurrung (Blake, Clark and Krishna-Pillay 1998: 71), but do not see these suffixes.

As with the Melbourne song (section 4.2.1), Thomas's 'translation' is more the context of the song rather than a translation. We have seen with a number of the songs performed by Stan Day (see section 2.2) that the story behind the song is much deeper than a word-by-word translation of the song would suggest. Also, both this song and the first song in the supplement of Melbourne songs in MS 6290 (section 3.5.1), as well as many of Stan Day's songs, and the Corroboree song (section 3.2.5), are about birds, a very common motif in these songs.

4.2.3 Bacchus Marsh song

The last of these songs is listed as being from Bacchus Marsh in MS 6290, but in RAIGBI MS 38, p. 133, it is written in blue ink that indicates it is from the Bayry-birrip tribe of Melbourne. The text of this song is presented as Box 4.6:

Box 4.6: Bacchus Marsh song

(Bacchus Marsh)
Nidyĕ-matty-mah-gāyring-ahkāy-āy-mangāy-
wēēn-nyāh-yōōky-mangy-lah-ah-Barrōō-
mattoo-mah-gnŷināy-wōōllang-ngah-ah-
ah-nidyē-matty-mah-gāyring-ahkay-āŷ-
mang-gāŷ-wēēn-nŷāh-yōōky-mangy-lah-
Barroo-mattoo-mah-gnyinnāy-wōōllang-
ngah-yah-ah-ah
Translation:
A Parroquet sipping from a tree blossom – Blackfellow threw a waddy at him and knocked him off his perch. He picked him up and showed him to his uncle. His aunt composed and sang this ditty.

Source: SLV MS 6290, p. 230; adapted by authors.

The song text is repeated in full, as becomes clearer when the 'lines' are rearranged as in (4.10):

(4.10) Nidyĕ-matty-mah-gāyring-ahkāy-āy-mangāy-wēēn-nyāh-yōōky-mangy-lah-ah-
Barrōō-mattoo-mah-gnŷināy-wōōllang-ngah-ah-ah-
nidyē-matty-mah-gāyring-ahkay-āŷ-mang-gāŷ-wēēn-nŷāh-yōōky-mangy-lah-
Barroo-mattoo-mah-gnyinnāy-wōōllang-ngah-yah-ah-ah

We suggest the following regularisation of the first line as (4.11):

(4.11) **Nitya mayt ma kerringakai ai manggai winya yuki manggi la a**
parru matu ma nginai wulang nga ya a a

Unfortunately, no convincing analysis can be given for this song. The only word we can recognise with any confidence is the word for parrakeet, regularised in Blake, Clark and Krishna-Pillay (1998: 127) as **yukip**, and realised in the song as *yōōky*.

More speculatively, the form **winya** might represent the word for 'what' (Blake, Clark and Krishna-Pillay 1998: 83). The first word of the song might be **nyita** 'hide' (Blake, Clark and Krishna-Pillay 1998: 114), perhaps suggesting that the blackfellow who knocked the bird of its perch was hiding.

None of the words we might expect in this song, such as **yung(ga)-** 'throw' (**yuma** in Eastern Kulin), **ngupa-** 'drink', or any of the Wathawurrung words for 'waddy', **kurr**, **wawarra**, **wirrawirr**, **liyangwil**, can be recognised here.

5

Gippsland songs

5.1 Background to the Gippsland songs

One of the largest collections of traditional songs from Victoria are those in the Gippsland languages. Most of these were documented with translation by A.W. Howitt (1830–1908), who has provided more than 20 songs (see section 5.2), and by Rev. John Bulmer (1833–1913) (see section 5.3). We are very fortunate to have one song recorded on an audio tape recorder by Luise Hercus, from Laurie Moffatt (section 5.5), but although we have made a transcription of both words and music for the song, unfortunately we have not been able to suggest a translation for this song.

The songs documented by Howitt in particular are made even richer because of the considerable amount of contextual background that he wrote about many of the songs, and about the song men who composed them. A number of these songs survive in multiple forms – published in Smyth (1878) or Howitt (1887a, 1904) or found in manuscripts in either the State Library of Victoria (MS 9356, particularly Box 1053/4) or Museums Victoria. Much of the knowledge collected by Howitt came from Tulaba (also known as Billy Macleod; see section 5.1.6).

The Gippsland languages were spoken by five tribes: Bratauolung, Brabralung, Braiakaulung, Krauatungalung and Tatungalung[1] (see Hercus 1986: 163). According to Howitt (SLV MS Box 1053/3 (b), p. 2), there were three languages, called *Mukthang* (spoken by Brabralung and Braiakaulung),

1 In a footnote, Howitt (1904: 73) notes the meanings of some of the morphemese that make up these names: '*Bra* is "male" or "man," *yak* is "west," and *lung* "of" or "belonging to." *Tatung* is the sea, sometimes spoken of as *gatching*; *gal* is a possessive suffix. *Muk* is "good," *thang* is "speech," *Krauat* is "east."'

Nūlit (spoken by Brataualung and Tatungalung) and *Thángŭai*[2] (spoken by the Krauatungalung). Surviving information about the languages of Gippsland is sketchy, but it is likely that these three languages were very similar. One difference that Howitt showed, for example, was that the word for the elopement song in *Mukthang* is *yenjin* (regularised as **yentjin(y)**) whereas in the *Nūlit*, the word is *yennin* (regularised as **yen(h)in(y)**) (Howitt SLV MS Box 1053/3 (b), p. 12).[3]

Hercus (1986: 163) pointed out that the five tribes 'were known collectively as the Ganai', a word spelled *Kŭrnai* by Howitt in various publications. The community today generally uses the name GunaiKŭrnai, with Kanai being used by Theatre (2024).

5.1.1 Musical terminology in Gippsland languages

A small amount of terminology relating to songs has survived. In Table 5.1, we present some terms relating to the songs and dance and the creators of those.

Table 5.1: Metalinguistic terms relating to songs and their creators

Term	Definition and source	Notes
yentjin(y)	'elopement spells' (Howitt 1904: 274)	See section 5.1.4
puntjil yentjin(y)	'medicine man' (Howitt 1904: 274)	The term **puntjil** refers to someone skilled in a particular art. It refers to males. See section 5.1.4
kunyeRu	'a term for those songs which accompany dancing' (Howitt 1904: 274)	See section 5.1.2
piRaRk	'(person who) composed the songs and dances' (Howitt 1904: 389)	See section 5.1.3
watj	'sing' (see also example 137)	–
muRantha	'dance' (Robinson *monedun*)	–

Source: Authors.

2 This name is preseved in the place name Tonghi Creek, in East Gippsland, just west of Cann River, at 37.6019836 South, 149.013689 East. There was also an old lady called Grandma Tonghi who remembered spells and cures and figured in the AIATSIS collection 'South Coast Voices'. She had obviously come to the South Coast from Krauatungalong country (Luise Hercus, pers. comm.).

3 Further research on the Gippsland language sources is needed to establish if this is a regular correspondence between intervocal /**nty**/ and /**n(h)**/. Theatre (2024) will provide a lot more information about the language.

5.1.1.1 'Corroboirè' dialogue from Gippsland

One potentially important piece of metalanguage about songs is the dialogue written down by the compiler of State Library of Victoria MS 6290, almost certainly containing information given by either Billy Clarke or Big Joe (see section 1.5.2). Box 5.1 presents the original text of the dialogue relating to 'Corroboirè' (corroboree). A second version of this dialogue is found in Royal Anthropological Institute of Great Britain and Ireland (RAIGBI) MS 38, pp. 131–32.

Box 5.1: Dialogue relating to 'Corroboirè'

Put on your pipe clay	4	Gō-gwāŷ-āh
Get ready to begin	4	Ŷap-pan
Now girls make a fire	4	Tōw-ŭr-waddy-dōōrt-do-bonahra-gwīrrāyl-gahterry
Now, women, sit down	4	Dōōrn-bōōgalla-behŭba-mŭrundimba-wahwŭrdy
You must sing	4	Waht-waht

Source: SLV MS 6290, p. 228; adapted by authors.

We have not been able to analyse most of these sentences. The first is what looks like a single word *Gō-gwāŷ-āh*, translated as 'put on your pipe clay'. This word does not resemble the word for 'pipe clay', written by Thomas as *Mallōōk* (MS 6290, p. 162), which Fesl regularises as **marlu** (Fesl 1985: G11, no. 71), and is also translated as 'dust' (Fesl 1985: G11, no. 70). Nor does this first sentence resemble the phrase 'paint red ochre', written as *Dōōngŭrro* in the same manuscript (SLV MS 6290, p. 164). Perhaps *Gō-gwāŷ-āh* related to the painting of a particular ochre, and is a verb unrecorded in other sources that have been identified so far. It might perhaps mean 'put on', 'rub' or 'mark', but no verbs with those meanings have been identified in any of the Gippsland sources.

Similarly, we are not able to offer any analysis for the second line of the dialogue, *Ŷap-pan*, translated as 'Get ready to begin'.

Our suggested analysis of the third line is presented as example (5.1):

(5.1) *Now girls make a fire*

Tōw-ŭr-waddy-dōōrt-do-bonahra-gwīrrāyl-gahterry

thaueRa	**waty**	**tut(pakan)**	**panha-Ra**	**kweRay(i)l**	**katjeRi**
fire	song?	daughter	sit-FORM	big	possum rug

'Daughters, having sat at the fire to sing, now (beat) the big possum rug.'

The words for 'fire' and perhaps 'sit' and maybe 'song' can be identified in this sentence, but no word for 'girl' or 'woman' is recognisable. We suggest that perhaps this sentence in combination with the next example (5.2), contains something about making fire, sitting and then singing. The word 'sit' has a form **panhunga** (Fesl 1985: P2, no. 7) based on R.H. Mathews[4] and presumably built from a root **panha-**.

Corey Theatre (2024) lists **tutpakan** 'daughter' **kweRayil** 'big' and **katjeRi** 'possum rug', original spelling *cuttarie* (Dawson and Pettit [1850s] cited in Theatre). As Theatre pointed out, this could refer to the big possum rug used for beating time.

(5.2) *Now, women, sit down*

Dōōrn-bōōgalla-behŭba-mŭrundimba-wahwŭrdy

tutpaka-la	**piyu-pa**	**muRanth-impa**	**wa(tj)-watj**
daughter-?	??-imp?	dance-IMP	sing.REDUPL

'Girls, … (you should) dance and sing!'

Notes

The first word seems likely to be **tutpaka-la** 'daughter-case?'.

The word for 'dance' is spelled *murndhan* by R.H. Mathews and *mone-dun* in MS 6290 (Fesl 1985: P5, no. 92). Our regularisation of a dental cluster **-nth-** is based on Mathews's spelling with *-ndh-*. Corey Theatre (pers. comm.) suggests **muntha-**.

The last sentence is a single word, given in (5.3):

(5.3) *You must sing*

Waht-what

watj-watj

sing.REDUPL

'(You must) sing!'

4 In this chapter, we have not always given the reference to the exact location in the R.H. Mathews papers for every word referred to. An examination of Fesl (1985) or Theatre (2024) will contain more detailed references.

Fesl (1985: R2, no. 13) gives a number of spellings of the word for singing, all based on a form **waty-**[5] but with a range of possible suffixes, the meanings of which are not known. These forms include: *watwaty* (R.H. Mathews); *witebalan* (Bulmer in Curr 1887, 3: 550); *white-pil-lung, wite-pil-lung* (Robinson); and *wat-wahn-gahrŭng-gahrŭng* (SLV MS 6290).

The word for 'sing' is also written down by Bulmer in Smyth (1878, 2: 30), presented as (5.4). As with the forms written by Robinson and Bulmer in Curr, there is a form **pil-** or **pal-** following the root.

(5.4) *Watbilimba*

Sing you a song

watj-pil-impa

sing-?-IMP.PL?

'(All of you), sing!'

Another example of **watj-pil** is found in a word written by Robinson as *whitepillung* in his 1847 Gippsland list (Clark 2002: 296).

5.1.1.2 An interesting set of word pairs

In the course of this study, we have identified an interesting pattern of word pairing, involving words that have some connection to the traditional songs or the rituals associated with those songs. These word pairs are comprising multisyllabic words in which a final nasal varies with a homorganic final stop. The examples so far recognised are presented in (5.5):

(5.5) **krauwan** 'female cross cousin' / **krauwat** 'east'

teteling 'bundle of thin rods'[6] / **tetelik** 'frog'[7]

kliyan 'water hen' / **kliyat** 'sinews under knee' (Fesl 1985: A19, no. 165) 'hamstring' (Fesl 1985: A17, no. 130)

prewin 'evil spirit, who is like the wind' (see section 5.2.4); **prewit** 'when the boys are already initiated and living with other young men' (see section 5.2.21.2).

5 This could also have been a final laminal dental, as **/wath/**. There may have been variation between the laminal dental and laminal palatal according to the language variety, as already mentioned in connection with the word **yentjin(y)/yen(h)in(y)** discussed in section 5.1.1.

6 In a pencil annotation to a copy of Howitt's paper on 'The Jeraeil, or initiation ceremonies of the Kurnai tribe.', Mathews spells this word as *deddeluñ* (NLA MS 8006/8/556).

7 Interestingly, Thomas lists the name of the tribe at 'Bukan' (i.e. Buchan) as the Teddalook Tribe (SLNSW MLMSS 214, Volume 05 Item 02, William Thomas journal of a journey to Gippsland, 29 November-23 December 1860). We do not know whether this tribal name is somehow related to these two words.

There may be a relationship between these words. For example, the **kliyan** 'water hen' is the patrilineal totem (see section 5.1.7.2) whose song involves 'straightening out the sinews' (see section 5.3.3). The word **kliyat** is glossed as 'sinew under knee'. Similarly, the **teteling** is a bundle of thin rods used in the **tjeRayil** or boys' initiation ceremony (see section 5.2.21), while **tetelik** is a frog, and part of that initiation ceremony is called 'Giving the boys some frogs'.

5.1.2 The types of songs

The deep knowledge of traditional songs passed on by Tulaba and others to Howitt included information naming two types of song, and mentioning a third:

i. **kunyeRu** (spelled *gunyeru* by Howitt and *koonyeroo* by Bulmer), a song that accompanied dancing
ii. **yentjin(y)** (spelled *yenjin* by Howitt and *yinginy* by Bulmer and called 'elopement songs' by Howitt and simply 'love songs' by Bulmer, but also termed 'spell'
iii. initiation songs (discussed in more detail in section 5.2.21).

There were songs composed in response to contemporary events (such as sections 5.2.2 and 5.2.3) or describing the feelings of the songster (such as section 5.2.1). One of these, the 'White Woman' song (section 5.2.3), is specifically described as a **kunyeRu** and it may be that all such songs were treated as **kunyeRu**.

Howitt's papers (SLV MS Box 1053/3 (b), hw0404.pdf, p. 50) have a section labelled *Yennin*, with McAlpine listed as the consultant, describing how these **yentjin(y)** songs were used to persuade women to elope with men, and the consequences of that. This is also discussed in detail in section 5.2.8 below.

Examples labelled as **yentjin(y)** are presented in sections 5.2.8, 5.2.9 and 5.2.10 (written by Howitt) and section 5.3.2 (written by Bulmer). Examples labelled as **kunyeRu** are presented in sections 5.2.3 and 5.2.5, both documented by Howitt. The song discussed in section 5.2.2 is probably related to that in section 5.2.3. The content of Song 4 (section 5.2.4), like

Song 5 (section 5.2.5), relates to *Brewin* (**Prewin**), a 'supernatural being' of generally evil intent.[8] Our assumption is that both of these songs were **kunyeRu**, even though only the second is specifically identified as such.

Among the other songs, some are labelled as 'charms' or 'spells', including one of the *Brewin* (**Prewin**) songs (discussed in section 5.2.4), the songs used against the *Barrn* (**Parn**) spirit (discussed in sections 5.2.6 and 5.2.7) and also the song discussed in section 5.2.13. It may be that these three songs were also **kunyeRu**, but this cannot be confirmed.

Howitt's more general discussion of the **kunyeRu** song (1904: 413–14) is given below. While this quote relates to Aboriginal groups beyond just the Gippsland groups, his use of the Gippsland term to refer to the songs, and the fact that he did most of his research in Gippsland suggests to us that the categories of song mentioned here were all found in Gippsland:

> The word 'corrobboree' probably meant originally both the song and the dance which accompanied it, which is the meaning of the word *Gunyeru* in the Kurnai tongue.
>
> The songs are very numerous, and of varied character, and are connected with almost every part of the social life, for there is little of Australian savage life, either in peace or war, which is not in some measure connected with song. Some songs are only used as dance-music, some are descriptive of events which have struck the composer, some are comic or pathetic. There is also an extensive class of songs connected with magic, and of these many are what may be called 'incantations' – words of power, chanted in the belief that supernatural influence is, not asked, but compelled, by them, an influence for evil, or for warding off evil.
>
> There are also songs which are only heard at the initiation ceremonies, and which are therefore not known to the uninitiated, or to women. To English ears, unaccustomed [p. 414] to the simple and somewhat monotonous airs to which the words are set, there seems but little melody in the chants. But with custom they grow upon one, until at length one feels in some measure the effect which they produce upon an aboriginal audience in so powerful a manner. …

8 Howitt (1904: 504) speaks of one man who, after coming into contact with Christianity, 'first identified Brewin with Jesus Christ, and afterwards with the Devil'. Howitt does not name the person or indicate whether he was a Christian convert.

> The makers of Australian songs, or of the combined songs and dances, are the poets, or bards, of the tribe, and are held in great esteem. Their names are known in the neighbouring tribes, and their songs are carried from tribe to tribe, until the very meaning of the words is lost, as well as the original source of the song. It is hard to say how far and how long such a song may travel in the course of time over the Australian continent.

This quote makes it clear that there was once a large body of songs with relationships to aspects of everyday life, including those that were 'descriptive of events' (for example, section 5.2.2), 'comic or pathetic' (we are not sure which songs exemplify this), and songs 'connected with magic' (for example, section 5.2.6).

In the third paragraph of this quote, he suggests that these songs are to be distinguished from songs only heard at (male) initiation ceremonies (see section 5.2.21). He states that at least some of these were not to be heard by uninitiated males or females. It is not clear whether he documented any of these restricted songs; what we can establish about this is discussed below in section 5.2.21. It would appear, though, that the **kunyeRu** songs were open to the whole community.

Other types of songs may include 'singing the rain'. Howitt (SLV Box 1053/3 (b), hw0404.pdf, p. 66) describes this:

> There were old men who were called 'Bunjil Willŭng' who could make rain come. They obtained their power in dreams. To produce rain one of them went down into a water hole and filling his mouth squirted in that direction which was appropriate to his tribe. He then 'sang [his so – crossed out] the rain'. Braiaka squirted water and sang towards the West the Krauŭn, the Brataua towards the west also, the Tatŭngalŭng towards the South – the sea, the Brabra and the Krauatun to the Belling – the South East wind. From these quarters their several rains came. When for instance a nearby rain came to the BraBra – it was the Braiaka who sent it and so on. The same 'BunjilWillŭng' could bring thunder.

Unfortunately we have no example of this song. In a Gippsland story about *Tidelik* 'the frog' drinking up all the water, Howitt records that '[t]he bullfrogs when [sing – crossed out] croaking in full chorus all said to be rain makers (Bungil wilŭng) singing for rain to come' (MV XM 615, page numbered 28, page 35 of the PDF). Bulmer described the *bungil willang* (**puntjil wilang**) as 'rain makers' (Campbell 1999: 28).

Bulmer also gave an example of men 'singing' a person (Bulmer to Howitt, 26 October 1881, MV XM 88):

> You ask if I refer to the Kurnai when I speak of a lot of men sitting around a rude figure of a man on the ground and singing some one who is is [oblivious??] to them. This only refers to the Kurnai.

We are not exactly sure what the function or form of this 'singing' was.

One final example that we have not included was shown by Howitt in Notes from J.C. McLeod (SLV Box 1049/3 (b), hw0024.pdf):

> My black boy and I both understood enough of their language to make them understand us and to understand them. They said there were no bullocks. They were in high glee, dancing and slapping their legs at us as a token of defiance.
>
> They thought they were out of reach so I gave them a shot, it struck in the mud and sent it all over them. They ran into the scrub frightened out of their lives.
>
> After a time out they came again, singing 'Knart bun, a burry burrya nyu, Knart bun jerrumbuddy boorlooka nyu' – that is – 'Don't shoot me, I didn't spear the bullock'. So we fired three rounds over their heads and they cleared out into a dense scrub and reeds.

We regard the use of the word 'singing' here as representing a way of speaking or indeed pleading. The word *knart bun* is the negative **ngatpun** 'no', the word for 'gun' is recorded by Pettit and Dawson as *boorooboorya*, and *boorlooka* is 'bullock'. So this is probably an example of language usage, but not a song in terms of this book.

5.1.3 The PiRaRk – the composers of the kunyeRu

According to Howitt, the composer of songs in Gippsland was the **piRaRk** (spelled *birraark* by Howitt and *birrararrk* by Bulmer). A great deal is written by both Howitt and Bulmer about the **piRaRk**, whose power and skills were considerable, and included the compositions of songs, certainly the **kunyeRu** and perhaps also the **yentjin(y)**. His functions are described by Howitt (1904: 389) as follows:

> … the functions of the *Birraark* are separated from those of the medicine-man (*Mulla-mulung*). The former combined the functions of the seer, the spirit-medium, and the bard, for he foretold future events, he brought the ghosts to the camp of his people at night, and he composed the songs and dances which enlivened their social meetings. He was a harmless being, who devoted himself to performances which very strikingly resembled those of the civilised 'mediums.'

Howitt and Fison (1880: 232) stated that all Kŭrnai (Gippsland people) had the same 'corroboree-songs and dances which enlivened their social gatherings were brought by the mysterious Birraarks from cloudland – the bright home of their dead ancestors'.

The **piRaRk** received his power from the **mratj**, usually translated as 'ghost' and spelled *mrart* by Howitt and *mraat* by Bulmer. This word was recorded by Fesl (1985: C1–2, no. 50) as being still in use and pronounced as [mraɖ] (**mrart**). Our regularisation, however, will follow that of Hercus (1986: 241) as **mratj**. The **mratj** is described in Howitt (1904: 389–90):

> A man was supposed to become a *Birraark* by being initiated by *Mrarts* or ghosts, when they met him hunting in the bush; but, that they might have power over him, he must at the time be wearing a *Gumbart* that is, one of those bone pegs which the Australian aborigine wears thrust through the septum of his nose. By this they held him and conveyed him through the clouds. Some say that he was conveyed hanging to a *Marrangrang*, which was described as being either like a rope or else something on which the *Birraark* can sit. But whatever it was like, the *Mrarts* went first and the *Birraark* last. It is said that, when they reached the sky, the leading *Mrart* gave a signal, and some one inside opened a hole and looked out. This, it is said, was a *Gweraeil-mrart*, in fact a Headman of ghostland, as a Kurnai man remarked to me when speaking of this matter, 'like a *Gweraeil-kurnai*.' As the *Birraark* climbs through the hole last, the *Mrarts* put a rug over his head, all but a place through which he can see the people there, the women beating their rugs, and the men dancing. Looking on, he learns new songs and dances (*Gunyeru*), which he afterwards teaches to the Kurnai. But he must not on any account laugh. One *Birraark* was away from his camp for a time, and on returning he told his people that when aloft with the *Mrarts* he could not help laughing, because two *Mrarts* caught hold of him by the sides and tickled him. As a penalty they kept him with them for some time, after which his tribes-people called him *Brewin*.

This last incident is described in more detail in Fison and Howitt (1880: 292), 'as nearly as possible, in my informant's words':

> 'I was once at Yūnthŭr. The Dinna Birraark Brewin was there with his wife. In the night she woke and shouted out that he was gone up to the mrarts. We all got ready, and some one shouted out, 'Where are you?' He replied, 'Here I am – I am coming down!' He said he had heard the mrarts having a corrobboree (gounyūrū), and making a great noise, and had gone up to them. Then the mrarts came down with him, and conversed with us about where the other mobs of Kurnai were, and whether any Brajerak were coming after us. When the mrarts went away, we found Brewin lying, as if asleep, where we had heard them speaking to us. The mrarts talked in very curious voices! This Birraark was once away with the mrarts for two nights and a day, and the Kurnai therefore gave him the name of Brewin.'

Another example of a **piRaRk** being taken by the **mratj**s is that of the most famous **piRaRk**, Mundauin, and his dream about a **kunyeRu** corroboree relating to the Kangaroo (Howitt 1904: 390; the manuscript notes on this are in SLV Box 1053/3 (b), hw0404.pdf, p. 43):

> One of the best remembered of the *Birraarks* was a man of the Brabralung clan named Mundauin. It is related of him that he became a *Birraark* by dreaming three times that he was a kangaroo, and as such participating in a kangaroo *Gunyeru*, or dancing corrobboree. He said that after dreaming of the kangaroos, he began to hear the *Mrarts* drumming and singing up aloft, and that finally one night they came and carried him away. A man who was in the camp on the occasion of one of his manifestations said as follows :–
>
> 'In the night his wife shouted out, "He is gone up." Then we heard him whistling up in the air, first on one side of us and then on the other, and afterwards sounds as of people jumping down on the ground. After a time all was quiet. In the morning we found him lying on the ground, near the camp where the *Mrarts* had left him. There was a big log lying across his back, and when we woke him and took the log off, he began to sing about the *Mrarts*, and all he had seen up there.'

We do not have any record of the text of the Kangaroo corroboree referred to here, but it is likely that the song that Mundauin sang on this occasion would have been a long one, if indeed he sang about 'all he had seen up there'. This is further evidence that the songs listed by Howitt from Tulaba and other people, and discussed below, are indeed only very tiny fragments of what must have been a much more substantial artistic and ritual tradition.

Howitt (1904: 392) described in more detail how the **piRaRk**, holding a pair of yamsticks (**kaniny**, spelling *kunnin* by Howitt and *kunniñ* by R.H. Mathews), led the **kunyeRu** performance:

> As the *Birraark* brought new songs and dances, he was the master of the ceremonies in the *Gunyeru*, and chose the place at which it was to be held. I remember how one of the Kurnai who was a noted dancer spoke with enthusiasm of the *Gunyerus* of the old times at which a *Birraark* officiated. He said, 'When the *Birraark* comes to the place, he has a *Kunnin* in each hand, which he beats together. All the men and women then say, "Hallo! we shall have some fun. We must dance; we must make our legs light." Each woman gets her rug to drum upon – a lot of blacks dancing.'

Bulmer adds about the **piRaRk** that '[t]he *birrarark* pretended they were carried about on a sort of ladder which was continually before their eyes. They could also get up trees without the ordinary mode of climbing …' (Campbell 1999: 28). A 'ladder' (probably **truRa** in the language) is also referred to in the extract about the **piRaRk** in Smyth below, and the term is used, perhaps, to refer to the sailing ships of the white men in the whitefellow's ship song (see section 5.2.2).

Smyth (1878, 1: 473–74) also contains a long description about the **piRaRk**, which probably has Howitt as its source:

> Connected with the *Mrarts* are the *Birra-arks*. There are no *Birra-arks* now living. The last one, *Dinna Birra-ark,* was a blackfellow who was shot near the Lakes when the country was first settled. *Dinna Birra-ark* is rendered as meaning *The Birra-ark*. Many blacks now living remember these people, and the following particulars are condensed fr om the account given to me by several Aborigines:– A *Birra-ark* was a blackfellow who was in communication with the spirits of the dead-of the *Bungil Wour-kunyey* (the old blackfellows). Any blackfellow may be made *a Birra-ark* who is found by *Mrarts* in the bush; but he must at the time be wearing one of the small bones of the kangaroo's leg, called *Goombert,* through the hole pierced in his nose. The *Mrarts* carry him off, it is said, up a ladder, which swings up into the clouds. There he is instructed, and when he returns to his friends he is a *Birra-ark.* The *Mrarts* teach him the corrobboree songs and dances, and he in his turn instructs the blacks. He seems to be the poet and magician of the tribe. Many of the songs used here were composed by the *Dinna Birra-ark* I have spoken of-the last of the bards. He was also consulted about many things-for instance, of the whereabouts and well-being of some

> friend whom the questioner had not heard of for a long time; or as to whether any strange blacks *(Borajerack)* were coming down 'on the war path;' and, when the country was first being settled, as to where cattle were to be found in the mountains. The mode of procedure was this: On the evening fixed, a little after dark, the *Birra-ark* goes out of the camp into the bush. All the blacks in the camp keep quiet, *very* frightened; one only 'cooyes' very loud for a long time; then a noise is heard. (The narrator here struck a book against the table several times to describe it.) This is *Bullun-Bowkan* (the great spirit) coming first. Then a loud whistle is heard up in the air at one side of the camp, then another loud whistle in the air on the other side; then is heard the sound of *Mrarts* jumping down on the ground one after the other. They can be heard talking together, but they cannot talk plainly. Next you hear the *Mrarts* marching past the camp after each other, and a voice calls out, 'Do not make a bright fire, or we shall go back.' Questions are now put to them, which they answer, and the replies are always found to be true.

Fison and Howitt (1880: 254) describe the same invocation of the spirits, which he termed a 'séance', told to them by 'one of the Tatūngolūng':

> On a certain evening, at dusk, the Birraark commenced his invocation. The audience were collected, and silence was kept. The fires were let go down. The Birraark uttered the cry 'Coo-ee' at intervals. At length a distant reply was heard, and shortly afterwards the sound as of persons jumping on the ground in succession. This was supposed to be the spirit 'Baukan,' followed by the ghosts. A voice was then heard in the gloom, asking, in a strange intonation, 'What is wanted?' Questions were put by the Birraark, and replies given. At the termination of the *séance*, the spirit voice said, 'We are going.' Finally, the Birraark was found in the top of an almost inaccessible tree, apparently asleep. It was alleged that the ghosts had transported him there at their departure. At this *séance* the questions put related to individuals of the group who were absent, and to the suspected movements of the hostile Brajerak.

The names of eight **piRaRk**, who were living in 1842, together with their clan/tribe affiliations, is given in Howitt (1904: 392):

> When the whites first came into Gippsland in 1842 the following were the *Birraarks*, of whom there was one in each clan. They were all called *Dinna-birraark*, the prefix implying age, and according to the old men, my informants, they were located as follows :–

> (1) Bunjil-brindjat[2] at Lake Tyers, that is, he was of the Wurnungati division of the Krauatungalung clan.
> (2) Mundauin at Bruthen-munji, that is, of the Bruthen division of the Brabralung clan.
> (3) Batti-batti at Dairgo, that is, of the Dairgo division of the Brabralung clan.
> (4) Takit-berak in the district round what is now called Rosedale, that is, of the Bunjil-kraura division of the Brayakaulung clan.
> (5) Brewin of the Ngarawut division of the Tatungalung clan.
> (6) Bunjil-narran at Boney Point, on the Lower Avon River, that is of the Bunjil-nullung division of the Brayakaulung clan.
> (7) Bunjil-bamarang at the Inlet from Lake Victoria called Newlands Backwater, of the Dairgo division of the Brabralung clan.
> (8) There was also at least one *Birraark* belonging to the Brataualung clan, but whose name I was unable to ascertain.
>
> Footnote: 2. *Brindjat* is a fish, the Flathead.

(Further information about some of these is given in section 5.1.6.)

Howitt never met a **piRaRk** as the last had died sometime before he arrived in Gippsland (1904: 392):

> The last *Birraark* was killed in the troubles which occurred in the early years of settlement in Gippsland. My information has therefore been derived from the old people, and such of the younger who were brought up in the primitive conditions of the tribe, and who saw the changes consequent upon the inroad of the white men into their country, and who still remembered the old beliefs and customs.

Bulmer (Campbell 1999: 28) also gives information about the **piRaRk**, naming two others: 'There were two *birrarark* at Yowang, one was named Maanyuk and the other was Bungil Koorambal'.

Bulmer goes on to give a good deal of information about the *Bunjil-narran*, the sixth named on Howitt's list above (Campbell 1999: 28):[9]

> Another lived at Boney Point, the father of Charley Foster. His name was Bungil Narran. Curious stories are told of this man, it appears on one occasion he was sailing in the air with his *mraat* (spirit) when passing over Lake Wellington he fell off the *marangirang*, this was the

9 Further information about the Bungil Narran is found in a letter from Bulmer to Howitt dated 10 June 1880 (Howitt, SLV MS Box 1053/3 (a), hw0392.pdf).

instrument needed for their aerial flights. He was most fortunately not drowned as the *mraat* fished him up with his *marriwan* (spear thrower) and put him again on his aerial carriage. Old Ellen tells me she often heard the noise of a multitude of *mraat* in the air passing the camp with Bungil Narran and they sometimes made a great noise as they got off the *marangirang*. She could hear the distinct sound of their feet on the ground as they went by. The noise was like a multitude talking I have not heard of a *birrarark* among the *krautungalung*, they tell me there were none.

5.1.4 The puntjil yentjin(y) – composers of the yentjin(y)

The second type of song, the **yentjin(y)**, was apparently composed and performed by a different person from the **piRaRk**. Howitt calls this person the **puntjil yentjin(y)** or 'medicine man' as discussed in (1904: 274). It is likely that this is same form as the personal name of Thomas Bungaleen (1847–1865),[10] who was the son of a 'Gippsland headman'[11] recorded as *Bungaleen*, but this seems to be compound of **puntjil** and **yentjin(y)**. Referring to the same chief, Thomas wrote that *Pundgil Ying Ying* was the '[n]ame of Black chief who is said to have white woman in Gippsland' (State Library of NSW MLMSS 214, Volume 23 Item 02, SLNSW_FL814574.jpg). This clearly suggests that the name later written as *Bungaleen* was originally **puntjil yentjin(y)**. Over time, the name *Bungaleen* and its pronunciation [bɐŋɐli:n] (first syllable rhyming with *sung*) has replaced the original which would have been pronounced something like [pʊɲɟɪl jeɲɟiɲ]:

> The second instance to be given is that of the *Bunjil-yenjin*, a medicine-man, whose specialty was the arrangement of marriages by elopement spells. *Bunjil* is a prænomen applied to men who have some special qualification; in this case the marriage spells were called *Yenjin*, as *Gunyeru* is the term for those songs which accompany dancing, usually called by us corrobborees. Probably the office of *Bunjil-yenjin* has been vacant since, if not before, 1855. Before that

10 See, for example, Victorian Naval Forces Muster Database for the Colony of Victoria, 'Thomas Bungalene', accessed 17 November 2021, www.cerberus.com.au/muster_dadabik/index.php?table_name=crew&function=details&where_field=ID&where_value=353, for further information about Thomas Bungaleen including an image of the wood carving created in his memory by Simon Wonga. This website suggests that his indigenous name may have been Marbunnun.

11 See Museums Victoria, 'Item X 6249: Grave marker. Yarra, Wurundjeri Woi Wurrung RAP. Coranderrk, Port Phillip, Victoria, Australia. 1865–1866', accessed 19 July 2024, collections.museumsvictoria.com.au/items/162920, for description of a memorial created for him.

> time there was at least one in each division of the tribe. Some men were more celebrated than others, and of them Bunjil-gworan, before mentioned, had a great name. The following account is derived from the statements of the Kurnai, and from those of old residents of Gippsland, who as boys in the early days were much with the blacks in their camps, and thus conserved and remembered many practices which are now obsolete.[12]
>
> It seems from these statements that almost the last time when the *Bunjil-yenjin* exercised their office on a large scale was at the holding of a *Jeraeil* on the south side of Lake Wellington, about the year 1855. At it ten or a dozen young couples ran off under the influence of love and the songs of the *Bunjil-yenjin*. Some of the people who were there were well known to me, and from them, and especially from a woman who was a girl at that time, and who then ran off with her future husband, I have received very full accounts of what was done.
>
> The substance of those statements is as follows. It was the business of the *Bunjil-yenjin* to aid the elopement of young couples. For instance, when a young man wanted a wife, and had fixed his mind on some girl, whom he could not obtain from her parents, he must either go without her, persuade her to run off with him, or call in the aid of the *Bunjil-yenjin*. In the latter case his services were retained by presents of weapons, skin rugs, or other articles. The *Bunjil-yenjin* then lay down on the ground in or near the encampment; next to him was the young man, and beyond him his comrades. The Bunjil-yenjin then sang his song, and the others all joined in with him.

The songs that are labelled as **yentjin(y)** are given in sections 5.2.8, 5.2.9 and 5.2.10 (recorded by Howitt) and section 5.3.2 (recorded by Bulmer). The song presented in section 5.2.1 may also be a **yentjin(y)** song. The quotations above are the introduction to the **yentjin(y)** presented in section 5.2.9. Howitt noted that Billy Wood said of these **yentjin(y)** songs that 'these songs always made the women run away in every direction' (SLV MS Box 1053/3 (b), hw0404.pdf, p. 27).

12 Howitt here has a footnote 'J. Macalpine and W. Lucas'. These were squatters in Gippsland, who we presume gave direct information to Howitt.

Singing could also be used to reverse an elopement. Writing about a situation in which a girl had already eloped, Howitt (1887b: 37–38) writes what happened when her parents awoke:

> After a time, according to my informant, the old people woke up, and finding their daughter gone, the old man summoned his kindred to assist him in singing a song which was believed would cause the youth's legs to become so weary that he would not be able to make his escape.

5.1.4.1 A note on the term puntjil

The term **puntjil**, used for elders and those skilled in some area of knowledge, combines with a range of terms to refer to male elders who had expertise in one art or another. Howitt (1904: 73) says of this word: '*Bunjil* is a designation applied to men of mature age, and always with a word which expresses some characteristic. For instance, one old man was called *Bunjil-barlajan*, being Bunjil-platypus,[13] he being a great hunter of that creature'. It seems likely that the word is cognate with the word for 'eaglehawk', also used for the creator and as a moiety term, in Eastern Kulin, which also has the form there spelled **bundjil** (see section 3.2.4).

Apart from the **puntjil yentjin(y)**, there were also **puntjil kunyeRu**. In a letter to Howitt, Bulmer states that 'Bobby Brown is Bungil Koonyoroo (corroborie) & I expect he was an expert songster' (MV XM 91).

More examples of the use of the term **puntjil** are given in Howitt and Fison (1880: 211). Bulmer also uses the term, spelling it as *bungil*. He gives examples of *bungil willung* 'rain makers' and *bungil krowero* 'having power over the winds' (Campbell 1999: 28).

5.1.5 Corroborees documented

Although we have a similar number of songs documented in Gippsland as were shown to have come from the Melbourne area, there are fewer references to corroborees; this is probably related to the fact that the Gippsland songs were mostly recorded at a later date when the traditional dances had already ceased.

13 He was also known as Timothy.

One corroboree that was recorded is in the William Thomas papers (SLNSW MLMSS 214, Volume 03 Item 07) in a footnote to his diary entry of 3 July 1849. It discusses the differences between a Gippsland corroboree and those of the Melbourne area, and gives detailed information about the dancing and attitudes of the dancers, but no information about any songs sung on that occasion (transcription from Stephens 2014, 2: 392):

> The Gipps Land Blks corroborry are no ways like the Melbourne Bls or other Blks visiting Melbourne. It is destitute of noise & Beeting of sticks, but little order & little daubing of body, the lubras as in ours only by the fire beets their rugs, 1 man with slight noise with 2 sticks, calls the dances who are in the bush preparing themselves. When in a disorderly group, the[y] come
>
> [next page]
>
> forward but soon may be seen in one strait line with a bough or [drawing of group of leaves] steps from Cockatoos feather in a stick as a painters brush, making a motion with the hands upward & downwards as the saw [moves?] in a sawyers pit, or some other attitude, when the dancer at head turns another attitude with hands, 5 takes another the dancers being on the quivive to see what attitude his hands are in sometimes they are hanging sometimes oblique, sometimes to the ground, some times in the air, no Shout [or shoot?] or [them?] stamp^{g} […?]

Note that quivive is an old word meaning 'alert, on the lookout'.

This piece of text has a small diagram that indicates the route followed by the dancers as they moved – 1. Lubra, 2. Fire, 3. Dancers. This diagram is reproduced in Figure 5.1, where 3 (Dancers) is found at the top right. The dancers therefore moved from side to side, turning and shortening the distance they moved in one direction with each turn as they get closer to the fire.

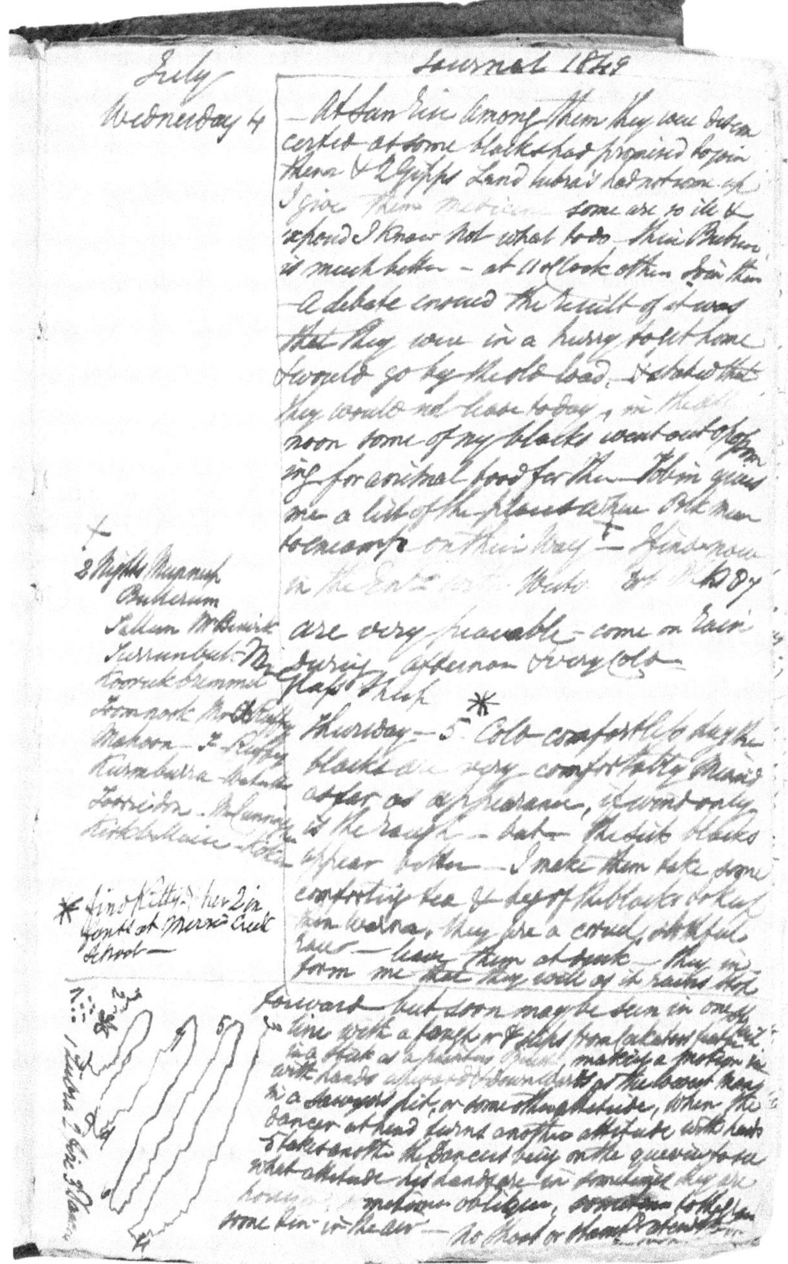

Figure 5.1: Drawing showing the route of the dancers in the Gippsland corroboree, William Thomas journal, 5 July 1849

Source: Courtesy of State Library of NSW (SLNSW MLMSS 214, Volume 03 Item 07; SLNSW_FL836202).

5.1.5.1 The 'silent corroboree'

Another corroboree type that is discussed in detail by Fison and Howitt (1880: 213–14) was the silent corroborees, performed with gestures. This was performed when the people had spotted some outsiders (*brajeraks*). Fison and Howitt wrote that the people:

> had a corroboree; they danced nearly all the night. But they did not sing. They were quite silent, and only made gestures and stamped their feet. In the middle of the night they all marched off well armed. They walked until they were about two miles from the Brajerak, then they had another silent dance.

5.1.6 The songsters

Howitt's main consultant for the songs appears to have been Toolaba, the informant for many songs, but each of the others discussed in this section had given information about songs or were known to be expert songsters.

Billy the Bull

Billy the Bull was born around 1840. He was of the shark totem (Yalmerai) (see section 5.1.7.2) and is known to have been able to send away sharks by singing to them (see section 5.3.3), and was probably the informant for **yelmeRai** (shark totem) song in Box 5.61.

He is listed in the William Thomas 1860 census of the Brutheron tribe with an Indigenous name, Turt-gu-a, and a given age of 20 (SLNSW MLMSS 214, Volume 05 Item 02).

In talking to Howitt, Billy Wambat said that 'Billy the Bull would be a head man and was much listened to years ago – it was because he was so strong and could talk and fight' (SLV MS Box 1053/3 (b), p. 16, hw0404.pdf, p. 39).

Though married at Ramahyuck to Emily Clark in 1873, he raised his family at Lake Tyers, where his own parents, Jemmy and Mary Bull, had settled.

He was present at the re-creation of the initiation ceremony (see section 5.2.21).

Billy Wood

Billy Wood died on 31 May 1887 at the Gippsland Hospital aged 55. There was an inquest into his death. His widow Sarah went on to marry William Barak.

It seems that his grandfather (*nakŭn* – **ngatjen** based on Hercus (1986)) was named by Howitt. Howitt stated that 'Billy Woods' Nakŭn was Bunjil Dauangŭn and Bunjil Barn was his elder brother' (SLV MS Box 1053/4 (a), p. 59, hw0404.pdf, p. 90).

He was present at the re-creation of the initiation ceremony (see section 5.2.21).

Bobby Brown

Bobby Brown, Indigenous name Boon-wool, is listed as aged 23 in the census of the Brutheron tribe collected by William Thomas in 1860 (SLNSW MLMSS 214, Volume 05 Item 02). He died on 5 November 1906 in the Bairnsdale Hospital at 70 years of age. Lily Brown who predeceased him by 20 years was probably his wife.

He was known to be an expert in composing corroboree songs (**kunyeRu**); as Bulmer wrote in a letter dated 8 February 1884, 'Bobby Brown is Bunjil Koonyorro (corroborie) so I expect he was an expert songster' (MV XM 91). He was present at the re-creation of the initiation ceremony (see section 5.2.21), but is not confirmed as the source for any of the individual songs presented here.

Bruthen Munyi

One of the major older experts was the Bruthen Munyi. Howitt (SLV MS Box 1053/3 (b), p. 16, hw0404.pdf, p. 39) recorded some information about him from Billy Wambat:

> Brūthen Mŭnyi was an old man and could talk nice – Billy Tulaba has his talk from him – Brūthen Mŭnyi was very strong and could fight well. He used to run after Brajerak and catch these with his hands and then Bernbuitel his brother would come up and knock these in the head.

He was probably born around 1800, and was still alive in 1860, being mentioned on one of Thomas's census lists (SLNSW MLMSS 214, Volume 05 Item 02), as being aged 60. In that same list his wife is named as *Year kun* (aged 52), which is the word for 'mother' (regularised as **yakan**) and was probably used as a generic term for married women who had children. In another portion of the Thomas papers (Census of the Brutheron Tribe, SLNSW MLMSS 214, Volume 05 Item 02), his Indigenous name is given as Bru-than-mun (aged 60), and his Western name as Bruthen Mandy King. His wife is named as Mary Queen, Indigenous name Bet-tur-look (aged 42).

Mundauin, the **piRaRk** mentioned in section 5.1.3 and discussed below, was listed in Howitt (1904: 392) as 'Mundauin at Bruthen-munji, that is, of the Bruthen division of the Brabralung clan'. We do not know if this was a title of Mundauin, or the two were different people.

Charley Rivers

Charley Rivers was Howitt's informant for the second **Parn** song (see Box 5.16 in section 5.2.7). He was born in 1832, was married to a woman named Lucy, also Nea-ron, from Lake King, and had at least three children. He was one of three brothers, another being William Flanner. Bulmer wrote of them that they were involved with a couple, Paddy (Tootloo Kaal) and Kitty (Brolga), who at first were not allowed to marry, leading to fights of 'daily occurrence'. Bulmer (in Campbell 1999: 80) goes on to say:

> He got badly wounded in every fight, till at last the people took pity on him and gave him the wife. Shortly afterwards Paddy and his wife with Flanner & Rivers and their wives went on a hunting expedition, their object being to get Swans' eggs. They were away about a month when Flanner & his brother Rivers returned to the station without Paddy & Kitty. They told me the couple had gone to Sale – Paddy's country, but it was found that they had not done so. I with the police made every inquiry which ended in finding the body of Kitty in a mud hole. Flanner & Rivers were never convicted of the murder but there is now no moral doubt they were the murderers.

The story of the finding the journey to find swan's eggs, the non-return of Paddy and Kitty, and the finding of Kitty's bones is told in language and English translation in Smyth (1878, 2: 32–33).

His third brother was Tommy Doughboy.

Lamby/Deal

Lamby was from Metung and died at Lake Tyers on 18 January 1895, aged 80. On the Gippsland Blanket List, his 'native name' was given as *Deal*, and he is listed as belonging to Swan Reach District (C. J. Tyers, 'Issue of Blankets to Aborigines, 1854-1858', SLNSW, Call No. A 842). In William Thomas's census from 1860, however, his name is given as Klu-em-bar (aged 36) and his (presumed) wife as Mary, or Yet-bin-kar-ly (aged 16). (SLNSW MLMSS 214, Volume 05 Item 02).

Although not an informant for a particular song, he was a senior leader and was present at the re-creation of the initiation ceremony (see section 5.2.21).

Mundauin

Mundauin was a very important leader of the Gippsland people. He was named by Howitt (1904: 392) as one of the **piRaRk** (see section 5.1.3):

> (2) Mundauin at Bruthen-munji, that is, of the Bruthen division of the Brabralung clan.

He may have been the same person as Bruthun Munyi mentioned above.

Mundauin is also known as King Barney and his son was Harry Stevens. Some additional information about him is found in a letter from Bulmer to Howitt containing some genealogical information, dated 23 April 1899 (SLV MS Box 1053/3 (a), hw0398.pdf, p. 3), where he is also termed a *Birrarark*. He says:

> 1. Birrarark was the father of Harry Stephens by his wife Dookalanem who afterwards married Barney his stepfather.

According to a family tree drawn on the next page (SLV MS Box 1053/3 (a), hw0398.pdf, p. 3), Barney, father of Harry Stephens was the elder brother of Tulaba.

Old Morgan/Mondabeet

Another important leader from the earliest times was known as Old Morgan. In the Gippsland Blanket List, his name is given as *Mondabeet*, and his district (Tribe) as Tarra (Tyers, 'Issue of Blankets to Aborigines, 1854–1858'. SLNSW, Call No. A 842).

Bulmer wrote of him in a letter of 8 February 1884 that 'Morgan was Bunjil Quarran (thunder) I suppose he said he could make thunder' (MV XM 91).

He is listed in another blanket list as 'Old Morgan' (here with his title Bun-geel-kor-reen) and being still alive in 1860 (Thomas manuscripts, SLNSW MLMSS 214, Volume 05 Item 02).

He is also mentioned in the Moravian Papers, referred to as a song man. His death is recorded as 'Morgen (an old man on 24.12.1864)', adding later that '[o]n the 24th of December 1864 the oldest black that belonged to us died. He was named Morgen and was reputed to be one of the most feared men, whose name was known far and wide' (Jensz 2001: 11; this comes from a letter written from Br Kuhn to Br Reichel on 17 January 1865).

There is a possible photograph of Old Morgan in the State Library of NSW with the catalogue description 'Picture of "Old Man Morgan" of the Yarram Tribe'.[14]

Tommy Hoddenit

Tommy Hoddenit (alias Arnott) was born at Port Albert in the early 1840s, the son of Tankly nee Warry (Squirrel) and Younga Youngoom (Laughing Jackass). His father had a second name of Kimbooroo or Nimbooroo meaning Honeysuckle. His mother had been taken by Gippsland men from Cranbourne, which may have enabled him to move more freely between Gippsland and central Victoria as an adult. Tommy travelled at a relatively early period and married three times. The date of his death is not known, but he was present at the re-creation of the initiation ceremony (see section 5.2.21).

Tulaba (1832–1886)

The most important single informant for songs in Gippsland was Tulaba (also spelled Toolabar) who was raised on the Macleods' property and is also known as Billy Macleod. He was Howitt's main consultant for information

14 The catalogue reference is from the State Library of NSW, 'Photographic Portraits of Aboriginal Australians, Victoria, approximately 1866-1870s', accessed 11 June 2019, primo-slnsw.hosted.exlibris group.com/primo-explore/fulldisplay?docid=ADLIB110353231&context=L&vid=SLNSW&lang=en_US&search_scope=MOH&adaptor=Local%20Search%20Engine&tab=default_tab&query=any,contains,Aboriginal%20Victoria,AND&sortby=rank&mode=advanced&offset=0. This link does not lead to an image of the photo.

about Gippsland and there is a detailed biography of him written by D.J. Mulvaney in the *Australian Dictionary of Biography.*[15] There is a photo of him in Howitt (1904: 344).

Mulvaney's biography discusses the various names that Tulaba had:

> Before the first stage of his initiation Tulaba (also spelt as Toolabar) was called Burrumbulk; he possibly never proceeded to his final initiation stage. He was also known as Karlbagwran and later as 'Billy McLeod'; his nickname 'Taenjill' meant incessant talker.

He is listed in Thomas's 1860 census of the Brutheron tribe as Billy, with the Indigenous name Tu-lar-bă, and age given as 26. His wife is listed as Kitty, with the Indigenous name Year-long, aged 24. He was a nephew of Bruthen Munji, mentioned above. As Howitt's collaborator and principal consultant, he was a very significant contributor to the anthropological research in the nineteenth century, as Mulvaney's (2005) biography of him discusses:

> Becoming the most prominent of Howitt's more than twenty Gippsland informants, in 1873 Tulaba supplied the key enabling Howitt's comprehension of the kinship system: following difficulty with abstractions, Howitt imaginatively asked him to arrange matchsticks to indicate the generational relationships and terminology of named individuals centred around him. This mode of interrogation became Howitt's standard. He compiled a circular genealogy to enable investigation of 'terms of consanguinity and affinity', printed in 1874 by the Board for the Protection of the Aborigines. The genealogical table that was provided used Tulaba as the exemplar, so 500 copies citing his model circulated around Australia.

5.1.7 A note on the totem systems in Gippsland

There were two main types of totem: (1) Sex totems and (2) Patrilineal totems. Bulmer (in Campbell 1999: 10) mentions that Billy the Bull insisted that 'there are only two divisions and that all men are *yarang* and all women *djeetgang*'. This is the sex totem system, discussed below (section 5.1.7.1). These terms occur in a number of **yentjin(y)** songs, such as in section 5.2.9.

15 D. J. Mulvaney, 'Tulaba (1832–1886)', *Australian Dictionary of Biography*, National Centre of Biography, The Australian National University, adb.anu.edu.au/biography/tulaba-13226, published first in hardcopy in 2005, accessed online 20 June 2019.

Bulmer went on to add that 'Another Aborigine, Harry, informed me that there were totems and that the child had the same totem as its father'. The informant here was Harry Daramung. This is the patrilineal totem system described in more detail below (section 5.1.7.2). Bulmer recorded songs that belonged to specific patrilineal totem groups, and these are discussed in section 5.3.3.

5.1.7.1 The sex totems, tjitkan 'blue wren' for females and yiRang 'emu wren' for males

The sex totems of the Gippsland tribes were two birds, **yiRang**, the southern emu-wren (*Stipiturus malachurus*), termed simply emu-wren by Howitt for males, and **tjitkan** the blue wren (*Malurus cyaneus*), which Howitt terms the 'superb warbler' for females. Howitt (1904: 148) explains the significance of these birds:

> There are two birds which the Kurnai reverence: the Emu-wren and the Superb Warbler, which, are the sex totems, and no man would think under any circumstances of injuring his 'elder brother,' *Yiirung*, or any woman her 'elder sister,' *Djiitgun*. Thus, as to these sex totems, the usual totemic taboo exists. The totem is the protector of the individual, and the individual protects his totem.

The importance of these birds in the culture of the Gippsland people cannot be understated. Together with a third bird, the **pulawrang**, 'scarlet robin' (*Petroica boodang*),[16] Howitt (1904: 619) writes that '[t]he birds *Bullawang*, *Yiirung*, and *Djiitgun* are said to be three of the "*leen muk-Kurnai*" ("real Kurnai ancestors")'.

We have regularised the names of these birds as **tjitkan** and **yiRang**. As mentioned above, they are named in some of the **yentjin(y)** songs, such as section 5.2.9, as well as in the **tjeRayil** (Boys' initiation ceremony), see section 5.2.21.

16 Howitt (1904: 618) names this bird as *Petroica multicolor*, but this species was split in 1999 between a rare robin on Norfolk Island and the much more common bird on the Australian mainland. Since the first specimen was collected on Norfolk Island, in common with the practice in animal and plant classification, it is the species on the mainland that receives a new name.

Howitt records fights between the sexes as a result of arguments over marriage (1904: 149):

> But the most remarkable feature of these fights over the killing of the man's brother or of the woman's sister, was when there were young women who were marriageable, but not mated, and when the eligible bachelors were backward. In this tribe, as I have explained in the chapter on Marriage, there was no practice of betrothal, the cases thereof being so rare as to prove the rule. Marriage was by elopement, and therefore the young woman had the power to refuse, unless constrained by the incantations of the *Bunjil-yenjin*.
>
> Under such circumstances some of the elder women went out, and having killed a Yiirung, returned to the camp and casually let some of the men see it, who became enraged at one of their brothers being killed. The young men and the young women then armed themselves with clubs and sticks and fought together. In this fight it was only those young men who had been made Jeraeil, and who were now allowed by the old men to marry, who took part in these affrays.
>
> On the following day the young men went out and killed a Djiitgun, which would occasion another fight when they came back. By and by, when the bruises and perhaps wounds received in these fights had healed, a young man and a young woman might meet, and he, looking at her, would say, for instance, 'Djiitgun ! What does the Djiitgun eat?' The reply would be, 'She eats kangaroo, opossum,' or some other game. This constituted a formal offer and an acceptance, and would be followed by the elopement of the couple as described in the chapter on Marriage.

This passage indicates the importance of these birds, as sex totems, to the process of marriage, and their connections to the **yentjin(y)** songs. The arguments that resulted from the killing of one of the totems is reminiscent of those reported for Wemba-Wemba by Stan Day in Hercus (1986: 61) (see section 2.2.2).

Hagenauer in Smyth (1878, 2: 191) records the Indigenous name of the McAlister River as *Wirnwirndook'yeerung*, translated as 'Song of some bird'. The bird referred to here is surely the **yiRang** 'emu wren' and it may be that *Wirnwirndook,* regularised as **wirnwirntuk**, represents the sound of the chirping of that bird.

5.1.7.2 The patrilineal totem system (thant(h)ang)

As mentioned above, Bulmer (in Campbell 1990: 10) collected information from Harry (Henry Daramung) about the patrilineal totem system. He stated that Harry gave several examples,[17] adding:

> A little later, I had a quiet talk with the old men and obtained six examples of the child being of the same totem or *jaak* as the father. I am of the opinion that the *jaak* were selected according to their plentifulness in a district.[18] For instance if the *glean* was to make a noise, they would say so & so is coming and at the *jerail* [initiation ceremony] they would only be intimate with those who had the same bird and at play of *dilk* (the purse [scrotum] of an old man kangaroo made into a ball) they would only throw to the person of the same *jaak*.[19]

The term used by Bulmer to describe this system is the word for 'meat', which we regularise as **tjak**. (Note that the use of the word for 'meat' to refer to a totem is also found in western Victoria, as told by Donald Cameron to Howitt.) Howitt, however, refers to this Gippsland system by another term, that of the **thant(h)ang**[20] or 'elder brother' as we see in the following from Howitt (1904: 135):

> Each Kurnai received the name of some marsupial, bird, reptile, or fish, from his father, when he was about ten years old, or at initiation. A man would say, pointing to the creature in question 'That is your *thundung*; do not hurt it.' In two cases I know of, he said, 'It will be yours when I am dead.' The term *thundung* means 'elder brother,' and, while the individual was the protector of his *thundung*, it also protected its 'younger brother,' the man, by warning him in dreams of approaching danger, or, by coming towards him in its bodily shape, it assisted him, as in the case of the man Bunjil-bataluk mentioned elsewhere, or was appealed to by song charms to relieve sickness.
>
> The *thundung* of the Kurnai known to me are as follows:
>
> | | |
> |---|---|
> | Narut | wombat |
> | Jirha | kangaroo |

17 The reference here is given in Campbell (1990) as 'Bulmer 1904, letter to A.W. Howitt of 11 March'.

18 The reference here is given in Campbell (1990) as 'Bulmer 1904, letter to A.W. Howitt of 21 March'.

19 The reference here is given in Campbell (1990) as 'Bulmer 1904, letter to A.W. Howitt of 11 March'.

20 This is an example of a word spelled by Howitt with <u> but for which, by comparison with other sources listed in Fesl (1985: B55), we regularise with /a/. Examples of spellings include *tandang* (Bulmer) and *dandang* (Hagenauer).

> Barlajan platypus
> Gliun water-hen
> Blit-buring a small bird
> Gwanamurrung eagle-hawk
> Thurung tiger-snake
> Bibing[21] sea-salmon
> Burra small conger-eel
> Noy yang large conger-eel
>
> The *thundung* are clearly the equivalents of the totems of other tribes, and form a vestigiary survival of a class system.

As will be demonstrated below (section 5.3.3), some songs were specifically related to particular **thant(h)ang**, and were presumably sung only by members of that **thant(h)ang**.

Box 5.2: Patrilineal totem (thant(h)ang) tables

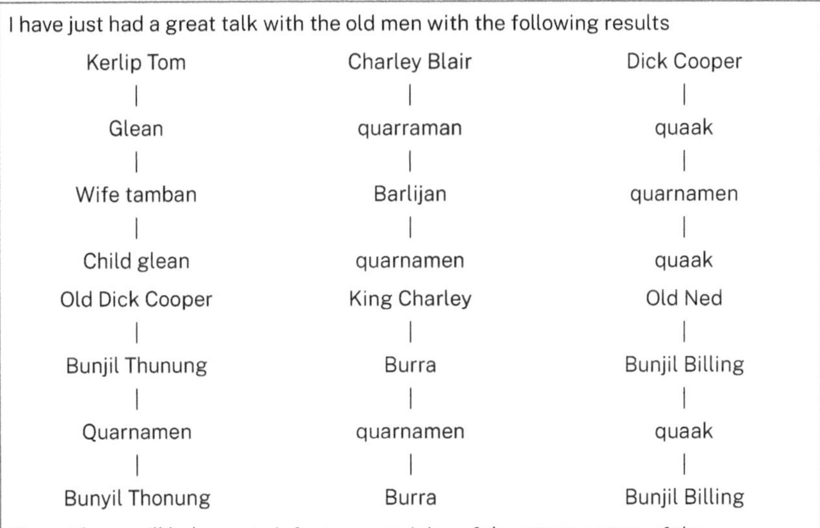

I have just had a great talk with the old men with the following results

Kerlip Tom	Charley Blair	Dick Cooper
|	|	|
Glean	quarraman	quaak
|	|	|
Wife tamban	Barlijan	quarnamen
|	|	|
Child glean	quarnamen	quaak
Old Dick Cooper	King Charley	Old Ned
|	|	|
Bunjil Thunung	Burra	Bunjil Billing
|	|	|
Quarnamen	quarnamen	quaak
|	|	|
Bunyil Thonung	Burra	Bunjil Billing

These I hope will help you to inform your opinion of the totem system of the people here.

It seems to me that they get these totems from the plentifulness of the particular Jaak.

Source: Letter from Bulmer to Howitt (MV XM 96); adapted by authors.

21 This word is elsewhere spelled *Billing* or similar. We believe that the spelling here is a typographical error or misprint.

In several letters to Howitt, Bulmer exemplified the **thant(h)ang** system by relating it to particular individuals. One example of this is shown in Box 5.2. On the top left, Kerlip Tom is named as having the patrilineal totem *glean* 'water-hen'[22] and his wife as *tamban* 'spangled perch'.[23] Their child, of either sex, would also be a *glean*.

There seems to have been an exception to the patrilineal descent when someone from outside the Gippsland community married into Gippsland. Bulmer (Campbell 1999: 9) recorded a discussion from Colin Hood, who originated from the Grampians but shifted to Gippsland to marry his second wife, Helen Rivers, also known as Honey, at Lake Tyers in 1898. Bulmer records the following:

> Colin Hood a very intelligent Aboriginal from the Western District tells me he is a *jallan* (whipsnake) … He himself has married a *yelmara* daughter but the children must be the same as her father [natural grandfather] that is *yelmara*.

What we understand from this is that Colin's wife was a *yelmara* 'shark' and that Colin's children would inherit their **thant(h)ang** from their maternal grandfather, presumably because Colin's own totem belonged to a different system. In addition, in western Victoria, where Colin Hood came from, totem inheritance was matrilineal, so that the inheritance of the mother's totem would be the norm.

There is more information about the totem system in different parts of both the Howitt and Bulmer papers; for example, Museums Victoria XM 524 and State Library of Victoria MS Box 1053/4 (a), hw0404.pdf, pp. 137–43, which is a small notebook.

5.2 Songs documented by A.W. Howitt

More than 20 separate song texts were noted by Howitt in the Gippsland languages. Most of these have been found in versions in the manuscript collection of the State Library of Victoria, but some were published and some are also recorded in the manuscripts at Museums Victoria. These songs are listed in Table 5.2 with their sources:

22 Possibly the Australasian swamphen (*Porphyrio melanotus*).

23 *Leiopotherapon unicolor*.

Table 5.2: Sources for Gippsland songs in Howitt's manuscripts and publications

Name of song (section)	Field notebooks (Museums Victoria)	Manuscript loose pages with PDF reference (State Library of Victoria)	Publications
Song 1 – Song of the bottle (5.2.1)	–	MS Box 1053/3 (b), hw0404.pdf, p. 1	–
Song 2 – The whitefellow's ship (5.2.2)	–	MS Box 1053/3 (b), hw0404.pdf, p. 5; and MS Box 1053/4 (a), hw0404.pdf, p. 149	–
Song 3 – White Woman song, a KunyeRu of the *Dinna Birraark* (5.2.3)	–	MS Box 1053/3 (b), hw0404.pdf, p. 5	–
Song 4 – **Prewin** song of Pruthen-Muntji (5.2.4)	–	MS Box 1053/3 (b), hw0404.pdf, p. 5	Fison and Howitt (1880: 246); Howitt (1904: 437); also Smyth (1878, 1: 472)
Song 5 – KunyeRu – **Prewin** song (5.2.5)	–	MS Box 1053/4 (a), hw0404.pdf, p. 121; MS Box 1053/3 (b), hw0404.pdf p. 29	–
Song 6 – **Parn** song (5.2.6)	–	MS Box 1053/3 (b), hw0404.pdf, p. 5	Smyth (1878, 1: 475)
Song 7 – **Parn** song (5.2.7)	–	MS Box 1053/3(b), hw0404.pdf p. 52	Howitt (1904: 377); also Smyth (1878, 1: 475)
Song 8 – **Yentjin(y)** – Elopement song (5.2.8)	–	MS Box 1053/3 (b), hw0404.pdf, p. 27; MS 1053/4 (a), hw0404.pdf, p. 91	–
Song 9 – **Yentjin(y)** – Elopement song (5.2.9)	–	MS Box 1053/3 (b), hw0404.pdf, p. 28	Howitt (1904: 275); Howitt (1887a: 334)
Song 10 – **Yentjin(y)** – Elopement song (5.2.10)	–	MS Box 1053/3 (b), hw0404.pdf p. 35	Howitt (1904: 275)
Song 11 – Nunga Nunga song (5.2.11)	–	MS Box 1053/3 (b), hw0404.pdf, p. 53	–
Song 12 – Woman's answer to the **Yentjin(y)** (5.2.12)	XM 653	–	–

Name of song (section)	Field notebooks (Museums Victoria)	Manuscript loose pages with PDF reference (State Library of Victoria)	Publications
Song 13 – Charm to drive away pains (5.2.13)	XM 761, p. 107	–	Howitt (1904: 388); Howitt (1887a: 334)
Song 14 – Song for stopping the wind (5.2.14)	–	–	Howitt (1904: 397)
Song 15 – Red Moon song (5.2.15)	–	MS Box 1053/3 (b), hw0404.pdf, p. 38	–
Song 16 – Bratualong song (5.2.16)	–	MS Box 1053/3 (b), hw0404.pdf, p. 15	–
Song 17 – Lullaby (5.2.17)	–	–	Howitt (1887a: 334)
Laments (5.2.18)	–	–	–
Ritual sayings (5.2.19)	–	MS Box 1053/3 (b), hw0404.pdf, p. 37, p. 38, p. 39	–
Three short texts in Howitt (5.2.20)	–	MS Box 1053/3-4, hw0404.pdf, p. 124	–
Boys' initiation ceremony (5.2.21)	XM 761, p. 101	–	–

Source: Authors.

5.2.1 Song 1 – Song of the bottle

The first song we treat here has, to date, only been found in the Howitt papers in the State Library of Victoria (MS Box 1053/3 (b), p. 1). It is named 'Song of the bottle'. The full text is given in Box 5.3.

Box 5.3: Song 1 – Song of the bottle

Nabungada-gada	gauan-gauanda	
	pull out cork	
bŭnyel	drarndu-willen	máyonga
you a(n)d I –	little warm place –	a little further

Source: SLV MS Box 1053/3 (b), hw0404.pdf, p. 1; adapted by authors.

At the bottom of the page, Howitt adds the note 'ngittal – mine – from Charly Alexander 23/6/72'. We do not know if this refers to the informant who gave Howitt this song. He may have been from South Gippsland.[24] Charles Alexander moved up to the Monaro, then on to Sydney, where he died (Bulmer in Campbell 1999: 69).

We believe that this song relates to two people who are about to drink together, and are talking about moving a bottle to a warm place that might be favourable for pulling out the cork and having a drink.

A suggested regularisation of this song is presented in (5.6):

(5.6)	*Nabungada-gada*	*gauan-gauanda*
		pull out cork
	napung(k)at(h)a-kat(h)a	**kauwan-kauwan-t(h)a**
	?	pull out?-REDUPL-?

bŭnyel	*drarndu-willen*	*máyonga*
you a(n)d I	*little warm place*	*a little further*
pa-nyal	**trant(h)u-wilan**	**mayung(k)a**
?-1DL.INCL	warm place	DEM?

'… pull out (the cork); you and I (will go) to a warm place, a little far.'

Notes

Both words in the first line of example (5.6) are partially reduplicated, and both contain a possible suffix *-d(h)a*. In the paradigm noted by R.H. Mathews (NLA MS 8006/8/7), *-dha* marks the 1st person singular in past tense, as *dhangadha* 'I spoke'. However, Fesl (1985: 120) made a study of all the sentences recorded by R.H. Mathews and found that the form *dha* appeared in sentences that were translated in past, present and future, although most of those sentences did have a 1st person singular subject. We cannot say if the final element in the first two words is this same suffix.

The second line is a little easier to analyse. The word *bŭnyel*, glossed by Howitt as 'you and I', surely contains the 1st person dual inclusive suffix, **-nyal**, also found recorded by R.H. Mathews in the word *Dhangginyal*,

24 Russell Mullet (pers. comm.).

translated as 'we incl. shall speak' (NLA MS 8006/8/7). A similar form, /**pa-**/ plus a pronominal is found in Song 8 (see section 5.2.8). It is likely that this song is actually an example of the **yentjin(y)** song.

The next word, *drarndu-willen*, is glossed by Howitt as 'little warm place'. This word bears no similarity to any words listed by Fesl (1985).

The final word *mayonga* is glossed 'a little further' and may be a demonstrative. There are a number of demonstratives in the Gippsland languages with initial **m-**, such as *moko* 'there' (see further discussion in section 5.2.3). Since Howitt's glosses are reliable for a number of other songs, we accept that the glosses are probably correct here.

5.2.2 Song 2 – The whitefellow's ship

Two versions of this song exist in the manuscripts, both held in the State Library of Victoria, Version 1 (Box 5.4) and Version 2 (Box 5.5). The page containing Version 1 contains a note 'Aug 23 1868, per J.C. Macleod', presumably John Campbell Macleod (1822–1889), the son of Archibald Macleod who took up a pastoral lease at Bairnsdale in 1844.

This song and the next are connected; both songs were probably composed by the same person, the Dinni Birrarrk (see section 5.2.3 for more discussion of the composer of these songs), and both appear to relate to the 'White Woman', the first describing a shipwreck and the second (see section 5.2.3) illustrating how she was welcomed by the people with a possum skin skirt and a blanket. The context given in the manuscript for this song, found at the top of the page containing Version 1 (SLV Box 1053/3 (b) p. 2; hw0404.pdf p. 5), is as follows:

> Blacks told him in the early days the white woman was wrecked in the coast with some men who were killed - the woman being saved. She was a tall woman, young with very long black hair in ringlets (some said the hair was fair). She was drowned in McLennans straits with her children. [She?] was [she?] Bessie Howard who was about 16 years of age when the vessel in which she was going to Melbourne was lost. Daughter of Commissary Howard. Part of the vessel was after picked up in the ninety mile beach.

Notes

Deputy Assistant Commissary General Charles Howard is listed in the 1839 Directory of the Port Phillip District.[25]

'McLennan's Strait is a long channel of water that connects Lake Wellington to Lake Victoria. On the northern side of the Straits there are extensive wetlands that are important bird habitats – so important, in fact, that they are international Ramsar Agreement sites.'[26]

Carr (2001: 19) names two brigs, the *Britannia* and the *Britomart*, that were lost in Bass Strait in late 1839, and confirms that 'in early 1840 … Aborigines had reported finding a small boat on the Ninety Mile Beach'. She adds that the '*Port Phillip Herald* reported on 24 March that Captain Moore had located the small boat (said to have belonged to the ill-fated *Britannia*)' and that documents assumed to belong to passengers of the *Britomart* had been found, and 'it was speculated that the *Britomart* had been plundered by pirates who had massacred the survivors' (2001: 20).

Carr (2001: 228f) also mentions Mary Howitt's story that refers to the white woman drowning in McLennan's Strait many years later.

This song relates the destruction of the ship referred to above. Both this song and the 'White Woman' song are examples of songs composed in response to a present-day event.

Box 5.4: Song 2 – The whitefellow's ship, version 1

Blaung-a-requa	drūraua	kŭllŭngŭka		
burn	ladder	whitefellow		
Wūrūng-	tūnkū	bŭdda-	tūnkū	pŭtta-ngaiu
boughs	from here	?	from here	me
tūka-pŭnta	kŭrnŭng-ŭka	ma-kŭrnung-ita		
muskduck-camp/nest	creek-down	I-leave it there		

Source: SLV MS 1053/3(b), hw0404.pdf, p. 5; adapted by authors.

25 A transcription of this is available at Port Phillip District, Victoria, Australia, '1839 Directory of the Port Phillip District', 2013, accessed 30 November 2018, www.portphillipdistrict.info/1839_Directory.htm. He is also mentioned in George Augustus Robinson's diary on Saturday, 16 November 1839 (Clark 1998, 1: 101).

26 Riviera Nautic, 'Interactive Guide to the Gippsland Lakes', accessed 21 January 2026, rivieranautic.com.au/materialis/gippslandlakes/.

Box 5.5: Song 2 – The whitefellow's ship, version 2

Blaung-aréqua	druráua
burn	ladder
Kúlung-úka	wurun-lunka
white fellow	boughs from here
buda-tunku	putta-ngaia
tuka-punta	kurnung-inna
muskduks-camp	down at the creek
makurnang-ita	(ita = I)
I leave from there	

Source: SLV MS 1053/4 (a), hw0404.pdf, p. 149; adapted by authors.

We have only been able to present a partial translation of this song in example (5.7). The reference to a ladder – a word otherwise not recorded for the Gippsland language – is reminiscent of some creation stories that Howitt (1904: 502) refers to, in which 'the first man' could go up into the sky by means of a ladder. The 'ladder' is also a magical device that the **piRaRk**, the composer of these songs, used to climb up into the air, as reported by Bulmer in both Campbell (1999: 28) and Smyth (1878, 1: 473–44) (see section 5.1.3).[27] It seems likely that this was used as a metaphor to compare with the rigging that was used to join the sails to the mast of a sailing ship. Howitt (1904: 493) earlier refers to a supernatural being *mungan-ngaua* 'our father' whose secrets were taught at the initiation ceremony (see section 5.2.21) and who could also go up to the heavens.

We suggest that the 'the ladder of the white man' refers to the rigging of a sailing ship.[28] The reference to the musk duck's nest relates this song to the next (section 5.2.3), because the term for 'white woman' in the language includes the word for musk duck.

27 In various manuscript notes, Howitt associates the word *Marangrang* with the device used for climbing into the air. In SLV MS Box 1053/3 (b), hw0404.pdf, p. 43, for example, in a discussion apparently with Mundauin (see section 5.1.7), he writes: 'When the mrarts take a man up they go up the Marangrang – I do not know what it is like but that it is very big and softer than a rope'.

28 Peter Sutton (pers. comm.) pointed out that the 'ladder' is more likely to refer to the rigging of the ship, perhaps the Dinni Birrarrk may even have seen people climbing up and down it. Probably the sails would have been down at the time of the shipwreck, and maybe the youngest sailors were sent up to try and stop the wrecking.

(5.7)

Blaung-a-requa	*drūraua*	*kŭllŭngŭka*
burn	*ladder*	*whitefellow*
plaunga-Rekwa	**truRa-wa**	**kulungak-a**
burn-?	ladder-POSS	white man-OBL

'The ladder of the white man … is burning.'

Wŭrūng-	*tūnkū*	*bŭdda-*	*tūnkū*	*pŭtta-ngaiu*
boughs	*from here*	*?*	*from here*	*me*
wuRung-	**t(h)ungku**	**pat(h)a-**	**t(h)ungku**	**pat(h)a-ngayu**
boughs	hence	?	hence	?-1SG

'From the boughs hence, from the … from there I.'

tūka-	*pŭnta*	*kŭrnŭng-ŭka*	*ma-kŭrnung-ita*
muskduck-	*camp/nest*	*creek down*	*I-leave it there*
t(h)uk-a	**pang-ta**	**ka(r)nang-aka-ma**	**ka(r)nang-itha**
muskduck-OBL	camp-POSS	hollow-?-POSS?	?-hollow-1SG.POSS

'… the musk duck's nest … down there, in my hollow … I.'

Vocabulary notes

The word **plaunga-** as a root meaning 'burn' is also found in SLV MS 6290 as *ballan-gŭn.*

The phrase *drūraua kŭllŭngŭka* is analysed as a possessive construction 'the white fellow's ladder'. This construction is discussed in detail in Morey (2016).

Howitt's list in Curr (1887, 3: 556) gives 'white man' as *loan, cullungurk.*

The word **thung(k)u** 'hence' (spelled in various ways) is found in several of the stories documented by Howitt (2016), and also in sentences recorded by Bulmer in Smyth (1878, 2).

The free pronoun form for 'I' in the Gippsland languages was written *ngaioo* by Mathews (NLA MS 8006/4, File 8d, Folder 18).

The word for *tūk* is given as the word for 'musk duck' (*Biziura lobata*) in Fesl (1985: J9, no. 108), the sources being Howitt. We have regularised this with an /u/ vowel, as **t(h)uk**, because of the use of the macron in the spelling. However, it may be an /a/ vowel, as in the next song Howitt spells this with the shortener as *tŭka*. The similarity of this word with English *duck* is purely coincidental given the role of this word in the legends discussed in section 5.2.3.1.

The phrase *tūka-pŭnta* also appears to be an example of a possessive construction. This also relates to the 'White Woman' (see section 5.2.3), who may have been a passenger on this ship who was rescued and cared for by the local people, as the song relating to her indicates.

The word for 'camp' or 'hut' is regularised by Fesl (1985: D1, no. 1) as /baŋ/, based on forms from multiple sources. It is possible that the form *pŭnta* in the song is this word marked as a possessum. We assume that this word is **pang-ta**.

The last part of the song is difficult to interpret. The word *kŭrnŭng* is the root of two separate 'words' that are glossed as 'creek down' and 'I leave it there' and glossed 'down there' by Howitt in SLV Box 1053/4 (b), p. 82. In Song 10 (section 5.2.10) it is glossed as 'the hollow (in the ground)'. The suffix *-ita* is interpreted as **-(ng)itha** and is a 1st person singular possessive suffx, as in *wangingitha* 'my boomerang', indicated by R.H. Mathews (NLA MS 8006/4, File 8d, Folder 18).

The prefix *ma-* on the last word is found in several places in the stories listed by Howitt; as a suffix, **-ma** marks the possessum in a possessive argument, possibly a marker of inalienable possession (see Morey 2016).

Given that we analyse this song as being about a shipwreck, it is interesting to mention that both Robinson and Thomas wrote down words meaning 'shipwreck', respectively *ke-re-wad-de* and *nag-wŭrr-pĕlly-gun* (Fesl 1985: D10, no. 134).

5.2.3 Song 3 – White Woman song – KunyeRu of the *Dinna Birraark*

This song relates to a persistent story in early colonial Victoria – that a young white woman had lived with the Gippsland Aborigines after being shipwrecked in the 1840s. The story has been often discussed, and was in described detail by Carr (2001), but the songs connected with this story do not appear ever to have been mentioned in any of these various publications.

As might be expected, most of the many sources that describe the White Woman story come from earlier settlers, but one is reported thus in Carr (2001: 199; original reference from Pepper with De Araugo 1985: 76):

> Phillip Pepper attributes one version of the White woman story to Kurnai oral history: 'they remember Lohan-tuka as a legend of "a big pale coloured woman with long flowing red hair who lived by herself. She came out of her cave to frighten the people and little children."'

The song exists in one manuscript form so far identified, State Library of Victoria, MS Box 1053/3 (b), p. 2r, following immediately after Song 2 (see section 5.2.2). The background, the story of the shipwreck and the white woman, identified as a Miss Howard, is given in section 5.2.2. As we can see from the meaning of the text, 'Give the white woman from over the sea the possum skin skirt, and that yonder blanket there' (see example 5.8), the song appears to record that the people comforted the woman after the shipwreck and provided her with clothing.

The song is stated to be a 'gūnyerū of Dinni Birraark'. Elsewhere, Howitt (1904: 391) points out that *Dinni* or *Dinna* simply means 'old', whereas Smyth (1878, 1: 473) said: 'The last one, *Dinna Birra-ark,* was a blackfellow who was shot near the Lakes when the country was first settled. *Dinna Birra-ark* is rendered as meaning *The Birra-ark*'. We are not sure which of the eight individuals mentioned above in section 5.1.3 in referred to here. One possibility is that he was the Bunjil Bamarang, named as one of the **piRaRk** by Howitt, and also named on the page following, under the heading 'per Billy Wood', where it is written (SLV MS Box 1053/3 (b), hw0404.pdf, p. 6):

> A Dargo man Bungil Bamaring had a tame brown snake (thūrŭng) which he fed in frogs. People were very much afraid because he sent it out at night to hurt people.

Bunjil Bamarang came from Newlands Backwater, just south of Eagle Point,[29] and is the most likely of the Birrarks to have been known to J.C. Macleod. When he composed this song, he could have been sitting in dunes that face both the ocean and the freshwater back lake, which is where the musk duck's nest would be (Russell Mullet, pers. comm.).

29 Given the distance between Eagle Point and Dargo, it seems unlikely that this refers to the same person.

As mentioned earlier, Howitt (1904: 274) wrote that a **kunyeRu** was a song that accompanied dancing, but there is no information about the dance that would have accompanied it.

The song itself is transcribed in Box 5.6. Howitt wrote numbers underneath the first four words and glossed the meaning, but did not do so for the words in the second line. However, the words 'rugs (blankets)' is certainly the translation of *nŭrrau-un-gŭl*, while 'there' is the translation of *mūndū*.

Box 5.6: Song 3 – White Woman song

U-auda	kai-ū	Lohan-tŭkan	móka kat-teir
1	2	3	4
nŭrrau-un-gŭl	mūndū		wánganna

(1) give, (2) a possum fur string, (3) white woman (4) over the sea
rugs (blankets), there, ?
A gūnyerū of Dinni Birraark

Source: SLV MS Box 1053/3 (b), hw0404.pdf, p. 5; adapted by authors.

Our analysis of the song is presented as (5.8):

(5.8)

U-auda	*kai-ū*	*Lohan-tŭkan*
give	*possum fur string*	*white woman*
yuwa-tha	**kaiyu(n)**	**lu(wu)n-t(h)uk-a**
give-?	possum skin skirt	white person-musk.duck-OBL

móka kat-teir	*nŭ́rrau-un-gŭl*	*mūndū*	*wánganna*
over the sea	*rugs (blankets)*	*there*	-
muku-katjing	**naRauang(k)al**	**muntu**	**wanga-na**
DEM.FROM-sea	blanket	yonder	LOCATIONAL-?

'Give the white woman from over the sea the possum skin skirt, and that yonder blanket there.'

Vocabulary notes

The verb 'give' seems to have two different stems **yuwa**, as in this example, and **yuka** found in section 5.2.4.

The words *kiung* (Gi-C3) 'skirt of possum skins' and *kaiun* 'female's skirt made of possum skins' (Howitt) are listed in Fesl (1985: D10, no. 135). Howitt describes this in more detail (SLV MS Box 1053/4 (a), hw0404.pdf, p. 88):

> the kaiŭng or bridda bridda was made of possum fur string 15 ft long and two kilts one in front = nit-tŭn and one behind = nit-gwannŭng. The kaiung of the women hung down to the knees in front.

Howitt (1904: 444) notes that the word for 'white woman' was 'Loantuka, the wife of Loan'. However, the words for 'wife' in Fesl (1985: B9, no. 45) are not the same as *tuka*. The words related to *Loan* are discussed further in detail below.

Fesl (1985: D9, no. 120) shows the word for blanket as *nartowngill*.

R.H. Mathews lists *mooga* as 'there' (NLA MS 8006/4, File 8d, Folder 18). Howitt's notes (SLV MS Box 1053/3 (b), hw0404.pdf, p. 64) suggest that the meaning of *moko*, **muku**, is either far distant, or is a demonstrative with motion attached, perhaps 'to there / from there'.

The word written by Howitt as *kat-teir* is clearly the word for 'sea'. Similar forms, with the meaning 'water', are listed in Fesl (1985: F1, no. 1), all from Curr (1887, 3: 553, 555, 557): *kailtung*, *katung* and *gattung*. Howitt (1904: 73n1) says: '*Tatung* is the sea, sometimes spoken of as *gatching*'. Hence we have regularised this as **katjing**.

5.2.3.1 Lu(wu)n and Lu(wu)nt(h)uka 'the white man and white woman'

Howitt (1904: 444) describes the meaning of **luwun** 'white man' as follows:

> The strange sight of ships sailing past their shores had been a wonder to them, and the white man when he arrived was recognised as a *Mrart*, or as Löan, and the white woman as Löantuka, the wife of Löan. When Tulaba described to me how the Kurnai first saw the white men when he was a boy, and cried out to each other, '*Löan* ! *Löan* !' I observed that he looked down, and moved his eyes from side to side, as if to avoid a blow. On inquiry I found that the belief was that the white man possessed a supernatural power of the eye, to flash death to the beholder, or to draw together the banks of a river, and to pass over it. This power was called *Ngurrung-mri* or 'sinew eye,' and I think that I have also heard it called *Mlang-mri*, meaning

> 'lightning eye.' Therefore when white men were near, the Kurnai would make off, crying to each other, 'Don't look ! don't look ! he will kill you.'

The **luwun** was known also to the Eastern Kulin speakers, as reported by Howitt (1904: 134):

> A Wurunjerri legend relates that long ago Loän, who may be described, in the words of Mr. Andrew Lang, as a 'non-natural man,' wandered from the Yarra River, following the migration of the swans, first to the inlets of Western Port Bay and then to Corner Inlet, between Wilson's Promontory and the mainland, where he took up his abode. This is far within the country of the Kurnai, whose legends also speak of him living there with his wife Loäntuka, as the guardian of the Brataua clan.

And also, Howitt (1904: 485):

> The Wurunjerri legend of *Lohan* is, that when he was cooking eels at the Yarra River he observed a swan's feather carried by the south wind. Walking in that direction, he at length came to Westernport Bay, where the swans lived. There he remained till they migrated to the east, and he followed them. Coming to Corner Inlet, he made his home in the mountains of Wilson's Promontory, and watched over the welfare of the people who followed him.
>
> Although the Kurnai had no legend of the migration of *Lohan*, they also believed that he lived in the mountains of Wilson's Promontory, with his wife *Lohan-tuka*. The Brataua clan, in whose country his home is, said that their old men had seen him from time to time marching over the mountains with his great jag-spear over his shoulder. They also believed that he watched over them, and that he caused their country to be deadly to strangers. It was therefore to him that they attributed the taboo which protected them against the visits of other tribes, from the eastern extremes of Gippsland to the lower Murray River.

He goes on to add:

> There is a legend that the first Kurnai man marched across the country from the north-west, bearing on his head a bark canoe in which was his wife *Tuk*, that is the Musk-duck, he being *Borun*, the Pelican.

In the manuscript notes, Howitt makes it clear that his information came from Tulaba and that the two terms for 'white man' were both in place before the arrival of white people (SLV MS Box 1053/3 (b), hw0404.pdf, p. 25), saying:

> Billy Tulaba says that long before the whitemen came into Gippsland, the Kurnai spoke of 'Loän' and of his wife 'Loäntŭkau' and that afterwards whitemen were called Loan & whitewomen Loantuckan. He also says that the name Kŭllŭngrŭk was also applied to Loan and afterwards to the whiteman.

5.2.4 Song 4 – Prewin song of Pruthen-Muntji

This song was composed by Tulaba's father's brother, Bruthen-munji, whose name is spelled Bruthenmungee in a family tree in the Fison papers (NLA MS 7080, Letter Book 4, p. 66). The term for 'father's brother' is *brebba mungan*. It would appear that this uncle is not one of the eight **PiRaRk** listed in section 5.1.3; he is not the same as Mundauin who lived at Bruthen-munji and was the father of Harry Stevens. In several family trees (SLV MS Box 1053/3 (b)), the son of Tulaba's uncle is named as Commening and it is noted that he had already died. Smyth (1878, 1: 476) reports that 'the last blackfellow reported to have been killed by *Barrn* was called *Bruthen-mungie*' (see Box 5.17). It is not clear whether this refers to the same person.

There are four versions of this song that we have found so far, given below in Boxes 5.7, 5.8, 5.9 and 5.10. Compare also the related song from Bulmer that also mentions the **Prewin** and the **maRiwan** (see section 5.3.1).

The **Prewin** is an evil spirit described in Fison and Howitt (1880: 250) as '"who is like the wind", and who, entering his victims, can only be expelled by suitable incantations. Howitt (1904: 429) added the following legend:

> A Kurnai legend about Brewin is as follows. 'Long time ago the moon (*Narran*) was a young man. He went out hunting, and found an emu on the other side of a creek. When he wanted to cross over on a log, Brewin twisted it round so that Narran fell into the water. Each time he tried to walk over, Brewin made him fall in.'

Fison and Howitt (1880: 254) name three spirits that are evil, adding that the other two (Būllūm-dūt and Baukan) are 'not so bad as Brewin'.

Box 5.7: Song 4 – Prewin song of Pruthen-Muntji, version 1

Tūndŭnga	Brewínda	nandū-ŭnga	yūgaringa
bark fibres	Oh Brewin	I think	(you) have given
mri	mūrriwŭnda	-	(da capo)
(with) eye	of boomerang		

Source: SLV MS Box 1053/3 (b), hw0404.pdf, p. 5; adapted by authors.

Box. 5.8: Song 4 – Prewin song of Pruthen-Muntji, version 2

Tulaba, whom I have elsewhere mentioned, said that his "other father"[1] Bruthen-munji came to him during sleep and taught him songs (charms) against sickness and other evils. One charm which he thus learned, and which I have heard him sing to cure pains in the chest, is as follows:–

Tundunga Brewinda nunduunga ugaringa mri-murriwunda

Tundung by *Brewin* – I believe – hooked by – eye of spear-thrower.

"The belief that *Brewin* has filled the sufferer's chest with the frayed fibres of the stringy-bark tree, called *Tundung*, by means of the hooked end of his spear-thrower. This hooked end is called the eye, *Mri*."

[Footnote]1. That is, the brother of his father.

Source: Howitt (1904: 437); adapted by authors.

Box 5.9: Song 4 – Prewin song of Pruthen-Muntji, version 3

Tulaba states that his "other father" Brūthen Mūnji, occasionally visits him when asleep, and communicates to him charms (songs), against sickness and other evils. He states, further, that if he could remember all his father teaches him in sleep, he should be a mŭlla mŭllung (doctor). One charm which he has thus learned, and which I have heard him use to cure pain in the chest, by singing monotonously over the sick person, runs thus:— "Tūndŭnga Brewinda nŭndū ŭnga ūgarinda mri mŭrriwŭnda;" or, freely translated — "Oh tūndŭng! I believe Brewin has hooked me with the eye of his throwing-stick."*

Footnote * Tūndŭng, supposed to be a substance like frayed stringybark, which the doctor sometimes professes to extract and exhibits as the cause of the disease; Brewin = an evil spirit; nŭndū ŭnga = to believe or think; ugarinda = to hook or catch; mri = eye; mŭrrawŭn = throwing-stick. The throwing-stick is supposed to have magical properties.

Source: Fison and Howitt (1880: 246); adapted by authors.

Box 5.10: Song 4 – Prewin song of Pruthen-Muntji, version 4

BOWKAN, BREWIN, AND BULLUNDOOT.

The Aboriginal natives of the neighbourhood of the Mitchell River, and of the Lakes in North Gippsland, believe in three spiritual beings-*Bowkan*, a beneficent spirit, *Brewin*, a malignant spirit; and with *Brewin* is associated *Bullundoot* - the term *Bullun* being 'two,' signifying a dual existence. *Bowkan* is also sometimes called *Bullun-Bowkan*. They are said to live in the clouds; and sudden attacks of illness are often attributed to *Brewin*. *Bowkan* is invoked to relieve from the influence of *Brewin*, who inflicts upon the blacks, as they believe, various forms of disorder, which are called, for instance, *Toondung*, seemingly a chest affection; violent pains in the abdomen, &c.; these may be caused by *Brewin* with the hooked part of the throwing-stick (*Murrawun*), or by actually passing down the afflicted person's throat. In the latter case it is attempted to drive out the intruder by shouting out abusive and threatening words to him.

One form of charm used is this :-

Toondunga Brewinda

Nandu-unga Ugaringa

Mrew murrawunda

Toondunga, &c., &c.

It is sung to a monotonous chant, and may be rendered, 'Oh, *Brewin*! I expect you have given *Toondung*, or the eye (sharp hooked end) of the *Murramun* (throwing-stick).'

Source: Smyth (1878, 1: 471–72); adapted by authors.

Note that further information about Bulun Baukun and Bulluntūt is recorded in the Museums Victoria MS XM 615, p. 27.

Further explanation of the *Toondung* is given in Smyth (1878, 2: 474), for which the information has presumably come from Howitt:

> A *Murla-mullung* is a doctor; a blackfellow becomes *a Murla-mullung by* being visited in the night, by some departed relative-as a father, uncle, or brother. The vision shows him the causes of disease, such as *Toondung*, the inner bark of a variety of ironbark, which is supposed to get into the chest; *Bulk*, an egg-shaped quartz pebble; *Groggin*, quartz fragments, to which may be added *Bottle*, that is broken glass; *Murrawun*, the magical throwing-stick, made of ironbark wood.
>
> For these and other ailments various charms and their appropriate tunes are taught, and the sleeper on awakening is a *Murla-mullung*. He can now charm out the *Toondung* by singing the appropriate remedy over the patient; and, placing his hand on the chest under the 'possum rug, draws out the offending *Toondung* in the shape of some of the inner bark of the ironbark called *Yowut;* it is said always to have blood on it. In the same way other cures are performed. If, for instance, the patient has had some quartz fragments or broken

> glass placed in his legs or arms by the enchantment of some enemy, the *Murla-mullung* straightens out the limb, smooths it down with his hands, and then, after singing his chant, sucks the quartz or glass out of the place, and removing it from his mouth, shows it to the patient, who is then cured.

Our analysis of this song is presented in (5.9):

(5.9)	*Tūndŭ́nga*	*Brewínda*	*nandū-ŭnga*
	bark fibres	*Oh Brewin*	*I think*
	t(h)untang-a	**Prewin-ta**	**nant(h)u-(a)nga**
	inner bark of ironbark-POSS	spirit-OBL	think?-1SG?

yūgaringa	*mrí*	*mūrriwŭnda*	-	*(da capo)*
(you) have given	*(with) eye*	*of boomerang*		
yuka-Ri-nga	**mri**	**maRiwan-ta**		
give(2)-?-?	eye	magic throwing stick-OBL		

'The ironbark fibres of *Prewin*, I think you have given (to someone), or the eye of the **maRiwan** throwing stick.'

Vocabulary notes

This song, along with a number of others in this chapter, employs the possessive construction described in Morey (2016).

Mathews's verb paradigm (NLA MS 8006/4, File 8d, Folder 18) gives a form **-nga** for the 1st person future, as *Dhangginga* 'I shall speak'. The translation of *nandū-ŭnga* has a 1st person subject, but that of *yūgaringa* has a second person subject. A very similar transcription of the word *nandū-ŭnga* is found in the Braiakaulung song analysed below (see section 5.2.12).

Fesl (1985: R2, no. 14) lists two forms for 'think', *kalandanngat* from Mathew (1899) and *gal-larn-da* from SLV MS 6290, which would suggest a root form of **kalanda** for 'think'. We cannot find any verb with a root similar to **nanda** (Fesl 1985: R2, no. 24 also lists *nguttay*, from Thomas, for 'understand').

The word for 'woomera' was regularised by Fesl (1985: D2, no. 13; D4, no. 38) as *mariwan* with an alternative form *miriwan*. The word is variously spelled by Howitt with <ū>, <ŭ> or sometimes <u> as the vowel in the first syllable. More information about the **maRiwan** is found below in Box 5.17.

Smyth (1878, 1: 476) described the **maRiwan**:

> The *Murrawun* is the magical throwing-stick, made of ironbark wood. The person who has learned to make these, and to render them, as the blackfellows describe it, 'big fellow poison,' is called a *Bungil-Murrawun*. He is said to make it 'carry poison' by rubbing kangaroo marrow on it, and by singing over it. The *Murrawun* is used to injure blackfellows by pointing at them, making a hissing noise at the same time; by tying a piece of some one's hair on it with some kangaroo fat and an eaglehawk's feather, and roasting the hair, &c., before the fire; in fact it is believed of potent effect in many ways.

5.2.5 Song 5 – KunyeRu – Prewin song

A second **Prewin** song, perhaps recorded from a different consultant, is found in two versions, both in manuscript form in the State Library of Victoria, given in Boxes 5.11 and 5.12.

In Box 5.11 it is described as a **kunyeRu**, which is defined in section 5.1.2 as a song that accompanied dancing, but Box 5.12 specifically describes this as being an ancient song that is not danced to. It is not clear whether this song was used for curing ailments in the way that the previous **Prewin** song (see section 5.2.4) was said to have been used. The sentences below the song (see Box 5.13) include the word for 'you tell a lie' *Jetbol álō*, which may relate this song to the Nunga Nunga song sung at ritual fights (see section 5.2.11).

Box 5.11: Song 5 – KunyeRu – Prewin song, version 1

Kurnai Gūnyerū

Míringŭna	dŭrŭgan
look point (mra = eye)	throwing stick
drt krawe´a	Brewinda
that way (east) (Krauat = east)	of Brewin
Kŭrnunga	niniwa
not far	Red bluff (at)

Source: SLV MS Box 1053/4 (a), hw0404.pdf, p. 121; adapted by authors.

Box 5.12: Song 5 – KunyeRu – Prewin song, version 2

Songs	A favorite song was this:–	
	Míringănda	dŭrrŭganda
	Look (see)	the throwing stick
	Brewíndū	mūnda
	of Brewin	there
	drtkrauéa	kŭrŭnga
	east ward	a little distance
	ninnewa	
	at Ninne (The Red Bluff – Lake Entrance)	
This is a very ancient song – it is not danced to		

Source: SLV MS Box 1053/3 (b), hw0404.pdf, p. 29; adapted by authors.

Our analysis is presented in (5.10):

(5.10)	*Míringŭna (-da)*	*dŭ́rŭgan (-da)*	
	look point (mra = eye)	*throwing stick*	
	miRinga-nta	**t(h)uRu(n)gan-ta**	
	point-?	throwing stick-OBL	
	Drt krawéa	*Brewinda*	*(munda)*
	that way (east) (Krauat = east)	*of Brewin*	*there*
	tRatkrauwe-a	**Prewin-ta**	**munta**
	east-POSS	spirit-OBL	yonder
	Kŭrnunga	*niniwa*	
	not far	*Red bluff (at)*	
	tarnang-a	**niniwa**	
	down there-OBL	Red Bluff.OBL	

‘With your eye (point) … with the throwing stick, yonder in Prewin’s east, not far down at Red Bluff.’

Vocabulary notes

The first word is unclear. As Howitt pointed out it contains the root **mri** ‘eye’. In view of the example in Box 5.13, analysed as example (5.11.2), we have regularised this as **miRinga-**. This is not the word for ‘look’, as shown by Howitt, probably based on the 'see' root **tha-** and taking the form **thayala**, exemplified in the sentences below (SLV MS Box 1053/3 (b), hw0404.pdf, p. 24):

> Look at that = Déala mundatti
> Look at that child = Déall leet mundatti

The word for 'throwing stick' is probably 'reed spear' *toorooknaroong* (Gi/Hag C3) (Fesl 1985: D3, no. 33), which would be regularised as **t(h)uRungaRung**.

The word Kŭrnung was found in section 5.2.2 where it was glossed as 'down at the creek'. In the manuscript (SLV MS Box 1053/4 (a), hw0404.pdf, p. 121), it is glossed as 'down there, not far away, a little way'.

The second version of this text is followed by a series of sentences that may be a partial explanation of the text. The transcription of these is presented in Box 5.13:

Box 5.13: Sentences following Song 5

Illustration of above					
	(1) Q	Miringátū	ngánda	mŭrriwŭnda	
		point you	to me	with the throwing stick	
	(2) A	Jetbol álō	(3) A	nanma	gūnūnjattū
		you tell a lie		that one (he)	not at all lies
	(4) Q	Ngándū	tūnga		
		Who	told you?		
	(5) A	Tūngam	Brabrolūng		
		tell me			
	Tŭrdi	Kŭrnai	Mūnda	drt Krauea	
	dead	blackfellow	over there up there	eastwards	
	'There is a blackfellow dead to the eastward'				
The four directions					
The direction	Where the sunrise - east - Drt Krauéa				
"	Where the sunset - west - Dé-aua				
"	North - Tŭrnb-brrra				
"	South - Kátter				

Source: SLV MS Box 1053/3 (b), hw0404.pdf, p. 29; adapted by authors.

These sentences are analysed and glossed in (5.11). The first of these (5.11.1) is clearly related to the song text.

(5.11.1)	*Miringátū*	*ngánda*	*mŭrriwŭ́nda*
	point you	*to me*	*with the throwing stick*
	miRinga-tu	**nganda**	**maRiwan-ta**
	point-?	1SG.DAT	throwing stick-OBL
	'Point … to me with the throwing stick.'		

(5.11.2)	*Jetbol álō*
	You tell a lie
	tjetpo-lo
	lie-?
	'(You) lie.'

(5.11.3)	*nanma*	*gūnūnjattū*
	that one (he)	*not at all lies*
	n(g)anma	**kunungyatu**
	what	?
	'What …'	

(5.11.4)	*Ngándū*	*tūnga*
	who	*told you*
	ngantu	**thanga**
	who	speak
	'Who said it?'	

(5.11.5)	*Tūngam*
	tell me
	thanga-m
	speak-?
	'Say …'

(5.11.6)	*Tŭ́rdi*	*Kŭrnai*	*Mūnda*	*drt Krauea*
	dead	*blackfellow*	*over there* *up there*	*eastwards*

'There is a blackfellow dead to the eastward'

terti	**kanai**	**munt-a**	**krauwe-a**
die	person	yonder-OBL	east-POSS

'There is a dead black fellow in yonder east.'

Vocabulary notes

The word *gūnūnjattū* 'not at all lies' cannot be related to other words so far identified in the Gippsland vocabularies. There is a form *kanitba*, shown by Thomas with the meaning 'thankful' (Fesl 1985: O4, no. 46).

We assume that *drt* is short for the English word 'direction' and perhaps indicates that at this point there was a gesture towards the east. It is possible that the phrase *Mūnda Krauea* in (5.11.6) is a possessive construction. See Morey (2016).

5.2.6 Song 6 – Parn song

This song and the next both relate to *barrn* (**parn**), which literally means 'she-oak', and is regularised by Fesl (1985: M8, no. 57) as *barn* with a retroflex final /rn/, a regularisation that we will follow, save that we will use initial voiceless **p**. In connection with the second song, to be presented in section 5.2.7, the tree is identified both as '*Casuarina leptoclada*: Miquel', and *Casuarina suberosa*, but this species is now known as *Allocasuarina littoralis* (Salisb.), commonly called 'black she-oak'. As indicated in the introduction to the discussion of this song in Smyth (1878, 1: 475), **parn** also refers to a type of spell or 'bewitchment'. There are two **parn** songs, the one presented here, used to counter the effects of the spell, and that in section 5.2.7, which was sung to cast the spell.

There are three versions of this song: a version with the text only from the manuscripts in the State Library of Victoria, presented in Box 5.14; a version with a considerable amount of context, from Smyth (1878, 1: 475), presented in Box 5.15; and a version in Howitt (1904: 377), which is included in Box 5.16 (section 5.2.7).

Box 5.14: Song 6 – Parn song, version 1

nŭmba	jellŭn	barnda
not (will)	point	of He oak (catch me)

Source: SLV MS Box 1053/3 (b), hw0404.pdf, p. 5; adapted by authors.

Box 5.15: Song 6 – Parn song, version 2

Barrn is the name of the he-oak* (forest oak), but it also means a certain kind of bewitchment by which the victim is killed. The mode of doing this is called 'making *Barrn*,' or 'to catch some one with *Barrn*.' There is a lesser and a greater process. The less is done by finding a place where the intended victim has sat on the ground – the place must be still 'warm.' The spot is then beaten with a *Barrn*, which is a piece of he-oak about an inch diameter and four inches long, cut to a blunt point at each end; an appropriate song is chanted at the same time. The *Barrn* thereupon goes mysteriously into the body of the victim, and unless got rid of by a *Murla-mullung*, kills him. One counter charm against *Barrn* is this :–

Noomba jellen Barrnda,

which means, 'The sharp *Barrn* is not to catch me,' and is sung over and over again.

Source: Smyth (1878, 1: 475); adapted by authors.

The version in Howitt (1904: 377) gives the text as '*Numba jellung barnda*; literally, "Never sharp barn," or anglicised, "Never shall sharp barn catch me."'

Our analysis is presented in (5.12):

(5.12)	*nŭmba*	*jellŭn*	*barnda*
	not (will)	*point*	*of He oak (catch me)*
	numpa	**tjilan(g)**	**parn-ta**
	?	tongue?	he.oak-OBL/ERG?[30]
	'… she-oak's tongue.'		

Vocabulary notes

Fesl (1985: X1–2, no. 2) regularises two forms for the negative, /ŋalgo/ and /ŋaɖban/, which we would spell **ngalko** and **ngatjpan**. Neither of these appears to be part of this text. If the literal gloss in the version of Howitt (1904) is correct, then **numpa** should be a negative, and the word **tjilan(g)**, there spelled *jellung*, should mean 'sharp'. However, the Howitt version also points out that the practice of casting this spell was termed '*Jellun-daiun*, or

30 Theatre (2024) will contain a discussion of the case markers that will help to better understand this.

tonguechoke' by the Brabralung, and therefore we have glossed the second word as 'tongue'. Perhaps the literal meaning of the whole song is 'never the **parn**'s tongue'.

Thomas has *dilba* for 'catch' (Fesl 1985: U1, no. 11) and *dillba* for 'toss' (Fesl 1985: U1, no. 9). It is possible therefore that the second word is the same root, meaning 'catch'.

5.2.7 Song 7 – Parn song

Whereas the previous song (in section 5.2.6) was the one sung to protect from the effects of a **parn** spell, this text appears to be an example of the spell. As Box 5.17 points out, it is sung by a group of men to 'get rid of' someone, to cast a spell on them. According to the account in Smyth (1878, 1: 475), these men were termed *Bungil Dowa-gunney* spelled *Bunjil Dauangŭn* by Howitt (SLV MS Box 1053/4 (a), hw0404.pdf, p. 90), which can perhaps be regularised as **puntjil thawangan**. In the account in Howitt (1904), in Box 5.18, these men were termed **puntjil parn** 'expert-she.oak/spell'. An important feature of this type of song appears to have been that it involved naming the person who was to be protected. Bulmer (in Campbell 1999), while not giving an example of this type of song, nevertheless gives some context of the use of names in songs, which is presented below (section 5.3).

Howitt stated that 'Billy Woods' Nakŭn was Bunjil Dauangŭn and Bunjil Barn was his elder brother' (SLV MS 1053/4 (a), hw0404.pdf, p. 90). The word *nakŭn* is the same as that recorded by Hercus (1986) as **ngatjen** meaning 'maternal grandfather'.

This second **parn** song has three versions, from Howitt's manuscript in Box 5.16, from Smyth (1878, 1) in Box 5.17 and from Howitt (1904) in Box 5.18. The informant is Charl(e)y Rivers, named in Box 5.16.

Box 5.16: Song 7 – Parn song, version 1 (Song 6 – Parn song, version 3)

A man can be caught with Barn & you can find the place where he has been sitting. But it must be directly after he has gone away. They must be at the place with the barn and sing

Rivers says Barn song is

Moonang ngi-ay (then name)

he is coming

Bee-ar lounganda barnda

the barn is swinging him along

Source: SLV MS Box 1053/3 (b), p. 29, hw0404.pdf, p. 52; adapted by authors.

Box 5.17, the version from Smyth (1878, 1: 475), describes the process of casting this spell in detail. Apart from the naming of the potential victim, there is also the drawing of an image of that person. The chanting itself is described as lasting 'for several hours', and the example that we have is only one of what were probably many songs that would be used in this way.

Box 5.17: Song 7 – Parn song, version 2

The other process is as follows:– A number of blackfellows join together to get rid of some person. They are called *Bungil Dowa-gunney*, and do as follows:– A place is found where a suitable he-oak grows, about six inches in diameter. The branches are cut off, so as to leave the stem smooth and pointed; the bark is chipped off smoothly; on the ground an extended figure of the victim is drawn, with the he-oak growing out of his head. Sometimes the outline is formed with he-oak branches, buried under the surface of the ground. A *Murrawun* is stuck into the figure. Three or four trees are then joined by lines marked on the ground from one to the other, and sometimes by stringybark cords, enclosing an area of perhaps eight or ten paces in the side; the surface, inside, is cleared up, and the grass and rubbish piled over the *Yambo-ganey* or 'double' of the victim, marked under the *Barrn* tree. This tree is also called *Tschu-duck*. Everything being thus prepared, the *Bungil Dowa-gunney* go to the place about two o'clock in the afternoon. They must be perfectly naked, rubbed with charcoal, and with their heads, bodies, and limbs wound round with stringybark cords. They hold the small *Barrns* I have spoken of in their hands. They then chant for several hours some song which is to have the effect of bringing the victim to the spot. It is believed that when the incantation has been strong enough, the victim finds himself impelled, by a power he cannot resist, to get up wherever he may be, and walk towards the *Barrn*. He is said to walk like a man asleep; he staggers from side to side, and his eyes goggle out of his head. One song describes them as being *Woorburru-mrew-nurrundu*, or a 'cranky eye like the moon.'

One of the songs used is this:–

> *Moon-aug ngi-ay* [here comes the name] ;
>
> *Bee-ar lounganda-Barrnda*

which may be rendered thus:–

> He is coming along [naming the person] ;
>
> The *Barrn* is swinging him about.

So soon as he comes in sight of the Barrn, he walks straight to it, and on entering the marked space the Bungil Dowa-gunney throw their Barrns at him.

* *Casuarina leptoclada*: Miquel

[p. 476]

He falls on his back; they then draw his tongue out of his mouth and separate it at each side from the throat. It is now put back, and he is roused. He stands stupidly looking about him. One of the *Bungil Dowa-gunney* says to him, 'You are only to live two days'–or whatever the time may be–to which he nods assent, not being able to speak. They then send him home, sometimes giving him a 'possum to eat on the road. At the end of the time he dies, as ordered.

Sometimes it is said they amuse themselves by throwing big 'sow-thistles,' which grow wild in places in the bush, at him; they go right through him, but are pulled out before he goes home, though the poison remains in him.

The last blackfellow reported to have been killed by *Barrn* was called *Bruthen-mungie*; but *Barrn* has been made for the purpose of 'catching' one of the Bony Point blackfellows during the past year. My informant says that Barrn trees have been several times found lately, but that the blackfellows finding them cut them up and throw them away.

Source: Smyth (1878, 1: 475–76); adapted by authors.

Box 5.18: Song 7 – Parn song, version 3

Death is attributed by the Kurnai not only to the action of evil magic, but also to the combination of evil magic and violence. Such is the magical proceeding called *Barn*, a practice much affected by the Kurnai, who called those who carried it out *Bunjil-barn*.

Here is an instance which took place in 1874. Some Brabralung Kurnai, among whom were Tankowillin and Turlburn, had a grudge against Bundawal, and they determined to catch him with *Barn*. They chose a young He-oak tree[3], lopped the branches and pointed the stem, then drawing the outline (*Yamboginni*) of a man as if the tree-stump grew out of his chest, they also cleared the ground for a space round the tree, making a sort of magical circle. Then they stripped themselves naked, rubbed themselves over with charcoal and grease, a common garb of magic, and danced and chanted the Barn song. They told me afterwards that they did this for several days, but that,

[Footnote]3: *Casuarina suberosa*

[p. 377]

as Tankowillin expressed it, they "were not strong enough." Under the influence of their magic spells, Bundawal was expected to rise from his camp and walk to them in a trance, "like it sleep." When the victim entered the magic circle the *Bunjil-barn* would throw small pieces of He-oak wood, shaped like the *Guliwils* before mentioned, at him. When he fell to the ground they would cut out his tongue, or rather, as the *Bunjil-barn* explained to me, would have pulled out a great length of it, cutting it free at each side as it was protruded, and so sent him home to die. The Brabra clan of the tribe called this practice *Jellun-daiun*, or tongue-choke. The great Headman Bruthen-munji is said to have been the last known victim of this form of evil magic. His tribal son Tulaba has repeated to me his counter charm against Barn, which runs as follows: "*Numba jellung barnda*" literally, "Never sharp barn," or anglicised, "Never shall sharp barn catch me." This was repeated in a monotonous chant.

The secrecy with which personal names are often kept arises in great measure from the belief that an enemy, who knows your name, has in it something which he can use magically to your detriment.

I have been told of a certain way of catching a person with Barn, namely, to find the place where he has sat down on the ground and left an impression on it. But the incantation must be commenced immediately after his departure.

One of the spells sung by the *Bunjil-barn* is as follows:–

Munang	ngiai	(then the person's name)
Coming	he is	
biar	lounganda	barnda
along	swinging him	barn is

Source: Howitt (1904: 376–77); adapted by authors.

The sentence in Smyth (1878, 1: 475), which is present in Box 5.17 above, is analysed in (5.13). It seems to be some kind of metaphor.

(5.13)	*Woorburru*	*mrew*	*nurrundu*
	cranky eye like the moon		
	wuRbuRu	**mri-u**	**naRan-tu**
	cranky	eye-ERG?	moon-ERG?
	'Cranky eye (like) the moon.'		

Vocabulary notes

The word **naRan(g)** 'moon' is well attested with many sources (Fesl 1985: G4–5, no. 28). Many of the sources spell this word with a final /n/ including the word for moon in the **yentjin(y)** song discussed in section 5.2.8. The song in section 5.2.13, however, has a word for moon that appears to have a final velar nasal /ng/.

No word resembling *woorburru* or with a meaning 'cranky' has been indicated by other sources. Thomas (Fesl 1985: O3, no. 13) gives *wangōōr-wangōōr-biddarŭk* with the meaning 'crazy' and 'mad'.

Our analysis of the song text is presented in (5.14):

(5.14)	*Munang*	*ngiai*	*(then the person's name)*
	coming	*he is*	
	munang	**ngi-ai**	
	DEM?	?	
	biar	*lounganda*	*barnda*
	along	*swinging him*	*Barn is*
	piR	**luwung(k)ant-a**	**parn-ta**
	move	?- -POSS	he.oak-OBL
	'(From) yonder … moving, the swinging of the *Parn*.'		

Vocabulary notes

The first word does not resemble any of the documented words for 'come', several of which are based on a root **ngawa** (see Fesl 1985: P2, no. 9). Hercus (1986) recorded a form **muntjap** 'he's gone' (past participle), the root of which is probably **muntja** that looks similar to some of the demonstratives, such as **muntu** 'yonder'. Perhaps the phrase *munang ngiai* means something like 'from yonder', and the motion is expressed by **piR** in the second line.

The word for 'swing' is given by Thomas as *bai-anga* (Fesl 1985: P5, no. 100). This form is unrelated to *lounganda,* which perhaps only refers to swinging the branches of the black she-oak. This latter word is probably related to *Lo-ungil* 'to entice or seduce', which is discussed in connection with the next song (in section 5.2.8). The word appears to imply enticement, as it does in the next song.

5.2.8 Song 8 – Yentjin(y) – Elopement song

The first of the **yentjin(y)** or elopement songs is presented here. As mentioned above, this song was used to seduce a woman into elopement, as described in the introductions to the two versions of this, both from the manuscripts in the State Library of Victoria and presented as Box 5.19 and Box 5.20.

The name given to the woman who is enticed away is given in a footnote in Fison and Howitt (1880: 259): 'a *Lo-ŭngil rūkŭt* is a term of reproach. *Lo-ungil* = to entice or seduce away; *Rūkŭt* = woman'. As mentioned in the previous section, the word *Lo-ŭngil* is similar to the word *lounganda* glossed as 'swinging him'.

The description in Box 5.19 mentions the *Nunga Nunga* fight that relates to the song presented in section 5.2.11. The location of this fight was Providence Ponds, north-east of Bushy Park and north of Lake Wellington and a well-known local site from at least the 1860s.[31]

31 Thanks to Amanda Lourie for pointing this out.

Box 5.19: Song 8 – Yentjin(y) – Elopement song, version 1

Among the songs of the Kurnai are some called Yĕnjin. As Billy says, these songs always made the women 'run away in every direction'. A man would sing one of these son(g)s entertaining until at length the women continually talking about it & him since the women would eye him knew through some friend of his – a male cousin of hers for instance – that she wanted him. And then the eloped would take place. If they escaped to some distant place he would be safe – if he & she were caught he would perhaps be killed. The men and women alike attacking him, the men with their weapons, the women with their yam sticks sharpened at the end for the purpose of stabbing him in the stomach. His own friends would endeavour to assist him by opposing the others and a severe fight would ensue. If the onslaught became too strong he might have at last to escape of tumult and take to flight. The woman if caught was treated as described in K & K -speared cut down with the Tundewung in the back and legs and perhaps killed. Yet this elopement of women married or unmarried constantly went on. This kind of 'free fight' differs entirely from the *Nunga Nunga* which is an arranged "ordeal of battle"

There are many of these songs inciting to elopements one of them thus:

Dilbŭn	kaiŭng	tūlūyanara
kick	womans apron	kicking walking
Balwŭt	blappande	malnarranme
	going	moonlight
Warrige mŭlla	Brabira	
rousing up	Brabras	

One old man of Providence Ponds was from his always singing such songs called Būnjil Yenjin. The man who ran off with a woman and who suffered in consequence is called Būnjil Rūkŭt

Source: SLV MS Box 1053/3 (b), hw0404.pdf, p. 27; adapted by authors.

Box 5.20: Song 8 – Yentjin(y) – Elopement song, version 2

Kurnai Yenjin per Toolaba

One of the Bunjil Yenjin was hanged by the whitemen in Melbourne about the white woman. He belonged to the Providence Ponds.

A funny song

Dilbŭn	kaiung	tūlū	yánowa
kick	womans apron	kick out	walking
bulwŭt	blappade		
all of us	going		
mal naranme	wărigemŭla		
moonlight	raise him up		
Brabira			
the Brabra man			

Source: SLV MS Box 1053/4 (a), hw0404.jpg, p. 91; adapted by authors.

Our analysis is presented in (5.15):

(5.15)	*Dilbŭn*	*kaiung*	*tūlū*	*yánowa*
	kick	*woman's apron*	*kick out*	*walking*
	t(j)ilpa-n	**kaiyu(ng)**	**tulu**	**ya-n(h)uwa**
	toss	possum skin skirt	kick?	walk-?

'Toss the possum skin skirt, kick it, walking …'

bulwŭt	*blappade*
all of us	*going*
pa-l-wart(u)	**plapa-te**
?-1PL.INCL	go-?

'All of us going'

mal naranme		*wărigemŭla*	*Brabira*
moonlight		*raise him up*	*the Brabra man*
mal	**naRan-ma**	**waRitja-ma-la**	**prapra**
GO	moon-POSS	raise up-?-?	tribal name

'With the going of the moon, raise up … the *Brabra* man.'

Vocabulary notes

Thomas lists the word *dillba* for 'toss' (Fesl 1985: U1, no. 9) and *dilba* for 'catch' (Fesl 1985: U1, no. 11), which are obviously the same root. We have suggested that the gloss for this word should be 'toss'.

The only other record of a word meaning 'kick' in the Gippsland sources is also recorded by Thomas with the form *dōōrdŭtbilly* (Fesl 1985: T1, no. 13). This might be the same root that we find here, which we have regularised as **tulu**.

In the second line we find a form *bulwŭt*, glossed by Howitt as 'all of us'. A root /**pa-**/ followed by a pronominal ending has already been seen in Song 1 (section 5.2.1), where *bŭnyel* was glossed by Howitt as 'you and I', /ba-/ plus the 1st person dual inclusive suffix **nyal**. The form wŭt is surely **-swaRu** found in the pronoun paradigms of R.H. Mathews with the meaning 1st person plural inclusive. Perhaps the **R** was pronounced as a trill or a tap in more rapid speech, hence *wŭt*.

5.2.9 Song 9 – Yentjin(y) – Elopement song (Brabralung tribe)

The second **yentjin(y)** song we are presenting is found in three versions, one from the State Library of Victoria manuscripts, transcribed in Box 5.21, and two from Howitt's publications, Box 5.22 and Box 5.23. This song names both of the sex totems, the male *yeerung* 'blue wren' and the female *djeetgun* 'southern emu-wren'.

Box 5.21: Song 9 – Yentjin(y) – Elopement song (Brabralung tribe), version 1

Another Yĕnjin is the following

Káiakjirai	yĕndu	
why cut off	beard	
Yīrŭng	málbretŭng	
Yeerung	long ago	
Jītgŭnjitgŭn	mŭna	bét-jūrŭnga
Djeetgun	there	the place
	at that place	where the
		young girl
		sleeps in
		her mother's camp

or

Why did the Yirung cut off his beard long
ago? The maiden Djeetgŭn sleeps in her camp.

This song is said by Toolaba to be a very favourite one to make women elope. He says that he has sung it effectively many times himself.

Source: SLV MS Box 1053/3 (b), hw0404.pdf, p. 28; adapted by authors.

It is not clear what it means that Tulaba had 'sung it effectively many times himself'. He is not known to have married many women, so it may be that he sang the song on behalf of another man to persuade a woman to elope with the other man.

Howitt (1904: 275) also gives a version of this song, for which W. Lucas is named in a footnote as the informant. Lucas is listed as William Lucas in the 1904 index, and named on page xi as a correspondent, and was probably a white man.

Box 5.22: Song 9 – Yentjin(y) – Elopement song (Brabralung tribe), version 2

Another of these songs, also said to be a most powerful charm, is as follows :—

Kaiaki-jirai	*yendu*	*Yiirung*	*malbretung*
Why cut off	beard,	Yiirung,	long ago ?
Djiitgun-djiittgun	*muna*		*betjurnnga*
Djiitgun	there (at that place)		the placc where the girl sleeps in her mother's hut.

Or, freely translated, "Why did the young man cut off his beard long ago? the maiden sleeps in her camp."

This performance-ceremony it might even be called-was well known to all the camp, for there was no concealment, and even if done at a little distance, there was always some female friend to carry the news to the girl, and say, "There is so and so singing a Yenjin about you."

When the *Bunjil-yenjin* thought his magic was strong enough, he ceased his song. In one case, when one of my informants was present, Bunjil-gworan was the *Bunjil-yenjin*, and the girl's parents covered themselves as if asleep.

Source: Howitt (1904: 275); adapted by authors.

The singer of this song was named *Bunjil-gworan*. He is described in Howitt (1904: 278) as a 'Headman', and his name incorporated the word for 'thunder'. This word will be regularised as **kwaRany**, with a final palatal nasal, after the spelling in R.H. Matthews of *gwurruñ* (Fesl 1985: G1, no. 11).

This song also appears in Howitt (1887a: 334), presented in Box 5.23:

Box 5.23: Song 9 – Yentjin(y) – Elopement song (Brabralung tribe), version 3

... to add another of the songs by which the Bunjil Yenjin of the Kurnai aided those in olden times married by elopement. This Yenjin is in the Mŭkthang dialect of the Brabra Kurnai

Kaiáka	*jirai*	*yéndū*	*Yírŭng*	*malbretŭng*
Why cut	off	beard	Yeerung,	long ago
Djitgŭn-djittgŭn	*mūna*	*betjūrŭnga*[1]		
Djeetgun	there	girl's sleeping place at		

The songs used by the doctors are merely spells chanted over and over again, in fact "incantations" in the old sense of the word.

Footnote 1. Betjūrŭk is the word applied to that part of the hut in which the unmarried daughter sleeps, that is to say, at her mother's back, and being thus next to the bough or bark shelter, her position gives opportunity for signalling to her from without by her youthful admirer.

Source: Howitt (1887a: 334); adapted by authors.

Our analysis of this song is presented in (5.16). It has some similarities with the **yentjin(y)** song recorded by Bulmer (see section 5.3.2).

(5.16)

Kaiáka	*jirai*	*Yĕndū*	*Yírŭng*	*malbretŭng*
Why cut	*off*	*Beard*	*Yerrung*	*long ago*
kaya-ka	**tjiRai**	**yen-tu**	**yiRang**	**mal pret(h)ang**
shave-?	?	beard-ERG?	MALE TOTEM	GONE-other?

'… shaved (your) beard, *yiRang* (boy) some time ago.'

Djitgŭn-djittgŭn	*mūna*	*betjūrŭnga*
Djeetgun	*there*	*girls sleeping place at*
tjitkan tjitkan	**muna**	**petjuRang-a**
FEMALE TOTEM	DEM	girls sleeping place-OBL

'The *tjitkan* (girl) is there in the girl's sleeping place.'

Vocabulary notes

We are not able to gloss the first two words *Kaiáka jirai*. Presumably these contain the word for 'shave off'. Thomas recorded a word *birdagāӯr* meaning 'scrape', which might contain the morphemes **piRa** 'move' and **kaya-** 'scrape'.

The word for 'beard' is regularised by Fesl as /jen/ (**yen**) with a final alveolar nasal. It is also glossed as meaning 'chin'.

We analyse the word *malbretŭng* as having several morphemes: **mal** 'gone' and **pretha-**, which may be related to **prepa** 'other'. The word for yesterday is listed as **malpukang** in Fesl (1985: V5, no. 63), which is literally 'gone night', where **pukang** is night (Fesl 1985: G7–8, no. 38).

5.2.10 Song 10 – Yentjin(y) – Elopement song

The third **yentjin(y)** song is found in two versions, one in a manuscript at the State Library of Victoria (Box 5.24) and one in Howitt (1904) (Box 5.25).

Box 5.24: Song 10 – Yentjin(y) – Elopement song, version 1

Yēnyin or in the Nūlit (Braiaka) language Yennin.

There were men called Bunjil Yenjin whose business it was to bring about a particular elopement. For instance when a young man wanted a wife and fixed his mind upon some particular girl he employed the Bunjil Yenjin to whom he gave, a rug, spears &c. This man then lay on the ground the youth next to him and next all his comrades. The Bunjil Yenjin then says his song accompanied by the young men. This might be in the camp, in fact usually was, for it was it seems essential that some friend of the girl or her female cousin should carry to her the news of which he sing on. Every one knew that was being done and the name of the girl, such as song is the following:–

Bára bŭrni	wangŭr		molla
roll up the twine	(Jaw) the human name		there (over there)
Tállo	bŭrni	tallo	káragan
the little	twine	little	sweetheart
ngellagálli	kárnang		
I go ahead	the hollow (in the ground)		
gōla	yinna		
before	you		

When the Bunyil Yenyin considers that his song has been sung long enough, he tells the youth '*that will do*', now you can go and move off with her. But before this a further incantation takes place, the Bunjil *Dauangŭn* is called in, and he is paid a rug, spears, proceeds to sing the parents of the girl to sleep. He does this with the aid of his throwing stick which is stuck in the ground, slightly slanting towards the camp of the parents. By it is placed his būlk and a little distance in front in the same direction are stuck in the ground his are Yirtŭng (the small leg bone of a kangaroo pointing which he injures people) and also his gūmbart. He then sings his song and when the Murriwŭn falls down, the parents are supposed to be fast asleep. The young man then goes up gently to the camp and from the back pushes the girl with a stick. She being ready pulls the end as a signal and quietly fills her battŭng (bag) with the things–[...?] her possum rug and joins him over where is waiting her.

By and by as the charm wears off the old people wake up and find the girl gone. The father collects his brother &c and they sing a song which is supposed to have the effect of making the young mans legs heavy so that he cannot travel. The father then takes his murriwŭn in his right hand held loosely between the fore & second finger and under the [...?]. And makes short blows to all points successively of the compass. When the blow falls in the direction in which the girl ~~is supposed to have~~ has run away–the murriwŭn is said to give a loud crack. The father and his 'posse' then pursue.

Source: SLV MS 1053/3 (b), hw0404.pdf, p. 35 and p. 36; adapted by authors.

This song is published in Howitt (1904: 275).

Box 5.25: Song 10 – Yentjin(y) – Elopement song, version 2

The following is one of these songs, of which there were very many used on such occasions, and it is said to have been a very powerful one. One of my Kurnai informants, whose wife was one of the girls that eloped at the *Jeraeil* above mentioned, said in speaking of it, "That *Yenjin* made the women run in all directions when they heard it."

Bara-burni		*Wangur*	*molla*	*tallo-burni*	
Roll up the twine,		Jaw,[1]	down	there little twine	
tallo	*karagan*	*ngella-galli*	*kernanga*	*gola*	*yinna*
little	sweetheart	I go first	the hollow (to)	before	you.

[Footnote] 1 Wangur is the name of the girl to whom this *yenjin* was addressed.

Source: Howitt (1904: 275); adapted by authors.

Our analysis is presented in (5.17):

(5.17)

Bára bŭrni		*wangūr*	*molla*
roll up the twine		*(jaw) the human name*	*over there*
paRa	**pani(k)**	**wang-uR**	**mula**
roll	string	jaw-?	DEM

'Roll up the sting for *Wangūr* over there.'

Tállo	*bŭrni*	*tallo*	*káragan*
the little	*twine*	*little*	*sweetheart*
t(h)al-u	**pani(k)**	**t(h)al-u**	**kaRakan**
small-ERG?	string	small-ERG?	sweetheart?

'(That) small string is like a small sweetheart.'

Ngellagálli	*kárnang*	*gōla*	*yinna*
I go ahead	*the hollow (in the ground)*	*before*	*you*
ngelagali	**karnang**	**ngula**	**ngina**
return home?	hollow	before?	2SG

'… return home to the hollow before you.'

Vocabulary notes

No words for 'roll' have been documented. We assume that the root form is **paRa**.

Fesl (1985: D8, no. 112) listed two words for 'string' – *par-nic* 'rope/string' (Robinson) and *bunnik* 'rope swing' (Dawson and Pettit). Both had a final **-k**.

The word 'jaw' and 'cheek' are both listed in Fesl (1985: A5, no. 32 and no. 33) as having forms like *wahng* 'jaw' (Thomas) and *wa-ang* 'cheeks' (Bulmer).

The word for little was shown by Hercus as **tala**, but by R.H. Mathews with an initial dental stop as *dhalliban*. It is not clear here if there is an ergative suffix **-u**.

No word similar to *káragan* has been recorded with a meaning 'sweetheart'. However, Hercus (1986) records a form **pra kalakRan** for 'young man' and Fison and Howitt (1880: 189) gives the word for 'girl' as *kuerejŭng*, while Dawson and Pettit list the word for 'sister' as *carrajung* (Fesl 1985: B13, no. 57). These are all likely the same root, perhaps with a meaning like 'young unmarried person'.

Bulmer (Smyth 1878, 2: 25) writes a word *mellagan* with the meaning 'homeward'. This may be the same root as the word **ngelagali**.

The word for 'hollow' has already been discussed in section 5.2.2.

Bulmer (in Smyth 1878, 2: 26) offers the word *nulla* for 'before', which may be the same form intended by *gula* here. We have regularised it as **ngula**.

The intended form of the 2nd person pronoun may be **ngina**.

5.2.11 Song 11 – Nunga Nunga song

The Nunga Nunga song was sung during a ritual fight, described in detail by Howitt (1904: 344–46), which contains the text of the song. The word *Wait-jurk* is glossed in a footnote as 'murderer'. In a section of the Howitt manuscripts (MV XM 692, p. 61) he refers to 'the aggressor who is called "Waitjŭrk"', and on page 64 of the same manuscript notes that the injured person is called 'Nūngi-nūng-it – which also gives the name to the ceremonial ordeal'. Howitt (1904: 344–46) has:

Among the Kurnai, when a man had been called upon to appear and submit to an ordeal by weapons, for some death which he had been supposed to have caused by magic, for instance by *Bulk*, *Murriwun*, or *Barn*, he was attended by his kindred and by that branch of the tribe to which he belonged. He was called *Wait-jurk* and the aggrieved person, that is, one of the near kindred, was called *Nungi-nungit*, which also applied to all his kindred who took part in the ordeal. They also were respectively supported by their section of the tribe.

In the proceedings, the aggrieved party and the accused were each at the ordeal accompanied by the *Gweraeil-kurnai* of their section of the tribe. The proceedings were conducted by the old men according to the ancient traditions, that is, as they would put it, 'as their fathers did.' An open and level piece of ground was chosen for the meeting. The two bodies of people assembled, facing each other, and some two hundred yards apart. The aggressor stood out in advance of his party, painted with red ochre over his face, with two broad stripes from the shoulders down the breast, where tliey met horizontal alternating bands of white and red across the stomach as far as the hips on each side. According to the rules, he was only armed with a shield, or in some cases with a club or a bundle of spears in addition. Some men presented themselves to their adversaries, dancing and twirling their shields in a defiant manner, others crouched down awaiting the attack. Beside the *Wait-jurk* his wife stood, if he had one, with her digging-stick, to help in turning aside or breaking the weapons discharged at him, and at one side of the ground the women sat beating their skin rugs in measured time. The body of people stood behind the women with the old men at hand to observe and direct the proceedings. At a distance of some two hundred yards were the aggrieved, who might be a numerous party, including widely ramifying relationships. These men were painted white in token of their kinsman's death. Each man was armed with his shield, a bundle of spears, several boomerangs, and various clubs used for throwing. Their women sat in front, drumming on their folded rugs, and singing at the same time some song appropriate to the occasion. In a Nungi-nungit, which I saw represented in an alleged case of death by magic, the following song was sung, while the wife of the accused made abusive speeches to the advancing party:–

Nana-mulk	*eed-janung*	*dinne-bra-mittel*
Why you	thought	old husband mine
waitjurk-jandu	*dinn-din*	*baia-quung*
to murder	you bad	orphan

> or, freely translated, 'Why did you think to murder my old husband, you worthless orphan?' *i.e.* 'person without any kindred.'
>
> The ordinary word used for 'orphan' is *Yetherun*, but *Baia-quung*, which also has that meaning, is one of the most offensive terms which can be applied to a Kurnai, and in the old times would require to be expiated by spear-throwing, or other recourse to weapons.
>
> After singing such a song, the women got up and went forward some thirty or forty paces, drumming their rugs as they carried them, and then sat down again and sang. As they walked forward, the men followed them closely, crouching down behind them, as if seeking concealment.
>
> All this time the aggressor was dancing his defiance, and the *Nungi-nungit* came on by short stages until about sixty yards from him, when the women moved off to one side, leaving them and the Wait-jurk face to face. While the latter continued to dance, or sat crouched behind his shield, the former extended their line in the form of a crescent so as to hem him in. The oldest of the *Nungi-nungit* now addressed him, with a formal statement, as for instance, 'Why did you kill our brother with *bulk*?' The reply might be, 'I never did anything to him; it is all *jetbolan*' (lies).

Howitt then goes on to describe the fight in more detail, adding later (1904: 347): 'A good instance of the *Nungi-nungit* was one in which the man Bunbra, otherwise *Jetbolan*, was the defendant, and which occurred about the year 1850'.

Note that in this description, there is reference to *bulk*, defined by Howitt (1904: 378) as 'practice of evil magic much practised by the Kurnai is that of *Bulk*. This is a rounded and generally black pebble, which the medicine-man carried about and occasionally showed to people as a threat'. This word is not recorded by other sources; the general word for stone in the Gippsland languages was **walang** (Hercus 1986).

The word for 'lies/lying', *jetbolan*, also occurs in connection with the sentences discussed below Song 5 in section 5.2.5. Song 5 is a **Prewin** song.

The SLV manuscript version of the song is presented in Box 5.26:

Box 5.26: Song 11 – Nunga Nunga song, version 1

Kurnai

Nunga Nungy Song

This song is in two verses

Nána mŭlk	ēdjanning	
what for	(you) thought	
dinne	Bramittel	waidjŭrk-gitjándu
old	husband-mine	murder
dinnin	baiëg ŭng	
bad	orphan	

(or) Why did you think to murder my old husband your worthless orphan – ie. person having no kindred

Waitchurk	Nunga-nunget	
nŭn-ma tari?		
what (he) do (to you)		
mŭk	lŭlia	ngŭn
		me

Source: SLV MS 1053/3 (b), hw0404.pdf, p. 53; adapted by authors.

The following page of the manuscript (SLV MS Box 1053/3 (b), hw0404.pdf, p. 54) gives some further context about the decoration of the participants in the Nunga Nunga fight. In this description we find reference to *Bullawreng*, elsewhere spelled *Bullawang*. This is literally **bula mri wrang** 'two-eye-black duck'. Howitt (1904: 619) writes that '[t]he birds *Bullawang*, *Yiirung*, and *Djiitgun* are said to be three of the "*leen muk-Kurnai*" ("real Kurnai ancestors")'. The other two birds are the sex totems (see section 5.1.7.1). The term Bullawang is also used to refer to the guardian of the boys undergoing the initiation ceremony (see section 5.2.21). Howitt (SLV MS Box 1053/3 (b), hw0404.pdf, p. 54) notes:

> In attending a 'set-fight' (nŭnge-nŭnger) e.g that of Lamby, the aggrieved are painted with murlu all over their head and faces in bodies while then aggressors are painted with naial. Also when a party went out to revenge a death by killing someone the members were painted with murlu. See the fight at *Nunulmungee*. For *corroboree* both red and white paint were used in marks on the face and body arbitrarily put on at the fancy of the wearer.
>
> At the Jeraiel the youths were painted with Naial on the face.

> The Mullamullung wore a white stripe across the face.
>
> The *Bulla wreng* was painted round each eye with murlu in resemblence to the black duck.
>
> … the black duck that the Bullawreng was named having reference to his eye.
>
> | Bulla – | (mree) – | wreng |
> |---|---|---|
> | Two | eyes | duck? |
>
> The black duck and the robin were both 'policemen' to look after the boys. Both of them were Bullawreng but this name was not spoken before boys or girls.

An example of a Nunga Nunga fight is described in a little later in the manuscript (SLV MS Box 1053/3 (b), hw0404.pdf, p. 56), with the words *Nunga Nunga* written on the side and McAlpine[32] given as the consultant:

> In 1856 a black boy called Benny was with McAlpine as stockrider. A girl called Sally was in the house as a servant. They ran away together to Snake Island & remained away 6 weeks. When they returned there was a great row. When McAlpine went down to the camp hearing the disturbance, he found Bennie standing naked about sixty yards off. He had only a turnmung in his hand. A number of his friends were standing behind him at a distance. There were a number of women beating rugs. Old Morgan, Darby and other men at the camp facing Bennie & the others with him. Much speechifying went on. Old Morgan made an oration, an old woman followed, then old Darby spoke then another old woman and so only for nearly two hours. Then several men stood out each having one spear and one boomerang. Each man in succession threw his spear and then instantly his boomerang at Benny, who however warded off or dodged all. When all had been thrown the matter ended. Benny was allowed to keep the girl. Benny was Darbys tribal brother; the girl was the tribal sister of Darby's wife.

32 McAlpine was a squatter in the South Gippsland area.

There is another reference to the Nunga Nunga fight in a letter from Howitt to Tylor, dated 21 February 1888.[33] In the online transcription, the name of the fight is spelled *Mingi nungil*, but we have corrected this in the quote below:

> (3) If however it happened that (for instance) an own or tribal brother of the man died under the suspicion of magical malpractices by some relation of his wifes father and that in consequence a Nungi nungit were formed. That is to say an arranged expiatory fight – The daughters husband would be on the opposite side to his wifes father and would be bound to revenge the death of his brother.

A second, shorter version of the song text (Box 5.27) is in Museums Victoria (XM 692, p. 62):

Box 5.27: Song 11 – Nunga Nunga song, version 2

Nanamŭlk	dina	bramitel
my (think of it)	old	husband mine
wa'itjŭk-gitjandū		
murder		
di'nin	ba'ïëgŭng	
worthless	orphan	
bad		

Source: MV XM 692, p. 62; adapted by authors.

The Nunga Nunga song is very difficult to analyse. Our attempt is presented here as (5.18):

(5.18)	*Nána mŭlk*		*ēdjanning*
	what for		*(you) thought*
	n(g)anma	**malk**	**etjaning**
	what	?	?
	'What …'		

33 Pitt Rivers Museum, 'Transcription of Box 12: Howitt Correspondence Tylor Papers Pitt Rivers Museum Manuscript Collections Part 2', transcribed April and November 2013, accessed 6 May 2016, web.prm.ox.ac.uk/sma/index.php/primary-documents/primary-documents-index/417-howitt-tylor-papers-prm-2.html.

dinne	*Bramittel*	*waidjŭrk-gitjándu*
old	*husband-mine*	*murder*
tini	**pra-m/ng?-ithal**	**waitja(R)k-kitj-antu**
old	man-FORM-1SG	aggressor-?-2SG?

‘(That) you murdererd the old man my husband’

dinnin	*baiëg ŭng*
bad	*orphan*

(or) Why did you think to murder my old husband your worthless orphan - ie. person having no kindred

tintin	**payakung**
bad	without kin

‘You worthless orphan!’

Waitchurk	*Nunga-nunget*	*nŭn-ma tari?*	
what did (he) do (to you)			
waitja(R)k	**nunga-nungit**	**n(g)anma**	**taRi**
aggressor	victim	what	do?

‘What did the *waitja(R)k* do to you (*nunga-nungit*)?’

mŭk	*lŭlia*	*ngŭn*
-	-	*me*
mak	**laliya**	**ngan**
good?	?	1SG?

‘(Do) good? … to me.’

Notes

The 1st person possessive suffix is documented in range of forms, possibly an underlying **(ng)itha(l)**. Some of the forms shown have a final **-l** and others (such as *Wangingitha* ‘my boomerang’, written by R.H. Mathews) lack this. We think it likely that the word for ‘my husband’ was in fact **pra-ngithal**, although both sources have **-m** as *Bramittel.*

The final suffix on the form *waidjŭrk-gitjándu*, spelled *waitjurk-jandu* in Howitt (1904: 346), may be **-ntu**. In a manuscript draft (NLA MS 8006/8/7), R.H. Mathews gives the following paradigm:

Singular	1st person	I speak or talk	Dhangganetch
	2nd person		Dhanggandu
	3rd person		Dhangga

This paradigm makes it appear that **-ntu** was a 2nd person suffix, also found in the 2nd person singular free pronoun form **ngintu**, included by many sources. A 2nd person singular interpretation is appropriate in this example, but the same suffix occurs on many sentence examples in the Mathews papers with a non-2nd person reference.

The insult word for 'orphan', which we have regularised as **payakung**, appears to be related to two words included by Dawson and Pettit: *omigorn* 'motherless (orphan)' and *jaigong* 'fatherless (orphan)' (Fesl 1985: B7, no. 19). The second of these certainly has the same final **kung**, which would a appear to be a suffix, and the first one also seems to have it. Perhaps **kung** meant 'without'. We cannot at present suggest meanings for *omi-* and *jai-* as these do not resemble the usual words for 'mother' and 'father', which are **yakan** and **mungkan** respectively.

The final syllable of the song, *ngŭn*, regularised as **ngan** is glossed by Howitt as 'me'. It is likely that the same form is found in a sentence recorded by Bulmer (Smyth 1878, 2: 15), presented as (5.19):

(5.19)	*Man*	*jilly*	*panda*	*ngan*	*poorko*
	He hit me head				
	man	**tjili**	**pantha**	**ngan**	**puRk-u**
	?	3SG	hit	1SG	head-ERG
	'He hit me on the head.'				

5.2.12 Song 12 – Woman's answer to a Yentjin(y), or elopement song

The only song that was reported by a female is found in Museums Victoria XM 653. The transcription of a section with the heading 'Marriage' on the left is presented in Box 5.28. The first draft of this transcription was done by Sharnthi Krishna-Pillay in a report prepared for the Victorian Aboriginal Corporation for Languages (VACL report on Howitt part 7.pdf, p. 16). Krishna-Pillay added a note relating to Nanny's father: 'Bunjil Nullung, the country between the Avon and Providence ponds, also name of a man, is a division of Brayakaulung (Howitt, 1996:76)'.

Box 5.28: Song 12 – Braiakaulung song

Old Nanny – the oldest woman now living among the Kurnai – was a widow with grey hair when Angus McMillan first discovered Gippsland. She says that it was the universal custom for a young woman to obtain a wife by running off with her. If a man wanted a second one it was the same. If the first wife did not object she would assist them, but if she thought she was going to be put outside the camp she might inform the parents of the intended second wife. If her husband suspected – he would probably not tell her anything but leave her behind when he ran off. Very rarely if two ~~young~~ men agreed to exchange sisters it would not be necessary to run off – if the girls had no partners or if the fathers consented. But she only remembered three instances – one of which was her own case. She was given away by her brother and her husband was not therefore expected to fight.

One very fine song brought back by the Birra ark

yeerunga'day	nganduang	woorlingita
yeerung	I think	before me

Source: MV XM 653; adapted by authors.

Nanny went on to give information about the Braiakaulung marriage customs.

We assume that this song is an example of the **yentjin(y)** (elopement song) but was perhaps sung by a female in response to the songs sung by the males. This seems to be the only song documented for which a female was the informant and the only example of a song sung from the female perspective.

Our analysis of this song is presented as (5.20):

(5.20)	*Yeerungaday*	*onganduang*	*woorlingita*
	Yeerung	*I think*	*before me*
	yiRang-at(h)ai	**nant(h)u-(a)nga**	**wu(r)li-ngitha**
	MALE TOTEM-?	think?-1SG?	front?-1SG.POSS

'The *YiRang* (male) is in front of me, I think.'

Notes

The word for 'I think' is also found in the **Prewin** song of Brudhen Mundyi (see section 5.2.4). In that song, the form is spelled *nandŭ-ŭnga*, but this is clearly the same word.

We assume that the word *woorlingita* is literally 'my front', and that a form like **wu(r)li** was a noun meaning something like 'front'.

5.2.13 Song 13 – Charm to drive away pains

A short charm referring to the moon and used to drive away pains is found in three versions. The first is from Howitt (1904: 388), presented here as Box 5.29; the second is from Howitt (1887a: 334), presented in Box 5.30. The manuscript version is in Museums Victoria (XM 761, p. 107), presented in Box 5.31. The Museums Victoria version was recorded as part of the detailed description of an initiation ceremony (see section 5.2.21.1.1). In that version, it was described as 'Billy's song', where 'Billy' refers to Tulaba. It was sung late on the Monday night of a ceremony that had commenced on the previous Thursday. Howitt wrote: 'Last night men returned late with wallaby – knocked up – Billy's song'. We have included the song here, rather than in the discussion of the initiation ceremony, because in Box 5.29 the function of the song is to drive away pains; in this case, those being experienced by Tulaba's wife. It thus appears that it is not a core part of the boys' initiation ritual.

Box 5.29: Song 13 – Charm to drive away pains, version 1

… I give a charm to drive away pains, which Tulaba learned from his deceased father in a dream. One evening when I was at the *Jeraeil* ceremonies I heard a most extraordinary song proceeding from his camp. I found that he was driving away pains which were troubling his old wife, and he told me that he was singing a most powerful song which his father Bruthen-munji had taught him while he slept. The words are as follows, an extraordinary emphasis being laid on the last word:–

Minyan	*bulunma*	*naranke*
Show	belly	moon to

Source: Howitt (1904: 388); adapted by authors.

In Howitt (1887a: 334) the text is slightly different (Box 5.30):

Box 5.30: Song 13 – Charm, version 2

Minyan	būlūn	ma naranke
show or point to	belly	the moon to

Source: Howitt (1887a: 334); adapted by authors.

The version in Museums Victoria is in Box 5.31:

Box 5.31: Song 13 – Charm, version 3

Billy's song

mínyan	būllūni	ma nárranke
show	belly	to the moon

Source: MV XM 761, p. 107; adapted by authors.

Our analysis is presented in (5.21). This is some kind of metaphor, related to driving away his wife's pains.

(5.21) *Minyan* *bulunma* *naranke*

show *belly* *moon to*

minyan **puluny-ma** **naRang-(k)a**

show belly-POSS moon-?OBL

'Show the moon's belly.'

Note that *minyan* is not recorded in other sources with a meaning 'show'. We think this word is likely related to **miRinga** 'point' found in the KunyeRu – **Prewin** song (Song 5) above (section 5.2.5).

5.2.14 Song 14 – Song for stopping the wind

A short song with which the **Puntjil KrauRa** (spelled Bunjil Kraura by Howitt) stopped the wind, is shown in Howitt (1904: 397), presented here in Box 5.32, and in Fison and Howitt (1880: 231), presented in Box 5.33. The 1880 version contains important additional information omitted from the 1904 version: the first two words of the song were repeated and a clearer explanation was given of the word wang, which in the 1904 version is translated with a misprint 'bond' in place of 'band'; the 1880 version makes it clear that this is a headband. We have not found a manuscript version of this song, but the ability of Puntjil KrauRa to control the wind is discussed in Museums Victoria XM 525.

Box 5.32: Song 14 – Stopping the wind, version 1

I have before spoken of one of the Brayaka Headmen who was credited with the power of calling up the furious west winds, whence he derived his name of *Bunjil-kraura*. His song by which he stopped the gales which prevented his tribes-people from climbing the tall trees in the western forest, ran thus –

Kutbuna-wang Kraura

from *Kutbun* to bear or carry, Wang a bond or something tied, and *Kraura*, the west wind. I did not hear the song by which he caused the western gales to arise, but I have no doubt that it was of the same character. When these gales came, he was propitiated by presents to send them away.

Source: Howitt (1904: 397–98); adapted by authors.

Box 5.33: Song 14 – Stopping the wind, version 2

... Bunjil Kraura, who is said to have had control over the winds. It was believed that he could call up the great west wind (gwera-ale, kraura) if he was not well supplied with food. He would make it so to rock the trees that the blackfellows could not climb in search of same. When duly propitiated, he would charm the storm to rest by tying a band of twisted stringy bark round his head and chanting this spell— "Kŭtbun-a-wang, kŭtbŭn-a-wang, kraura, &c, &c."

(Kŭtbŭn= carry or wear ; wang=a band or string).

Source: Fison and Howitt (1880: 231); adapted by authors.

Our analysis is presented in (5.22):

(5.22)	*kŭtbŭn-a*	*wang*	*kŭtbŭn-a*	*wang*	*kraura*
	carry, wear	*band, string*	*carry, wear*	*band, string*	*west wind*
	kartpa-n(h)a	**wang**	**kartpa-n(h)a**	**wang**	**krauRa**
	take-?	headband	take-?	headband	west

'Wearing a headband, wearing a headband, the west (wind).'

Notes

The word for 'wear' is regularised as **kurtpa** /guḍba/ in Fesl (1985: U2, no. 18), based on the form *kurtba*, written by R.H. Mathews. However, on the basis of the spelling in Fison and Howitt (1880) and spellings like *kart-bur* in Robinson, we feel the first vowel should be /a/.

5.2.15 Song 15 – Red Moon song

The song presented in this section was sung when a red moon was seen. This presumably refers to what is usually termed a blood moon, which happens during a total eclipse of the moon or lunar eclipse.[34] As the manuscript notes point out, it was believed that such a moon had devoured people. The informant for this information is named as Billy Macleod (Tulaba). The only version we have found is in a State Library of Victoria manuscript, presented in Box 5.34:

34 Some information about blood moons can be found at Daisy Dobrijevic, 'What is a Blood Moon and When Can You See the Next One in 2026?', space.com, accessed 21 January 2026, accessed 1 May 2022, www.space.com/39471-what-is-a-blood-moon.html.

Box 5.34: Song 15 – Red Moon song

When the Kurnai saw the moon red they believed that it had then devoured a number of dead men (turdegŭni kŭrnai) in another country; being supposed to have sneaked upon these while they were busy searching sow thistles upon which they were supposed to feed. When the moon was thus seen, the following song was sung

Yakwa	Yakwa	Yakwa
(nest)		
Tari-gwando	bringwana	
avid	bone excrement	
Bēnbalai		
a place west of Lindenow flat		

This song is said to have been composed by the Ngūl'ŭmbra Kŭrnai (ancient blacks) (old time blacks)

Source: SLV MS Box 1053/3 (b), hw0404.pdf, p. 38; adapted by authors.

The word *Ngūl'ŭmbra* would appear to be a compound word containing the word **pra** meaning 'human, man'. We have not been able to find any word similar to *Ngūl'ŭm*, which we would regularise as **ngulam**, in the various word lists consulted. It appears that the whole compound had second syllable stress, as **ngulámpra**.

Our analysis of this song is presented in (5.23):

(5.23)	*Yakwa*	*Yakwa*	*Yakwa*
	(nest)		
	yakwa	**yakwa**	**yakwa**
	?	?	?

Tari-gwando	*bringwana*	*Bēnbalai*
ovid	*bone excrement*	*A place west of Lindenow flat*
taRi-kwantu	**pring-kwana(ng)**	**penpalai**
void?	bone-faeces	PN

'Void? the faeces of bones, at *Penpalai*.'

Notes

We are unable to offer any analysis for the word *yakwa*, which is glossed as 'nest'. Bulmer (Smyth 1878, 2: 29) gives the sentence *Thununa ngi woorngan togä jacka*, with the meaning 'Going to I seek nest bird', where the phrase *togä jacka* is to be translated as 'nest(ing) bird', a possessive construction in which the second element is the noun **tjak** 'meat'. It is possible that this is an exclamation, similar to that uttered by the women in the initiation ceremony as '(2 women) ya! qua -yeh!' (MV XM 615, p. 100). We regularise this as **ya kwa ye**.

The word *Tari-gwando* is glossed as 'void', which we presume refers to defecation. The word appears to contain the **kwa-** root, but we cannot analyse it further.

The place name *Bēnbalai* is not included in the list of place names provided by Howitt in Smyth (1878, 2: 188).

The word for 'sow thistle' is listed as *thalak* in Fesl (1985: M10, no. 122), the source being Bulmer. This word does not appear to be in the song.

5.2.16 Song 16 – Brataualong song

A short song, for which no contextual information was provided, and no suggested translation, is found on an unnumbered page in the State Library of Victoria manuscript Box 1053/3 (b). When examined by us, it was between pages 9 and 10. The informant is given as J. McAlpine, and the transcription is presented in Box 5.35:

Box 5.35: Song 16 – Brataualong song, version 1

Brataua
song
Per J. McAlpine
    Dinni ma dinni ma
    Gi naul naul worein

Source: SLV MS Box 1053/3 (b), hw0404.pdf, p. 15; adapted by authors.

A second version is found in notes by Howitt on Omeo tribe, presented here in Box 5.36:

Box 5.36: Song 16 – Brataualong song, version 2

Old corroberry song (Gūnyerū)
Dinni ma Dinni ma
Gi baul baul worein (McAlpine)

Source: SLV MS Box 1054/2 (b), hw0436.pdf, p. 11; adapted by authors.

Our suggested analysis is given in (5.24):

(5.24)	*Dinni ma*	*dinni ma*	*Gi naul*	*naul*	*worein*
	-	-	-	-	-
	tini-ma	**tini-ma**	**ki(ka)-nyal**	**nyal**	**waRing**
	old-?	old-?	-1DL.INCL	1DL.INCL?	sea

'We two the old ones, (our) going to the sea.'

This translation is indeed very tentative. It may be that the two instances of the word *ma* are examples of the possessum marker (see Morey 2016). We are tempted to suggest that the form *Gi naul* is a form of the verb 'go', listed by Hercus (1986) as **gigan**.

5.2.17 Song 17 – Lullaby

A short lullaby is recorded in Howitt's article of songs (1887a: 334), the text of which is presented as Box 5.37:

Box 5.37: Song 17 – Lullaby

Finally, I may conclude these notes by staying that there are also "lullabys" and "children's songs", of which the following will serve as samples

Wa!	*Wa!*	*Wa!*	*lelándū*	*mri ngū*
Stop!	Stop!	Stop!	sleep	eye thine

Source: Howitt (1887a: 334); adapted by authors.

Our analysis of this is presented in (5.25):

(5.25)	*Wa!*	*Wa!*	*Wa!*	*lelándū*	*mri ngū*
	Stop!	*Stop!*	*Stop!*	*sleep*	*eye thine*
	Wa	**wa**	**wa**	**lela-ntu**	**mri-ngu**
	EXCL	EXCL	EXCL	sleep?-2SG	eye-?

'Eh, Eh, Eh, you are sleeping, … eye.'

Notes

The first three words of this song, all written as *Wa!*, are glossed by Howitt as 'stop'. Fesl (1985: P4, no. 64) lists two words glossed as 'stop': *wellbunite*, recorded by Dawson and Pettit; and *ngalla lōōrbin*, clearly a negative phrase, recorded by Thomas. We suggest that the three repetitions of *wa* are in fact exclamations such as those found in the initiation ceremony (see section 5.2.21).

The most commonly recorded word for 'sleep' in Gippsland was **pernta-** (Fesl 1985: S4, no. 36). The root word here is presumably **lela**, combined with the suffix -**ntu** that appears to have been a 2nd person singular suffix in the Nunga Nunga song (see section 5.2.11).

The final phrase *mri ngū* is glossed 'eye thine', where *ngū* corresponds to 'thine' (2nd person singular possessive). In Mathews's papers, the form for this is usually -**ngina, as** in *wangin-ngina* 'thy boomerang' (**wangkin** 'boomerang'). Bulmer includes a form **ngingal** translated as 'thy' (in Smyth 1878, 2: 15), and *Koothoula* 'thine' (in Smyth 1878, 2: 25). No form similar to **ngu** has been shown in the other sources with a 2nd person singular possessive meaning.

5.2.18 Laments

Howitt (1904: 459) gives examples of a number of laments, some translated only into English, but with one formulaic lament of the form 'my spouse is dead' or 'my child is dead'. The texts of these and the context are presented in Box 5.38:

Box 5.38: Laments

Among the Kurnai, when a man died, his relatives rolled him up in a 'possum rug and enclosed it in a sheet of bark, cording it tightly. A hut was built over it, and in this the mourning relatives collected. The corpse was placed in the centre, and as many of the relatives as could find room lay with their heads on it. There they lay lamenting their loss, saying, for instance, "Why did you leave us?" Now and then their grief would be intensified by some one, for instance, the wife, uttering an ear-piercing wail "*Penning-i-torn*" (my spouse is dead), or a mother would say "*Lit-i-torn*" (my child is dead). All the others would then join in with the proper term of relationship, and they would cut and gash themselves with sharp stones and tomahawks until their heads and bodies streamed with blood. The bitter wailing and weeping continued all night, only the more distant relations rousing themselves to eat until the following day.

Source: Howitt (1904: 459); adapted by authors.

The text in language is of the form 'kinship term-*i-torn*'. The kinship terms in this example are regularised as **pen(h)ang** 'husband' (see Fesl 1985: B8–9, no. 44 for examples) and **litj** 'child'. The form meaning 'is dead' is unfamiliar from other sources, where the word for 'die' is **tertika**- (Fesl 1985).

Bulmer also talks about the laments in Campbell (1999: 35):

> Mourning by the Gippslanders was touching. The widow cried for her husband, *mian etcha*, my husband, repeated over & over again and each person would show their connection with the dead man, as

> *brammun*, brother too. When it was a child the cry was very plaintive and always reminded one of David's lament, it was *leethi*, *leethi*, my child, my child. The mourning would always be accompanied with head chopping, the women tearing their faces, leaving permanent marks for the rest of their lives. The men's heads were all bald on top, which was caused by this chopping.

The form of 'my husband' here, *mian etcha*, is unfamiliar from other sources.

5.2.19 (Ritual) sayings

This next section contains two short sections of words that are spoken, possibly in a ritual and certainly a formulaic way, in two circumstances, first, when the aurora australis is seen (section 5.2.19.1) and second when a messenger brings news of the death of someone (section 5.2.19.2).

5.2.19.1 Sayings relating to the aurora australis

The story of the origin of the aurora is given by Howitt (1904: 493), and relates to the initiation ceremony discussed in section 5.2.21, some part of which was restricted:

> When some one impiously revealed the secrets of the *Jeraeil* to women, and thereby brought the anger of *Mungan-ngaua* on the Kurnai, he sent his fire, the Aurora Australis, which filled the whole space between the earth and the sky. Men went mad with fear, and speared each other, fathers killing their children, husbands their wives, and brethren each other. Then the sea rushed over the land and nearly all mankind was drowned. Those who survived became the *Muk-kurnai*. Some turned into animals, birds, reptiles, fishes, and *Tundun* and his wife became porpoises. *Mungan* left the earth, and ascended to the sky where he still remains.

When the people saw the aurora (**wiRa**), they would speak a ritual saying. There are two versions of this, the first from Tulaba in Box 5.39 and the second from Billy Macleod in Box 5.40:

Box 5.39: Sayings relating to the aurora australis, version 1

When the Kŭrnai saw the Wíra they were much frightened and held out each *one hi* "Brétakŭrnai and said "send it away or I will "Jíbŭn a móko (threw in the fire)

Source: SLV MS Box 1053/3 (b), hw0404.pdf, p. 37; adapted by authors.

Box 5.40: Sayings relating to the aurora australis, version 2

The aurora was called Wira. When they saw it they were much alarmed and holding out their [dead?] hands would say for instance "Jibbŭn a moka" as is I will burn in fire, if it did not send the aurora away.

Source: SLV MS Box 1053/3 (b), hw0404.pdf, p. 38; adapted by authors.

Our analysis is presented in (5.26):

(5.26) *Jibŭn a móko*
threw in the fire
tjilpa-na muku
throw-? DEM.into
'Throw it in (to the fire).'

The word **muku** is a demonstrative with an allative meaning 'to that, thither'. This word is also discussed by Howitt (SLV MS Box 1053/3 (b), hw0404.pdf, p. 64).

5.2.19.2 Sayings relating to the dead

Howitt also wrote down the words that were spoken when the death of someone was announced by a messenger. These words were termed **lewin** 'message, news' and were carried by the *Daiaur* 'messenger', a word that can perhaps be regularised as **tayau(R)**. The formulaic saying spoken at that time is presented in Box 5.41:

Box 5.41: Sayings relating to the dead

In the olden time Lewin was sent by words only. The Daiaur carried the words but did not carry any thing like a stick. I think the Kurnai learned from the Brajerak to send Bommerangs and spears.
When a Baiaur brought word that someone was dead he would say when coming into the camp "Father (as the case might be) of that one (pointing to someone or other) is
Tŭrdegatū būlū tūndū
Tŭrdegatū-dead, būlūt = above-tūndū-there
or he might ...
[written on the side]
... might sit down near the camp till his friend went to him-took him to his camp and gave him food. Then all being assembled the Baiaur sometimes told his message to all-sometimes to person to whom he was sent who in a loud voice repeated it to all

Source: SLV MS Box 1053/3 (b), hw0404.pdf, p. 39; adapted by authors.

Our analysis of this saying is presented as example (5.27):

(5.27)	*Tŭrdegatū*	*būlū*	*Tūndū*
	dead	*above*	*these or he might be*
	tertika-tu	**pulu**	**Tuntu**
	dead-ERG?	above	DEM
	'He is dead … above.'		

Notes

The root for the word for 'dead' was given as **tertika** in Fesl (1985: S4, no. 42, see also N11–12, no. 113). However, in Song 5 (section 5.2.5) the form is **terti-**, which is presumed to be the root form. The form **tertika** might mean 'dead one' and it is possible that the suffix in this word and in *tūridū* are the ergative **-tu**, examples of which can also be found in the Brewin song documented by Bulmer (see section 5.3.1).

Bulmer shows *booloot* as 'above' (Smyth 1878, 2: 26).

5.2.20 Three short texts in Howitt

This section includes short texts from Howitt's papers; they may relate to marriage customs or be examples of words spoken at the time of men or women moving to be married. Because the texts given in both Box 5.43 and Box 5.44 finish with *yah*, which looks like a song language cry/exclamation, found frequently in the Boys' initiation texts (see section 5.2.21), we think it likely that these are song-like texts, and have therefore included them here.

The first two texts (Boxes 5.42 and 5.43) are similar:

Box 5.42: Short text no. 1

Woornin-gin
Ginan ga gan
workut

Source: SLV MS Box 1053/3-4, hw0404.pdf, p. 124; adapted by authors.

Box 5.43: Short text no. 2

Wū nin-gin
Yangi wūnmatu brawa (she says) mūna mūngie
Kikanat lūlūi yah

Source: SLV MS Box 1053/3-4, hw0404.pdf, p. 124; adapted by authors.

Underneath this second text is written the following:

To Chas Riv Yangi wūnmatū brawa-mūnda [taerta?]

Our analysis of this first text is given in (5.28):

(5.28)	*Woornin-gin*	*Ginan ga gan*	*workut*
	wun-ingin	**kina-kikan**	**wuRgat**
	where-2SG	?-go	woman
	'Where do you go, woman!'		

Linguistic notes

The word **kina** may be some kind of grammatical word. Bulmer showed two short utterances with a form *kinna*, of uncertain meaning:

> *Kinna guani* 'Or' (Smyth 1878, 2: 26)
> *Kinnat gan yarrowa* 'I am fightable (I was angry)' (Smyth 1878, 2: 29).

The analysis of the second text is given in (5.29):

(5.29)	*Wū nin-gin*
	wun-ingin
	where-2SG
	'Where are you?

yangi	*wūnmatu*	*Brawa*	*mūna*	*mūngie*
yangi	**wunmatu**	**pra-wa**	**muna**	**muntji**
I say	where	male/man-OBL	DEM?	DEM?
'I say, where is the man's …				

kikanat	*lūlūi*	*Yah*
kika-n(h)atj	**luluwi**	**ya(h)**
go-1SG	EXCL?	EXCL
'I have gone … ya!'		

Linguistics notes

The form *wūnmatu* may be marked for 2nd person.

Box 5.44: Short text no. 3

[aun?]	[nang?]	mūnda	Beera watūn	(Bruthen)
	Don't know	there at		
Nabbūnda	brebba?	tūntu	yah	
How many	more	that way	[next]	

Source: SLV MS Box 1053/3-4, hw0404.pdf, p. 124; adapted by authors.

The analysis of this text is presented as (5.30):

(5.30.1)	*nang*	*mūnda*	*Beera watūn*
	don't know	*there at*	*(Bruthen)*
	nan(g)	**munta**	**piRawathan**
	who	DEM	PN
	'Who is there at Bruthen?'		

(5.30.2)	*nabbūnda*	*brebba*	*Tūntu*	*yah*
	how many	*more*	*that way*	
	n(g)apunt(h)a	**prepa**	**Tuntu**	**ya(h)**
	how many?	other	DEM	EXCL
	'How many more are there?'			

Notes

This suggests that the name Bruthen derives from a form meaning 'move possum', **piRa-wathan**.

Maybe *nang* is actually related to the form *nan* recorded by Bulmer meaning 'who'.

5.2.21 The Boys' initiation ceremony (TjeRayil)

As mentioned earlier, apart from the **kunyeRu** and **yentjin(y)**, the third main type of song was that sung during the ceremony of the initiation of boys, the term for which we have regularised as **tjeRayil** (spelled variously *jeraeil* and *jerryale*). Descriptions of this ceremony are found in six different sources, laid out in Table 5.3. The songs sung at these ceremonies were cries and exclamations for the most part, as well as calls to the sex totems (see section 5.1.7.1). The song texts as written down by Howitt will be presented and analysed below (section 5.2.21.2).

The word **tjeRayil** is stated by Howitt (1904: 617) to mean 'leafy' or 'having leaves or twigs', being connected with the word *jerung* (**tjeRang**) meaning 'leaf or twig'. The ceremony was 'staged' at Howitt's request in 1884, and he kept detailed notes on that performance. The background to that performance and the identification of its location are discussed in Gibson and Mullett (2020).

Table 5.3: Sources for information about the TjeRayil (Boys' initiation ceremony)

Source	Contents	Reference to section
MV XM 761, pp. 29–30, 32, 97–102, 105–7	Detailed description of a 'staged' ceremony, possibly held in January–February 1884, with consultants/participants named	5.2.21.1.1
Howitt in Smyth (1878, 1: 62–63)	Descriptions of the ceremony written prior to the holding of the staged ceremony	5.2.21.1.2
Fison and Howitt (1880: 194–98)	Descriptions of the ceremony written prior to the holding of the staged ceremony	5.2.21.1.3
Howitt (1904: 617–33)	Description of the ceremony	5.2.21.1.4
Bulmer in Campbell (1999: 6–7)	Brief notes on the ceremony	5.2.21.1.5
Howitt MSS in SLV	Tulaba's recollection and Jimmy Scott's recollections	5.2.21.1.6

Source: Authors.

We will not go into detail about all the aspects of the **tjeRayil** ceremony here as readers who want to learn more can visit the sources cited above, as well as more recent work such as Gibson and Mullett (2020). Nevertheless, some introductory remarks are needed to set the context for the songs presented in section 5.2.21.2.

Origin of the ceremony

Fison and Howitt (1880: 194) stated that when they performed this ceremony, the men were '*Kŭrnai* – the descendants of Yeerŭng – performing a ceremony handed down to them through their ancestors from the mystic pair, Yeerŭng and Djeetgun'. This refers to the two birds that are the sex totems of the Gippsland people, **yiRang** 'southern emu-wren' for males and **tjitkan** 'blue wren' for females.

Restrictions on participation in the ceremony

All the Gippsland people would participate in these ceremonies.

Howitt (1904: 617) makes it clear that the ceremony should be led only by those who are fully initiated, but that in his staged performance, two men, including the then head of the Krauatungalung, would be allowed to participate even though they were not fully initiated (i.e. they had not undergone the full ceremony themselves), because there were otherwise not enough men to perform the ceremony.

On the other hand, those who were termed 'half-castes' were not permitted to attend that staged performance. As will be mentioned below, some parts of the ceremony are restricted to only fully initiated men and those who are undergoing initiation.

Howitt (1904: 322) writes that he was himself 'initiated in the Yuin tribe', and this initiation seems to have been accepted by the Gippsland people, as per this quote in Howitt and Fison (1880: 198):

> It was from Tūlabā that I first obtained particulars of this custom, and who afterwards arranged the rehearsal of the ceremony. I said jokingly to him, 'I am jerra-eil now.' He replied, 'Yes, now you are my brogan.' Being his brogan, it followed, as I have said, that a peculiar relation was established, and in accordance with the custom, his wife often addressed me as 'brā bittel' (my husband), whilst I spoke to her as 'rūkut bittel' (my wife).

Howitt also details how, at the most delicate and restricted stage of the ceremony, he was asked to prove that he had been properly initiated by producing sacred objects that he had been given (1904: 627). While his acceptance as an initiate was apparently based on his possession of a bullroarer that he had collected in Queensland for the Pitt Rivers Museum in Oxford, it has been questioned.[35] As Petch and Gibson (2013)[36] wrote: 'According to Mulvaney (1970: 207–14), it was this object that Howitt produced to prove his "credentials" with the senior men during the Jeraeil ceremony'.

35 The 'bullroarer' from Queensland is 1917.553.461 at the Pitt Rivers Museum, documented as being bequeathed by Tylor after his death in 1917 and described in the PRM accession book as 'bull-roarer, bribbun, swung at initiation ceremonies, Chepara tribe, south Queensland coast (south of Brisbane)' (Petch and Gibson 2013).

36 They go on to point out that Howitt had collected three bullroarers from Gippsland, one catalogued at the Pitt Rivers Museum as 1911.32.10, and described in the PRM accession register as 'Bull-roarer, "large Tundun", Kurnai, Gippsland, Victoria'. There were two additional smaller ones numbered 1911.32.11 and 1911.32.12 described as '2 Bullroarers, rukut tundun' (Petch and Gibson 2013).

Participants in the ceremony

The boys who are to undertake the ceremony experience it in three stages, as Howitt describes it 'the stages of *Tutnurring* and *Brewit* to *Jeraeil*' (1904: 617). The first stage, which we can term 'initiate' or 'novice', is regularised as **tutnaRing** or **tutnaRang** (see discussion in section 5.2.21.1.1). The second stage, **prewit**, refers to when the boys are already initiated and living with other young men. Howitt (1904: 622) indicates that this stage is reached before the boys have the secret knowledge given to them. The final stage, **tjeRayil**, refers both to the ceremony and to those who have fully passed its processes.

Three other groups of people are mentioned in this ceremony. The **krauwan** 'female cross cousins' play an important role of support for the boys in the early parts of the ceremony. The **pulawrang**, usually spelled *Bullawang* in Howitt (1904) is the male guardian of the boys during the ceremony. The **pulawrang** has already been mentioned in connection with the Nunga Nunga song (see section 5.2.11).

The other participant who is named is the *Gweraeil Rukut*, an old woman who summons all of the women to drill the boys (**tutnaRing**) and the **krauwan** in their performances (Howitt 1904: 617), and leads dancing and singing at various stages in the ceremony. The name *Gweraeil Rukut* can be regularised as **kweRayil rukat**, literally 'big woman', where the second word is spelled by Hercus (1986: 241) as ['rukət]. Fesl (1985: B7, no. 18) notes that John Mathew gave the term for 'old woman' as *kwerailmina*, *wurukot*, which confirms the initial **kw-** in this word.

The restricted portions of the ceremony

These are described in Howitt (1904: 625–31) and will not be discussed in detail here. Howitt's letter to Tylor on 2 February 1884 makes it clear what is to be restricted:

> (3) The secret ceremony called by the Kurnai 'shewing the grandfather' is the exhibition of the Tundun to the youths and at this time they are duly instructed in the local knowledge of the tribe.

In the same letter, Howitt makes it clear that 'Death is the penalty in time past for unlawful revelation of these secrets. The old men refused to admit me to them until I fully satisfied them that I had already been initiated elsewhere'.

None of the song texts that we will be presenting here relate to this restricted/secret portion of the ceremony.

In their early 1880 book, Howitt and Fison (1880: 198) also describe the exhibition of the *tundun* and add:

> They stare at the strange sight – a wonderful thing, such as they have never seen before. Each boy is held by an old man by the back of the neck with the left hand, while in the right he points a spear to the boy's eye, and says, 'If you tell this to any woman you will die – you will see the ground broken up and like the sea; if you tell this to any woman, or to any child, you will be killed.'

Ceremonies held in traditional times

Howitt (1904: 617–18) mentions that the ceremonies fell out of use after the first 20 years of white settlement, being revived at his request in 1884:

> After the occupation of Gippsland by the white people in 1842, these ceremonies were held at intervals for some twenty years. They then fell into disuse, and were only now revived in response to the message which I had sent round.[1] The old men said they were glad to receive my message, and to hold the *Jeraeil*, for the reason that the Kurnai youth 'were now growing wild. They had been too much with the whites, so that now they paid no attention [p. 618] either to the words of the old men or to those of the missionaries.'
>
> 1. Those to whom the message goes accompanied by the *Tundun* must obey the call. Two of the Brayaka clan failed to attend after being summoned, having remained at one of the missions for a wedding. The old men were very indignant, and said, 'When that *kalk* (wood) goes to a man he *must* come, he cannot stop away.' In olden times this non-attendance would have had serious results for the two Brayakas.

The revived ceremony of 1884

This ceremony is described in detail in a notebook in Museums Victoria (XM 761). Page 29 lists all of the old men involved in organising the ceremony, headed by Billy McLeod (Tulaba), and page 30 lists which of the wives of the old men were involved (see Box 5.45).

The dating of this re-created ceremony is somewhat uncertain. While we follow Gibson and Mullett (2020) in accepting the date of January–February 1884, two letters of Howitt's dated 13 February and 25 March

1882 (MV XM 89 and XM 90) seem to suggest the ceremony was held in that year; it was certainly held before a letter to Tylor[37] written on 2 February 1884, which also seems to confirm that the re-creation of the ceremony had occurred before that date.

However, this date is later than the publication of both Smyth (1878) and Fison and Howitt (1880). The latter suggests there may have been an earlier re-creation of the ceremony, as in this quote from Howitt (1880: 194):

> In order to ascertain as clearly as possible what the ceremonies were, I prevailed upon some of the Brabrolung and Tatungolung men to give me a representation. I regretted it was not a dress rehearsal; nevertheless, the actors were in their parts con amore. The past seemed to revive in them.

Foods

This ceremony involved restrictions on foods that could be eaten; a detailed list of foods and who could eat what is found in the State Library of Victoria (MS Box 1053/3 (b), hw0404.pdf, pp. 31–34; also Box 1053/4 (a), hw0404.pdf, p. 74).

Messengers

Smyth (1878, 1: 62) makes the point that all of the five tribes of Gippsland would attend these **tjeRayil** ceremonies, and these would be summoned by messengers. Fison and Howitt (1880: 192) describe these messengers:

> Two messengers were sent from the division or the clan taking the initiative to the division or the clan nearest to it. These men were called lewin, or specially lewinda-jeira-alla, that is, the messengers of the jerraeil or initiation.

This term *lewinda-jeira-alla*, which we regularise as **lewin-ta tjeRayil-a**, is another example of a possessive construction; the possessor here marked with the suffix **-ta**, which follows a noun with final **-n** (see Morey 2016). The literal meaning is therefore 'the messenger's ceremony'.

37 Pitt Rivers Museum, 'Transcription of Box 12: Howitt Correspondence Tylor Papers Pitt Rivers Museum Manuscript Collections Part 1', transcribed 2013, accessed 6 May 2016, web.prm.ox.ac.uk/sma/index.php/primary-documents/primary-documents-index/414-howitt-tylor-papers-prm.html.

5.2.21.1 Descriptions of the ceremonies

5.2.21.1.1 Museums Victoria, Howitt papers

Manuscript XM 761, a notebook of over 100 pages, appears to be a detailed description of the re-creation of the **tjeRayil** ceremony apparently performed in early 1882. The location of this re-creation was at McLennan's Strait (see section 5.2.2).

This ceremony ran over five days (from late Thursday through to Monday, and we have divided the notebook text relating to these five days into five separate sections: Box 5.46 (Thursday), Box 5.47 (Friday), Box 5.48 (Saturday), Box 5.49 (Sunday) and Box 5.50 (Monday).

The list of participants and some background to the organisation of the ceremony is given in Box 5.45. Page 29 lists the old men who were the organisers of the event, and page 30 also includes the details of which of their wives were involved. Page 29 also includes, under note 5, a list of the five stages of the ceremony. This is to be compared with the seven stages in Howitt (1904), see section 5.2.21.1.4.

Page 29 commences with a list of participants with the amount of money that they were paid in shillings. The two main participants seem to have been Tulaba (Billy Mcleod) and Lamby, as each was paid 2 shillings a day. Their wives were also involved as W means that the wife of the person named was present.

Box 5.45: Boys' initiation ceremony, list of participants

Billy Mcleod --W ---------------------.	2
Lamby ----W ----------------.	2
Billy Wood ---------------------	
Dick Cooper ---------------------	
Billy Bull ---------------------	1
Joe ---------------------	1
Toby ---------------------	
Larry---------------------;	
Billy Clark ---W ---------------------	1
Johny ---W---------------------	1
Charley Blair --W ---------------------	1
Kangaroo Jack--W ---------------------	1
Bobby Brown --W ---------------------	
King Charley ---------------------	1

Johnny Fidgett--------------------	1
William Barak--------------------	1
Dick Richards--------------------	1
McKay--------------------[serf??]	1
	--
	15
	5
	--
	75 /-
ten fares a 5/-	50 /-
	--
	125 /-

[p. 29 second part]

Contents

(1) organising the meeting [through??] my action

(2) calling of meeting

(3) meeting – delays - difficulties in deciding when to go on

(4) Secret council of old men – the nyak bŭrmaim – the proceedings commence

(5) 1st scene the performers

2nd scene ditto then bough performance – putting boys to sleep

(3) the bundle of rods

(4) waking the boys

(5) showing the Waintwin

(6)

[p. 30]

Billy – wife

Lamby – wife

Billy Wood – wife

[Johny Hoddenot – wife – crossed out]

Kangaroo Jack – wife

Charly Blair –

King Charly – wife

Billy Bull – wife

Larry

Joe –

Toby –

Billy Macdougall – wife

Neddy Rourke – wife

? Jimmy Fidgett –

? McKay

Source: MV XM 761, pp. 29–30; adapted by authors.

As Box 5.45 shows, there was a secret council of the men, presumably held before the event was undertaken in order to arrange the ceremony. The name of this council is given as *nyak bŭrmaim*; the second word is likely to be **burdany** 'old man' (Fesl 1985: B5, no. 13, spelled in R.H. Mathews as *burdain*). This term, which we would regularise as **nyag burdany**, is in the form of a compound noun, rather than a possessive construction.

The 'showing the *waintwin*' referred to is the euphemism for the most sacred and restricted portion of the ceremony, 'Showing the Grandfather' (see below). The word *waintwin* is the word for 'father's father' (Fesl 1985: B14, no. 62). We would regularise this as **waindhwin**. A very similar form was shown by Hercus (1986: 242) as **webwen** ['webwən] 'grandfather (paternal)'.

Later in the notebook, on page 93, there are the words 'Mungan-aur my father'. Bulmer (in Smyth 1878, 2: 34) gives the form for 'our father' as *Mungan oura*. As far as we know, the only occurrences of 1st person plural possessive suffixes reported for the Gippsland languages relate to this word. On page 94 and 94b of the notebook, it is made clear that the most sacred and secret part of the ceremony originates from this figure, the creator. The transcription of the notebook (MV XM 761) is not always clear:

> [p. 94]
>
> If the women were allowed to see the Turndun the Big fellow up above would be so angry that he would send fire. The air & sky and earth would be all fire and the blacks would be so terrified that they would all kill each other out of sheer fright
>
> [p. 94b]
>
> [??] the fire & hence the dread at its appearance. The Big Fellow up above is called by no name except – mūngan nginaur – i.e. 'our father' – and Tulabar spoke of him [??] 'that fellow' pointing up with his fore finger. He said that it was his father who told him all this when he [??] Jerrail. It was M.N. who first made the Jerrail – made the Tundoon, taught the Blacks all [??]to eat [??] Then their personal names eg Tanbullun, Warkukanda, [??] &c. The boys are told about him at the Jerail.

The *tundun* is mentioned by Fesl under the heading 'bullroarer' (1985: C1, no. 43, also listed under 'wooden instrument' at C3, no. 73). There is also a mention of a female version, *rukut-tundun* from a story of Mary Howitt, 'Come Wind Come Weather' (two of these *rukut tundun* are preserved at the Pitt Rivers Museum, accession numbers 1911.32.11 and 1911.32.12, see Petch and Gibson 2013).

The description of the actual ceremony itself commences with Box 5.46:

Box 5.46: Boys' initiation (Thursday evening)

[p. 97]

Thursday evening about sundown the Tūtanaring were placed on the ground the Krauan behind them and Old [Mary??] represented all the mothers. Jonny Fidgett waited with the boys as master of the ceremonies. Old William & Dick [??]about. The men all went away to [??] and after a time – William gave the signal to be ready.

[p. 98]

The boys were then placed in front of their Krauan and the mother behind them. In the distance was heard the reverberatory sound of heavy blows struck answered by shouts of Huh! The men appeared in a long winding row striking the strip of bark which each had held in each hand on the ground. The movement was a sinuous one as [hole??] line of men. Old Lamby running in a winding course towards the boys – at each step he struck a resounding blow on the ground – first on the right side then on the left. The others did the same [shouting huh! – inserted] Then at about the [fifth??] stride all

[p. 98a]

halted & struck the ground several times with a long Huh!

The boys and Krauan at this time were standing wavering from side to side the boys keeping their eyes down and any seeing glimpses of the strange procession as his head being at one side brought him into view. The men were dressed as in the sketch. After passing twice in front of the Tūtanaring the procession halted – the men sank on their knees in a semi-circle in front of the boys and struck the ground by hand shouting Huh! All then returned to the camp.

Source: MV XM 761, pp. 97–98; adapted by authors.

It is clear that this part of the ceremony was open to all, including and especially females, since the female cross-cousins (**krauwan**) play a significant part in this.

The word *Tutanaring*, found in various spellings, is the term for the initiates at this stage of the ceremony. Fesl (1985: B3, no. 8) glossed this as 'novice/ initiate'. We suggest a regularisation of **tutnaRing**, although in Fison and Howitt (1880) the word is spelled *tūtnŭrrŭng*, which would suggest **tutnaRang**.

The second day of the ceremony is described in Box 5.47. This is the day in the ceremony in which the largest number of songs and cries were performed.

Box 5.47: Boys' initiation (Friday)

[p. 99]

Friday morning. While I was sitting with Lamby & Jonny Fidget talking about the arrangement of 1st scene we heard a distant hail from across the river and then a gunshot. The expected contingent had arrived and we all heard their shouts. Four men soon stood [??] King Charley, Big Joe, McKay & _______ But the sundown was very bright & the [shores??] too rough – our canoe both small and [useless??]. After mending it, it was decided not practicable [to cross the river – inserted] and the men started out to send for another - one which Old Lamby an expert canoeist [arrived??] with some tea & sugar and part of a damper. As the black with the usual improvidence had no more

[p. 99b]

[cooked??] them & had eaten at breakfast I gave the arrivals most of the damper which I had baked for myself. Charley Blair and I went out but only found a possum & no canoe. The other men came back and at 2 o'clock nothing had been done but cross one of the boys they brought and two swags. The men over the straits had by this time procured a small canoe and proceeded to render it as serviceable as possible. By __ o'clock all were over, i.e. King Charley, Joe and two boys - the others having remained [??]at Bairnsdale.

[p. 100]

They got over by coming in the big canoe attended by a boy in a small one who towed back the other and so da capo

Jirŭng = bough – Huh!

[This page also includes a rough chart of the location of the ceremony]

(1) scene – Tedeling

(1 men) yehi wah-yeh

[sleek?? offering – crossed out]

(2 women) ya! qua -yeh!

(3) bulling chong

(4) yūī yui-nga!

Raising up boys ...

By [Bullawrang??] long drum

Leave them over there.

The men hold up sticks with bough at end.

(5) then the same done [will be Bullawrang??] on each

Each bulling faces his own country.

(6) laying down boys

He! (guttural) – Nye!

Leaves sprinkled over them.

Lie on back side by side

arm crossed on breast.

Covered all over with rags

(7) Tedeleng all beaten round-wati yah yeh!
Boys told not to speak any more women & men paramount.
Round women's fire by about 20 minutes The [tundon??] sticks [??] by & bye boys told to be silent & go to sleep.
A large fire lit in front home camp just behind [??] this time [carried?? out??] this is [family??] around [??] female [??]
Cannot eat porcupine or wild dog.
Old men stood round & and tell them this-
[p. 101b]
[??] Arrange then comfortable.
When T. [??] any thing [??]
yeering, note, Bul[lawrang?] says [??] you want
Songs are:
Yahi wahi-yeh
Kaiŭng-yah!
Yeerŭng yah!
When boys want anything [??]-yer = several

Source: MV XM 761, pp. 99–101b; adapted by authors.

Notes

On page 99, the dashes have been put in by Howitt. It seems that he has forgotten the name of the fourth man who stood up.

On page 100, in the first section, the words 'Jirŭng = bough – Huh!' are written. It is unclear whether the word *Jirŭng* (regularised as **tyeRang**), 'bough', already mentioned as being the source of the word **tjeRayil**, was part of the song/cry or not. The *huh* is certainly one of the cries uttered in the ceremony.

This section of the manuscript also has a small chart of the locations of the participants during the ceremony, including boys' camp, men's camp. Howitt uses the Wiradjuri word *burbung* to describe this.

Box 5.48 presents the events of the ceremony on the third day (Saturday):

Box 5.48: Boys' initiation (Saturday)

[p. 101b continued]

Saturday

Yearing - yeh! Commenced by women, old men & doctors - mulla mulla -

Feeling stomach by Dr so they should not in future be too greedy or hungry.

This was done.

NB because boys had been with the Loan.

[p. 102]

Then gradually brought round - each covered by his blanket and instructed to look towards fire and [??] down.

They then had a little [??] fire then and were allowed to sleep and if the old men went to shoot a kangaroo.

Saturday

Up at [??] head station

Big Joe, Larry, [??] remained to watch the boys.

About 10am [Billy??], Toby, Billy Bull, Billy Wood came.

At 11am the men returned unsuccessful.

Council in scrub.

At 1pm started out to hunt - [??] men preparing the place for the next scene [mixed??]

the boys into a camp - see sketch.

When they sit up must do so covered up by blanket and not stare about. Jemmy & Larry watching them.

As Old [Billy??] says, "it is like it Sundays".

At about 3pm Jimmy came back from a visit to the men who were arranging the next scene and said [sit??] here to [the??] boys up there.

[Note: very faint till end of page - and virtually unreadable and not transcribed]

Source: MV XM 761, pp. 101b–2; adapted by authors.

Notes

This section mentions *loan* (regularised as **lu(wu)n**) which means 'white man', but also refers to a spirit whose existence pre-dated the arrival of whites (see section 5.2.3.1). It seems likely that this refers to the fact that the young men being initiated had been in contact with white people, and hence the doctor (**malamalang**) examined them.

The manuscript is unclear at this point as the next section commences from 'Saturday morning'. We presume that this is actually the fourth day, Sunday, or perhaps there were two sets of events on the same day. Perhaps no part of the ceremony was performed on the Sunday out of respect for the Christians. This second set of Saturday events, which restarts in the morning and might have actually been on Sunday, is given in Box 5.49:

Box 5.49: Boys' initiation (Sunday??)

[p. 105]

Saturday morning.

The men rather late after yesterday. About 8am went up to young men camp, found all Kurnai there. Tatanaring camped further away to be out of sight of women. Joe then complained that boys were out hunting and with no one to mind them–great argument [??]eloquent & Billy waited indignant [??] Boys sought out. General council-I speak - boys return [??]I address them. Men go out [??]& game and I went King Charley, Dick Cooper, [??]mind the boys. Boys are spoken to impressively as to their duties. M[en] change to be out of sight of women. Jimmy tells [??] and says [??] when he had I had ordered Jerail be begun he thought about what the old men had told him when he was made young man and said to himself "that was just like what the Minister says".

[p. 106]

Saturday afternoon

The camp where the tootanaring are is 2000 paces from the women's camp on the border of the teatree and effectively hidden from view as well as affording no view itself.

The object of giving the boys the Kangaroo meat and the conger eel is to make "them free of it" for unless this is done these also are prohibited.

Source: MV XM 761, pp. 105–6 of the PDF; adapted by authors.

Notes

Page 105: Jimmy is telling what he was told by the elders.

Page 105b, which has not yet been transcribed, contains information about food restrictions and other rules.

On page 106b, the transcription of which is omitted here, the following words are found underneath a drawing of a man dressed in colonial clothes and top hat lying on his side: 'A good road [??]= Laen wauŭng-būllokji'. This is certainly in the Gippsland language. It appears likely that this piece of language is not connected with the initiation ceremony.

Page 107a includes the text: 'Visitor was also obliged to learn to speak the dialect before he could go further into the country'. We do not know if this was a general comment on the situation, or whether it applied only to the time of the **TjeRayil** ceremony.

Page 107 contains the song discussed in section 5.2.13. As mentioned earlier, it was probably sung because Billy Tulaba's wife was unwell. We suggest that it was probably not part of the ceremony.

The events of the fifth and final day, Monday, are given in Box 5.50:

Box 5.50: Boys' initiation (Monday)

[p. 107 continued]
Monday
Last night men returned late with wallaby - knocked up - Billy's song at day break got ready the Dūra scene - then more painting - the mrarts - the boys stand - Old Di[nni] [Birr]ark addresses them.
Waiting for the steamer - card playing - the song of Mumbulla - the Tangbulla jerail. The steamer full of people.
Water ceremony -
The vessel is a gillūng made of wattlebark.

Source: MV XM 761, p. 107f; adapted by authors.

Notes

Some of the things listed on page 107 seem to relate to the previous day. This includes what is likely to have been the painting of pictures of the **mratj** 'ghosts' onto bark.

The '*Dūra* scene' relates to the part of the ceremony after the secret portion described by Howitt (1904: 632, 634) as 'Giving the boys some frogs'. (See also section 5.2.21.1.4.)

One feature mentioned in this document that was clearly not traditional is the card playing. Perhaps this is a reminder that at times in the ceremony there would have been moments for relaxation and recreation.

The 'water ceremony' was also one in which the whole community took part, discussed in more detail in Howitt (1904: 636). The *gillūng* is not referred to in the published description, but the word was recorded by Hercus (1986: 241), spelled as **kilang** ['gɪlaŋ] with the meaning 'billy can'.

In the Howitt papers in Museums Victoria, there are also plans of the **TjeRayil** ground.

The reference to Mumbulla on page 107 relates to Mumbulla Mountain on the South Coast of New South Wales in Yuin territory.

5.2.21.1.2 Howitt's description in Smyth

A detailed description of the ceremony is included in Smyth (1878, 1: 62–64), where the information is shown as having come from Howitt.

This account explains the purpose of the initiation as 'the severance of the boy from his mother's influence and control, and also possibly of his future married state', and that this ceremony was attended by all the Ganai groups ('from Lake Tyers to the Tarra in South Gippsland'). Howitt's description explained that the young men to be initiated were sitting down around 30–40 yards from the camp, and married women were sitting at the camp beating 'rugs folded up' (1878, 1: 63).

Box 5.51 gives the section of text commencing with the point where the boys are sitting with their **krauwan** (female cross cousins) sitting behind, the first point in the ceremony that included cries and songs:

Box 5.51: Boys' initiation ceremony

... the *Jerryale* sits cross-legged with his arms folded on his breast, and the *Growun* sits behind him, close to him, in a like attitude. When there are more *Jerryale* than *Growun*, one of the latter sits half-way between two of the former. Thus – J for *Jerryale*, G for *Growun*:–

(G) (G) (G) (G)

(J) (J) (J) (J) (J)

At this time the men are arranged at a little distance in a row fronting the *Jerryale*. At a signal, they run forward and halt just in front of them. They beat up the soil or sand in front of the *Jerryale* with sticks, shouting '*Ai-eeee- ee-ei*;' at each cry they strike the ground so as to make soil fly up towards the *Jerryale*. These say nothing, but slowly incline the head – the arms being folded first on the left breast, then on the right. The *Growun* exactly imitate the gestures of the *Jerryale*. The men have a stalk of grass thrust through the perforation in the cartilage of the nose instead of the bone *goombert*. They are also rubbed round the eyes with charcoal-dust. This ceremony is performed every evening, from about four o'clock to ten o'clock, for two weeks; and it is moreover done at different places, thus progressing through the tribes from one limit of the district to the other. In addition to the cry of '*Ai- ee-ee*,' the words '*Bu-ee-bu-ee-bu-ee*' are also used, but no explanation can be given of these terms. During the fortnight that this ceremony continues, the mothers of the youths go down to the young men's camps (called *Brew-it*), which are apart from the main camp, and beat upon folded 'possum rugs there – their sons the meanwhile sitting silent in front of them in the manner above described. The mothers go from camp to camp in this way. The ceremonies now change; the *Jerryale* stand in a row at the camp, naked; behind them all the gins stand naked, except an apron of emu feathers round their waists, and cords made of stringybark round their heads; they hold upright in front of them their yam-sticks with boughs tied on the end. The men come up with bundles of wood-splinters a foot long in each hand, singing '*oo-oo-oo-oo-yay-yay-yay-yay*,' &c., &c. When they come near, they, while chanting '*oo-yay*,' throw the splinters one by one to the gins, who gather them up, and beat the bundles on

[p. 64]

"each other in time, singing also *'oo-oo-oo-yay-yay yay.'* Then the men come forward. Each *Jerryale* has a blackfellow to take charge of him, a kind of sponsor, called *Bullera-wreng*. Two of the *Bullera-wreng* take hold of the *Jerryale*, one by one, by the ankles, and launch him up in the air as high as they can, calling out at the same time "*nurt*."* The *Jerryale* holds his arms, palms forward, straight up above his head. They then lie down upon a couch of green boughs, side by side, each one attended by his sponsor. These *Bullera-wreng* watch them, and if they are compelled from any cause to leave the place, attend them, covering the heads of the *Jerryale* with a rug, and surrounding him so that his mother may not catch a glimpse of him. The *Bullera-wreng* watch all night by the *Jerryale*, who has to lie extended on these boughs for two, three, or four days. All this time the *Bullera-wreng* and the mothers are chanting *yay-yay yay-oo-oo-oo*, &c., &c.† On concluding this, the old gins sing *djeetgun-djeetgun-djeetgun-eering-eering-eering*, beating the ground with bundles of small saplings. *Djeet-gun* is the superb warbler; the *eering* the emu wren; the former is called the 'gins' sister,' the latter the 'blackfellows' brother.' The *Bullera-wreng* paint the faces of the *Jerryale* with pipeclay or *murloo*, so as to resemble the duck *nurt*, i.e., with a white circle round each eye, and a white band across the cheek-bones or eyebrows. The *Jerryale* stand together; the *Bullera-wreng* a little way in front of them. Then the latter cry out *nurra*, or ready, shaking boughs and vibrating their legs. The *Jerryale* run off to them, who catch them by the arms, then let them pass, and they run off into the bush; as my informant said, 'my mother see me no more.' After a month spent in the forest, the *Jerryale* one day kill two kangaroos and leave some of the meat on the top of a log. They then go down to the camp of the tribe a little before noon. The *Growun* is on the look-out for her *Jerryale*, and holds out to him a fish, *too-rook*, which he takes in his hand, throws down, and runs off about a hundred yards. His mother is standing near. The *Bullera-wreng* picks up the fish and follows the *Jerryale*, who eats it. In the afternoon, all the *Jerryale* go to where the kangaroo meat was left, the men of the tribe forming a circle round. These, when they see the kangaroo meat on the log, cry out *Wa-a-a-on*, this being the cry with which they drive that game in hunting. The *Jerryale* go up with their 'possum cloaks over their heads, and eat the kangaroo flesh; all the men look on, and, after a little, join in the feast. This is about two or three o'clock in the afternoon, and ends the ceremony of *Jerryale*."

Source: Howitt in Smyth (1878, 1: 62–64); adapted by authors.

5.2.21.1.3 Fison and Howitt's description

Fison and Howitt (1880: 194–98) also contains a substantial description of the whole ceremony, which is not presented in full here. The portion containing cries and songs commences, as in the Howitt notes in Smyth (1878, 1: 62) (see section 5.2.21.1.2), when the boys are seated with the **krauwan** (female cross-cousins) sitting behind them. The section that includes the cries and songs is presented in Box 5.52:

Box 5.52: Boys' initiation ceremony

[p. 195]

At a signal, given by the remainder of the women beating their rugs in slow time, the mothers stamp their yamsticks, and each youth and girl reclines the head sharply towards one shoulder; at the next beat of the rugs and stamp of the yamsticks the heads sharply recline over the other shoulder. But the body remains unmoved, the arms are still crossed, and the boys still keep their eyes to the front, while the girls keep theirs cast down. Then is heard the sound of slow chaunting in the forest. The sounds come nearer, and all the men appear in line. They keep step and time with their

[p. 196]

chaunt. They are thickly smeared with charcoal. Their heads are ornamented with feathers, and painted with naial. Down to the waist they are all wound round with frayed stringybark in thick folds. From the waist downwards they are naked. Each man has a thick bushy tuft of grass passed through the perforated septum of his nose. In one hand each bears a long flat strip of thick bark. As they wind rapidly forward, each one beats his strip of bark on the ground with a hollow sound. They chaunt – "Yeh! yeh!* Wah! wah! wah! Yeh! yeh! Yeerŭng! yeerŭng!" When they reach the space in front of the seated line of youths and girls, the men run round in a ring, beating their strips of bark on the ground and chaunting as before. Then they form before the line, a man before each pair, and again the chaunt commences. The ground is beaten, the boys and girls move their head from side to side, the mothers stamp the ground with their sticks. It is faster, but the time is perfectly kept.

The man facing the boy is his "bŭllerwang," who has to look after him during the ceremony, and he is painted about the eyes to resemble the "black duck," after which he is named. The next part of the ceremonies is that the boy rises to his feet, and, at a given signal, each bŭllerwang raises his boy up into the air, the boy aiding by giving a spring. He is now no longer a wot-wotti, but a tŭtnŭrrŭng.

Boughs are now spread on the ground, and on them the boys are laid side by side on their backs. They neither move nor speak, but when they are in want of anything, they call the bŭllerwang by imitating the chirping note of the yeerŭng. The boys lie there all night, there is no sleep in the camp, the chaunting continues, the women beating

* This is sounded like the termination of our Hurray! and is said by the Kŭrnai to be an exclamation of triumph.

[p. 197]

time on their rugs. Next morning, about ten o'clock, there is a respite, and they get breakfast. About noon the ceremonies recommence. So it continues for two or three days. At length, early in the morning, about daybreak, the old women are heard chaunting "Yeh! yeh! Wah! wah! wah! Yeh! yeh! Djeetgŭn! djeetgŭn!"

Source: Fison and Howitt (1880:195–97); adapted by authors.

5.2.21.1.4 Howitt's published description

The description of the ceremony in Howitt (1904: 617–36) is the most substantial surviving description; it also includes a good deal of background, some of which has already been mentioned.

Howitt divides the description of the **TjeRayil** ceremony into stages, of which there seem to have been eight, which are summarised below:

1. First day: **telping** 'Preliminary ceremony', pp. 618–20. This, 'the first ceremony of the *Jeraeil*, called *Telbing*, or "wattle-bark"' (Howitt 1904: 618).
2. 'Laying the Boys down to sleep' (Howitt 1904: 620); This second part of the ceremony commences a little before sundown on the next day. A couch of boughs is prepared and the same ceremonies as the previous day are repeated. This ceremony marks 'the separation of the boys from the women', at which point the boys become *brewit*. The boys are then laid down in the couch of boughs. They may not move or sleep but: 'If one of them wanted anything, he was to signify this to his *Bullawang* by chirping like an Emu-wren (*Yiirung*)' Howitt (1904: 623). Howitt (1904: 624) goes on to say:

> The *Bullawang* had first to stoop down and ask the boys in the neighbourhood whence the chirp came, 'Is it you? Is it you?' until he questioned the right one, when an affirmative chirp replied. Then he had to find out what the boy wanted, which he could only do by a series of questions, the boys not being allowed to speak. Several times he was completely posed; and, after a number of ineffectual queries, such as 'Are you too hot?' 'Is there a stick sticking into you?' 'Do you want to be moved?' 'Do you want to drink?' he had to wait, and scratch his head, in the hope of thinking of the right question.

Following this was a ceremony performed by the women, led by the *Gweraeil-Rukut*. This ceremony involves chanting that leads the boys to being put into a magic sleep, from which they will wake as men. Finally, the following morning, the women, led by the *Gweraeil-Rukut*, leave, again to singing (it is not clear by whom).

3. The restricted sections of the ceremony (Howitt 1904: 625–31). This includes the fact that Howitt himself was asked to prove that he had been fully initiated before the ceremony that was performed for him could be taken further. He showed them objects he had received in ceremonies performed in other tribes and this satisfied the men. This description of the restricted section of the ceremony includes details of investing the boys with decorations and other ritual objects, a section called 'Showing the Grandfather', including the mysteries of the *tundun* 'bull-roarer' (listed in Fesl 1985: C1, no. 43) and the revelation of ancestral beliefs. There are no song texts in this section of the description.

4. Playing of the 'opossum game' (Howitt 1904: 631), which represents a possum hunt. Howitt said that he regarded 'this "opossum game" as most probably a survival from a time when the Kurnai had a class-system with numerous totems'.
5. 'Frightening the Women'. This stage is described by Howitt (1904: 631–32):

> At about eight o'clock in the evening the *Bullawangs* took their charges, each carrying a *Tundun*, for the purpose, as they put it, of 'frightening the women.' The women and children are always told that at the secret parts of the *Jeraeil*, *Tundun* himself comes down to 'make the boys into men.' The hideous sounds which the uninitiated may chance to hear from a distance they are told is *Tundun's* voice, and they are warned not to leave their camp while he is about, lest he should kill them with his spears.

6. 'Giving the Boys some Frogs' (Howitt 1904: 632, 634). This part of the ceremony is less strict and apparently open to all. It relates to the eating of *Dura* (*Typha angustifolia*), a rush also known as 'Narrow-Leaved Cattail'.
7. 'Seeing the Ghosts' (Howitt 1904: 635). The boys are told to come and see the **mratj** 'ghosts'. A large kangaroo is hunted, and the boys are told to go and look at 'where "the ghosts had caught a kangaroo"' Howitt (1904: 635). After this the boys are dressed as men with the red ochre (*naial*).
8. 'The Water Ceremony' (Howitt 1904: 636). Involving the whole community, the boys are led by their *Bullawang* to a creek, where:

> As they came up, each woman stooped to drink, and her son splashed the water over her with a stick which he held in his hand. She, appearing enraged, filled her mouth with water several times, and squirted it over his face and head. The novices then walked off to the young men's camp, and the women went to their own. One of them was crying at the loss of her son.

This completed the ceremony. Howitt (1904: 632–33) also gives a list of rules that the boys are expected to follow.

Songs are only found in the first two sections, the **telping** and the 'Laying the Boys down to sleep'. The songs found are detailed below.

During the **telping** preliminary ceremony the boys are seated with the *Krauun* behind, and a procession of men comes into sight from afar. Their dress and decorations are described in detail. The cries uttered in this part of the ceremony, and their context, is presented as Box 5.53:

Box 5.53: Boys' initiation ceremony – Preliminary

The line of men came rapidly forward from the bush in a series of short runs, following and imitating the actions of their leader, who came on in a serpentine course, shouting "*Huh! Huh!*" beating the ground in time with his strips of bark, first on the one side and then on the other. After every fifteen or twenty paces the men stopped, and raising their strips of bark, set up a loud shout of "*Yeh!*" (Hurrah!).

As soon as the men appeared, the women began to beat their rugs, the mothers kept time by stamping their yamsticks on the ground, and the seated rows of *Tutnurring* and *Krauun* swayed in perfect unison alternately to right and left. The men, having run in a winding course once or twice past the boys, formed a semicircle in front and near them; and, kneeling down, struck the ground violently with their bark strips, shouting "*Huh! Huh! Yeh!*" This continued some little time, and then the men walked off to the camp, after having stripped off their disguising costumes.

Source: Howitt (1904: 620); adapted by authors.

The second section of the ceremony, termed 'Laying the Boys down to sleep' by Howitt (1904), included a number of songs. The first section involving songs comes at the point in the ceremony where the boys are 'placed standing in a row with their faces toward the camp, the *Krauun* being in another row behind them, and behind them again were the mothers' Howitt (1904: 621). This is presented in Box 5.54:

Box 5.54: Boys' initiation ceremony – 'Laying the Boys down to sleep' (1)

After a short time of waiting, we heard in the distance a curious rattling sound accompanying the words "Ya! Wa! Ya! Wa!"[1] At intervals there was a pause, followed by shouts of "Yeh!" The men came in view, led by the old Headman, slowly marching in line. Each man held a bundle of thin rods, called Teddeleng, in each hand, which he struck together to the words "Ya! Wa!"

[Footnote]1. No meaning can be given for these words. I was told in reference to them, "Our fathers always said and did thus to make the boys into men."

Source: Howitt (1904: 621); adapted by authors.

Later in this section of the ceremony, the boys, now in the care of the *Bullawang*, are raised up (Howitt 1904: 622). The songs and cries performed at this time appear in Box 5.55:

Box 5.55: Boys' initiation ceremony – 'Laying the Boys down to sleep' (2)

With loud shouts of "*Huh!*" and the rustling of bunches of leaves, each group of three Bullawangs raised their boy several times high in the air, he extending his arms towards the sky as far as possible.

Source: Howitt (1904: 622); adapted by authors.

Howitt speculates that this could be a reference to *Mungan-ngaua*, 'the equivalent of the Murring *Daramulan*'. Note that Murring is a term that Howitt uses to describe one of the Yuin tribes. For further discussion of Daramulan, see below in the songs from the Yorta Yorta (section 9.6) and Dhudhuroa (Chapter 10).

The boys are then laid down, with some cries, presented in Box 5.56:

Box 5.56: Boys' initiation ceremony – 'Laying the Boys down to sleep' (3)

Each one was led by three old men to the enclosure wherein the couch of leaves had been prepared, and was there carefully laid down with exclamations of "*He! Nga!*"[1]

[Footnote]1. "*He!*" may be translated here "Well," or "Good." The aspirate has a nasal sound which cannot be represented in writing. "*He!*" is also used affirmatively as we use the sound "*Hm!*" *Nga* = yes.

Source: Howitt (1904: 623); adapted by authors.

A further ceremony is performed by the old lady *Gweraeil-Rukut*. The songs and cries led by her are presented in Box 5.57:

Box 5.57: Boys' initiation ceremony – 'Laying the Boys down to sleep' (4)

The ceremony commenced by the *Gweraeil-Rukut* standing up at her fire with a bundle of rods in each hand, and slowly beating them together to the words "*Ya! Wa!*" and "*Yeh!*" at intervals. All the women joined in, and the Headman, with all the men, followed suit at their fire. After this had gone on for perhaps a quarter of an hour, the old woman moved off, and marched round the enclosure to the tune of "*Ya! Wa!*" followed by the women, and these were followed by the men. This went on for hours, the only sounds being the soft tramp of the people walking round the enclosure, the regular rattling of the rods, and the monotonous utterance—I cannot call it chant—of the words "*Ya! Wa! Yeh!*" This was sometimes varied by the words "*Yiirung!*" and "*Kaiung!*" instead of "*Ya!*"

[p. 625]

and "*Wa!*" but the expression of exultation "*Yeh!*" was in all cases used at intervals.

Source: Howitt (1904: 624–25); adapted by authors.

Howitt (1904: 625) went on to add:

> Anything more monotonous than this part of the ceremony I cannot conceive; but the Kurnai seemed to derive great satisfaction from it. … It is supposed to have the effect of putting them to some kind of magic sleep, not like the ordinary sleep of mankind, from which they may waken into manhood.

The women now depart, and the songs sung as they leave, taken over by the men, are presented as Box 5.58:

Box 5.58: Boys' initiation ceremony – 'Laying the Boys down to sleep' (5)

> Just before dawn the old Headman woke, and called out to the *Gweraeil-Rukut* to rouse the women. Very soon the proceedings recommenced just where they left off the night before. The slow marching round to the monotonous beating of the rods, and the cries of "*Yiirung! Yiirung! Yeh!*" went on for about half-an-hour, when the women ceased, leaving the men standing in a crowd at the feet of the prostrate, motionless *Tutnurring*, still beating their rods to the same old song, and invoking *Yiirung*, the "men's brother," for the last time.

Source: Howitt (1904: 625); adapted by authors.

5.2.21.1.5 Bulmer's description in Campbell

Bulmer's brief notes on the boys' initiation ceremony, presented below, do not include any songs (Campbell 1999: 6–7):

> Among the Gunai/Kurnai the young men were made as follows: They were in a circle surrounded by the women. When the old men approached and took them, a bed of leaves was prepared for them on which they were put by their attendants – *boolerwrang*, this name was given from the peculiar way they were painted white around their eyes by making their eyes look like those of a black duck, hence the name for eyes like a duck. While the young men were on the bed covered up with their rugs, they were not allowed to move, or get up on any pretext and without permission. Should they require to get up they had to signal their attendants, they were then lifted out of bed and afterwards carried back again. They would sometimes lie for two or three days, at all events they were under the control of the initiators. After they had lain on the beds, some of the old men approached with *turndun* [bull-roarers], a piece of oval shaped wood with a string attached to one end. This was swung around when a boomerang noise was made. As the old men were approaching uttering words, which I cannot write even in their language, sufficient to say it was all in keeping with the blackfellows' character, and was calculated to make the young men true blackfellows in every respect.

5.2.21.1.6 Howitt papers, State Library of Victoria

The papers in the State Library of Victoria include a significant amount of information about the initiation ceremony. For example, information is provided by Jimmy Scott, described as 'a Būnjil Nellŭn Braiaka', who told Howitt about a Jeraeil 'at which I was made a young man' (SLV Box 1053/3 (b), hw0404.pdf, pp. 41–43). This includes the following description of the announcement:

> it was ordered to be held by Bruthen Mŭnji and Keŭng and it was they and their Kŭrnai who got the ground ready. Bruthen Mŭnji had sent Lewin (news) by a Bai-aurn (messenger)
>
> [Note on the side] The Bai-aurn carried a jagged spear (Boron) having suspended to the point a Kaiŭng (man's belt) and a Budda Brulda of Kangaroo rat skin (ngallŭn)

This description also includes a plan showing the boys being laid down to sleep.

Tulaba's recollections of a **tjeRayil** are given in the same section of the manuscript (SLV MS Box 1053/3 (b), hw0404.pdf, p. 26):

> Toolaba's first recollection of a Jeraeil was one held at where Mr Bell lives on Reeves River beyond Shaving Point. He was then about ten years old and his elder brother Harry was made Turtnuning. *There were so many boys. At the sun as they were laid on the ground extended* for about twenty paces long. Lamby was made a young man then. The next was at *Brinyerra* and at that a great number of people attended. The whitemen had first settled in Gippsland at that time. Toolaba was then about fifteen or sixteen. At the Jeraeil a white lot of girls eloped – among others Tommy Hoddinot's *Mary & her two* sisters *according to* Toolaba then. Must have been a dozen of elopements of young people. He says *this was* because the old people would not give their consent to any of the girls being married.
>
> The next jeraeil was at Bairnsdale about the time that '*the girl came about dinner time*'.
>
> After that there was another at B'dale where the township now is – *Mr* Macleod & Jones lived at the Mitchell then
>
> After that there was a large jeraeil at Bushy Park, and then no more until ones at *Weniál*

5.2.21.2 Songs in the initiation ceremony

In this section, we will present the original texts of the songs and cries that are found in the sources, together with information about who performed the songs and cries, and the context of their performance.

Songs and cries are found in four of the descriptive texts: Museums Victoria (XM 761), presented in Table 5.4; Howitt in Smyth (1878, 1: 62–64), in Table 5.5; Fison and Howitt (1880: 194–98), in Table 5.6; and Howitt (1904: 621–23), in Table 5.7.

In all of these texts, the only cries/songs that have been written down are those that are uttered and performed in the public sections of the ceremony, before the secret ceremony known as 'Showing the Grandfather'. Some of these cries and songs are specifically noted as having been sung by women, and many of them were sung at the point in the initiation ceremony in which the boys are seated, or standing, in front of their **krauwan** 'female cross-cousins' and often with their mothers present also. We thus conclude that these songs and cries were intended to be heard by the whole community.

Some of these cries have an initial **h** sound, which is generally not a phoneme in Victorian languages. Luise Hercus pointed out that words with initial **h** are found in the Eagle and Crow myths in Maraura (Tindale 1939: 252). The initial **h** might represent an /h/ sound, which is otherwise not a phoneme, or it may be a reflection of the fact that these exclamations have initial /h/ in English and do not actually reflect a [h] sound.

Table 5.4: TjeRayil song, text 1

Who performs the cries/chants	Form of chant	Context and notes
Men moving from afar in a long winding line, striking the ground with a strip of bark	*Huh!*	First day of the ceremony, boys are sitting with the **krauwan** behind
Men coming across by a big canoe	*Huh!*	Second day of the ceremony (Note: The words *Jirŭng* = *bough* are written here. It is not clear if this is a part of the song)
Various participants	(1 men) *yehi wah-yeh* (2 women) *ya! qua -yeh!* (3) *bulling chong* (4) *yūī yui-nga!*	Second day of the ceremony. Section involving *Tedeling* ('bundle of thin rods')
Unstated	unclear, possibly the same as the previous	Second day of the ceremony; repetition of the same with the bullroarer

Who performs the cries/chants	Form of chant	Context and notes
Unstated	*He!* (guttural) – *Nye!*	Second day of the ceremony, laying down of the boys
Men?	*Wati yah yeh!*	Second day of the ceremony, when the *Tedeleng* is beaten all around
Unstated	*Yahi wahi –yeh* *Kaiŭng –yah!* *Yeerŭng yah!*	Second day of the ceremony; uncertain at which point
Commenced by the women, with the old men and 'doctors' (**malamalang**) joining	*Yearing –yeh!*	Third day of the ceremony

Source: Howitt notebook, MV XM 761; adapted by authors.

Table 5.5: TjeRayil song, text 2

Who performs the cries/chants	Form of chant	Context and notes
Men fronting the seated boys who run forward crying	*Ai-eeee-ee-ei bu-ee-bu-ee*	Performed when the boys are sitting with the **krauwan** behind; 'no explanation can be given of these terms'
Men with bundles of wood-splinters a foot long in each hand;	*oo -oo-oo-oo-yay -yay-yay-yay*	When the boys are standing in a row at the camp
While chanting they throw the splinters one by one, the women gather them and beat them. The women also sing	oo-oo-oo-yay-yay yay	–
The *bullera-wreng* and the mothers are chanting	*yay-yay yay-oo-oo-oo &c &c* Footnote: 'This resembles the chant for the dead'	While the boys are lying on a couch of green boughs, surrounded by the *bullera-wreng* 'sponsor' so that their mothers cannot see the boys
After this, the old women sing, while beating the ground with bundles of small saplings	*djeetgun-djeetgun-djeetgun-eering-eering-eering*	–
The men cry out	*Wa-a-a-on*	After a month in the forest, the boys kill kangaroos and leave their flesh on a log. The boys go to see it and are surrounded by the men. This is the conclusion of the ceremony

Source: Howitt in Smyth (1878, 1: 62–64); adapted by authors.

Table 5.6: TjeRayil song, text 3

Who performs the cries/chants	Form of chant	Context and notes
All the men in a line, coming from afar, slow chanting, winding rapidly forward, beating a strip of bark on the ground with a hollow sound	*Yeh! Yeh! Wah! Wah! Wah! Yeh! Yeh! Yeerŭng! Yeerŭng!*	Performed when the boys are sitting with the **krauwan** behind. Noted that *yeh* rhymes with the last syllable of 'hurray'; said by the Kūrnai to be an exclamation of triumph
The old women	*Yeh! Yeh! Wah! Wah! Wah! Yeh! Yeh! Djeetgŭn! Djeetgŭn!*	Several days later, about daybreak

Source: Fison and Howitt (1880: 194–98); adapted by authors.

Note that here the men sing **yiRang**, which is the male sex totem, and the females sing **tjitkan**.

Table 5.7: TjeRayil song, text 4

Who performs the cries/chants	Form of chant	Context and notes
A procession of the men from afar, following a 'serpentine course'	*Huh! Huh!*	During the **telping** ceremony, preliminary ceremony, when the boys are seated with the *Krauun* behind them
After having reached the boys and run past them twice, the men in a semicircle in front of them, strike the ground with bark strips	*Huh! Huh! Yeh!*	**Telping** ceremony
The men, coming from afar, holding a bundle of thin rods (teddeling)	*Ya! Wa! Ya! Wa!* At intervals there was a pause, followed by shouts of 'Yeh!'	Laying the Boys down to sleep ceremony; the boys standing in a row with the *Krauun* behind them. Howitt asked for the meaning of the words and was told: 'Our fathers always said and did thus to make the boys into men.'
The Bullawang	*Huh!*	Laying the Boys down to sleep ceremony; the boys in the care of the bullawang are raised up.

Who performs the cries/chants	Form of chant	Context and notes
Three old men, leading one boy at a time	*He! Nga!*	Laying the Boys down to sleep ceremony; the laying down of the boys. '*He!*' may be translated here 'Well' or 'Good'. The aspirate has a nasal sound that cannot be represented in writing. '*He!*' is also used affirmatively as we use the sound '*Hm!*' *Nga* = yes.
Presumably the *Bullawang* lead this, but are joined by others, including the women	'*Ya! Wa!*' and '*Yeh!*' at intervals. Sometimes varied by the words '*Yiirung!*' and '*Kaiung!*' instead of 'Ya!' and '*Wa!*'	Laying the Boys down to sleep ceremony; after the boys have been lain down.
The women led by the *Gweraiel-Rukut*; joined by the men; eventually the women cease	*Yiirung! Yiirung! Yeh!*	Laying the Boys down to sleep ceremony; on the morning of the next day.

Source: Howitt (1904: 621–23); adapted by authors.

Most of the cries and chants were either the syllables **wa, ya** or **ye**, or invocations to the two sex totems **tjitkan** and **yiRang**.

A mysterious syllable *huh!* is found frequently in the sources, particularly in the Museums Victoria manuscript and also in Howitt (1904). We presume that this was a breathy syllable, perhaps pronounced with an initial /h/ that is otherwise not found as a phoneme in the Gippsland language. We tentatively regularise this as **hah**.

A second cry, used only at the time that the boys were actually laid down, is written by Howitt as *he!* and explained as follows (1904: 623n1):

> '*He!*' may be translated here 'Well,' or 'Good.' The aspirate has a nasal sound which cannot be represented in writing. '*He!*' is also used affirmatively as we use the sound '*Hm!*' *Nga* = yes.

In the Museums Victoria manuscript (XM 761), this sound *he!* is described as 'guttural'. It does not appear that Howitt is confusing the sound, which he writes <h> with a velar nasal **ng**, as in the section where this exclamation occurs it is immediately followed by **nga** (Howitt 1904: 623n1). In MV XM 761, it is followed by **nye**. The description he has given here perhaps suggests that the initial consonant was a velar fricative sound followed perhaps by a nasalised vowel, [ɣẽ].

There are some other cries and words that were shown on page 100 of the Museums Victoria manuscript (XM 761). We suggest the regularisation of these in Table 5.8:

Table 5.8: Regularisation of song texts and cries

Spelling in Howitt	Our regularisation
(1 men) yehi wah-yeh (2 women) ya! qua -yeh! (3) bulling chong (4) yūī yui-nga!	(1 men) **yayi wa ye** (2 women) **ya! kwa-ye!** (3) **puling tjong** (4) **yuwi yuwo nga!**
(6) laying down boys He! (guttural) - Nye!	(6) laying down boys **ɣē! nye!**
(7) Tedeleng all beaten round - wati yah yeh!	(7) **teteling** all beaten round **wati ya ye!**

Source: MV XM 761, p. 100; adapted by authors.

5.3 Songs documented by Rev. John Bulmer

Rev. John Bulmer (1833–1913) was a Church of England missionary who worked first at Yelta on the Murray River (now a suburb of Mildura), from 1855, and later was instrumental in setting up the Lake Tyers Mission in 1862, which he managed until 1908 (Campbell 1999: xvii).

Although a keen observer of Aboriginal culture, Bulmer's papers frequently mix information from Gippsland with that from other parts of Victoria; we cannot always be sure where the information in his papers originates from. We are very fortunate that the late Alastair Campbell transcribed much of the Bulmer material at Museums Victoria (Campbell 1999). Where possible, those sections relating to traditional songs have been rechecked with the original manuscripts.

Bulmer made some general observations about songs (Campbell 1999: 56):

> These are various. There are war songs and love songs. Some are handed down from very early days, and I may remark, the older the songs the more they expressed. Some of their mythological songs were of greater length than any of modern times, indeed, the songs now in use do not generally have more than six to twelve words, these are repeated as long as required …

It is much to be regretted that none of these long mythological songs have been written down, though we must be grateful to Bulmer for confirming their existence. In the manuscript papers in Museums Victoria, he speaks about the **kunyeRu** and about the spread of songs from other areas (MV XM 922, pp. 24–25):

> But their great festival was when they held their corroborie (koonyero), this was generally in the summer time when food was plentiful and travelling easy. Then strangers came from different parts, perhaps one had brought a new song, and he was going to teach them how to dance to it. The song might be to them in an unknown tongue, but that was no hinderance to them learning it. All they wanted to know the song and time and the figure of the dance, and all would be complete, and very much looked up to for the time being, as all were eager to learn.

A slightly different version of this was printed in Bulmer (1888: 31).

We cannot be sure that these comments relate to the Gippsland area, because although he uses the Gippsland word for corroboree, he goes on to talk about the widely travelled corroboree song discussed below (section 13.2).

Bulmer's papers include the texts of songs from a range of locations. In this section, we will examine only those that are clearly related to Gippsland. These are listed in Table 5.9:

Table 5.9: Sources for Gippsland songs in Bulmer's manuscripts and in Campbell

Name of song (section)	Manuscript source	Campbell page reference
Prewin song (5.3.1)	not yet identified	29
Love song (**Yentjin(y)**) (5.3.2)	MV XM 925, p. 45	–
Songs of the **Thant(h)ang** (patrilineal totems) (5.3.3)	MV XM 96; SLV MS Box 1053/4 (b), hw0404.pdf, p. 141	29
Song in the Story of the Big Eagle's Children (5.3.4)	MV XM 925, p. 45	47–48
Prophetic song (5.3.5)	not yet identified	57–58
Coastal song (5.3.6)	not yet identified	58

Source: From Bulmer's manuscripts and Campbell (1999); adapted by authors.

Bulmer wrote about the use of songs in some detail. For example, the following passage (Campbell 1999: 24) deals with the casting of spells by song:

> To cause death in this manner several Aborigines would meet in a secret place and draw a rough figure of the victim on the ground. They chant a song, freely using the victim's name. This was supposed to bring up the spirit, *mraat*, of the person. Under the spell the person is told that he must die in a certain time. If such a ritual had been performed and the person happens to die shortly afterwards, death would be attributed to the spell. The friends of the dead man would then seek revenge, either by counter plotting or by secret murder.

The use of names in song, exemplified in the **parn** (spell) song in section 5.2.7, is further discussed by Bulmer based on information from Eliza O'Rourke (Campbell 1999: 25) about action taken against a young woman called Mary[38] who had eloped with William McBryde. This marriage was 'against their law' and it was determined that she should be punished, which was carried out without the knowledge of Mary's parents. In the words of James Perry, Eliza's then husband (Campbell 1999: 24–25):

> I went with Jack and Charley to a lonely place a little distance from the camp. I asked them why they had come there they told me I should soon see. They commenced singing a peculiar chant in which the real name of the girl Mary was used freely. From the tone of the song I understood they expected Mary to come to them. I told them I did not think she would come but they told me to wait & see. I looked in the direction of the camp, at first I thought I heard the sound of a bird singing, but at last I to my great astonishment saw Mary coming along. She came and stood before the singers. They had a stick made from she-oak with this they hit her several times they also pointed at her with an iron bark *marriwan*, or spear thrower (Fig. 7). They put their hands on her. She in the meantime seemed dazed or as the blacks say *narutban* (stupid), after treating her so they gave her a small possum telling her to roast and eat it, but that she would die in a few days. She only nodded her head but never spoke a word. When she returned to the camp she seemed to have no recollection of having been away or any idea of what or who had done anything to her. However she took a fit of vomiting and in a short time she died. Her parents knew nothing of this, but the two men Charley & Jack were looked upon with suspicion.

Later, Bulmer points out of the charm song 'the name of the person they wished to practice upon was freely used. It must be the real name *maak thar*' (Campbell 1999: 25).

38 Daughter of Keslop Tom, who is surely the same as Kerlip Tom, mentioned in connection with the patrilineal totem (see section 5.1.8.2).

5.3.1 Prewin song

Like Howitt, Bulmer also records a **Prewin** song, presented in Box 5.59. This is presumably a **kunyeRu**, as are the **Prewin** songs recorded by Howitt. See, for example, Song 5 (section 5.2.5), which is named as a **kunyeRu**, and Song 4 (section 5.2.4), which also mentions both *Brewin* and the **maRiwan**.

Box 5.59: Prewin song

The *malamulang* or medicine man was supposed to be able not only to see but also to extract the poison. The great idea was to exorcise the evil spirit, hence they sang a chant which sounded like the following: *brewin do murrawan do*, and the doctor would call out loudly for the evil spirit to depart, not being very complimentary as to the names he gave him.

Source: Bulmer in Campbell (1999: 29); adapted by authors.

Our linguistic analysis is presented in (5.31):

(5.31)	*brewin do*	*murrawan do*
	prewin-tu	**maRiwan-tu**
	evil spirit-ERG	magic throwing stick-ERG
	'The *Prewin* does it, the magic throwing stick does it.'	

Notes

The ergative marker is recorded by Mathews (1902a: 94) in his Brabirrawulung language notes as **-(t)u** as in *Kunnaio waddhan dhânda* 'a man an opossum eats' and *Waddhando dyerring dhânda* 'an opossum leaves eats', where the form of the ergative is **-u** after a vowel and **-tu** after the final /n/. This pattern parallels the morpho-phonology of the oblique marker described in Morey (2016). We have regularised the vowel to **u**.

Example (5.31) is thus clearly an example of the use of the ergative.

5.3.2 Love song (Yentjin(y))

The next song is a **yentjin(y)** song written down by Bulmer in a manuscript at Museums Victoria (MV XM 925) on page numbered 45. This song is not found in Campbell (1999).

The text is presented with its context in Box 5.60:

Box 5.60: Yentjin(y) song

There were also love songs was the Kurnai called them Yinginy. Some were pretty decent but others were mere filth. I give one of the most decent as a sample. It was made by an old man who died a few years ago.

Deah	baak	thundha	birrawangan	kooki
See	breasts	there	going to + fro	wonderful
Muruk gnopa		yingna	yain munju gnarlo ngetu	
Truly you ought not to cut your beard before come I				

The burden of the whole is a swain has fallen in love with the dangling breasts of a woman, the expression kooki is just what a black makes when he is surprised he is surprised by the beauty of her form, and she is equally enraptured with him only he has made a mistake in cutting his beard before she saw him. Perhaps these specimens will give a fair idea of what blacks can do in the poetic line.

Source: Bulmer, MV XM 925 p. 74;[39] adapted by authors.

Our analysis is presented in (5.32):

(5.32)	*deah*	*baak*	*thunda*	*birrawangan*	*kooki*
	see	*breasts*	*there*	*going to + fro*	*wonderful*
	thaya	**pak**	**thuntu**	**piRa-wanga**	**kuki**
	see.IMP	breast	there	move-LOCATIONAL	EXCL
	'See her breasts there, moving up and down, wow!'				

muruk	*gnopa*	*yingna*	*yain*	*munju*	*gnarlo*	*ngetu*
Truly you ought not to cut your beard before come I						
muRuk	**ngatjp(a)**	**yingna**	**yen**	**muntyu**	**ngauwa-lo-ngithu**	
truly?	NEG	cut?	beard	DEM?	come-?-1SG	
'Truly (you) ought not to have cut (your) beard before I came.'						

Notes

Most of the words in this song are found in multiple word lists recorded by Fesl (1985). The form **piRa** is analysed by us as a verb meaning 'move', also found in the *Barn* **(Parn)** song recorded by Howitt and presented above (section 5.2.7).

39 This is page 74 of the PDF, the page is numbered 45.

We assume that the word *ngopa* represents the negative, represented by Hercus (1986) as /ŋaɖban/, and that consequently *muruk* is the word that conveys the meaning of 'truly' and 'ought'. We have not found any word in the other Gippsland sources to confirm this.

The words shown by Fesl (1985: T1, no. 29) for 'cut' do not resemble any of the forms in example (5.32). One of them is specifically a verb meaning 'cut with tomahawk' (*ti-lou-wurt*) and we assume that a specialist verb meaning 'cut a beard' would have been present in the language, and that *yingna* is this verb, but there is no confirmation of this from other sources.

5.3.3 Songs of the Thant(h)ang (patrilineal totems)

Several songs that related to particular **thant(h)ang** or patrilineal totems were written down by Bulmer, and references to them are also found in the Howitt papers. In the State Library of Victoria (MS Box 1053/4 (b), small notebook p. 12), Howitt makes it clear that these songs belong to a particular totem, as we see in Box 5.61:

Box 5.61: YelmeRai (shark totem) song

Yalmerai when sick sing the Yalmerai song
Thruwungunda clean your teeth
Ngourabindi the open sea

Source: Howitt, SLV MS Box 1053/4 (b), hw0404.pdf, p. 141; adapted by authors.

The source for information about these patrilineal totem songs appears to have been Bulmer. In a letter from Bulmer to Howitt dated 29 March 1884 (MV XM 93), he makes it clear that these songs have curative powers:

> We see this in the powers even now they attribute to the Yelmire & Glean in being able to cure diseases. They seem to have had an animal for the cure of every disease. In headache they would use the teeth of the Yelmir and in diseases of the limbs they would look to the Glean to straighten the strings so animals having the power it would be no wonder of they identified themselves with them and thus become their totems. Of course it will perhaps always remain a mystery as to the origin of the totem system and I suppose all we can do is to speculate on the subject.

In the Howitt papers in Museums Victoria, there is a typescript that contains further information about the patrilineal totem and the words 'Billy the Bull is a Yalmerai (shark). When there are too many about the Lakes Entrance, he sends them away by singing to them. He belongs to Lake Bunga' (XM 524). These two functions of curing people, and of sending away dangerous animals, are two examples of the functions of these songs.

Bulmer's notation of these songs came because of his enquiries into *jaak*, literally 'meat', which is the word that his consultants gave for the patrilineal totems and Howitt recorded as *thundung* (**thant(h)ang**) (see section 5.1.7.2). Clearly neither Howitt nor Bulmer fully understood how this system worked, because in a letter dated 11 March 1884 (MV XM 92), Bulmer wrote that he found Billy the Bull 'very obscure on this subject' and that:

> he now tells me that Yelmire was not his father's Jaak but the reason he was called by that name was because he once dreamed about a Yelmire and made a song about it.

What does seem to be the case is that the **malamalang** (medicine man) would sing a different song according to his **thant(h)ang** (patrilineal totem), however he acquired that totem. Apart from the brief reference in the Howitt papers in the State Library of Victoria (see Box 5.61), the main source for information about these songs is an incomplete letter from Bulmer (MV XM 96), part of which is transcribed in Box 5.62:

Box 5.62: Totem songs, version 1

XM 96, p. 2 [continuation of letter about the patrilineal totems]

... in the district belonging to them [was?? Noorala??] and the Snowy River is Noyang. His wife from same district is Billing (salmon) just as old Yelmri who lived at Lake Tyers got that name. The song they sing over the sick was

Thunang gnardrak clean your teeth

Gnark a bundha the sea or the back of a thing. The back of the world. Thus they always call the sea.

They tell me that when the Mala malang sang over the sick he always sang his Jaak. The song of the Glean would be Toot toot ba gnarang that is straighten the strings. They had some idea when a man was sick he needed straightening out hence the song.

...

PS I [??]was told the reason they sang the Yelmri song they sing clean your teeth is they have the teeth of Yelmri tied to the forehead of the patient so that clean your teeth will refer to Yelmeri is so that he may be able to remove the disease & do it cleanly &c.

Source: Bulmer, MV XM 96; adapted by authors.

Campbell's transcription of the same passage is presented in Box 5.63:

Box 5.63: Totem songs, version 2

> The song they sang over the sick was *thurnang gnardaak*, clean your teeth, *gnark a bundha*, the sea or the back of the world. This they always call the sea. They tell me that when the *malamulang* sang to the sick he always sang his *jaak* [totem]. The song of the *gleean* would be *toot toot ba gnarang*. That is straighten the strings, they had some idea when a man was sick he needed straightening out.
>
> For headache they would use the teeth of the *yelmara* and in disease of the limbs they would look to *gleean* to straighten the strings[16].
>
> [Footnote 16 Chapter 3: Bulmer 1904, 29 March (this refers to MV XM 93)]

Source: Bulmer in Campbell (1999: 29, 100n16); adapted by authors.

Howitt (1904: 135) shows that the *gleean* **kliyan** is both a kinship term and an animal term, literally 'water-hen' (see section 5.1.1.2).

As we will see in the analysis of the second song, example (5.34) below, the 'strings' here refer to sinews, or other body parts. The word *gnarang* is elsewhere recorded as meaning 'sinew' or 'tendon', and Howitt (1904: 474) also refers to the straightening out of limbs as part of the process of the cure (see section 5.2.4). As we have pointed out earlier, a word **kliyat** is glossed both as 'hamstring' (Fesl 1985: 130) and 'sinews under the knee' (Fesl 1985: 165). This word is similar in form to the word **kliyan**, which is the name of a patrilineal totem whose members can sing this song. Perhaps the **kliyan** 'water hen' was particularly associated with this part of the body, and perhaps some of the dances illustrated, showing the stretching of the legs, were related to this.

We presume from this that the song documented by Bulmer was only sung by a *malamulang* who was of the *gleean* totem. Since there are at least a dozen other totems shown by both Bulmer and Howitt and discussed in section 5.1.7, we presume that each of these probably had its own song to be sung when a cure was needed.

Our analysis of the first song is presented as (5.33):

(5.33)	*Thurnang*	*gnardaak*
	clean your teeth	
	tha(r)nang	**nga(r)tak**
	Clean	tooth
	'Clean your teeth.'	

gnark a *bundha*
sea of back of the world
ngaRak-a **pantha ?**
back-POSS world.OBL ?
'(The sea is) the back of the world.'

There is no word for 'clean' or similar recorded in Fesl (1985). This word, which we have regularised as **tha(r)nang**, is translated with an imperative 'clean' where perhaps /**-ang**/ is a suffix otherwise not indicated. There are several words with initial **tha-** that relate to the mouth; the root word for 'eat' is **tha-**, while **thanthampa** is 'kiss' (written as *dhurndhumba* by R.H. Mathews, Fesl 1985: S2, no. 17), and the word for 'talk' 'language' is **thang**. The words for 'tooth' and 'back' were documented by Hercus (1986) as / ŋandag/ ['ŋandak] and /ŋarag/ ['ŋarak] respectively.

There is no word recorded in Fesl (1985) for 'world' or 'earth' that is similar to *bundha*. The most usual word for 'earth' is **wrak** (Fesl 1985: G8–9, no. 40 and no. 41).

The analysis of the second song, the *gleean* totem, is presented in (5.34):

(5.34) *toot toot ba gnarang*
Straighten the strings
t(j)ut(j)ut(j)pa **ngaRang**
Straighten sinew
'Straighten the sinew(s).'

Fesl (1985: U3, no. 61) records a verb *dōōrt-dōō-baya* 'twist' (in Thomas), and we consider that this is the same verb as found in example (5.34) since 'twist' and 'straighten' have related meanings and refer to same process, manipulation of a long thin element like a sinew or a string, or perhaps a verb reserved for the ritual action involved in this healing process.

Howitt (1904: 444) gives the word *ngurrung-mri* 'sinew-eye' when discussing names Gippsland people gave to the white men:

> white man possessed a supernatural power of the eye, to flash death to the beholder, or to draw together the banks of a river, and to pass over it. This power was called *Ngurrung-mri*, or 'sinew eye,' and I think that I have also heard it called *Mlang-mri*, meaning 'lightning eye.'

The same word was listed by Thomas with the meaning 'tendon' and the form *ngahrang* (Fesl 1985: A19, no. 165).

5.3.4 Songs in the Story of the Big Eagle's Children: Song 1 – Mother's mourning song

The following story written down by Bulmer is also transcribed in Campbell (1999: 47–48). Our transcription has been checked with the original manuscript and differs slightly from that in Campbell. It is presented in Box 5.64:

Box 5.64: Songs in the Big Eagle's Children story

Some more stories of the Mythology of Aborigines. A big eagle had a lot of grown up children. One the youngest one, last she had. She thought much of the youngest one. All the brothers would go out to hunt for meat, but she hid the youngest, indeed the brothers did not know of his existence. When the brothers went out to hunt, the youngest would go another route to get *gnallu* (meat for his mother). The brothers would often bring nothing but the mother was never hungry, this puzzled the brothers as to how their mother got fed, so they determined to watch her. They pretended to go hunting but hid themselves in various parts. They saw the young fellow go out and bring meat to his mother. So they determined to outwit him. They got two young women to enter into the plot. They got a kangaroo bone, and sharpened it, and stuck it into the ground covering it up so that it looked like a bandicoot's nest. They watched him the next time he went hunting. They went up to him in the bush getting him away to the nest. They asked him to kill the bandicoot for them. Oh said he, I will spear it. Oh no said they, that will spoil the meat, he said I will kill it with my club. That said they, will bruise the meat. I will lay on the top of it and catch it in my hands, but this would not do, so he said he would put his foot on it, doing this he was impaled on the kangaroo bone, he now fell down. They carried him away, but he seems to have got away with the two women who had caught him with the bone. The mother now mourned her son as follows:

Dah ning ga	*Dah ning ga*	*Narrin*	*than daan*
My son	My son	gone	my son
Billin billindu		*Karo gan thargo*	
Some one must have killed him		My husband's child.	

[SM: The first letter of Karo is unclear, it might be *Tharo*]

Then the mother sings across the sea and her son answers her from the Island he is on

Koolin bang wa Birringa Wanmunga

I am coming home I am away with somebody.

Referring to the women he had taken.

Gnallu coro winyu

Meat I am bringing

> After singing for her son and getting an answer from him across the sea she kept on singing and he answering her all the way home. When he was coming all sorts of birds met him, for then men were represented by birds which might have been their totem. him even crowds of birds congregated to stop his progress. He was able to brush them all aside when he got close to the landing place. As soon as they landed the mother hawk had to strike the two women who had by their cunning taken away her son. But he walked through the crowd still brushing them all aside. There were two brothers at the camp waiting. He could manage the crowd but the two brothers overcame him and he had to undergo his punishment for his misadventure.

Source: Bulmer, MV XM 923, pp. 77–78;[40] adapted by authors.

Some words in this story, notably *gnallu* 'meat', are in the Gippsland languages; this word having been shown by Hercus as /ŋale/ 'meat'.

In the case of the first two lines, sung by the mother, our analysis is presented here as (5.35). We have not been able to suggest a linguistic analysis with confidence.

(5.35)	*Dah ning ga*	*Dah ning ga*	*Narrin than daan*	
	My son, My son, gone my son			
	t(h)aningka	**t(h)aningka**	**n(g)aRin-than-than**	
	?	?	-1SG??	
	Billin billindu	*Karo*	*gan*	*thango*
	Some one must have killed him, my husband's child			
	pilin pilin-tu	**kaRu**	**kan**	**thangu**
	?-ERG	perhaps?	?	?

Notes

We are unable to offer much analysis for this section of the song. It is possible that the form *daan* is the same as a 1st person singular suffix sometimes written as *-down* that is found in forms like *Dahgŭn-yakindown* 'I'm going to see my mother' recorded by William Thomas, where **thaka-** is the root for 'see' and **yakan** is 'mother'.

The last word in the first line might be a kinship term. 'Daughter's husband' is given by Howitt as *ngaribil* (Fesl 1985: B10, no. 51), but only when a male is speaking, and this song is in the voice of a female. Perhaps the root **n(g)aRi-** is a kinship term.

40 These pages are not numbered in the manuscript, these are the numbers of the PDF file.

The other possible word in this section is **pilin** that might be the same as **piling** 'salmon', which is recorded as one of the **thant(h)ang** or patrilineal totem terms. If we are correct that this term is combined with the ergative -**tu**, it may be that the singer is suggesting that the killing was done by a member of that patrilineal totem. If this is correct then the meaning 'kill' should be found inside the words *karo gan thango*, but none of the 'kill' words indicated by Fesl (1985) bear any similarity to these.

We can also speculate that the form *garru* should be **kanyu** 'perhaps', spelled *kanno* by Bulmer in Smyth (1878, 2: 26).

The second song is the son's answer, presented as (5.36):

(5.36)	*Koolin*	*bang*	*wa*	*Birringa*	*Wanmunga*
	I am coming home, I am away with somebody				
	kulin	**pang-wa**		**piR-wanga**	**wanmung(k)a**
	?	camp-OBL		move-LOCATIONAL	?
	'To the camp … moving about …'				

Notes

There is no documented word for 'coming' with a form like *Koolin*. We have the exclamations 'come' on, which is *koo-e-a* and *go-ir* (Fesl 1985: X2, no. 3), probably **kuwiya**. The usual word for 'come' is based on **ngau(w)a-**.

The form looks like an oblique case marker. It is already observed in Morey (2016) that the form was **-wa** after a vowel.

We suggest that the form *Birringa* is actually the same as **piRa wanga**, already seen in the **yentjin(y)** song presented in section 5.3.2.

The last song is also sung by the son, referring to the women he has captured. Our analysis is presented in (5.37):

(5.37)	*Gnallu*	*coro*	*winyu*
	Meat I am bringing		
	ngalu	**kuRu**	**wanh-u**
	meat		fetch-?
	'… fetching … meat.'		

Notes

The word for meat was shown by Hercus (1986) as ['ŋale]. Perhaps there is a -u suffix here.

R.H. Mathews documented the form of 'fetch' as *wannhai*.

5.3.5 Prophetic song

A song that was claimed to have prophesied the arrival of the white men was written down by Bulmer (Campbell 1999: 57–58). This is presented in Box 5.65:

Box 5.65: Prophetic song

The one I now give has some pretensions to prophetic power. A black once lived named Bungil Noorook. I am told it was some time before the advent of the white man. He is said to have had a foresight of the white man -*loorn*- who would come in ships sailing about the sea (*nerkabundha*). The song is as follows:

mundhanna loornda kathia prappau

There are white men long way off with great noise

muraskin mundhanna yea a main

Guns there sailing about.

[p. 58]

Which would be: There are at present white men sailing about on the sea, making a great noise with guns.

I suspect this song was made after the advent of white men; or, at all events, the Bungil Noorook must have heard of *loorn* having landed further east, and that they had ships to sail about; and also muskets, as *muraskin* is only muskets pronounced by an Aboriginal.

Source: Bulmer in Campbell (1999: 57–58); adapted by authors.

Note that Howitt also documented a song relating to white men sailing, the song that appears to refer to a shipwreck, see section 5.2.2.

Our analysis is presented in (5.38):

(5.38) *mundhanna* *loornda* *kathia* *prappau*

There are white men long way off with great noise

muntha-na **lu(wu)n-ta** **katji-ya** **prepau**

far off-OBL white man-POSS sea-OBL other?

'The white man far off, (on) the other sea.'

Muraskin	*mundhanna*	*yea a main*
Guns there sailing about		
muRaskin	**muntha-na**	**yeyamany**
musket	far off-OBL	sailing?
'The musket far off, sailing? …'		

Notes

The word **muntu** 'yonder' is found in a number of sources. We suggest that this word (with a nasal cluster **-nth**) is here marked for oblique case, and forms a phrase with the possessor **lu(wu)n-da**, literally 'the white man's (being) far away'.

We cannot find any words relating to 'great noise'[41] that have similarity to *kathia prappau*; however, these two words could mean 'on the other water'. Bulmer, for example, writes 'another man' as *Preppa kani* (Smyth 1878, 2: 27).

As already discussed in relation to the 'White Woman' song (section 5.2.3), a form meaning 'sea' that we have regularised as **katying** is found in a number of sources, all from Curr (1887, 3): *kailtung*, *katung* and *gattung*. Howitt (1904: 73n1) says: '*Tatung* is the sea, sometimes spoken of as *gatching*'.

We presume that *yea a main* means 'sailing'.

5.3.6 Coastal song

Bulmer also documented a song from the people on the coast. This is presented in Box 5.66:

Box 5.66: Coastal song

The following song was famous among the Gunai/Kurnai. It was made by one who lived mostly on the sea coast:

yenna kunyero nganjo winna barrajute,

Lift song I always rivers

panda ngaliwan mali thunga, thunga,

Spearing seals in water, water, water.

41 For example, Thomas gives noise as *gillöö-galla-mĕraht* (Fesl 1985: C1, no. 26).

The translation of which would be: "I lift up my voice to sing of the spearing of seals on the waters of the river." Certainly a most ambitious and classical commencement, but the poet gets no further. Like the tones of a beautiful organ which is suddenly stopped by the bursting of a pipe. So the poet suddenly collapses, and leaves you to imagine what followed, perhaps the *ngaliwan* got into their native element and left the poet suddenly.

Source: Bulmer in Campbell (1999: 58); adapted by authors.

Our analysis is presented in (5.39):

(5.39)	*yenna*	*kunyero*	*nganjo*	*winna*	*barrajute*
	lift	*song*	*I*	*always*	*river*
	yena	**kunyeRu**	**ngayu**	**wina**	**paRatjut**
	lift	dance.song	1SG	?	?
	'I lift up a song …'				

	panda	*ngaliwan*	*male*	*thunga,*	*thunga*
	spearing	*seals*	*in water, water, water*		
	pantha	**ngaliwan**	**mal**	**thung(k)a**	**thung(k)a**
	strike	seal	GO?	hence	hence
	'Striking the seals going hence hence.'				

Notes

We have been unable to suggest any analysis for the word *winna* and *barrajute*. The only word relating to water remotely similar to *barrajute* is the word *praryoong* 'water hole', written down by Robinson (Fesl 1985: F2, no. 8). This word could have a root form **paRatja-**. It is also similar to the Melbourne-area place names *Prahran* and *Birrarung Marr*, which both derive from the Indigenous name of the Yarra River.

The word *male* may be the form **mal**, discussed in Morey (2016), which appears to relate to motion and is glossed as GOING.

5.4 Gippsland song

As discussed above (section 1.5.2), State Library of Victoria MS 6290, previously ascribed to William Thomas, was written down in Pentridge Prison under the guidance of the Inspector General of Pentridge, Col. W. Champ. According to Andrew Tanner (pers. comm.), the language consultants for

Gippsland were Big Joe and Billy Clarke. Big Joe, whose native name was Ton-wylean, is mentioned multiple times in William Thomas's journals. He was born at Boi-boi in about 1830 and died at Lake Tyers in 1891. Billy Clark(e) was also one of A.W. Howitt's consultants and was present at the 're-creation' of the Boys' initiation ceremony in 1884 (Gibson and Mullett 2020).

If this song was told to the compiler of this manuscript by Billy Clark(e), who came from the Sale area and was a Brayakaulung man, the song may represent that language. 'Big Joe', the Gippsland person who gave information probably came from further to the east.[42]

Big Joe is also mentioned multiple times in the journals of William Thomas (Stephens 2014, 3), and William Thomas visited him in jail at Pentridge in 1861. Thomas names his father as Tee-go-bar, aged 52, so Big Joe may have been about 30. Thomas wrote that on 11 July 1862, people came to ask him 'to let Big Joe out of Prison. I pacify them by saying in one moon Big Joe come home' (Stephens 2014, 3: 386).

The manuscript includes a single song from Gippsland with the context of its meaning (which is termed 'Translation'). The text and this 'translation' are presented in Box 5.67. A second version of the manuscript of this song is in the Royal Anthropological Institute of Great Britain and Ireland MS 38, p. 133.

Box 5.67: Gippsland song

(Gippsland)
Bōman-dai-lallan-billy-minya-ōōlōbei-bah
marrōōmba-kāŷkyōōbara-bah-barōōmba-bah
marrōōmba-bah-kāŷkyōōbara-bah-marrōōmbah
bomen-dai-lallan-billy-minnŷa-ōōlōbēi-bah-
maroombah-kaykyoobara-bah-baroomba-bah-
marrōōmba

Translation:

A blackfellow meeting a whitefellow in the Bush asked him for some tea. The white man refused him, and he turned away, ejaculating, "Poor man".

Source: SLV MS 6290, p. 229; adapted by authors.

42 We are grateful to Russell Mullett for providing this information, Big Joe may have been associated with the Rosedale area, also Brayakaulung.

It is clear that the song is in two sections, with considerable repetition. The extent of this parallelism is realised when we rearrange the presentation of the text, shown in (5.40):

(5.40) Bōman-dai-lallan-billy-minya-ōōlōbei-bah marrōōmba-kāŷkyōōbara-bah-barōōmba-bah marrōōmba-bah-kāŷkyōōbara-bah-marrōōmbah

bomen-dai-lallan-billy-minnŷa-ōōlōbēi-bah-maroombah-kaykyoobara-bah-baroomba-bah-marrōōmba

A suggested regularisation is presented as (5.41):

(5.41) **puman-tai lalan-pili minya-wulupai-pa**
maRumpa kaikyupaRa-pa paRumpa-pa
maRumpa-pa kaikyupaRa-pa paRumpa-pa

puman-tai lalan-pili minya-wulupai-pa
maRumpa kaikyupaRa-pa paRumpa-pa
maRumpa

Notes

The only word that we believe we can recognise in this is **pili**, which is perhaps the word for 'billy', used for preparing tea.

We might expect exclamations to be part of the song text, but there is nothing in the song resembling the two most appropriate exclamations as recorded in Fesl, the exclamation of despair *jukka-dom*, from Dawson and Pettit (Fesl 1985: X2, no. 7), and the exclamation of hurt, *ko-ki*, from Howitt (Fesl 1985: X3, no. 20).

It is possible that the form **kaikyupaRa**, spelled *kāŷkyōōbara*, is the verb 'to drink'. In the word list in MS 6290 this is recorded as *grō-gŭr-wah*, and several words glossed as 'drink' seem to be based on a root something like **klukp-** (*glookban*, Curr C4; *klurkpan*, Hagenauer) (Fesl 1985: S3, no. 24).

5.5 Laurie Moffatt – boat song

On 30 January 1963, Luise Hercus recorded Laurie Moffatt[43] singing a song about a journey by boat to go hop picking. The song is recorded on field tape 79/1. The AIATSIS digitisation of this recording is named HERCUS_L02-012786.tmp, and the recording of Laurie Moffatt singing commences at 22:04. A recording of this song has been cut and uploaded to YouTube at youtu.be/xJTQEuqaMw8.

AIATSIS staff have partly transcribed the discussion between Luise and Laurie Moffatt following the singing of the song. This transcription is given below (HERCUS_L02_12786-12788_TranscriptB.pdf):

> LH: Yes … what did it mean?
>
> LM: That's a boat on the river. Yes, going down, you see. They used to sit up there and know all the old people at () you know, they all used to have a boat running up and down. The old () Gippsland, Gippsland and all that lot. And they used to be there hop picking and they made that song up, yes.
>
> LH: Who taught it to you, actually?
>
> LM: Oh I heard them singin' it () well that's how I come to pick it up, really.
>
> LH: Oh, that's wonderful. I think it is the only song from Gippsland in the lingo that has been recorded. Do you remember any others?
>
> LM: Oh no, no no no. That's the only one. Used to be the-well, we'd all have a go at it. All the boys and the girls would sit down and hit the (claps). That's when we were-there used to be hop picking, you know, just going up there on the river there on the right hand side-you might have … the Mitchell River? They all were there.

A.W. Howitt owned a hop farm at Eastwood, which is now a suburb of Bairnsdale on Clifton Creek. It is possible that the original song was composed at the time that Gippsland people used to travel up to Howitt's

43 A biography of Laurie Moffatt is at Joanne Bach, 'Moffatt, Lawrence Francis (Laurie) (1897–1966)', *Australian Dictionary of Biography*, National Centre of Biography, The Australian National University, adb.anu.edu.au/biography/moffatt-lawrence-francis-laurie-13105, published first in hardcopy in 2005, accessed online 6 February 2023. There is a large photo of Laurie Moffatt in the Donald Thompson collection at the State Library of Victoria. This collection is owned by the University of Melbourne but kept at the library. It is believed that Laurie participated in one episode of the ABC TV series *Alcheringa* in 1962.

farm to pick hops. Note that the hops industry in Gippsland was wiped out about 1904 and the song was therefore presumably composed before that date.

In 2015, Luise Hercus and Stephen Morey made a tentative transcription of the words of this song, which we present as (5.42):

(5.42) [gəi gəduŋ bəm lɐŋ gən daŋ ŋa læŋ ge]
[yɐŋ na mɐn də gɜ læŋ ge]
[gən gəde wə bəle ə diŋ ma]
[ye kʰa daŋ mɜŋ ŋa ləŋ gə de ŋa laŋ gə de]
[bərr liŋ bə la læŋ ge wə ge]
[ge men ɲə ŋe]
[bərr]

The final word [bərr] was uttered with a falling pitch and a long final rhotic trill. It was perhaps an invocation to dance.

The song is notable for bisyllabic forms that seem to have stress, or at least lengthening, on the second syllable. For example, the form [gə de] occurs several times, each with clear stress on the second syllable.

We cannot recognise any words in this song and cannot offer a suggested translation. It is possible that the first word, which we have transcribed as [gəi], is in fact the word for 'canoe' **kri**, extended to refer to whatever boat the people travelled up to the hop farm on.

We might have expected the word for Mitchell River to be included in the song. According to Hagenauer (in Smyth 1878, 2: 191), this is *Wahyang*, 'literally 'spoon-billed duck', but we cannot find that form in the song, unless the form [yɐŋ] at the beginning of the second line represents this.

The word for the Snowy River, written as *Karang Gil* by Bulmer (Smyth 1878, 2: 191), and glossed by him as meaning 'from great quantities of water-weed about' might be present in the song as [kʰa daŋ] in the fourth line of the song.

A musical transcription of this song, with the words from example (5.42), is presented in Figure 5.2:

Laurie Moffatt's Song

Figure 5.2: Musical analysis of Laurie Moffatt's song

Source: Grace Koch.

In this song, Laurie Moffatt sings in long-breathed phrases with a clear tone.

The song encompasses a major third. Pitches are F, G and A, with each verse ending on a syllable with an extended 'e'. The form follows an A, B, A, B1 structure with the B1 section resembling a longer version of the earlier B section. On the final descent of the G to F in the B1 section, the singer uses a combination trill and turn on the G immediately before the final descent to F. The song mainly follows a triple metre. A call, possibly a dance call, is sounded at the end, with a trill descending an octave. The range of the trill is not included in the general pitch range as it only hints at pitches.

6
Bunganditj songs

The language of the Mount Gambier area is variously known as **Bunganditj** or **Booandik**. Blake (2003a: 3) discusses the variations in the form of the name; here we will use the variant Bunganditj. Altogether, 10 songs are documented as being connected to this community, but the vocabulary of the six songs from Tindale are not easily reconciled with the other Bunganditj sources (see section 6.2). The others are one written down by William Thomas (see section 6.3), two songs documented by Christina Smith (section 6.4), and a song published in the Mount Gambier *Border Watch* newspaper in 1903, recorded by 'Panangharry' (see section 6.5).

There is some information about the process of corroboree in the Bunganditj area recorded by 'Panangharry' in a newspaper article in the *Border Watch*, 22 July 1903.[1] The name 'Panangharry' may have been used by a white settler who wished to have a native nom de plume. It is almost certainly the Bunganditj word for 'brother-in-law', **panang**, with an unknown suffix.[2] The article commences with the song (see section 6.5), followed by the description of the corroboree that is given here:

> For the corroborree (Bruneyah Trual), or blackfellows' dance, all the Truals (or black fellows) who were to take part in one of those performances, which always took place at night, spent nearly all the previous day in arranging their toilet. Scanty though it was, they took

1 Panangharry, 'Early Recollections of Glen-Coe, Lake Leake, and the South-East No. 4', *Border Watch* (Mount Gambier), 22 July 1903, 4, accessed 30 June 2017, trove.nla.gov.au/newspaper/article/77159439/7602235.

2 In this chapter we will use basically the same regularisation as that in Blake (2003a), though using only voiceless stops throughout (with the exception of stops following nasals). We have retained Blake's notation of words with initial clusters having an apostrophe as **p'rr-**.

great pride in the devices of white paint with which they painted their faces, bodies and legs. A girdle of opossum skin round the loins, with strips of the skin hanging down in front and behind; some gum-boughs tied round the ankles; two short sticks with which to beat time; a boomerang or waddy (Wirring) stuck in the girdle; and the one-time lord of Australia was ready for the ball. A clear place is chosen and some firewood and dead boughs collected, some round holes dug and the spot made ready before dark. As soon as it is quite dark the fires are lit. Four or five strong lubras squat down in front of the holes, which are generally near the best fire, with a part of an opossum rug rolled up very lightly, each one beating this over the hole with her right hand, which acts as a drum. The master of ceremonies then makes his appearance with two short sticks for beating time. He takes his place near the lubras and starts a sing-out (song), keeping time with the two sticks, the lubras also beating time. This is a signal that all is ready. The blackfellows now seem to be coming in from all directions, and the boughs can be heard rustling as they come running up in the dark from their mia-mias (Gnoorlaha). They all make for the cleared place, a good distance from the M.C, and stand there in a body. They are not kept waiting long, the M.C going out to them singing in a loud voice, lifting first the right then the left hand and partly turning the beating sticks. At the same time they all, facing him, lift their beating sticks the same as the M.C., the latter walking backwards towards the lubras, followed by all the rest lifting first one leg and then the other, keeping time with their hands. On arriving at a spot near the lubras, at a particular time of the M.C.'s sing-out, they all strike their individual sticks together, and continue beating, the M.C singing, gradually getting faster and faster, finishing by all except the M.C throwing both arms up in the air as near together as possible. This finishes Act No.1. They then trot back, yabbering to one another. Sometimes this is repeated two or three times. Then the brune-yah proper commences. First a few will start singly, then all will get in a kind of a semicircle not far from the fire, stride out their legs, nearly touching each other's feet, lifting the heels of their feet, bringing them down with a jerk, and shaking the muscles of the thighs. This is the step of the dance. They way this is done is most extraordinary, and requires a deal of practice to acquire. Some of the good ones at it will actually make the muscles whirr again. It cannot be kept up long. While doing this they all utter a kind of grunt, hum, hum, hum. After dancing a short time some will utter a yell, first lifting one leg very high then another, thus shaking the boughs around their ankles and bolting into the darkness, reappearing almost immediately and doing another brune-yah, being greatly applauded by all the kine-kine-yals and truals (lubras and blackfellows) who are spectators. The swarthy

> bodies of about 200 blackfellows, all painted white in different devices, doing the brune-yah in a continuous line or semicircle, with the weird effect of the light of the fire flickering upon them, and their various other evolutions, is a sight never to be forgotten by any person who has witnessed it. Kine-kine-yal brune-yah, or the lubras' dance, is altogether different. They are not so much adorned with paint as the blackfellows. They have a small bunch of boughs in each hand, and commence by sliding each foot along the ground, first one and then the other, both feet being kept together. The arms are extended at right angles, and are shaken in time with the feet, with a kind of jerk. This forms a kind of track in the ground. After many have done this, which forms the first step in the dance, the track being about 10 yards long, generally on a slight incline, they each then commence the second step, by each one staring on the top of the track, sliding both feet together with a jerk, keeping time with their arms. Others are singing and beating the drum the same as the blackfellows, but no beating sticks are used.

There are several words in Bungaditj found in this description. These are presented in Table 6.1:

Table 6.1: Bunganditj words in the description of the corroboree by 'Panangharry'

English version in 'Panangharry'	Bunganditj word as spelled by 'Panangharry'	Regularised spelling (after Blake 2003a)
Corroboree	Bruneyah Trual	**p'rruniya truwal**
boomerang or waddy	Wirring	–
mia mia	Gnoorlaha	**ngula**
lubra's dance	Kine-kine-yal brune-yah	**kan(kan)yul p'rruniya**

Source: *Border Watch* (Mount Gambier), 22 July 1903, p. 4; adapted by authors.

The word for 'dance' is related to the word for 'play', regularised by Blake (2003a) as **p'rrun.nga**. This is the same root, **p'rrun(a)**-, as the word for corroboree in Table 6.1 but with a different suffix. As we will see in section 6.1, a third suffix occurs with this word in the word recorded by Stewart to mean 'native dancing', which is **p'rrunanban truwal**, where **truwal** means 'man'. Thus there are three suffixes found with this root of unknown meaning, presented in example (6.1):

(6.1) **-nga**
-anban
-iya

6.1 Musical terminology in Bunganditj

In this section, we will present the surviving examples of Bunganditj language used in connection with dance and song.

Tindale (1941: 239) gave some fairly detailed information about the names of different types of songs relating to the emu songs. After the last of these (see section 6.2.8), he wrote the following:

> These three emu songs (Disc 4 and Disc 5) form a suite which was sung at an emu dance. The names applied to them have the following significance and the same terms are, in general, used for the three recognised types of dancing songs.
>
> ['kupanbina] – imitative dances in which the performers simulate the movements of the emu, prancing about, growling and making noises; the song is a general accompaniment.
>
> ['wakan'ŋadeik] the ['menpurumi] of Tanganekeld, also called ['ŋuluŋulukana:mb] because each part of the song is enacted. In the present case they dramatise the behaviour of the emu and the eagle when in opposition.
>
> ['wire'wiruk] – the songs of the true dancing climax; the men stand in one place with legs outspread, vibrate their legs and give loud grunts as the chorus of women chant the ['wire'wiruk].

The words given here cannot be related to the other sources for Bunganditj, save for the last form ['wire'wiruk], which is related to the word for dance written down by Mathews, *wirrawa*, regularised as **wirriwa**.

Other words relating to song and dance listed in Blake (2003a) are presented in Table 6.2:

Table 6.2: Glossary of words relating to singing in the Bunganditj language

English	Blake regularisation	Sources
Corroboree	marrapina	murapena Christina Smith
Corroboree	wirrani	wir-un-ne Thomas
Dance	wirriwa	wirrawa R.H. Mathews
'native dancing'	p'rrunanban truwal	proon-an-ban druol Stewart (literally 'play man')
Sing	nhiwiya	ngai-winyay 'song' Thomas
Sing	nurripa	nurip-nurip 'song' Stewart

Source: Blake (2003a); adapted by authors.

6.1.1 Corroboirè dialogue from Mount Gambier

Our other principal source for language relating to songs and dances is the dialogue in State Library of Victoria MS 6290 (see section 1.5.2 for a discussion of this manuscript). The manuscript includes language information from both Mount Gambier (Bunganditj) and Wonnin (Warrnambool). As already discussed above, Andrew Tanner (pers. comm.) has established that the language consultants for these two languages were Monkey Neddy, King Tom's Billy and Jackey White, the first two being from Mount Gambier and the last from the Wonnin area.

Unlike the first two informants, we do know something of Jackey White's background. He was born in approximately 1824, so would have been 37 when tried, convicted and imprisoned. He was married and his wife Louisa was born in 1833, and going by their children's records, they lived between the 'Wannon district' and pastoral runs and towns such as Strathdownie, Dartmoor and Digby. Both parents and their children, John, Flora, Albert, William and Daniel, appear to have died and been buried at Lake Condah Mission, which may reflect the narrowing of life options for Aboriginal people in the district as time went on. Importantly, we know that Flora was of the Krokitch or White Cockatoo moiety and, given matrilineal moiety descent, Jacky would have been of Gamadj or Black Cockatoo moiety.

Because the language information in this dialogue appears to mix information from both these languages, we present both here, with the original Mount Gambier material presented as Box 6.1 and the original Wonnin material as Box 6.2.

Box 6.1: Dialogue relating to 'Corroboirè' labelled Mount Gambier

Put on your pipe clay	5	Gŏt-inŷaŷ-pēē
Get ready to begin	5	Wot-grōōng-ngāŷ
Now girls make a fire	5	Ngrang-gŭrk-mring-a-ween
Now, women, sit down	5	Ninya-ka-ngrang-gŭrk
You must sing	5	Laūrt-big-gah

Source: SLV MS 6290, p. 228; adapted by authors.

Box 6.2: Dialogue relating to 'Corroboirè' labelled Wonnin

Put on your pipe clay	6	Gŏt-āŷ-gat-kar-witty-wan
Get ready to begin	6	Yōō-arp-pawan-mot-tay-ngyat-māŷring
Now girls make a fire	6	Bŭlla-bŭllay-warrōōnēē-*wirram*
Now, women, sit down	6	Ngyāŷng-gang-ngŭn
You must sing	6	Nei-wee-ah

Source: SLV MS 6290, p. 228; adapted by authors.

The last three lines of each of these appear to have been mixed up. For example, in the third line, the word for 'woman' (translated by the compiler of the manuscript as 'girls') is given as *Ngrang-gŭrk* for Mount Gambier and *Bŭlla-bŭllay* for Wonnin. An examination of all the records listed in Blake (2003a, 2003b) makes it clear that the Bunganditj word for 'woman' is **pa(r)la-pa(r)la** and the Warrnambool word is **n(g)arang-kurk**. On the basis of this, we suggest that the third to fifth sentences in these dialogues have been confused; however, the first and second sentences appear to be correctly assigned.

In Bunganditj the word for 'clay' is **pi**. This word is regularised by Blake (2003a) as **piyi**, but the original sources are spelled *bee* or *pee*. Stewart (1880: 127) says of this word '*Be* – pipeclay (pronounced short)', suggesting **pi**. The Warrnambool form is **pik**, so the first sentence of the Mount Gambier dialogue in Box 6.1 is therefore probably Bunganditj. Our analysis of it is presented in (6.2):

(6.2) *Put on your pipe clay*

Gŏt-inŷaŷ-pēē

kutin(y)-i **pi**

paint-IMP (pipe) clay

'Put on your/the pipe clay!'

We are unable to offer an analysis of the second line of the Mount Gambier dialogue.

For the third to fifth lines, we take the Bunganditj forms to be those listed by the compiler of the manuscript as 'Wonnin'. Our analysis of the third line is presented as (6.3):

(6.3) *Now girls make a fire*

Bŭlla-bŭllay-warrōōnēē-wirram

pa(r)la-pa(r)la-i	**warrun-i**	**warnam**
woman-?	light-IMP	fire

'Women! Light the fire!'

Note

The compiler gives the form *Warrŏōnee-wirram* in an earlier sentence in the Mount Gambier dialogue as meaning 'make a fire'.

Our analysis of line 4 is given as (6.4):

(6.4) *Now, women, sit down*

Ngyāŷng-gang-ngŭn

nging(g)a-ngan

sit-?

'(They) sat down.'

Our analysis of the fifth line of the dialogue (also erroneously listed under Wonnin) is given as (6.5):

(6.5) *You must sing*

Nei-wee-ah

nhiwiya

sing

'Sing!'

Note that Mathews (1903a) gives *nēwia* 'sing'.

6.2 Songs recorded by Norman Tindale

In 1941, Norman Tindale published two articles with related recordings of songs sung[3] by Milerum (Clarence Young) from the South East region of South Australia (Limestone Coast). While most of the songs recorded here were from the Tangane or Tanganekald language of South Australia, there

3 The recordings, originally made on wax cylinders and later transferred to disc, are held in the South Australian Museum in Archive Collections / Dr Norman Barnett Tindale / Series AA338/11 / Clarence Long series (SA) 1937-38.

are eight songs associated with the 'Buandik ['Buŋanditj] tribe' recorded on 22 November and 2 December 1937. In an earlier article, Tindale (1937) had listed eight types of songs recorded from Milerum:

a. 'Dream' Songs or Pekere
b. Magical Songs
c. Songs associated with Sickness and Death
d. Totemic Songs
e. Hunting Songs
f. Dramatic Songs and Epics
g. Fighting Songs
h. Songs Demonstrating Public Opinion.

In the 1941 paper, he stated that:

> The older (pre-European) songs of the present series are associated with: 1. sickness and death; 2. hunting; 3. mythological and totemic stories; 4. magic; 5. personal experiences and adventures; 6. drama. They touch on many aspects of native life which throw much light on the culture of the vanished folk, memory of whom has lingered only in the minds of a few survivors of the aborigines.

Ellis (1964) contains a section of musical commentary of the whole group of songs collected by Tindale, presumably including the Bunganditj. She does not present any musical transcriptions in the book, but states that 'there seem to be no specific differences in the music of the various types of songs listed here' (1964: 338).

In more detailed comments (1964: 339–40), Ellis went on to observe that:

> The general characteristics of the music are entirely different from those of the sacred music of Central Australia. These differences are particularly noticeable during the process of transcribing. While in the Aranda music great difficulty was experienced in achieving any satisfactory method of notating pitch, the Tanganekald music fits well in Western notation. But the ease of transcribing isorhythmic music has been replaced by the difficulties arising from the great freedom and irregularity of rhythm in this music from the Coorong.

Ellis published a musical transcription of one of the Tanganekald songs, which is number 15 in Ellis (1966: 186–88). It appears that she did not transcribe any of the Bunganditj songs.

Other observations that Ellis made about the whole group of songs were that 'the downward trend of melodies … is present to a certain degree', though she added that the descent (i.e. vocal pitch descent) 'is less consistent and more gradual' than that observed for Central Australia. She went on to add that 'the songs do not end in the low register', by which we take it to mean the songs do not end on the lowest note of the melodic range. Ellis also added that the songs tended to be divided into sections (as we also observe with Stan Day's songs, see section 2.2). Furthermore, she noted that the songs included a descending passage that 'is often glissando', by which we take it she refers to what we have called a pitch slide observed in some of Stan Day's songs and also in those recorded by von Luschan (see section 2.8). She also observed that these songs included leaps of an octave or around an octave (1964: 339–40), also observed in the Stan Day and von Luschan songs.

The fact that she writes about the 'process of transcribing' suggests that her transcriptions of at least some of these songs may exist. At present, these have not been identified.

The songster who sang these songs was Milerum. He died at the age of about 72, shortly before the publication of the 1941 paper. Tindale described him as 'one of the last links with the old life of the people of the South-East of South Australia'. His biography, written by Norman Tindale, describes him as an Australian ethnologist whose grandparents had avoided contact with white people for as long as possible.[4] Milerum's recordings, now held in the South Australian Museum, are of high quality, performed with clarity and precision, and we regret that we cannot present musical transcriptions and musicological analysis of them, save for the Guichen Bay song for which we have Alice Moyle's transcription (see section 6.2.1).[5]

We present the text of each of these songs as they were published by Tindale. Despite Tindale's glossing of these songs, in most cases we cannot relate most of the words in these songs to the other sources of the language that are found in Blake (2003a). As Barry Blake (pers. comm.) observed, 'none of the Bunganditj songs in Tindale seem to be Bunganditj, although several have a few Bunganditj words'. Does this suggest a special song language?

4 Norman B. Tindale, 'Milerum (1869–1941)', *Australian Dictionary of Biography*, National Centre of Biography, The Australian National University, published first in hardcopy in 1986, accessed 2 July 2019, adb.anu.edu.au/biography/milerum-7572/text13217.

5 Some of Milerum's songs have been arranged into Western notation by Becky Llewellyn (1998) with the words set in English rather than language. None of the Bunganditj songs were included.

Or perhaps these songs were sung by the Bunganditj but the language was actually from a remote place. One possible clue to explaining this is found in Tindale (1974: 67), which has a map of the 'place names of seven of the clans of the Tanganekald on the Coorong of South Australia'. In the clan closest to Bunganditj territory, the Nankandoli, there is a place name spelled by Tindale as ['Puŋanditjiŋ].[6] Perhaps this place name indicates a connection between the Bunganditj and the Ngarrindjeri (including the Tanganekald) that is not well understood.

Tindale (1941: 239) was able to classify the three emu songs into three different types (see section 6.1). They are surely rich in cultural and linguistic information, and it is much to be regretted that we cannot give a better analysis of these songs.

Table 6.3: Bunganditj songs recorded in Tindale

Name of song	Tindale page reference	Section
Song of Guichen Bay	236	6.2.1
Song of Baudin Rocks	236	6.2.2
A Bunganditj Mimikur (or Bullroarer) song from Mt Gambier	236	6.2.3
A Bunganditj Hunter's song from Millicent	237	6.2.4
Bunganditj Dancing song from Millicent	237	6.2.5
Bunganditj Emu song from Mount Benson	238	6.2.6
A second Bungaditj Emu song, called Kupabina, from Biscuit Flat	238	6.2.7
A third Bunganditj Emu song, called Wirewiruk	239	6.2.8

Source: Tindale (1941); adapted by authors.

The list of songs as Tindale named them, with their sources, is presented in Table 6.3. Note that although the first two songs are not explicitly named as Bunganditj, the 'Song of Guichen Bay' is identified as originating with a Bunganditj speaker, Patpul, and both it and the 'Song of Baudin Rocks' refer to places that are within Bunganditj territory on Tindale's map (albeit only just) and by the description of Smith (1880: ix) that states that Bunganditj went up to Lacepede Bay. Thus both songs are included here.

6 This refers to a place on the Coorong that is named on Google Maps as 'Stinking Waterhole' at lat 35.956349 S, long 139.455076 E.

The section containing these songs is introduced by Tindale (1941) as follows:

> *Disc No. 4* – Same Series. Songs of the Buandik ['Buŋanditj] Tribe, Robe, South Australia, 2 December 1937.

6.2.1 Song of Guichen Bay

The first song, the 'Song of Guichen Bay', was composed in colonial times and relates to the construction of a new road to Guichen Bay. The text and Tindale's notes are presented as Box 6.3:

Box 6.3: Song of Guichen Bay

'Endjeligatjun	ŋarum	gamun 'ga:wun (repeat)	'mola'pan
Place name-at		stand-and-look-around	(mo:lakinju
			to turn when walking)
'Wiŋgau	'gaduba	'kutjubei	
Place name	moving towards	Guichen Bay	

"Standing on the hill (at Watul, swamps on Section 472, Hundred of Waterhouse), we see the winding track. To walk around to Wingau we head for Kutjubei."

This song of the Post-European period tells of the old road to Guichen Bay (Kutjubei, as pronounced in this song) and was originated by Patpul, of the ['Buŋanditj] Tribe, whose home was at Robe.

The old native track from Watul to Wingau wandered through the sandhills and along the beach. White men cut a new road to the Salt Lakes where it turned west towards Wingau. The construction was authorised in 1865 and this dates the song as in the late '60's. ['Wingau] is the old native camp, within the present township site of Robe, beside the fresh water lake. The Tanganekald called the place Windau. ['Kutjubei] = ['Kutjubeia] (native acceptance of Baudin's name Guichen Bay) was applied by the natives to the vicinity of the salt lake near Section 299, Hundred of Waterhouse, its former name having been lost or discarded. Incidentally [Pa'rame:ja] or ['Purami'ja] was the name for the Bluff at Robe, the former camp where the old jail stands.

Source: Tindale (1941: 236); adapted by authors.

Linguistic notes

Since most of the words in the song are place names, comparison with the other sources of the Bunganditj language recorded in Blake (2003a) is only possible for the words *gamun 'ga:wun* 'stand-and-look-around', *'mola'pan* 'to turn when walking' and *'gaduba* 'moving towards'. Nothing resembling these forms with similar meanings is found in Blake (2003a).

Although we can say very little about the linguistics of the song, there is a musical analysis done by Alice Moyle (1968). This transcription has been entered into the Finale program, as is presented here as Figure 6.1:

Figure 6.1: Musical analysis of the Song of Guichen Bay by Moyle

Source: Moyle (1968); Collection of the Queen Victoria Museum and Art Gallery, Launceston, Tasmania.

This song has a tonal centre of B, and form similar to a minor scale.

Moyle's version had a slightly different text from that published in Tindale. For example, the first two words in Tindale are *'Endjeligatjun ŋarum*, whereas Moyle had *en-dje-li ŋa-rum*. In the transcription presented here, <ŋ> has been changed to <ng>.

Based on Moyle's transcription, the full text in the recording might be expected to have taken the form given in example (6.6), where the opening phrase *Endjeli ngarum gamun gawun mo* is repeated a different number of times before the line final *molapan*. Moyle's transcription also includes similar final vocables to those that we heard when we listened to the recording of the Marditjali song, also sung by Milerum (see section 2.12).

(6.6) Endjeli ngarum gamun gawun mo x 3 molapan
Winggau gaduba kutjubei
Endjeli ngarum gamun gawun mo x 2 molapan
Winggau gaduba kutjubei
Endjeli ngarum gamun gawun mo x 6 molapan
Winggau gaduba kutjubei
Endjeli ngarum gamun gawun mo x 4 molapan
Winggau gaduba kutjubei
Ga (puramin) ei hei wo whi

Alice Moyle made a number of observations about the music of this song, comparing it to the music of Tasmanian people. She noted a distinction between the melodic direction of the Tasmanian songs that she described as 'bi-directional', whereas the mainland examples (including the Song of Guichen Bay) 'descend more or less directly from the highest not to the lowest' (1968: 5). We can add that the melody appears to follow a minor key structure and could be regarded as being in B minor.

Moyle established the presence of a tonic note in the song of Guichen Bay, writing that (1968: 5):

> after this level has been affirmed (by repetition and short, appogiatura-like descents) in the Bunganditj sample, there is an immediate rise to a tone at the upper boundary. It would seem then that the 'tonic', more strongly emphasised in the Australian [i.e. mainland] examples, is a sign for re-commencement of the main (descending) melodic movement. Moreover in any one Australian song 'item' … there may be more than one such melodic re-commencement.

Moyle also observed that the word for Guichen Bay, *kutjubei*, was a borrowed word, and that its use was 'reserved for the lowest (as well as the uppermost) terminating tones'. In other words, it is found on the lowest note, B2, as in bars 8, 9 and 22, as well as on the highest note, C4#, in bars 36 and 37 near the end of the song. We add that there is a descending glissando of approximately an octave followed by three calls.

The rhythmic structure of the song is enhanced by percussion, performed by sticks, which are also notated by Moyle in Figure 6.1. We assume that the sticks were clapped on the stressed beats of the song, and that, as a consequence, this song had a very regular metre.

We have had the opportunity to listen to some of the Tanganekald (Ngarrindjeri) songs that Milerum sang, discussed by Ellis (1964) (and also transcribed by Llewellyn 1998). The Tanganekald songs that we have been able to listen to contain several songs with octave leaps as well as sections where there is a rapid repetition of pitches sounding a minor third. Differences between those songs and the song of Guichen Bay are some short phrases on one or two pitches after longer phrases, especially for songs 1, 4 and 5, and the number of octave leaps. They also lack the final vocables present in the song of Guichen Bay and the other songs discussed in this section.

6.2.2 Song of Baudin Rocks

This song is presented as Box 6.4. The Baudin Rocks are two small 'islands' off Boatswain Point, at the north end of Guichen Bay. They are located at 37.0881499 S, 139.72299 E.

Box 6.4: Song of Baudin Rocks

'Tunuŋa		'bial ' bial	'ŋawurinje
Look out (from Kripangulu,		Place name	"big island"
near Mount Benson)		(Baudin Rocks)	
'gari bu:l	(h)'edno	'garibi'o:ŋi	'maiba
a few long steps	etenoija	and stepping out	
(emu strides)	full of rage	(gari = emu)	

The meaning of this song, word for word, was obscure to Milerum. It has only a few words in it but "a great deal of meaning". It is connected with a legend of the "Emu and Native Companion." The song tells how the emu people were trapped on Baudin Rocks by a sudden rise of water, supposed to have been caused by the native companions, who watched out from Kripangulu and saw the enraged male parading about ("stepping out") in a display of anger at the trick played on him by his traditional enemies.

Source: Tindale (1941: 236); adapted by authors.

Linguistic notes

Blake (2003a) regularises the word for 'emu' in a number of forms, **kapir**, **kawir**, **krapa**, **krawer**, all of which have initial **k-**. He also lists the form **karipun** based on the forms in the third emu song (see section 6.2.8). Otherwise we can find no words in this song that relate to the other sources for Bunganditj listed in Blake (2003a).

Tentative observations based on listening to the recording[7]

On the recording, Milerum sang the first line up to and including *garibul* four times, with the fourth singing of that line being higher in pitch. Then, commencing with a long note on the syllable o, he sang the second line.

This was followed by a fifth singing of the first line up to and including *garibul*, and then a sixth singing finishing with something that sounded like *tununga nge*.

This was followed by a set of vocables that we noted down as mm *mm mm mm we wo wi*, similar in rhythm to those in the Marditjali song – see Figure 2.25 in section 2.12. These final vocables are similar to those transcribed by Alice Moyle for the Song of Guichen Bay (see Figure 6.1).

6.2.3 Mimikur (Bullroarer) song

The third of Tindale's songs is presented in Box 6.5:

Box 6.5: A Bunganditj Mimikur (or Bullroarer) song from Mount Gambier

'Matujeire	'wat paiju	baŋara:na:	'anjaŋ	'koinja
A woman's name			came home at last	
'mor	'waŋunjup	'je:garam	'muŋungein	
they've come together		woman departs from camp (seen by husband)		
'weijan'gori	dolamboinja	anjeŋkoiŋja	repeat	Ne'rokan.
weijankar	refuses	come back to her home		Die!

7 One of the authors (Stephen Morey) was able to spend a relatively short time listening to each of these recordings and make some tentative notes that we hope will be useful for future researchers. A more detailed analysis will hopefully follow when these songs can be transcribed with the same care as the Song of Guichen Bay.

This song has come down from the remote past. It tells of an ancestral woman, Matujeire, who abandoned her husband and went with another man; it is a bullroarer-magic-song, sung whenever there is any trouble between man and wife which may lead to boning and revengeful killings. Matujeire left her husband; she went with another man; her friends said "Carry on, we will keep your husband's anger away." A quarrel developed. Other friends said, "Listen to your husband, you have a good man, don't heed those bad men friends of yours." The incidents of this traditional event were enacted as a dance, made topical by being applied to new instances. "pieces" being put in to "make it fit" "Old songs properly used mean a great deal" and make the new troubles "come right". In singing the song, Milerum ended in with an appropriate expression of condemnation.

As remarked previously, the force of community control was strongly fortified by the use of song and the power of ridicule in them.

Source: Tindale (1941: 236–37); adapted by authors.

Most of the words as glossed by Tindale do not correspond with other sources. However, we suggest that the word ['weijan'gori] that refers to the woman may be the same as **witjiniya** 'white woman', for which there are two sources: *witchinear*, recorded by Stewart in Curr (1887, 3: 460); and *wei-ginya* (which could possibly be regularised as **wikiniya**). Note that this word has a final [-ri] on a word relating to a human, which is also found in the name *Panangharry* that is based on the word for 'brother-in-law', **panang**. (See discussion at beginning of chapter.)

The word [Ne'rokan] 'Die!' is also based on the root **nra/nera** 'die'.

Tentative observations based on listening to the recording

On the recording, Milerum sang the text at least four times, but not all parts were repeated. There were a number of cries/vocables followed by one more repetition.

6.2.4 Hunter's song

The fourth of Tindale's songs is presented in Box 6.6:

Box 6.6: A Bunganditj Hunter's song from Millicent

'Wialpunul	'gurinje	'galpe'mun	'wareindji
Rise-early	good hope, full of hope	crawling	thighs and knees, crawling on knees
'buri:n	bar'elinje	danbalawan	
(could not get clear)	something follows (bad spirit or bad will of someone on camp)		
'galajeir			
pick up (weapons, galajera) for a quarrel			

Early morning, rising full of hope for game, crawling on knees all in vain, evil wishes are following; pick up weapons for a quarrel.

An old song, first heard by Milerun [sic] when a youth. It was sung by old men of Reedy Creek, who obtained it from the Bunganditj people at a gathering at Millicent. It describes how early in the morning a man goes out hunting full of hope; he smokes himself over a fire to remove scent and evil influences, prepares and smokes his weapons also; with sufficient weapons to ensure good fortune, he sets out in high spirits; unable to come near game even by crawling, he returns to his camp in quarrelsome mood. With its staccato and impressionistic recording of the changing moods of a hunter's day, this native song reveals a mature, if primitive, style.

Source: Tindale (1941: 237); adapted by authors.

This hunting song was followed by an associated dancing song, presented in section 6.2.5.

Barry Blake (pers. comm.) examined the text of this song and suggested that there are some resemblances that are 'not too strong' with Tanganekald. The words that bear some similarity to Tanganekald are *galajeir* 'pick up (weapons, *galajera*) for a quarrel'. This may be related to Tanganekald *kaieŋgl* 'weapon'. The first word of the second line may be Tanganekald *puri* 'attacks, one who challenges'.

Tentative observations based on listening to the recording

The first verse lower pitch, with a word similar to *[w]angal* spoken before the first verse. It was repeated six more times at a higher pitch.

This was followed by a set of vocables that we transcribed as *he he wo* similar to those transcribed by Alice Moyle for the song of Guichen Bay (see Figure 6.1).

6.2.5 Dancing song

The third of Tindale's songs is presented in Box 6.7:

Box 6.7: A Bunganditj Dancing song from Millicent

'Wiraŋinj	'go:ta	'Moro'bia		Moto:n		
What's wrong		I'll fight him		come here		
(says the wife)		(says the man to himself)				
'golen'en	'waðaware	'iŋama:	'denmau			
man's name	everyone	watches	comes out			
			(the other man)			
laŋenje	'warai	'warai	denbula	'waŋan	'warai	'warai
rush together			what's the trouble about (they ask)			
'denbula	wananji	bulinji				
what's the trouble		dust				
(others come to fight)						

"What's wrong?" asks the wife. "I'll fight them!" he mutters. "Come here, Golangolan." Everyone watches; out they step; they step together. "What's the trouble?" they cry. All rush to fight. "What's the trouble?" Dust flies.

The song describes how the unsuccessful hunter vents his spleen and causes a general fight among those in camp; some rush into the scrimmage even before the have learned its origin.

Source: Tindale (1941: 237–38); adapted by authors.

We can find no resemblances between any of the words in this song and any existing vocabulary lists for either Ngarrindjeri or Bunganditj (Barry Blake, pers. comm.).

Tentative observations based on listening to the recording

The singing starts with a long vocable **o**. We did not note down how many repetitions were sung, but did note that the singing finished with a long final note sung on a vocable **e**. A final word that was something like *nyango* was then sung.

This was followed by a set of vocables that we noted down as mm *mm mm mm we mm he wo*, similar in rhythm to those in the Marditjali song – see Figure 2.25 (section 2.12). These final vocables are also similar to those transcribed by Alice Moyle for the song of Guichen Bay (see Figure 6.1).

6.2.6 Emu song from Mount Benson

This song, together with the other two emu songs, is stated to be from Mount Benson, which is located on the coast at 37.1059946 S, 139.7509372 E. This location is at the northernmost end of the Bunganditj territory. Nevertheless, only a very small number of words can be recognised from the other Bunganditj sources.

The first emu song is presented in Box 6.8:

Box 6.8: Bunganditj Emu song from Mount Benson

'Waŋaja:ndjelaŋ	'waiga'waren		'gol'gol	repeat
Early-morning	I cannot travel far		eggs	
	(says emu female)		(within me)	
liŋamun	'ŋidia	'gindawiri:ŋ		'ga:wen
beware	eagle	don't go far away		be careful
'waŋejaindjelaŋ	'waiga'waren	'gulu:r	'liŋamun	'ŋidia
early morning	not travel far	eggs	beware	eagle
		(gol gol)		
'gandawereiŋ	'ga:wen			
don't go far	be careful			

This describes incidents in the "Story of the Emu" an important myth of the Buandik people. Two emus were walking along the Mount Benson Range. The female was heavy with eggs.'

"We will go to that range and make a nest," she said. It was a rather open place with a few mallee trees and bushes. From the next range she saw a place with bracken ferns ['mol:ari], "That will do." At the same moment she saw an eagle's nest above it in the trees.

"He will not harm us," they said to themselves and made their nest. One egg came. The male eagle swooped down and looked at the emu woman. The other egg came. She used to feed all day while the male sat on the nest. He went out at night to feed, returning by devious tracks to the nest at dawn. With the young ones came trouble; the emus were kept busy defending their young from the eagle. This song is one of warning. "Women, beware of the eagle who comes to look at you."

Source: Tindale (1941: 238); adapted by authors.

Underneath the transcription is written: 'Disc No. 5 – "Tanganekald Tribe, Coorong, South Australia, 21 December 1937"'.

Blake (pers. comm.) has pointed out that there are two words in this song that can be related to other Bunganditj sources. ['ŋidia] 'eagle' is found in several sources as **ngirri**, and ['gol'gol] 'egg' is **kula**.

Tentative observations based on listening to the recording

The first line was introduced with a set of vocables that we noted down as **o o o ngal** and the line was sung as far as the word *lingamun*. Then the same line was sung twice more at a higher pitch as far as the word *golgol*. Then the remaining section was sung, speeding up.

This was followed by a set of cries/vocables similar to those described in the previous song.

6.2.7 Second emu song (Kupabina)

The second emu song is presented in Box 6.9:

Box 6.9: A second Bunganditj Emu song, called Kupabina, from Biscuit Flat

'waŋa	'jandjelaŋ	'waigawaren	'golu:r	a:n	'dakinjin
early-in-the-morning (hear noise of eagles)			eggs	look around quickly	
'jira	'dumaŋi	'ŋiraŋgo:nj	jondinj	'baŋar 'baŋar	
start up (to guard)	rush-in	fighting	jumps (eagle)	determined	
ŋawei we:r		'dakinjin		'jira	
return to attack (giving no peace)		look around (as if surprised)		start up (take up position of guard when surprised)	
dumaŋi	'ŋiraŋgo:nj				
rush-in	fighting				

This is a short song; sung through once. Sticks were used to beat time. It ends with the [wi! Wo!] flourish common to several other songs.

Both male and female emu had to share in the defence of their young; the female broke her rule of staying away and feeding all day, for both birds had to protect their young against the onslaughts ("jumps") of the eagle. The emu man who sang it was Parpul's brother (sociological) who was also a brother to Wati, the hero of several songs mentioned in Part .1 of this series.

Source: Tindale (1941: 238–39); adapted by authors.

The word ['golu:r] glossed by Tindale as 'eggs' is similar to Bunganditj **kula** 'egg', but this is the only resemblance to other Bunganditj sources (Blake, pers. comm).

Tentative observations based on listening to the recording

Milerum sang the verse in full, starting with a word that we notated as **angurr** before the initial *wanga*. The pitch rose after singing the word *yandjelang*.

At the end of the full verse, Milerum sang a vocable *ho* and then the words *wangai dakinjin jira dumangi niranggonj*, finishing with a set of vocables that we noted down as *mm mm mm mm he wo wi*, similar in rhythm to those in the Marditjali song – see Figure 2.25 (section 2.12). These final vocables are also similar to those transcribed by Alice Moyle for the song of Guichen Bay (see Figure 6.1).

6.2.8 Third emu song (Wirewiruk)

The third emu song is presented in Box 6.10:

Box 6.10: A third Bunganditj Emu song, called Wirewiruk

Bapindj	garapun	maŋin	ŋidi	bapindj	garapun
mother	emu	hovering	eagle	mother	emu
warawara	garibun	moribi ŋawuru			
legs	emu	defeated			
(legs fighting)					

Sticks were used to beat the time; the tempo slows towards the end and terminates with the wi! Wo! Flourish.

When an emu falls down on its back and strikes out with its feet it can hit with considerable effect. The emu man who made this song watched one in combat with the eagle and sang this song about the adventure.

"The mother emu and the hovering eagle; the mother emu and her fighting legs. The emu has defeated it."

Source: Tindale (1941: 239); adapted by authors.

Three words in this song have a resemblance to other Bunganditj sources: [bapindj] 'mother', which is **pap** in Bunganditj; [ŋidi] 'eagle', which is **ngirri**; and [garibun] 'emu', which allowing for metathesis, is **kapir** in Bunganditj (Blake, pers. comm.).

Tentative observations based on listening to the recording

Milerum's singing commenced with a vocable **o**. Our impression was that the text was sung twice and then three more times on a higher pitch gradually heading downwards in pitch.

It slowed down at the end, followed by a set of vocables that we noted down as mm *mm mm mm wi mm e wo wi*, similar in rhythm to those in the Marditjali song – see Figure 2.25 (section 2.12). These final vocables are also similar to those transcribed by Alice Moyle for the song of Guichen Bay (see Figure 6.1).

6.3 Mount Gambier song

As discussed above (section 1.5.2), MS 6290, once believed to have been written by William Thomas, was in fact produced at Pentridge Prison under the guidance of Col. Champ. One song, headed Mount Gambier, was probably sung by Monkey Neddy or King Tom's Billy. We have not been able to learn much more about them, save that they were in prison in 1861. The song is also found in the Royal Anthropological Institute of Great Britain and Ireland MS 38, p. 357.

The text of this song as found in MS 6290 is presented as Box 6.11:

Box 6.11: Mount Gambier song

(Mount Gambier)

Ng-āŷ-marrōōnāŷ-banyŭll-walbin-gŏroŭn-

wirrāŷ-dadŷai-gŭinan-ngamāī-walpin-

gŏbarrāŷ-ba-tahgŏnōōn-bŭnbal-la-kalōīgn

min-karŏin-bŏ-yōw-wa-gōōlŭrŭ-gōōlōōrŭ-

dogÿlōōrma-ŷarra-marrōōnay-banyŭll-

walbin-gŏrŏŭn-wirray-dadŷai-yinnanng-

amāī-walpin-gobarray-ba-tahgōnōōn-bŭnbal-la-kaloign-min-kŭrŏm-bŏ-yōw/-wa-

gōōlŭrŭ-gōōlōōrŭ-dŏgȳlōōrma-yarra

Translation

Blackfellow dreams that he goes out to fish in a large freshwater lake-and that he sees the water in waves like the sea, splashing about in the boat.

Source: SLV MS 6290, p. 231; adapted by authors.

It has two rather long lines that are almost identical. Example (6.7) presents the text rearranged into these two lines.

(6.7) Ng-āŷ-marrōōnāŷ-banyŭll-walbin-gŏroŭn-wirrāŷ-dadŷai-gŭinan-ngamāī-walpin-gŏbarrāŷ-ba-tahgŏnōōn-bŭnbal-la-kalōīgn min-karŏin-bŏ-yōw-wa-gōōlŭrŭ-gōōlōōrŭ-dogȳlōōrma-ŷarra-

marrōōnay-banyŭll-walbin-gŏrŏŭn-wirray-dadŷai-yinnanng-amāī-walpin-gobarray-ba-tahgōnōōn-bŭnbal-la-kaloign-min-kŭrŏm-bŏ-yōw-wa-gōōlŭrŭ-gōōlōōrŭ-dŏgȳlōōrma-yarra

A suggested regularisation of the song line is presented as (6.8):

(6.8) **ngaimarru nai panyul walpin kurun(y) tatyai yinang-amai walpin kuparai pa takunun(y) panpal-a kaluny min karuny-po-yowa kulurru kulurru tukilurma yara**

We cannot recognise many words in this song as being similar to the other Bunganditj sources. It is likely that the word spelled *gōōlŭrŭ-gōōlōōrŭ*, which we have regularised as **kulurru-kulurru**, is a form of the Bunganditj word for 'fish' regularised by Blake as **kulal**.

6.4 Songs documented by Duncan Stewart

In her 1880 book, Christina Smith gives two songs. The actual collector of the information was Duncan Stewart, her stepson. Of songs in general, she wrote, '[t]he Booandik have no songs, properly so called. The following are two fair specimens', going on to give the songs presented as Box 6.12 and Box 6.13 (Smith 1880: 128). A full analysis of the second song is given in Blake (2003a: 141).

6.4.1 Song 1 – About the Birds

The first of the two songs, 'About the Birds', is presented in Box 189. It is a list of birds and other flying creatures. Perhaps it was a corroboree song, similar to that from central Victoria given in section 3.2.5.

Box 6.12: About the Birds

Yul-yul, thumbal
Kallabal, moonarebal
Nana nan molanin
Korotaa, king nal
Yongo birrit

This is repeated over and over.

Translation of the foregoing:–

Fly March fly, beetle
Fly beetle, bat, night
Parrot, little parrot
Wattle bird, minah bird

Source: Smith (1880: 128); adapted by authors.

Our analysis is presented as (6.9):

(6.9) *Yul-yul, thumbal*
Fly March fly,

yul yul	**thumbal**
house fly	march fly

'House fly, March fly.'

Kallabal, moonarebal
Beetle, Fly Beetle

kalapal	**munarapal**
beetle	flying beetle

'Beetle, flying beetle.'

Notes

Both of these words, and also the word for 'march fly' in the previous line, carry a final syllable **-pal**, which may have been a suffixal form relating to small creatures.

The word 'centipede' in Blake (2003a) is **kala-mana** – analysed as literally **kalayi** 'many' + **ma(r)na** 'hand'. However, the word given in the song as 'beetle' also has an initial **kala-**, and we would not expect this to be a word for 'many'. It may be that the initial of 'centipede' and 'beetle' is the same element.

The word for 'flying' beetle' in this song is similar to two other words for animals, **muna** 'penguin' and *moon-o-erp* 'mosquito' (also documented by Stewart in Smyth 1880).

Nana nan molanin

bat, night

nganin nganin	**mula-nin**
bat	night-?

'Bat, night.'

Notes

The Bunganditj word for 'night' is **mul**. There is a suffix **-(a)nin**, which is also present on the word for 'bat'. It is possible that this line refers to a single animal.

Korotaa, king nal

parrot, little parrot

korrota	**kayingal**
parakeet	parrot

'Parakeet and parrot.'

Note

The word for 'parrot' seems to have had two forms, **kalingal** from the spelling *kal-ingal* (Stewart in Smith 1880) and **kayingal**, spelled *gai-ing-al* by Thomas.

Yongo birrit
wattle bird, minah bird

yunggu	**pirrit**
wattle bird	minah

'Wattle bird, Minah.'

6.4.2 Song 2 – About the Whale

The song 'About the Whale' is presented in Box 6.13. The story of this song may well be related to the Kondoli dreaming of the Ngarrindjeri. Kondoli was a man with fire, but while he was dancing, the skylark (**krilbalu**) speared him and ran away with the fire. Then the whale, shark, stingray and seal dived into the water (Berndt and Berndt 1993: 450, Appendix 4: 104).[8] The words **kantapul** and **kondoli** ('whale' in Ngarrindjeri) are somewhat similar.

Box 6.13: About the Whale

Waton aa young naa
Konterbul walonaa
Young naa konterbul

This also is repeated over and over. Translation:–

The whale is come,
And thrown up on land.

Source: Smith (1880: 128); adapted by authors.

Our translation is presented as example (6.10). This is based on that in Blake (2003a: 141), but we have put in the full root form of the word 'throw'.

(6.10) *waton aa young naa*

watha-nha	**yungga-nha**
come-PRF.PART	throw-PRF.PART

'(It is) come and thrown.'

8 This story is being reanalysed by Mary-Anne Gale with Phyllis Williams under the title *Kondoli Dreaming*.

konterbul walonaa
The whale is come
kantapul watha-nha
whale come-PRF.PART
'The whale is come.'

young naa konterbul
And thrown up on land
yungga-nha kantabul
throw-PRF.PART whale
'Thrown (up) is the whale.'

Milerum also sang a whale song for Tindale (1937: 112). This song has been transcribed (but set with English language text) by Becky Llewyllyn (1998).

6.5 Song sung by 'Panangharry'

The last of the Bunganditj songs treated here was documented by 'Panangharry' in an article in the Mount Gambier *Border Watch* on 22 July 1903.[9] The text is presented in Box 6.14. Glencoe is around 20 kilometres north-west of Mount Gambier.[10]

This article is one of several written by 'Panangharry'. In the first of this series in the *Border Watch*, dated 30 May 1903, the author commences with 'Panangharry is partly English and partly Boandick and is intended to convey that all speaking these languages are included in these recollections'. Beyond this, the source of this information is at present not identified.

9 The full text is available online at Panangharry, 'Early Recollections of Glen-Coe, Lake Leake, and the South-East', *Border Watch* (Mount Gambier), 22 July 1903, 4, accessed 30 June 2017, trove.nla.gov.au/newspaper/article/77159439/7602235.
10 Coordinates: 37.6784812 South, 140.0503244 East.

Box 6.14: Boandik song, from 'Panangharry'

EARLY RECOLLECTIONS OF GLENCOE, LAKE LEAKE, AND THE SOUTH-EAST. (By Panangharry) No. 4.

Bring Bring Wadyoeng,

Bellum und gad yah,

Yore ang mo you ba yong,

Gran bo yun gal lee.

Repeat ad lib. This is a Boandik song, but I am unable to put it into English. There may possibly be someone in the South-East who would remember it, and be able to explain its meaning.

Source: *Border Watch*, 22 July 1903, p. 4; adapted by authors.

Our suggested regularisation of this song is given as (6.11):

(6.11) **p'rring p'rring wat(j)ayang**
palam-an katja
yuriyang moyu payung
krambu yung(g)ali

Notes

On the first line, the first word *bring* could be the word for 'dog, kangaroo catching', regularised by Blake as **p'rring(g)a**.

The second word *wadyoeng* could be a form of **watayi** 'come'. If so, the first line might be **p'rring(g)a p'rring(g)a watayang** 'the kangaroo hunting dogs are coming'.

The first word of the second line may be **palam**, a form that is found in one of the Bunganditj place names – Mount Gambier, Peak of, *Ereng balam* 'eaglehawk' given by Stewart in Smith (1880: 132). The more frequent Bunganditj word for 'eaglehawk' is **ngirri**. There is a Bellum Hotel halfway between Mount Gambier and the coast to the south at Port MacDonnell.

In the last line, the first word *gran bo* might **krambu** 'vomit' and the second word *yun gal lee* might be based on the root **yung(g)a** 'throw'.

7

Warrnambool songs

Only two songs were documented in the Warrnambool language(s). Dawson (1881), whose records of this group of languages are the most substantial, named two varieties/dialects of the language as *Kuurn kopan noot* 'small lip' and *Peek whurrong* 'kelp lip'. Blake (2003a: 2, 7–12) lists and discusses the names of the other varieties that were listed by Dawson. The term Gunditjmara is widely used by the community today, and was spelled Guṇḍidj by Hercus (1986: 100), with a retroflex stop-nasal cluster medially. Blake (2003a: 2) discusses the use and documented history of this word. Following Blake (2003a), we will use the term Warrnambool language(s).

Although there are very few songs recorded in these languages, some information about the use of song in the area was given by Stähle in information sent to Fison (Tippett collection, TIP 70/10/37 item 3, pp. 3–4):

> The Gournditch-mera believed that the spirits of the deceased father or grandfather occasionally visited the male descendants in dreams and imparted to them charms (songs) against disease or against witchcraft. There were also among them persons who professed to communicate with the spirits of the deceased and to learn from them corrobboree songs and dances and to enquire from them concerning future events. This tribe had no ceremonies of initiation of the young men or young women to manhood or womanhood.

The two songs that we have are a song about the construction of the telegraph written down in State Library of Victoria MS 6290 (see section 7.2), who termed the language *Wonnin*, and the Barnmitt song written down by Isabella Dawson (see section 7.3). This latter song was likely in either the *Kuurn kopan noot* or *Peek whurrong* variety.

In our regularisations of the Warrnambool languages, we will use voiceless stops throughout, following Blake (2003b).

7.1 Musical terminology in the Warrnambool languages

Words relating to song and dance from Dawson (1881) are presented in Table 7.1. Note that these forms were also presented together with the Tjapwurrung words above (section 2.1.2).

Table 7.1: Glossary of words relating to singing in the Warrnambool languages

English	Kuurn kopan noot (small lip)	Peek whurrong (kelp lip)	Blake regularisation of Kuurn kopan noot
Dance, name of	Karweean	Kurween	**karwiyan**
Dance, to dance	Karweean neut	Kurween	**karwiyan**
Dance of gigantic crane	Yakeapeean	Kurween	**yakiyapiya**
Sing	Lærpeean	Lærpeen	**lirpi(ya)**
Song, a song	Lirpeean	Lirpeen	**lirpi(ya)**
Song of bird	Lirpeean	Lirpeen	**lirpi(ya)**
Song of piping crow, or organ bird	Kaaruman	Gnark kueaa	**ngakuwiya**
Stick for beating time	Popok	Popok	**pakap** 'fire stick'
Whistle	Tirng kærann	Wuinja	**thirng kiran, wuindja**
Whistle, by holding the lower lip	Tækærann	Teewirna	**tikira, tiwirna**

Source: From Dawson (1881); adapted by authors.

Robinson (transcribed in Clark 2002: 281) wrote down words in two Warrnambool language varieties, *Tjarcote* (Tc) (spelled **Tjaku(r)t** in Blake 2003a: 12) and *Manemeet*, a variety that Blake was not able to ascribe to one of the language varieties he discussed (2003a: 7–12), but which means 'wild black'. Robinson's words are given in example (7.1):

(7.1) *cone.de.an.nut* (Tc); *car.re.we.nut* (M): little corrobbery at the huts.

undoc.er.de (M); *car.re.we.ar.noot* (Tc): big corrobbery

The second form in each of these lines, *carre we nut* and *car-re-wee-ar-noot*, can be analysed as the root **karwiyan** 'dance' with **-ut,** a third plural subject bound pronoun (Blake 2003a: 37). We thus analyse both of these forms as **karwiyan-ut**, literally 'they (pl.) are dancing'.

Blake also lists the word **muwiyn** for 'corroboree/dance', originally spelled *mo-ein* (SLV MS 6290).

Robinson also wrote *wone de un nun* 'dance', regularised by Blake as **wuindja**. This is similar in form to the Peek whurrong word for 'whistle' written down by Dawson and listed in Table 7.1. We are unsure what the significance of this is, but it may suggest the use of whistle in some dances.

7.1.1 Corroboirè dialogue from Wonnin

As already mentioned (section 6.1.1), the compiler of MS 6290 appears to have confused the Bungaditj (Mount Gambier) and Warrnambool (Wonnin) sentences for the 'Corroboirè' dialogue. We regard the first two sentences from 'Wonnin' as being Warrnambool language, and the final three sentences from the Mount Gambier dialogue as being Warrnambool. The first two lines are presented in Box 7.1 and the last three in Box 7.2.

Box 7.1: 'Wonnin' dialogue relating to 'Corroboirè'

Put on your pipe clay	6	Gŏt-āŷ-gat-kar-witty-wan
Get ready to begin	6	Yōō-arp-pawan-mot-tay-ngyat-māŷring

Source: SLV MS 6290, p. 228 (first two lines); adapted by authors.

Box 7.2: 'Mount Gambier' dialogue relating to 'Corroboirè'

Now girls make a fire	5	Ngrang-gŭrk-mring-a-ween
Now, women, sit down	5	Ninya-ka-ngrang-gŭrk
You must sing	5	Laŭrt-big-gah

Source: SLV MS 6290, p. 228 (last three lines), adapted by authors.

We are unable to offer any analysis of the first line, save that it contains a form similar to **kutin(y)-i**, which was analysed as the imperative of a verb meaning 'paint (pipe-clay)' in Bunganditj. See example (6.2) above.

Our analysis of the second line is presented in (7.2):

(7.2) *Get ready to begin*

Yōō-arp-pawan-mot-tay-ngyat-māŷring

yuwa	**pawa-n**	**mutj-ai-ngatj**	**merring**
hasten	burn-TENS	smoke-?	ground

'Hasten to burn (the fire) and … smoke … the ground.'

The words **pawa** 'burn', **mutj** 'smoke' and **merring** 'ground' are all attested in the Warrnambool sources, but **yuwa** for 'hasten' has been found in only in Bunganditj sources. Nevertheless, we are assuming that the word was also in use in Warrnambool.

The third line is presented as (7.3):

(7.3) *Now girls make a fire*

Ngrang-gŭrk-mring-a-ween

ngarang-kurk	**miring-a**	**wiin**
woman	ground-LOC?	fire

'Women, (make) fire on the ground.'

Blake (2003a: 32) listed **-a** as an ergative suffix and **-i** as a locative suffix, which we would expect here. In Dawson (1881), the locative is written as *-æ* but his illustration of the use of this suffix suggests the form should be /-i/ (see further discussion in Blake 2003a: 32).

The fourth sentence is presented as (7.4):

(7.4) *Now, women, sit down*

Ninya-ka-ngrang-gŭrk

ngingga-ka	**ngarang-kurk**
sit-IMP?	woman

'Sit down, women!'

The most frequently mentioned imperative in Dawson (1881) is *-kæ*, which Blake (2003a: 47) realises as **-ki**. Clearly an imperative is intended in example (7.4), and it is interesting that the case suffix in example (7.3) and the imperative here both have final *-a* in Thomas's transcriptions that correspond to Dawson's *-æ*. Perhaps this represented a dialectal difference.

The fifth sentence, *Laūrt-big-gah* 'you must sing', appears to contain a word for 'sing' that may be related to **lirpi(ya)**, given by Dawson (1881). (See Table 7.1.)

7.2 Wonnin song

As discussed above (section 1.5.2), SLV MS 6290, once believed to have been written by William Thomas, was in fact produced at Pentridge Prison under the guidance of Col. Champ. We think that one song, headed 'Wonnin', was most likely sung by Jackey White, though it might also have been sung by either Monkey Neddy or King Tom's Billy. We have not been able learn much more about Jackey White, save that he was in prison in 1861. The song is also found in the Royal Anthropological Institute of Great Britain and Ireland MS 38, p. 358. The text of this song as found in MS 6290 is presented as Box 7.3:

Box 7.3: Wonnin song

(Wonnin)
Bat-in-yŏ-yĕhrahn-man-tallāŷ-grap-mōōn-
an-ni-yŏ-wenn-ga-than-parrōōp-pangah-
tōōn-baht-in-yŏ-yĕrahuman-tally-grap-
moon-an-in-yo-wenn-ga-than-parōōp-pangahtīm
Translation:
A song about white men using the telegraph, it cannot be translated literally

Source: SLV MS 6290, p. 231; adapted by authors.

The text here contains two lines that are almost identical, but the second commences with a syllable *tōōn*. The rearrangement into two lines is presented as (7.5):

(7.5) Bat-in-yŏ-yĕhrahn-man-tallāŷ-grap-mōōn-an-ni-yŏ-wenn-ga-than-parrōōp-pangah-
tōōn-baht-in-yŏ-yĕrahuman-tally-grap-moon-an-in-yo-wenn-ga-than-parōōp-pangahtīm

A suggested regularisation of the song line is presented as (7.6):

(7.6) **pat-iny-u yerranyman telegraph mun-an ni-yo-weng(g)athan parrup-panga**
tun-pat-iny-u yerranyman telegraph mun-an ni-yo-weng(g)athan parrup-pangat-im

Notes

The word for 'telegraph', spelled by Thomas as *tallāŷ-grap*, is clearly recognisable here. We are not able to suggest glosses for any other words, beyond some speculation, such as that the last word of the line is somehow related to **paruparn** 'Sirius', in some way connecting the telegraph with the stars.

The last word in each line may be intended to be **pangat**. There is a word **pang(g)at** 'sandhill' in Blake (2003a: 142)[1] and perhaps the telegraph line into Warrnambool ran along the sand dunes at some point.

7.3 Barnmitt song, documented by Isabella Dawson

The song recorded by Isabella Dawson is found in an article published in the newspaper *The Australasian*, dated 19 March 1870.[2] The song relates to an evil spirit that attacks children. (For another example of a similar song, see the Hairy Beka chant in section 9.5.1.) The full text of the song is presented in Box 7.4:

Box 7.4: Barnmitt song

WORDS OF A SONG

Barnmitt barnmitt tung-ang koorooketch.

Barnmitt barnmitt tung-ang koorooketch.

Ba'roong tookooenoong.

Yah wirng kah wirng ah.

Yan kaloom ee Nitt.

TRANSLATION, OR MEANING

Evil spirit, evil spirit, come and eat orphans

Evil spirit, evil spirit, come and eat orphans.

Many many children.

Hark to me many many children.

The devil will take you into a dark scrub.

Source: *The Australasian*, 19 March 1870, p. 8; adapted by authors.

1 Thanks to Corey Theatre (pers. comm.) for pointing this out.

2 Isabella Dawson, 'Tha Language of the Aborigines', *Australasian* (Melbourne), 19 March 1870, p. 8.

A fairly complete analysis of this song is possible because of the translation given by Isabella Dawson. This analysis is presented in (7.7):

(7.7) *Barnmitt barnmitt tung-ang koorooketch*
Evil spirit, evil spirit, come and eat orphans
pa(r)nmit pa(r)nmit thang-ang ku(ru)k(a)itj
evil spirit evil spirit eat-PART? orphan
'The *Pa(r)nmit* (evil spirit) is eating the orphans.'

Barnmitt barnmitt tung-ang koorooketch
Evil spirit, evil spirit, come and eat orphans
pa(r)nmit pa(r)nmit thang-ang ku(ru)k(a)itj
evil spirit evil spirit eat-PART? orphan
'The *Pa(r)nmit* (evil spirit) is eating the orphans.'

Ba'roong tookooenoong
Many many children
parung thukuwi-n(y)ung
Many child-3SG.POSS[3]
'(So) many his/her children.'

Yah wirng kah wirng ah
Hark to me many many children
ya wirng ka wirng a
EXCL ear EXCL ear EXCL
'*Ya!* (use your) ear, *Ka!* (your) ear, *A!*'

Yan kaloom ee Nitt
The devil will take you into a dark scrub.
yan(a) kalum?-i ngut
Go scrub?-LOC devil
'The Devil (will) go into the scrub.'

3 This analysis was suggested by Corey Theatre; this suffix is discussed further in Theatre (2018).

Notes

The word *Barnmitt*, regularised as **pa(r)nmit** is not found as one of the many spirits and ghosts listed in Blake (2003b). It is assumed to be the name of the spirit.

The word for 'orphan' is given by Blake (2003b) as **kukitj**, with Dawson's spelling being *kokaitch*. In the song there is an additional **-ru** syllable. We cannot be sure if the word has final **-itj** or **-aitj**.

The words given in Blake (2003b) for 'scrub' – **yarowi**, **wuru-wuruk** and **tarun** – do not resemble the word in the last line of the song. It is possible that the whole word *yan kaloom ee* is a single word **yang(g)alumi**.

8

Maraura and other Paakantyi songs

The Paakantyi group of languages was spoken on the lower Darling, and across the border into Victoria at Yelta. While most of the speakers of Paakantyi languages were in New South Wales, the songs that we have from this area are mostly in the Maraura (Marawara) variety from the south and indeed were mentioned first by Rev. John Bulmer at Yelta in Victoria. Our principal linguistic sources for these languages are outlined in Hercus (1982, 1984 and 1993).

This chapter includes five songs originally documented by Rev. John Bulmer, at Yelta in Victoria. Some of these were also published in Smyth (1878), and they are discussed in section 8.1. In addition, there are two songs recorded by Berndt and Berndt, one sung by Dan Limberry and the second by Jacko; a sound recording of the latter song was made and these two songs are discussed in section 8.2. Third, there is a song from Menindee, collected by Hermann Beckler during the Burke and Wills expedition, and published with a musical transcription in 1868 (section 8.3). Furthermore, there is a song sung by Fletcher, recorded by E.H. Davies and Norman Tindale, for which a sound recording also exists (section 8.4), and finally there is a song published in a newspaper, which is mixed English and Maraura, discussed in section 8.5.

There is in addition some background context about the songs of the Maraura, also termed Wimbaio. Howitt (1904: 366) describes some of the skills of the medicine man, *Mekigar*:

> One of the practices of the Wiimbaio *Mekigar* (medicine-man) was to step among the crowd at a corrobboree, and pick up something off the ground, saying that it was a piece of *nukalo* (quartz) which some *Mekigar* at a distance had thrown at them.

Note that in Bulmer's manuscript, the word for 'doctor' or 'seer' is spelled *makeega* (Campbell 1999).

The medicine-man was called *Mekigar*, from *Meki*, 'eye', or 'to see', otherwise 'one who sees' (Howitt 1904: 380). The making of these medicine men is described in Howitt (1904: 404). The Mekigar had many powers. He could knock down a man in the night with 'a club called *Yuri-battra-piri*, that is, ear-having-club, a club having two corners, i.e. ears', in order to take away kidney fat (Howitt 1904: 367).[1] This word is **Yuri-pathara-pira**, literally 'ears-wide-club'.

Rev. John Bulmer describes a song that he heard performed by Maraura people (Howitt 1904: 416), when referring to well-travelled songs:

> Another instance is a song that was accompanied by a carved stick painted red, which was held by the chief singer.This travelled down the Murray from some unknown source. The Rev. John Bulmer tells me that he saw this performance in the Wiimbaio tribe. Such a song, accompanied by a red stick, was brought into Gippsland from the Melbourne side, and may have even been the above-mentioned one on its return.

One ritual utterance that has been recorded is the word of the messenger of death, who, when bringing the news of death (Howitt 1904: 686):

> walks in a dejected manner on nearing a camp, holding his spear in one hand and letting it rest in the hollow of the other arm. When close to the camp he says '*Dau*' (death) twice, which is the formula suited to the occasion. His face is painted with a little pipe-clay. He walks through the encampment, repeating the word '*Dau*' at each hut, before he sits down, apart from the others, waiting till some friend brings him some food. After a time he again goes into the camp and delivers his news.

1 Howitt (1904: 367) adds that there were two kinds of 'men of other tribes who, they believe, prowled about seeking to kill people. They called them *Thinau-malkin*, that is, "one who spreads a net for the feet," and *Kurinya-matola*, "one who seizes by the throat"'.

8.1 Songs collected by Rev. John Bulmer

The songs recorded by Bulmer were collected when he was based at Yelta, now a suburb of Mildura, in the 1850s. The songs he collected there are listed in Table 8.1:

Table 8.1: Sources for Maraura songs recorded by Bulmer

Name of song (section)	Manuscripts	Campbell (1999) page references	Smyth (1878) page references
Moiety song (8.1.1)	MV XM 94; MV XM 923, p. 7	43	423–24
Sun song (8.1.2)	MV XM 923, pp. 2–3; NLA MS 8006/2, File 9	40	430
Kangaroo song (8.1.3)	NLA MS 8006/2, File 9	-	-
Moon song (8.1.4)	XM 923, pp. 2 and 3	40 and 41	431
Riding across the Murray (8.1.5)	Howitt papers, SLV Box 1054/2 (a), hw0436. pdf, p. 22	27	-

Source: Authors.

8.1.1 Moiety song

The first song recorded by Bulmer is a song related to the moiety system, which in the Paakantyi area was **makwarra** 'eaglehawk' and **kilparra** 'crow'.

Tindale also published a detailed linguistic analysis and context of a story told by Peter Boney about the Eagle and Crow (Tindale 1939). We assume that this Moiety song was one of many that is related to this and other stories.

An important creation figure unnamed in the song but mentioned in the introduction to it is *Nooralie*. Tindale (1939: 245) wrote that:

> ['Wa:ku], or Crow, a man of the ['Ki:lpara] Moiety, formerly lived at one end of Manara Range and ['Ka:nai], or Eagle, a man of the ['Makwora] Moiety, lived at the other. There were noth ['nu:rili] ancestral beings.

In her 1993 dictionary, Hercus gives the name of this being as **Nhuurali**, defined as 'Ancestral Being, particularly the main Creator Ancestor, Crow'. Another story collected by Hercus (1982: 246), 'Eaglehawk and Crow: The Crow's Revenge', also mentions **Nhuurali**, though this story does not directly relate to the song. Berndt and Berndt (1993: 221) pointed out that *Nooralie* might be related to *Nguril*, the creator figure in the language of the Murray River languages (see below the discussion of Pound's song – section 12.4), and *Ngurunderi*, the principal character in the Creation Dreaming of the Ngarrindjeri people of the mouth of Murray River (Berndt and Berndt 1993).[2]

Bulmer (in Campbell 1999: 40) gives the definition of *nooralie* as 'ancient of days', adding that 'an old man would say *nooralipilli ngio* "I am an old man"' (see also Table 8.1). Bulmer's longer description of *Nooralie*'s importance is presented below in Table 8.4, in his introduction to the Sun song.

The similarity of the names of these three 'Creator Ancestors' suggests connections that surely need to be further researched. Our suggestion is that the four songs recorded by Bulmer, this Moiety song, and also the Sun song (section 8.1.2), Kangaroo song (section 8.1.3) and Moon song (section 8.1.4), are all in some way related to these Creation stories.

There are three versions of the Moiety song: one in Smyth (1878, 1: 423–24), clearly based on Bulmer, presented in Box 8.1; another in the Bulmer papers, Museums Victoria, XM 923 (also published in Campbell 1999), presented in Box 8.2; and a third version in a letter from Bulmer to Howitt, MV XM 94, presented in Box 8.3.

Box 8.1: Moiety song, version 1

The Aborigines of the northern parts of Victoria say that the world was created by beings whom they call *Nooralie*–beings that existed a very long time ago. They name a man who is very old *Noorālpily*.† They believe that the beings who created all things had severally the form of the Crow and the Eagle. There was continual war between these two beings, but peace was made at length.

[Footnote on p. 423]

† *Nooran-an-ya* means "far off."

"The Murray natives believe in a Being with supreme attributes, whom they call *Nourelle*; that he lives in the sky, and is surrounded by children born without the intervention of a mother; that *Nourelle* never dies, and that blackfellows go to him, and never die again. They also believe that *Nourelle* created a great serpent, and gave him power over all created things."–*Aboriginal Natives of New South Wales*. Pamphlet by a Colonial Magistrate, 1846.[3]

2 Also see, for example *Ngurunderi, and Aboriginal Dreaming*, South Australian Museum, accessed 26 August 2019, www.samuseum.sa.gov.au/gallery/ngurunderi/.

3 The name of this magistrate appears to have been William Hull. In Smyth (1878, 1: 244), the title of this pamphlet is given more fully as *Remarks on the probable Origin and Antiquity of the Aboriginal Natives of New South Wales*. This was published probably in Melbourne in 1846.

They agreed that the Murray blacks should be divided into two classes – the *Makquarra* or Eaglehawk, and the *Kil-parra* or Crow. The conflict that was waged between the rival powers is thus preserved in song:–

Thinj-ami	*balkee*	*mako*
knee	strike	crow
Nato-panda	*Kambe-ar*	*tono*
Spear	father	of him

The meaning of which is: "Strike the Crow on the knee; I will spear his father."

The war was maintained with great vigor for a length of time. The Crow took every possible advantage of his nobler foe, the Eagle; but the latter generally had ample revenge for injuries and insults. Out of their enmities and final agreement arose the two classes, and thence a law governing marriages amongst these classes.

Source: Smyth (1878, 1: 423–24); adapted by authors.

The second version (Box 8.2) is that in the Museums Victoria manuscript XM 923, p. 7, also published as Campbell (1999: 43). Note that our transcription varies slightly from that in Campbell.

Box 8.2: Moiety song, version 2

I may here remark that this story is common to all the tribes of the Murray as well as Gippsland. Over 46 years ago I heard it at the junction of the Darling. The Aborigines used to repeat it in a sort of epic poem. The story opened with this content and the blacks used to repeat it with great excitement.

thingame bakla wako

on the knee strike the crow

nato panda kambeartona

I spear his father

The hawk was determined to break the knees of the crow and also to destroy the whole family as the above would indicate.

Source: MV XM 923, p. 7; Campbell (1999: 43); adapted by authors.

Bulmer adds a very interesting observation in a letter that he sent to A.W. Howitt on 22 April 1887 (see Box 8.3), namely that the words in the songs could be changed if the language was changed due to the death of a person. This contains only the first line. We would regularise this as **thingami palka nani**.

Box 8.3: Moiety song, version 3

I dare say you are aware that the language undergoes great changes as they so often have to alter words on the death of someone whose name even rhymed with the words used by them. For instance when I was among them they used to recite the legend as follows.

Thingami balku wakoo

The knee strike crow

but on the death of one of the people they change Wakoo to Nanee so they used to say

Thingami balku nanee

Source: MV XM 94; adapted by authors.

Our linguistic analysis is presented as example (8.1):

(8.1) *Thinjami* *Balki* *mako*

knee *strike* *crow*

thing-ami **palka** **waaku**

knee-? strike crow

'Strike the crow on (the) knee.'

Nato-panda *Kambe-ar* *tono*

spear *father* *of him*

ngathu-panta **kampiya-ithu-n(h)a**

1SG-spear father-this-3SG

'I (will) spear his father.'

Notes

This is most definitely Marawara because of the form **kampiya** 'father' while other Paakantyi dialects have **kampitya**.

The Paakantyi word for 'knee' is **thingi**.[4]

The suffix on the last word is analysed as -**nha**, 3rd person singular, rather than the genitive which is -**na** in Paakantyi but -**n** in the other Maraura song texts. See, for example, the Kangaroo song (section 8.1.3).

4 This word is omitted (by mistake) from the Paakantyi dictionary (Hercus 1993), but is found in Hercus (1982).

8.1.2 Sun song

The second song is the Sun song; there are at least five versions: in the Bulmer papers in Museums Victoria XM 923, p. 2, presented in Box 8.4; one in Smyth (1878, 1: 430), presented in Box 8.5; one in the Howitt papers, Museums Victoria XM 605, presented in Box 8.6; one in McAllister (1878: 148), presented in Box 8.7; and another in a letter from Bulmer to R.H. Mathews, presented in Box 8.8. This last version also contains the Kangaroo song, to which the Sun song is thus presumably related (see section 8.1.3).

In this song, the sun is addressed by the creator **Nhuurali** and asked to disappear at times. The idea of talking to the sun is not unfamiliar in Aboriginal thinking. In certain central desert myths, for example, a character talks to the sun to get it to burn someone or something.

Box 8.4: Sun song, version 1

The people of the Murray believed that *nooralie*, the spirit being which had the form of an eagle, arranged the universe as it is today. Unlike the Christian Creator who made all things by the word of his mouth, *nooralie* was able to employ others to do his will. Everything including inanimate objects was under his command. The story of creation as an epic poem had been taught to the children by their parents for many generations.

For instance in the beginning the sun did not go down but was always shining, but at the command of *nooralie* it was taught to rise & set. The order given to the sun was as follows:

yukho warri yukho warri

yarrara yarama wanedilyu

yuntho yunthoma wanedilyu

tull tull

Meaning hot sun hot sun. Wood your wood burn

bowels your bowels burn & go down.

Source: MV XM 923, p. 2; Campbell (1999: 40); adapted by authors.

Box 8.5: Sun song, version 2

At the beginning the Sun did not set. It was at all times day, and the blacks grew weary. *Nooralie* considered and decided at length that the Sun should disappear at intervals. He addressed the Sun in these words:-

Yhuko warrie, Yhuko warrie,

Yarrarama wane dilya,

Yantha, Yanthoma wane dilya,

Tull Tull.

Which being interpreted means: "Sun, Sun, burn your wood, burn your internal substance, and go down."

The natives believe that because the Sun gives heat it needs fuel, and that when it descends below the horizon it reaches vast depths whence it procures fresh food for its fires.

Source: Smyth (1878, 1: 430); adapted by authors.

The version in the Howitt papers is a typescript, and the text is presented in Box 8.6. It contains glosses of the individual words given by Howitt.

Box 8.6: Sun song, version 3

The Wembaio said that at one time the sun never [set-crossed out] [moved -inserted]. Nūreli being tired of the eternal day, order it to go down [to the next-inserted] by the following song:

Yŭkowarri	yarara-yanama	wendilye
Sun	wood-yours	burn
Yŭntho-yŭnthama	wendilye	tūl-tūl
entrail	burn	go-away

Source: Howitt, MV XM 605; adapted by authors.

It seems as if in the section of the Howitt manuscripts the letter u written with a breve *ŭ* represents /u/ and that with macron *ū* is /a/, the opposite of the usual practice. This is because the words for 'sun' and 'entrail' clearly have a /u/ vowel in the first syllable, and the word spelled *tūl-tūl* seems to be related to the word glossed as 'crash' in the Eagle and Crow stories (Tindale 1939: 252).

The version in McAllister (see Box 8.7) is glossed a little differently from the other versions, and in particular includes 'you' as the gloss for *Warry*. There is no documented word with a form similar to **wari** meaning 'you' in Paakantyi, but there are two words **wari** 'move about' and **warra** 'direction, side' which could possibly be intended here.

Box 8.7: Sun song, version 4

The natives along the Murray and Edwards Rivers, and in many other localities, believed that the sun is simply a large fire, which is renewed every morning and extinguished every evening; but from their traditions, it is evident that they believed that, at one time, the sun's fire burned constantly both day and night – the very words used when the change was being made still preserved in some of their songs, of which the following is a translation of one verse, furnished me by the Rev. Mr. Bulmer:–

Yhuko	Warry	Yhuko	Warry
Sun	*You*	*Sun*	*You*
Yarra	Yarroma		Warredilyee
Wood	*Wood of yours*		*Burn*
Yuntho	Yunthoma		Warredilyee
Bowels	*Bowels of yours*		*Burn*
Tule!	Tule!		
Go down!	*Go down!*		

Since the utterance of these mystic words, the rising and setting of the sun has been constant.

Source: McAllister (1878: 148); adapted by authors.

The fifth version (Box 8.8) is in a letter from Bulmer to R.H. Mathews that also includes a song 'referring to the creation of the kangaroo'.

Box 8.8: Sun song, version 5, together with Kangaroo song

Minna minna Booloola

Minna minna Booloola

Nartagan Koombadjan

Titte Bock bock

'This refers to the creation of the Kangaroo. It is asked what's to be done for the kangaroo. He is told to throw himself forward and bock bock. The sound he is supposed to make in moving another was:

Yuckoo warri yuckoo warri

Yurrara Yurrama Wandela

Yuntho yunthoma wandela

Tull tull

This refers to the sun it seems to have required to know its movements so it is told to burn all its wood and even its internal parts and go down. So it goes down to get more wood.

Source: Letter from Bulmer to R.H. Mathews, NLA MS 8006/2, File 9; adapted by authors.

Note that both songs in Bulmer's letter finish with a repeated word, *Bock Bock* and *Tull Tull*. These are probably onomatopoeic.

Our analysis is presented in (8.2):

(8.2) *Yhuko warrie, Yhuko warrie,*
yuku wari yuku wari
sun move about sun move about
'The sun is moving about, the sun is moving about.'

Yarrarama wane dilya
yarr-aama waarnti-la
wood-2SG.POSS burn-TOP
'Your wood is burning.'

Yantha, Yanthoma wane dilya
yunthu yunth-oma waarnti-la
entrail entrail-2SG.POSS burn-TOP
'Your entrails are burning.'

Tull Tull.
thul thul
ONOM.crash
'Crash crash.'

Notes

Our spelling of **yunthu** for 'entrails' is suggested by the spelling in the Howitt version and also the Kurnu word **yurtu** 'kidney', Kurnu being a Paakantyi variety some distance to the North.

We suggest that the last word, *tūl-tūl*, is the same as a form *Tal! Tal!*, glossed by Tindale (1939: 252) as 'crash', in the Eagle and Crow story.

8.1.3 Kangaroo song

A song that may have been paired with the Sun song is the Kangaroo song, already given above in Box 8.8. The portion relating only to the Kangaroo song is presented here again as Box 8.9.

Box 8.9: Kangaroo song

Minna minna Booloola Minna minna Booloola Nartagan Koombadjan Titte Bock bock This refers to the creation of the Kangaroo

Source: Letter from Bulmer to R.H. Mathews,NLA MS 8006/2, File 9; adapted by authors.

Our analysis is presented as (8.3):

(8.3) *minna* *minna* *booloola*
minha **minha** **pululya**
what what kangaroo
'What (is this), what (is it), a kangaroo?'

minna *minna* *booloola*
minha **minha** **pululya**
what what kangaroo
'What (is this), what (is it), a kangaroo?'

nartagan *koombadjan*
nharta-ka-n **kumpatya-n**
down-LOC-GEN big-GEN
'Big one down there.'

tittel *bock bock*
thithi **pok pok**
bottom ONOM?
'Bottom, …'

Notes

The word **pululya** is the western grey kangaroo.

The suffix **-ka** 'in, at' usually conveys location, but may also have a directional meaning; **mirika** 'in front', **waraka** 'at the side'.

The form **pok pok** might be some kind of onomatopoeia.

8.1.4 Moon song

Like the Sun song above (section 8.1.2), the Moon song was one in which the creator **Nhuurali** sings in order to get the moon to behave as required. The various contexts given below suggest different reasons why the song was sung. Bulmer (in Campbell 1999: 41) suggesting that it was a condemnation of men to death, and Smyth (1878, 1: 431) suggesting it was an order to the moon to appear at appropriate intervals. We cannot know, but it is surely possible that this song had multiple functions.

There are four versions of this song, two in the Bulmer papers in Museums Victoria (MV XM 923, p. 2 and p. 3), also in Campbell (1999: 40 and 41), presented in Boxes 8.10 and 8.11; a version in Smyth (1878, 1: 431), presented in Box 8.12; and a version in Howitt (1904: 428), presented in Box 8.13.

Box 8.10: Moon song, version 1

The moon also had to be taught so nooralie ordered it thus:

pilou puckamalemba, penahpithenba

benah bulgar bulgaroo

The literal translation is moon, you die, your bones go white, your bones go to dust to dust.

Source: MV XM 923, p. 2; also Campbell (1999: 40); adapted by authors.

A few lines later, in the story of *Bonelya*, the bat, Bulmer gives a second version. The word for 'bat' is **panhatya** in Paakantyi, though Bulmer's spelling here would be regularised as **panhalya**, where the -**ty**- ~ -**ly**- correspondence may be an example of a regular sound correspondence between Paakantyi and Maraura.

The association of the bat with death is discussed in Smyth (1878, 1: 428), writing:

> The first created man and woman were told not to go near a certain tree in which a Bat *(Bon-nel-ya)* lived. The Bat was not to be disturbed. One day, however, the woman *(Nonga)* was gathering firewood, and she went near the tree in which the Bat lived. The Bat flew away, and after that came death. Many amongst the Aborigines died after that.

In a footnote, Smyth (1878, 1: 428) added that while there was some similarity to the Christian story, Bulmer had written:

> it may have been invented by the Aborigines after they had heard something of scripture history; but he [Bulmer] says – 'The blackfellow who told me the story was by no means sharp. I should not give him credit for inventing such a story. I believe it to be a genuine tradition of their own.'

Another story that may relate to this song is a story of a Bat, his two wives, the mosquito and the wood lizard and the moon. This story involves the moon singing and locking the Bat's wives in stone. The story is in a notebook in the R.H. Mathews papers (NLA MS 8006/3/7.2, Languages, initiation &c, p. 16). The story was probably told to Mathews by Maraura man Harry Perry. The first part of the story reads as:

> Bŭnnŭlnya, a bat Kilparra – had 2 wives – musquito Kundhi and wood lizard burnu – they lived by themselves on yams. Moon lived near them – on yams also. The moon and 2 gins [pulled??] yams & spread them out till they dried. After that the gins pissed on all the yams. The moon came back & gathered up the yams and started to eat the yams, and they tasted salt. No good – What has happened my yams – he went away 200 yards, having [spewed??] out the yams the second time. In the night he went and stripped some bark. He made the gins sleep. When they slept, he stood the bark up all round them. He sang to the bark to turn it into stone, & he went away.

It is possible that the song sung by the moon is in fact the same song that is being discussed here, or one very similar.

As already mentioned above in connection with the Moiety song, we regard all these four songs written down by Bulmer as related to the traditional stories of the Ancestor Creator and other beings.

Box 8.11: Moon song, version 2

The bat plays a very important part in the subsequent fate of mankind. It was through his being disturbed that death entered the world. I give the account as I heard it from the people of the Murray. The bat after his work was done was very much exhausted, so he went to rest in a hollow tree. *Nooralie* told every one to keep clear of that tree under severe pains & penalties. It appears a woman gathering sticks allowed one of the sticks to touch the tree, this disturbed *bonelya*, who at once flew away. This raised the ire of *nooralie* who condemned men to death as follows:

Puck a malimba

Penah pithenba

Penah Bulga Bulgarro

The same sentence as pronounced against the moon and so men have died.

Source: MV XM 923, p. 3; also Campbell (1999: 41); adapted by authors.

Box 8.12: Moon song, version 3

The Moon was aberrant before her motions were regulated by *Nooralie*. *Nooralie* had much to remember and to consider before he could decide what should be the times of the appearance of the Moon, and how she should appear, but at length he addressed her in these words :–

Puk-a	*Mal-imba*	*Penah-pethanba,*	
Die	you	bone	whiten,
Penah	*Bulga*	*Bulga.*	
bone	powder	powder.	

In other words: "Die ! your bones whiten – and your bones go to powder."

The Moon obeyed Nooralie. She dies at regular periods – and re-appears – and does her duty to the Aborigines as Nooralie in times long past commanded her to do.

Source: Smyth (1878, 1: 431); adapted by authors.

The final version (Box 8.13) is in Howitt (1904: 428).

Box 8.13: Moon song, version 4

According to the Wiimbaio, the moon did not die periodically, as it does now, until Nurelli ordered it to do so by the following song :–

Puka-malimba	*puta*	*paithanha*	*pina*	*bulga-bulgara*
Die you	bone	whitened	bones	dust-dust-to.

Source: Howitt (1904: 428); adapted by authors.

Our analysis is presented in (8.4):

(8.4) *Puk-a* *Mal-imba* *Penah-pethanba,*
Die *you* *bone*
puka-ma-l(a)-imba **piRnha** **paatya-na-ba**
dead-VERBALIZER-OPT-2SG bone white-?-?
'You are made dead, your bones are made white.'

Penah *Bulga* *Bulga.*
bone *powder* *powder.*
piRnda **pulka** **pulka**
bone powder powder
'Your bones are (gone to) dust, to dust.'

Notes

In Paakantyi, 'white' is **paatyirka**, and the word for 'moon' was recorded **paartyira**, spelled by Tindale as *patyira*.

We are unclear what the final suffix on the word for 'white' is. It may be a single suffix **(a)nba**, or a combination of either the locative or genitive **-n** with an unknown suffix **ba**.

8.1.5 Riding across the Murray – Jamieson's song

The last of Bulmer's songs is 'Riding across the Murray', sung by one of the ritual songsters named Mr Jamieson. He was described by Bulmer as a *birrarark*, a Gippsland word referring to a powerful expert whose skills included 'the seer, the spirit-medium, and the bard' (for more detail, see section 5.1.3). We do not know what term would have been used in Maraura for this person, though Hercus (1993) included the words **pityi** and **pityika** 'senior, most important ritual leader' in her Paakantyi dictionary.

Mr Jamieson came from downstream of Yelta. He was a big man, both physically and as an influential member of his community. His original name is not known, but he was named after one of the Jamieson Brothers who had runs at Mildura and further downstream. This Mr Jamieson is mentioned by Bulmer as being at Yelta, telling in particular about a trip to Adelaide moving stock and the tales of wonder he brought back after it. As an expert songster and in control of magic, he was reputed to be able to ride in the air.

There is a version of this song text in MV XM 92, a letter from Bulmer to Howitt, 11 March 1884 (Box 8.14):

Box 8.14: Riding across the Murray, version 1

I think many of the songs were the result of dreams. I remember once an old man on the Murray made such a song, it was

Thoopee Nappu

Karo Koora

Murlu Rintee

That is it was carried to another country on the other side other Murray, so I expect Yelmire's connection with the Shark arose from the same cause.

Source: MV XM 92; adapted by authors.

The version in Box 8.15 is also based on the Museums Victoria manuscript XM 92, p. 21.

Box 8.15: Riding across the Murray, version 2

Another class of men were called *birrarark*, these men were harmless fellows, they were supposed to ride in the air like our witches on a broom stick. They must have possessed ventriloquial powers as they could make their voices sound as from above. They generally keep the camp amused during the evenings as the camp would suddenly hear voices in the air and it would appear as if several persons were sailing about. These men had great influence they did not injure people, but their powers were rather awesome to the tribe. One of them (Mr Jamieson, a *birrarark*) I remember on the Murray who had made a corroboree song after this fashion:

> Rode I another country
>
> *thopie nappu karo kara*
>
> otherside Murray
>
> *murlu rintu*

I rode to another country on the other side the Murray.

Source: Campbell (1999: 27); adapted by authors.

Another version of the song is found in the Howitt papers in the State Library of Victoria, presented in Box 8.16:

Box 8.16: Riding across the Murray, version 3

I know a cure among the Murray
Blacks where an old man named
Mr Jamieson dreamt that his soul
went away to a distant place on the
other side of the Murray. He made
a Corroborie about it which had
this beginning

> Thopie Nappu
>
> Karo Kara
>
> Murli Rentie (Murray)

Which being translated would mean
I rode to another country on the
other side of the Murray, This man
may have been a Birrarark but
I do not know. However I feel
[back side]
certain that the Murray Blacks had culden
of the possibility of the soul (Kone gerie) being
able to leave the body in dreams.

Source: Howitt Papers, SLV Box 1054/2 (a), hw0436.pdf, p. 22; adapted by authors.

Our analysis is presented as (8.5):

(8.5) *Rode I another country*

thopie nappu karo kara

thupa(i)-ngapa	**kaRu**	**kaRa**
jump-1SG	other	Ground

'(I) jumped (to) another country'

otherside Murray

murlu rintu

mu(r)lu	**rintu**
across?	Murray river

'Across? the Murray'

Notes

The word **thupa-thupa** is 'jump, hop' in Paakantyi. Having the full pronoun **ngapa** instead of the bound form was common as an emphatic form in Maraura.

Curr's Paakantyi lists (1886, 2: 238–41) contains two words for 'ground' recorded by Bulmer and give as coming from 'the confluence of the Darling and the Murray', viz 'Ground: *kara, murndi*'.

The second line may be another language. Hercus (1986: 232) has shown rind ['ri:nd] as the Tarti-Tarti word for the Murrumbidgee River, and 'also a general term for "river"'. Given the fact that there were speakers of the Murray River language Yerri-Yerri nearby to Yelta, it is perhaps the case that Jamieson used the Murray River word for 'river' here. The general word for 'river' in Paakantyi is **paaka**, which is also the word for the Darling River. No word for the Murray River was documented by Hercus (1983).

The word *murlu* may not be a Paakantyi word, but like the following word *Rintu* may be from one of the 'Murray River languages', possibly Tarti-Tarti. None of the sources in Horgen (2005) give a word like **mu(r)lu** as meaning 'across'. There is a form *murlong* meaning 'small' in the list given by Peter Beveridge (in Smyth 1878, 2: 72). The nearest form in Paakantyi is **mulu**, explained by Hercus (1983) as:

> The **Mulungga** corroboree (which Grannie Moisey learnt and participated in). This corroboree originated in the Northern Territory among the Wampaya, and became popular in northern SA at the turn of the century. Grannie Moisey's account shows that it was popular also in the Far West of NSW.

If the word *murlu* is from a Murray River language, then the two lines of the song are in different languages, the first line in Maraura or another Paakantyi variety and the second perhaps in Tarti-Tarti.

8.2 Songs documented by the Berndts

Two songs documented by Ronald and Catherine Berndt and published in 1993 are included here as being in Maraura language. The first is the song sung by Dan Limberry but made by 'the Barindyi man Monkey' (section 8.2.1) and the second is a song sung at Wentworth made by Jacko (section 8.2.2).

8.2.1 Song sung by Dan Limberry but made by the Barindji man Monkey

The song shown by Berndt and Berndt (1993, Appendix 7.8) was sung by Dan Limberry, also known as 'Up the river Dan', who died at Wentworth in 1911, aged 68.[5] Whether there is a surviving sound recording of this song is not known at this stage.

However, the song was not composed by Dan, but, as Berndt and Berndt (1993: 216) explained:

> Another song was sung by a Darling River man named Dan when he visited the Lower Murray area. The composer, however, was a man called Monkey, also from the Darling, belonging to the Banreindji (Barindji) language group, whose country ran parallel to and east of that river. The subject was an old woman who was travelling along and saw a dead body (see Appendix 7.8). Pinkie learnt this song as a young woman, and she was also able to be present at the ceremony.

Jeanette Hope, in an unpublished 'Historical database of Aboriginal people on the Murray River: An Aboriginal biographical dictionary', quoting unpublished diaries of Armourer Forster, discussed the details of where

5 New South Wales Death Certificate 1911/8135.

particular Aboriginal people were at particular times, adding that '[t]hese examples also indicate the networks between people: Monkey and Dan (McGregor) knew each other – and both probably also knew Minduk Jack'.

The E.B. Scott papers[6] mention a man called Monkey 15 times as working at Moorna, just west of the Darling River mouth in New South Wales, in the period 1862–66, but it is always possible that there could have been a second person with that name.

Although Berndt and Berndt (1993: 216) state that Monkey belonged to 'the Banreindji (Barindji) language group', now termed Parrintyi, our analysis is that the language of this song is Maraura, not Parrintyi. However, because of the paucity of records of Maruara, unless otherwise stated, the data used in comparison are from the best known dialect, Southern Paakantyi. The Berri-ait (Parrintyi) word list by Cameron (1884) is almost identical with Southern Paakantyi. The language of this song is close to Southern Paakantyi, but there are also words from elsewhere, and unknown words. There is loss of final vowels as is found in Maraura (see Hercus 1982, 1984).

None of the Paakantyi dialects have words beginning with vowels, except for a few pronominal forms, so words beginning with 'a' are likely to have had an initial nasal, mainly **ng**, which has probably been misheard. The text contains a number of separate vowels; these can be interpreted as being 'just song language'.

The main difference between the spelling used by Berndt and Berndt (1993) and the spelling now used for Paakantyi is that Berndt and Berndt generally, but not always, used the voiced consonants **b**, **d**, **g** and **dj**, whereas the modern spelling is **p**, **t**, **k** and **ty**.

The text of Monkey's song is presented in Box 8.17:

Box 8.17: Monkey's song

First Part					
1	*A beringet e ina*	*mikei a*	*beringet*	*a a a*	*mikei*
	I'm going	down	I'm going	down	
	akangangga	*anggera*	*tilelipan.*		
	stream	staying the night	you must listen.		

6 Scott, E.B. (1822–1909). (n.d.) Papers of Edward Bate Scott, State Library of South Australia, on microfilm at PRG 608.

(After coming down a number of creeks from Ned's Corner, the woman reaches a place called Anggera, meaning 'stop the night', but also named Wolwol, probably in the vicinity of Wookool Bend.)

Second Part

1	*Wongkuna a*	*kalingul ei ya*	*wongkuna ei*	*kalingul.*
	Howling	of wild dogs	howling	of wild dogs.
2	*Pure-ura*	*amang*	*minggin*	*telpaiang.*
	Right awa	among	those	samphire bushes.

(Near where she camps for the night, there is a dead human body covered with boughs. 'Strangers don't know of this form of corpse disposal', Pinkie Mack added, and the woman did not. The wild dogs are howling, calling for their young because they smell the dead body.)

Third Part

1	*Paraiyu ai*	*yunggamandi i ai*	*paraiyu*	*yunggamandi*	
	Old woman	kind	old woman	kind.	
2	*Paraiyu ai*	*yunggamandi*	*yunggawa*	*angger.*	
	Old woman	kind	kindness	staying at night	
3	*A a ngarimp*	*a ai Putangat*	*Yunggawa.*		
	Lying down	Putangat	kindness.		
4	*Kangandan-ga*	*kailpunet*	*awak*	*putunanda a*	*pundun.*
	From here	I will go directly	trouble	I saw it	head.

The old woman is 'kind', which implies diffidence, not wishing to make trouble. She stays a night at Wolwol where the dead body is. She decides to go north to Putangat in the desert, west of the Darling. The song ends with her saying she saw trouble, she saw the head of a wild dog coming to the corpse.

I'm going down, downstream, [where I will] stay the night. You must listen!

Wild dogs howling, wild dogs howling.

Diffident old woman ...

Diffident old woman, sleeping at night

Lying there thinking of Putangat; diffident.

From here I will go directly. I saw trouble, saw a dog's head.

Source: Berndt and Berndt (1993: Appendix 7.8); adapted by authors.

Our analysis is presented in examples (8.6) to (8.8):

First Part

(8.6)	1	*A*	*beringet e ina*	*mikei a*	*beringet e ina*
			I'm going	*down*	*I'm going*
		a	**paringka-thu-inha**	**miki**	**paringka-thu-inha**
		EXCL	go.away-?1SG.TRANS-here	?	go.away-?1SG.TRANS-here

mikei a		*akangangga*	*anggera*	*tilelipan*
down		*stream*	*staying the night*	*you must listen*
miki	**a**	**kanka-ngka**	**nhaangka-ra**	**thalti-pani**
?	EXCL	here-their	sit-?	listen-INTENS

'Ah, coming away here … coming away here … for staying here in this place, listen carefully!'

The locations referred to in this song are Ned's Corner,[7] Anggera (**nhaangka-ra**), meaning 'stop the night', said to be 'also named Wolwol,[8] probably in the vicinity of Wookool Bend'.

Note that this location may not have been traditional Maraura land, being on the Victorian side of the Murray River. The local language spoken there would probably have been one of the Murray River languages; the area is marked as Ngintait by Tindale (1974), a language for which very few records remain.

Notes on the translation

The first word *beringet e ina* is interpreted as **paringka-thu-na**, where -**thu** is a 'bound form of 1 sg. tr. subject pronoun' (Hercus 1993). We would expect a 1st person singular subject here, but the transitive form is perhaps surprising. A similar suffix, written *-tono* is observed in the Moiety song recorded by Bulmer (see section 8.1.1). Songs commencing with words like 'I'm going away from here' are common in Aboriginal languages, as we see in the Wemba-Wemba Dingo song (section 2.2.7).

The word *ina*, is **inha** 'that one, there'; but we have glossed it as 'here' in the context of this song.

There is no known Paakantyi word similar to *mikei*, with the meaning 'down'. There are three Paakantyi words that could sound like *mikei* in song, **miiki** 'eye'; **mika** 'sick, sickness, pain'; and **miki** 'name'. It is possible that the word might refer to names of places. It is also possible that it may be **miityi** 'to set (sun)'.

7 Ned's corner can be found on Google Maps, 'Neds Corner', accessed 14 December 2017, www.google.com.au/maps/place/Neds+Corner/@-34.2230151,141.1934749,10z/data=!4m5!3m4!1s0x6ac3e7de08a08acb:0xd562140321440c8d!8m2!3d-34.2230518!4d141.4736264.

8 Wolwol is found on Google Maps, accessed 14 December 2017, www.google.com.au/maps/place/Neds+Corner/@-34.1810261,141.179227,14z/data=!4m5!3m4!1s0x6ac3e7de08a08acb:0xd562140321440c8d!8m2!3d-34.2230518!4d141.4736264. It is now called Lake Wallawalla.

There is no word resembling *akangangga* with the meaning 'stream' in the available Paakantyi sources. Assuming that the initial *a* is a song language particle (which may have actually been realised as **nga**), we have analysed this as **kanka** 'here' and **-ngka** 'belonging to them', possibly meaning 'in other people's country'.

The word *anggera* is the verb **nhaangka** 'to sit, to stay' in the adjacent Paaṟuntyi dialect of Paakantyi. A formative -**ra** may mean 'for'.

The word *tilelipan* is **thalti** that means 'to listen, to hear' in all the Paakantyi dialects and **-pa** 'completely', which also has the form **pani**, an aspectual suffix expressing thoroughness as well as intensity. The loss of the final vowel is a *-pani* (*-pan* with loss of the final vowel) has a similar function 'listen carefully'.

Second Part

(8.7)	1	*Wongkuna*	*kalingul ei ya*	*wongkuna ei*	*kalingul*
		Howling	*of wild dogs*	*howling*	*of wild dogs*
		wangka-na	**karli-ngul-iya**	**wangka-na-e**	**karli-ngul**
		make noise-CONT	dog-DUAL-?	make noise-CONT	dog-DUAL

2	*Pure-ura*	*amang*	*minggin*	*telpaiang*
	Right away	*among*	*those*	*samphire bushes*
	Pururu	**?**	**mingki-n(a)**	**thalypa-n(a)**
	further on	among?	dawn?-LOC	near-LOC

'The two wild dogs are howling, the two wild dogs are howling … further on, nearby at dawn?'

Linguistic notes

The word *wongkuna* is translated by Berndt and Berndt as 'howling'. We suggest that this might be the word **wangka** 'to speak', sometimes also meaning 'to make a noise', not previously found in the Paakantyi languages, but well attested in the Thura-Yura languages, e.g. Kaurna **wanggandi** 'to speak'.

The suffix **-ana** is a participle implying continuous action.

The form *Kalingul ei ya* is translated as 'of wild dogs' by Berndt and Berndt, consisting of a widespread root **karli** 'dog' and the dual suffix **-ngulu** in Paakantyi, but here showing the final vowel deletion that is typical in Maraura.

The word *pureura* translated as 'right away' by Berndt and Berndt could be **purur̲u** 'further on'.

The word *amang* is unknown in Paakantyi. It may be the English *among*.

Although the last two words are glossed by Berndt and Berndt as 'those' and 'samphire bushes', we have not been able to relate these forms to words known in Paakantyi. There is no Paakantyi deictic pronoun that looks anything like *minggin*, translated as 'those' by Berndt and Berndt. We[9] think this form could be the Paakantyi word **mingki** meaning 'dawn, first light' with the locative suffix and final vowel deletion, as **mingki-n(a)** 'at dawn'.

The last word in this section, *telpaiang*, is probably **thalypa** 'nearby', with the locative suffix **thalypan(a)** 'in the vicinity'.

Note that the word for 'samphire bush' (*Sarcocornia quinqueflora*) in Paakantyi was not documented.

Third Part

(8.8)	1	*Paraiyu ai*	*yunggamandi i ai*		
		Old woman	*kind*		
		paraiyu-ai	**yungka-manti ai**		
		old woman-1SG.POSS	self-DAT- ?		
		paraiyu ai	*yunggamandi*		
		old woman	*kind*		
		paraiyu-ai	**yungka-manti**		
		old woman-1SG.POSS	self-DAT		
	2	*Paraiyu ai*	*yunggamandi*	*yunggawa*	*angger*
		Old woman	*kind*	*kindness*	*staying at night*
		paraiyu-ai	**yungka-manti**	**yungka-wa**	**nhaangka-ra**
		old woman-1SG.POSS	self-DAT	self-EMPH	sit-?for

9 This suggested analysis was made by Luise Hercus based on her considerable knowledge of Paakantyi.

3	*A a*	*ngarimp*	*a ai Putangat*	*yunggawa*
		lie down	*Putangar*	*kindness*
	a a	**nhari-imp**	**a ai Putangat**	**yungka-wa**
	EMPH	lie.down-2.SG	EXCL-PN	self-EMPH

4	*Kangandan-ga*	*kailpunet*	
	from here	*I will go directly*	
	kanka-nt(u)-ngka	**kayilpu-na-t**	
	here-from-their	directly-?LOC-1SG?	
	awak	*putunanda a*	*pundun*
	trouble	*I saw it*	*head*
	ngawak	**putunanta a**	**puntu-na**
	trouble	silent-ABL-?	smoke-LOC ??

'The (my) old woman, by (her)self, the old woman, very alone is staying. You are lying down by yourself at Putangat. Directly from here, silently. There is trouble …'

Berndt and Berndt (1993) commented that 'The old woman is "kind"'. The ideas of 'kindness' and 'diffidence' are perhaps implied by the words **yungkamanti** and **yungkawa**. The song is poetic and metaphorical: it does not tell us what the old woman saw, it is much more effective, keeping the horrible truth unexpressed.

Linguistic notes

The word *Paraiyu ai* is translated by Berndt and Berndt as 'old woman'. The only Paakantyi word resembling this is Kurnu **paraka** 'old woman', which was perhaps **paraiyu-** in Maruara. **-ai** is the 1st person possessive marker that could be used in a friendly fashion, or as an emphatic. In preparing the analysis of this song, Luise Hercus observed that there is a number of similarities between Maraura and Kurnu.

yungka in Paakantyi means 'self', 'by oneself', 'on one's own', and it is commonly used in the expression **yungkaaku** 'alone', 'by oneself', **yungka mala-** means 'to make oneself alone', 'to abscond', 'to move away from a group of people'. The form in the song, *yunggamandi* is analysed as **yungka-manti**, with a suffix meaning dative-purposive. This has the same meaning of 'by oneself', 'on one's own'. **yungka-wa** is an even more emphatic way of saying this, 'absolutely alone' as **-wa** is an emphatic clitic, used mainly with pronouns.

ngari- means 'to lie down', 'to go down' (of the sun), and **-imp(a)** is the bound form of the 2nd person singular intransitive pronoun: **ngarimpa** means 'you are lying down'.

The form *Kangandan-ga* reflects the form from Verse 1, *kangangga*, but with an additional suffix **-ant(u)** 'ablative'. Thus **kanka-nt(u)** means 'away from here', followed by **ngka** 'belonging to them'.

kayilpu 'directly' is followed by the locative **-n(a)** and *et*, the latter of which was seen in the first line, example (8.6). In both cases *-et* is translated with 1st person reference by Berndt and Berndt.

The word *awak*, translated by Berndt and Berndt as 'trouble', is presumably from a Paakantyi word **ngawak(a)** meaning 'something dreadful'. There is a Paakantyi verb **ngawala** 'to be in a very bad way'.

The word *putunanta* does not appear to be a verbal form, as the 1st person is marked on the previous word. There is a Paakantyi word **putu** that means 'still, not moving, silent', and **-anta** may indicate an ablative case. **pami** is the usual verb for 'see' in Paakantyi.

The last word, *pundun*, is translated by Berndt and Berndt as 'head', but there is no evidence for such a word meaning 'head' in Paakantyi or any nearby languages. There is, however, a Paakantyi word **puntu** meaning 'smoke' and if the final **-n** represents the locative case marker **-na**, with final vowel dropping, the whole of this would mean 'in the smoke'.

We cannot find the meaning 'seeing the dog's head' out of the words that are in the song; it is possible that the meaning that we can interpret is some form of metaphor.

8.2.2 Wentworth song made by Jacko

The second song documented by Berndt and Berndt (1993) is Jacko's song, for which we have both the Berndt and Berndt published transcription and translation (see Box 8.19) and the recording.

The name Jacko or Yaku from Wentworth is descriptive. Tindale (1974: 251) gives *yaako* as meaning 'no', and *Yaaku-Yaaku* as an alternative name for the language name of the Maraura area. The language names in the area are reduplicated names for 'no'. Therefore Jacko, alias **Yaaku**, probably meant 'the Maraura man'. We presume that the tribal name *Jakəmal'da:k* is also related to **Yaaku**.

This song is not an old one, being composed after the arrival of Europeans. Berndt and Berndt (1993: 220) wrote of it that 'this song is from the *Patangi* category, which is "related to a special kind of dancing"'.

In the 1950s, 13 cylinders recorded by Berndt and Berndt were re-recorded as audio on tape by the musicologist Alice Moyle, who also made musical transcriptions of some of them. This tape recording was later digitised by AIATSIS and given the name BERNDT_RC01-004244A. There are two sets of metadata notes relating to these held at AIATSIS. The first is a document headed as follows:

> R.M. Berndt
> Cylinder Collection
> East Wellington, South Australia, 1943
> For Australian National Research Council

This document goes on to state that on Cylinder 12 there were two songs recorded, the Up River initiation song (see section 14.1) and Jacko's song. The actual metadata reads as follows (Box 8.18):

Box 8.18: Details of Cylinder 12 recorded by Berndt and Berndt

No. 12.
1st part: an Up River initiation song 'pa:ta 'winəma ...
2nd part: A 'Jakəmal'da:k tribal song from up the river 'dugdugədo 'ja:na

Source: AIATSIS BERNDT_RC01-004244A; adapted by authors.

This portion is on the AIATSIS WAV file from 18:48 to 21:29, commencing with the words spoken by Alice Moyle: 'No. 12 slightly mildewed at commencement'.

Both sound recordings have considerable background noise and are not fully audible. In particular, we cannot make out the words that are being sung. A musical transcription of the Up River initiation song, made by Alice Moyle, and presented as Figure 14.1 (section 14.1), may include a musical transcription of this song too.

There is a restart that may be the actual beginning of Jacko's song, at 0:58 into this section of the recording (19:46 on the AIATSIS recording). It is possible that the first syllable after the restart, an upward slide in pitch, is in fact something like **thak-** (corresponding to Berndt and Berndt's *dug*). If this is the case, it means that Pinkie Mack either sang these words at least four times, or there were additional words not translated.

In addition, we have been unable to match the Alice Moyle transcription with what we hear at 18:48 of the AIATSIS digitisation. It would appear that Alice Moyle's transcription is the whole of Cylinder 12, so it would presumably include Jacko's song.

The full text of Jacko's song is given in Box 8.19:

Box 8.19: Jacko's song

Jacko or Yaku from Wentworth composed a song which told of a European barmaid who served Jacko at a wineshop across from Wentworth. As she poured the wine from one bottle to another, she talked and laughed with him, spilling some and pouring some of it back. She was said to be cheating Jacko, pretending she had given him too much.

1	Dug-dugedo		yana	anganinama	ga'lalpai	yunelo.
	Spilling		yarn	to me	talking	stop.
2	Bero-berolin		bureminin	nganbai	rumelban	waki
	She's laughing		pouring it	into the other	too much	in that
	buremin-ai	yana	anganinama	dug-dugedo.		
	pouring	yarn	to me	spilling.		

Spilling the wine while yarning with me!

She's laughing, pouring too much into the other bottle,

Spilling it as she yarns with me.

The translation of this song differs from that mentioned in R. and C. Berndt 1951:86.

Source: Berndt and Berndt (1993: Appendix 7.25); adapted by authors.

Our linguistic analysis of this song is presented in example (8.9). The glosses of the words are based on forms recorded in other sources; their interpretation is discussed in the notes below example (8.9).

(8.9)	1.	*Dug-dugedo*	*yana*	*anganinama*	*ga'lalpai*	*yunelo*
		spilling	*yarn*	*to me*	*talking*	*stop*
		thakthak-atu	**yana**	**-aanha-ninama**	**gulpa-la-**	**yuna-lu**
		pierce.REDUPL-?	yarn	1SG.OBJ-?	speak	then

'It is coming out … (while she) is yarning, speaking (to me).'

2.

Bero-berelin	*bureminin*	*nganbai*	*rumelban*	*waki*
She's laughing	*pouring it*	*into the other*	*too much*	*in that*
piripiri-lin	**pura-minin**	**nganba-i**	**rumelban**	**waki?**
laugh-?	drop out-?	to bone-?	?	

'She is laughing … while pouring out …'

buremin-ai	*yana*	*anganinama*	*dug-dugedo*
pouring	*yarn*	*to me*	*spilling*
pura-minai	**yana**	**-aanha-ninama**	**thakthak-atu**
drop out-?	yarn	1SG.OBJ-?	pierce.REDUPL-?

'It is coming out … while she is yarning, speaking (to me).'

Notes

The word *dug-dugedo* appears to be based on the root **thaka** 'pierce, write', also found in **thak-mala** 'to float, to drift loose'. We assume that the form *dug-dugedo* means something like 'stuff is coming out'.

We assume that the form *yana* is the English word 'yarn'.

We suggest that the first part of the form *anganinama* is the bound 1st person singular object/possessive form **-aanha**. The second part of this word presumably contains other bound morphemes. Alternatively, the word may contain the alternate free form of the 1st person singular object pronoun, **nganha** followed by the oblique suffix **-na**.

The word *galalpai* is the root **kulpa** 'to talk', possibly with a further **-la** suffix.

The word *yunelo* contains the root **yuna** 'then' with a suffix, possibly the purposive **-lu**.

The word *Beroberolin* is probably connected with **piri**, the name of a malicious mythical creature who has a cackling laugh. The usual Paakantyi word for 'laugh' is **kiinta**.

The word *puremin* contains the root **pura**, 'to fall out, drop out'. A word built on this root is also recorded in the story told by Peter Boney about the Eagle and Crow (Tindale 1939). In that story the form is written by Tindale (1939: 248) as *'purabalit'pili*, with the meaning 'I am going over' (*pili* is glossed by Tindale as 'now' later on the same page). Note that the form **pururu** 'further, over there' is found in the song composed by Monkey and sung by Dan Limberry (see section 8.2.1).

The word *nganbai* is glossed as 'into the other'. We suggest that this may be a root **nganba-**, which is also found in the Eagle and Crow story (Tindale 1939: 246) in the form *nan 'ŋanbar'du:ma* glossed as 'I will catch you with a bone'; *ŋanba* is glossed by Tindale as 'magic bone'.

The word *rumelban* is curious. There is only one r- initial word listed in Hercus's Paakantyi dictionary, **raltha-raltha** spurwing plover. Tindale shows several other r- initial words in the Eagle and Crow story (1939: 250). It is tempting to think that the word is used in connection with English 'rum'.

8.3 Song documented by Hermann Beckler

A song was written down by Dr Hermann Beckler at Menindee in 1861, during the Burke and Wills expedition.[10] Beckler published this song in 1868 as part of group of songs collected in Queensland, together with words, some explanation of the meaning and a musical transcription. The transcription is given in Box 8.20.

Box 8.20: Song transcribed by Beckler

text: *Bai indi bai indi balema balegna onbai indi bai indi gan on bale*

gloss: "Hier möge nur noch der den Anfang machende Gesang, eine Hymne, wenn man will, Musik und Text treu wiedergegeben, Platz finden. Ich ließ mir nachher sagen, es sei ein Gebet, eine Bitte an ihren Gott, um ein großes Uebel, vielleicht eine Krankheit, von ihnen abzuwenden" (Beckler 1868, 84): "Here there is only space for the opening song, a hymn, if you like, with music and text faithfully represented. I heard from later enquiries that it was a prayer, a request to their god, to avert a great evil, perhaps an illness."

Source: Beckler (1868); adapted by authors based on transcription in Skinner and Wafer (2016).[11]

10 We are grateful to the excellent website, Graeme Skinner and Jim Wafer, 'A Checklist of Colonial Era Musical Transcriptions of Australian Indigenous Songs', *Australharmony* (an online resource toward the early history of music in colonial Australia), 11 January 2016, accessed 28 July 2017, sydney.edu.au/paradisec/australharmony/checklist-indigenous-music-1.php, for drawing our attention to this. This song is listed as 18.3 on the website.

11 Skinner and Wafer, 'A Checklist of Colonial Era Musical Transcriptions of Australian Indigenous Songs: 18.3 Darling Downs Corroboree 2', accessed 28 July 2017, sydney.edu.au/paradisec/australharmony/checklist-indigenous-music-1.php#018.

The musical transcription of this song as it appears in Beckler (1868) is given as Figure 8.1:

Figure 8.1: Musical transcription of song documented by Beckler

Source: Beckler (1868).

The only linguistic analysis that we can suggest is that the words *balema, balegna and bale* may be based on a single root **pal-**. Luise Hercus suggested that this could be related to a group of words having meanings similar to 'good', such as **palii-mala** 'well' and **palirika, paliira** 'nice, good beautiful' (see Hercus 1993).

A musical analysis shows an A, A1, B, A, B with coda form for the rhythm. The rhythmic cells are:

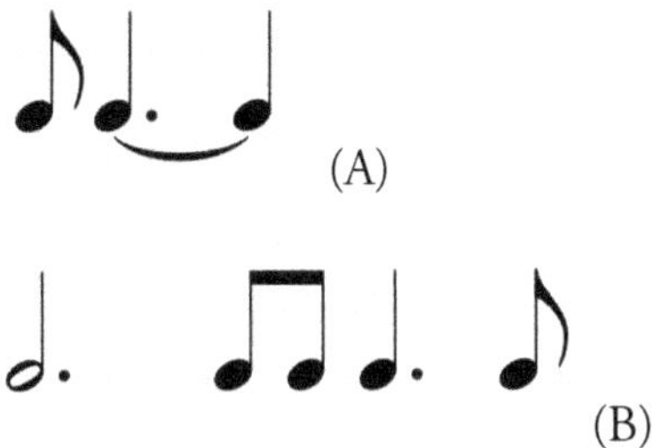

with a brief coda a

(C).

Schematically, we have:

A (x6) rest A (x2) rest A (x1) rest B + A(1)

A (x6) rest B + C (Coda)

Generally, the song is in two verses with short sections in between. The melody descends gradually by semitones for the first verse, then rises to descend again on the final verse.

The melody for the A section descends a semitone for the first three repetitions (G–F#), then descends a minor third G–E), reverting to the semitone pattern (F–E) for the next four repetitions. One repetition of this pattern with an extra E at the start is sung, then, after the rest, the B section begins with a dotted minim on E followed by a pattern of F–D–G and F#. The A section begins again with a G–F#, followed by a rise (A–F#), then a descending pattern of A#–F#, A–F#, G–E, F–E, F–E. The upper note of the two pitches descends thus chromatically. After a rest, the B pattern occurs, followed by the C coda on G–F#–E.

8.4 Fletcher's song

Another song for which there is a sound recording is that made of the singer Fletcher at Swan Reach on 20 March 1927. The head of the expedition that made the recording was Prof. E.H. Davies, and the expedition was reported in the *Murray Pioneer and Australian River Record*, 8 April 1927, where the singer is named as Frank Fletcher. He was born near Wentworth and was of the Kilpara moiety, and his totem was a silver fish. He moved 'down river' as a young man after a 'wrong' marriage and never returned to his country. He was interviewed by Norman Tindale a number of times.

Although the report in the newspaper does not say so, we believe that Norman Tindale was also present on this occasion, and that there is a single recording of this song, made on that day. The AIATSIS audition text for this recording[12] includes a transcription of the introduction, which is believed was spoken by Norman Tindale, saying:

> Record of a song made by Fletcher at Swan Reach on March the 20th 1927. Fletcher's name is Ilya-Marrina. The song originated about 50 years ago and was composed by another blackfellow of the Wentworth district. The song itself has a reference to places in neighbourhood of Broken Hill.

The recording is listed as being part of Tape No. 9567 (collection SAM_01 at AIATSIS). The portion of the recording that includes Fletcher's song commences at 10:46. The sound on the recording is too unclear to produce a linguistic transcription, but a musical transcription is possible. The song is arranged into what sound like verses. In total there were five verses, but the fifth is incomplete because the cylinder ran out.

Only the first verse (11:28 to 11:45 on the original recording) is transcribed here. The subsequent verses contain basically the same musical material as the first. It sounds as if it might be based on some non-Indigenous song with a 6/8 rhythm. It shares none of the musical features of the other songs for which we have musical transcriptions in this volume.

12 SAM_01-009567_audition.pdf.

Figure 8.2: Musical notation of the first verse of Fletcher's song
Source: Grace Koch.

The melody proceeds in a 6/8 metre until the last two measures changing to a 5/8 metre.

8.5 Steamer song: Taken from an old newspaper

The final song that we present here is not a traditional song, but is included here to make a more-or-less complete list of songs in languages related to Paakantyi. It was found by Jeanette Hope (pers. comm.) in an old newspaper[13] who passed it on to Luise Hercus. Given Luise's detailed knowledge of Paakantyi, she was effectively the only person who could present a linguistic analysis of this song. The steamer referred to is apparently the PS *Warrego*.[14]

The text of the song is presented in Box 8.21:

13 We have not been able to trace the source of this through Trove.

14 A photo of the *Warrego*, taken on the Darling, is found at State Library of SA, 'P.S. Warrego on the Darling [PRG 1258/1/3968] Photograph', accessed 26 August 2019, collections.slsa.sa.gov.au/resource/PRG+1258/1/3968. According to Wikipedia, the *Warrego* was destroyed by fire in 1900. Wikipedia, 'List of Murray–Darling Steamboats', accessed 25 September 2019, en.wikipedia.org/wiki/List_of_Murray%E2%80%93Darling_steamboats.

Box 8.21: Steamer song

Teemer, teemer, tumble down, Wimbie a bogie kitchie toorie no good, Bale give em blanket, Bale give em flour, Bale give em tobacco, Kumbooka witchie gamma moora, Good morning, old woman.

Source: Jeanette Hope (pers. comm.) in an old, unidentifed newspaper; adapted by authors.

This song is partly in English, partly in pidgin (words shown in bold italic) and partly in Paakantyi (words shown in bold). Our analysis is presented in (8.10):

(8.10)

Teemer	*teemer*	*tumble*	*down*
steamer	steamer	tumble	down
steamer	steamer	tumble	down

'The steamer, the steamer is tumbling down.'

Wimbie a	*bogie*	*kitchie*	*toorie*	*no good*
wimpiya	***bogie***	**kityi**	**thuri**	no good
person	bathe	this one	rise up	no good

'The people are bathing, this one is rising up and it's no good.'

Bale	*Give*	*em*	*blanket*
bale	give	em	blanket
no	give	them	blanket

'(No one) gives them blankets.'

Bale	*give*	*em*	*flour*
bale	give	em	flour
no	give	them	flour

'(No one) gives them flour.'

Bale	*give*	*em*	*tobacco*
bale	give	em	tobacco
no	give	them	tobacco

'(No one) gives them tobacco.'

Kumbooka	*witchie*	*gamma*	*moora*
kumpaka	**wiitya**	***gamma***	**muRa**
wife	drink	give me	quickly

'The old woman gives me drink quickly.'

Good	*morning*	*old*	*woman*
good	morning	old	woman
good	morning	old	woman

'Good morning old woman.'

9

Yorta Yorta songs

A number of Yorta Yorta[1] songs have come down to us from a range of sources. Songs in this language were both traditional songs and Christian songs, such as the well-known Bura Fera 'Pharoah' that is a translation reportedly made by Thomas Shadrack James, a teacher at the Maloga mission school. Bura Fera was recently highlighted in the 2012 film *The Sapphires*.[2] In this present study, we are not including a discussion of these Christian songs (Bowe and Morey 1999: 117 discuss these in detail), along with several songs of English mixed with some Yorta Yorta words (see further Bowe and Morey 1999: 116).

One of these mixed songs was introduced in Bowe and Morey (1999: 117) as 'in the single manuscript sheet of A. Edwards, he mentions the following song: "Coroboree Song of the Moira Lake tribe of blacks, composed by Johnny, their chief, on first seeing a breech-loading gun, about the year 1875"'. Bowe and Morey (1999) describe this source as 'material given to the Rutherford family of Deniliquin, who historically had attachment to the Ulupna Homestead, and passed on to members of Geraldine Briggs' family'. Unfortunately, we do not know anything about the chief named Johnny.

1 We use this spelling because it is the one adopted by the community. We do not wish to claim, by this spelling, that there is a retroflex stop. Hercus (1986: 239) recorded this word as ['yo·ta].

2 For a description of the film, see Wikipedia, '*The Sapphires* (film)', 10 April 2012, accessed 21 July 2017, en.wikipedia.org/wiki/The_Sapphires_(film).

The full text of this song is presented as Box 9.1:

Box 9.1: Corroboree song of the Moira Lake tribe

Boung ang ah! Boung ang ah! Melbourne
Ah! dunning ah! cartridge, breech-loader,
webalung oh! gebero, jedero, powder, ah pucka
wunga kingen kat, mungino, weri weri
jah mung oh! De, bung ang ah!

Source: Edwards (c. 1875); adapted by authors.

Most of the words in this song are either English or probably onomatopoeic. Bowe and Morey (1999: 117) noted that 'none of the words in the song accord with the word listed by Robinson for "gun" or "musket", *po.mid.er.re. ger*'. We have included its text here because it was a corroboree song, but we are not able to offer any further analysis of it.

We are pleased, however, to be able to present several song texts that were not known to Bowe and Morey (1999) and which have either never been published or have been out of the public view for many years. These are the corroboree song published in the *Riverine Herald* on 21 December 1892, the version of the 'Down the railway' song sung by Camelia Satchell, and the songs, cries and chants as part of the Boys' initiation ceremony, part of John Atkinson's statement that was written down by R.H. Mathews (NLA MS 8006/3/4.1, Notebook 1) in the last decade of the nineteenth century.

The traditional songs presented can be grouped into (1) corroboree songs, (2) a hunting song, (3) a chant relating to tribal territory, (4) a song about an evil spirit, the Hairy Beka chant, and (5) a song sung as part of the initiation ceremony. A list of the songs that are discussed here is presented in Table 9.1:

Table 9.1: List of Yorta Yorta traditional songs

Song	Source	Bowe and Morey page references	Section
Corroboree song	*Riverine Herald*, 21 December 1892	-	9.2.1
Corroboree songs	Locke in Smyth (1878, 2: 335)	112	9.2.2
Hunting song	Curr (1887: 579)	112	9.3
Chant relating to tribal territory	Eastman MS: 8	116	-
The Hairy Beka chant	Margaret Tucker singing, recorded by Luise Hercus	113	9.5.1

Song	Source	Bowe and Morey page references	Section
Down the railway	As recorded by Wayne Atkinson, and also Camelia Satchell singing, recorded by Luise Hercus	-	9.5.2
Cries and songs from the Boys' initiation ceremony	John Atkinson's statement (R.H. Mathews, NLA MS 8006/3/4.1, Notebook 1, pp. 166–72)	-	9.6

Source: Bowe and Morey (1999); adapted by authors.

Note that in our linguistic analyses, we follow the regularised spellings used by Bowe and Morey (1999). In most cases the rhotic is written as a double **rr** here; however, Bowe and Morey did not use that consistently (see for example, 1999: 52), although in the word list (1999: 164–274), double **rr** is usually employed.

9.1 Musical terminology in Yorta Yorta

Words listed in Bowe and Morey (1999) relating to song and dance are presented in Table 9.2:

Table 9.2: Words for 'song' and 'dance' in Yorta Yorta

Regularised spelling	Sources[3]
damánmu-	*tumman'muty* 'corroboree' (R.H. Mathews); *dum num mitter* 'dance' (Robinson)
garra-	*kurradhan* 'dance' (R.H. Mathews); *cur.re.yae, cur re yuc* 'corroboree' (Robinson)
watjúka gorrkara	*warchūka kōrkora* 'drive away by means of a song' (Curr) (compare gorrkara 'rain')
bayi-	*bayiya, bâ-ee-ya* 'sing' (R.H. Mathews)

Source: Bowe and Morey (1999); adapted by authors.

We do not have any information about the process of 'driving away by means of a song', but we assume that this refers to evil or otherwise undesirable spirits and entities, and the likely related phenomenon of driving away illness.

3 We have not listed all the sources here, just a selection. Readers who want to see all the sources should consult Bowe and Morey (1999).

9.2 Corroboree songs

9.2.1 Corroboree song 1

The corroboree song presented here was published in the *Riverine Herald*, a newspaper read both in Echuca and Moama, in 1892.[4] It is the reminiscences, written in the first person, of an (as yet unidentified) man who states that he left the Bendigo Goldfields in 1850[5] with his 'mate Bill Symons' and arrived in Echuca just as it was being founded, staying in a pub 'kept by a man named Hopwood'. This Hopwood is Henry Hopwood (1813–1869), a former convict who made his way to the Murray River in 1848 and set up a hotel and a punt. The post office of Echuca was known as 'Hopwood's Punt' until 1855. The writer of this story would have arrived in Echuca in the early 1850s, and the corroboree that he described must have been performed around that time.

The location of the corroboree was at what is now the Echuca Post Office, at 226 Pakenham Street.[6] It is close to both the Murray and the Campaspe rivers, but is not at the junction of the two.

The text relating to the corroboree is presented as Box 9.2.

Box 9.2: Corroboree song 1

One night the blacks held a "corroboree" just about where your post-office now stands. If I live till I am as old as Methuselah I'll never forget that night. The blacks, some two hundred of them, were all painted like living skeletons, each rib being re-produced on the outside by means of white or yellow ochre. Their faces wore hideously marked, and as the gleams of the dew fell on their forms they looked like ... [some words obscured in online version] fanatical devils. As they danced around, clashing their sticks together, and chanting a sort of verse, they were for all the world like a lot of demon's let loose. I'll give you an idea of their song.

Here he got into the centre of the bar floor, and beating both heels together on the boards, he capered nimbly around, chanting the following : —

"Yama nong a neepeeah

Anortha to tha teeno ;

4 The whole article from which this was taken can be seen at 'Echuca – Then and Now', *Riverine Herald*, 21 December 1892, 2, accessed 21 July 2017, trove.nla.gov.au/newspaper/article/114694538?searchTerm=Echuca%20then%20now&searchLimits=exactPhrase|||anyWords|||notWords|||requestHandler|||dateFrom=1892-12-21|||dateTo=1892-12-21|||l-advtitle=311|||sortby.

5 This is not accurate, as gold was not discovered in Bendigo until September 1851.

6 Located at 36.1293316 South, 144.7489861 East.

Nai mine, crah bien, crah bine,

Crah bone, crah boo !

Yah — r-r-r-r-r-r — rah ! !

The old fellow danced around with much gusto, finishing off with a great rattle of "r's," and concluding with a "rah !" like the snap of a rat trap.

Source: *Riverine Herald*, 21 December 1892, p. 2; adapted by authors.

Our suggested regularisation of this song is given as (9.1):

(9.1) **yama nong(g)a n(h)ipiya**
(ng)anorrtha dotha d(h)inu
n(h)ai main grapin grapain
grapon grapu
da rrrrrr ra(h)!

Notes

Without any information about the meaning of the song, we can only speculate at what the words here might mean. The first word might be **yama** 'to run', and it is possible that the first phrase *yama nong a* means 'run from', which was recorded as having the form *yamin noynuck* (Barry 1867). Note also that one of the songs translated by Ludwig Becker as being from 'the Lower Murray' is named as Yaam-song (see section 14.2).

There is no word in the various sources for Yorta Yorta listed in Bowe and Morey (1999) that is of the form *neepeeah*, but G.A. Robinson did record *nite yer* 'creek'. If this line meant either 'run away to the creek' or 'run away from the creek', we would expect either an allative suffix or an ablative suffix, but there does not appear to be one (see Bowe and Morey 1999: 58 for discussion of those suffixes).

The last part of the song appears to be vocable or onomatopoeic. There do not appear to have been initial clusters in Yorta Yorta, and so the section of the song *crah bien, crah bine, crah bone, crah boo*, which we have regularised with initial **grap-**, would not meet the usual phonotactic rules of the language, as also the rhotic trills *r-r-r-r-r-r* and *rah*. It is possible that *crah bine* and so on actually represents English 'grab him'.

9.2.2 Corroboree songs reported by Locke

Three songs were written down by Locke (Smyth 1878, 2: 335), who introduced them thus: 'The three following were their favourite corrobborees'. They are presented as Box 9.3:

Box 9.3: Corroboree songs written by Locke

1.	Berri berri ma, jildomba
	Berri berri ma, jildomba
	Berri berri ma, jildomba-naga
	Athen jindema, no goi-eela;
	Jindema, jindema, o-en-dethen-o.
	Warrim bang-e, berri berri ma jildomba-a,
	Berri berri ma jildomba, berri berri ma jildomba.
2	Aree muthe-e, aree mutho-o
	Aree mutha, comang-a thalitanga magoonba
	Malang-oree, malang-oree
	Mullin mullin jing-a magoonbang-a jiltang-a
	Jing-a jing-a, gothanga, magoontanga thalato
3.	Thunda irra tha, thunda ra-oo,
	Gra imalang-a imee-a;
	Thunda irra tha, thunda re-e,
	Gra imalang-a, imme-e-e

Source: Smyth (1878, 2: 335); adapted by authors.

We are not able to add further to the analysis beyond that done by Bowe and Morey (1999: 113) who suggested the following:

> Song 1, lines 1–3, 7; *berri berri ma*; may be the Yorta Yorta expression **birrama** 'go away'
>
> Song 1, line 4; *goi-eela*; possibly **Gaiyila** 'Goulburn River'
>
> Song 1, line 6; *bang-e*; may be the Yorta Yorta past participle **banga**
>
> Song 1, line 6; *warrim bang-e*; possibly **worrwa** 'climb' + **banga** 'PAST'
>
> Song 2, line 2; *mutha*; possibly **matha** 'canoe'
>
> Song 2, line 4; *magoon*; possibly **makun** 'fish, perch'
>
> Song 2, line 4; *bang-a*; may be the Yorta Yorta past participle **banga**

Song 2, line 4; *mullin*; may be the Yorta Yorta word **malin** 'beat'

Song 3, lines 2, 4; *imalang*; appears to be the Yorta Yorta word **(y)imilang** 'today' (which also appears in the corroboree song recorded by Curr).

9.3 Hunting song

The hunting song documented by Curr (1887, 3: 579) also included a translation. The text with Curr's translation is presented in Box 9.4:

Box 9.4: Hunting song recorded by Curr

Ngoe immilang kai-i-mer,	Yes, today (we will have) kangaroo,
Yoorta yanna yooringa,	Not go sun (or before sundown),
Wanama wai panama,	...
Yoorta purra wollikthia.	Not red kangaroo fat.

Source: Curr (1887, 3: 579); adapted by authors.

The analysis from Bowe and Morey (1999) is presented as (9.2):

(9.2) *Ngoe immilang kai-i-mer*

Yes today (we will have) kangaroo,

ngowe **imilang** **gaiyimarr**

yes today kangaroo

'Yes, today (we will have/hunt) kangaroo.'

Yoorta yanna yooringa

Not go sun (or before sundown),

yota **yana** **yurrnga**

NEG go sun

'Not going (before) sun (down).'

Wanama wai panama

...

wanama **wayi** **banama**

Curr did not suggest a translation for this line. Bowe and Morey (1999: 112) suggested that the first word might be 'eagle', based on a form *wanmir* 'hawk', recorded in the *Exposition Internationale Melbourne* (Barry 1867).

Yoorta purra wollikthia
Not red kangaroo fat.

yota	**barra**	**walitja**
NEG	red kangaroo	fat

'Not red kangaroo fat.'

Bowe and Morey (1999: 112) further observed that '[t]he language used in the song shows considerable economy of word usage. The vocabulary is standard but the only verb that is recognisable is in a non-inflected form (perhaps because it occurs in a nominal context.)'.

9.4. Chant relating to tribal territory

Another text discussed by Bowe and Morey (1999: 23) is listed as follows (Box 9.5):

Box 9.5: Eastman text

(xiv) c. 1890 Eastman MS

(EA) The Aborigines – their life and contact with the whites'. Manuscript, contained in Riverina Records, Mitchell Library, Sydney. Microfiche CY 1249. Four-line lyric, one word, and some discussion of Yorta Yorta/Yabula Yabula relations.

Source: Bowe and Morey (1999: 23); adapted by authors.

This included a four-line song, in mixed English and Yorta Yorta, which is discussed in Bowe and Morey (1999: 117). The original source is the typescript version (MLMSS 130, B 1341)[7] that contains a reference to the usage of traditional song, on page 8. These comments are presented in Box 9.6.

Box 9.6: Chant relating to tribal territory

The education of the youth included a boundary line direction by the elders who would accompany the pupils – Various notable spots on the boundary chain give a name – later to be memorized into a whole, into a sing song reputedly bird-like chant. I can only recall an odd spot or name on a round, I once heard run over by an aboriginal the significance of which made appeal possible in these two instances. The one "Thuggera-munnera" given a clump of trees one of which had been struck by lightning, the word meaning Thunder which then treated in pure Abo it rather resembles.

Source: Eastman MS, p. 4, adapted by authors.

7 This can be looked up at State Library of NSW, 'Hugh Malcolm Eastman Memoirs, ca. 1850 – ca. 1952', MLMSS 130, B 1341, accessed 27 August 2019, archival.sl.nsw.gov.au/Details/archive/110319508.

Bowe and Morey (1999: 234) list the word for 'thunder' as **munarra**, a word attested in a number of sources. We cannot offer any explanation of the meaning of *thooggera*.

The Western Kulin word for 'thunder' is **marndarr** in Wemba Wemba. Eastman was based at Morago, which is west of Deniliquin in Kulin territory; but he does also talk about the Yorta Yorta speaking areas. We assume that this text is indeed in Yorta Yorta.

9.5 Songs recorded in the 1960s

9.5.1 Hairy Beka chant

The Hairy Beka chant is a rare example of a traditional song that survived in the 1960s and continues to be sung until the present day.

Bowe and Morey (1999: 113) wrote of it that:

> The Hairy Beka chant is the best known traditional story fragment known today for which we can confidently provide an analysis. There were apparently many stories of a hairy creature called the Beka of whom children were afraid. Curr gives the meaning of Beka as 'ghost' (pĕk-ka Cb, pekka Ct). Lois Peeler recalls hearing stories from her grandmother (Theresa Middleton Clements) about the Hairy Beka which had a strong odour. It had long white hair, long arms and legs and when it walked its bones made a creaking sound (Bowe, Peeler and Atkinson 1997:23).
>
> When speaking to Luise Hercus, Priscilla McCrae (Hpmc) recounts a story in which an old woman, an old witch, (the Beka) is said to have been left at home to mind the children while their fathers and mothers went out hunting.

There are two versions of the text of this chant, both recorded by Luise Hercus, one from Priscilla McCrae, presented in Box 9.7, and the second from Margaret Tucker, presented as example (9.3). There is also a related song, 'Down the railway', in two versions, discussed in section 9.5.2. Howitt (1904: 289) also describes how the counting out of parts of the body was done, and in his manuscript describes counting out information relating to ceremonies (SLV MS Box 1053/6 (b), hw0421.pdf, pp. 25–26).

The text of the chant, spoken but not sung, by Priscilla McCrae was recorded by Luise Hercus in July 1963, on the recording digitised by AIATSIS as HERCUS_L04-000217A.wav (original name field tape 21/14). The discussion of the Hairy Beka chant commences at 52:31, with an explanation of the context. A cut file of this recording has been uploaded to YouTube at youtu.be/_NKS0G_TkZ8.

This text arose when the parents of some children went off hunting for a whole day and their children were left with an old lady, whose task was 'to have a hole dug and a fire made and this oven heated up for the prey that they'd bring, and then they'd have a good cook up and a good meal'.

The detailed explanation of the chant as given by Priscilla McCrae is presented in Box 9.7 (this portion commences from 54:08 on HERCUS_L04-000217A.wav). Our transcription is largely based on Bowe and Morey (1999: 114) but slightly altered following another opportunity to listen to the recording.

Box 9.7: Hairy Beka chant as explained by Priscilla McCrae, context and text

Then the story goes on. It's sort of a twist up. The story goes on that while the mother and father were away, this old lady, real old lady the witches like, you know, she got very nasty to the children, cos the mother and father was all away, this is a horrible thing. So she said to them 'Come and get some sticks and we'll make a (they call fire ***bitja***, see), bring us some wood we'll make a big ***bitja*** now and make this oven hot for your mother and father cause they'll be running, throwing it in and throwing it in, and so she said I'm going to go away from here, and these children come on, all go round now, go right round this hole. Sit down and lean over, lean over like that' And she came along, it is a fable, but this is the yarn they used to tell, see, and some of the language came into this, she'd start at this one and she'd say: ***Woningenda, gɔruminda, deewin ngangabrawin***. ... then she'd get that one there see, and that one'd fall in.

Source: Bowe and Morey (1999: 114), adapted by authors.

Priscilla McCrae went on to explain the meanings of the expressions in the counting out chant. The transcriptions presented in example (9.3) have been slightly adjusted from Bowe and Morey (1999: 114) after listening to the tapes again.

(9.3)	[wonigənda]	'this one here'
	[gɔɹʊmənda]	'you here'
	[de:jawɪn]	'this one'
	[ŋaŋa brawɪn]	'you too'

The word [gɔɹʊmənda] does not accord with our other knowledge of the Yorta Yorta language, and so Bowe and Morey (1999: 114) suggested it was based on the root **mumin-** 'seize', as shown by their analysis, presented as (9.4):

(9.4) *Woningenda gomenda deewin ngangabrawin?*

womigin-da	**muman-da**	**deyawin**	**ngangaburrayawin**
where-3SG	seize.NON.FUT-3SG	this one	that far one

'Which one is (s)he seizing, this one, that far one?'

It is also possible that the second word is based on **buraya-** 'far'; that is, referring to you over there.

Curr (1887: 578) documented a sentence that has a related meaning. The linguistic analysis is presented as (9.5):

(9.5) *Which one will you take or seize*

womigin ngia mommon

womigin	**ngina(k)**	**muman**
which	you	seize.PRES

'Which one will you seize?'

A second version of the chant was sung by Margaret Tucker, recorded by Luise Hercus on 1 August 1962 at Broadmeadows, on field tape 21/2, which has been digitised by AIATSIS as HERCUS_L04-000211A.wav. The Hairy Beka chant is found at 54:27 on this recording. A cut file of this recording has been uploaded to YouTube at youtu.be/t_n9E9KOhFc.

The linguistic analysis is presented as (9.6):

(9.6) *Ngangaburai, ngangaburai, ngangaburai, deyawin*

o	**ngangaburraya**	**ngangaburraya**	**ngangaburraya**	**deyawin**
EXCL	that far (one)	that far (one)	that far (one)	this one

'That one, that one, that one ... this one!'

The musical analysis, as done by Grace Koch, is presented as Figure 9.1. The word **deyawin** is spoken clearly and loudly rather than sung.

Hairy Beka Song

Sung by Margaret Tucker to Luise Hercus

HERCUS_L04-000211A_MargaretTucker_HairyBekaChant_SongOnly

Range: Octave (G# - G#)

Figure 9.1: Musical analysis of Margaret Tucker's version of the Hairy Beka chant

Source: Grace Koch.

The song is a chant mostly on one pitch with an octave leap towards the end followed by a spoken phrase. The song maintains a triple metre throughout.

9.5.2 Down the railway

A longer song, containing English words but also the same material as the Hairy Beka chant, was documented by Wayne Atkinson (1981: 64) from Priscilla McCrae. The explanation and song are presented as Box 9.8:

Box 9.8: Down the railway as sung by Priscilla McCrae

the old people taught us the corroboree song and we used to sit down with our legs crossed and a pillow in our laps, beating the pillows and singing while they'd be corroboreeing. We used to sing …

Down the railway, goobya goobya (go away)

narabri	*der yuh win*	*ngungarbri win*
you	this one	here
woolba woolba	*woothamayi*	
that one	there look	
derya wyn	*ngungabri wyn*	
this one	here look	

Source: Bowe and Morey (1999: 115), adapted by authors.

The analysis based on Bowe and Morey (1999: 115–16) is presented here as (9.7):

(9.7) *Down the Railway*

goobya goobya	
go away	
gabai	**gabai**
come.IMP	come.IMP

narabri	*der yuh win*	*ngungarbri win*
you	*this one*	*here*
ngangaburraya	**deyawin**	**ngangaburrayawin**
that far (one)	this one	that far one

woolba woolba	*woothamayi*
that one	*there look*
wulba wulba	**wuthamayi**
?	?

derya wyn	*ngungabri wyn*
this one	*here look*
deyawin	**ngangaburraya**
this one	that far one

'Down the railway, come, come, that one, this one, that one there, … this one, that one there.'

A second version of this song, with different words, was sung by Camellia Satchell for Luise Hercus on 28 November 1965 at Bendigo. This was originally recorded on Hercus field tape 21/40, and digitised by AIATSIS as HERCUS_L03-001002B.wav. This song is found at 8:59 on the digitised recording. A cut file of this recording has been uploaded to YouTube at youtu.be/IkdHovT52OA.

Our transcription of the words is given in (9.8):

(9.8) *Down the Railway*

yagabai o

girri bang o

gilau

She went on to say that the song was learned from Cummeragunja Mission and 'all used to sing it'.

We are not able to offer any analysis of the meaning of this song. We have not included a transcription of the music, as this song does not appear to be traditional music.

9.6 Songs and cries from the Boys' initiation ceremony

In this section we present John Atkinson's statement, a section of six pages in R.H. Mathews (NLA MS 8006/3/4.1, Notebook 1). The statement includes very clear detail about the Boys' initiation ceremony, and three short songs as well as some cries and several short songs. Much of the information contained in this statement was published by Mathews (1904: 306–22)[8] under the heading 'The Wonggoa or Wongupka Ceremony'. In that publication, Mathews combined into a single account information about the Yorta Yorta ceremony with those about the Dhudhuroa Wanggo'a and Dyibbau ceremonies (see Chapter 10), and probably other ceremonies, without clearly indicating the sources (see further section 9.6.1).

This is one of several documents relating to the initiation ceremonies in the R.H. Mathews notebooks, the others of which are information about the *Wonga'a* ceremony, described on pp. 62–64, the *Jibâga* (pp. 66–68), and the *Wôngŭmŭk* (pp. 69–73). It is not clear who the informants for these three descriptions were, nor in what order they were performed. Since these descriptions do not contain text, transcriptions of these are not presented here.

John Atkinson was one of the leaders of the community. He is probably the same John Atkinson who died on 24 December 1912 at the age of 58, his parents having been named in his death certificate as John Atkinson and Kitty Erran. His place of death was Moira Station.

8 Reprinted as a book in 1905. We believe the text of the 1905 book is largely the same as the 1904 article.

The full text of John Atkinson's statement is given in Box 9.9:

Box 9.9: John Atkinson's statement

p. 166

Wūngupga Ngunnē as sweetheart looks after a boy

R-Rirt! Yeh! Wah! I stamp one foot

Boys muster in ring every afternoon for 2 or 3 weeks

Ye! Yeh! Wirr! This lasts for about a week

At the end of this time they say Birr! Weh! Woh! Wir!

Kā'lurtē' one old man sings out while they are dancing round

repeating that word

Yēbok! and the old fellow sings out and repeated by mob

Bu! i! = no more and then fellow sings out and they repeat

Yeh ! and then fellow & repeat and that finishes it

Last moon, boys put in goanga & and sit round him

His mother is outside in direction by country. She gets one of his ngorea [kilt - inserted] & swings it round her head & dances round. Presently cover boys with [lots of-inserted] rugs, [sewn together-inserted], furry side up. Some men prop the middle up. Man in the bark shovels throw hot ashes & coals on top of rug. Men propping rug sing out Bir-Bir-Bir! and turn boys round until all the ashes thrown up. The boys put sitting in same spot. All the men gather up the swags. After the boys leave the women scrape up the ashes which are thrown

p. 167

on the boys into a heap in the goanga. The boys mother has the boys Ngore tied on the end of a reed spear and stand it in the side of the heap-all mothers do the same. A boys mother's sister [might-crossed out] [would-inserted] also have a ngore in a similar manner. The mothers & female relatives dance round the heap while the boys are going away but a crowd of men prevent them from seeing the boys.

The boys are led out of the goanga into the bush

Your great grandfather is coming directly to take you along on the dry land in a canoe (muttha). They throw a bit of bark and it makes a whirring sound. On they travel & camp they are thirsty. Lets give the boys a drink of water. They make a little papal'war (little for water) [& heat-crossed out] bend a rod over it with a few leaves attached -They cut some rush-grass and put it flat on top of the water. Then they go and chop a dhūlpaka out of a tree & make it into a bullroarer, with a string attached. When all is ready they fell one and then. All the time little bits of bark are whirled about. The men say

p. 168

"They'll be with you presently" A big fire is made - A very large one. Even as fire is blazing up well the men start swinging bullroarer in different places around. Keep away they'll get inside the boat directly. At that the blankets are taken off. And at that they hand the boy his great g f who was going to sail him in the canoe [put under around - inserted]. They caution boys

Dharamulan - Bĭng'algä - Baraina

When Dharamulan was burnt he pulled at his tongue and threw it into all the trees.

Next thing all the boys are brought to the waterhole and kneel down with elbows on ground & take a mouthful each, and all the men do the same. They all go [to th - crossed out] round the fire with mouthfulls of water and squirt the water into it & quench it & pull the boys aside to that it won't blaze on the dance. Now if you open mouth you will be killed like the fire is put out. Then they sing Dh. song

Bing'alga wanha wurrana

Bing'alga wan'ba warrana yeh! woh

This is sung in day time

p. 169

They leave that place and go on to a camping place where they play antics. Women in family way. [song of it - crossed out] [spears shake in ground all around her in night time - inserted]

[Banggorba - crossed out] Bandha'nggorba anborba

Wirragĭñ ngaia

This is sung in night time

Any time men go back to woman's camp, two women go run to meet them with spears and tails and pass tail round head & run back to goang'a & dance.

After all this boys are brought in with about a rate of a run or jog. All boys painted with forked bough over each shoulder led with string in front. The mothers come out a short distance to meet them, with each a bunch of boughs or twigs, a mother and her sister meet the lad and one goes each side - They all in a string as the mothers run along with the boy, they sing yer! yer! and strike him on the side - hips - with the boughs, until the first boy is

p. 170

[Here is a small drawing of a circle, with a dot in the middle, slightly towards the left, marked 'fire' and an image of a fire, with a wavy line leading from the right of the circle]

they are plucked this day they are brought back to fire

at the fire at the bott of a tall tree and stand - all the others stand round they throw the leaves on the fire, and push the boys in - the men do this - the mothers stand back as the boys stand on the green bushes in the thick smoke till nearly suffocated. the guardian takes him to 20 feet away where there are logs laid together with leaves on top for a seat. The boy is put sitting down on the top of the bag. All the mothers go back to the camp. After that they are taken off the seat (Karkaria) they are taken to a bough shed where they sleep that night.

Next morning they are taken away before sunrise by two old men and camp out in the bush till after sundown when they are brought back to the bough hut.* They go like this for a week or two, then they can come near to the ngu'-lumbar'a or young men's camp and are smoked again. They are now allowed to come into the young man's camp

* [Insert] They must not let a woman's shadow fall on them or walk on a pathway used by women.

p. 171

Ban'upka

Tyibbauga

In a few months, or perhaps a year, they [shave-crossed out] [pluck-inserted] the hair off his face & paint him as for a corroboree, they put ngoree (several ngores). He goes about among the people carrying wood or water-he brings mud-he brings a little stick & [groans?? wader??] it-if they ask him for food will give them the bones. He has a bag slung over his shoulder with a live snake in it with the poison broken up with a stick rubbed on it. He sits down & dungs close to the young woman. [When-crossed out] This goes on for several weeks. He goes to bed and he wakes in the morning all right and goes about quickly and does not go near the women nor more generally with men.

Ban'upka-is the same as Tyibbauga-but they put clay on the centre of his head & shave the hair up into it till it forms [wiya-crossed out] winya or ridge from forehead to back of neck.

Source: R.H. Mathews, NLA MS 8006/3/4.1, Notebook 1, pp. 166–71; adapted by authors.

We can recognise a number of words in this text as being Yorta Yorta. The words in the statement that are not contained in the songs are given in Table 9.3:

Table 9.3: Words in Yorta Yorta language in John Atkinson's statement

Spelling	Translation given	In Bowe and Morey (1999)	Notes
goanga	refers to the camp	**gundja** 'home'	The spelling with *oa* suggests perhaps **gong(g)a** or **gondja**.
ngorea	'kilt'	**ngorra** 'kilt'	The spelling suggests **ngorre**; similar to the Western Kulin *ngouratch* (see section 2.3.4)
muttha	'canoe'	**matha** 'canoe'	-
papal'war	'little for water'	-	babálwa; this is explained in Mathews (1904: 313): 'The men set to work and dig several little holes, papal'wa, about the size of a wash-basin, and bend a small green rod, with some leaves attached, over each hole.' He goes on to explain that the boys will suck the water out of this 'through a net-like covering of loose rush-grass floating on the surface'.
karkaria	'seat'	-	perhaps gagarriya. The root ga- means 'to sit'

Spelling	Translation given	In Bowe and Morey (1999)	Notes
ngu'-lumbar'a	'young man's camp'	–	ngulámbarra
Ban'upka	refers to boy undergoing initiation	banupka 'young man, 16 years'	–

Source: R.H. Mathews, NLA MS 8006/3/4.1, Notebook 1, pp. 166–71; adapted by authors.

The text materials contained in John Atkinson's statement consists of several shouts and short cries that are given at the front of the statement on page 166. These are presented with notes as Table 9.4:

Table 9.4: Cries in John Atkinson's statement

Text of cry/shout	Background information in the statement	Notes
Wūngupga Ngunnē	'as sweetheart looks after a boy'	**wong(g)a** is term for 'a partially initiated boy'. Mathews added 'boy whose tooth is not to be knocked out'. The suffix **pka** is found in a number of words in the language, but its meaning is not clear (Bowe and Morey 1999: 97). It might refer to the state of partial initiation. **ngune** may be a 2nd person singular possessive pronoun, given as **nguni** (Bowe and Morey 1999: 64).
R-Rirt! Yeh! Wah!	'I stamp one foot'	These words cannot be translated. Note that *r-rirt* is an /r/ initial word, an initial phoneme only found in a very small number of words. It probably represents a cry that does not follow the usual phonotactics of the language.
Ye! Yeh! Wirr!	'This lasts for about a week'	–
Birr! Weh! Woh! Wir!	Prior to these words, Mathews writes 'At the end of this time they say'	The word **birr** might be the verb meaning 'go away', a very common word in Yorta Yorta (Bowe and Morey 1999: 94).
Kā'lurtē'	'one old man sings out while they are dancing round repeating that word'	Mathews's notation indicates second syllable stress, as **galúrrte**. Bowe and Morey (1999: 52) point out that the addition of a suffix can lead to stress shift. It may be that this word contains a root **galu-** with a final suffix. (Note: we assume the final consonant is not a retroflex **rt** but is a cluster **rrt**.)
Yēbok!	'and the old fellow sings out and repeated by mob'	–

Text of cry/shout	Background information in the statement	Notes
Bu! i!	'no more and then fellow sings out and they repeat'	–
Yeh !	'and then fellow & repeat and that finishes it'	–

Source: R.H. Mathews, NLA MS 8006/3/4.1, Notebook 1, p. 166; adapted by authors.

The use of cries in ceremonies is also found in the Boys' initiation ceremony from Gippsland (see section 5.2.21.2). They are not uncommon throughout Australia, having been recorded in many places. In Maningrida in the Northern Territory, for example, people report that in funerals of long ago there were a range of types of cries appropriate for certain points in the ceremony.[9]

John Atkinson's statement also contains three longer texts, which may have been songs. The first of these, from page 168, is from the point in the ceremony where the boy is handed to a grandfather who is going to sail him in a canoe, and he cautions the boy against Dharamulan. The text and regularisation are presented as example (9.9). Note that this is not listed as a song in Mathews (1904) and may have been a piece of spoken text.

(9.9)	*Dharamulan*	*Bĭng'algä*	*Baraina*
	dharramulan	**bing(g)álka**	**Barraina**
	PN	?	?
	'Dharamulan …'		

It is possible that the line written underneath this text conveys the meaning or the context: 'When Dharamulan was burnt he pulled at his tongue and threw it into all the trees'. We cannot find the attested Yorta Yorta words for 'burn', 'pull', 'tongue' or 'throw' in this song, and can only recognise the word for Dharamulan in example (9.9). The second word has stress marked on the middle syllable, suggesting that it is a root **bing(g)a**- followed by a suffix **-lka**. No such suffix was recorded for the language, though this combination of consonants is found frequently in Yorta Yorta. This word is also found in the next song and may be connected with fire or burning in some way.

9 Margaret Carew, pers. comm.

Dharamulan is a mythological figure well known in New South Wales.[10] He is strongly associated with the Wiradjuri, and was male and the son of Baiame, the creator. He is also referred to in the Dhudhuroa Dyibbau ceremony (see section 10.2). This raises the possibility that part or all of these songs are actually using Wiradjuri language or some kind of common ceremonial language. In relation to the second song, which with its introduction, an explanation or translation, is presented in Box 9.10, the word *bing'alga* that we are not able to interpret may be related to the form *Bing-gil-bee*. This word is found in a song that Mathews noted, presumably from Wiradjuri, and which is found with musical notation in the Mathews papers (NLA MS 8006/4/7). The full text of that song is *Dhar-ram-oo-loon Dhar-ram-oo-loon Bing-gil-bee moon-da-nun-a gum-mer-ra-wa.*

Box 9.10: Song in John Atkinson's statement

Now if you open mouth you will be killed like

the fire is put out. Then they sing Dh. song

Bing'alga wan'ba warrana yeh! woh

Bing'alga wanha wurrana

Source: R.H. Mathews, NLA MS 8006/3/4.1, Notebook 1, p. 168; adapted by authors.

The 1904 published version of this song is given in Box 9.11:

Box 9.11: Song in Mathews's publications

Men and boys now approach the fire already mentioned and squirt the water out of their mouths upon it – as many as possible squirting at the same moment. The men then jump round and sing

"Bingalga wanba wan-ana! yen! won!"

This chant is repeated over and over again for some time, and when it is finished the novices are allowed to drink a few mouthfuls of water by crouching down beside the papalwas, or water-pans, as before. They are also given some human ordure11 and animal flesh. In a little while both boys and men go to rest for the night.

Source: Mathews (1904: 314); adapted by authors.

10 See for example Wikipedia, 'Daramulum', accessed 25 July 2017, en.wikipedia.org/wiki/Daramulum, and Dharug and Dharawal Resources, 'Biiami', accessed 25 July 2017, dharug.dalang.com.au/plugin_wiki/page/Biiami.

11 We have not been able to find references to the eating of human excrement in the manuscript sources, an additional reason to doubt the accuracy of the information in Mathews (1904). There is mention of this type of custom in Mathews (1905b), relating to ceremonies in other parts of Australia.

Our analysis is presented as (9.10):

(9.10)	*Bing'alga*	*wan'ba*	*warrana*	*yeh!*	*woh*
	bing(g)álka	**wanha**	**wurru-na**	**ye**	**wo**
	?	WH	mouth-ABL?	ONOM	ONOM
	Bing'alga	*wanha*	*wurrana*		
	bing(g)álka	**wanha**	**wurru-na**		
	?	WH	mouth-ABL?		

'... where ... (your) mouth, *ye! wo!* ... where ... from? (your) mouth.'

Note that the word *bing'alga* was also found in example (9.9) above. It may mean 'extinguishing'. We believe that the two other words in this song are probably the interrogative **wanha** and **wurrana**, the word for 'mouth' with an unknown suffix. Perhaps the overall translation was something like 'extinguishing the fire, like (your) mouth …'.

The third song and its context is presented in Box 9.12, repeated from above.

Box 9.12: Song in John Atkinson's statement

> They leave that place and go on to a camping place where they play antics. Women in family way. [song of it - crossed out] [spears shake in ground all around her in night time - inserted]
>
> [Banggorba - crossed out] Bandha'nggorba anborba
>
> Wirragīñ ngaia
>
> This is sung in night time

Source: R.H. Mathews, NLA MS 8006/3/4.1, Notebook 1, p. 168; adapted by authors.

In the version in Mathews (1904: 315), it is written as *Bandhanggorba wirralgiñ ngaia* without the division of the first word.

The text with a suggested regularisation is presented in (9.11):

(9.11)	*Bandha'nggorba*	*anborba*	*wirragiñ*	*ngaia*
	bandhanggó(rr)ba	**(ng)anbó(rr)ba**	**wirrakiny**	**ngaiya**

Notes

We cannot propose any translation for this song. The first word is likely a root **bandha-** with a suffix **-nggó(rr)ba**. Most probably there is no **rr** here, and the spelling <or> is indicating vowel quality. There is no root **bandha-** recorded in the old sources; the nearest form is *bandola* 'how', recorded by Curr (1887). There are also no roots with an initial **wirr-**.

9.6.1 Comparison with Mathews's published articles

As discussed above, Mathews (1904: 306–22) and its reprint (Mathews 1905a) contain a long description of the Wongg'oa or Wongupka ceremony that is partly based on John Atkinson's statement, but also includes information gained from Ned Wheeler about Dhudhuroa ceremonies. Mathews (1904) is a widely available source,[12] and we thus regard it as important that the more accurate and nuanced descriptions in the notebooks be made available.

Mathews (1904: 306) generalised these ceremonies, which may have been similar in various groups, stating that what he was presenting was 'an account of the initiation ceremonies of the native tribes who originally occupied that portion of the Upper Murray, Mitta Mitta, Kiewa, Ovens, King and Broken Rivers. These rites were also in ... on the upper Goulburn, Yarra and Saltwater rivers'. The article includes the various cries presented above in Table 9.4, at (1904: 309), and the song presented above in Box 9.10 at (1904: 314). The versions of the songs and cries given in the published text are often different from those in the manuscript notebook.

There is some information in Mathews (1904) that is not found in John Atkinson's statement. This relates, for example, to the construction of the *papal'wa* and the way in which the water is taken from it (see Table 9.3). Given that this information is not found in the original manuscript, we are unclear what is the source of this information, or whether there may be other information in the Mathews papers about this that has not yet been identified.

12 R.H. Mathews, 'Ethnological Notes on the Aboriginal Tribes of the New South Wales and Victoria: Part I', in *Journal and Proceedings of the Royal Society of New South Wales for 1904* 38, edited by the Honorary Secretaries. www.biodiversitylibrary.org/page/41579064#page/9/mode/1up.

Another example of something that we cannot attest in the manuscripts is that after discussing the two Yorta Yorta songs, Mathews moves to a description of 'the burlesque of "Thunder," *muri-muriwa*' (1904: 315). Thus it seems that this source is an amalgam of multiple sources, including John Atkinson and Ned Wheeler, and others besides.

A possible clue to Mathews's methodology is contained in a manuscript sheet in the National Library of Australia (NLA MS 8006/8/397), which is included in an offprint of Mathews (1905b). This is headed 'Scheme – Wongupka' (with the word Wongupka added in blue pencil, possibly at a later time). Our suggestion is that this list is Mathews's collation of information about the initiation ceremony from several sources, and it was this collation that led to the 1904 publication.

This document is transcribed in Box 9.13.

Box 9.13: Wongupka scheme

Scheme–Wongupka [this word added in blue]			
√	Contingents arrive with novices in centre of ring		
√	Women & children muster close by		
√	Men call out names of places &c		
√	Disperse & erect camps		
√	Corrobborees held till all the people arrive		
√	Breaking up arranged for		
√	At daylight all the boys are mustered out of entire camp		
√	Strings tied round arms–painted		
√	Fire throwing	√	Small roarer
√	Teeth out–p 338	√	Mother & Women
√	Story of canoe		
	[Holes in clay and water–crossed out]		
√	Must not walk under leaning tree, through water		
√	Women in family way		
√	Thunder		
√	Women rush out to meet a man with oposs tail		
X	Scarring of bodies		
√	Return of boys first time & [smoth??]		
√	Camp made for boys [and corrobboree–crossed out and linked by pencil to the line 'Holes in clay and water']		

√	Pantomime [Performances - crossed out] - [Possums - word added in blue]
	Semi dramatic
√	Dharamulan on bank , with roars [& his song - added in blue]
√	Boys must not speak
	[Small roarer bringing boys home - added in blue]

Source: R.H. Mathews, NLA MS 8006/8/397; adapted by authors.

Note that in one copy of Mathews (1905a), held in the National Library of Australia, he makes significant pencil margin notes expanding on the information in that source. These pencil notes have not yet been transcribed, but are found in NLA MS 8006/8/105.

10

Dhudhuroa songs

A number of short songs and cries were listed by R.H. Mathews in notes taken down from Ned Wheeler and recorded in NLA MS 8006/3/4.2, Notebook 6. The songs documented were accompanied by some detailed contextual information, which is presented here in full.

The information collected from Ned Wheeler later formed part of the description of the 'Wonggoa or Wongupka Ceremony' in Mathews (1904: 306–22), which was later reprinted in Mathews (1905a). This description, however, combines aspects of the initiation ceremony from the Yorta Yorta (see section 9.6) based on information from John Atkinson.

While Neddy Wheeler was clearly an important cultural figure and referred to in a number of sources, in common with many other Indigenous people of his time little reliable information on him remains. We do know that he was born around 1840 at Narragang in the Mitta Mitta district and died at Lake Moodemere in 1908, after often camping there over the years with other Aboriginal people, such as Tommy McRae – the well-known painter – and his brother Billy, and their friends and relations. His wife Charlotte died at Lake Tyers in 1908.

Mathews (1904: 306) stated that the 1904 description was 'an account of the initiation ceremonies of the native tribes who originally occupied that portion of the Upper Murray, Mitta Mitta, Kiewa, Ovens, King and Broken Rivers. These rites were also in force on the upper Goulburn, Yarra and Saltwater rivers'. This suggests that the features of the ceremony were similar across a wide part of Victoria. However, the songs that were sung on those occasions would presumably have differed from language to language. The songs presented in this section are those collected from Ned Wheeler and presumed to be in Dhudhuroa language.

The list of songs and cries is summarised in Table 10.1.

Table 10.1: List of Dhudhuroa traditional songs

Text/ceremony	Contents	R.H. Mathews page reference	Section
Wanggo'a ceremony ('man-making')	A couple of short cries	34–35	10.1
Dyibbau ceremony (boy's initiation)	One short song (glossed)	36–37	10.2
Revenge	One short song (unglossed)	37–38	10.3

Source: R.H. Mathews, NLA MS 8006/3/4.2, Notebook 6; adapted by authors.

10.1 The Wanggo'a ceremony as told by Ned Wheeler

The Wanggo'a ceremony, also described as 'man-making', appears to have been one of at least two ceremonies related to the initiation of young men. It contains some short cries, uttered when the *tyibbauks*, presumably young men who are at a higher stage of initiation, come out 'with bark and boughs' and 'run into the camp', crying Oh! Oh Wa! Ho.

The full text relating to the ceremony is presented as Box 10.1:

Box 10.1: Dhudhuroa Wanggo'a ceremony

[p. 34]

Wanggo'a ceremony

Boy sits in mother's lap. A ring is made on the ground and boys put sitting in it on the grass. His mother is near him. The boys are then taken away into the bush, and a tooth taken out.

Kubbi marries Butha or Murri.

Kubbi is a porcupine. His father was Ippai, possum

mother was Kangaroo also whipsnake mother

Muddyigang is the bullroarer

Yirragaminnarnga, small roarer

After teeth out swing the roarer within hearing of boys

Smoke boys when bought in out of bush

sup. 36&37

Tyibbo-Ring hair off head except central line. Paint him. Boughs in belt all round. After all the men come home from hunting-The other men bring the jibbouk close & plant them. Some will be roasting others making [burn??]. [p. 35]

Wanggoa is name of man making. Nurmang is a man who is through Wanggoa

The tyibbauks come out with [furry??] bark and boughs run into camp. Oh! oh wa! ho. A tyibbo will catch a boy and [throw-crossed out] pretend to throw him into the water He will hit the bark and make sparks fly. He has a net over his shoulder. He will pick up any possum and put it in net bag. Expose arse to women & genitals also. For about a week continue. Then feed. They go and camp at ngooloobooloo after jibbauk. After that they get a Koo scrotum & fill it with grass and sew it up with sinew.

See p.36

Source: R.H. Mathews, NLA MS 8006/3/4.2, Notebook 6, pp. 34–35; adapted by authors.

This specifically includes the cry 'Oh! oh wa! ho' that does not appear in Mathews (1904), although at the end of the ceremony, when the initiates have almost finished, Mathews (1904: 325) writes:

> He passes on to another camp where a man or woman will perhaps call out 'Tyibbauga! fetch me some water.' He answers, 'waho !' and taking the vessel offered to him, scampers off to the creek or water-hole and brings back a small quantity of water with dirt in it. The person refuses this, and then the novice goes and brings good water. Several different persons may make the same request, and be similarly responded to.

It is unclear whether this information relates specifically to the Dhudhuroa ceremony or has been generalised from information about a range of ceremonies held in different parts of Victoria. (For a further discussion of the problems in Mathews's (1904) and (1905a) description of this ceremony, see section 9.6.1.)

The description of the Wangg'oa ceremony in Box 10.1 is followed by the description of 'Making young women'. Ned Wheeler was also the informant for this. There are no songs or cries given here, and we include this as Box 10.2 primarily because transcriptions of this information may not have been published before.

Box 10.2: Dhudhuroa 'Making young women'

<table><tr><td>Making young women – N. Wheeler
Put girl up a sapling & put green bushes under over in smoulding fire & smoke her. About 10 feet high old women do it. They camp with the girl for a couple of days and smoke her at the finish. Paint girl with possum's fat & raddle. Put apron her dyabēng, put strings around arms, made of fur [& skin – inserted] of the ringtail possum. Cut skin in thin slices & twist, with the fur on it. He has a snake, a sleing (blue tongue) lizard. After a young woman has her first child, she and her babe are smoked.</td></tr></table>

Source: R.H. Mathews, NLA MS 8006/3/4.2, Notebook 6, p. 35; adapted by authors.

10.2 The Dyibbau ceremony as told by Ned Wheeler

A second ceremony related to initiation, but which seems to refer to a later stage than Wanggo'a is the Dyibbau ceremony. The word *Dyibbau* is clearly related to the word *Jibauk*, referred to in connection with initiation in the Djadjawurrung tribe (see section 2.3.2).

The description of the Dhudhuroa Dyibbau ceremony also includes a short song that names Dharramulan, a mythological creature well known in New South Wales.[1] He was male and the son of Baiame, the creator. Dharramulan is also referred to in one of the songs in the Yorta Yorta initiation ceremony reported in John Atkinson's statement (see section 9.6).

The full text of the Dyibbau ceremony, as told by Ned Wheeler, is presented in Box 10.3:

Box 10.3: Dhudhuroa Dyibbau ceremony

<table><tr><td>[p. 36]
Dyibbau ceremony – Ned Wheeler
He carries a guralie or shield. He drags some of the things on the ground. He carries a piece of green stick about 4 feet long. In passing a camp he will throw a sleepy lizard or a snake in among the women, who scatter in all directions. They mix up strukes mushroom, shit, & mix it & throw among the people. He comes along pretending to cry & people come out & he throws filth at them
The last of it, all the women & girls will be swimming in the river. He comes with a bush close to them till within reach. He lets go the bough and dives under a girl & all the girls run away. Some old men bring them spears pretending they think some wild man has attacked them.</td></tr></table>

1 See for example, Wikipedia, 'Daramulam', accessed 25 July 2017, en.wikipedia.org/wiki/Daramulum; and Dharug and Dharawal Resources, 'Biiami', accessed 25 July 2017, dharug.dalang.com.au/plugin_wiki/page/Biiami.

At conclusion the gibbouks go into the water and wash themselves

At man making – a figure of Dharamula on the ground in bark & painted – a bullroarer lying on top. All the men dance and sing the following song:–

[p. 37]

In Dhudhuroa tribe

	cover a little	
Dharamulan	ngun'ninga-wa,	ye! ye! ye!
shoving		
nundhannga		

Source: R.H. Mathews, NLA MS 8006/3/4.2, Notebook 6, pp. 36–37; adapted by authors.

In the 1904 article, Mathews gives another version of this song (1904: 318) with some more detail:

> Lying on the top of the human figure are two real bullroarers, one being the muddyigang or larger kind, and the other the yirraga-minnunga, which is supposed to be the wife of Muddyigang. The novices are brought up and shown the image of Dharamulan, with his two descriptions of bullroarers, and are invited to carefully observe them. The men then dance round and sing:-
>
> Dharamulan ngunning-a-wa
>
> Nundhunna, yen! yeh! yeh!
>
> After this exhibition, the youths are warned against revealing anything which has been said or done in the bush, under terrible penalties seized with fearful maladies from which it is impossible to recover.

Using the Blake and Reid system of regularisation, employing voiced consonants, and assuming that Mathews's glosses are correct, we suggest the following analysis of this song, presented as example (10.1):

(10.1)	*Dharamulan*	*ngun'ninga-wa,*	*ye! ye! ye!*	*nundhannga*
		cover a little		*shoving*
	dharramulan	**ngunging(g)a-wa**	**ye! ye! ye!**	**nundhana**
	PN	cover-?	ONOM	shove

'Covering the (image) of Dharramulan, *Ye! Ye! Ye!*, Shoving …'

10.3 Revenge ceremony and song

In addition to the two texts relating to initiation, Ned Wheeler also wrote about the processes followed when a revenge party headed out. This description also includes a short song that is, unfortunately, not glossed by Mathews. The text of the story including the song is presented as Box 10.4:

Box 10.4: Dhudhuroa Revenge ceremony

[p. 37]

Revenge - N Wheeler

Gūr're or killing an enemy. They mark a tree. A party is picked and starts away and mark at tree at first camp Spit at the tree as they dance round & sing

"Wūre Bunningandha [urru - crossed out] [dumbu - inserted] balladha"

Mark a tree every night wherever they camp. A couple of scouts go on to locate the enemy. A couple of fellow go up to the victim and attack him with spears. His wives are also forbidden to flee. They hack pieces of skin off his buttocks and down to his knees, from the shoulders - in short all his back. Take his kidney fat also.

That night at camp of victors they cut the skin & flesh into smaller pieces & divide among kindred of [diccans??] also his friends. The hands were mostly cut off the victim also.

The last night before the murder, they make a little mia by putting green boughs on end, boughs end up, with a bough terminating it. Small pieces of wood were put on the fire under this cover. Men danced round this all night - about half danced while other half slept and changed about. A tree also marked being the last tree.

Doubled a dead body up. Dug a hole in sand, with a ledge in one side. Lay the body on its side with head toward sunrise, and fill it

- heap it up a couple of feet above the ground.

- He took a message stick about 2 feet long and about 2 inches wide to muster for the gurē' marked with devices with possum tooth & painted with red ochre. White stone - emu bones & kangaroo bones nicely marked.

Source: R.H. Mathews, NLA MS 8006/3/4.2, Notebook 6, pp. 37–38; adapted by authors.

A suggested regularisation of the song is presented as (10.2), together with the original text:

(10.2) *Wūre Bunningandha dumbuballadha*

wurre banhingandha d(h)ambabaladha

Notes

The first word is perhaps the word for 'sorcerer', written by Mathews as *wurrăwe* (NLA MS 8006/8/227), regularised by Blake and Reid as **warrawe**, but for which we suggest **wurrawe/wurre**, based on the form here. The presence of the word for 'sorcerer' in a song of this type would seem to be appropriate. It is possible that this word is also connected with the word for 'moon' **wurrayu**.

It may be that the third word is **dhumbaba** 'smoke', which is spelled as *toombaba* by Mitchell in the 'Barwidgee vocabulary' (Mathew 1899: 214).

11

Pallanganmiddang songs

There is a song/chant that was published in Smyth (1878, 1: 62) in the description of the Narra-mang, an example of a 'coming of age ceremony'.[1] Smyth neither identifies the 'correspondent' who gave him this information, nor indeed where the ceremony was from, save that it was part of custom of tooth evulsion, the knocking out of the upper incisor teeth, practised on 'the Murrumbidgee, Murray, Ovens and Goulburn'. Note that Mathews (1898) also mentions the 'Narramang' but states that it is the ceremony of 'the tribes speaking the Darkinung, Wannerawa, Warrimee, Wannungine, Dharrook and some other dialects'. This area is well to the north and east of the locations mentioned by Smyth.

Possible evidence for its identification is found in the text of the description of this ceremony, where two animals are named, *My-ioa* 'black swan' and *Joh-gah* 'musk-duck'. The first word is found in the Pallanganmiddang language (Blake and Reid 1999: 28), regularised as **mayiwa**, with forms written down by G.A. Robinson and Thomas Mitchell, who gave the form as *miewa* (in Curr 1877, 3: 562–63). Since Mitchell was also a correspondent with Smyth, we suggest that the information about the Narra-mang ceremony and the accompanying song may have been provided to Smyth by Mitchell, and we have, consequently, included it as an example of a Pallanganmiddang song, the Ovens River also being part of the Pallanganmiddang territory.

1 Note that Narramang is mentioned as an alternative name for the Burbang in the R.H. Mathews notebook titled 'The Burbang of the Darkinjung Tribe' (NLA MS 8006/3/8). At one point the word Burbang is crossed out and Narramang is written (see Mathews 1897: 11). The Darkinjung territory is the Hunter region and Hawkesbury River; and the Darkinjung word for black swan is *Mulgwa*. While this is plausibly related to *My-ioa*, given the location stated for the Narra-mang we are assuming that this song was used by the Pallanganmiddang and have kept discussion of it in this chapter. Jesse Hodgetts (pers. comm.) confirmed that 'Ngarramang was practised by both the Darkinyung and Awabakal around the Hawkesbury, Hunter and Central Coast of NSW' but that he did not recognise the words for 'black swan' and 'musk duck'.

There is one more possible word in language in the text, the word *coradjes* that presumably refers to older, already initiated males who took care of the young boys in the ceremony. This word, also spelled **kuradji**, refers to a 'clever man' in some languages of New South Wales, and was probably in widespread use in the nineteenth century. This word has some similarity to *guritch*, who had a similar function in the initiation ceremony of the Djadjawurrung, according to Howitt (1904: 613). See section 2.3.3 for a longer discussion of the song associated with initiation in western Victoria.

If we are correct in assigning this as a Pallanganmiddang song, it is the only surviving text in the language. It is much to be regretted that we can offer no analysis of it.

The full text of the description of the ceremony with the song is presented as Box 11.1:

Box 11.1: Narra-mang ceremony and song

One of my correspondents gives this account of the ceremonies practised on the "making of young men":- *Narra-mang* – the name given to a custom of the blacks of the Murrumbidgee, Murray, Ovens, and Goulburn tribes – consists essentially in the knocking out of two of the incisor teeth of the upper jaw. It may perhaps be regarded as a religious ceremony, in the performance of which many mystic rites are observed – rites that no white man is permitted to witness unless he be one who has the confidence and regard of the old men. The operation is performed at the age of puberty, and the teeth of the males only are knocked out. When a lad has to be initiated, he is removed to some remote and secluded spot, and when it is night, the coradjes (priests and doctors), painted and decorated with feathers, &c., begin their operations. A ring is marked out, and in this the youths are placed, one at a time; incantations are uttered by the priests; and, finally, one of them, holding in one hand a piece of wood shaped like a punch, and in the other a tomahawk, approaches the youth and knocks out two teeth. When this has been done, the young man is placed in a gunyah, formed of, so closely interwoven as to be nearly impervious to light, and then the wild songs of the women are heard, who approach and walk round the gunyah, each holding in her hand a lighted brand. For the space of one moon the youths are prohibited from seeing any one except the coradjes. If they are seen by a female, they will surely die. When this ordeal is passed, and not before, they are permitted to eat of the flesh of the *My-ioa* (black swan), and that of the *Joh-gah* (musk-duck), and they may then also eat of the emu. Some of the chants are of this kind:–

Therr-an-jee-gar jabery-mah Johans Joh-gah–&c.

'Tis now that you are sick,

But soon will grow your beard,

And on the magic musk-duck

With the men you shall feed.

Source: Smyth (1878, 1: 62); adapted by authors.

A possible regularisation of this text is presented in example (11.1):

(11.1) **dherrandji-ga djaberri-ma djowa-na djoga**

Blake and Reid (1999) noted that 'a suffix **-ga** appears on some human nouns'. It may be that this suffix is present on the first word of this song, and perhaps the first word is related to the word for 'human', **djerri**. We can speculate that, since this song is about the initiation, the first word may be referring to a human, namely the boy who is to undergo initiation.

It is possible that the word written as *Johans* has a misprint in the last letter as *s* for *a* and this may suggest a suffix **-na** that is discussed in Blake and Reid (1999: 22).

The word *Joh-gah* is glossed in the text as 'musk duck', for which we have suggested a regularisation of **djoga**. No word for 'musk duck' has been documented in Pallanganmiddang or its neighbour Dhudhuroa, but the fact that the word is glossed in contextual explanation above the song and present in the text of the song, and the translation 'musk duck' is in the translation, suggests that this song does indeed include mention of the 'musk duck'. It is possible that the 'musk duck' (*Biziura lobata*) was an important animal in the moiety system of the Pallanganmiddang.[2]

The translation contains more material than the text, which unfortunately is cut off by '&c.'

2 The musk duck is also mentioned in two Gippsland songs, both related to the 'White Woman' story. In Gippsland, the word for 'white woman' included the word for 'musk duck' (see sections 5.2.2 and 5.2.3).

12

Songs in the Murray River languages

Very little linguistic information about the Murray River languages spoken in Victoria and just across the border in South Australia has survived. Our comments on the four songs discussed in this chapter can only be preliminary at best.

The most comprehensive study of this group of languages from the Victoria perspective, Horgen (2004), gathered together information about a range of languages in the Lower Murray area, including Yaraldi (Ngarrindjeri/ Narrinyeri), Ngayawang, Yu-Yu, Keramin and Yitha-Yitha, although it was not a comprehensive study and did not include the information gathered by Berndt and Berndt (1993: 12). Of the languages studied by Horgen, Yu-Yu, Keramin and Yitha-Yitha are the languages that will be referred to in this chapter. Our analysis of these songs will draw on Horgen, and also the word list headed Lyart from the William Thomas papers (State Library of NSW, MLMSS 214, Volume 21 Item 17), which was not included in Horgen's study.

The languages as named by Berndt and Berndt (1993) are (1) Yakamuldak, for the songs sung by Minduk Jack, and (2) Yeyu, for the song sung by Pound. Berndt and Berndt (1993: 220) said of Yakamuldak that it was a 'variation of or an alternative for either the Kureinyi (Ke-mendok) who originally occupied country on the Murray near Wentworth or the Maraura (Yako-Yako)'. Our analysis is that these songs are not Maraura, and therefore belong to Kureinyi, which is a variant form of Keramin.

Yeyu is stated by Berndt and Berndt (1993: 221) to be 'probably an alternative name for the Yite-yite' (the latter is assumed to be Yitha-Yitha). However, it is more likely to be the language Yu-Yu (see Horgen (2004) for further discussion of these groups).

It is not known if these 'Murray River languages' form a linguistic subgroup. Dixon (2002: 669) referred to them as the 'Lower Murray Small Linguistic Area', referring to them as the 'Lower Murray Areal Group' elsewhere (for example, 2002: xxxvi). While observing that the languages shared certain features, Dixon (2002: 669) observed that it was 'most unlikely that all five languages could be shown to constitute a genetic subgroup'.

Hercus (1986), in her map, associated Yitha-Yitha, Tarti-Tarti and Keramin with the Upper Murray languages (Dhudhuroa and Pallanganmiddang).

There is a large number of tribal names for the groups in this area, which have been assessed by Clark and Ryan (2008). Clark and Ryan (2008: 27) included a comparison of Tarti-Tarti (which they spelled Dadidadi) and Yari-Yari, the language recorded by Thomas (SLNSW MLMSS 214, Volume 21 Item 17, pp. 273–85). While there are differences between these word lists, there may be enough common forms to suggest a connection between them.

12.1 The songsters – singers and composers

While the information about these languages is very sketchy, the four songs presented here, all documented by Berndt and Berndt (1993), are rich examples of traditional songs, and if they are indeed in the Murray River languages, they represent the most substantial texts surviving in these languages. All the songs in this chapter were sung by the Yaraldi tradition bearer Pinkie Mack.

Confusingly, Berndt and Berndt (1993: 517) also said that John Mack, first husband of the well-known Pinkie Mack, came from east of Mildura 'in Munpul clan territory of the Yakamuldak language group'. Our analysis is that these songs are not Maraura and nor are they in John Mack's own Letyi-Letyi language (see further Blake et al. (2011) for more detailed discussion of the Letyi-Letyi sources; the song composed by John Mack in Letyi-Letyi is presented in section 2.10).

Only a small number of the words in the songs could be confirmed by the other sources in the language (mostly given in Horgen 2004). There are, however, enough of these to confirm that all of these songs are indeed in the Murray River languages.

We are able to say a little about the two men who composed these songs. Geographical locations often formed part of Aboriginal peoples' public names in the colonial period and Minduk Jack's personal name shows his place of origin in the area of Minduk Creek (various spellings), which lies in what is now the northern reaches of the Mallee Cliffs National Park, NSW, some 20 kilometres south-east of the Victorian town of Red Cliffs.[1]

Minduk Jack remained throughout his life in his home district and was working on Mailman and Tapaulin stations on the New South Wales side of the Murray in the early 1880s and Mildura Station in Victoria as late as 1885.[2] The year 1885 also saw the founding of the Mildura Irrigation Settlement that featured as locale and source material for the first of Minduk Jack's songs as recounted below. Based on Pinkie Mack's testimony, the Berndts viewed 1890 as a probable date for the events depicted in this song, but as a Parliamentary Commission enquiring into the operation of the settlement definitely saw members of parliament visit in 1896, we believe the latter date is more likely. As Pinkie and John Mack's family was based in Mildura around this time[3] it is possible that Pinkie's detailed knowledge of the song stemmed from her personally seeing the events Minduk Jack described in his song. Certainly this is a very rare instance of such direct knowledge of the composition and transmission of a particular song.

Unlike Minduk Jack, Pound is an elusive figure and does not feature in any of the historical sources from the area, other than in Berndt and Berndt (1993). It is unlikely then that he remained in his home district, but we are unable to determine whether he died young or moved down river like people who would have been known to him such as Bob McKinlay (Yu-Yu) and Frank Fletcher (Maraura) did.

1 State Records of New South Wales, MacCabe FP, Surveyor General's Crown Plans 1792-1886, Lower Darling Squatting District Map No. [2544], plan 3 of 5 of map of Murray River between Taila Creek and the Darling River.

2 Mallee Cliffs Cash Book 1883–1885, Mildura Genealogical Society.

3 Victorian Death Certificate 1895/2881.

12.2 Musical terminology in the Murray River languages

A small number of words for 'sing', 'dance' and 'corroboree' were documented in the Thomas papers, SLNSW MLMSS421, Volume 21 Item 17.[4] This is the section containing words listed as belonging to the Lyart Tribe. Clark and Ryan (2008: 29) point out that *Lyart* or *Lutt* is the name for the Murray River, and that these words were collected in August 1860 from Kulkyne Bobby and Young Man Tommy who were at the time on trial.

The words for 'sing' and 'dance/corroboree' that were collected are presented in Table 12.1.

Table 12.1: Words for 'sing' and 'dance/corroboree' in Thomas's Lyart word list

Page number	English	Language	Suggested regularisation
281	'to sing'	Eure-re-vein	**yurriwin**
281	'corroberry'	Young-lun	**yang(g)ilan**
284	'Let us corroberry'	Wag-ge-men Young-lann	**wakamin yang(g)ilan**

Source: SLNSW MLMSS 214, Volume 21 Item 17; adapted by authors.

12.3 Minduk Jack's songs

Three songs sung by Minduk Jack to the Berndts are presented in this section. In *A World That Was* (1993: 220–21), in the section about the *Patangi* style of songs, Berndt and Berndt described these songs as follows:

> Three songs that were sung to us were composed by Minduk Jack of the Yakamuldak language group in the vicinity of Mildura and Wentworth. This language name is a variation of or an alternative for either the Kureinyi (Ke-mendok) who originally occupied country on the Murray near Wentworth or the Maraura (Yako-Yako) whose territory was on the northern side of the Murray from Wentworth and included part of the western side of the Darling River.

These three songs are presented in sections 12.3.1, 12.3.2 and 12.3.3.

4 These papers are available online at the State Library of NSW website, 'Volume 21 Item 17: William Thomas "Language Murry Tribe from Kulkyne Bobby & Young Man Tommy, 1860, Trial etc. 1868"', accessed 4 January 2016, acmssearch.sl.nsw.gov.au/search/itemDetailPaged.cgi?itemID=1148277.

12.3.1 Song 1

Berndt and Berndt (1993: 220) describe this song as follows:

> One of Minduk's songs describes how he was sitting on the bank of the River Murray watching Europeans arriving by steamer in order to establish the township of Mildura (see Appendix 7.26). This was said to be a party of parliamentarians coming to look at the project site. The party arrived by steamer, was taken in a buggy to inspect the site and eventually returned to the boat. Pinkie Mack, who sang this song for us, added that more than one buggy was involved and that these belonged to the 'Chaffey Brothers'; the date of the visit by the Europeans was about 1890. The song was sung when the up-river and the down-river people met for their ceremonies.

For this song there is also a recording of Pinkie Mack singing it, recorded by Berndt and Berndt on to a wax cylinder at East Wellington in South Australia in 1943. In the 1950s these cylinders were played and transferred onto magnetic tape at the behest of Alice Moyle and this recording is now digitised by AIATSIS as BERNDT_RC01-004244A.wav. This consists of 13 cylinders, of which Cylinder No. 9 contains the following (Box 12.1; from BERNDT_RC01-004244_listing.pdf):

Box 12.1: Details of Cylinder No. 9 recorded by Berndt and Berndt

1st part: John Mack's song from ˈLaitʃum ˈBanreinʤi – Upper Murray. ˈKim ˈŋala ...
2nd part: Minduk Jack's song: ˈJakəmulˈda:k tribe, Upper River Murray. ˈna:ŋgili ...

Source: AIATSIS BERNDT_RC01-004244_listing.pdf; adapted by authors.

The section of the recording containing the two songs from Cylinder No. 9 appears to commence at 13:00 on this recording and run until 15:41, including a back announcement by Alice Moyle that 'No. 9 showed very little sign of mildew but No. 10 is badly mildewed'.

The first of these songs is discussed in section 2.10. The words are very difficult to make out on the recordings, and we cannot even be sure when the first of these songs finishes and the second commences. It may be that the second song, that of Minduk Jack, commences at about 14:47 on the original recording and runs for about 45 seconds. We cannot easily make out the words to confirm that this is indeed the song.

The full text and translation of the song from Berndt and Berndt (1993) is presented as Box 12.2:

Box 12.2: Minduk Jack's Song 1

1.	*Nanggili*	*bugi*	*gudawal gudawa*	*maimana gudawa*
	Going on	buggy	climbing hill road	looking around
2.	[line 1 repeated]			
3.	*Maimana gul*	*wilkin a gudawal*	*gulnga*	
	looking around	going right around	and returning	
4.	[line 1 repeated]			
	Going on the buggy, climbing the hill road, looking around			
	Looking around, going climbing around, and returning			
	Going on the buggy, climbing the hill road, looking around			

Source: Berndt and Berndt (1993: Appendix 7.26); adapted by authors.

The only word that can be certainly associated with the Murray River languages is *maimana* 'look'. In Keramin, *maima* is given as 'see' by McFarlane in Curr (1886, 2: 282–83), and in Thomas's Lyart list, *my-mull* is listed with the meaning 'seeing' (p. 276). We suggest that there is a root **maima-** 'see'.

The words for 'go' and 'road' in Horgen (2004) do not resemble the words found in this song.

12.3.2 Song 2

The second song is described by Berndt and Berndt (1993: 221) as follows:

> In another song, Minduk Jack told of his boss from the sheep station on which he worked going away from his own camp (see Appendix 7.27). Minduk was brooding about the manager, who had gone out looking for sheep without telling him. 'He could have stopped back and talked to me; he could have said goodbye, and told me when he would return!'

The full text and translation of the song from Berndt and Berndt (1993) is presented as Box 12.3:

Box 12.3: Minduk Jack's Song 2

1.	*Natangun*	*amaima*	*kula*	*wildja-matja*
	he left	without seeing me	gone on	to the other side
	idenap a	*leun a*	*ininpan-ngara*	
	I would have	sat down	been talking they would	
2.	*Ida*	*pundingari*	*narimia*	*kaipi*
	me would	he have found there	left me	he could have said
	yu-gubaii	*ngaii-towa*	*wilka*	*kaipi*
	you goodbye	my 'white man'	return	he could have said
	He left without seeing me, he went to the other side.			
	We could have sat talking together.			
	He could have found me there in my camp. But he left me. He could have said			
	'Goodbye you!', My 'white man', he could have said, I"[sic] come back!'			

Source: Berndt and Berndt (1993: Appendix 7.27); adapted by authors.

There are a number of words in this song that correspond to other sources in the Murray River languages.

Line 1

amaima 'without seeing me' contains the root **maima-** 'see', already discussed in connection with Song 1 (section 12.3.1).

leun a 'sat down' is the root regularised by Horgen (2004) as **lew-a** 'sit', found widespread in this group, found as *lewa* in both Keramin (McFarlane in Curr 1886, 2: 282–83) and Yitha-Yitha (J.A. Macdonald in Curr 1886, 2: 285–89), as well as in Thomas (SLNSW MLMSS 214, Volume 21, p. 284) as *Laven-nal-ly* 'let us sit down'.

Line 2

kaipi 'he would have said' is found in Ngayawang as *kappun, kaptun* (see Horgen 2004).

ngaii 'my'. Thomas (SLNSW MLMSS 214, Volume 21, p. 284) records *ngar-gee-woon* as meaning 'my knife', writing 'my' underneath *ngar-gee.*[5]

thowa 'white man' is found in Keramin as *thow-wur* 'white man' (McFarlane in Curr 1886, 2: 282–83).

5 The meaning of *woon* is uncertain. On page 279, Thomas (SLNSW MLMSS 214, Volume 21) gives a list of weapons and implements and names the boomerang as *woone*.

12.3.3 Song 3

The last of Minduk Jack's songs is discussed by Berndt and Berndt (1993: 221) as follows:

> Minduk also wrote a song which focused on one of his tasks as a shepherd (see Appendix 7.28): dragging sheep out of a bog. The sheep were covered Bunwith maggots but still alive. The maggots would come crawling out of the mud towards the sheep.

The full text and translation of the song from Berndt and Berndt is presented as Box 12.4:

Box 12.4: Minduk Jack's Song 3

1.	*Betulun*	*aruka*	*ambal*	*beru-itj*	*tjang-itjang*
	fly eggs	becoming	that are	maggots	crawling
	ailiminai		*ilimindi*	*tjang-itjang*	
	following in streams		trying to	crawling	
2.	*Yamilin-o*	*beru-itj*	*tjang-itjang*		
	Writhing	maggots	crawling		
3.	[lines 1 and 2 repeated]				
	Fly eggs becoming maggots				
	crawling, following in streams				
	[to infest sheep]				
	Writhing, crawling maggots.				

Source: Berndt and Berndt (1993: Appendix 7.28); adapted by authors.

Notes

In this song only one word is recognised from the Murray River language sources: in line 1, the word *betulun* 'fly eggs', contains the form of the word for 'egg' found in Yitha-Yitha, recorded as *báte* and *beit* and in Keramin, recorded as *bet, bit, bert* and *bart* (Horgen 2004).

This word also contains the form *loane*, recorded in Keramin with the meaning 'housefly'. We therefore suggest that this word is a compound, literally 'egg-housefly'.

The word listed by Horgen for 'maggot' (Ngayawang *yeltirri* 'maggot, applied to rice') does not resemble the form found in this song.

12.4 Pound's song

Unlike the songs of Minduk Jack, the song presented here has a much more traditional theme, telling the story of Nguril, an Ancestor Creator.

Berndt and Berndt (1993: 221) stated that Nguril was identified with Ngurunderi, the chief ancestor being of the Yaraldi (Ngarrindjeri) of the Murray mouth, and that Ngurunderi had originally come down from up river. They refer to the Maraura narrative Norman Tindale (1939) took down, relating how 'Ngurunderi followed his two wives down river'. Tindale's Maraura informant Peter Bonney did not name Ngurunderi directly in this narrative, and it is unclear from a reading of it which of a range of male figures might represent him. Peter Bonney did say, however, that the Nurili are ancestral beings; very old men, the ŋurunderi of the river is one, also Wa:ku and Ka:nau – Crow and Eagle. He was thus aware of Ngurunderi and equated him as an ancestral being along with figures from his homeland as 'Nurili' – a term that clearly correlates to Nguril of the Yu-Yu as featured in Pound's song. While there is little detail in this song beyond a general confirmation of Nguril creating the land, we read the absence of specifics as emblematic of the conventions and limitations of song as opposed to story.

In terms of further context, Berndt and Berndt published a story from a Yu-Yu speaker, Mrs Carter, recounting what was a Bareindji narrative from the scrubland out from the Darling but referring to Crow and Eaglehawk rather than other ancestral beings. Its focus on Crow and Eaglehawk paralleled that in Peter Bonney's story (Tindale 1939) and also referred to overlapping locations on the lower Darling and nearby reaches of the Murray.

Overlapping motifs and linked ancestral beings occur in stories from areas further apart, however. Albert Karloan recounted how 'in the early days of the Dreaming Ngurunderi followed the great Murray Cod down the river, poling his canoe', with the Cod's actions forming the landscape (Berndt and Berndt 1993: 223). Like many of the ancestors who are linked, he had two wives.

This parallels a story taken down by R.H. Mathews (NLA MS 8006/3/4.1, Notebook 1, p. 153) from Werkaya speakers of the Victorian Mallee in which *Datyukul* (literally 'arm-having') pursued the giant Cod down the Murray, again forming the landscape as they went. In the Werkaya version the Cod was pursued from Swan Hill down to Murray Bridge before the narrative swept across country to the east, while in the Yaraldi story the Cod was pursued down through the lower lakes. The same figure appears as **Thathakwil** in a Mathi-Mathi account of Orion taken down by Luise Hercus from Jack Long (Blake et al. 2011: 130), showing an even greater spread of linked stories across land as well as in the night sky. We see how these links extended even further again as R.H. Mathews notes that 'Thattyukwil some fellows call him Būndyal' (NLA MS 8006/3/4.2, Notebook 6, p. 6[6]) and 'Bunjil is "Datyukul" from Datyuk is the arm' (NLA MS 8006/3/4.1, Notebook 1, p. 153), 'Bunjil' being the major creation figure for Eastern Kulin speakers of central Victoria (see section 3.2.4 for a song relating to **Bundjil**).

In his story 'Narroondarie's Wives', David Unaipon (1990) told of how Ngurunderi came from the north, where he 'was known or called Boonah, hence the initiation ceremonies'.

Unaipon, a devout Christian and much influenced by Christian teaching, went on to say that 'Narroondarie and Boonah are names by which he is known as a good man, as a Sacred Man who is endowed or guided by the will of the Great Spirit, the Nhyanhund or Byamee, the our father of all'. Baiame, another Ancestor Creator, is mentioned in connection with Dharamulan (see sections 9.6 and 10.2).

Unaipon (1990) says: 'After coming from the Northern part of Australia down into various parts of New South Wales and Victoria, he found his way into South Australia, dwelling mostly in and around the shores of Lakes Alexandrina and Albert'.

Thus it appears that Pound's song is in fact a part of much greater story, part of a very long 'songline' that is only very fragmentarily recorded, but for which we do have the song that related to the Ned's corner area.

The Berndts' fuller description of the background to the song is given below (Berndt and Berndt 1993: 221):

> A further *patangi* came from Ned's corner of the Victorian side of the River Murray (see Appendix 7.29). It was sung by a man named Pound of the Yeyu language group. This was probably an alternative name for the Yite-yite who originally occupied part of the northern side of the Lachlan River. This song was of particular

6 We are grateful to Harley Dunolly-Lee for pointing out this reference.

> significance since it referred to Nguril who is identified as the mythic Ngurunderi. Roughly, the song was translated as 'This is where Nguril has been walking; this is what he has been doing; these are his tracks across plain after plain, with flowing creeks making their way down to the River'.

They went on to say:

> This is the only direct Aboriginal statement we heard at that time about Ngurunderi's linkage with the upper reaches of the Murray, except the statement that he came down the Murray from this direction in mythic times (see Chapter 15). However, Howitt (1904: 489) referred to the Wiimbaio people speaking of Nurelli, which could well be a variation of Nguril. This mythic being was said to have made the whole country and eventually gone into the sky from a point located on the north side of the Murray, at Lake Victoria, about fifty miles from Wentworth. Two songs about Nurelli are set out in Howitt (ibid.: 428). The patangi was performed at night, when decorated men and women danced. Pinkie Mack herself was a participant when she married John Mack, who came from this general area.

The two songs referred to here are the Maraura Sun song (section 8.1.2) and the Moon song (section 8.1.4). Perhaps it is possible that these two are part of the same song series/dreaming/songline that also involves Ngurunderi and Nguril? We might also mention here that the Kangaroo song (section 8.1.3) and the Moiety song (section 8.1.1) are also possibly related to a similar 'dreaming'.

The full text and translation of the song from Berndt and Berndt (1993: Appendix 7.29) is presented as Box 12.5:

Box 12.5: Pound's song

1.	*Imanei*	*ipana*	*Nguril al*	*anggitjin*	*imanei*
	Look here	he did this	Nguril	that is what	look here
	ipana	*Nguril ai*			
	he did this	Nguril			
2.	[line 1 repeated]				
3.	*Waral-waral waral-waral*		*amalivin livin*		
	Plains after plains		creeks flowing through		
	a mukuluwei				
	River water				

Look here! Nguril did this! That is what Nguril did. Plain after plain, with flowing creeks, To the river's water.

Source: Berndt and Berndt (1993: Appendix 7.29); adapted by authors.

Notes

The word *imanei* in line 1 might be based on the root **maima-** 'see' that is found in two of Minduk Jack's songs and discussed in section 12.3.1.

In line 3, the word *mukuluwei* 'river water' is probably based on the word **nguk-** 'water', found in a number of sources. Hercus (1986: 232) wrote ['ŋu:k], which would be spelled as **nguuk** with a long vowel. Thomas (MLMSS 241, Volume 21 Item 17, p. 276) gives *noourk* for 'water', and Horgen (2004) lists a range of similar forms from all five languages in his study.

The word *mukuluwei* is glossed as 'river water' and it is possible that this compound contains a form of the word for Murray River *lut*/*ludt* in Keramin and *lutte* in Yitha-Yitha (Horgen 2004), also spelled *lyart* by Thomas (MLMSS 214, Volume 21 Item 17, p. 273).

We also speculate on the possibility that the forms *-al* and *-ai* written after the word Nguril are intended to be the same suffix and are actually ergatives.

13
Widespread songs

A number of the nineteenth-century sources refer to songs that were known by a wide range of people, and had often come from far away. They were sung by Aboriginal people, even though the meaning was not known to the singers.

In general we are not able to translate these, as often we have neither any suggested meaning, nor any clear idea of what the original language of the song was.

Table 13.1: Widespread songs

Name of song (section)	Source of text	Other references	Notes
Ma-le song (13.1)	Georgiana McCrae (1966: 201); George Gordon McCrae (1917: 170)	Perhaps the same as the *Mallæ malææ* song referred to by Dawson (1881: 80)	If the song referred to by Dawson is the same as that recorded by the McCraes, it is a commemoration of the ravages of smallpox.
Corroboree song, said to originate in the Yass area (13.2)	Bulmer, MS letter (MV XM 81); Bulmer in Campbell (1999: 56); Bulmer MS (MV XM 922, pp. 24–25); Smyth (1878, 1: 170); Howitt SLV MS 1053/4 (a)	–	Language unknown. In the Howitt MS, it is suggested the song originated at Yass and Tumut, so may be Wiradjuri.
Song brought down the Murray (13.3)	Bulmer in Campbell (1999: 56); MS (MV XM 925, p.44)	–	The song was presumably collected by Bulmer at Yelta. It could have been in any of a number of languages.

Name of song (section)	Source of text	Other references	Notes
The platypus, a far-travelled song (13.4)	Howitt (1904: 414); Howitt MS (SLV MS Box 1053/4 (a), p. 57)	–	This song may have come from NSW, possibly from the Richmond River.

Source: Authors.

We are not able to offer linguistic analysis of any of these songs, save to present the original texts and any small observations on them we have been able to make.

13.1 Ma-le song

There are three versions of this song. In her diary entry dated 5 January 1847, Georgiana McCrae writes 'Eliza told me the words of a few native songs I noted them down. There was one which the Goulburn blacks' tribe sing when one of their number is sent to jail', following which she gives the text of the song, the name of which we have regularised as **ma-le**, which we write with a hyphen so that it will not be misread as English *male/mail*. The version from Georgiana's journal (McCrae 1966: 201) is presented as Box 13.1:

Box 13.1: Ma-le song, version 1

Malay nyar wara goma malay a a
nyar wara a rindia a a malay
wara goma a a a malay a rindia
a a malay a a wah wara goma etc.

Source: Georgiana McCrae's journal, 5 January 1847; McCrae (1966: 201); adapted by authors.

The second version is from a notebook that forms the first part of George Gordon McCrae's manuscript journal of reminiscences 'Experiences not Exploits'. It is dated by the State Library of Victoria's McCrae papers Finding Aid as 1840–41, but although perhaps referring to that time, it was composed much later. The full text of the song with introduction is presented as Box 13.2:

Box 13.2: Ma-le song, version 2

Now, we first began to spell out native names and barter such small treasures as we had, for boomerangs, waddies and leangls, not to say canoe-paddles, spears, nulla-nullas and wee-a-weets or throwing sticks beside womeras or spear propellers. Here too we learned our first (and last) Australian boat or rather canoe song, but of which only a solitary couplet and the chorus survive in my memory

Mahlay, O, O, Ryndya

Ryndya, O, O, gomay

Mahlay, Mahlay, wah!

A really pretty melody with a chorus fading away by degrees

Source: George Gordon McCrae manuscript, SLV MS 12018, Box 2523/3 (a), p. 140;[1] adapted by authors.

A third version is in the published notes from George Gordon McCrae (1917: 170) and is presented as Box 13.3:

Box 13.3: Ma-le song, version 3

MAH-LAY

Mah-lay nya ware gomay.

Wara a, a, a, gomay-wara

Mah-lay nya Ryndia Mah-lay

Wah … Ah! wara.

Source: George Gordon McCrae (1917: 170); adapted by authors.

In McCrae (1917), the song associated with jail is the one given above (section 3.7.1) as having been composed by Ningolubbel. It is possible that the **ma-le** song may be the widely travelled song relating to smallpox, mentioned by Dawson (1881: 80):

> A lament called 'Mallæ malææ', composed in New South Wales in commemoration of the ravages of small-pox, is known all over the Australian colonies and is sung in a doleful strain, accompanied with groans and imitations of a dying person.

It may also be that the song is the same as the one mentioned by Teichelmann and Schürmann (1982 [1840], Vocabulary: 34).[2] Note that *palti* means 'song; play':

1 McCrae has numbered only those pages that are written on; but not those which are blank (mostly recto) or have a drawing pasted on them (also recto). Sometimes, however, the recto page is written on and numbered.

2 Thanks to Corey Theatre for pointing out this reference.

> Nguya. *s.* pustule; the disease of smallpox, from which the aborigines suffered before the Colony was founded. They universally assert that it came from the east, or the Murray tribes, so that is not at all improbable that the disease was at first brought among the natives by European settlers on the eastern coast. They have not suffered from it for some years; but about a decennium ago it was, according to their statement, universal; when it diminished their numbers considerably, and on many left the marks of its ravages, to be seen at this day. They have no remedy against it, except the *nguyapalti.*
>
> Nguyapalti, small-pox song, which they learnt from the eastern tribes, by the singing of which the disease is believed to be prevented or stopped in its progress.

Both Dawson and Teichelmann and Schürmann mentioned that this is a widespread song, and Dawson named it, but only Georgina McCrae wrote down the words.

All three versions contain a word with initial /r/, *rindia*, which suggests that the song has travelled from another place. Initial /r/ was not found in the Eastern Kulin languages, and this suggests that the song may be from one of the Murray River languages, as Hercus has recorded **rind** ['ri:nd] as the Tarti-Tarti word for the Murrumbidgee River, and 'also a general term for "river"' (1986: 232).

Note that in Box 13.2, George Gordon McCrae did specifically state that this was 'an Australian boat or rather canoe song' and made no mention of the possible connection with smallpox. If our suggestion that this is a Murray River languages song is correct, then the fact that it contains the word for 'river' may be the reason why McCrae's consultant, Bed-be-endgeer or Ben (see section 3.1.2), categorised it as a 'boat song'.

Another possible connection is a reference noted down by Howitt in his manuscript notebooks 'Corroboree beginning "Mally Mallay – tariarara" for which Murray Jack had heard formerly at Lambing Flat but heavy rain set in and prevented it' in Museums Victoria (XM 760, p. 15). Murray Jack was from the Yuin tribes.

We cannot offer any translation of the meaning of this song, and if it is indeed the same song that Dawson (1881) and Teichelmann and Schürmann (1982 [1840]) were referring to, it is likely that people in the Melbourne, western Victoria and Adelaide areas would not have understood it either.

13.2 Corroboree song, said to originate in the Yass area

The corroboree song recorded here is found in a range of versions. The first, presented as Box 13.4, occurs in a letter of Bulmer's relating how a stick would be sent to a tribe when a corroboree was to be held, informing people of the coming corroboree. This version also describes the text as being 'the burden of the song'. In the nineteenth century, *burden* meant 'the refrain or chorus' and it may be that these words were only part of the whole song.

Other versions of this song are found in Bulmer in Campbell (1999: 56), see Box 13.5; the manuscript version that Campbell used as the basis for this transcription (MV XM 922, pp. 24–25), presented as Box 13.6; a report from Bulmer in Smyth (1878, 1: 170), see Box 13.7; and also in the Howitt manuscripts, State Library of Victoria (MS Box 1053/4 (b), page numbered 5, hw0404.pdf, p. 86), see Box 13.8.

Box 13.4: Corroboree song, version 1

Many years ago when I was on the Murray a stick about 3 feet long was sent to the tribe at Yelta. It was marked with their usual marks and was an object of great interest to the tribe. I[t] was held in the hand of the time keeper at the corroborie and was struck with a bough of a tree at intervals. The burden of the song was as follows: *Wilpon tha wilpon me gra*. At the *gra* the stick was struck. All the men held sticks in their hands but only the one who taught the song held the stick which had travelled, the blacks said a very long way. Indeed, it must have travelled far for I found the same song was quite familiar to the Kurnai here so that it must have been known all along the arms of the River Murray and up the Darling and through Gippsland and indeed I have no doubt it was known in the greatest part of NSW.'

Source: Bulmer, letter of 15 April 1880, MV XM 81; adapted by authors.

Box 13.5: Corroboree song, version 2

Corroborees

Their great festival time was when they held a corroboree (*koonyeroo*). This was generally in the summer time when food was plentiful and travelling easy. Then the strangers came from different parts, perhaps one had brought a new song, and he was going to teach them the figures of the dance belonging to it. All they wanted was to know the song which could be learned in five minutes and the figures of the dance.

The corroboree songs travelled a long way, one song which was sung on the Murray in 1857 I heard sung at Lake Tyers in 1862. It was only a very few words; *wilpore tho wilpore me garaw*. When it was brought to Yelta it was accompanied by a stick of about a yard long. This stick was held in the hand with one end on the ground. It was struck by the dancer with a bough, at each sound of the word *garaw*.

Source: Bulmer in Campbell (1999: 56); adapted by authors.

The part of this description relating to this widely travelled song is found in the Bulmer papers (MV XM 922, pp. 24–25), and our transcription is here presented as Box 13.6. There are some differences between this and Campbell's transcription:

Box 13.6: Corroboree song, version 3

These corroboree songs travelled a great many miles. At the junction of the Darling in 1857, a song came down from the Upper Murray. It was accompanied by a stick of about a yard long, well carved. This was held in the hand while the song was being performed. For in some corrobories they did not use their legs

[p. 25]

but merely their hands. In this case the stick was held in the hands of the singers and was struck with a small bough. The song consisted of but five words. It was as follows: *wilpon tho wilpon me gra*.

But the tune was much more musical than any I had heard. In 1861 when I came to Gippsland I found this same song had gone all over that part of Victoria.

Source: Bulmer papers, MV XM 922, pp. 24–25; adapted by authors.

Box 13.7: Corroboree song, version 4

"The corrobboree," says the Rev. Mr. Bulmer, a Missionary at Lake Tyers, in Gippsland, "is a simple affair. The tune is the best part of it. In fact the tune is the chief feature, the poetry being generally poor. The song which made a great stir at the last corrobboree I witnessed was composed of about five words. It was of a language I did not understand, and indeed the blacks themselves did not understand it ; but that did not matter to them. All they desired was the tune and the figure of the dance. The words were as follows:–

Wilpon

Tho Wilpon

Me

Gra.!

"The sound of *gra* was carried on to a great length, while all the men made a very graceful bend of the body, and thus it was repeated at pleasure. In the corrobboree the blacks sometimes use their legs as in a regular dance, always keeping time remarkably well. At other times they only, bend their bodies in a very graceful way. When the dance consists in using the legs freely, then, as a rule, they never use any particular stick, but carry in the hand a boomerang or a tomahawk, as in a war-dance ; but when they present themselves in figure only bringing the body into play, they mostly have something in the shape of a stick, which it is presumed belongs to that particular kind of dance. Sometimes the stick is held in the left hand, to support the performer while he sways his body backwards and forwards. At each forward movement he strikes the stick in his left hand either with a bough or with another stick. It is astonishing to see with what soldier-like regularity the body of each man bends to the time. On certain occasions, when the legs have been mostly exercised in the dance, some of the men would assist the women in the singing, and would use their sticks in beating time."

Source: Bulmer in Smyth (1878, 1: 170); adapted by authors.

Box 13.8: Corroboree song, version 5

Imported Corroboree

Billy the Bull and Lambi heard the following corroboree at Sale some years ago. Melbourn blackfellows brought it over. It was said to have come from Yass & Tumut, thence to the Murray and to Melbourne. Mr Bulmer heard it at the junction of [the] Darling & Murray in 1860. It was sung by a man who stood facing a line of men (audience) so that the firelight shone on him. In his hand he held the message (corroboree) stick - which was about 30 in. long by 3 wide and say ¼ in. thick. Marked by diagonal bands of alternate red ochre and pipe clay. In his other hand he held a bough which he waved over the stick as he sang thus:

When Mr Bulmer saw it the stick was round with diagonal bands.

The words as follows:-

Wilpontho - wilpontha - jŭro-o-o

jŭra-a-a

The meaning of the words is unknown.

Source: Howitt, SLV MS Box 1053/4 (b), page numbered 55; hw0404.pdf, p. 86; adapted by authors.

Billy the Bull is one the elders of the Gippsland tribes. For further information about him, see section 5.1.6.

We are unable to offer any translation for this song.

13.3 Song brought down the Murray

Bulmer also wrote down this song, stating that it was 'brought down the Murray'. There are two versions presented here, that transcribed by Campbell from the Bulmer papers, presented in Box 13.9, and the manuscript version from Museums Victoria (XM 925, p. 44), presented in Box 13.10.[3] The Campbell transcription differs slightly from ours.

3 The page numbering of some of the Bulmer papers is very confusing. The PDF file which we were able to work from contains two pages numbered 44 in succession. This piece of text is on the second of those, and the previous page does not contain the section of text in [] brackets.

Box 13.9: Song brought down the Murray, version 1

> The songs now in use do not generally have more than six to twelve words, these are repeated as long as required, thus:
>
> *dilli mi generay*
>
> *tharamba lanuma*
>
> *ngio*
>
> The above was brought down the Murray, and though it was in an unknown language to the blacks, yet they sang it very often.

Source: Bulmer in Campbell (1999: 56); adapted by authors.

Box 13.10: Song brought down the Murray, version 2

> [the songs now in] use do not generally have more than 6 to 12 words, these are repeated over and over again thus:
>
> *dilli mi genera tharamba lanuma ngio*
>
> This was repeated as long as the singing was required. They state that the [ulni?] is in a language that was not known to the tribe where it was used & had travelled a long way before it got to the people they could sing it.

Source: Bulmer, MV XM 925, page numbered 44, p. 73 of PDF; adapted by authors.

Since we do not know anything about the meaning of the song, or where it originated from, we cannot suggest any translation.

13.4 The platypus, a far-travelled song

The final song presented in this chapter is about a platypus. Here, we have a word-by-word gloss, and a word for platypus written as *Malla-malle* and *Mulla-mulle*, which we would suggest can be regularised as **mala-mala**. We do not know any language in which the word for 'platypus' is similar to this form.

There are two versions, that in Howitt (1904), presented here as Box 13.11, and the manuscript version from the State Library of Victoria, presented as Box 13.12. Howitt (1904: 414) mentions that the song was heard in Narrinyeri country, but it does not originate there.[4]

4 According to Wikipedia, 'Platypus', accessed 29 October 2017, en.wikipedia.org/wiki/Platypus, the platypus range does not extend into Narrinyeri territory.

Howitt mentioned that it was heard in the Geawe-gal tribe, which is the name of a clan of the Dharawal that lived on Botany Bay, NSW. Later in the same text he mentions that a Wolgal speaker had said that this text came originally from the Richmond River. We are not at present able to say from where this song originated, but it was presumably in a place where platypus live, and the word for them is something like **mala-mala**.

In his manuscript version of the song, Howitt names Murray Jack, a Yuin man, as the consultant, using his Indigenous name Yibai-malian in the 1904 book.

Box 13.11: The platypus, a far-travelled song, version 1

The makers of Australian songs, or of the combined songs and dances, are the poets, or bards, of the tribe and are held in great esteem. Their names are known in the neighbouring tribes, and their songs are carried from tribe to tribe, until the very meaning of the words is lost, as well as the original source of the song. It is hard to say how far and how long such a song may travel in the course of time over the Australian continent.

A good example of such far-travelled songs is the following, of which I have heard two versions. One runs as follows:–

Malla-malle	*taria-rara*	*uananga*
Ngumberanga	*ye-yandaba*	

I heard it first sung by one of the Narrinyeri in 1861, and afterwards Mr. G. W. Rusden sang it for me from memory, having heard it in the Geawe-gal tribe many years before. In neither case was the meaning of the words known.

The second version I heard sung at the Murring Kuringal in 1880 by Yibai-malian, who said that it came to his tribe, the Wolgal, many years before, having been, he believed, originally brought from the Richmond River in New South Wales. The air to which it was sung was the same as I had before heard, but the words differed from those of the first version given, being:–

Mulla-mulle	*kuruitba*	*tarria-rara*
Platypus	large rock	bend of river
Guiltura	*nanga*	*ebermeranga*

[p. 416]

He said the words spoke of a platypus sitting on a rock in the river, but he could not explain the second line.

Source: Howitt (1904: 414, 416); adapted by authors.

Box 13.12: The platypus, a far-travelled song, version 2

Australian Aborigines

Corroborree Song

Mŭlla-mŭlle′	*Kūrūi′tba*	*tā′ra-irā ta′ra-ira′*
platypus	big rock	river bend
gūialtūra	*nauga*	*ebermernang*
big water hole		

Mŭ′ri Jack couldn’t remember the remainder of the song

Source: Howitt, SLV MS Box 1053/4, hw0404.pdf, p. 88; adapted by authors.

14

Songs in unknown languages

In this chapter we present two songs whose languages we have been unable to establish. The first of these is the Up River initiation song, documented in the Lower Murray area by both Radcliffe Brown and Berndt and Berndt.

14.1 Up River initiation song

This song was sung by both Pinkie Mack and Albert Karloan, neither of whom knew the language in which it was sung. Two versions of the text have come down to us, one from Berndt and Berndt (1993) (see Box 14.1), and the second from Radcliffe Brown (Box 14.2).

There are also surviving recordings of this, and a transcription of the music for the Berndt and Berndt recording by Alice Moyle. As with the other songs recorded by Berndt and Berndt onto a wax cylinder at East Wellington in South Australia in 1943, the singer was Pinkie Mack. Berndt and Berndt (1993: 172) wrote that:

> (We tried to record this on part of an Edison wax cylinder recording at Brinkley, East Wellington, in 1943. Pinkie Mack was the singer. This collection of cylinders is now in the Australian Institute of Aboriginal and Torres Strait Islander Studies, AIATSIS, in Canberra.)

These wax cylinders were played and transferred onto magnetic tape at the behest of Alice Moyle, and this recording is now digitised by AIATSIS as BERNDT_RC01-004244A.wav. This consists of 13 cylinders, of which Cylinder No. 12 contains the following (Box 14.1; from BERNDT_RC01-004244_listing.pdf):

Box 14.1: Details of Cylinder No. 12 recorded by Berndt and Berndt

1st part: an Up River initiation song 'pa:ta 'winəma ...
2nd part: A 'Jakəmal'da:k tribal song from up the river 'dugdugədo 'ja:na

Source: AIATSIS BERNDT_RC01-004244_listing.pdf; adapted by authors.

This portion is on the AIATSIS WAV file from 18:48 to 21:29, commencing with the words spoken by Alice Moyle: 'No. 12 slightly mildewed at commencement'.

The musical transcription made by Alice Moyle is in pencil, and (apparently) kept at AIATSIS.[1] We have been able to access a PDF copy of it; one of around 13 transcriptions of songs from the Berndt and Berndt collection made by Alice Moye. In Figure 14.1, we present a clear version of the transcription done by Alice Moyle of this song. In the document containing this transcription there are multiple songs and it may be that the one immediately following the double bar line in the original represents a transcription of the second part of Cylinder No. 12, the Wentworth song, sung by Jacko (see section 8.2.2). We are not including that musical transcription in this volume.

Figure 14.1: Alice Moyle's musical analysis of the Up River initiation song
Source: Grace Koch.

1 The PDF file from which we derived Figure 14.1 was called BERNDT_RC01-004244_supplementary1.pdf. Using the Adobe Photoshop program, we extracted a JPG file and decreased the brightness until all of the writing was readable.

Range: Major 9th (C–D)

The two text versions of the song are presented below. Box 14.2 is the version in Berndt and Berndt (1993), and Box 14.3 is the version as notated by Radcliffe Brown.

Box 14.2: Up River initiation song, version 1

Unfortunately Karloan and Pinkie Mack did not know the meaning of the dancing and the songs. They were said to have been introduced to the Yaraldi in the middle of the nineteenth century by visiting Walkandi-woni, but the specific language in which the song was rendered was unknown. Pinkie Mack, who had some knowledge of up-river languages, was unable to identify it. (We tried to record this on part of an Edison wax cylinder recording at Brinkley, East Wellington, in 1943. Pinkie Mack was the singer. This collection of cylinders is now in the Australian Institute of Aboriginal and Torres Strait Islander Studies, AIATSIS, in Canberra.)

The songs words were as follows, and our rendering is directly from actual field notes taken at the time Pinkie Mack discussed the words with us; it was not taken from the song recording:

Part One

1 Pata winema ngama leiwuninang ania akaka.

2 Maria pailpata mani mani tjatu-pulanda waipali ai malo-a.

Part Two

1 Pata winema ngama leiwuninang a ai …

2 Mani-mani tjatu-pulanda waipali ai malo angk.

3 Pata winema ngama leiwuninang ei a …

4 Mani-mani tjatu-pulanda waipali ai malo a.

The above two parts were repeated and followed by the concluding words:

Pata winema ngama leiwuninang malo tr tr tr

Songs of this kind always began and ended with three beats.

Source: Berndt and Berndt (1993: 172); adapted by authors.

Box 14.3: Up River initiation song, version 2

Informant Albert Kaláwan

'corroboree coming from up the Murray river'

Partawineme name láwinana

ania:ka:ka:

maria paitjpa:ta:

(Murray)

mani mani tartubarlanda*

alpeli au ma:lauwang

partwinema

----

ya:mbalan

*metre has been indicated on this line.

Source: Radcliffe Brown Papers, AIATSIS MS 995; transcribed by Peter Sutton.

We do not know what language this song is, but we can be confident that it is not Ngarrindjeri (Narrinyeri), because if it had been, both Albert Karloan and Pinkie Mack would have been able to translate it, whereas neither of them knew the meaning and Pinkie Mack could not identify the language.

It has been suggested (Mary-Anne Gale, pers. comm.) that the initial word *pata* could be related to the song type *patangi*, one of the song types discussed in Berndt and Berndt (1993) (see also the discussion of Jacko's song, which was a *patangi*, in section 8.2.2). She also suggested that *winema* could be *winmun* 'construct/work' or *winamun* 'beating time' from 'wiñam-in, v.s., beating time' (Meyer 1843: 107) and *winamin* Taplin (1879).

However, Berndt and Berndt (1993) noted that the song was brought down to the coastal areas by *Walkandi-woni*, who were a 'generic Grouping of non-Yaraldi people further up river. Compound is based on "North Wind"', adding (1993: 213) that:

> Pinkie Mack also mentioned that the Walkandi-woni people were the main source, in later days, of various ceremonies when Kukabrak ones were held less frequently or not at all. Upriver people, she said, sent a prigi (messenger) who came to Mannum and continued by canoe with a companion.

This would suggest that the language is less likely to be Ngarrindjeri.

There is a similarity between this song and another initiation song documented by Howitt in section 2.3.3, which we have included in the Western Kulin languages section. Both of these songs commence with the word *pata* and both are initiation songs. As seen in section 2.3.3, Howitt glossed *pata* as 'wait a while', but this meaning is not found in any of the language sources for Western Kulin. It is possible that both this Up River initiation song and the Initiation song in section 2.3.3 are in the same unknown language.

We note that the form *leiwuningang* is found in the Berndt and Berndt version (Box 14.1), and a corresponding *láwinana* in the version recorded by Radcliffe Brown (Box 14.2). Both of these forms are similar to the Murray River word **lewa-** 'sit' (see discussion of Minduk Jack's second song, section 12.3.2). If this song were in one of the Murray River languages, however, we would have expected Pinkie Mack to understand its meaning, since she was able to interpret the meaning of Minduk Jack's songs.

Note that the word for 'father' in Keramin is recorded with the spellings *pate* and *bait* (Horgen 2004), which could be realised as *pata*.

However, beyond these speculations, we cannot say much about this song, neither being able to offer any translation of it or even any certainty as to which language it is.

14.2 Anaruka song (Creek song)

On 27 November 1860, Ludwig Becker, who was one of the members of the Burke and Wills expedition, sent a letter to Dr Macadam, MLA, Hon. Secretary, Royal Society, Victoria, and the letter was read at a meeting of the society in December 1860 and published in *The Argus* on 11 December 1860.[2] Becker included 'A specimen or two of a song and tune of one of the Murray Tribes'. He introduced this as follows:

> Remark.—I had not had much opportunity as yet to converse sufficiently with the natives so as to offer something new or of great interest to others unacquainted with the Lower Murray and the Upper Darling tribes. However, I was fortunate enough to hear from an intelligent native some-thing which may prove interesting enough to lovers of primitive songs and tunes. It is a translation of a corroboree song, and which that young Murray black dictated to me in English. I wrote it down word for word. The same young man also favoured me with a love-song, repeatiug it several times, so as to enable me to note correctly words and melody.
>
> LUDWIG BECKER.
> Darling Depot, Nov. 27.

2 'Royal Society of Victoria', *Argus*, 11 December 1860, accessed 30 April 2017, trove.nla.gov.au/newspaper/article/5694801?searchTerm=aboriginal%20melodies&searchLimits=l-state=Victoria. The text is also published in Tipping (1979: 190), where we first became aware of it.

The translation of the corroboree song, also described as Yaam song, is given in Box 14.4:

Box 14.4: Yaam song (Corroboree song)

(Lower Murray.)
"I am with the white people,
But all my tribe in the camp at home,
And I am living with the white people ;
And I am amongst other blacks,
And cannot understand their speaking.
Wheregara was my country,
But I am covering myself with the blanket now,
And I am not covered with the opossum rug,
And I cannot make it :
Cannot get the opossum to make the rug,
I am with the white people now.
And I cannot go to my home yet.
I cannot get married to my colour.
Being now with the white people ;
And if I want to marry my colour
I must go home.
And if I marry to my colour,
And if I go to another country
With the white people,
And leave behind my lubra,
Perhaps white people take her,
And give her to another black.
And this I do not like ! Ugh !"

Source: Recorded by Becker (1860); adapted by authors.

We do not know of any language in which **yam(a)** means 'corroboree' or 'dance', and cannot therefore associate this song with any known language group. Note, however, that the first word of the corroboree song reported in the *Riverina Herald*, discussed in section 9.2.1, has **yama** as its first word.

The form and sentiment of this Yaam song raises questions about the status of this song.

Becker's discussion of the Anaruka song is presented in Box 14.5, and the full text with music (from Tipping 1979: 190) is presented as Figure 14.2.

Box 14.5: Anaruka song (Creek song)

> Note.—'Anaruka' is the word for 'creek,' but often given as a name to girls. There is a truly poetical conception in the double meaning of the word. "Walwallim (name of a black fellow) sings—
>
> "Anaruka ! you must be quick, come down,
>
> I cannot wait for you long;
>
> No man can wait for you long.
>
> I am going to sleep (to die)."

Source: Recorded by Becker (1860); adapted by authors.

Figure 14.2: Musical analysis and text of the Anaruka song recorded by Becker

Source: Becker (1860) in Tipping (1979: 190); courtesy of Melbourne University Press.

Range: Augmented 5th (B–F)

Becker has put the song into a 4/4 metre. The semitone drop from C to B and the diminished 5th rise in the 6th bar suggest an underlying Lochrian mode.

The full text is given in (14.1):

(14.1) *Anaruka walli-walli madin haana-ruk carrol-gunnage allsan-u-ri wai ki-waiki yen dailombnai geng nadami.*

We presume that the first word could be regularised as **nganaruka**. This does not resemble any words in Paakantyi or Maraura and so we cannot offer any analysis of the song's meaning or suggestions as to which language it is in.

15

Reflections on these songs into the future

Stephen Morey and Russell Mullett

What we have done in this book is to gather in one place every piece of information that the authors could find relating to what we are thinking of as traditional songs in Indigenous languages of Victoria. We did not include Christian hymns translated into language, such as the well-known Bura Fera,[1] in Yorta Yorta language, mentioned in Chapter 9.

This chapter is co-written with Kurnai traditional custodian Russell Mullett from Gippsland and aims to add his Indigenous perspective on the contents of this book. It is intended as a short reflection on the place of these songs and the role that we hope this book will have in the reclamation and revitalisation of language and, in particular, song traditions among the Indigenous people of Victoria. There can and surely will be other Indigenous perspectives, and we hope this book will facilitate and encourage further examination of these songs in communities and discussion about the place of these songs.

1 This was sung in the popular film *The Sapphires* (2012). An extract from the film can be found at ABC Indigenous, 'One Song's 130-Year Impact on Australian Music', YouTube, accessed 1 June 2022, www.youtube.com/watch?v=vDZ2NQkkOAk.

15.1 What kind of songs are in this book?

We group the songs in this book as 'traditional' because they relate to or were performed in traditional ceremonies (for example, the Ye-pen-ni pie-kai dance, section 2.4), or were part of the everyday customs (for example, **YelmeRai** the shark totem song, section 5.3.3). We also include songs that Indigenous people wrote responding to modern events, such as the Telegraph song (section 7.2) and the songs relating to the 'White Woman' (sections 5.2.2 and 5.2.3).[2] As Russell Mullet observed:

> In traditional society, when something interesting happened, you would create a song about it and memorise it. Songs of this kind are similar to the tradition of storytelling except that songs do so very concisely; it is story pulled down to its basic structure.

Thus, in the 'White Woman' song (section 5.2.3), the text is very short, translated as: 'Give the white woman from over the sea the possum skin skirt, and that yonder blanket there'. In story form this would have been told in much greater detail. Unfortunately we do not have the story form of the rescue of the 'White Woman' from a shipwreck, and her being comforted and clothed by the people as the song suggests.

Nor do we have the melody for this song, just the words. Russell Mullett has also observed:

> The song may be reduced but the sounds of the song, the beat, the rhythm and the singing style would also communicate meaning.[3]

2 See also Stephen Morey and Jason M. Gibson, 'Recovered Aboriginal Songs Offer Clues to 19th Century Mystery of the Shipwrecked "White Woman"', *The Conversation*, 11 December 2018, theconversation.com/recovered-aboriginal-songs-offer-clues-to-19th-century-mystery-of-the-shipwrecked-white-woman-108070.

3 The extent to which non-linguistic features, such as melody, rhythm and accompanying dance style may have conveyed additional meaning to the listeners is not known, but such things have been observed by one of the authors (Morey) in the songs of the Tangsa people on the border of India and Myanmar. There we can see the same words used in different styles of songs with different meanings. Thus, the words 'my rice granary is so full I cannot push it over' in a song dedicated to the spirit of the earth in thanks for the harvest (Wihu song) would convey thanks the spirits, whereas the same words (but different melody) in a love song, with a different melody, sung by a boy would convey to the girl listening that the boy was wealthy and a good prospect for marriage (Morey and Schöpf 2018).

15.2 What is the approach of this book?

This book is written in the Western Academic Tradition, which we have spelled with capital letters because it is a particular style of writing that involves careful and detailed study of every aspect of the songs, with multiple references. In addition, we identify or suggest possible links with other songs and reference previous academic studies of songs in Indigenous Australia and other places. This is the academic way of doing things, and these songs are of interest in this Western Academic Tradition, but they are surely of greater importance to the Indigenous communities from which the songs originate.

Many of these songs have not been known in their communities for a long time, most are found only in manuscripts or in nineteenth-century books and journal articles that can be difficult to obtain, and the passing on of this kind of knowledge has been interrupted.

The invasion of what is now called Victoria by white people, commencing in 1834, very quickly disrupted many aspects of traditional life, but these songs are evidence of the maintenance of knowledge and continuation of traditions. For example, many of the songs written down in State Library of Victoria MS 6290 (see section 1.5.2 for a discussion of this manuscript) are commenting either on what we might call 'everyday events' (a boy tripping on an anthill, section 4.2.1) or on recent events in the general society, such as the arrival of the telegraph in south-western Victoria (section 7.2). We suggest that these songs, although commenting on recent events, have their roots in Indigenous culture since time immemorial. These songs are a documentary record of culture that did not disappear and was and continues to be maintained.

As already mentioned, even though some of these songs have only come down to us as written words on a page, there was music and melody, and action, such as dance and accompaniment by musical instruments, associated with these songs. What was being conveyed by these songs is more than just the words, and the listeners would have shared with the singers an understanding of the deeper cultural meanings.

For example, the **Yentjin(y)** (elopement) songs in Gippsland, composed by people like Tulaba, carried with them context that was shared between composer and listeners; context that may have been conveyed by particular melodies as well as by words and a context that was confirmed by the time and place of the singing. All the members of the community in traditional times understood the place of this **Yentjin(y)** song, and if they did not want to hear it, they might pretend not to hear and move away (see section 5.2.8). This is an example of the way that Indigenous people understood all the context of these songs and much more beside.

In some cases we have considerable information about the context, and some songs have a long history of being remembered. Perhaps the most detailed information relates to the Gaiggip song (section 3.4.1) first known to have been performed in 1843. This song is important because it contains information about the following aspects of the song and its performance:

i. multiple contemporary detailed descriptions of the performance
ii. known dates of performance
iii. names of some of those involved
iv. text of the songs sung
v. drawings and paintings that likely depict the performance
vi. description of some of the objects that were present at the performance and
vii. description of the dances performed.

Two important features were described, first the music, the melody used in the singing, and second the meaning of the words. We have some hints about the first, since McCabe's description does include that the women 'had just commenced singing in a more plaintive manner than I can recollect to have heard them before' and that 'a few of the men were with them beating time with their sticks'.

Gaiggip is significant also because it was remembered for a long time – Barak probably spoke about it with Arthur Baessler in 1892 (see Vanderbyl 2019b: 42), remembering a performance two generations before. As discussed in section 3.4.1, at least one of Barak's paintings is said to relate to the Gaiggip. We need to say that one area in which our book is certainly incomplete, largely due to the lack of knowledge by the authors, is the relationship of these songs to art works done by Indigenous artists that depict dance performances.

Some of the songs sung by the late Stan Day in 1962 to Luise Hercus also have a long history. The song 'Going to the land of the dead' (section 2.2.4) was passed down, in part, to Stan Day from his grandfather Marrərt, who had learned it from an elder man, Tommy, who said that the song was composed for Tommy's grandmother's death.

So although we have presented as much detail as we could in this book, clearly one of the tasks in the future is to engage in a deeper discussion with community members about these songs. As already mentioned in connection with the Gaiggip, there are a number of aspects of these songs that it would be ideal to know about. We have developed a list of these here:

1. Detailed description of the context of the song, when it was performed, night or day, at what time of the month or in connection with what ceremony or other community event
2. Who composed the song
3. Who performed the song, who had the right to sing it
4. Whether the song was performed with dance, and if so, a description of the dance
5. Whether the song was performed with ceremonial or other objects and if so, a description of those objects
6. A full text of the song words
7. A translation and if available word-by-word gloss of the meaning of the song
8. Whether the song is related to traditional stories
9. Whether the song is part of a larger network of songs (also referred to as songlines)
10. A musical transcription to indicate the melody and rhythm of the song, or if it was after 1900, a sound recording
11. Whether the song was performed with instrumental accompaniment, such as clap sticks and if so information about the rhythm of those instruments
12. Drawings and/or paintings of the ceremony in which the song was performed.

Most probably we do not have any songs for which answers to all of these 12 points exist.

As Russell Mullett observed about the meaning and context of these songs:

> The words of the songs are important, even more so is understanding the deeper meaning and context of the song. We may be given the language words and the English meaning, but it's the deeper meaning that tells the story, and some or all of the twelve aspects listed above

> contribute to that deeper meaning. These 12 aspects are like prompts to our community to further investigate and understand what that deeper meaning might be.

In the next section, we will make some preliminary observations on the reclamation of song traditions that this book, or at least the data in it, will hopefully assist.

Before doing that, however, we must observe that the academic style of this book, the substantial detail and the presentation of multiple versions of the same text may not be easy for some people to read. Perhaps what is also needed is another version of this that is written to be more community friendly – but that is essentially another task.

15.3 Reclamation of song traditions

There is a reasonably long history of the repatriation of sound recordings of songs and their reclamation by communities. As Treloyn, Dembal and Charles (2019), writing about songs in the Kimberley, say: 'Repatriation has become almost ubiquitous in ethnomusicological research on Australian Indigenous song', going on to present an example of 'repatriation-centered song revitalization'. In some cases, this type of repatriation has occurred in communities where song traditions are still in place, and where access to earlier recordings can assist in confirming or strengthening those traditions (other references include papers in Wafer and Turpin 2017; Harris, Barwick and Troy 2022).

One of the authors (Koch) has been involved in a reclamation project in the Torres Strait involving materials collected during the 1898–99 Cambridge Anthropological Expedition to the Torres Strait Islands, led by Alfred Cort Haddon.[4] Some of the materials collected in 1898–99 are songs that are still known. As Grace Koch explained:

> According to the wishes of the descendants, only family members of the people recorded by the Expedition were present at playback of their ancestors' voices. Some of the melodies were still known by the descendants, and one person sang some of the songs after hearing the recordings. All were greatly moved by hearing the recordings and

4 Rebekah Hayes and Grace Koch, 'Alfred Cort Haddon 1898 Expedition (Torres Strait and British New Guinea) Cylinder Collection (C80)' Torres Strait Islands Cylinders Research Document, True Echoes, British Library, doi.org/10.23636/0z5f-ww40.

> thankful that their ancestors had been recorded by the Expedition in 1898. Reactions to playback can be found on the following website under the AIATSIS section. (True Echoes, www.true-echoes.com/)

Unlike in the Torres Strait or the Kimberley, in most parts of Victoria traditional songs have not been performed for a long time. We hope that our book is a prelude, a preliminary step that brings these songs and their context more to the attention of communities. Repatriation in this case is a different process.

That said, some revitalisation of traditional songs is occurring, of which the best example known to us is the corroboree song sung by Barak to Dr Torrance (section 3.2.5). For several years prior to the COVID-19 pandemic, this song was sung at the annual performance of the Tanderrum ceremony (see section 3.4.1.1) at the opening of the Melbourne International Arts Festival.[5] This song was one of few from the nineteenth century that was published with a musical transcription; in general most of these songs exist only as words, and the music that once accompanied them, which was not noted down, is now silent.

So, while there is an increasing interest in the languages of Victoria, as witnessed by translating Australian Football League (AFL) songs into language,[6] there is yet to be a complete reclamation of the songs in this book by the many communities represented here. This is not surprising because these songs come from multiple mostly nineteenth-century sources, many of them difficult to identify. Moreover, these songs have never been gathered in a single location before.

The reclamation of cultural heritage takes many forms, including the repatriation of cultural property. One recent example is the purchase by the Wurundjeri community, with financial support from the Victorian Government, of a painting by Barak that depicts women in possum skin cloaks at a corroboree.[7] This painting and others by Barak depict some of the corroborees or other dance performances that are discussed in this book (see section 3.4.1).

5 In 2018 this was recorded by a member of the public, who put up a copy of their recording on YouTube. Dirty Pierre, 'Tanderrum Festival 2018', YouTube, 24 May 2019, www.youtube.com/watch?v=B8EPgwRUr0E.

6 One example of this is the Melbourne Football Club song, 'Melbourne Theme Song | Woiwurrung', YouTube, accessed 1 June 2022, www.youtube.com/watch?v=KcvXrsEXg_0.

7 Margaret Paul, 'Descendants of William Barak Buy Two of His Works at New York Auction', *ABC News*, 26 May 2022, www.abc.net.au/news/2022-05-26/william-barak-art-auction-new-york/101100606.

Reclamation will certainly involve continuing discussions with community members, bringing together a range of expertise to better understand these songs. Over the last decade, as this book has slowly been completed, we have shared earlier versions of parts or all of it with community members that we have come to know in all parts of Victoria. One example of building such connections is with the Earthquake song (see section 3.8) and two stories, that of Mombulark and that of Thadagŭn, both involving the Echidna. The Earthquake song was published in 1878 (Smyth 1878, 2: 111) and the Mombulark story in the 1940s (Shaw [1940s?]), while the Thadagŭn story written down in the 1880s remained in the unpublished A.W. Howitt papers. It was only in 2021 at an online presentation attended by several elders of the Wurundjeri community that the link between the song and these stories emerged; the discussion of the song led to an understanding that these two stories and the song are perhaps the same narrative but in different media (song and story) and written down by different people (John Green, Ethel Shaw and A.W. Howitt). Further, in discussion of the last but one word of the song, written by Green as *karwen* and relating to the shaking of the ground, the stories tell of the way that the Echidna dug into the ground and shook it up to help release a kidnapped boy trapped under a big stone. The connection of the Echidna, **gawarn** in the Woiwurrung language, with thunder and earthquake was not obvious to the authors at first, until pointed out. We are very grateful to Auntie Joy Wandin Murphy and also to Andrew Tanner for the knowledge they both added to the understanding of this song.

It may also be that more than one interpretation of the meaning is not only possible but desirable as an artistic effect. One of our anonymous reviewers suggested this, writing that 'the possibility of holding multiple possible parsings (glossings) produces an aesthetic result that is pleasurable and memorable; and it is one only possible in orally transmitted traditions (like songs)'.

Thus, discussions with community might lead to reinterpreting some of the song analyses in this book. As Russell Mullett observed:

> There might be surprises in what comes out of this. It might lead to the discovery of more sources (manuscripts or recordings) or it might head in directions of community reclamation that we can't predict. That's up to the communities, it's their choice on if or how they proceed with the knowledge in this book.

Reclamation may include communities coming together to discuss and 'workshop' these songs to fully reclaim their ownership of them. New music may be created to sing the songs with music that may be similar to some of the nineteenth-century styles (i.e. the corroboree song discussed above) or the music may be completely new and different. Similarly, other of the 12 points listed above, such as the detail of the dances and dance steps, the settings of the performances, the instrument accompaniment, may have to be re-created or adapted from other places.

Because the melody of songs is an integral part of the song, we have included musical transcriptions of songs wherever possible. These transcriptions are both those made in the nineteenth century, such as by Dr Torrance (section 3.2), and those based on available sound recordings made in the twenty-first century by Grace Koch (for example, section 2.2). Where possible we have placed links to sound recordings in this book that allow readers to listen to original recordings from 1914 and the 1960s.

By gathering all of these materials – the words of the songs, the music (if known), the context of its performance and information about its composers – together in a single location, we are hopeful that a process of community reclamation of these songs can now commence, and the authors are happy to be involved as much, or as little, as communities wish. As Russell Mullett explained:

> The cultural knowledge (Indigenous communities' current knowledge) and the scientific knowledge (in this case linguistic/musicological/historical) should work together – in the form of strong relationships based on mutual respect, acknowledging the values of each other to produce an outcome.
>
> Science – in this case this book – does its job but then the community discussions and consultations about what to do with these take it to the next stage (or not, as the communities decide). There may not be a next stage, or there might be – community might leave that for a time, maybe years, there's no need to rush, when the community is ready, that's their decision.

We hope that by providing as much information about these songs as we can, communities are better able to decide what they want to do.

As we mentioned earlier, some songs, such as the Gaiggip and the songs known by Stan Day, survived for a long period in the colonial era. One song that might have been in consistent use throughout the colonial era, up until today, is the Hairy Beka chant, recorded by Luise Hercus, and known in the time that Dr Heather Bowe recorded Mrs Geraldine Briggs (see section 9.5.1). This is possibly the only traditional song that had a continuous history of use. As Russell Mullett pointed out:

> In general there's a total interruption to transmission, and given that all the resources here are historical sources then there is no urgency to reclaim, that can be done as community wishes in its own time.

Although there is interruption, song is also an important part of language documentation and revival. This is another reason why we believe the discussions of words and their meanings in this book is so important. Even in one's own language, understanding poetry and song requires lengthy discussion of the symbolism, alliteration and poetic features.

15.4 How might reclamation proceed?

In this section we just wish to put down a few ideas, things that may or may not be taken on by communities when reviewing the songs given here.

Communities may reincorporate these songs into their cultural events, as is already occurring with the corroboree song sung by Barak.

Communities may decide that some of these texts should have some restrictions placed on them, but as Russell Mullett said:

> This book is a capture of all things. The community will need to decide what to do and how to contextualize, but in this book everything is there for people to see and make further decisions about. For example, the material related to initiation, if you pull that out, you'd be losing important knowledge. What this book includes is the social context of song, it is music of the past still connected to today and we can't separate anything out of that, which is why this book has everything in it.

We do not know for sure what restrictions may have been placed on these songs in the past. They were told by Indigenous people, presumably mostly the elders, to white people like William Thomas and A.W. Howitt. We know that this was done at a time of massive change in communities and in a situation where the balance of power was with the white man. Thus, it has been suggested that A.W. Howitt, for example, was told some secret information after he had tricked people into believing he was initiated (Mulvaney 1970; Gibson and Mullett 2020). As Russell Mullett said, however:

> Even if that was the case, the information from Howitt has been there in the public arena for more than a century in several publications and this book adds information about things such as the Initiation Ceremony in Gippsland [section 5.2.21.2]. The added information is often clarification, and is about who gave the information to Howitt and potentially helps to correct what might otherwise be errors or misunderstandings.

One example of what we regard as problematic scholarship from the early twentieth century is the description by R.H. Mathews, published in 1904 and 1905a, of 'The Wonggoa or Wongupka Ceremony'. In the published version, information about ceremonies from both the Yorta Yorta and the Dhudhuroa have been grouped together in a description that reads as if it is a single ceremony. Only by rechecking the original manuscripts was it possible to disentangle the confusions that would arise from reading Mathews as it stands. As was the usual practice in 1904, he did not name his consultants, in this case John Atkinson and Ned Wheeler in the published versions, but they are named in the manuscripts. The problem is compounded by the fact the published versions, with their inaccuracies, are easily accessed online, while the manuscripts are not. In our opinion, Indigenous people need to have such access, online, to these manuscripts and to the transcriptions of them.[8]

While we have aimed to provide as much information in each of the 12 aspects listed in section 15.2, in many cases we do not have the information we would like to have. Consider again the **Yentjin(y)** songs of Gippsland: these may well have been sung in private such as by a young man to a young woman; we do not know if all the community would have been permitted to hear them. But we do know that older men such as Tulaba remembered these from his youth and passed them on. Maybe there were people that you could not sing these in front of. We do not know. As Russell Mullett said:

8 The Nyingarn project aims to achieve access to images of manuscripts that are linked to searchable, readable transcriptions (/nyingarn.net/). Two examples of projects already achieving this are Digital Daisy Bates (bates.org.au/) and Howitt and Fison Archive (howittandfison.org/), the latter of which contains the manuscript images for all the Howitt manuscripts discussed in this book.

> This book and the words and songs that are in it are the starting point for discussions about these type of things and how people want to engage with this song book. Similarly, once Howitt (1904) became more easily available, a lot of people bought it. Early than that it was harder to know about.
>
> More recently we have the Howitt and Fison website. For many years, the materials in there lay in public institutions without us knowing what was there. Now that it's transcribed, it has made it very much easier for people to read it and talk about it and make decisions about it.

One big difference between a book like this and an online website like the Howitt and Fison Archive is that this book allows linking of all the different sources that give context about particular songs, such as the Earthquake song (section 3.8), and it offers the chance for scholars to suggest linguistic and in some cases musicological analysis that a project of presenting transcriptions would not allow. Our suggested translation of the corroboree song in section 3.2.5 posited that this was a song about birds, possibly about birds that were totems. We could do this because of the linguistic expertise of some of the authors and the information about the language that had been collected and published over many years.

As Russell Mullett wrote:

> The focus of this book is on a subject matter, whereas the Howitt and Fison Archive website is everything that Howitt wrote. So, to extract just the songs is fantastic because it deals with one subject matter which is something that links all the groups in Victoria – indeed beyond.

Communities may find errors/misinterpretations in this book that need to be corrected, and if there are errors then the published book will continue to contain those on into the future. As authors whose expertise is limited, we sometimes miss signals about the song. As Russell Mullett puts it:

> The academics need to do the interpretation that they can do, even if in future it turns out that a better interpretation is identified, because otherwise it's just words on paper that the community can't easily interpret. This book is a step in the stage towards better knowledge, and like all such steps, it might not be perfect but it allows for better work in the future that wouldn't happen if this foundational work wasn't done first.

15.5 Some final comments

Songs are a powerful aspect of culture. In a public lecture in May 2022, John Bradley spoke about the Yanyuwa people of the Gulf of Carpentaria and how they consider songs:

> In a Yanyuwa way of understanding, these songs are thoughts that provoke … they should arouse in the hearer's mind a deeply 'subjective' response … (they should) make demands of the listener … (they are) to be heard not read.[9]

We should not expect the songs of Victoria to be all that very different. They are meant to be heard by whoever the community deems fit. We hope this book is a step towards that.

9 Seminar entitled 'Yanyuwa Song Poetry: An Intimate Window into Kin and Country', presented by John Bradley, Research Unit for Indigenous Language, University of Melbourne, 24 May 2022.

References

Archival sources

Australian Institute of Aboriginal and Torres Strait Islander Studies (AIATSIS)

Moonahcullah Ration Books, 2 vols. MS 5056.

The Moravian Mission in Australia Papers, 1832–1916: First Mission at Lake Boga. AIATSIS microfilm MF 165.

Radcliffe Brown Papers, MS 995.

Berlin Phonogramm-Archiv

Von Luschan, Felix. Berlin Phonogramm-Archiv Collection VII WS 209.

Mildura Genealogical Society

Mallee Cliffs Cash Book 1883–1885.

Museums Victoria (MV)

A. W. Howitt papers, XM 524, XM 525, XM 605, XM 615, XM 615, XM 653, XM 653, XM 692, XM 746, XM 755, XM 759, XM 760, XM 761, XM 775, XM 922, XM 923, XM 925, XM 925.

Charles Officer papers relating to Mt. Talbot, XM 1530.

John Bulmer papers, XM 81, XM 88, XM 89, XM 90, XM 91, XM 92, XM 93, XM 94, XM 96.

National Library of Australia (NLA)

Fison Papers, MS 7080.

Papers of Robert Hamilton Mathews, MS 8006, MS Acc09.011.

Royal Anthropological Institute of Great Britain and Ireland (RAIGBI)

Champ, W. Aboriginal vocabulary, comprising the Ballaarat, Bacchus Marsh, Melbourne and Gipps Land: dialects with a selection of dialogues and familiar phrases. Pentridge, 1862. MS 38.

Royal Historical Society of Victoria

Box 118-14 (MS 011271), 'A Vocabulary of the "Western Port" Aboriginals by George Gordon McCrae with an introduction and notes by A. A. Kenyon' – 7 pages typewritten with handwritten corrections. Includes 'Copied from remains of a Vocabulary of the Tribe sometimes called "the Western-Port" but inhabiting the country about Arthurs Seat Port Phillip in the Forties and Fifties'.

St Mark's National Theological Centre, Canberra

Tippett collection. TIP 70/10/37, item 3. Howitt Documents: Howitt Schedule, data for eight different aboriginal tribes. Bairnsdale material arranged by Fison. n.d.

State Library of New South Wales (SLNSW)

Hugh Malcolm Eastman memoirs, ca. 1850 – ca. 1952, MLMSS 130.

G.A. Robinson papers, A 7086.

William Thomas papers, 1834-1868, 1902, MLMSS 214.

Tyers, C.J. 'Issue of Blankets to Aborigines, 1854-1858'. A 842 Crown Lands: Squatters' runs, Gippsland, 1844-1867. [Charles James Tyers papers, 1831-1870].

State Library of South Australia

Scott, E.B. n.d. Papers of Edward Bate Scott, on microfilm at PRG 608.

State Library of Victoria (SLV)

Dawson, W.T. and J.H.W. Pettit. [1850s]. 'Gippsland Vocabularies and Place Names Obtained and recorded in the Fifties by W.T. Dawson, District Surveyor, and J.H.W. Pettit, Surveyor'. Unpublished manuscript and typescript. MS Box 1054/2 (c), Alfred W. Howitt Collection.

Howitt, A. W. Manuscript papers, MS 9356 and 10241 (Boxes 1044–1055).

Le Souëf, A.A.C. 'Personal Recollections of Early Victoria', MS 8719.

McCrae family papers [not after 1958], MS 12018.

Robert Brough Smyth papers, MS 8781.

Unknown compiler. 1862. 'A Lexicon of the Australian Aboriginal Languages in the Six Dialects of Ballarat, Bacchus Marsh, Melbourne, Gipps Land, Mount Gambier and Wonnin'. MS 6290.

State Records of New South Wales

MacCabe FP, Surveyor General's Crown Plans 1792-1886, *Lower Darling Squatting District* Map No. 2544; plan 3 of 5 of map of Murray River between Taila Creek and the Darling River. INX-33-5385.

University of Cape Town Libraries

Special Collections (Manuscripts and Archives), BC151 Bleek and Lloyd Collection, Series E Unpublished Notes, File E3.1 Australian and other dialects: E3.1.9-E3.1.22 Letters to Dr Bleek and Lucy Lloyd giving information about Australian Aborigines, dialects, customs, folklore, etc., from George Gordon McCrae, c.1875-1877. Illus. MSS 14.

Other sources

Apted, Meiki E. 2010. 'Songs from the Inyjalarrku: The Use of a Non-translatable Spirit Language in a Song Set from North-West Arnhem Land, Australia'. *Australian Journal of Linguistics* 30, no. 1: 93–103. doi.org/10.1080/07268600903134053.

Atkinson, Wayne. 1981. 'A Picture from the Other Side: Cummeragunga and Its Historical Connections with Coranderrk from Written and Oral Sources'. Typescript. Melbourne. MS 1598, Australian Institute of Aboriginal and Torres Strait Islander Studies.

Australischer Christenbote: Monatsblatt für die evangelische-lutherische Kirche in Australien. 1860–1917. Melbourne: Gedruckt von F. Gelbrecht.

Barry, Sir R., ed. 1867. *Exposition Internationale Melbourne: Vocabulaire des dialects des Aborigènes de l'Australie.*[1] Melbourne: Masterman.

Barwick, Diane. 1984 'Mapping the Past: An Atlas of Victorian Clans 1835–1904. Part 1'. *Aboriginal History* 8, no. 2: 100–131. doi.org/10.22459/AH.08.2011.08.

Barwick, Linda. 2005. *Jurtbirrk: Love Songs of North Western Arnhem Land.* Batchelor: Batchelor Press.

Barwick, Linda, Bruce Birch and Nicholas Evans. 2007. 'Iwaidja Jurtbirrk Songs: Bringing Language and Music Together'. *Australian Aboriginal Studies* 2007, no. 2: 6–34. hdl.handle.net/1885/23241.

Beckler, Hermann. 1868. 'Corroberri: Ein Beitrag zur Kenntnis der Musik bei den australischen Ureinwohnern', *Globus: illustrierte Zeitschrift für Länder-und Völkerkunde* 13: 82–84.

Berndt, R. M. 1987. 'Other Creatures in Human Guise and Vice-Versa: A Dilemma of Understanding'. In Clunies Ross, Donaldson and Wild, *Songs of Aboriginal Australia,* 168–91.

Berndt, Ronald M. and Catherine H. Berndt with John E. Stanton. 1993. *A World That Was: The Yaraldi of the Murray River and the Lakes, South Australia.* Carlton: Melbourne University Press at the Miegunyah Press.

Besold, Jutta. 2012. 'Language Recovery of the New South Wales South Coast Aboriginal Languages'. PhD thesis, The Australian National University.

Blake, B. J. 1991. 'Woiwurrung, The Melbourne Language'. In *The Handbook of Australian Languages,* Vol. 4, edited by R. M. W. Dixon and B. J. Blake, 30–122. Melbourne: Oxford University Press Australia.

Blake, B. J., ed. 1998. *Wathawurrung and the Colac Language of Southern Victoria.* Canberra: Pacific Linguistics.

Blake, Barry J. 2003a. *The Bunganditj (Buwandik) Language of the Mount Gambier Region.* Canberra: Pacific Linguistics.

Blake, Barry J. 2003b. *The Warrnambool Language.* Canberra: Pacific Linguistics.

1 This publication was issued in French and English, but it is the French version that was first made available to us via R.M.W. Dixon.

Blake, Barry J. 2011. 'Dialects of Western Kulin, Western Victoria Yartwatjali, Tjapwurrung, Djadjawurrung'. Unpublished draft.

Blake, Barry J., Ian Clark and Shamthi H. Krishna-Pillay. 1998. 'Wathawurrung: The Language of the Geelong-Ballarat Area'. In *Wathawurrung Language and the Colac Language of Southern Victoria*, edited by Barry J. Blake, 59–154. Canberra: Pacific Linguistics.

Blake, Barry J., Ian Clark and Julie Reid. 1998. 'The Colac Language'. In *Wathawurrung Language and the Colac Language of Southern Victoria*, edited by Barry J. Blake, 155–77. Canberra: Pacific Linguistics.

Blake, Barry J., Luise Hercus, Stephen Morey with Ted Ryan. 2011. *The Mathi Group of Languages.* Canberra: Pacific Linguistics.

Blake, Barry J. and Julie Reid. 1998. 'Classifying Victorian Languages'. In *Wathawurrung Language and the Colac Language of Southern Victoria*, edited by Barry J. Blake, 1–58. Canberra: Pacific Linguistics.

Blake, Barry J. and Julie Reid. 1999. 'Pallanganmiddang: A Language of the Upper Murray'. *Aboriginal History* 23: 15–31. doi.org/10.22459/AH.23.2011.02.

Blake, Barry J. and Julie Reid. 2002. 'The Dhudhuroa Language of Northeastern Victoria: A Description Based on Historical Sources'. *Aboriginal History* 26: 177–210. doi.org/10.22459/AH.26.2011.08.

Blake, L. 1977. *Place Names in Victoria.* Melbourne: Rigby.

Bowe, H. and S. D. Morey. 1999. *Yorta Yorta (Bangerang) Language of the Murray-Goulburn including Yabula Yabula.* Canberra: Pacific Linguistics.

Breen, M. 1989. *Our Place Our Music.* Canberra: Aboriginal Studies Press.

Bride, Thomas Francis, ed. 1898. *Letters from Victorian Pioneers.* Melbourne: Trustees of the Public Library.

Broome, Richard. 2005. *Aboriginal Victorians: A History since 1800.* Crows Nest: Allen and Unwin.

Bulmer, John. 1888. 'Some Account of the Aborigines of the Lower Murray, Wimmera, Gippsland'. *Transactions and Proceedings of the Royal Geographical Society of Australia (Victorian Branch)* 5: 15–43.

Bunce, Daniel. 1857. *Australasiatic Reminiscences.* Melbourne: J.T. Hendy.

Cahir, Fred. 2012. *Black Gold: Aboriginal People on the Goldfields of Victoria, 1850–1870.* Canberra: ANU E Press. doi.org/10.22459/BG.09.2012.

Cahir, Fred and Ian D. Clark. 2009. 'The Case of Peter Mungett: Born Out of the Allegiance of the Queen, belonging to a Sovereign and Independent Tribe of Ballan'. *Journal of Public Record Office Victoria* 8: 15–34.

Calder, Winty. 1997. *Classing the Wool and Counting the Bales: The Wragges of Tulla and Yallambie.* Mt Martha: Jimaringle Publications.

Cameron, A. L. P. 1884. 'Notes on Some Tribes of New South Wales'. *Journal of the Anthropological Institute* 14: 344–70. doi.org/10.2307/2841627.

Campbell, Alistair, comp. 1999. *John Bulmer's Recollections of Victorian Aboriginal Life. 1855–1908.* Edited by Ron Vanderwal. Melbourne: Museum Victoria.

Carr, Julie. 2001. *The Captive White Woman of Gipps Land: In Pursuit of the Legend.* Melbourne: Melbourne University Press.

Carter, Samuel. 1911. *Reminiscences of the Early Days of the Wimmera.* Melbourne: Norman Bros.

Chapman, F. R. 1917. '"South Suburban Melbourne, 1854–1864", From the Reminiscences of Frederick Revans Chapman, Judge of the Supreme Court of New Zealand'. *Victorian Historical Magazine*, no. 5: 171–88.

Clark, Ian D., ed. 1998. *The Journals of George Augustus Robinson.* 3 vols. Ballarat: Heritage Matters.

Clark, Ian D., ed. 2000. *The Journals of George Augustus Robinson.* 6 vols. Ballarat: Heritage Matters. (vols 1–3, previously published as Clark 1998, were republished).

Clark, Ian D., ed. 2002. *The Papers of George Augustus Robinson, Chief Protector, Port Phillip Aboriginal Protectorate. Vol. 2: Aboriginal Vocabularies: South East Australia, 1839–1852.* Ballarat Ian Clark through Heritage Matters.

Clark, Ian D. 2014. 'Multiple Aboriginal Placenames in Western Victoria, Australia'. In *Indigenous and Minority Place Names: Australian and International Perspectives*, edited by Ian D. Clark, Luise Hercus and Laura Kostanski, 239–50. Canberra: ANU Press and Aboriginal History Inc. doi.org/10.22459/IMP.04.2014.13.

Clark, Ian D. and Fred Cahir. 2004. *Tanderrum 'Freedom of the Bush': The Djadjawurrung Presence on the Goldfields of Central Victoria.* Castlemaine: Friends of Mount Alexander Diggings.

Clark, Ian D. and Toby Heydon. 2002. *Dictionary of Aboriginal Placenames of Victoria.* Melbourne: Victorian Aboriginal Corporation for Languages.

Clark, Ian D. and Edward Ryan. 2008. 'Aboriginal Spatial Organization in Far Northwest Victoria – A Reconstruction'. *South Australian Geographical Journal* 107: 15–48.

Clark, Ian D., Rolf Schlagloth, Fred Cahir and Gabrielle McGinnis. 2020. 'Kurrburra the Boonwurrung *wirrirrap* and Bard (1797–1849) – a Man of High Degree'. *Australian Journal of Biography and History*, no. 4. doi.org/10.22459/AJBH.04.2020.04.

Clunies Ross, Margaret, Tamsin Donaldson and Stephen A. Wild, eds. 1987. *Songs of Aboriginal Australia*. Sydney: University of Sydney Press.

Curr, Edward M. 1886–87. *The Australian Race: Its Origin, Languages, Customs, Place of Landing in Australia and the Routes by which It Spread Itself Over That Continent.* 4 vols. Melbourne: John Ferres, Government Printer.

Dawson, James. 1881. *Australian Aborigines: The Languages and Customs of Several Tribes of Aborigines in the Western District of Victoria, Australia*. Melbourne: George Robertson.

Dixon, R. M. W. 2002. *Australian Languages: Their Nature and Development*. New York: Cambridge University Press. doi.org/10.1017/CBO9780511486869.

Dixon, R. M. W. and Grace Koch. 1996. *Dyirbal Song Poetry: The Oral Literature of an Australian Rainforest People.* St Lucia: University of Queensland Press.

Donaldson, Tamsin. 1987. 'Making a Song (and Dance) in South-Eastern Australia'. In Clunies Ross, Donaldson and Wild, *Songs of Aboriginal Australia*, 14–42.

Ellis, Alexander John. 1848. *The Ethnical Alphabet, or, Alphabet of Nations: Being an Extension of Messrs Pitman and Ellis's English Phonetic Alphabet.* Bath: Phonetic Printing Offices.

Ellis, Catherine. 1962. 'Ornamentation in Australian Vocal Music'. *Ethnomusicology* 7, no. 2: 88–95. doi.org/10.2307/924544.

Ellis, Catherine. 1964. *Aboriginal Music Making*. Adelaide: Libraries Board of South Australia.

Ellis, Catherine. 1966. 'Aboriginal Songs of South Australia'. *Miscellanea Musicologica* 1: 137–90.

Fels, Marie Hansen. 2011. *'I Succeeded Once': The Aboriginal Protectorate on the Mornington Peninsula, 1839–1840*. Canberra: ANU E Press. doi.org/10.22459/ISO.05.2011.

Fesl, Eve. 1985. 'Ganai: A Study of the Aboriginal Languages of Gippsland Based on 19th Century Materials'. Master's thesis, Monash University.

Fison, Lorimer and A. W. Howitt. 1880. *Kamilaroi and Kurnai: Group-marriage and Relationship, and Marriage by Elopement, Drawn Fhiefly from the Usage of the Australian Aborigines: Also the Kurnai Tribe, Their Customs in Peace and War.* Melbourne: George Robertson.

Fox, Paul with Jennifer Phipps. 1994. *Sweet Damper and Gossip: Colonial Sightings from the Goulburn and North-East.* Exhibition catalogue. Benalla: Benalla Art Gallery.

Garde, Murray. 2006. 'The Language of *Kun-borrk* in Western Arnhem Land'. *Musicology Australia* 28, no. 1: 59–89. doi.org/10.1080/08145857.2005.10415278.

Gibson, Jason and Russell Mullett. 2020. 'The Last Jeraeil of Gippsland: Rediscovering an Aboriginal Ceremonial Site'. *Ethnohistory* 67, no. 4: 551–77. doi.org/10.1215/00141801-8579216.

Griffiths, Billy. 2018. *Deep Time Dreaming: Uncovering Ancient Australia.* Carlton: Black Inc.

Harris, Amanda, Linda Barwick and Jakelin Troy, eds. 2022. *Music, Dance and the Archive.* Sydney: Sydney University Press. doi.org/10.30722/sup.9781743328675.

Haydon, G. H. 1846. *Five Years Experience in Australia Felix.* London: Hamilton, Adams and Company.

Hercus, Luise A. 1965. 'The Survival of Victorian Languages'. *Mankind* 6, no. 5: 201–6. doi.org/10.1111/j.1835-9310.1965.tb00347.x.

Hercus, Luise A. 1982. *The Bagandji Language.* Canberra: Pacific Linguistics.

Hercus, Luise A. 1984. 'The Marawara Language at Yelta: Interpreting Linguistic Records of the Past'. *Aboriginal History* 8, no. 1: 56–62. doi.org/10.22459/AH.08.2011.05.

Hercus, Luise A. 1986. *Victorian Languages – a Late Survey.* Canberra: Pacific Linguistics.

Hercus, Luise A. 1992. *Wembawemba Dictionary.* Canberra: Published by the author.

Hercus, Luise A. 1993. *Paakantyi Dictionary.* Canberra: Published by the author.

Hercus, Luise A. and Grace Koch. 2017. 'Lone Singers: The Others Have All Gone'. In *Recirculating Songs: Revitalisation the Singing Practices of Indigenous Australia,* edited by Jim Wafer and Myfany Turpin, 102–18. Canberra: Asia-Pacific Linguistics.

Hercus, Luise A. and Stephen Morey. 2008. 'Some Remarks on Negatives in Southeastern Australia'. In *Morphology and Language History: In Honour of Harold Koch*, edited by Claire Bowern, Bethwyn Evans and Luisa Miceli, 139–54. Amsterdam: John Benjamins. doi.org/10.1075/cilt.298.14her.

Horgen, Michael. 2004. 'The Languages of the Lower Murray'. MA thesis, La Trobe University.

Howitt, A. W. 1887a. 'Notes on Songs and Songmakers of Some Australian Tribes'. *Journal of the Anthropological Institute of Great Britain and Ireland* 16: 327–35. doi.org/10.2307/2841521.

Howitt, A. W. 1887b. 'On Australian Medicine Men; or, Doctors and Wizards of Some Australian Tribes'. *Journal of the Anthropological Institute of Great Britain and Ireland* 16: 23–59. doi.org/10.2307/2841737.

Howitt, A. W. 1904. *The Native Tribes of South-East Australia.* London: McMillan and Co. reprint, 1996. Canberra: Aboriginal Studies Press.

Howitt, Richard. 1845. *Impressions of Australia Felix.* London: Longman, Brown, Green and Longmans.

Hull, William. 1846. *Remarks on the Probable Origin and Antiquity of the Aboriginal Natives of New South Wales Deduced from Certain of Their Customs, Superstitions, and Existing Caves and Drawings, in Connexion with Those of the Nations of Antiquity. By A Colonial Magistrate.* Melbourne: William Clarke.

Jensz, Felicity. 2000. *Moravian Papers Project Final Report Stage 2.* Report prepared for the Victorian Aboriginal Corporation for Languages.

Jensz, Felicity. 2001. *Moravian Papers Project Final Report Stage 3.* Report prepared for the Victorian Aboriginal Corporation for Languages.

Kenyon, A. S. 1917. 'Introduction and Notes'. In McCrae, *A Vocabulary of the 'Western Port' Aborigines.*

Laughren, Mary, Myfany Turpin and Gemma Turner. 2017. 'Songs Performed by Willie Rookwood at Woorabinda in 1965'. In *Recirculating Songs: Revitalising the Singing Practices of Indigenous Australia*, edited by Jim Wafer and Myfany Turpin, 122–45. Canberra: Asia-Pacific Linguistics.

Lhotsky, John. 1834. *Song of the Women of the Menero Tribe Arranged With the Assistance of Several Musical Gentlemen For the Voice and Pianoforte, Most Humbly Inscribed as the First Specimen of Australian Music, to Her Most Gracious Majesty Adelaide, Queen of Great Britain & Hanover, by Dr. J. Lhotsky, Colonist N. S. Wales.* Sydney: John Innes.

Llewellyn, Becky. 1998. *Clarence Long (Milerum) Songs: Transcriptions by Becky Llewellyn with Assistance from Major Sumner and Betty Sumner*. Sydney: Australian Music Centre.

Locke, William. 1878. 'Notes on the Language and Customs of the Tribe Inhabiting the Country Known as Kotoopna'. In Smyth, *Aborigines of Victoria and Other Parts of Australia and Tasmania*, 2: 333–35.

Lydon, Jane. 2009. *Fantastic Dreaming: The Archaeology of an Aboriginal Mission*. Lanham: AltaMira Press.

McAllister, D. 1878. 'The Australian Aborigines'. *Melbourne Review* 3.

McCrae, George Gordon. 1917. 'A Vocabulary of the "Western Port" Aborigines (with an Introduction and Notes by A.S. Kenyon)'. *Victorian Historical Magazine* 5, no. 4: 164–70.

McCrae, Georgiana Huntly (Gordon). 1966. *Georgiana's Journal, Melbourne, 1841–1865*, edited by H. McCrae. 2nd ed. Sydney: Angus and Robertson.

McDonald, Barry. 2017. 'A Survey of Traditional South-Eastern Australian Indigenous Music'. In *Recirculating Songs: Revitalising the Singing Practices of Indigenous Australia*, edited by Jim Wafer and Myfany Turpin, 146–77. Hamilton: Hunter Press.

Marett, Alan. 2005. *Songs, Dreamings, and Ghosts. The Wangga of North Australia*. Middletown: Wesleyan University Press.

Massola, Aldo. 1968. *Aboriginal Place Names of South-East Australia and Their Meanings*. Melbourne: Lansdowne.

Massola, Aldo. 1969. *Journey to Aboriginal Victoria*. Adelaide: Rigby Limited.

Mathew, John. 1899. *Eaglehawk and Crow: A Study of Australian Aborigines Including an Inquiry into Their Origin and a Survey of Australian Languages*. London: David Nutt; Melbourne: Melville, Mullen and Slade.

Mathews, R. H. 1897. 'The Burbung of the Darkinung Tribes'. *Proceedings of the Royal Society of Victoria* 10, no. 1: 1–12.

Mathews, R. H. 1898. 'Initiation Ceremonies of Australian Tribes'. *Proceedings of the American Philosophical Society* 37: 54–73.

Mathews, R. H. 1902a. 'The Aboriginal Languages of Victoria'. *Journal and Proceedings of the Royal Society of New South Wales* 36: 71–106. doi.org/10.5962/p.359381.

Mathews, R. H. 1902b. 'Languages of Some Native Tribes of Queensland, New South Wales and Victoria'. *Journal and Proceedings of the Royal Society of New South Wales* 36: 135–90. doi.org/10.5962/p.359384.

Mathews, R. H. 1903a. 'Language of the Bungandity Tribe, South Australia'. *Journal and Proceedings of the Royal Society of New South Wales* 37: 59–74. doi.org/10.5962/p.359399.

Mathews, R. H. 1903b. 'Notes on Some Native Dialects of Victoria'. *Journal and Proceedings of the Royal Society of New South Wales* 37: 243–53. doi.org/10.5962/p.359413.

Mathews, R. H. 1904. 'Ethnological Notes on the Aboriginal Tribes of New South Wales and Victoria'. *Journal and Proceedings of the Royal Society of New South Wales* 38: 203–381. doi.org/10.5962/p.359439.

Mathews, R. H. 1905a. *Ethnological Notes on the Aboriginal Tribes of New South Wales and Victoria.* Sydney: F.W. White General Printer.

Mathews, R. H. 1905b. 'Some Initiation Ceremonies of the Aborigines of Victoria'. *Zeitschrift für Ethnologie* 37, no. 6: 872–79.

Merlan, Francesca. 1987. 'Catfish and Alligator: Totemic Songs of the Western Roper River, Northern Territory'. In Clunies Ross, Donaldson and Wild, *Songs of Aboriginal Australia*, 142–67.

Meyer, Heinrich August Edward. 1843. *Vocabulary of the Language Spoken by the Aborigines of the Southern and Eastern Portions of the Settled Districts of South Australia.* Adelaide: James Allen.

Morey, Stephen. 1998. 'The Verbal System of the Central Victorian Language, the Aboriginal Language of Melbourne – an Investigation into the Manuscripts of Rev. William Thomas (1793–1867)'. Honours thesis, Monash University.

Morey, Stephen. 1999. 'Previously Unexamined Texts in Victorian Languages – The Manuscripts of Rev. William Thomas (1793–1867)'. *Monash University Linguistic Publications* 2, no. 1: 45–60.

Morey, Stephen. 2004. 'Transcriptions of the Linguistic Data Relating to the Language of the Melbourne Area'. In Byrt, *The Thomas Papers in the Mitchell Library: A Comprehensive Index*. Melbourne: Monash University Faculty of Arts.

Morey, Stephen. 2016. 'Two Traditional Stories in the Ganai Language of Gippsland'. In *Language, Land and Story in Australia. Studies in Honour of Luise Hercus*, edited by Peter Austin, Harold Koch and Jane Simpson, 377–91. London: EL Publishing.

Morey, Stephen and Jürgen Schöpf. 2018. 'The Language of Ritual in Tangsa – The Wihu Kuh Song'. In *Ritual Speech in the Himalayas: Oral Texts and Their Contents*, edited by Martin Gaenszle and Michael. Cambridge: Harvard University Press.

Mulvaney, D. J. 1967. 'Thomas, William (1793–1867)', Australian Dictionary of Biography, National Centre of Biography, The Australian National University, adb.anu.edu.au/biography/thomas-william-2727/text3845, published first in hardcopy 1967.

Mulvaney, D. J. 1970. 'The Anthropologist as Tribal Elder'. *Mankind* 7, no. 3: 205–17. doi.org/10.1111/j.1835-9310.1970.tb00409.x.

Mulvaney, D. J. 2005, 'Tulaba (1832–1886)', Australian Dictionary of Biography, National Centre of Biography, The Australian National University, adb.anu.edu.au/biography/tulaba-13226, published first in hardcopy 2005.

O'Keeffe, Isabel. 2010. '*Kaddikkaddik ka-wokdjanganj* "Kaddikkaddik Spoke": Language and Music of the Kun-barlang *Kaddikkaddik* Songs from Western Arnhem Land'. *Australian Journal of Linguistics* 30, no. 1: 35–51. doi.org/10.1080/07268600903134012.

O'Keeffe, Isabel. 2016. 'Multilingual manyardi/kun-borrk: Manifestations of Multilingualism in the Classical Song Traditions of Western Arnhem Land'. PhD thesis, University of Melbourne.

Petch, Alison and Jason Gibson. 2013. 'The Ablest Australian Anthropologists, Two Early Anthropologists and Oxford'. *Journal of the Anthropological Society of Oxford* 5, no. 1: 60–85.

Robinson, George Augustus. 1998. *The Journals of George Augustus Robinson, Chief Protector, Port Phillip Aboriginal Protectorate*. 6 vols. Edited by Ian D. Clark. Melbourne: Heritage Matters.

Ryan, Edward. 2016. 'Under Sentence of Death, Melbourne Jail'. In *Language, Land and Song: Studies in Honour of Luise Hercus*, edited by Peter K. Austin, Harold Koch and Jane Simpson, 468–79. EL Publication. www.elpublishing.org/book/language-land-and-song.

Schmidt, Wilhelm. 1919. *Die Gliederung der Australischen Sprachen*. Vienna: Mechitharisten Buchdruckerei.

Shaw, Ethel. [1940s?]. *Early Days among the Aborigines: The Story of Yelta and Coranderrk Missions*. Fitzroy: W. & J. Barr.

Skinner, Graeme and Jim Wafer. 2016. 'A Checklist of Colonial Era Musical Transcriptions of Australian Indigenous Songs'. Australharmony. sydney.edu.au/paradisec/australharmony/checklist-indigenous-music-1.php.

Smith, Christina. 1880. *The Booandik Tribe of South Australian Aborigines: A Sketch of Their Habits, Customs, Legends, and Language*. Adelaide: Spiller, Government Printer.

Smyth, Robert Brough. 1878. *Aborigines of Victoria and Other Parts of Australia and Tasmania*. 2 vols. Melbourne: John Ferres, Government Printer. Facsimile of the first edition, 1972. Melbourne: John Currey O'Neil.

Standfield, Rachel. 2015. '"Thus Have Been Preserved Numerous Interesting Facts That Would Otherwise Have Been Lost": Colonisation, Protection and William Thomas's Contribution to The Aborigines of Victoria'. In *Settler Colonial Governance in Nineteenth-Century Victoria*, edited by Leigh Boucher and Lynette Russell, 47–62. Canberra. ANU Press. doi.org/10.22459/SCGNCV.04.2015.

Stephens, Marguerita and Victorian Aboriginal Corporation for Languages. 2014. *The Journal of William Thomas, Assistant Protector of the Aborigines of Port Phillip & Guardian of the Aborigines of Victoria, 1839–1867*. 4 vols. Melbourne: Victorian Aboriginal Corporation for Languages.

Stone, A. C. 1911. *The Aborigines of Lake Boga, Victoria*. Melbourne: Royal Society of Victoria.

Sutton, Peter. 1987. 'Mystery and Change'. In Clunies Ross, Donaldson and Wild, *Songs of Aboriginal Australia*, 77–96.

Tanner, Andrew. Forthcoming. 'The Eastern Kulin Languages: A Comprehensive Analysis of Archival Sources'. PhD thesis, La Trobe University.

Taplin, George, ed. 1879. *The Folklore, Manners, Customs, and Languages of the South Australian Aborigines / Gathered from Inquiries Made by Authority of South Australian Government*. Adelaide: E. Spiller, Acting Government Printer.

Teichelmann, C. G. and C. W. Schurmann. 1982. *Outlines of a grammar, vocabulary and phraseology of the Aboriginal language of South Australia spoken by the natives in and for some distance around Adelaide*. Facsimile reprint, Largs Bay: Tjintu Books. First published, 1840. Adelaide: Thomas and Co.

Theatre, Corey. 2018. 'Lirrpa-ki Ngutjung: Subconscious Transference of Morpho-syntactic Patterns through Song.' MA thesis, Department of Linguistics, University of Adelaide.

Theatre, Corey. 2024. 'Mak Thang: The Aboriginal Language(s) of Gippsland'. PhD thesis, Department of Languages and Linguistics, La Trobe University.

Thompson, Tommy Kngwarraya. 2003. *Growing up Kaytetye: Stories*, compiled by Myfany Turpin. Alice Springs: Jukurrpa Books.

Tindale, Norman B. 1937. 'Native Songs of the South-East of South Australia. Part I'. *Transactions of the Royal Society of South Australia* 61: 107–20.

Tindale, Norman B. 1939. 'Eagle and Crow Myths of the Maraura Tribe, Lower Darling River, New South Wales'. *Records of the South Australian Museum* 6, no. 3: 243–61.

Tindale, Norman B. 1941. 'Native Songs of the South-East of South Australia. Part II.' *Transactions of the Royal Society of South Australia* 65, no. 2: 233–43.

Tindale, Norman B. 1974. *Aboriginal Tribes of Australia, Their Terrain, Environmental Controls, Distribution, Limits, and Proper Names*. Berkeley and Canberra: University of California Press.

Tipping, Marjorie, ed. 1979. *Ludwig Becker: Artist and Naturalist with the Burke and Wills Expedition*. Melbourne: Melbourne University Press.

Torrance, G. W. 1887. 'Music of the Australian Aboriginals'. *Journal of the Anthropological Institute of Great Britain and Ireland* 16: 335–40. doi.org/10.2307/2841522.

Treloyn, Sally, Matthew Dembal and Rona Googninda Charles. 2019. 'Moving Songs: Repatriating Audiovisual Recordings of Aboriginal Australian Dance and Song (Kimberley Region, Northwestern Australia).' In *The Oxford Handbook of Musical Repatriation*, edited by Frank Gunderson, Robert C. Lancefield and Bret Woods, 591–606. Oxford: Oxford University Press. doi.org/10.1093/oxfordhb/9780190659806.013.42.

Troy, Jakelin and Linda Barwick. 2020. 'Claiming the "Song of the Women of the Menero Tribe"'. *Musicology Australia* 42, no. 2: 85–107. doi.org/10.1080/08145857.2020.1945254.

Turpin, Myfany. 2007a. 'Artfully Hidden: Text and Rhythm in a Central Australian Aboriginal Song Series'. *Musicology Australia* 29, no. 1: 93–108. doi.org/10.1080/08145857.2007.10416590.

Turpin, Myfany. 2007b. The Poetics of Central Australian Song. In *Studies in Aboriginal Song: A Special Issue of Australian Aboriginal Studies*, Vol. 2, edited by Allan Marett and Linda Barwick, 100–115. Canberra: Aboriginal Studies Press.

Turpin, Myfany with Grace Koch. 2008. 'The Language of Aboriginal Songs'. In *Morphology and Language History*, edited by Claire Bowern, Bethwyn Evans and Luisa Miceli, 167–83. Amsterdam/Philadelphia: John Benajamins.

Turpin, Myfany and Jenny Green. 2011. 'Trading in Terms: Linguistic Affiliation in Arandic Songs and Alternate Registers'. In *Indigenous Language and Social Identity: Papers in Honour of Michael Walsh*, edited by Ilana Mushin, Brett Baker, Rod Gardner and Mark Harvey, 297–318. Canberra. Pacific Linguistics.

Unaipon, David. 1990. 'Narroondaries Wives'. In *Paperbark: A Collection of Black Australian Writings*, edited by Jack Davis, Stephen Muecke, Mudrooroo Narogin and Adam Shoemaker, 19–32. St Lucia: University of Queensland Press.

United Brethren in Christ. 1861. *Periodical Accounts Relating to the Missions of the Church of the United Brethren Established among the Heathen*, Vol. 24. London: Brethren's Society for the Furtherance of the Gospel.

Vanderbyl, Nikita. 2019a. 'William Barak's Paintings at State Library Victoria'. *La Trobe Journal* 103: 6–23. www.slv.vic.gov.au/sites/default/files/La-Trobe-Journal-103-Nikita-Vanderbyl.pdf.

Vanderbyl, Nikita. 2019b. 'Artist and Statesman: William Barak and the Trans-Imperial Circulation of Aboriginal Cultural Objects'. PhD thesis, Department of Archaeology and History, La Trobe University.

von Sturmer, John. 1987. 'Aboriginal Singing and Notions of Power'. In Clunies Ross, Donaldson and Wild, *Songs of Aboriginal Australia*, 63–76.

Wafer, Jim and Myfany Turpin, eds. 2017. *Recirculating Songs: Revitalising the Singing Practices of Indigenous Australia*. Canberra: Asia-Pacific Linguistics.

Wild, Stephen A. 1987. 'Recreating the jukurrpa: Adapation and Innovation of Songs in Warlpiri Society'. In Clunies Ross, Donaldson and Wild, *Songs of Aboriginal Australia*, 97–120.

Song index

Note: Page numbers in **bold** indicate figures and tables. Page numbers with 'n' indicate footnotes.

www.ingramcontent.com/pod-product-compliance
Lightning Source LLC
LaVergne TN
LVHW020500100826
845148LV00003B/682

* 9 7 8 1 7 6 0 4 6 7 1 1 1 *